HEART STOPPERS
AND HAIL MARYS

HEART STOPPERS AND HAIL MARYS

THE GREATEST COLLEGE FOOTBALL FINISHES (SINCE 1970)

TED MANDELL

FOREWORD BY DOUG FLUTIE

Hardwood Press
South Bend, Indiana
2006

Manufactured in the United States of America

1 2 3 4 5 6   11 10 09 08 07 06

Library of Congress Cataloging in Publication Data

Mandell, Ted.
    Heart stoppers and Hail Marys: the greatest college football finishes
(since 1979) / Ted Mandell; foreword by Doug Flutie. – 1st pbk. ed.
             p. cm.
       Includes index.
    ISBN 0-89651-559-1 (pbk.: alk. paper)
    1. Football - United States - History - 20th century. 2. College sports
– United States - History – 20th century. 3. Radio broadcasting of sports
– United States - History – 20th century 4. Television broadcasting of sports
– United States - History – 20th century.   I. Title.
    GV950.M26 2006
    796.332'63 – dc22   2006023765

∞ The paper used in this publication meets the minimum requirements of the American National Standard for Information Sciences — Permanence of Paper for Printed Materials, ANSI Z39.48-1948.

Hardwood Press
www.staugustine.net

CONTENTS

CONTENTS

COMPACT DISC CONTENTS

DISC/ TRACK	GAME	ANNOUNCER / STATION
1-01	Yale • Harvard	Ken Coleman / Harvard Football Radio Network
1-02	Kentucky • Vanderbilt	Caywood Ledford / University of Kentucky Radio Network
1-03	Mississippi • Louisiana State	John Ferguson / LSU Sports Network
1-04	Auburn • Alabama	Gary Sanders /Auburn Network
1-05	Pittsburgh • West Virginia	Jack Fleming / Mountaineer Sports Network
1-06	Oklahoma • Ohio State	Gary Johnson / University of Oklahoma Radio Network
1-07	Clemson • South Carolina	Jim Phillips / Clemson Sports Network
1-08	Duke • North Carolina	Woody Durham, Bob Holliday / Tar Heel Sports Network
1-09	Indiana • Michigan	Bob Ufer / WJR Radio, Detroit MI, Michigan Football Network
1-10	Michigan • Notre Dame	Tony Roberts, Al Wester / Westwood One
1-11	Alabama • Mississippi State	Jack Cristil, John Correro / Mississippi State University Radio Network
1-12	Florida • Georgia	Larry Munson, Loran Smith / The University of Georgia Athletic Association/Collegiate Images
1-13	Brigham Young • Southern Methodist	Tony Roberts, Al Wester / Westwood One
1-14	Oklahoma • Southern California	Tom Kelly / University of Southern California Radio Network
1-15	Stanford • California	Joe Starkey, Jan Hutchins / KGO Radio, San Francisco
1-16	Southern California • UCLA	Fred Hessler / UCLA Football Radio Network
1-17	Nebraska • Miami	Sonny Hirsch / University of Miami Football Radio Network
1-18	Bloomsburg (Pa) • West Chester	Jim Doyle, Charlie Chronister / WHLM Radio, Bloomsburg PA
1-19	Boston College • Miami	Dan Davis / Kelley Communications
1-20	Auburn • Alabama	Paul Kennedy, Doug Layton /Alabama Sports Network
1-21	Northern Iowa • Eastern Illinois	Ken Wooddell, Doug Bock / WLBH Radio, Matoon IL
1-22	Auburn • Florida	David Steele, Norm Carlson / Florida Gator Radio Network
1-23	Northeast Louisiana • Northwestern State	Frank Hoffmann / Univ. of Louisiana at Monroe Athletics Dept.
1-24	Marshall • Louisville	Bill Roth / Marshall University Thundering Herd Network
1-25	Iowa • Ohio State	Jim Zabel / WHO Radio, Des Moines IA
1-26	Holy Cross • Princeton	Bob Fouracre / WWTM Radio, Westboro MA
1-27	Miami • Notre Dame	Tony Roberts, Tom Pagna / Westwood One
1-28	North Texas • Kansas State	Mitch Holthus, Stan Weber / Kansas State University Radio Network
1-29	Florida • Auburn	Jim Fyffe /Auburn Network
1-30	Utah • Minnesota	Bill Marcroft / KALL910 Radio, Salt Lake City UT
1-31	Mississippi • Arkansas	David Kellum, Lyman Hellums / Ole Miss Radio Network
1-32	Ohio State • Iowa	Terry Smith, Jim Karsatos / The Ohio State University, WBNS Radio, Columbus, OH
1-33	Southern California • UCLA	Pete Arbogast / University of Southern California Radio Network
1-34	Colorado • Notre Dame	Tony Roberts, Jack Ham / Westwood One
1-35	Tennessee • Notre Dame	John Ward / USA Vol Network
1-36	Northeast Louisiana • Eastern Kentucky	Greg Stotelmyer, Webber Hamilton / Eastern Kentucky University Radio Network
1-37	San Jose State • Wyoming	John Shrader / San Jose State University Football Network
1-38	Appalachian State • James Madison	Brian Estridge, Steve Brown /Appalachian Sports Network
1-39	Northwestern • Illinois	Dave Eanet / WBBM Radio Chicago, IL and Northwestern University
1-40	Virginia Tech • Rutgers	Pat Scanlon, Bob Casciola / New Jersey Network

2-01	Penn State • Notre Dame	Tony Roberts, Tom Pagna / Westwood One
2-02	Mississippi State • Mississippi	David Kellum, Lyman Hellums / Ole Miss Radio Network
2-03	South Carolina • Georgia	Bob Fulton, Tommy Suggs / Gamecock Sports Network
2-04	Florida • Kentucky	Mick Hubert, Lee McGriff / Florida Gator Radio Network
2-05	Illinois • Michigan	Neil Funk, Jim Grabowski / Illini Sports Network
2-06	Thomas More • Defiance	Gary Ball, Bill Harmon / Northern Kentucky Sports Network
2-07	Nevada • Arkansas State	Randy Rainwater / Arkansas State University Radio Network
2-08	Boston College • Notre Dame	Dick Lutsk, Peter Cronan / Kelley Communications
2-09	Colorado • Michigan	Larry Zimmer / KOA Radio, Denver CO, Colorado Football Network
2-10	Virginia • Michigan	Larry Henry, Jim Brandstatter / WWJ NewsRadio 950, Detroit MI
2-11	Arkansas • Alabama	Paul Eels, Rick Schaefer / Arkansas Razorback Sports Network

COMPACT DISC CONTENTS

DISC/ TRACK	GAME	ANNOUNCER / STATION
2-12	Auburn • Louisiana State	Jim Hawthorne / LSU Sports Network
2-13	Florida State • Virginia	Warren Swain, Frank Quayle / The Virginia Sports Network
2-14	Penn State • Michigan State	Fran Fisher, George Paterno / Clear Channel Sports
2-15	Colorado State • Air Force	Steve Anderson / Colorado State Sports Network, Clear Channel Sports
2-16	Ohio State • Arizona State	Terry Smith, Jim Karsatos / The Ohio State University, WBNS Radio
2-17	Wisconsin • Northwestern	Matt LePay / Wisconsin Badger Network from Learfield Sports
2-18	Amherst • Williams	Steve Epstein, Jason Hehir, Matt Marvin / WCFM, Williams College
2-19	Nebraska • Missouri	Warren Swain, Adrian Fiala / Pinnacle Sports Network
2-20	Washington • Arizona State	Bob Rondeau / KOMO Radio, Seattle WA, Husky Football Network
2-21	Virginia Tech • Syracuse	Doug Logan, Jim Ridlon / WSYR Radio, Syracuse NY
2-22	Kansas State • Texas A&M	Dave South, Dave Elmendorf / Clear Channel Sports
2-23	UNLV • Baylor	Tony Cordasco, Hunkie Cooper / KXNT Radio, Las Vegas NV
2-24	Louisiana Tech • Alabama	Dave Nitz, Dan Newman / KXKZ Radio, Ruston LA, and Louisiana Tech Athletic Media Relations
2-25	Arizona • Washington State	Brian Jeffries, Les Josephson / KNST Radio, Tucson AZ, Arizona Wildcat Network
2-26	Northwestern • Minnesota	Dave Eanet, Ted Albrecht / WGN Radio, Chicago, IL
2-27	Central College • Linfield	J.B. Connoley, Al Dorenkamp / KRLS Radio, Pella, IA
2-28	Akron • Miami (OH)	Steve Baker / Miami University
2-29	Michigan • Michigan State	George Blaha, Larry Bielat / TBC Sports/ Spartan Sports Network
2-30	Furman • Appalachian State	David Jackson, Avery Hall /Appalachian Sports Network
2-31	Louisiana State • Kentucky	Jim Hawthorne / LSU Radio Network
2-32	Ohio State • Miami	Paul Keels, Jim Lachey / The Ohio State Radio Network
2-33	Columbia • Princeton	Phil Wallace, Todd Keryc / WKCR Radio, New York NY
2-34	Iowa • Louisiana State	Gary Dolphin, Ed Podolak / Hawkeye Sports Properties/ Learfield Communications
2-35	Texas Tech • Nebraska	Brian Jensen, John Harris / Texas Tech Sports Network
2-36	Penn State • Michigan	Frank Beckmann / Host Communications and The Michigan Sports Network
2-37	Southern California • Notre Dame	Pete Arbogast, Paul McDonald / 1540 "The Ticket" and The Trojan Radio Network
2-38	Texas • Southern California	Craig Way, Keith Moreland / Host Communications/The University of Texas/Collegiate Images

Digitally mastered at Sweetwater Sound, Fort Wayne, Indiana, Larry Pester, sound engineer.

ACKNOWLEDGMENTS

This project was a wonderful two-headed monster.

First, The CD. The audio compact disc was compiled with the assistance of numerous kind souls across the country who guided me on a nostalgic telephone ride covering dozens of radio stations, networks, announcers, engineers, and sports directors, as I tried to track down recordings more elusive than I ever could have imagined. But it was well worth it.

So many have been so helpful. First and foremost, my deepest thanks to John Miley, a man who should be given a lifetime achievement award for the Miley Collection, an endless archive of irreplaceable sports broadcasts, collected, preserved, and nurtured for over fifty years- truly a national treasure of sports memories in Evansville, Indiana. I cannot thank John enough for his generosity and kindness.

Thanks to the following individuals, companies, and universities for their help and cooperation in assembling the audio material and granting permission for its use.

John Veneziano, *Harvard University;* Kyle Moats, *University of Kentucky Athletics Association;* Jim Hawthorne, *LSU Sports Network;* Jon Cole, *Auburn Network, Inc.;* Heidi Saffel, *Mountaineer Sports Network;* Rick Hart, *University of Oklahoma;* Timothy Bouret, *Clemson University;* Tim Noonan, *Vilcom Sports, Inc.;* Michael Fezzey, *WJR Radio, Detroit;* Bennie Ashford, *Mississippi State University;* Tim Tessalone, *USC Sports Information;* Joe Starkey, *University of California Football Broadcaster;* Marc Dellins, *UCLA Athletics;* Patrick Nero, *Athletic Department, University of Miami;* Jim Doyle, *WHLM Radio, Bloomsburg PA;* Paul Kelley, *Kelley Communications;* Larry White, *University of Alabama;* Ken Wooddell, *WLBH Radio, Matoon IL;* Steve Babik, *University Athletic Association, University of Florida;* M. Cory Rogers, *University of Louisiana at Monroe;* Clark Haptonstall, *Marshall University Department of Athletics;* Jim Zabel, *WHO Radio, Des Moines IA;* Tim Young, *WGMC-TV, Worcester MA;* James O. Epps, *Kansas State Athletic Department, Kansas State University;* Brad Stone, *KALL 910 Radio, Salt Lake City UT;* Langston Rogers, SID, *University of Mississippi;* Richard Van Brimmer, *The Ohio State University;* Steve Early, *USA Vol Network;* Greg Stotelmyer, *WTVQ-TV, Lexington, KY;* Lawrence Fan, SID, *San Jose State University;* *Appalachian Office of Sports Information;* Alan Cubbage, *Northwestern University;* William Jobes, *NJN Public Television;* S. Scott Powers, *Gamecock Sports Marketing;* David Johnson, *University of Illinois;* Todd Asalon, *Thomas More College;* Barry Dowd, *Arkansas State University;* Larry Zimmer, *KOA Radio, Denver, Colorado Football Network;* Larry D. Henry, *WWJ NewsRadio 950, Detroit MI;* Mark Meadors, *Arkansas Razorback Sports Network;* Mac McDonald, *Cavalier Sports Marketing, The Virginia Sports Network;* Tom Stevens, *Clear Channel Sports;* Matthew Toombs, *Colorado State Sports Network, Clear Channel Sports;* Rick Stoneking, *Learfield Communications;* Dick Quinn, *Williams College;* Paul Aaron, *Pinnacle Sports Network;* Bob Rondeau, *KOMO, Husky Football Network;* Ted DeLuca, *WSYR Radio, Syracuse NY;* Charles Cavagnaro, *University of Nevada-Las Vegas;* Malcolm Butler, *Louisiana Tech Athletic Media Relations;* Brian Jeffries, *KNST Radio, Tuscon AZ, Arizona Wildcat Network;*

David Jackson, Appalachian Sports Network; Chris Kesicke, Collegiate Images; Anita Thielen, Eric Buchanan, Hawkeye Sports Properties; Dale Arens Univ. of Iowa Trademark Licensing; Steve Wright, Host Communications; Wendy Hart, TBC Sports; Ann Beebe, Broadcast Operations, USC; Skip Mosic, RadiOhio, Inc.; Steve Pitts, Texas Tech Sports Network.

Special thanks to Larry Michael and Westwood One for their permission and generosity.

Thanks to Larry Pester at Sweetwater Sound for his expertise in mastering the CD, and Julie Doust for all her assistance.

Thank you to all the announcers, whose unabashed on-air excitement captured these thrilling moments for generations to come.

Secondly, The Book. The text was written and researched with the help of numerous university libraries, sports information departments, and countless interviews with broadcasters, coaches, and players. The following individuals were especially helpful, providing research materials, photos, and personal insight into the games. I apologize to those I've inadvertently left out.

Scott Quintard, UCLA Photography; George Rugg, Joyce Sports Research Collection, Univ. of Notre Dame; Kentucky Media Relations; Jim Fyffe; Sally Jirik, Auburn University Archives; Auburn Athletic Media Relations; Debbie Landi, Univ. of Missouri Archives; Bob Brendel, Univ. of Missouri ; Michigan State University Sports Information; David Bartlett, West Virginia University Libraries; Shelly Poe, West Virginia Sports Communications; University of Oklahoma Western History Collections; Jim Phillips; Rick Brewer, University of North Carolina SID; Woody Durham; Charlie Fiss, Southwestern Bell Cotton Bowl; David Ablauf, Univ. of Michigan Athletic Media Relations; Carol Kaesebier, Univ. of Notre Dame; Michael Bennett; Ken Berthelot, Tulane University; Mississippi State Sports Information; Bruce Binkowski, Culligan Holiday Bowl; Paul J. Schneider; Alan Virta, Boise State University Special Collections; Ken Thompson, *Lafayette Journal and Courier*; Jack Dale; Bob Condron; Joe Starkey; Rod Searcey; University of Miami Department of Sports Publicity; Jennifer Wallace, Univ. of Delaware Archives; Dan Wakely, College of William & Mary Athletic Department; Earl Gregg Swem Library; Jay Colley; N. Avery McLean, Univ. of Georgia; Jim Doyle; Robert Dunkelberger, Bloomsburg University Archives; Danny Hale; Mike Stewart; Tom McGuire, Bloomsburg Sports Information; Boston College Athletics; Jim Martz, 'Cane Sports; Phil Webster, Principia College; Jim Murphy, Illinois College SID; Hayner Public Library, Alton IL; Dan Sellers; Jon Hinds; Tom Rowland; Taylor Watson, Paul W. Bryant Museum; Tom McClellan, Georgia Southern Athletic Media Relations; Mike Ferlazzo, Susquehanna SID; Lycoming College/Snowden Library; Rob Sochovka; Al Bucci; Dave Kidwell, Eastern Illinois SID; University of Northern Iowa Archives; North Carolina State Athletics Media Relations; Catherine Jannik, Northwestern State University, Cammie G. Henry Research Center ; Frank Hoffmann; Jim Zabel; Roger Maxwell; Steve Tosches; Bob Fouracre; Jo Anne Carr, Holy Cross Archives; Kristen Turner, Seeley Mudd Library, Princeton NJ; Rod Commons, Washington State University SID; Kansas State Athletic Department; Mitch Holthus; Norm Burge; Scot Dapp; Bub Parker, Juniata College; D.F. Durnbaugh, Juniata Archives; John Cox, University of Southern Mississippi; University of Louisville Archives; Shayne Wasden; Paul Mogren, University of Utah Marriott Library; Univ. of Minnesota Athletic Media Relations; Allison George, Georgia Tech Athletics; Eric Kaelin, WBNS; Terry Smith; Gary Migdol, Stanford University SID; Hal Ramey; Bob Murphy; John Hopkins; Pete Arbergost; Greg Davis; Eastern Kentucky University Archives; Helen Chaney, Monroe News Star; University of Wyoming Libraries; Cecilia Mullen, San Jose State University Special Collections; Appalachian State Sports Information; Dave Eanet; John Beisser, Rutgers Sports Media Relations; Rutgers University Archives; Donald Forbes; Tom Ransom; David Witvoet; David Parry; Univ. of Mississippi Sports Information; South Caroliniana Library; Bruce Mills, Univ. of Florida SID; Greg Stofko; Leonard Reich, Defiance College SID; Don Weber; Ted Kiep; Randy Rainwater; Arkansas State Sports Information; Jason Wolfe, WEEI Radio; Larry Zimmer ; Miami University Department of Athletics; Dan Lopez, *The Cavalier Daily*; Stan Savron; George Paterno; Fran Fisher; Guido D'elia; Frick Weber; Richard Wynne; Steve Berry; Wyatt Thompson; Ohio State Athletic Communications; Liana Yamasaki, Pasadena Tournament of Roses; Matt LePay; University of Wisconsin Sports Information; Mark Bain; Steve Marovich, Carthage SID; Dave Johnson, Millikin SID; Tim Rucks; Kris Norton; Eric Corbett; Dick Quinn, Williams College SID; Jason Hehir; Matt Marvin; Warren Swain; University of Washington Intercollegiate Athletics Media Relations; John Rooke; Steve Terrill; Kevin Rogers; Doug Logan; Syracuse Athletic Communications; Dave South; Mark Wallington, UNLV; Fr. William Simmons; Sean Cangelosi; Randy Beckham, Compaq Plays of the Week; Marc Boucher, Ripon College.

Robby Edwards, Arkansas SID; Larry Happel, Central College SID; Joe Ritzert; Reid Evans; Todd Kennedy, Columbia SID; Phil Wallace; Jeff Otis; Bill Allen, NJ Sport Action; Terry Hoeppner; Steve Baker; Michael Harris, Miami University; Alan Wasielewski, Notre Dame Sports Information; Mike Wolf, Northwestern; Chris Cook, Assistant AD Texas Tech; Jake Knott; Chris Creighton; Ryan Short; Kurt Casper; Matt Cashore; Mike Karwoski.

Thanks to Jill Langford for guiding me along the path, answering my never-ending stream of publishing questions, and being a wonderful editor, and to her husband Jim for his advice. Thanks also to Juanita Dix for her design and layout. An extra special thanks to Kent Stephens,

ACKNOWLEDGMENTS

at the College Football Hall of Fame, for all his help, expert input, and friendship, and for allowing me to swim through scores of media guides, books, and videotapes. (Visit the College Football Hall of Fame in South Bend, Indiana!!!)

Special thanks also to my good friend, and ace historian on Notre Dame athletics, Charles Lamb at the University of Notre Dame Archives. I'm also very grateful to my departmental colleagues at ND, Don Crafton, Jill Godmilow, Bill Donaruma, Joe Buttigieg, Valerie Sayers, Mary Mitchell, and Jim Collins for their support, patience, and advice along the way.

Thanks to all the internet surfers who emailed me for over five years with their favorite finishes. Their selections were the seeds that began this project.

Last, but certainly not least, a huge thank you to my mother and father, Louise and Maurice Mandell, for their endless support and overflowing enthusiasm for this project... and thanks to my brother Steve who made me a Notre Dame fan at the age of nine, and sisters Chris, Jocelyn, and Melinda, who probably couldn't care less about college football, but still seem interested in the book.

This book was written from February 1999 to April 2000, a period of time in which my beautiful wife KeriAnn carried our first born for nine months, then, with God's help, gave birth to a precious 9 lb., 10 oz. son, Joel Theodore Mandell, on December 7, 1999. Without a doubt, *that* was the greatest finish of all time!

This book is for KeriAnn and Joel.

Updated May 2006

Six years, two more children, and 16 additional chapters later.....This book is now for KeriAnn, Joel, adorable Riley, and sweet, sweet Emma. Never could I imagine being blessed with such a beautiful, loving family...and never could I imagine Reggie Bush pushing Matt Leinart into the Notre Dame end zone. For giving me my family and the opportunity to witness frantic college football finishes... win or lose....I thank God.

Additional thanks for this edition to Bruce Fingerhut and Benjamin Fingerhut of Hardwood Press. Thanks guys for your enthusiasm, your ideas, your expertise and your willingness to take this book the extra yards.

Thanks also to my band of indexers, Breana Leader, Kate Leszkowicz, Vince Amatuzzi, Ray Jarosz, Amelia Hirschauer, Mary Fisher, John Klein, Mary Hannan, and Eddie Song. Thanks to Patrick Ryan for his stellar author photo work on the back cover.

And a huge thank you to Marty Schalm, for his wonderful cover design work on the new edition.

Last but certainly not least, Steve Boda began working for the NCAA in 1949. With the OK from his boss Homer F. Cooke, Jr., Steve took it upon himself to start compiling college football statistics in a loose-leaf folder for twenty years. In 1969, the NCAA released the first NCAA Records book, a 177-page manual of individual and team records. Today that book is a two-volume set with over 1000 pages of records and anecdotes. It contains an invaluable section called Cliffhangers, an annual list of games won on the final play of regulation. Without it, many of the smaller school games in this book would never have been unearthed. Steve invented the Cliffhangers section in 1971. He is the father of the NCAA Football Records Book and for his priceless statistical work for over half a century, all of us as college football fans should be forever thankful. Thank you Steve Boda.

FOREWORD

It's the signature play of my career. It's something that I will always be remembered for. It's the first thing most people think of when they hear the words "Doug Flutie."

It's The Pass. My 48-yard Hail Mary completion to Gerard Phelen that beat Miami in 1984. You've seen it, haven't you?

You know, it was a lucky play. It does take skill to have a good shot at it. But it's really luck to actually complete it and have it happen. So many stars have to align. Little things. For instance, initially there was a blown whistle on the play as we lined up over the ball. On the original alignment, our wide receiver Kelvin Martin was uncovered, and there was a Miami defender jamming Gerard. And then when we got restarted and I got under center, the guy who was on Gerard walked back out and tried to jam Kelvin, allowing Gerard to be the first guy down the field, and the one to catch the pass.

Actually, I didn't throw the ball to Gerard. I threw it to an area of the field. In fact, I really didn't know who caught the ball until five minutes after the game ended. After the celebration, after shaking hands, just before I went into the tunnel towards the locker room, I bumped into our strong safety Dave Pereira. "Who caught the ball?" I asked. "Gerard," he said.

I assumed it was Gerard, but I couldn't see who caught it. I never made it to the big pile in the end zone. Maybe that's not such a bad thing. Fortunately, I've never been at the bottom of one of those game-winning piles where you can't breathe and the entire team is jumping on you. I've been under piles of maybe five guys playing sandlot football as a kid where I got really scared. But I can't imagine having twenty 280-pounders on top of me.

We had done it before, Gerard and I, completing a Hail Mary at the end of the first half against Temple earlier in the year, which basically won that game for us. So when this pass happened, we thought, "Oh my God, we did it again." It was a great play. We won the game. We were excited it happened. But we didn't realize at the time that it would get all of the national attention that followed. Because it was Thanksgiving weekend, I believe it was the highest TV rating the network had all year for a college football game. Consequently, after that play, the media blitz was wild.

Things were crazy before that play. I was already being hyped for the Heisman, so I was dealing with lots of media attention all year long. But The Pass just took it to another level. The next two weeks, I was burned out on the autographs and the attention. It seemed like 10 years worth of signing autographs in those two weeks. That year for Christmas, everybody on the Boston College campus wanted to get their *Sports Illustrated* cover signed. They dropped them off at my place. I had stacks and stacks, thousands of copies of *Sports Illustrated* in my apartment to sign, and get back to the students for Christmas.

A week or two after the game, I remember the skit on *Saturday Night Live* where I was being interviewed. They played the highlight over and over again, and asked the same questions over and over again. The guy playing me got so frustrated he ended up yelling, "I wish that never had even happened! It was a stupid pass! It was lucky!" During that brief period of time after The Pass, sometimes I actually felt that way.

But you know, I wouldn't have changed that for the world.

Winning the heart stoppers. That's also been a signature of my career. It's the way that I play the game. In Canada, in college, in the NFL, I've had many last second victories. Too many to count. Because that one pass is ingrained in people's minds, the fans believe I'm going to pull a game out. We get the ball with a minute and a half to go, down by a few points, they think, "Oh, here comes that magic Flutie thing."

That's a great reputation to gain, to have both your teammates and the fans anticipating a last-second comeback. But, there's no magic here. It's hard work to pull out a come-from-behind win. Actually, it's a long odds situation, and many times, I don't succeed. And when I fail, the fans are surprised.

But I like it that way. I like the fact that they anticipate something good happening. That goes a long way with my teammates in the huddle—that they anticipate succeeding, that they believe in me.

When we're trailing in the final minutes and I run onto the field, I don't do anything different to rally my team. But I can tell you this. I remember talking to John Havlicek, the great Boston Celtics' guard. He said that in those last-second situations, in the last minutes of a game, it always seems like everyone else is moving in slow motion.

It's true. All of a sudden, time slows down. I think the intensity level goes up, the concentration level goes up. Maybe I'm thinking more clearly, maybe at a slightly quicker clip. But it always seems like I have all day to make those critical decisions.

And when I have more time to make those decisions on the field, it just seems easier. Easier to lead my team down the field. Easier to win those heart stopping games. Easier to put my team in the position to complete The Pass.

I'm happy to have made the cut for Ted Mandell's collection of 100 of the greatest finishes from the past 30 years. I'm even happier to hear Dan Davis' thrilling radio call of The Pass on the compact disc. Listening to these unbelievable audio clips really brings the moments back to life. **Heart Stoppers and Hail Marys** captures the excitement of college football for just about every fan, and any school you can think of from around the country.

After reading **Heart Stoppers and Hail Marys**, you'll realize that I'm not the only guy who's ever thrown a Hail Mary pass. Mine just happened to be on national television.

Doug Flutie

The Doug Flutie, Jr. Foundation for Autism

The Doug Flutie, Jr. Foundation for Autism was established in April 1998 by Doug and his wife, Laurie, in honor of their eight-year-old son, Doug, Jr., who was diagnosed with autism at age three. Autism is a neurological disorder that impacts the normal development of the brain in the areas of social interaction and communication skills and affects over one-half million people in the United States.

The goals of the foundation are to aid financially disadvantaged families who need assistance in caring for their autistic children, fund research and education into the causes and consequences of childhood autism, and serve as a clearinghouse and communications center for new programs and services developed for children with autism.

*For more information or
to make a donation, please contact:*
The Doug Flutie, Jr. Foundation for Autism
c/o The Giving Back Fund,
54 Canal Street, Suite 320
Boston, Massachusetts 02114
(617) 557-9910
www.dougflutie.org

From Nausea to Nirvana

November 14, 1998. Syracuse, NY. Two seconds remained on the clock as Donovan McNabb staggered over to the sidelines, wearily looked up at the 60,000 panicked fans in the Syracuse Carrier Dome, then vomited at the feet of coach Paul Pasqualoni. McNabb then wandered out on the field to perform a miracle in orange.

Somewhere... before McNabb's dramatic last gasp pass beat Virginia Tech 28-26.

Sometime... after tight end Stephen Brominski squeezed the football, buried beneath a mob of hysterical Orangemen players.

Someplace... in a sports bar or dorm room in Blacksburg, Virginia... a few thousand Hokies fans probably vomited too.

That's the beauty of college football.

On the evening of January 2nd, 1987, I went to a restaurant in Cincinnati with some friends to watch the Fiesta Bowl between Penn State and Miami. My best friend from high school, Richard, bleeds Nittany Lion blue. As the game was being played, Richard frequently ran back in forth between the bar area, which had the television, and the restaurant, which did not. When the game boiled down to the final few seconds, he refused to watch, listen, or even profess to be interested in the outcome. That winter evening in 1987, while Richard was face down, eyes closed on the restaurant table, I personally told him that Pete Giftopoulis intercepted a Vinny Testeverde pass to clinch Penn State's national championship. When he lifted his head, I couldn't tell whether he was nauseous or ecstatic. Perhaps both.

My friend Mike from South Bend, Indiana, videotapes every Notre Dame football game. In his blue and gold family room, decorated with various Fighting Irish memorabilia, he has the complete library of Notre Dame victories from 1988 through 1999 on VHS tape. What about the losses? He records over them immediately, refusing to watch even part of the game. There is no room in the loyal fan's closet for heartbreaking memories.

I won't lie to you. I'm an avid Notre Dame fan, tamed down quite a bit over the years.

I've attended every Notre Dame home game, except one, since 1988. The exception, my sister's wedding in New York, September 20, 1997. Not coincidentally, the Irish loss to Michigan State that day, marked a consistent pattern of Notre Dame losses corresponding with Mandell family weddings. 0-3 to be exact. Recognizing this trend I scheduled my own wedding to fall during an off week for the Irish during the 1998 season. I felt confident that not only would this be better for the success of the Notre Dame team, but my local friends, Mike included, would actually attend the wedding instead of going to the Notre Dame game.

Much to my chagrine, a few months before our wedding, the University announced that the September 19th game with Michigan State had been moved to my wedding date, September 12th, to accommodate ABC television. The result: Michigan State 42, Notre Dame 23. Another Mandell wedding/Notre Dame loss.

I never took the time to look back and see how the Irish fared the day my parents took their vows. But after the ND debacle on my own wedding night, I felt it necessary to examine history. My parents were wed on October 5th, 1950. It was a Thursday. Two days later, Notre Dame played host to Purdue. The Irish were sporting a 39-game unbeaten streak under coach Frank Leahy.

Final score: Purdue 28, Notre Dame 14. I feel sick.

I'm sure you can recite your exact location, what you were wearing, and what you had for lunch the day your favorite school caught the miracle catch, made the impossible comeback, or choked in the final seconds. I can too.

I bounced around my house, screaming uncontrollably when Joe Montana hit Kris Haines with no time remaining in the 1979 Cotton Bowl to give Notre Dame a 35-34 win over Houston. I was a fourteen year-old in ecstasy.

In 1980, I had a six inch AM radio pasted to my ear, sitting on a Kentucky hillside at a high school marching band contest when Tony Roberts screamed over the Mutual Broadcasting Network, "It's Goooooood!!!!!" Harry Oliver's 51-yard field goal on the last play of the game had just given Notre Dame a 29-27 victory over Michigan. It still gives me chills to this day when I hear it.

In 1988, I ran onto the field and kissed the ground after Pat Terrell knocked down Steve Walsh's two-point conversion attempt and the Irish beat Miami 31-30. After Reggie Brooks' diving two-point conversion catch in 1992 beat Penn State 17-16, I high-fived everyone in section 18 of Notre Dame Stadium. Everyone, that is, except my Nittany Lion friend Richard, who was quite pale at the time.

I've also stood chilly and dumbfounded as Boston College's David Gordon booted the Irish from the number one ranking in 1993 with a 41-yard field goal as time expired. I was there when an evil yellow flag went floating across the Orange Bowl grass as Rocket Ismail streaked down the sideline with the "punt return for a TD that never was" in the final minute against Colorado in 1991. My first Notre Dame game ever was Purdue's amazing/depressing 15-14 victory over the Irish at Ross-Ade Stadium in 1981.

I've been nauseous. I've reached nirvana. I'm a college football fan.

Great finishes are not necessarily great games. In fact, many remarkable endings came at the conclusion of rather dull or sloppily played contests. Likewise, many "Games of the Century" had very anti-climactic finishes. The 1971 Nebraska-Oklahoma game is generally regarded as one of the greatest ever played. But the game essentially ended with 1:30 remaining. The famous 10-10 tie between Notre Dame and Michigan State in 1966 ended when Ara Parseghian decided to run out the clock instead of risking a loss. These were legendary games, not legendary finishes.

You'll notice there aren't many overtime games in the book. Essentially, overtimes ruin drama, like a motion picture that's twenty minutes too long. Admit it, when you played football in your backyard as a kid, you didn't yell, "It's the fourth overtime and if they score here and hold the Tigers' on their four downs they'll win the championship!" No, it was something like this..."Three seconds left, two seconds, one second, he throws it to the endzone....It's caught! Touchdown! Touchdown!!"

Division I-A adopted overtime in 1996. The other divisions have had overtime since 1981 for conference-only games and tournament ties, and 1996 for all games. The few overtime games in the book are remarkable specifically for their regulation ending, in addition to the overtime finish.

Before you choke on your beer, upset about the games I've left out of the book, please remember this. Approximately 600 teams currently play NCAA college football. That's around 200,000 games played in the past 30 years. Which means that this book covers 5/100ths of one percent of all the games played in the past three decades.

There's some room for debate, don't you think? That's why the games in the book are not ranked, they are chronicled. They are the unbelievable, the astounding, the improbable moments that make college football so special.

This book is for you- the loyal, rabid fan who bleeds crimson and cream, garnet and black, green and white, maize and blue, and every other combination of alma mater colors. For you to remember those moments of soaring jubilation and utter despair. Chances are, there's a finish in this book that will make you sick. I'm sorry.

Just remember, for every distraught, losing fan throwing up in the bathroom, there's another ecstatic, winning one playing the CD over and over and over.

Update May 2006

Six years have gone by, and many more heartburn-inducing finishes have transpired, since the first edition of this book was released. If there's one question that I've been asked most about the book, it's "Why didn't you rank them?"

Well, I didn't think it was possible to do justice to these games by ranking one higher than another. To me, they all were fascinating. All worthy of their own special spot in this paper time capsule of college football.

But really, that's un-American, isn't it?

We want rankings! Especially college football fans. Let's face it, without rankings, what would we argue about? Who could we curse? Why would we listen to sportstalk shows? Without rankings, bloggers would be out of business.

Rankings are a necessary part of the U.S. economy!

So to appease the insatiable appetite of Americans to rank every possible artifact of society, as well as save the value of the dollar, I've done my part and polled 85 members of the Football Writers Association of America.

I asked them to rank their Top Ten Heart Stoppers, the greatest college football finishes since 1970, using the following criteria.

- Division I-A game since 1970
- Improbable dramatic ending
- A game on a "National Stage"
- High drama in the final five minutes

So here it is America. Start typing those angry emails. Get on your cell phones. Call the closest sportstalk jock immediately.

These are the Top Ten Heart Stoppers. You can read all about them in the pages that follow. (Ten points awarded for first place, nine for second place, and so on. First place votes in parentheses.)

1.	Stanford – California, 1982	(47)	736
2.	Boston College – Miami, 1984	(17)	621
3.	Texas – USC, 2006	(6)	447
4.	Miami - Nebraska, 1984	(3)	406
5.	USC – Notre Dame, 2005	(4)	390
6.	Ohio State – Miami, 2003	(2)	365
7.	Colorado – Michigan, 1994	(1)	251
8.	BYU – SMU, 1980	(1)	212
9.	Colorado – Missouri, 1990	(1)	142
10.	Auburn – Alabama, 1972		119

A total of 109 different games received votes. Here are the ones that received more than 30 points.

Florida – Georgia, 1980	(1)	102
Notre Dame – Houston, 1979		77
LSU – Kentucky, 2002		76
Nebraska – Missouri, 1997		66
Iowa – LSU, 2005		66
Penn State – Miami, 1987		46
Notre Dame – Miami, 1988		45
Michigan State – Ohio State, 1974		38

My thanks to the following journalists who participated in the poll and to the others who chimed in with memories rather than rankings.

Beano Cook	ESPN	Ken Costlow	Arlington Morning News
David Wharton	Los Angeles Times	John Harris	CollegeFootballNews.com
Tom O'Toole	College Editor, USA Today	John Lukacs	Author/Historian
Pat Forde	Columnist, ESPN.com	Jason Kelly	South Bend Tribune
Ivan Maisel	Senior writer, ESPN.com	Joe Hornstein	Orange Bowl Committee
Teddy Greenstein	Columnist, Chicago Tribune	Mike Goodman	Author, Pythagoras' College Football Book
Edwin Pope	Columnist, Miami Herald		
Dennis Dodd	Senior Writer, CBS Sportsline.com	Eric Hanson	South Bend Tribune
BJ Schecter	Sports Illustrated	Donnie Collins	The Times-Tribune, Scranton PA
Tom Dienhart	Columnist, The Sporting News	Charles Durrenberger	Arizona Daily Star
Chris Fallica	Producer, ESPN	Don "Fox" Bryant	Univ. of Nebraska (emeritus)
Bruce Feldman	Senior Writer, ESPN the Magazine	Braden Gall	Producer- Rivals Radio
		Bobby Burton	Executive Vice President, Rivals.com
Tony Moss	NFL Editor/Head Columnist, The Sports Network	Craig Barnes	South Florida Sun-Sentinel
Ralph Russo	Associated Press	Jeff Rapp	Columbus Sports Publications
Mark Snyder	Detroit Free Press	Tim Carmody	Football Today
Bob Condotta	Seattle Times	Embele Awipi	Columnist, The Salinas Californian
Irv Moss	Columnist, Denver Post	David Unkle	Slam! Sports
Mike Kern	Philadelphia Daily News	Mike Wachsman	Buckeye Sports Bulletin
Dave Hooker	Knoxville News Sentinel	Ryan Wood	Lawrence Journal-World, Lawrence KS
Ron Higgins	Memphis Commercial Appeal		
Tim Griffin	San Antonio Express News	Calvin Watkins	Columnist, Dallas Morning News
Corky Simpson	Tucson Citizen	Buck Turnbull	Des Moines Register (retired)
Chris Murray	Philadelphia Tribune	Tommy Hicks	Mobile Register
Ron Maly	Des Moines Register	Don Borst	Lindy's Sports Annuals
Andrew Logue	Des Moines Register	Vince Thompson	American Football Coaches Association
Alan Schmadtke	Orlando Sentinel		
Jimmy Burch	Ft. Worth Star Telegram	Harold Vigodsky	Clemson University
Jon Solomon	The Birmingham News	Vahe Gregorian	St. Louis Dispatch
Tony Duarte	Editor, CougZone, Rivals.com	Jordan Burchette	Maxim/College Sports TV
Tim Schnettler	The Bryan-College Station Eagle	Mark Wangrin	San Antonio Express News
		Joseph Person	The State
Tom Murphy	Columnist, Mobile Register	Mike Lopresti	Gannett News Service
Jim Johnson	Columnist, SouthernPigskin.com	Don Whitten	The Oxford Eagle
Rex Lardner	Managing Editor, American Football Monthly	Tim Gayle	Montgomery Advertiser
		Murray Olderman	National Columnist/Author
Pete Fiutak	CollegeFootballNews.com	Jerry Hogan	Freelance, New York
Paul Falewicz	Columnist, D2Football. Com	Nick Vista	Michigan State Univ. (retired)
Patrick Smith	Paul Finebaum Radio Network	Gregg Ellis	NE Mississippi Daily Journal
Ted Miller	Seattle Post-Intelligencer	Jeff Rapp	Buckeye Sports Bulletin
E. Lee North	Historian	Rich Kaipust	Omaha World Herald
Mike Babcock	Freelance writer, Nebraska	Todd Jones	Columbus Dispatch
Mike Huguenin	Orlando Sentinel	Dave Max	SportsPedia, Inc.
Mark Chalifoux	SportsFan Magazine		
Lindy Davis	Lindy's Sports Annuals		
Larry Cathey	Freelance writer, Detroit MI		
Jack Kerwin	National Columnist		
Kent Stephens	College Football Hall of Fame		

Yale vs. Harvard

"Never in my lifetime will I ever see another ending like that one. It just doesn't happen."—John Yovicsin

THE BACKGROUND

OK, so I lied. The book doesn't start at 1970.

But you can't write a book documenting the greatest college football finishes unless you start with *The Game.*

Harvard-Yale 1968. The founding father of great finishes from the past three decades.

The Yale Elis (8-0) entered the finale of the 1968 season with a 16-game winning streak, hoping to capture their second straight Ivy League Championship with a win over arch-rival and undefeated Harvard (8-0). The Crimson, seeking their first-ever outright Ivy title, boasted the nation's best scoring defense, allowing just 7.6 points per game.

But led by future NFL star runningback Calvin Hill and record-setting quarterback Brian Dowling, who hadn't lost a game he finished since sixth grade, Yale shocked Harvard in the first half. Dowling ran for one TD, threw to Hill for another (making Hill the all-time leading scorer at Yale), then threw to Del Marting for a third score. The Elis led 22-0 in the second quarter.

The highly anticipated 85th meeting between the two schools had turned into a rout even before halftime.

Harvard coach John Yovicsin, desperate to stir up his team's offense, benched quarterback George Lalich in favor of junior Frank Champi midway through the second quarter. Champi, a javelin thrower who started the season as a fourth-string QB, had just five completions the entire season.

"He looked scared to death," recalled his offensive lineman and future Academy Award-winning actor Tommy Lee Jones. "It all looked overwhelming to him." But the wide-eyed Champi quickly overcame his butterflies, drove the team 64 yards in 12 plays, and capped it off with a 15-yard touchdown pass to Bruce Freeman with 44 seconds remaining in the half. The Crimson botched the extra point. Yale took a 22-6 lead into the locker room.

Not a bad job by the nervous Champi. But not good enough to keep him in the game.

Yovicsin sent Lalich back on the field to start the second half, but the senior QB could muster nothing in three plays. Harvard punted back to Yale, but the Elis fumbled on the Yale 25. Harvard's Freeman recovered. Champi then re-entered for good. When Crimson fullback Gus Crim scored on a one-yard TD run to cut the margin to 22-13, Harvard had hope.

But not for long.

Intent on placing an exclamation mark on his illustrious Yale career, Dowling marched the Elis downfield on eight plays early in the fourth quarter. He scorched the Harvard defense with his fourth TD of the game, a five-yard run off the right side to make the score 28-13 with 10:44 to play in the game.

Feeling no need to go for a two-point conversion, Yale coach Carmen Cozza elected to kick the extra point and the Elis had a nearly insurmountable 29-13 lead. "I just didn't figure it was possible for Harvard to come back," he said. "There was just no way it could have happened."

Indeed, the Yale defense held, and, as Dowling marched the Elis toward another score, the Yale fans waved white handkerchiefs in Harvard Stadium screaming, "We're No.1, You're No.2."

With under four minutes to play, Yale wanted more. Dowling threw a screen pass to fullback Bob Levin who took it to the Harvard 14-yard line, but then fumbled. The Eli's sixth fumble of the game. Harvard's Steve Ranere recovered with 3:34 remaining, giving the Crimson the ball but hardly a chance, down by 16 points.

Champi did move Harvard to the Yale 38, where he faced third-and-18. Stepping up in the pocket, Champi was buried by two Yale linemen. But as he fell to the ground, the ball squirted out to his left where tackle Fritz Reed picked it up and rambled diagonally downfield 25 yards to the Yale 15-yard line. "I think he was trying to lateral," recalled Reed, "and the ball came out on the ground. It was just lying there."

The ball started to take on a crimson color. Champi's arm suddenly appeared golden.

From the 15, Champi rolled right and zipped a completion to Freeman at the Yale 5. The sophomore split end turned and bulled his way into the end zone for the score. Yale 29, Harvard 19.

Forty-two seconds on the clock. Champi looked for Peter Varney on the two-point conversion. The ball fell incomplete. But a flag flew. Yale was called for pass interference, giving the Crimson another chance. This time Crim barreled over for the two points and the score was 29-21.

Harvard Stadium shook. The Crimson tried the onside kick. Ken Thomas squibbed it across the 50-yard line where Yale's Brad Lee, an offensive guard, tried to pounce on it. But as he fell to the ground, another Yale defender tripped over Lee's helmet and the ball popped free at the Yale 49. Harvard's Bill Kelly recovered it.

Suddenly the impossible seemed plausible, if still improbable.

Harvard had the ball again. Dowling got anxious on the Yale sidelines and asked to play defense. "On the last series, I asked Carm if I could go in," remembered Dowling."As a quarterback, you should have a good idea of defenses. I had defensive experience in high school and had 32 interceptions."

Cozza kept Dowling on the sidelines. They watched as Champi ran around left end for 14 yards to the 35, before being tackled by Mike Bouscaren. Then another flag on Yale. Bouscaren was called for a face-mask penalty. The ball was moved to the Yale 20.

Thirty-two seconds left. Champi tried Freeman in the end zone. Incomplete. Then he threw for running back Jimmy Reynolds. Incomplete again. Twenty seconds remained.

Third down and 10. Champi and the Crimson surprised the Elis with a draw play to Crim who burst through a gaping hole to the Yale six-yard line. Harvard quickly called timeout with 0:14 on the clock.

It was too ridiculous for the Harvard fans to hope for another Crimson touchdown and two-point conversion to tie the game. Wasn't it? Sixteen points in 42 seconds? C'mon.

Champi looked to throw, but was sacked at the eight-yard line by Yale's Jim Gallagher. The Crimson called their final timeout with three seconds left.

The Harvard substitute quarterback had one final chance.

THE PLAY
CD 1—Track 1—*Ken Coleman,* Harvard Football Radio Network

A play that lives forever in Ivy League folklore.

Champi took the snap, dropped back to the 15, pump faked twice, ran up to the 10, faked a throw to the left, then to the right, shook off a tackle, ran back to the 16, looked right, turned left, then just as he was pounded by a Yale defender, launched a toss to the left side of the end zone where runningback Vic Gatto had sneaked open.

Champi described it his way. "I got hit. I thought someone was breathing down my neck. I scrambled. I threw off my wrong foot. Gatto was open for a moment. After that, I remember feeling a sense of inevitability. I thought, 'We've come this far.' I was very confident. It was inevitable.

"I just threw it in his general direction," he said.

Harvard fans flooded the field not once, but twice in the frantic final seconds. Photo courtesy of Harvard Athletics

Those fans who hadn't hyperventilated watching Champi dance around for almost 10 seconds, saw Gatto, the first 2,000-yard rusher in Harvard history, playing with a bad left knee, gather in the touchdown pass as he fell backward in the end zone with no time remaining. Astoundingly, Harvard trailed 29-27.

Gatto was picked up by his teammates. Crimson fans stormed the field. Harvard had miraculously scored two touchdowns in the final 42 seconds. After a long delay to clear the field of fans, the Crimson would now go for the two-point conversion, a 29-29 tie, and a share of the Ivy League title.

Could there be any doubt what would happen next? Yale was playing against fate.

It was almost anti-climactic. Champi rolled right, stopped, looked left, then threw to Pete Varney who ran a slant pattern from the left over the middle into the end zone. He had inside position. He had the ball. Harvard had the 29-29 tie. It certainly felt like a Crimson victory.

Hordes of Harvard faithful re-flooded the field, celebrating perhaps the most thrilling tie in the history of college football.

THE AFTERMATH

The two teams shared the Ivy League title with identical 8-0-1 records, but it seemed that Harvard's piece of the pie was a little bigger. The headline of the student newspaper, the *Harvard Crimson*, read "Harvard beats Yale 29-29."

"I don't know who said, 'A tie is like kissing your sister,' but I'll take this game just the way it ended," said Yovicsin.

"It was almost like a nightmare, really," said Cozza." I don't know how else to explain it. We feel like we lost it, even though we didn't. Something like that won't happen again in 1,000 years."

Dowling was bitter. "I don't want to take anything away from Champi, but he fumbled once and his tackle ran 23 yards, and that facemask penalty wasn't any of his doing either. He didn't pull it out, his team did."

Champi was king for a day. The next year, two games into his senior season at Harvard, he quit football to concentrate on track.

Dowling, who passed up offers to play at Ohio State and Michigan and instead enrolled at Yale, finished his senior year holding both season and career records for most touchdowns, yards passing, and total offense in his four years at Yale. After graduation, he spent a decade bouncing around numerous NFL teams as a back-up quarterback in Minnesota, New England, Green Bay, Washington, and Los Angeles.

Carmen Cozza retired in 1996 after 10 Ivy League championships and 32 years as head coach of the Elis.

Yale	7	15	0	7	-29
Harvard	0	6	7	16	-29

YALE	Dowling 3 run (Bayless kick)
YALE	Hill 3 pass from Dowling (Bayless kick)
YALE	Marting 5 pass from Dowling (Marting pass from Dowling)
HARV	Freeman 15 pass from Champi (kick failed)
HARV	Crim 1 run (Szaro kick)
YALE	Dowling 5 run (Bayless kick)
HARV	Freeman 15 pass from Champi (Crim run)
HARV	Gatto 8 pass from Champi (Varney pass from Champi)

Attendance 40,280

Oregon vs. UCLA

"That was the greatest comeback I've ever been around."—*Jerry Frei*

THE BACKGROUND

If ever there was one week when it truly hurt to be a UCLA fan, October 3-10, 1970 was the time. Could anything be worse than the fate bestowed on the Bruins in back-to-back games?

October 3rd, the No.2-ranked Longhorns of Texas hosted UCLA. Riding a 22-game winning streak, Texas was an overwhelming 21-point favorite to roll over Tommy Prothro's 13th-ranked Bruins. That's not the way it happened.

Led by the sizzling arm of quarterback Dennis Dummit, UCLA shocked Texas by collecting a school record 340 yards passing, and by slowing down Darrell Royal's vaunted Longhorn wishbone attack. The Bruins held a 17-13 lead late in the fourth quarter when Texas took the ball with just 58 seconds remaining.

On the fifth play of the final series, quarterback Eddie Phillips fumbled out of bounds at the UCLA 45. Only 20 seconds were left.

Down by four, facing third-and-19, and with their winning streak in jeopardy, Phillips threw a desperation pass over the middle to Cotton Speyrer at the UCLA 20. Speyrer jumped, along with two UCLA defenders. The Texas receiver was the only one standing as he came down with the ball. Speyrer ran the final 20 yards untouched for the stunning 45-yard touchdown reception with :12 left, and Texas won 20-17 as Memorial Stadium in Austin, Texas went berserk.

One week later, the Bruins (3-1) regrouped to host the Oregon Ducks (2-2). Head coach Jerry Frei had assembled an up-and-coming staff in Eugene, featuring offensive coach John Robinson, and defensive backs coach George Seifert. He also had a sparkling sophomore quarterback by the name of Dan Fouts, and a record-setting tailback in Bobby Moore (later known as Ahmad Rashad). The Ducks had the second-best passing attack in the country.

The Bruins fell behind 21-10 in the second quarter as Fouts scored on two TD runs, then handed off to Moore for another 15-yard touchdown to offset an early 62-yard romp by UCLA tailback Marv Kendricks.

But then Dummit, a senior who set both career and season passing records at UCLA, carried the Bruins on his back. After a shaky start, he scored on a one-yard sneak at the end of the second quarter, then came out in the second half by throwing a 31-yard strike to Gary Campbell for a 26-21 UCLA lead.

When Fouts fumbled a bad snap at the UCLA one-yard line, Dummit marched his squad 96 yards down the field, hitting Terry Vernoy with a 26-yard touchdown pass to make it 33-21 Bruins.

Dummit continued his aerial assault. In the fourth quarter, he hit Campbell again, this time for a 15-yard score and UCLA was cruising with a 40-21 lead.

"He's not only the best quarterback I've seen this year," said Frei about Dummit. "But there were periods when he was the best quarterback I've ever seen."

Meanwhile with just 4:38 left and the game seemingly lost, Frei pulled his own quarterback Fouts, and replaced him with senior captain Tom Blanchard, whose injured knee had prevented him from more playing time in his final season.

It took Blanchard 33 seconds to put the Ducks on the scoreboard. Moore caught a Blanchard toss at the UCLA 15, then avoided a tackler en route to a 29-yard score to make it 40-28 UCLA with four minutes left.

Despite the quick score, Prothro still felt the game was on ice, and sent in back-up QB Jim Nader. "We thought we had the game won and weren't going to throw anyway," said the Bruins' coach. Three plays after taking the ball at the UCLA 47, Nader fumbled. Oregon's Delton Lewis recovered at the Bruins' 40.

Blanchard came back in and continued the rally. On the second play, Moore broke down the sideline, hesitated, then beat the coverage of linebacker Max Kuppner. Blanchard connected with him, Moore spun away from two UCLA defenders at the 10-yard line and raced into the end zone, completing a 40-yard touchdown pass.

In 12 seconds, the Ducks had scored again.

Suddenly it was 40-35 with 2:10 left and the Bruins fans in the LA Coliseum were suffering from an acute case of déjà vu.

There was no remedy.

The Ducks tried an onsides kick. Ken Woody chipped the ball just beyond the 10-yard minimum where Dan Frease pounced on it. It was Oregon's ball again.

On second-and-eight from the UCLA 45, Moore took a sweep right with Blanchard as a lead blocker. The Bruins stuffed it for no gain.

Blanchard separated his shoulder on the play.

Frei called time-out. "Tom came over to the bench," said Frei. "He had a pained look in his eye and we asked if he was hurt and wanted out."

Blanchard wanted in. He came back on the field and on third down, threw long down the sideline for Leland Glass. Bruins Jerry Jaso and Allan Ellis went up for the jump ball with Glass. Both Glass and Jaso came down with it. The officials ruled a simultaneous catch and awarded Oregon the first down at the UCLA 11.

After the pass, Blanchard walked over to the sidelines and told Frei, "It's gone...my shoulder."

The senior who led the furious comeback, had to leave the game. Re-enter Dan Fouts.

Moore carried up the middle for six to the UCLA five-yard line. But then linebacker Rob Scribner sacked Fouts for a 10-yard loss. The Ducks were faced with third-and-14 at the UCLA 15 with under a minute remaining.

THE PLAY

Assistant coach John Robinson had called the offensive plays from the press box during the fourth quarter Oregon comeback. Forced to pass, he expected the Bruins to look for Moore (who had 103 yards rushing and 131 yards receiving) to be the primary receiver, remembering how the tailback beat the linebacker coverage for the previous touchdown.

"Robby figured that the UCLA cornerback would take Moore this time instead of leaving him isolated on a linebacker," said Frei.

Fouts took the snap. Moore broke down the left sideline, while leading Ducks receiver Bob Newland went down the right sideline. As Robinson predicted, Bruins cornerback Reynaud Moore drifted over to help the linebacker covering Moore. That left tight end Greg Specht open over the middle.

Before safety Ron Carver could pick up Specht, Fouts rifled a bullet into the end zone.

Specht grabbed it with 0:30 on the clock. A 15-yard touchdown reception. Shockingly, Oregon had scored 20 points in the final four minutes to take the lead 41-40.

Dummit did get one last chance, and re-entered the game in the final seconds. But after moving the ball to midfield, his Hail Mary pass on the last play was intercepted by Bill Brauner as time expired.

UCLA had lost for the second week in a row in the cruelest of fashions. "I've never seen one like it," said Prothro of the Oregon comeback.

Frei concurred. "Tonight's game has to top anything that's ever happened to me," he said.

THE AFTERMATH

Nineteen-seventy was Prothro's last year at UCLA. After the Bruins finished 6-5, he resigned to take the job as head coach of the Los

Angeles Rams. Prothro was replaced the next year by Franklin Cullen Rodgers, Jr., better known as Pepper Rodgers, who brought with him from the previous three-year stint at Kansas, assistant coach Terry Donahue.

The following week, Moore became Oregon's all-time leading scorer in his junior year with a touchdown run against Idaho. Fouts, rather skinny at 6-3, 187 lbs, broke 10 school passing records during the '70 season, including a season best 2,390 yards in the air. But the Ducks finished the year 6-4-1 after winning just one of their final four games of the season. Then, after a disappointing 5-6 campaign in '71, Frei was replaced as Oregon head coach by Dick Enright.

Fouts, Moore, and Blanchard, all were NFL draft picks. Blanchard went to the NY Giants in the 12th round of the '71 draft, and ended up using his punting skills in the NFL. Moore, a first-round pick of St. Louis in '72, later turned into a successful wide receiver for the Minnesota Vikings, and Fouts, chosen in the third round of the '73 draft by San Diego, became a Hall-of-Fame NFL quarterback.

October 10, 1970 — Los Angeles, California

ORE	14	7	0	20	- 41
UCLA	7	11	15	7	- 40

UCLA	Kendricks 62 run (Barnes kick)
ORE	Fouts 14 run (kick failed)
ORE	Fouts 1 run (Moore pass from Fouts)
UCLA	Barnes 24 FG
ORE	Moore 15 run (Woody kick)
UCLA	Dummitt 1 run (Kendricks run)
UCLA	Campbell 31 pass from Dummitt (Christiansen pass from Dummitt)
UCLA	Vernoy 26 pass from Dummitt (Barnes kick)
UCLA	Campbell 15 pass from Dummitt (Barnes kick)
ORE	Moore 29 pass from Blanchard (Woody kick)
ORE	Moore 40 pass from Blanchard (Woody kick)
ORE	Specht 15 pass from Fouts (run failed)

Attendance 44,722

Kentucky vs. Vanderbilt

"I knew the fans would make them throw."—John Ray

THE BACKGROUND

Two miserable teams on a miserable, rainy, see-your-breath-through-the-plastic-parka kind of day in Nashville, Tennessee.

Only 19,833 fans showed up at Vanderbilt Stadium for the Commodores' homecoming game against SEC doormat Kentucky. Only a handful of them stayed for the dumbfounding finish, which turned an afternoon nap into an unforgettable nightmare... or a delirious dream ending, depending on which side of the Tennessee-Kentucky border you lived.

This was a game for only true fans of the two schools. Vanderbilt (3-4-1, 1-3 SEC), sported an anemic offense that hadn't scored a point at home in the last 12 quarters. Kentucky (2-6, 0-5 SEC) had lost 17 straight conference games. In his third year as head coach, John Ray's Wildcats had never won two consecutive games, a streak that dated back to 1967, two years before Ray arrived in Lexington after leaving his assistant head coaching position under Ara Parseghian at Notre Dame.

Against Vandy, the 'Cats had a chance for an actual winning streak, fresh off a 33-27 victory over Virginia Tech. Sophomore safety Darryl Bishop intercepted Tech's Don Strock (the nation's leading passer), twice in the first four minutes of that game to help UK to a 20-0 first-quarter lead they barely held on to for the win.

Not surprisingly to the fans in Nashville, the first half of the UK-Vandy struggle ended in a 0-0 tie. The Wildcats missed two first-half field goals. Commodores kicker Hawkins Golden

blew a 25-yarder of his own. This was ugly. Mercifully, on the third play of the second half, UK's Jim Reed broke loose on a 44-yard touchdown run, giving the visting Wildcats a 7-0 lead.

With Vandy's home scoreless streak up to 15 consecutive quarters, the Commodores finally broke through in the fourth period on a 69-yard drive capped by a four-yard run by Jamie O'Rourke with 10:21 to play in the game. The score was tied 7-7.

Then Vandy looked to take the lead for good. But with 2:29 to play, Golden missed another attempt, this time from 42 yards. Kentucky took over, but failed to threaten. Faced with a fourth-and-eight on the UK 44 and just under 50 seconds left in the game, Ray elected to punt the ball away.

"I didn't want Vandy to get within range and kick a field goal," he explained. "With the slippery football, due to the rain, and the field position, we decided to give them the ball and hope we could get a fumble and kick a field goal."

As remote of a chance as that sounded, especially since UK kicker Tom Kirk had already missed three field-goal attempts in the game, what actually occurred was even more implausible.

Vandy's Walter Overton took a fair catch of the UK punt at the Commodore 30-yard line. On first down, quarterback Steve Burger ran a keeper for a four-yard loss. The clock kept runnning, ticking down toward 0:00. Apparently, Vanderbilt had chosen not to risk a turnover and settle for the 7-7 tie.

Game 3

THE PLAY

CD 1—Track 2—*Caywood Ledford,*
University of Kentucky Football Network

The few loyal fans remaining, probably wet alumni, cascaded a cold mist of boos down toward coach Bill Pace on the Vandy sidelines.

Ray was disappointed. "We felt they would try to throw since it was homecoming and they wanted to win," he said.

But then, as if to appease the home crowd, Burger came to the line of scrimmage, took the final snap of the game from his own 26-yard line, and dropped back to pass.

At that moment, after a dull, mistake-filled game on a dreary day, a bolt of lightning struck Vanderbilt Stadium.

"We were trying to go long, intended for Gary Chesley," said Pace, "but the ball was underthrown."

By 10 yards. It was so far off target that UK's Darryl Bishop thought it was intended for another receiver. "What happened, I think, was that the dude ran a post [pattern]," said Bishop, "but [Burger] thought he was going to curl." Either way, Bishop found himself with a gift-wrapped interception headed his way, and open sailing in front of him.

As the final seconds ticked off the clock, the UK safety picked off the errant throw at the Vandy 43-yard line, then streaked left with a head of steam, storming toward the Vanderbilt goal line.

After three frustrating years as head coach, Ray watched hopefully as the impossible finish unveiled before him. But at the same moment, he contemplated the worse. "I was afraid that he might go out of bounds," Ray thought to himself as Bishop barreled toward the end zone, and the UK players boiled over with excitement on the sidelines.

The clock expired. Only Burger stood a chance of stopping Bishop. But at the Vandy five-yard line, he was knocked down by defensive end Cecil Bowens. Bishop raced in for the score. Touchdown Kentucky. No time left. In unforgettable fashion, the Wildcats had finally won two games in a row for the first time in almost four years.

UK's happy coach credited the home crowd

with influencing the wacky ending. "I knew the fans would make them throw," Ray said. "We needed that one. It has been two and one-half years of frustration. Maybe this is a sign that we're going to have some more good luck."

THE AFTERMATH

Unfortunately for Ray, his ray of hope faded quickly as Kentucky lost their final two games of the year to Florida and Tennessee, finishing with a 3-8 record. Ray lasted one more season at Kentucky before he was replaced in 1973 by Fran Curci. In his four years as head coach, Ray compiled a 10-33 record.

Vanderbilt concluded its season 4-6-1 after a 10-7 victory over Tampa and a season ending 19-7 loss to rival Tennessee. Bill Pace coached for six years at Vanderbilt, compiling a 22-38-2 record. He then went on to be an assistant coach with the New England Patriots, before returning to college as an assistant at Georgia Tech, Georgia, and Tennessee, then retiring in 1982. Pace died suddenly of a heart attack in May 1990.

Darryl Bishop had an illustrious career at Kentucky, finishing in 1973 with a school record 14 career interceptions, three for touchdowns. He was named first-team All-SEC in 1973 and became a sixth-round draft choice of the Cincinnati Bengals in 1974.

Kentucky	0	0	7	7	- 14
Vanderbilt	0	0	0	7	- 7

UK	Reed 44 run (Kirk kick)
VAND	O'Rourke 4 run (Stokes kick)
UK	Bishop 43 interception return (Kirk kick)

Attendance 19,833

Mississippi vs. Louisiana State

"We had only one second left and only one play left."
—Bert Jones

THE BACKGROUND

The sixth-ranked LSU Tigers were riding a 10-game winning streak, the longest current streak in major college football. Ole Miss (4-3), had just captured their first SEC win of the year the previous week against Vanderbilt 31-7. Although the two teams were bitter rivals, the Tigers, a pre-season No.1 pick by *Sports Illustrated* and 17-point favorites against the Rebels, must have had one eye on Ole Miss and the other on the next week's opponent, Alabama. Looming on the horizon for Charlie McClendon's Tigers was a trip to Birmingham for an SEC showdown with the undefeated No.2 Crimson Tide.

The Rebels, led by second-year coach Billy Kinard, took advantage of the situation, hanging close to LSU all evening. After trailing 10-6 at the half, Ole Miss quarterback Norris Weese capped a 69-yard drive with a one-yard TD run with 5:17 left in the third period. The Rebels led 13-10. Steve Lavinghouse's third field goal of the game with 14:17 to play in the game made it 16-10. Then, with 7:18 remaining, Lavinghouze set up to kick his fourth field goal of the game, a 27-yarder which would have broken a school record for most field goals in a game.

He missed.

A renewed sense of urgency and opportunity swept through the LSU crowd as the Tigers took over and Heisman Trophy candidate Bert Jones marched his team downfield.

Jones had LSU at the Rebel 34 with only four and a half minutes to play. However, on fourth-and-nine, he was sacked by Reggie Dill for an 11-yard loss and the Rebel players celebrated as Ole Miss took over at the 45.

Death Valley turned deathly silent. But the LSU defense quickly turned up the volume, forcing a Rebel punt after three plays. Ole Miss booted the ball through the end zone.

With 3:02 left, LSU took over on their own 20. A second chance for the Tigers.

Jones sparked another rally with a 23-yard toss to Gerald Keigley, moving the ball to the LSU 43. Soon, the Tigers faced fourth-and-two at the Ole Miss 49. Jones kept the Bayou Bengals alive, hitting Jimmy LeDoux for 10 yards along the sideline to the Ole Miss 39.

The drive continued.

Again LSU faced fourth down. This time they needed just inches. Chris Dantin burst through right tackle for six yards to the Ole Miss 24. The drive continued, but the clock suddenly became a factor.

A huge factor. "I'd rather fight any football team in America than that clock," said McClendon. "That clock, fellows, just doesn't give you any consideration."

Oh really? Well, it did this night. Just ask the Ole Miss fans.

Jones connected with Keigley for six more yards. The clock stood at 0:10. The ball sat at the Ole Miss 20. Trailing by six points, LSU took their last timeout.

Jones came back on the field and looked for Keigley over the middle. His pass fell incomplete. But Ole Miss linebacker Bob Bailess was called for pass interference. The ball was moved to the 10-yard line. Four seconds remained.

Jones had one more shot at the end zone. From the 10, he dropped back near the 20, pumped left, then fired for LeDoux over the middle. The pass was batted away by a diving Mickey Fratesi, triggering a massive celebration of the Rebels contingent who had traveled from Oxford to Baton Rouge.

Only one problem. The clock at Tiger Stadium still read 0:01. Somehow, to the amazement of the Ole Miss coaches and players, Jones' pass took only three seconds.

"We had started celebrating because we figured the game was over—there was no way Jones could have done what he did and still have a second remaining," remembered Ole Miss safety Harry Harrison.

Apparently clock operator James W. Campbell, Jr., had a bad view of the field. He said he started the clock by looking through a gap of people at Jones' feet.

The Tigers were given another chance.

THE PLAY
CD 1—Track 3—*John Ferguson,* LSU Sports Network

Ole Miss called timeout to try and set their defense. Jones went over to McClendon. The LSU coach decided on a play the Tigers used for two-point conversions, "Halfback Flat."

"Son, this is it," McClendon told his senior QB. Jones winked back at his coach, then trotted onto the field. Across the field, the Rebel QB could only watch and hope. "When they had only four seconds left, I didn't think they'd score," said Weese. "Then with one second left, I was afraid they would."

Three receivers lined up left. Sophomore halfback Brad Davis lined up as a split back to the left. LSU ran their third play in the final 10 seconds. Jones took the snap. The clock immediately hit 0:00.

Davis ran out of the backfield, straight to the left corner of the end zone. Keigley cut to the middle, playing the role of decoy. "When I turned inside, I kept screaming for the ball to take the heat off Brad," said Keigley.

Jones looked right at Davis, then tossed it

to the back of the end zone. "It may have been the worst pass I ever threw, an end-over-end job," recalled Jones.

"It was the type [of a pass] a kid would throw over a house going straight up and over," Harrison recalled.

Davis looked up for the ball. "I thought Brad lost it somewhere up there in the lights," said Jones.

He did.

"I lost the ball in the lights," said Davis. "I put my hand up there and I felt it. That was the first time I knew where the ball was."

At the corner end zone flag, Davis bobbled the ball, trying to stay in bounds.

Harrison came over to try and jar the ball loose. "He wasn't my man, but I came up and hit him. I knocked him out of bounds."

The Tiger fans held their breath. Did Davis hold on to the ball? The offical made an immediate signal. Touchdown LSU.

A tidal wave of frenzied LSU fans poured onto the field, forgetting that an extra point still remained. The score was tied at 16-16. After three minutes of scooting them off the field, Rusty Jackson came on and knocked through the winning PAT. LSU had escaped, 17-16.

"What happened to us was just unbelievable, said Harrison. "We beat them for 59 minutes and 59 seconds, and then..."

Kinard was crushed. " How many plays did they run in 10 seconds," he said. "It just wasn't fair. It just wasn't."

McClendon was overjoyed. "You'd have to call this one victory one of the all-time thrills in Tiger football history," he said.

They still do in Baton Rouge.

THE AFTERMATH

A sign was erected at the Mississippi-Louisiana border that read, "You are now entering Louisiana. Set your clock back four seconds." The 1973 Ole Miss media guide recapped the game with the headline, "Ole Miss 16, LSU 10 + 7."

Jones finished fourth in the 1972 Heisman Trophy balloting, which was won by Nebraska's Johnny Rodgers. Twenty years later, Jones joked about the last play. "If you find that clock operator, thank him for me."

LSU's Bert Jones throws for Brad Davis as the clock finally reaches 0:00. Photo courtesy of LSU Sports Information

The 17-16 victory was the last game of the winning streak for the Tigers who lost to undefeated Alabama the following week 35-21. The Tide was also the last team to beat LSU before the streak started in '71. LSU finished the season 9-2-1, losing to Tennessee 24-17 in the BlueBonnet Bowl.

Ole Miss finished the year 5-5, 2-5 in the SEC, marking the school's first losing record in the conference since 1964. After a 17-13 loss to Memphis State the following season left the Rebels 1-2, Kinard was fired and replaced by former Ole Miss coach John Howard Vaught, whom Kinard had replaced in 1971 when Vaught stepped aside for health reasons after 24 years as the Ole Miss head coach. Vaught and the Rebels finished out the '73 season with a 6-5 record, before Vaught stepped aside again, ending his coaching career with a 190-61-12 record.

Mississippi	3	3	7	3 -16
LSU	7	3	0	7 -17

MISS	FG Lavinghouze 42
LSU	Jones 6 run (Jackson kick)
LSU	FG Jackson 29
MISS	FG Lavinghouze 38
MISS	Weese 1 run (Lavinghouze kick)
MISS	FG Lavinghouze 40
LSU	Davis 10 pass from Jones (Jackson kick)

Attendance 70,502

Auburn vs. Alabama

"You'd think memories would fade, but people still tell me exactly what they were doing that day."—David Langner

THE BACKGROUND

Alabama brought a 10-0 record and 21-game regular-season winning streak into Legion Field for their annual battle with Auburn (8-1), a bitter season-ending rivalry for state bragging rights started in 1893 and played every year since 1948.

The '72 season was supposed to be a rebuilding one for Ralph "Shug" Jordan's Tigers. With the loss of Heisman Trophy winner Pat Sullivan and consensus All-American Terry Beasley from a 9-2 squad in 1971, Auburn was picked to finish near the bottom of the SEC in '72.

That's not what happened. "The Amazin's," the nickname given to the overachieving Auburn squad, had slipped up only once all year, a 35-7 loss to a powerful LSU team.

Although ranked No.9 in the polls, Auburn was still a 16-point underdog to the No. 2-ranked Crimson Tide, coached by Paul "Bear" Bryant.

Bryant provided Auburn with some bulletin board material the week before the game. "I'd rather beat that cow college than beat Texas ten times," he said, referring to their upcoming Cotton Bowl game against Texas.

Auburn University boasts a very prominent College of Agriculture. Alabama was quite bullish when it came to recent post-season bowls, winless in their last five attempts.

But this day, the Tide plowed through Auburn for three quarters, with an offense made up of 99 percent ground game, 1 percent pass. Steve Bisceglia capped a 71-yard drive with a three-yard TD run in the second quarter to put the Tide up 6-0. However, Auburn defensive back Roger Mitchell blocked Bill Davis' extra point attempt. As the second quarter wound to a close, Alabama's defense, which held the Tigers to one first down in the half, got the Tide in scoring position again as Lanny Norris intercepted a Randy Walls pass at the Auburn 41 and returned it 28 yards to the 13.

But the Tigers scratched and clawed, holding Alabama to a Davis 14-yard field goal. The half ended with Alabama leading 9-0.

'Bama upped it to 16-0 when Wilbur Jackson scored from six yards out behind the blocking of John Hannah early in the third quarter. Meanwhile, Auburn had no offense. The Tide's defense, led by Wayne Hall and John Mitchell, held Jordan's Tigers to a miniscule 80 yards in total yardage for the entire game. In contrast, Alabama ran up 235 wishbone yards on the ground.

Tide quarterback Terry Davis threw just seven times, completing three. Unfortunately for Alabama, two of them were to Auburn defensive back David Langner.

Langner's first interception at the Alabama 35 resulted in a 22-yard Gardner Jett field-goal attempt that was botched after a bad snap. The Tiger offense couldn't get on track.

Their only productive drive of the afternoon came after Alabama's Greg Gantt missed a 50-yard field-goal attempt wide left at the end of the third quarter. The Tigers pieced together four first downs in a six-minute drive

An eery case of déjà vu for Crimson Tide fans as Bill Newton blocks Greg Gantt's punt...

that stalled at the Alabama 24. With only 9:15 to play, Jordan settled for a 42-yard field goal by Jett. Auburn still trailed 16-3.

"I remember the crowd booing when we went for the field goal," said Jordan. "We went for the field goal to create enthusiasm. We had some but we needed more."

About two touchdowns more.

Alabama took the kickoff, ran off another three and a half minutes on the ground, then lined up at midfield to punt the ball back to Auburn. Gantt waited for the snap, the sixth 'Bama punt of the game. His last punt traveled 72 yards.

This one went nowhere. It was blocked.

Linebacker Bill Newton, along with Ken Bernich, barreled into the 'Bama backfield. Newton smothered the ball with his body. Langner, who already had a superlative defensive day, was also rushing on the play. He found himself five yards behind the punter, all alone with the bouncing ball coming right at him. He picked it up in stride and scampered 25 yards untouched into the end zone. The clock read 5:30. Auburn was on the board again, slicing the lead to 16-10.

Still, Alabama just had to run out the clock, finish the season undefeated, and move onto the Cotton Bowl with a shot at the national championship.

The Tide got two first downs, one less than they needed. On third-and-four at the Alabama 48, linebacker Mike Neel caught Davis for a five-yard loss.

The Auburn defense, which held the Tide to 175 yards under their average total offense of 425 yards per game, had forced another Alabama punt.

Under two minutes remained.

THE PLAY
CD 1 - Track 4 —*Gary Sanders,*
Auburn Network

With their offense unable to move the ball, Auburn realistically had one chance.

Try to block the punt again.

Newton, a former walk-on, lined up in the exact same spot he had just a few minutes earlier. So did Langner.

Gantt took the snap again. Newton blew into the 'Bama backfield again. Newton blocked the kick again. It bounced to Langner again,

Game 5

...twice in the fourth quarter and David Langner (28) scores both times for Auburn. Photos courtesy of Auburn University Archives

who picked it up in stride again, and raced 20 yards for the touchdown...again.

Bizarre, improbable, stunning. Two identical blocked punts. Two identical Auburn touchdowns.

Langner was just as shocked as everyone else. "I didn't know what to think, it scared me to death. Both balls looked the same to me. They just bounced into my hands. All I had to do was pick it up and run."

Newton was equally surprised. "I was just trying to get through the same hole again. When they didn't touch me, and I saw the fullback go for somebody else, I knew I had it again."

(On the radio call, Auburn announcer Gary Sanders initially thought Mitchell made the second block, but actually it was Newton.)

Jett kicked the extra point with 1:34 on the clock. Auburn led by one point.

Deflated and without benefit of a passing attack, the Tide tried to get within field-goal range. But as if Langner hadn't done enough, he collected his second interception of the game at the Auburn 42 with 55 seconds left to seal the win. The Tigers' fantasy finish had turned reality. Auburn 17, Alabama 16.

Bryant took responsibility for the end of the game, forever known in Auburn football history as "Punt, 'Bama, Punt." "I've always said, and I mean this sincerely, that mistakes are head coaching. And of course, you saw what happened out there. The best coached team won. I did a lousy job," said Bryant.

"It was by far the greatest thrill I've ever had," said Langner, who hoarded the twin prized pigskins after the game, hoping to take them back to Auburn with him.

"You know, Langner has both balls, and he won't give me one," said a joking Newton. "I told him I should get one of those footballs. And I get half those points too."

THE AFTERMATH

'Bama still captured the SEC crown in '72, but they lost the Cotton Bowl game to Texas, 17-13, and ended the year ranked No. 7 with a 10-2 record.

The loss to Auburn was the only confer-

15

ence game Alabama did not win from 1971-1975 and their only regular season loss from '71-'74. The Tide won five straight SEC titles during that period with a conference record of 34-1.

The Tigers knocked off Colorado 24-3 in the Gator Bowl and finished the '72 season 10-1, ranked No.5 in the AP poll. Jordan was named UPI Southeastern Coach of the Year. In 1975, Jordan retired after 25 years as head coach at Auburn, the winningest coach in school history (176-83-6). Jordan passed away July 17, 1980.

Ten years passed before Auburn defeated Alabama again, a 23-22 win in 1982. It was Paul Bryant's last regular-season game as a head coach. Like Jordan, he also retired after 25 years at Alabama. The legendary Bryant was 232-46-9 as leader of the Crimson Tide. Four weeks after coaching his final game, a 21-15 Liberty Bowl victory over Illinois, the Bear died at age 70.

Auburn	0	0	0	17	-17
Alabama	0	9	7	0	-16

ALA	Bisceglia 3 run (kick failed)
ALA	FG Davis 14
ALA	Jackson 6 run (Davis kick)
AUB	FG Jett 42
AUB	Langner 25 blocked punt return (Jeff kick)
AUB	Langner 20 blocked punt return (Jeff kick)

Attendance 72,386

Nebraska vs. Missouri

"Any more thrills like this and I'll have ulcers."
—Missouri center Scott Anderson

THE BACKGROUND

National Champions 1970. National Champions 1971. The Nebraska Cornhuskers were coming to the end of an era. The Bob Devaney era. Devaney coached Nebraska from 1962-1972. After a 40-6 thrashing of Notre Dame in the 1973 Orange Bowl, Devaney retired, appointing his youngest assistant coach, 36-year-old Tom Osborne, the new leader of the Huskers.

Osborne started his head coaching career in 1973 with a 4-0 record, leading Nebraska to a No. 2 ranking. Then, in his very first Big Eight game as head coach, Osborne took the Huskers into Faurot Field to face the 14th-ranked Missouri Tigers, also 4-0.

Al Onofrio became head coach of Missouri in 1971. In his previous two games against Nebraska, Onofrio's Tigers had been outscored 98-0. The memories of those recent debacles hadn't slipped past the Missouri players. "I didn't mention last year's score once," said Onofrio.

He didn't have to. It's hard to forget 62-0. After two years without scoring a point against Nebraska, no one expected the Tiger offense to mount much of a threat this time around.

They didn't. Instead, the Missouri defense did.

Holding a potent Huskers offense to just two Rich Sanger field goals in the first half, the Tiger defense caught a break late in the second quarter. With Nebraska leading 6-3, Huskers quarterback David Humm bumped into his own pulling guard and fumbled the ball at the NU 24. Missouri middle guard Herris Butler recovered it with 1:04 left.

But the Nebraska defense, even more stingy than Missouri's, held the Tigers to a 31-yard field goal by Greg Hill with 31 seconds left in the half to tie the game at 6-6.

That's the way it remained through most of the second half. While Missouri managed just two first downs in the last two quarters, Nebraska moved up and down the field, rolling up a huge statistical advantage over the Tigers—21-7 in first downs and 440-170 in total yards.

The Missouri offense had a miserable seven yards passing for the entire game. But their defense had more lives than a cat reincarnated.

Somehow, in the second half, the Huskers could not score. Midway through the third quarter, after the Nebraska offense failed to cash in on a first-and-goal from the six, Sanger lined up for a short 21-yard field goal. It was blocked by Missouri's Butler.

Early in the fourth quarter, Humm drove the Huskers 69 yards to the Missouri 17 where he hit tailback Tony Davis with a pass. Davis coughed up the ball. Cornerback John Moseley recovered it.

Three plays later, the Tigers fumbled it back to Nebraska at the Missouri 19.

Surely, Nebraska would capitalize this time...No.

The Tiger defense held again. Sanger came on for a 33-yard attempt with 6:56 left. He missed it. The score remained 6-6.

With 4:08 left in the game, Humm moved

Missouri coach Al Onofrio was all smiles after his defense stymied Nebraska's final try. Photo courtesy of University of Missouri Archives

Nebraska into Tiger territory again. But Moseley made another huge play, intercepting Humm's pass at the Missouri 35 and returning it to midfield. Nebraska was left empty-handed for yet another time.

It was like a hockey game played entirely in the Missouri zone. Four Nebraska power plays. No goals.

Still, the Missouri offense was caught in neutral. Unable to move the ball, the Tigers were forced to punt from their 48 with 2:35 to play. Punter Jim Goble booted the ball high, over the head of Nebraska safety Randy Borg, a defensive star in the game who caught just as many passes from Missouri QB John Cherry (two interceptions) than Cherry completed to his own receivers (2 of 9).

But at this critical point, Borg may as well have taken out a gun, aimed it at his foot, and pulled the trigger.

In an ill-fated move, he retreated inside the Huskers' 10-yard line. "I debated for a moment whether to call for a fair catch and decided not to." Instead, Borg caught it, then bobbled it, then fumbled it. "I tried to run with it too soon, and the ball just slipped between my elbows," he said.

Missouri center Scott Anderson, streaking down the field after the snap, pounced on the loose ball at the Nebraska four-yard line. "I snapped the ball and nobody held me up. I went down the field hard and nobody touched me," said Anderson.

It took the Tigers two plays to score. Fullback Tom Mulkey bulled over right tackle from the one with 2:01 left. A four-yard scoring drive. A short-handed, breakaway goal. Missouri led 13-6. Faurot Field was shaking.

After the kickoff, Nebraska got the ball

back on their own 28. Facing a desperation situation, Humm tried one last time to get the Huskers in the end zone. This time, he caught fire.

Humm found wingback Rich Bahe for 31 yards. On the next play, he connected with tight end Larry Mushinskie for 20. Tailback Tony Davis then lost a yard. But at the Missouri 22, Humm struck again. He hit Bahe at the eight-yard line. Bahe cut over the middle then slipped into the end zone for the touchdown.

Just like that. Lightning. Four plays. Seventy-two yards. The Missouri lead was sliced to one point, 13-12.

Exactly 1:00 left on the clock. Now, for the first time as a head coach, Tom Osborne was faced with THE decision. "I knew it was coming as we moved downfield," he said.

Go for two, or take the tie.

THE PLAY

With a quarterback as hot as Humm (who happened to be from Las Vegas), Osborne rolled the dice.

The plan was for Humm to quickly roll left and look for Davis who had lined up just behind the tight end on the left side. Humm took the snap. Davis broke to the goal line then slid left, running parallel to the line of scrimmage. Humm ran a few steps to his left.

The left-handed quarterback rolled directly toward sophomore defensive end Bob McRoberts, who was going to drop off into pass coverage. He changed his mind. "David Humm rolled toward me and I thought 'Hey, he may run the ball.' So I came up to contain on the outside," said McRoberts.

Humm threw on the run, right in front of McRoberts. "He threw the ball right at me," said the surprised Tiger, who quickly thrust his hands up and got a piece of the ball.

Stripped of its velocity, the ball floated toward the goal line where 175-pound Tony Gillick was hovering in a zone defense. "I was looking for that exact play," said Gillick. "I knew they'd throw but I didn't know which way. Humm throws better going to his left so I just cheated over that way a little."

He cheated perfectly.

Gillick stepped in front of Davis, snatched the wounded pass, and set off a July 4th-like celebration in the state of Missouri. After running a few yards, Gillick was tackled to the ground at the 10 where his fellow teammates hugged him endlessly. The Tigers had upset Nebraska 13-12.

It was the first game Tom Osborne ever lost as a head coach. (Ten years later he would face the exact same situation at the end of a game. Only this time for the national championship, see Miami vs. Nebraska '84).

"It was probably as good a percentage play as we had," said Osborne. "If I had to do over, I would have called timeout and thought about a couple other plays."

Onofrio was glad he didn't. "What a day," the elated coach said. "It's just a great day."

THE AFTERMATH

After beating Texas 19-13 in the Cotton Bowl, Nebraska ended the '73 season 9-2-1 ranked No. 7 in the AP poll. The Huskers finished in the top 10 every year during the 1970s with the exception of 1977 when they were ranked No. 12.

Missouri's promising season, which started out 6-0, ended up 8-4 after the Tigers dropped four of their last five regular season games. However they did bounce back with a 34-17 Sun Bowl victory over Auburn to end the year ranked No.17, the only time during the decade that the Tigers were ranked in the AP Top 20 at the end of the season.

Al Onofrio was fired as the Missouri head coach after the 1977 season and replaced by Warren Powers. Onofrio was known for the many upsets his Tigers pulled off in the 1970s. Besides Nebraska in '73, they slayed eighth-ranked Notre Dame 30-26 in 1972 and, in an even more memorable game, stunned No.2 Ohio State 22-21 in 1976.

In that contest, Missouri, 19-point underdogs, rallied from a 21-7 halftime deficit in Columbus. Reserve quarterback Pete Woods, filling in for injured starter Steve Pisarkiewicz, drove the Tigers to the Ohio State two-yard line in the final moments. With 12 seconds left,

Woods hit Leo Lewis with a two-yard TD pass to bring Missouri within a point, 21-20.

Onofrio decided to go for the win. Brooks threw to the right corner of the end zone for tailback Curt Brown. The ball fell incomplete. Woods dejectedly turned and started walking off the field as the 89,000 fans celebrated in Ohio Stadium.

But then a late flag fell. Ohio State was called for defensive holding on the play. The Missouri coaches waved to Brooks to stay on the field. The Tigers had another chance. This time, Brooks ran the ball on a sprint option left. He dove between Buckeyes Kelton Dansler and Nick Buonamici into the end zone and the Tigers pulled off the stunning 22-21 upset.

| Nebraska | 6 | 0 | 0 | 6 | -12 |
| Missouri | 0 | 6 | 0 | 7 | -13 |

NEB	FG Sanger 42
NEB	FG Sanger 29
MU	FG Hill 35
MU	FG Hill 31
MU	Mulkey 1 run (Hill kick)
NEB	Bahe 22 pass from Humm (pass failed)

Attendance 68,170

Ohio State vs. Michigan State

"Until the films come out, we won't know who won."—Woody Hayes

THE BACKGROUND

The Ohio State Buckeyes were undefeated (8-0) and No. 1 in the country, an offensive juggernaut averaging over 40 points per game while outscoring their opponents 360-75.

How good was the Ohio State offense? They scored 24 of the last 26 times they had the ball.

Legendary Buckeyes coach Woody Hayes had just reached the milestone of his 200th victory, a 49-7 pasting of Illinois the week prior to traveling to Michigan State. While his team flourished, it was a tough year physically for Hayes, his 24th season as OSU's head coach. He suffered a heart attack on June 6, 1974, which temporarily slowed him down, but didn't keep him off the sidelines once the Buckeyes opened up their schedule.

Michigan State was 4-3-1 in head coach Denny Stolz' second year since taking over for longtime MSU coach Duffy Daugherty. Entering the Ohio State game as 25-point underdogs, the Spartans were hoping to duplicate their 1972 upset of the No.1-ranked Buckeyes, 17-12.

This was classic "three yards and a cloud of dust" Big Ten football.

Led by junior tailback Archie Griffin with 140 yards on the ground, the Buckeyes amassed 333 yards rushing while Michigan State had 230 yards. In contrast, Spartans quarterback Charlie Baggett completed just 5 of 13 for 98 yards while OSU's Cornelius Greene connected even fewer times (3 of 11 for 44 yards).

With OSU leading the defensive struggle 6-3 early in the fourth quarter, Baggett, whose 30-yard scramble led to MSU's only points at the end of the first half, broke off another long run. But in the clear at the MSU 44, he lost control of the ball and fumbled. Ohio State's Steve Luke recovered. "I was just about to tuck it under my arm and turn on the speed," said the junior quarterback. "And, somehow I dropped the ball."

The Buckeyes capitalized. In seven plays they moved to the MSU one-yard line where fullback Harold "Champ" Henson took it in for the score and OSU led 13-3 with nine minutes to play.

On the next possession, Baggett redeemed himself. He drove the Spartans from their own 20 to the Ohio State 44. There, he hit senior split end Mike Jones for a 44-yard touchdown pass. After a missed two-point conversion, the score was 13-9.

The Buckeyes' offensive machine then bogged down, gaining only nine yards in the next possession, and forcing a Tom Skladeny punt. Michigan State got the ball back with 3:30 left to play, trailing by four.

On first down at their own 12-yard line, Stolz called "44 veer," a quick opener to sophomore fullback Levi Jackson up the middle. "It's a simple fullback power play," explained Stolz.

Jackson broke free.

"After I got through the hole, I made a shoulder fake to the outside, then went straight through the secondary until I cut for the sideline," said Jackson. Down the right sideline sprinted Jackson, with safety Tim Fox giving chase. Fox made a desperate dive at the OSU 10

Levi Johnson's 88-yard TD run with just over three minutes to play game gave the Spartans the lead over No. 1 Ohio State. Photo courtesy of Michigan State University Sports Information.

but came up empty. Jackson had run 88 yards for an electrifying TD, putting the Spartans up 16-13.

Spartan Stadium was a madhouse. Players and fans mobbed Jackson. Play was delayed to clear the end zone.

After the kickoff, from their own 29, the Buckeyes began a final march downfield to preserve their No. 1 ranking.

It appeared to last one play. Greene threw on first down. Spartans linebacker Terry Mc-Clowry stepped in front of the pass and made a diving interception. At least that's what linesman Ed Scheck ruled. But umpire Frank Strocchia waved off the turnover, claiming the ball hit the ground. "There was no question about it that I picked it off cleanly, rolled over and showed it to the referees," said McClowry.

The official didn't buy it. The Buckeyes were given another life.

They took full advantage of it. On the next play, Griffin ripped off 31 yards on a draw up the middle. Seven plays later, Ohio State was at the MSU six-yard line. With the clock now

under a minute, Henson smashed forward for five yards, down to the one.

Twenty-six seconds remained and the Buckeyes had no timeouts left.

THE PLAY

Down three points, Hayes wasn't sending in his field goal unit. He called for Henson to try and blast it over from the one.

Henson didn't make it. There was a massive pile-up at the one-yard line. Fourteen seconds. The clock was running.

The Buckeyes desperately tried to get up. The Spartans defenders wouldn't let them off the pile. The clock kept dwindling.

Finally, the two teams separated and Ohio State scrambled to run another play, but would there be time?

The snap went through Green's legs. The clock read 0:00.

Wingback Brian Baschnagel picked up the loose ball. He then busted into the end zone. Linesman Scheck raised his hands indicating touchdown.

But at the same time field judge Robert Daganhardt and back judge William Kingzett were waving their arms. Was it a touchdown? Did Ohio State score and win the game? Or had time expired before the snap and Michigan State held on for the massive upset?

"The linesman held up two hands for a touchdown, that's all I know," said Baschnagel. "I scored."

Total confusion reigned. MSU fans flooded the field, jumping on the goalposts. Ohio State players streamed onto the field in celebration. So did Michigan State players. Both teams thought they had won.

The scoreboard still read MSU 16, OSU 13 as the players and coaches tried to figure out what happened. In the melee, the officials told the teams to go to their locker rooms. An announcement was made over the public address system that the result of the game was being held up pending clarification.

Clarification by Big Ten commissioner Wayne Duke, who was celebrating his 46th birthday at the game. After trying to make sense of the situation, Duke had to telephone the officials who had left the stadium via limousine for a nearby campus hotel.

Duke spoke with head referee Gene Calhoun, gave his decision to both coaches in the locker room, then returned to the press box and made an official statement to the press.

Meanwhile the emotionally wrought fans on the field were beside themselves. "If they give it to Ohio State, Wayne Duke better not come out of that press box 'cause I'd shoot him," one MSU fan on the field said.

After 46 minutes, the first delirious, then confused Spartan Stadium crowd heard the result over the P.A. system.

"Ladies and gentlemen. Michigan State has been declared the winner by the score of 16-13."

They were delirious again.

Duke explained his decision as a reaffirmation of the officials' ruling. "At the end of the game, the Ohio State players were attempting to unpile and it was ruled by the back judge and field judge, whose responsibility it is to maintain time on the field, that time had expired before the last play started."

In addition, replays showed that some of the Buckeyes were not set before the snap.

"Had time not expired, Ohio State would have been charged with a penalty for not being set on the line of scrimmage for one full second before the start of the play," said Duke.

However, there was much debate by those in attendance whether or not a fraction of a second was still on the clock when the final snap was made. In that case, OSU would have been assessed a five-yard penalty for illegal procedure and given one final play.

Hayes was furious. "It's ridiculous, they can't take this game away from us," he said. "I'll appeal, that's what I'll do, I'll appeal."

Duke squashed that idea. "That's the end of it," he said. "I don't want to discuss the subject further."

An apparently pesky reporter took the wrath of Hayes' anger in the locker room. "Unless you quit bothering me, I'm going to put my fist down your [expletive] throat!" shouted Hayes.

Once he calmed down, the Buckeyes head coach addressed the play.

"There were 25 seconds left when he ran the play with Henson. The referee should have called time out when they laid on the ball and would not let us run the play," he argued.

"That's the way the game is played," countered Spartans defensive tackle Jim Taubert, who was lying on the ball in the last frantic seconds. "When there's that little time left we just naturally take our time."

Stolz was simply overjoyed. "This was the greatest victory of any I ever had, the greatest day of my life," he exclaimed.

THE AFTERMATH

It was Ohio State's only defeat of the regular season. After knocking off Michigan 12-10, the Buckeyes won the Big Ten title, and positioned themselves for a shot at the national title when they faced USC (9-1-1) in the Rose Bowl.

Trailing the Trojans 10-7 in the fourth quarter, Ohio State rallied with two consecutive scoring drives to take a 17-10 lead. But USC's Pat Haden threw a 38-yard touchdown strike to J.K. McKay with 2:03 left to rally the Trojans to within 17-16. Then coach John McKay chose to go for the two-point conversion. Haden rolled out, looked for McKay again, but instead found Shelton Diggs in the end zone, who snagged the pass and USC led 18-17. A 62-yard FG attempt by the Buckeyes' Tom Skladeny fell short on Ohio State's final drive and USC took the Rose Bowl title, as well as a share of the national title.

The Buckeyes finished 10-2, ranked 3rd in the UPI poll, 4th in the AP.

Griffin captured the Heisman Trophy at the end of the '74 season, easily outpointing USC's Anthony Davis. He repeated the feat in 1975 to become the only two-time winner of the prestigious award.

Michigan State won their final two games and finished 7-3-1, Stolz's best season at MSU, earning him Big Ten Coach of the Year honors. He had a 19-13-1 record at Michigan State from 1973-75, then later coached at Bowling Green from 1977-85, and San Diego State from 1986-88.

Ohio State	3	0	3	7	-13
Michigan State	0	3	0	13	-16

OSU	FG Klaban 22
MSU	FG Neilsen 39
OSU	FG Klaban 20
OSU	Henson run (Klaban kick)
MSU	Jones 44 pass from Baggett (pass failed)
MSU	Jackson 88 run (Nielsen kick)

Attendance 78,533

Pittsburgh vs. West Virginia

"I don't think my feet hit the ground for a year."—*Bill McKenzie*

THE BACKGROUND

It's a 77-mile drive between Pittsburgh, Pennsylvania, and Morgantown, West Virginia. The two neighbors don't get along on the football field.

The Backyard Brawl is a bitter rivalry that has taken place nearly every fall since 1895.

Bobby Bowden knows about it. In 1970, Bowden's first year as head coach of West Virginia, he took his Mountaineer team into Pittsburgh to face the Panthers. West Virginia blasted out to a 35-8 halftime lead only to see Pitt rally for a remarkable 36-35 victory.

The Mountaineers fans were not happy. They banged on the doors of the West Virginia locker room, screaming obscenities. Bowden later called it one of his worst losses.

Beating Pitt was paramount in Morgantown and WVU hadn't done it in three years when they hosted the Panthers in 1975. Although West Virginia was 6-2 at the time, they were only 10-12 the previous two seasons, had a dreadful 16-14 homecoming loss to Tulane, and there were rumblings on campus about the head coach's job.

The Pittsburgh Panthers, also 6-2, rolled into Mountaineer Field heavily favored, ranked No.20, and sporting a star by the name of Tony Dorsett. Entering the game, the junior tailback ranked eighth in NCAA history with 3,599 career rushing yards. Earlier in his career he had already tied a NCAA record by rushing for 100 yards or more in nine games as a freshman.

It wouldn't be his last record.

On this day, however, Dorsett was matched run-for-run by WVU's Artie Owens. Dorsett had 107 yards on 22 carries. Owens rushed 17 times for 101 yards. Owens rambled for a 23-yard touchdown to give WVU a 14-7 lead in the fourth quarter. Dorsett countered by catching a nine-yard TD pass from quarterback Matt Cavanaugh to tie it up at 14-14.

That's where it stood with one minute left in the game. Perhaps the most famous minute in Backyard Brawl history.

With West Virginia deep in Pitt territory, needing only a field goal to win, fullback Ron Lee took a handoff from quarterback Dan Kendra. He fumbled.

Panthers linebacker Tom Perko recovered the ball at the Pitt 17 with 57 seconds left. The air went out of Mountaineer Field and Pittsburgh seemed to have salvaged a tie.

But Pitt coach Johnny Majors had a plan. Get a safe first down in the final seconds, then roll the dice with a long pass to get into field-goal range for a last second kick. The Panthers moved into a hurry-up offense.

Dorsett took a handoff from Cavanaugh on first down but was stuffed by tackle Rich Lukowski for a one-yard loss. On second down from the 16, Cavanaugh threw short to Gordon Jones who was knocked out of bounds at the 20 by WVU's John Schell. The clock stopped with 31 seconds left.

Still third-and-seven.

This time, Cavanaugh looked for Jim Corbett near the first-down marker. The pass was low. Corbett came back for the ball, caught

25

The goalposts came down in Morgantown with a small piece of the upright given to coach Bobby Bowden on his 46th birthday. Photo courtesy of West Virginia Intercollegiate Athletics

it, but fell to the ground two yards shy of the first down.

It was now fourth-and-two at the Pitt 25. The clock was running. The teams were scrambling. Suddenly a confused Cavanaugh called out a play, a sideline pass.

"Cavanaugh lost track of the down," said Majors. It wasn't third down, it was fourth down. Panic on the Pitt sideline.

Cavanaugh rushed the Panthers to the line of scrimmage. The crowd was screaming. The coaches were frantically trying to get the junior quarterback's attention. Nothing worked.

So in a moment of sheer desperation, both Majors and offensive line coach Joe Avezzano ran onto the field!

Flags flew. Whistles blew. The clock stopped with 18 seconds remaining. Pittsburgh was called for unsportsmanlike conduct and penalized half the distance to the goal.

"We had to stop him from running another play," said Majors. "We just had to take the penalty. There was no other way." If the Panthers failed on fourth down, West Virginia would have taken possession, already in field-goal range.

After the penalty moved the ball back to the 13-yard line, the Panthers finally got their punt team on the field. Larry Swider booted the ball. It was caught by Mark Burke, and downed at the Pitt 48 with just 10 seconds left.

West Virginia had no timeouts left. Bowden sent in the play.

Quarterback Kendra changed it.

While Kendra's No. 1 receiver, junior Tommy Bowden (the coach's son and future head coach), would probably get most of Pitt's attention, tight end Randy Swinson was supposed to run into the flat and look for the ball.

"I told him to run the 'snake.' That's where he turns upfield," explained Kendra. "The bench didn't know I was going to do it."

Kendra dropped back, threw down the left sideline, then got blasted just after he released the ball. "I never saw the pass," he said. Swinson did. He caught it, and at the Pitt 22 fumbled the ball out of bounds to stop the clock with 0:04 left.

Bowden was pleasantly shocked at his quarterback's veto power. "This is one time I don't care two cents for discipline," said the head coach.

After a tumultuous final minute of play, West Virginia now had an unbelievable chance to win the brawl.

Game 8

THE PLAY

CD 1—Track 5—*Jack Fleming,*
Mountaineer Sports Network

Sophomore Bill McKenzie, a former walk-on as a freshman, trotted onto the field. McKenzie's chip shot 20-yard field goal two weeks prior had beaten Virginia Tech 10-7.

From 38 yards, this one was no chip shot.

"I would say that he had about a 30 percent chance of making the field goal," said Bowden. "We had McKenzie practicing from the left and right hashmarks all week. He kicks the ball through on most of the attempts from the right, but he is lucky to make two out of five from the left."

Well, he was two out of five lifetime, from any hashmark.

So, depending on whether you believe Bowden or the stats, McKenzie had a 30 or 40 percent chance of making the dramatic kick.

The ball sat on the left hashmark. The snap came to backup quarterback Tom Loadman.

The straight ahead kicker approached the ball. McKenzie didn't want to look up. "I just kept my head down and kicked. By the time I wanted to look up, I couldn't. Everyone was on me."

The kick was good, straight through the uprights. Time expired. West Virginia 17, Pittsburgh 14.

"All hell broke loose," recalled McKenzie. "Fans swarmed the field and the whole team celebrated in a pile-up. I was at the bottom, wondering if I was ever going to get out of there alive."

He did, as a hero in West Virginia football history.

THE AFTERMATH

The rowdy chaos in Morgantown after the game resulted in 46 arrests made by local police. After the jubilant fans tore down one goalpost and mangled the other, Bowden, who celebrated his 46th birthday with the victory, was actually given a piece of one of the posts as a birthday present.

The following week, Pittsburgh stunned Notre Dame, 34-20, in one of Dorsett's most fa-mous games as a college player. He ran all over the Irish defense, for a total of 303 yards, the most ever by a Notre Dame opponent. The same day, the Panthers accepted a bid to play in the Sun Bowl where they defeated Kansas 35-19 to end the season 8-4.

Dorsett finished fourth in the Heisman Trophy voting at the end of the '75 season. He then won the award in 1976 after setting the NCAA record for most career rushing yards (6,082), and leading Pittsburgh to a 12-0 season and national championship.

The Mountaineers finished the '75 season 9-3, after upsetting Lou Holtz' North Carolina State squad 13-10 in the Peach Bowl. WVU ended the year ranked No.20 in the AP poll, three spots behind Pittsburgh. It was Bowden's last game as the West Virginia coach after six seasons and a 42-26 record.

He resigned and became the head coach at Florida State in 1976.

"I have always felt sorry the West Virginia fans had to suffer while I was learning what to do and what not to do as a head coach," he said years later in his book, *More Than Just a Game*. Bowden called the '75 victory over Pitt, the most exciting win of his career.

Although McKenzie finished a solid career in 1977 (he held the WVU record for most consecutive extra points made—39), he connected on just 4 of 12 field-goal attempts in '75. "Thank goodness nobody remembers that," he joked years later. "They just remember the one I made against Pitt."

Pittsburgh	0	0	0	14	-14
West Virginia	0	0	7	10	-17

WVU	Lee 1 run (McKenzie kick)
PITT	Jones 28 pass from Cavanaugh (Long kick)
WVU	Owens 23 run (McKenzie kick)
PITT	Dorsett 9 pass from Cavanaugh (Long kick)
WVU	FG McKenzie 38

Attendance 35, 298

November 8, 1975 —Morgantown, West Virginia

Oklahoma vs. Ohio State 🏈

"The hell with a most exciting game. I'd rather be drab as hell and win."—Woody Hayes

THE BACKGROUND

Third-ranked Oklahoma and fourth-ranked Ohio State. The two tradition-rich schools had never met on the gridiron and the buildup to this battle was enormous. In fact, the largest collection of media members ever at an Ohio State game gathered to watch the early season "dream game" between the Big Ten and Big Eight conference powers, both 2-0 early in the season.

Oklahoma's wishbone offense was orchestrated by junior quarterback Thomas Lott, whom coach Barry Switzer called, "the greatest wishbone quarterback I've ever seen."

"If that's true," Lott said, "it's because I'm not a quarterback, but a runningback in the quarterback's position." The elusive Lott was the catalyst to a diverse Sooner attack. But entering the Ohio State game, Lott was hurting. He missed OU's opening win over Vanderbilt with a bruised nerve in his leg. He played just one series of downs the following week in a 62-24 rout of Utah. But against the Buckeyes, Lott would have to perform.

He did. Running the wishbone to perfection, Lott masterfully managed the Sooners to an early 20-0 lead on TD runs by Elvis Peacock and Billy Sims. Even Lott's mistakes turned into gold for OU. His first quarter fumble squirted into the hands of Peacock who ran it in for a 33-yard TD.

But just when the game looked like a rout, Lott sprained an ankle in the second quarter. The Sooner offense blew a gasket. "We are a dif-ferent team without Lott," said Switzer. "The game changed when he wasn't in there."

Indeed, the Buckeyes roared back, helped by a half dozen Sooner turnovers (two interceptions and four lost fumbles). Ohio State scored 28 unanswered points. Tailback Ron Springs and quarterback Rod Gerald each had second-quarter TD runs. And when tight end Jimmy Moore pulled in a deflected pass off the hand's of OU's Bud Hebert in the end zone, the Buckeyes took a 28-20 third-quarter lead. Still, the margin could have been larger had OSU converted three other scoring chances set up by Sooner fumbles in Oklahoma territory.

Gerald left the game in the third quarter with a head injury, turning the Buckeye offense over to back-up QB Greg Castignola (who had previously thrown the TD pass to Moore). Nursing an eight-point lead with just a few minutes to play in the fourth quarter, Castignola was hit by OU's Dave Hudgens and fumbled the ball. Standout defensive lineman Reggie Kinlaw recovered it for Oklahoma at the OSU 43.

Back-up quarterback Dean Blevins finally got the Sooner offense moving again, down to the Ohio State 13 where they faced fourth-and-three. The Buckeyes, minus star linebacker Tom Cousineau who was injured in the first quarter, rose to the occasion. Fullback Kenny King was stopped short of the first down.

But a flag was thrown. The Buckeyes were offside on the play and Oklahoma had new life. Moving the ball down to the two, Oklahoma faced another fourth down. This time Peacock took it in with 1:29 left, and the score was 28-26.

28

September 24, 1977—Columbus, Ohio

Uwe von Schamann kicked it...

Switzer went for two, but Peacock was stopped cold. Ohio State maintained their two-point lead and appeared on their way to the victory.

The Sooners had one chance, recover the onside kick. Kicker Uwe von Schamann squibbed it sideways across the Ohio Stadium turf. The ball eluded OSU sophomore Ricardo Volley who tried to cover it. Instead, Oklahoma's Mike Babb pounced on it at the 50-yard line. The Sooners had possession again.

A frustrated Woody Hayes had prepared his Buckeyes for OU's kick alignment. "We knew exactly what they were going to do," he said. "and we worked on it three days this week."

"It was a miracle to get that onside kick," said Switzer. Suddenly, Oklahoma had a chance to win the game. Blevins quickly hit Steve Rhodes for 17 yards. Three running plays moved the ball down to the OSU 24 and with six seconds remaining, the Sooners called time-out.

THE PLAY
CD 1 - Track 6—*Gary Johnson,*
Oklahoma Radio Network

Von Schamann trotted onto the field and began his pre-kick ritual. The teams lined up for the 41-yard game-winning attempt.

Then Hayes called for a timeout.

"Obviously Woody was trying to ice me," remembered von Schamann. The 21-year-old native of West Berlin walked back to the Ohio State 35 and knelt down by himself to collect his thoughts.

The Ohio State fans began chanting, "Block That Kick! Block That Kick!" The roar was deafening.

"I knew what the crowd was trying to do," he said. "I didn't want it to bother me." So von Schamann stood up, lifted his arms, and mockingly waved them back and forth as if to conduct the Ohio State cheers from the field.

"I don't know why I did it," von Schamann said. "I was bored and a little pissed off. I guess I wanted to show them that they didn't get to me."

"It was a remarkable thing, watching a kid face up to 90,000 fans," recalled ABC broadcaster Keith Jackson.

After the ball was put back in play, von Schamann readied himself for the kick. "The snap was perfect and I hit it right on the nose," he said. The ball split the uprights with :03 on the clock and Oklahoma had rallied to defeat Ohio State 29-28.

Afterwards, von Shamann admitted, "I was scared to death. The pressure was tremendous."

Oklahoma's coach felt it too. "This game had more drama, more tension than any game I've been associated with," said a happy Switzer.

But the Ohio State coach was still pondering what had happened. "I thought we had it won, and we didn't," lamented Hayes.

THE AFTERMATH

Overjoyed with the victory, Governor David Boren, who attended the game, proclaimed the following week "Uwe von Schamann and Sooner Victory Week" in the state of Oklahoma.

As the years passed, von Schamann became amazed as to the significance of his kick to Sooner fans. "People still remember it," he said 20 years later. "People still want to talk about it. That's the only thing they talk to me about. They tell me where they were. What they were doing. Some people have even told me—this is really bizarre—it's like when John F. Kennedy died. They knew exactly where they were. That's really bizarre to hear them say that. When they compare a kick to one of our presidents getting assassinated, that's pretty amazing."

The Sooners defeated Kansas the week following the Ohio State game, but then were tripped up in their next game by Texas, 13-6, in Dallas. Winning their remaining games, OU finished the season 10-1, ranked No. 2 behind the undefeated 11-0 Longhorns and Heisman Trophy winner Earl Campbell.

When Texas lost to Notre Dame in the Cotton Bowl, 38-10, the Sooners had a shot to win

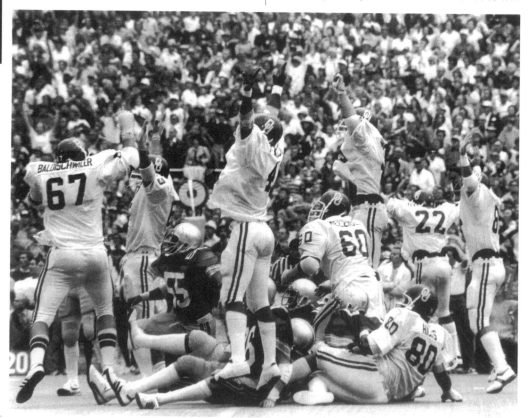

...and the Sooners partied after his 41-yard game winning FG.

Game 9

the national championship by beating sixth-ranked Arkansas in the Orange Bowl. Not only were Switzer's Sooners favored, they were heavily favored to beat the Razorbacks after first-year coach Lou Holtz suspended leading rusher Ben Cowins, leading receiver Donny Bobo, and reserve runningback Michael Forrest from the team after a dormitory incident involving the undressing of a coed. According to the *Washington Post*, the woman agreed to not press criminal charges against the players if disciplinary action was taken against them.

The three players, in turn, asked for a temporary restraining order in a U.S. District Court to force Holtz to allow them to play against Oklahoma in the Orange Bowl, claiming they were being discriminated against. The players were black, the woman was white. The situation tainted the bowl.

Three days before the game, the players dropped their suit. Bill Clinton , then Arkansas state attorney, whose staff represented the university in court, said the players withdrew their request "because they knew they could not prove their case."

Astonishingly, the Razorbacks ignored all the distractions and buried Oklahoma 31-6 in a huge upset. One game away from a possible third national championship in four years ('74 and '75), the Sooners ended up ranked seventh in the country.

Ohio State bounced back to win seven straight games before losing to Michigan 14-6 in the season finale for the Big Ten championship. The Buckeyes played Alabama in the Sugar Bowl where they lost 35-6, finishing 11th in the AP poll.

Thomas Lott ran circles around the Buckeyes before spraining his ankle in the second quarter. Photos courtesy of Chance Brockway

Oklahoma	17	3	0	9	- 29
Ohio State	0	14	14	0	- 28

OKL	Peacock 33 run (von Schamann kick)
OKL	Sims 14 run (von Schamann kick)
OKL	von Schamann 23 FG
OKL	von Schamann 33 FG
OSU	Springs 30 run (Janakievski kick)
OSU	Gerald 19 run (Janakievski kick)
OSU	Payton 1 run (Janakievski kick)
OSU	Moore 16 pass from Castignola (Janakievski kick)
OKL	Peacock 1 run (conversion kick)
OKL	von Schamann 41 FG

Attendance 88,113

Clemson vs. South Carolina

"I've never been in [a game] like that. I don't care to be in another one, either."—Mark Heniford, Clemson defensive end

THE BACKGROUND

The first meeting between the Tigers and the Gamecocks was in 1896. Make a list of the greatest finishes in this century-old battle for state bragging rights, and the 1977 game in Columbia will surely be near the top.

Underdog South Carolina (5-5), losers of four of their last five games, hosted their intrastate rivals from Death Valley. Clemson was ripe with confidence. After narrowly missing a huge upset victory against eventual national champion Notre Dame the previous week, the 7-2-1 Tigers hoped for an eighth victory which would guarantee their first bowl appearance in 18 years.

First-year coach Charley Pell had turned around a Clemson program that was just 5-15-2 the previous two years. He had a trio of talented juniors to lead his offense. All-American QB Steve Fuller and receivers Jerry Butler and Dwight Clark (the first two became first-round NFL draft picks, the third was a future All-Pro) posed a potent passing attack.

Through two and a half quarters, this was no contest. When runningback Ken Callicutt rambled 52 yards for a touchdown with 7:15 left in the third quarter, Clemson took an overwhelming 24-0 lead.

But then, on a fair weather day, lightning struck Williams-Brice Stadium.

Gamecock tailback Spencer Clark took a pitch from QB Ron Bass and raced down the left sideline 77 yards to put USC on the scoreboard. Then after moving the ball to the USC 27,

Clemson fumbled on the next drive. Again Carolina struck. A 40-yard pass from Bass to Philip Logan set up fullback Steve Dorsey's 11-yard TD run. With just 37 seconds elapsed in the fourth quarter, Clemson's lead was down to 24-14.

Clemson's offense stumbled again. Starting at their own 19, three plays failed to gain a first down. Then punter David Sims shanked a 10-yard punt off the side of his foot. USC took over at the Clemson 39. The Tigers were unraveling.

Eleven straight rushes for the Gamecocks and Dorsey scored again, this time from one yard out to cut the lead to 24-20. Coach Jim Carlen decided to go for two with 7:02 left in the game, but Bass' pass was incomplete and the margin remained four.

Trying to establish a running attack, Clemson's offense stalled a third straight time. On came Sims to punt from his own 34. This time he hit it straight up in the air. It traveled a mere 18 yards to the USC 48, where the Gamecocks took over with 4:01 on the clock.

Two minutes later, South Carolina faced a fourth-and-10 at the Clemson 40. After a timeout, Bass found Logan again over the middle at the Clemson 25. He jumped high, made the catch, and slipped several Clemson defenders to score the go-ahead touchdown with just 1:48 remaining.

Bedlam in Columbia. In a furious rally that took just over one quarter, South Carolina scored 27 unanswered points on four consecutive possessions to take the lead 27-24.

Could Clemson regroup?

Willie Jordan returned the Gamecocks'

kickoff to the Clemson 33. Fuller, who hadn't thrown a pass the entire fourth quarter, was left with 1:39 to rally the Tigers. After two short gains, Clemson faced third and seven at the 36. The poised Fuller found flanker Rick Weddington for a 26-yard gain to the USC 38.

Clemson fans had hope. Then Dwight Clark got open. Fuller connected with Clark, dumping the ball over the middle for 18 more yards. The Tigers were at the Gamecocks' 20 and the clock kept running with under a minute to play.

THE PLAY

CD 1—Track 7—*Jim Phillips,*
Clemson Sports Network

On first down at the USC 20, split end Jerry Butler lined up to run an "out" pattern to the sideline designed to stop the clock. But reading the defense, he suddenly decided to break off course and cut long over the middle toward the end zone.

Fuller recognized the change in plans. "The two of us have developed a sort of sense for what the other guy's gonna do, and Jerry was on his own to make up a route on that play," said Fuller.

"We've been waiting to use that all year long, and we finally had to," added Butler.

The streaking Butler was open. But Fuller sailed the ball off target, slightly behind him and high, almost too high.

Clemson broadcaster Jim Phillips remembered, "Butler, with his back to the end zone, went up in the air and arched his back. I can still see him arching that back and reaching up with both hands, and came down with the ball. And when he fell, he fell into the end zone."

"I knew I was in the end zone," said Butler. "I just worried about holding on to it."

He did. A breathtaking reception. Sixty-seven yards in 50 seconds. Clemson had scored with 0:49 left, taking the lead 31-27.

That moment, to be known forever in the state of South Carolina as "The Catch," carried a humorous anecdote as told by Phillips.

"I remember a woman calling me up and telling me her husband in Spartanburg was listening to the game," said the Clemson announcer. "He got so excited that he jumped up

in the air on the touchdown catch. There was a chandelier overhead and she ended up having to take him to the hospital to get quite a number of stitches in his head where the chandelier split his head open...It got quite a number of people's emotions going."

The Gamecocks did get the ball back one final time. But South Carolina's last gasps failed miserably, with Bass unable to complete a pass on four desperation downs in their own territory. The game was over.

THE AFTERMATH

After the game, Clemson officials accepted the offer to play defending national champion Pittsburgh in the Gator Bowl, the Tigers first bowl appearance since 1959. The Panthers overwhelmed Pell's squad, 34-3. But the 8-3-1 finish in '77 provided the foundation for Clemson's sparkling 11-1 record and No. 6 ranking the following season.

When the regular season ended in '78 and before their bowl game, Pell left Clemson after just two years, to take the head coaching position at the University of Florida. Interim coach Danny Ford was left to lead the Tigers back to Jacksonville, Florida, for a repeat performance in the Gator Bowl, this time versus Ohio State. It was Woody Hayes' last football game.

With Clemson hanging onto a 17-15 lead late in the game and OSU driving, Tiger defensive lineman Charlie Bauman picked off an Art Schlichter pass with 1:59 remaining, ruining the Buckeyes' chance at a game-winning field goal and preserving the Clemson victory. Bauman's momentum took him over to the Ohio State sidelines where, as he was getting up off the ground, a furious Hayes grabbed Bauman and hit him under the helmet with a roundhouse right forearm.

Bauman wasn't hurt, but at age 65, Hayes' legendary career was over. He was fired the next day after 28 years, two national championships, and 13 Big Ten titles at Ohio State.

Jerry Butler makes "The Catch" of Steve Fuller's 20-yard touchdown pass. Photo courtesy of Larry Cagle

November 19, 1977 —Columbia, South Carolina

Clemson	10	7	7	7	-31
South Carolina	0	0	7	20	-27

CL	Ratchford 4 run (Ariri kick)
CL	FG Ariri 18
CL	Brown 1 run (Ariri kick)
CL	Callicutt 52 run (Ariri kick)
SC	Clark 77 run (Parrish kick)
SC	Dorsey 11 run (Parrish kick)
SC	Dorsey 1 run (pass failed)
SC	Logan 40 pass from Bass (Parrish kick)
CL	Butler 20 pass from Fuller (Ariri kick)

Attendance 56,410

William & Mary vs. Virginia Tech

"I hope Tech locked the gates and charged the folks to leave, because they sure couldn't have seen a more exciting game."
—*William & Mary head coach Jim Root*

THE BACKGROUND

When Bill Dooley arrived at Virginia Tech in 1978 as the new head coach and athletic director, he made an immediate change to the struggling football program. He got rid of the traditional Gobbler head, which sat atop the scoreboard with its Tech beanie hat, "gobbling" out loud after each Hokies touchdown. Instead, Dooley had the new silent "fighting Gobbler" placed above Lane Stadium.

The new coach meant business. The uniforms were changed. The grass on the field was replaced. The locker rooms were remodeled.

But after the first three games of the season, Tech was 1-2. They had lost both home games, and the official "turkey caller" noise makers, sold to the home fans to substitute for the retired talking Gobbler head, apparently weren't working.

On the other hand, Dooley, who had just finished 11 seasons at North Carolina, knew the rebuilding at Tech would take a few years. The Hokies were 3-7-1 the previous season.

Jim Root was in his seventh season at William & Mary where he took over the program after Lou Holtz left following the '71 season to become head coach at North Carolina State. The Tribe was 3-0 when they took the bus trip from Williamsburg to Blacksburg for the continuation of a series that started in 1904. Led by senior quarterback Tom Rozantz, W&M rallied from 17 points behind the week before to beat Villanova 21-17.

"This is our first game of the season against an in-state opponent and we realize they will come in here sky-high," said Dooley. The Tribe did just that, leading 9-0 at the half on the strength of a 40-yard pass from Rozantz to Joe Manderfield late in the second quarter, which set up a one-yard TD run by Andy Banks. The Hokies missed two first-half field-goal attempts and the turkey callers were silent.

Tech finally scored on their second possession of the third quarter, driving 67 yards with junior runningback Kenny Lewis taking it in on a three-yard TD run. After a Tribe field goal, Lewis' second TD run of the game, this time from eight yards out, put the Gobblers ahead 15-12 with 10:59 remaining in the fourth quarter. It was Lewis' ninth TD in just four games. He also racked up 147 yards on 31 carries for the afternoon.

Rozantz tried to rally the Tribe. But Tom Franco fumbled, and Tech recovered with 4:18 left to thwart the W&M drive. Leading by three, the Hokies wanted to run out the clock. Instead, two minutes later, they fumbled the ball right back to the Indians on the Tech 45 with 1:53 to play.

This time Rozantz wasted no time. On the first play, he hit Manderfield for a 45-yard touchdown pass. W&M regained the lead. Or did they? Manderfield was flagged for offensive pass interference, negating the score, backing up the Tribe 15 yards, and enraging the Tribe coaching staff.

Rozantz tried again. On the next play he connected with Ed Scheilfelbein on the same identical pattern as the previous pass, only now from 59 yards out and the go-ahead touchdown.

But wait, another flag. This time, however, it was defensive pass interference and W&M regained the lead 19-15 with only 1:29 remaining. Free safety Matt Mead was the Tech defender beaten on the play. "I lost him for just a second and that's when he got away from me," he said. "I couldn't stop crying when I went to the sidelines."

With the distraught Mead on the sidelines, Tech senior QB David Lamie moved the ball to the 50-yard line with under 30 seconds to go. Down four points, needing a touchdown to win, he threw a bomb to senior wingback Ellis Savage. Incomplete. Then Lamie threw another desperation pass to freshman Henry Smith. Incomplete again.

Now only eight seconds remained and Lamie tried his third and last Hail Mary.

THE PLAY

"The play was called Purple 98," said Lamie. "The receivers do various cuts and wind up in the same area. When I came to the line and was calling signals, I noticed the free safety was standing at his 5-yard line."

By the time sophomore split end Ron Zollicoffer ran down to the goal line, three W&M defensive backs converged on him, waiting for Lamie's last gasp. After rolling right, Lamie threw it long for the third straight time. The 6-0 Zollicoffer leaped high, expecting to fight for the ball amongst many hands. "I thought the defensive backs would deflect it," he said.

But no one did. Zollicoffer, squeezed between all three Tribe players, grabbed the ball in mid-air, then juggled it as his legs flew up, parallel to the ground. He fell toward Dooley's newly planted bermuda grass.

Crossing the goal line, Zollicoffer hit the turf. Instantaneously, the ball squirted out of his hands. The clock read 0:00.

Ron Zollicoffer hauls in a Hokie Hail Mary from quarterback David Lamie...

Game 11

...as the William & Mary defenders desperately try to pull the ball loose. Photos courtesy of Gene Dalton

"The ball popped loose when I hit the ground. I could see the white stuff [goal-line chalk]. I didn't know if it was a touchdown or not," said Zollicoffer. It was a touchdown, or so the officials ruled. The Hokies were ecstatic. The Indians were irate.

"There is no doubt in my mind that Zollicoffer scored on the final play. Once you have possession of the ball in the end zone, you can let the air out of the ball, kick it into the air or do anything you want to with it. It's still a touchdown," said Dooley in his post-game remarks.

"It goes down as a hard fought loss regardless of the controversy over whether the ball was caught or not," said W&M's Root. "My kids say absolutely no catch. I honestly did not see the play."

Tech's Mead did, and he was happy not to be the goat for allowing W&M's last score. "When I saw the touchdown at the end, I just fell on my knees and went crazy," he said. "I don't ever want a game like this again."

Neither did Root. "There just are not words to describe the hurt," the coach remarked.

An unidentified W&M assistant coach, quoted in the Tech student newspaper, may have found the phrase eluding Root. "We were screwed," he said.

THE AFTERMATH

Virginia Tech finished the '78 season 4-7. The Hokies were 5-6 the following year, which was Dooley's last losing season at Tech. He reeled off seven straight winning seasons before leaving Blacksburg with a 64-37-1 record, and taking the head coaching job at Wake Forest in 1987.

Jim Root coached one more year at William & Mary before he was fired at the end of the 1979 season, eight years as head coach, and replaced by Jimmye Laycock.

William & Mary	0	9	3	7	-19
Virginia Tech	0	0	7	15	-22

W&M	Libassi 47 FG
W&M	Banks 1 run (kick failed)
VT	Lewis 3 run (Engle kick)
W&M	Libassi 41 FG
VT	Lewis 8 run (Lamie run)
W&M	Schielfelbain 59 pass from Rozantz (Libassi kick)
VT	Zollicoffer 50 pass from Lamie (Engle kick)

Attendance 34,000

37

Duke vs. North Carolina

"I just didn't know how we could go that far without a timeout."
—*Bob Loomis, UNC tight end*

THE BACKGROUND

Dick Crum's first season at North Carolina was not supposed to be like this. Crum had replaced Bill Dooley in 1978, who left to take the head coaching and athletic director's job at Virginia Tech. But the Tar Heels, defending ACC champions, were a disappointing 4-6 as they entered their final game of the '78 season against arch-rival Duke. Included in those five losses were unexpected upsets at the hands of Miami (OH) and Richmond. The loss to Miami was especially difficult for Crum since that was where he started his head coaching career four years prior in 1974, leading the Redskins to a blistering 21-1-1 record in his first two years in Oxford, Ohio.

The Duke Blue Devils were also at the end of a losing campaign. Coach Mike McGee's squad had an identical 4-6 record, and had only beaten Carolina once since McGee took over the head coaching job in Durham in 1971.

Crum played musical quarterbacks during the season, trying to find a rhythm with his new offense. Junior Matt Kupec, who led his team to a Liberty Bowl berth in '77, started the year behind center, only to be replaced later by freshman Chuck Sharpe. A similar scenario occurred in the finale versus Duke. Kupec got the start against the Blue Devils at UNC's picturesque Kenan Stadium, but was lifted for Sharpe midway through the second quarter with the Heels mustering only three first-half points and trailing 9-3 at the half.

Kupec was not pleased to be pulled. "I don't know why I had to come out of the game," he said. As the second half progressed, Sharpe faired worse than Kupec, completing as many passes to Duke defenders (three Blue Devil interceptions) as he did to Carolina receivers (3 for 9, 44 yards). Meanwhile, Duke senior QB Mike Dunn directed his team on the ground. Led by freshman runningback Bobby Brower, who had 124 yards rushing in the first three quarters, the Blue Devils looked to extend their lead to nine points early in the fourth quarter. But kicker Scott McKinney, who already connected on three FGs, missed wide right on a 36-yard attempt.

The score remained 9-3, when Crum sent Kupec back onto the field with 14:11 to play in the game. A determined Kupec quickly made a point, hitting three passes, the last one a 26-yarder to tight end Bob Loomis, to move the ball to the Duke 35. But on the next play, sophomore star runningback Amos Lawrence fumbled, and Duke recovered. After an exchange of possessions, and now without their leading rusher Brower who was on the bench with leg cramps, Dunn took over. The Blue Devil quarterback got loose around the right side and scampered in for a 29-yard score, the first touchdown of the game with just 4:20 remaining. The Blue Devils missed the conversion attempt but still led 15-3 in the waning minutes.

"You could probably say none of us were real confident at that point," noted Kupec. Nevertheless, with many of the UNC partisans filing out of the stadium, Kupec completed three quick passes, then converted a fourth-

38

and-six toss to Loomis at the Duke 23. Two plays later he hit Loomis again for a 10-yard touchdown pass. On the PAT, UNC had only 10 players on the field and were forced to call a costly timeout. Jeff Hayes then kicked the extra point and Duke's lead was trimmed to 15-10 with 2:46 remaining.

A fired up Tar Heel defense held Duke on downs, but in the process, used all of their remaining timeouts. After a Ricky Brummitt 25-yard punt, the Heels regained possession on their own 39 with 1:42 on the clock.

UNC went nowhere fast. Kupec's first pass to Lawrence lost two yards, while the next pass was incomplete. Third-and-12 on their own 37 with no timeouts.

Crum surprisingly called for a draw play to Lawrence. It worked. "Famous" Amos shot up the middle for 18 yards. New life.

"It was a play they weren't looking for," said Crum. "We caught 'em looking for the sprint draw pass we'd run quite a bit."

But three more downs and the Heels were faced with fourth-and-one at the Duke 36. Again the call was to Lawrence. He busted up the middle on a "blast" play for 21 yards down to the 15. The drive was alive, but the clock was winding down. Kupec hit wide receiver Jim Rouse on a four-yard sideline pattern to stop the clock with 18 seconds left.

On second down, Kupec ran a sprint out pass, threw to Loomis in the end zone, but then watched the ball slip through the tight end's outstretched fingers in the chilly November air.

Third down from the 11-yard line. Sixteen seconds on the clock. UNC down by five.

THE PLAY

CD 1—Track 8—*Woody Durham,*
Bob Holliday,
Tar Heel Sports Network

Unexpectedly, for the third time in the drive, the call came for Lawrence. "I thought it would be a pass play to stop the clock," said the surprised sophomore. But Crum gambled, knowing that he ran the risk of the clock running out if Lawrence was tackled in bounds. He called "Right-7."

Kupec, who had come off the bench to rally his team, explained the design, "I'd run out on the corners, then hand off to Amos on the sprint draw. The defense was loosened up."

It was the same play that worked earlier in the drive for big yardage. Crum was ready to take the blame if the gutsy call failed. "The play was sent in by me because only one man can take responsibility for a call like that," said the Tar Heels' first-year coach. "We ran it because I had confidence in Amos and so did every person on that field."

Lawrence, the ACC Rookie of the Year in '77 with 1,211 his freshman season, had just surpassed the 1,000-yard mark for the '78 campaign on the final drive. "When they called my number, I was a little stunned," he said. "But if the coaching staff has that much confidence in me, well, I wasn't going to let them down."

With the Duke linemen in a full pass rush, Lawrence took the delayed handoff and shot up the middle. "I had a wide hole to the left and I saw one Duke guy near the goal line. I also saw a couple more out of the corner of my eye," he said. Lawrence dodged tackler after tackler, four in all. Blue Devils Andy Schoenhoft, Rick Sommers, and Jim McMahon each had a shot at him. "I was hit at about the two-yard line but I just said, 'No way can we lose this now,'" said Lawrence.

With a burst of second-effort, he tumbled into the end zone for the winning touchdown.

Thirteen seconds were still on the clock in the now wildly, raucous Kenan Stadium. After Kupec's two-point conversion pass was incomplete, Duke's Dunn tried two desperation passes, one incomplete, the other intercepted as time expired, and North Carolina had finished the "Famous" rally to win 16-15.

Lawrence's run has become one of the most memorable moments in Tar Heel football history. Unfortunately, many UNC fans missed the moment.

"A lot of the fans, when it became 15-3, they started piling out," recalled North Carolina broadcaster Woody Durham. "I got a lot of cards and letters later from people who had stopped along the highway, leaving Chapel Hill to listen. When Carolina scored the touchdown to get within a touchdown, they pulled off on the side of the road and were listening on the radio. That's where they were when they heard it."

THE AFTERMATH

The end of Crum's first season in Chapel Hill was also the end of McGee's eight-year tenure at Duke. The Saturday evening following the game, McGee, the 1959 Outland Trophy winner as a Duke player, was fired as the Blue Devils' head coach after a 37-47-4 record.

Crum coached North Carolina through the 1987 season, returning the Tar Heels to the top of the ACC in 1980 with a 6-0 conference record, 11-1 overall, and No.9 ranking in the AP poll. He resigned and returned to his native Ohio as the winningest coach in UNC history with a 72-41-3 record. The Tar Heels won four straight bowl games under Crum from 1979-82, and made six bowl appearances in his 10 years as coach.

Amos Lawrence completed his college career in 1980 with four straight 1,000-yard seasons, joining Pittsburgh's Tony Dorsett as the only major college players (at the time) to ever to hit the 1,000-yard mark four times.

Duke	3	6	0	6	-15
North Carolina	3	0	0	13	-16

UNC	FG Hayes 32
DUKE	FG McKinney 26
DUKE	FG McKinney 39
DUKE	FG McKinney 41
DUKE	Dunn 29 run (run failed)
UNC	Loomis 10 pass from Kupec (Hayes kick)
UNC	Lawrence 11 run (pass failed)

Attendance 45,000

Notre Dame vs. 🏈 Houston

"When Joe came back to the field, I started thinking this was a fairy tale." —Kris Haines

THE BACKGROUND

An emotional Notre Dame coach Dan Devine faced a group of reporters. "You saw one of the most remarkable comebacks in the history of the sport," he said following the Irish's last regular season game of the 1978 season, a heart-stopping 27-25 loss at USC.

Apparently, Devine forgot that Joe Montana still had one college game left to play.

Montana had rallied ND from a 24-6 fourth-quarter deficit against the third-ranked Trojans. His touchdown pass to Pete Holohan with 46 seconds left in the game capped a furious 19-point rally, giving the Irish a 25-24 lead. But Trojans quarterback Paul McDonald, after a controversial fumble-called-incompletion with 19 seconds left, hit Cal Sweeney with a 35-yard pass to the Irish 26. Charles White ran for four more, and Frank Jordan kicked a 39-yard field goal with two seconds left for the dramatic USC win, one of the greatest games ever in the storied rivalry.

Notre Dame (8-3) would have to regroup to face the ninth-ranked Houston Cougars (9-2) in the Cotton Bowl.

Architect of the multi-faceted veer offense, Houston coach Bill Yeoman had his Cougars atop the Southwest Conference. The school joined the SWC in 1976 where they made an immediate impact, winning the conference championship in their first year, and finishing No.4 in the nation. They again were SWC champs in '78. Leading the way in Yeoman's vaunted veer attack were runningbacks Randy

Love and Emmitt King, both 1,000-yard rushers during the '78 season.

The air temperature at game time was 20 degrees with a wind chill of minus 6, following a bone chilling ice storm that hit the Dallas area. Maybe half of the sellout crowd of 72,000 even showed up for the game. The frozen field conditions and gusty winds contributed enormously to the 10 turnovers and two blocked punts in the game. Whoever had the 20 MPH wind at their back, had a huge advantage.

After building a 12-0 lead, Notre Dame went downhill fast in the second quarter. Montana fumbled a snap. Houston scored. He threw an interception. Houston scored. Another interception. Another Houston score. The Cougars led 20-12 at the half and Montana, who was recovering from a battle with the flu, fell ill again in the locker room.

"When we came in from halftime, I just got the chills and couldn't stop shaking," said Montana. The team doctors wrapped him in blankets to try and increase his body temperature which had dropped to 96 degrees. Montana stayed in the locker room as the second half started.

Houston rolled on. With the wind at their back and the temperature dropping, the Cougars cashed in on two short drives. Quarterback Danny Davis scored on touchdown runs of two and five yards. The second TD came after Bobby Harrison blocked Dick Boushka's punt at the Irish 19. The score was 34-12, and, for some reason, there were about 15,000 people in the stands who still hadn't gone home.

While back-up Tim Koegel was leading the

Joe Montana was only 13 of 34 for 163 yards with four interceptions on the day...
Photo courtesy University of Notre Dame Archives

...but the last pass of his Notre Dame career to Kris Haines is a permanent part of Fighting Irish folklore.
Photo courtesy of Cotton Bowl Athletic Association

Irish offense nowhere against the wind, team doctor Les Bodnar was feeding Montana warm chicken soup to raise his body temperature.

"They told us Joe was not coming back in the second half and we thought it was over," said Irish center Dave Huffman.

"I was coming back no matter what," maintained Montana. He did, with 4:40 left in the third quarter.

The chicken soup may have warmed Montana's body, but his arm was still ice cold. He re-entered the game playing no better than when he left, completing just one pass in 11 attempts. He threw interception number three. Then, as the fourth quarter started, a fourth interception.

The score was still 34-12 with 7:37 left in the fourth quarter when Houston dropped back to punt into the wind and two Notre Dame freshmen came together to shift the momentum of the game.

Tony Belden flew in untouched and blocked Jay Wyatt's punt. Steve Cichy grabbed the loose ball, shook off a would-be tackler, and scored from 33 yards out. It was 34-18. Montana returned to hit Vagas Ferguson with the two-point conversion pass and the lead was cut to 34-20.

Notre Dame's comeback had begun.

The Irish got the ball back with 5:40 left and suddenly Montana, a fifth-year senior, got his touch back. From the ND 39, he found tight end Dean Masztak for 17 yards, then Jerome Heavens out of the backfield for 30 more.

Montana capped the 61-yard, five-play drive with a three-yard TD run, then hit Kris Haines for the two-point conversion. Suddenly it was 34-28 with 4:15 still to play.

Those who stayed to watch were glad they did.

Again the Cougars struggled on offense, punting the ball back to Notre Dame with 2:25 left. Montana moved the Irish. Scrambling from the rush, he sprinted up the middle 16 yards down to the Houston 20. But at the end of the run, defensive MVP David Hodge knocked the ball out of his hand. The Cougars recovered with 1:50 left.

Apparently, Houston had weathered the storm.

"I was afraid that was it," said Montana. "But then I realized we had some timeouts left and I also remembered the defense was playing fantastic. I didn't want to lose the game on that fumble."

Down by six points, the Irish used up all their timeouts, held the Cougars without a first down, and forced a short Houston punt on fourth-and-six. But Notre Dame was offsides.

In a bold move, Yeoman chose to take the penalty, then sent his offense back on the field with 35 seconds remaining. It was fourth-and-inches at the Houston 29. Instead of risking another punt into the wind, the Cougars tried to wrap up the game by getting one yard. They didn't make it.

Davis handed to King up the middle. He

Game 13

was met head on by freshman Joe Gramke, who stood him up, then got help from senior Mike Calhoun to stop the Cougars short of the first down.

Montana now had 28 seconds and 29 yards to go. He scrambled out of bounds for 11 yards to the 18. He found Haines for 10 yards along the sideline to the eight. Six seconds left.

Montana took a quick drop and looked for Haines in the right corner. "If I see it's not there, I'm suppose to get rid of the ball right away," the Irish quarterback said. For a moment, Haines was covered. Montana threw it away. But then Haines got free. Too late, the ball was already gone. "Just as I got rid of it, I saw Kris break off his man," said Montana.

With 0:02 on the clock, the ball was still at the Houston eight-yard line.

THE PLAY

It would be Joe Montana's last pass as a college player.

Given the option of running a quick slant-in by the receivers, or a quick turn out, Montana chose the latter. It was called "91 out." The exact same play he had just missed.

Haines recalled the conversation in the huddle. "Joe asked me if I could beat him again, and I said yes," the senior wide receiver explained. "He smiled and said 'Let's do it.'"

This time Montana dropped back and rolled right, giving Haines a few more seconds to run his route. He threw low to the front right corner of the end zone. Haines came back to the ball, sliding on his knees as he approached the out of bounds line.

"He throws it. It is incomp....It's a touchdown! It's a touchdown!" yelled broadcaster Connie Alexander over the Cotton Bowl Radio Network.

Blocked from the line of sight of cameras and announcers by a group of media members huddled near the end zone, Haines just got his feet in bounds before skidding across the frozen turf. A delirious Notre Dame bench erupted. The score was tied 34-34 as time expired.

Joe Unis came on to kick the winning extra point. It was good, but Notre Dame was called for illegal motion. Unis, the walk-on kicker from Dallas filling in for an injured Chuck Male,

calmly hit the second kick from 25 yards out and Notre Dame completed the wild 23-point comeback with a 35-34 victory.

THE AFTERMATH

"We should have won that game, but we forgot to play 60 minutes," said Cougars tackle Melvin Jones, the following year when Houston returned to the Cotton Bowl after winning their third SWC crown in four years. "It's been tough to live with." Houston made amends by defeating Nebraska 17-14.

Yeoman continued at Houston until 1986 when he retired to take a fundraising position with the university after 25 years as head coach. At the time, Yeoman's career coaching record of 160-106-8 was the fourth best among all active coaches in intercollegiate football.

Montana's statistics in his last game were atrocious—13 of 34 for 163 yards and four interceptions. But the scintillating 23-point rally he engineered in the fourth quarter will forever be the highlight of his legacy under the Golden Dome, and the greatest comeback in the history of Notre Dame football.

Notre Dame	12	0	0	23	-35
Houston	7	13	14	0	-34

ND	Montana 3 run (kick failed)
ND	Buchanan 1 run (pass failed)
UH	Adams 15 pass from Davis (Hatfield kick)
UH	Love 1 run (Hatfield kick)
UH	Hatfield 21 FG
UH	Hatfield 34 FG
UH	Davis 2 run (Hatfield kick)
UH	Davis 5 run (Hatfield kick)
ND	Cichy 33 return of blocked kick (Ferguson pass from Montana)
ND	Montana 2 run (Haines pass from Montana)
ND	Haines 8 pass from Montana (Unis kick)

Attendance 72,000

Michigan vs. Indiana

"If I were him, I'd be crying."—Bo Schembechler, referring to Indiana coach Lee Corso

THE BACKGROUND

The 10th-ranked and heavily favored Michigan Wolverines entered their homecoming game against Indiana sitting atop the Big Ten Conference with a 4-0 conference record, 6-1 overall.

Across the field, future ESPN analyst Lee Corso and his Hoosiers hobbled into Ann Arbor missing five starters because of injuries (2-2 conference, 5-2 overall). But it was a second-quarter shoulder injury to Wolverine starting quarterback B.J. Dickey that had Michigan coach Bo Schembechler concerned. That, and the fact that Indiana outhustled and out-muscled his team in the first 30 minutes of play. Halfback Lonnie Johnson's 14-yard scamper with 1:09 left in the second quarter gave the Hoosiers a 14-7 lead and a truckload of momentum they took with them into the locker room at halftime.

Early in the second half, with back-up quarterback John Wangler (6-3, 192 lb. junior), taking the snaps, Michigan relied on its power running game and took control. Runningbacks Butch Woolfolk (30 carries for 127 yards) and Lawrence Reid (12 carries for 99 yards) both scored third-quarter touchdowns, with Reid's 50-yard romp giving Michigan a 21-14 advantage heading into the fourth quarter.

Indiana responded.

Playing, according to Corso, "one of the greatest games an Indiana football team has ever played," the Hoosiers rallied late in the fourth quarter. With time running out, quarter-back Tim Clifford hit Nate Lundy with a 54-yard desperation pass to move the ball deep into Wolverine territory. Then Clifford found Dave Harangody in the end zone from three yards out, and with 55 seconds remaining, Michigan's lead was cut to 21-20. (While calling the touchdown catch on the radio, IU announcer Don Fischer became so excited he caught himself on fire from a cigarette ash, burning the sleeve of his sport coat.)

With a chance now to take the lead, Corso bypassed the two-point conversion attempt and elected to go for the tie. Kevin Kellogg's PAT kick made it 21-21. Corso later explained, "I wanted to come out of this game with something. As a coach I've never had a team effort like I got today." His team's post-season chances were also on his mind. "A tie would have still given us a chance for the Rose Bowl," he said.

It appeared Indiana's defense would hold up in the final minute.

Woolfolk took the ensuing kickoff and returned it to his own 22-yard line. From there, the Hoosiers held Michigan to just nine yards in three plays. Schembechler was faced with a monumental decision. Fourth and one at the 31 with 36 seconds remaining. The Michigan coach gambled. "We could have lost the game, and maybe the Big 10 title, if we had missed on that fourth down play," said Schembechler. Fortunately, for the 104,832 nervous Michigan faithful in the stands, they didn't miss. Woolfolk got the first down with a four-yard run to the 35.

But only 25 seconds remained.

Game 14

Freshman Anthony Carter (1) at the end of his 45-yard catch and run on the game's final play. Photo courtesy of Bob Kalmbach

Two plays later, Indiana safety Tim Wilbur, playing with fractured ribs, picked off an errant Wangler pass. But he couldn't get a foot in bounds and the play stood as an incomplete pass.

Fourteen seconds left.

With no timeouts remaining, facing third-and-one at the Michigan 44, and desperate to get into field-goal range, Wangler hit Lawrence Reid for six yards. But Reid could not get to the sidelines to stop the clock, so he intentionally **lateraled the ball out of bounds...right to Corso! Ball in hand, the IU coach questioned the play. "I doubt seriously if the ball went backward,"** he said. "It's legal if it's a lateral, but I thought it was a little in front of him."

"Reid made one smart play; there's nothing illegal about fumbling the ball backward," said Schembechler.

With just six seconds now on the clock and the ball at midfield, the Hoosiers jumped offsides. Even with the ball moved to the Indiana 45, Michigan was still out of field-goal range.

The Wolverines had time for just one play.

THE PLAY

CD 1— Track 9 —*Bob Ufer,*
WJR Radio,
Michigan Football Network

"We were in a situation where we had been going deep and widening the areas by sending our receivers toward the sidelines," said Schembechler. "We had to go inside now; it was our only chance."

Freshman Anthony Carter, who had caught only one pass in the game, brought in the play from the sideline. Wangler, an efficient, if not spectacular 9 of 13 passing for 118 yards on the day, recognized Indiana's prevent defense. So did Carter. "Anthony said he knew he could beat the defense by running a post pattern," said Wangler. Yes, but could he get into the end zone?

Carter ran the post to the Indiana 20 where Wangler's pass met him. Indiana's Dart Ramsey hit the 155-pound Carter immediately, but so did teammate Stoner Gray, who collided with Ramsey and left the Michigan receiver still standing.

"I didn't think I had a chance to score when the first guy hit me," said the future two-time All-American, "but I was still on my feet so I kept going."

Carter stumbled forward and broke toward the goal line when Indiana's Wilbur made a last-ditch effort. "He grabbed at my left leg. But I just took it away from him," said Carter. "Still I almost went down at the 2, and that would have been the ball game." Carter crossed the goal line, the stands emptied, and the Wolverines won 27-21, electing to skip the moot extra point.

"I saw the safety come up in the middle, and I thought he had Carter," said Wangler. "I thought maybe we'd still have time to try for a field goal, but I guess time had run out. And then he went into the end zone. I was in heaven!"

So was Michigan announcer Bob Ufer, whose delirious call of the final seconds was like listening to the radio broadcast of the apocalypse. "Oh my God, Carter scored! " he screamed, between gasps for air.

Schembechler was ecstatic too. "Seventy-eight yards in 55 seconds...how about that," he said. I can't ever remember any of my teams doing something like that."

And for Indiana's Corso? "I thought one of our guys could stop him, but they didn't," the Indiana coach remarked.

"I didn't say much to Corso after the game," said Schembechler. "How many times will he have a chance to come in here and tie us, then have it taken away from him like that? If I were him, I'd be crying."

THE AFTERMATH

Two weeks later, the Wolverines began a season-ending skid which saw them lose three of their last four games and end the year with a 8-4 record. It began against Purdue when with 11 seconds remaining, Michigan found themselves down 24-21. Once again Anthony Carter's number was called, but this time the desperation pass was incomplete and the Boilermakers pulled off the upset. Losses to Ohio State and North Carolina in the Gator Bowl ended the campaign for the Wolverines. Nine-

teen-seventy-nine marked the first season that a Schembechler-coached Michigan team lost three regular-season games. Anthony Carter finished the season averaging 27.2 yards per catch. Three years later he finished fourth in the Heisman Trophy balloting after his senior season.

Lee Corso's Hoosiers wound up the season on a high note, winning three of their last four games, including a 38-37 Holiday Bowl victory over previously undefeated and ninth-ranked Brigham Young. BYU had a chance to win with seven seconds left, but Brent Johnson's 27-yard field-goal attempt missed the mark and the Hoosiers prevailed. Indiana finished with an 8-4 record.

Indiana	0	14	0	7	- 21
Michigan	7	0	14	6	- 27

MICH	Reid 3 run (Virgil kick)
IND	Harangody 3 pass from Clifford (Kellogg kick)
IND	Johnson 14 run (Kellogg kick)
MICH	Reid 50 run (Virgil kick)
MICH	Woolfolk 2 run (Virgil kick)
IND	Harangody 3 pass from Clifford (Kellogg kick)
MICH	Carter 45 pass from Wangler (no kick)

Attendance 104,832

Michigan vs. Notre Dame

"This is by far the greatest moment of my life."—Harry Oliver

THE BACKGROUND

It's an indisputable fact. Michigan taught Notre Dame how to play football.

Back in 1887, two former Notre Dame students who had transferred to Michigan, William Harless and George DeHaven, wrote a letter to Brother Patrick Connors, the director of the intramural sports program at Notre Dame. Harless and DeHaven had joined the Michigan football team. They wanted to bring the new game to ND. Connors invited the Michigan team to South Bend to teach the Notre Dame students how to play. An informal contest took place. It was Notre Dame's first football game and first loss, 8-0.

Since then, the two schools have played the game better than any others. Well, at least statistically. Michigan owns the most victories in the history of college football. Notre Dame is second. Notre Dame has the highest winning percentage. Michigan is second.

After playing nine times from 1887-1909 (Michigan won all but one game), the two teams met only twice again before the series was renewed in 1978. It's a storied rivalry which has been played just 29 times, Michigan leads the series (16-11-1).

In 1980, the Wolverines (1-0) entered Notre Dame Stadium ranked No. 14, while the Fighting Irish (1-0) were No. 8. As it turned out, this game would set the standard for all future ND-Michigan nail-biters.

Notre Dame controlled the first half, gobbling up 18 of the first 25 minutes of posses-

sion time. Sophomore Phil Carter scored on a six-yard TD run, and senior quarterback Mike Courey found Pete Holohan for a 10-yard TD pass. With just five minutes left in the first half, the Irish were dominating, 14-0.

Enter Michigan QB John Wangler. The 192-lb. senior had suffered a serious knee injury in the '79 Gator Bowl against North Carolina. This was his first time back on the field since that game.

Taking over for the struggling sophomore Rich Hewlett, Wangler quickly brought the Wolverines back. Michigan drove 68 yards in eight plays as Wangler hit Lawrence Ricks out of the backfield for an eight-yard TD to cut the lead to 14-7 with 1:50 left in the half. Then defensive back Marion Body picked off a Courey pass headed for split end Tony Hunter and returned it 20 yards to the ND 27.

With Michigan unable to gain a first down, Wolverine coach Bo Schembechler caught the Irish by surprise. Facing fourth down, UM faked a field-goal attempt and holder Hewlett threw 12 yards to Stanley Edwards. Seconds later, Wangler found Norm Betts for a nine-yard touchdown with just 0:31 to go in the half. The score was tied 14-14.

The Wolverines rolled on in the third quarter. Speedster Anthony Carter returned the opening kickoff of the second half 67 yards to the Irish 32. Six plays later, Edwards plunged in from the two and Michigan surged ahead 21-14.

The Michigan defense (orchestrated by defensive coordinator Bill McCartney) shut down Notre Dame, holding the Irish to zero first downs in the third quarter.

But as the quarter was winding down, it was the Irish defense that turned the tide. Wangler, looking for an open Carter near midfield, misread the coverage and was picked off by junior cornerback John Krimm who returned it 49 yards for a touchdown. ND looked to tie, but junior kicker Harry Oliver missed the extra point. Michigan maintained the lead, 21-20.

It stayed that way as the Wolverines marched downfield midway through the fourth quarter to put the game away. But Butch Woolfolk, playing injured but forced into duty when Ricks left the game with bruised ribs in the second half, fumbled at the ND 26. Dave Duerson recovered for the Irish with 7:33 left to play.

"I've made a lot of mistakes in my life but that may have been the worse," said Woolfolk.

The Irish immediately capitalized. An 11-play drive was capped off by a four-yard Carter TD run. The conversion failed, and with 3:03 remaining Notre Dame led 26-21.

The game was far from over.

Starting at their own 22, Michigan rallied and Woolfolk got redemption. He caught a 12-yard pass, then ran a draw play for 13, then another draw for 37 yards. Woolfolk and the Wolverines were at the Irish four-yard line with 1:06 left.

Facing third down at the one, Wangler went back to pass. "The ball was supposed to go to the fullback or the tight end," he said. Instead, it went to both.

Woolfolk and freshman cornerback Chris Brown reached high for the ball in the middle of the end zone. It caromed off Woolfolk's fingers. Tight end Craig Dunaway, cutting behind the play, dove for the rebound and caught it, just before the ball hit the ground. It was a stunning Michigan touchdown with just 41 seconds left.

Wangler's two-point conversion pass to Dunaway failed, and the Michigan lead stayed at 27-26.

After the kickoff, with the ball at the ND 20, Coach Dan Devine made a huge decision. He sent in strong-armed freshman Blair Kiel, the only Irish quarterback who had practiced a shotgun formation that suddenly Notre Dame unveiled for the first time. Kiel, also the team's

punter, took his first snap and threw a shaky floater towards midfield.

"It was a duck," said intended receiver Tony Hunter. "I was waiting for it and as I got ready to jump, a guy hit my side." It was Marion Body, who had previously picked off an Irish pass. Right in front of the Michigan bench, he was called for pass interference, a 32-yard penalty moving the ball to the UM 48.

"I'm not going to comment on the officiating," said Schembechler about the pivotal call. He paused and continued. "That usually says enough."

Now in Michigan territory, Kiel's second pass was nearly intercepted by Jeff Reeves. His third pass again barely escaped Michigan's hands.

After three plays, Devine's decision to use his freshman QB was looking shaky.

But on third down, Kiel finally connected to Carter out of the backfield. He stretched nine yards out of the play to the UM 39. Still, it was fourth-and-one. Just nine seconds remaining.

With no timeouts left, Kiel threw a quick out to Hunter who caught it for a five-yard gain, but then turned upfield instead of immediately getting out of bounds. Fortunately for Devine and the Irish, his foot stepped out at the UM 34.

Four seconds to play. On came the Notre Dame field-goal unit.

THE PLAY
CD 1—Track 10—*Tony Roberts, Al Wester,* **Westwood One**

The wind was reported to be blowing from the south at 15 MPH...right into the face of Harry Oliver, a left-footed kicker from Cincinnati Moeller High School (home of the next Notre Dame coach Gerry Faust).

As the Irish drove downfield, Oliver waited, pacing back and forth. "I was praying on the sideline. I was asking Mary, may the best thing happen," he said.

He had made one field goal in his entire Notre Dame career, an inconsequential 26-yarder, in a 31-10 victory over Purdue two weeks prior. The year before, Oliver kicked a 39-yarder on the junior varsity squad.

Game 15

Harry Oliver tries to make the second field goal of his Notre Dame career, a 51-yarder into the wind against Michigan. Photo courtesy of University of Notre Dame Archives

This was different. With four seconds left, Oliver scurried onto the field to try a 51-yarder...against Michigan.... into the wind.

As the Irish lined up for the field-goal attempt, broadcaster Al Wester checked the blowing flags atop Notre Dame Stadium. "The flags went limp. The wind had shifted," he said.

Devine sent in a signal. "I used a famous sign that I've used for a long time. It's called in the name of the Father and the Son," he said.

With the famed Touchdown Jesus mural over his shoulder, and 59,075 prayers behind him, Oliver kicked the ball. A low liner that sailed, and sailed, and sailed. Time expired.

"It issssssss..." Mutual Radio's Tony Roberts extended the word "is" for 51 yards.

"Good!" The ball snuck inside the left upright just a couple of feet over the crossbar. Simultaneously, the stands emptied, the Irish bench stormed the field, and the wind probably started blowing again.

"I didn't know it was good because someone had jumped on me and I was on the ground," said Oliver. That someone was holder Tim Koegel who screamed to Oliver, "It's good. It's good!" His teammates mobbed him.

"I've never seen Oliver kick one that far, but it went through today and that's all I care about," said Devine.

The scoreboard read "Notre Dame 29, Michigan 27." The following Monday, the *Michigan Daily* newspaper read "Michigan 27, Notre Dame 26, God 3." Perhaps both were right.

Schembechler put the game into perspective. "When you've coached as long as I have, you've had them worse than this," he philosophized. "This is the type of game that you win 20 times and lose 20 times. You've got to win this kind of game one more time than you lose it."

Wangler wished this game was that one time. "This probably would have been the highlight of my career if we had won," he said.

THE AFTERMATH

Last-second field goals (made and missed) have since become commonplace in the ND-Michigan series. Harry Oliver made it in '80, John Carney missed it in '86. Michigan's

Remy Hamilton made it in '94, Mike Gillette missed it in '88.

Notre Dame stayed undefeated throughout most of the 1980 season. They were No. 1 in the country before Georgia Tech tied the Irish 3-3 early in November. ND finished the regular season 9-1-1 after a 20-3 loss at USC. Then, in Dan Devine's last game as Notre Dame coach, top-ranked Georgia knocked off the Irish 17-10 in the Sugar Bowl to win the national championship.

Michigan was stunned the following week by South Carolina 17-14, but then rebounded to win their final nine games of the season, the Big Ten championship, and the Rose Bowl with a 23-6 victory over Washington.

It was Bo Schembechler's first bowl game victory ever and his first Rose Bowl triumph in six tries. The Wolverines finished No.4 in the AP poll, while Notre Dame was No. 9.

Michigan	0	14	7	6	-27
Notre Dame	0	14	6	9	-29

ND	Carter 6 run (Oliver kick)
ND	Holohan 10 pass from Courey (Oliver kick)
UM	Ricks 8 pass from Wangler (Haji-Sheikh kick)
UM	Betts 9 pass from Wangler (Haji-Sheikh kick)
UM	Edwards 2 run (Haji-Sheikh kick)
ND	Krimm 49 interception return (kick failed)
ND	Carter 4 run (pass failed)
UM	Dunaway 1 pass from Wangler (pass failed)
ND	Oliver 51 FG

Attendance 59,075

Kentucky vs. 🏈Tulane

"Gentlemen, I ain't got no comment."—Fran Curci

THE BACKGROUND

Fran Curci was not a crowd favorite at Tulane. And with good reason.

In 1972, Curci, in his second year as head coach at Miami (FL), led his Hurricanes into battle against the Green Wave at the Orange Bowl. With Tulane leading 21-17 late in the fourth quarter, Miami drove to the TU 18. The following sequence of plays occurred.

First-and-10 at the 18. Chuck Foreman gains two yards. Second-and-eight at the 16.Ed Carney throws incomplete, intended for Foreman. Third-and-eight at the 16. Carney's pass to Foreman is complete but Miami is penalized for illegal procedure.

After the penalty, third-and-13 at the 21. Carney's sacked for an 11-yard loss. Fourth-and-24 at the 32. Carney throws incomplete to Phil Corrigan.

Tulane takes over on downs, right? Wrong. Miami was mistakenly given an extra down.

Fifth-and-24 at the 32. Carney hits Witt Beckman for a 32-yard TD pass with 1:05 to play.

Miami, benefiting from an official's mistake, shocked the Green Wave and won the game 24-21. Tulane president Dr. Herbert Longnecker meticulously articulated the opinion of his school. "Had Tulane won a game under these conditions, the alleged victory would have been rescinded by our own actions and the game's outcome would have been reversed with the score reverting to that existing at the time of the illegal play," he said.

The rest of the Tulane faithful were more succinct.

"We got screwed," was probably the prevailing response in New Orleans. Either way, Miami kept the victory and Tulane kept a chip on their shoulder for Curci, who the following year, took the head coaching position at Kentucky.

Eight years later, Curci brought his Wildcats to the New Orleans Superdome on All-Saints Day to face Tulane, a school that was seemingly cursed against Curci-coached squads (Tampa, Miami, and Kentucky)...winless in five tries.

But this time, the Green Wave (5-3) looked golden against Kentucky (2-5). Led by the combination of senior QB Nickie Hall and senior WR Marcus Anderson, Tulane jumped out to a 21-3 second-quarter lead. Hall found the fleet Anderson three times for touchdowns of 48, 14, and 4 yards in the first half.

Then, something came over the Green Wave. They blew a huge opportunity. After Tulane's Lionel Washington intercepted UK quarterback Larry McCrimmon and returned the ball to the UK six-yard line, the Green Wave, looking to blow the game open, failed to score. First-year coach Vince Gibson skipped a sure field-goal attempt, only to fall short on fourth down, turning the ball over to the Wildcats shy of the goal line. Curci's 'Cats responded as Tom Griggs banged home a 35-yard FG as the first half expired making the score 21-6.

In the second half, the Tulane offense stumbled when UK switched to a nickel defense to slow down Hall. In the meantime, the UK offense rallied. First, Griggs connected again from 39 yards. Then Charlie Jackson scored from the one-yard line with 11:22 to play, inching the 'Cats closer at 21-16. Tulane fumbled at the UK 39 and McCrimmon brought Kentucky all the way back with an 18-yard TD pass to Greg Wimberly. With 4:05 left in the game, UK led 22-21.

Still, the Tulane offense struggled, forced to give up the ball as time ticked away. The Wildcats ran the clock down, then UK's Randy Jenkins punted, pinning the Green Wave back to their eight-yard line with just 0:12 on the clock.

There were no plays in the Tulane playbook designed to gain 92 yards in 12 seconds.

So Hall just dropped back into the end zone and launched a long prayer toward Anderson across midfield. "They were playing a prevent defense," said Hall. "Coach told me, 'Let Marcus run across the field,' and I told him I'd throw it as far as I can."

Hall heaved it. Anderson reached for it. The ball fell incomplete.

Seconds later, a flag fell. Defensive back Chris Jacobs was called for pass interference on Anderson, a spot infraction at the time, translating into a whopping 46-yard penalty against the Wildcats.

Now, five seconds remained on the clock. The ball was placed at the UK 46. Tulane had one more chance.

Or did they?

THE PLAY

Tulane used their final timeout. Then Hall tried Anderson again, hoping for a miracle at the end of another Hail Mary pass.

He didn't get a miracle. He got another flag. Pass interference again on Kentucky.

This time, defensive back Venus Meaux had been singled out, making contact with Anderson before the ball arrived at the four-yard line. A 42-yard penalty. Tulane had been mystically swept from their eight-yard line to the UK four-yard line on a magic yellow carpet ride.

The clock read 0:00. Since the game cannot end on a defensive penalty, Tulane was given one extra play. Beside himself on the sideline, Fran Curci knew what one extra play can mean. Perhaps this was his penance, eight years removed.

With the ball now sitting on the four-yard line, courtesy of 88 yards in penalties on two plays, Tulane kicker Vince Manalla came on to attempt a 19-yard field goal with no time on the clock. It was the football equivalent of a technical foul in basketball.

Manalla made it. Tulane won 24-22.

The Wildcats felt cheated. "It's all that fifth down stuff," said UK reserve halfback Terry Henry. "No wonder Tulane is 6-2 (actually 6-3)," added disgruntled runningback Richard Abraham.

Curci was too mad to talk. "Gentlemen, I ain't got no comment," he muttered to the media before slamming the door behind him. His team was penalized 169 yards for the game.

Call it redemption. Call it righting a past wrong. But at Tulane, they call it the "Miracle of All-Saints Day."

THE AFTERMATH

"I'm going to find time to go to church Sunday," said a thankful Gibson, his squad moving to 6-3 and breaking the curse of Curci. The Green Wave defeated Memphis 21-16 two weeks later to clinch a berth in the Hall of Fame Bowl. They then lost to LSU 24-7 at the end of the regular season, and Arkansas 34-15 in the Hall of Fame Bowl, to end the year 7-5.

Kentucky finished 3-8. Fran Curci coached one more season at Kentucky. After nine years at the helm in Lexington, he was fired after refusing to resign in 1981. Curci, a former standout quarterback at Miami, coached the University of Tampa to a No. 1-ranking among small colleges before coaching at Miami from 1971-72, then Kentucky from 1973-81. Later, he returned to Tampa where he led the Tampa Bay Storm to the championship of the Arena Football League in 1991.

Game 16

Kentucky	3	3	3	13	- 22
Tulane	7	14	0	3	- 24

TU	Anderson 48 pass from Hall (Manalla kick)
UK	FG Griggs 19
TU	Anderson 14 pass from Hall (Manalla kick)
TU	Anderson 4 pass from Hall (Manalla kick)
UK	FG Griggs 35
UK	FG Griggs 39
UK	Jackson 1 run (Griggs kick)
UK	Wimberly 18 pass from McCrimmon (pass failed)
TU	FG Manalla 21

Attendance 42,139

November 1, 1980—New Orleans, Louisiana

53

Alabama vs. Mississippi State

"Maybe the good Lord planned things this way as a test."
—Paul "Bear" Bryant

THE BACKGROUND

Emory Bellard created the "wishbone" offense. In 1968, as an assistant under Darrell Royal at Texas, Bellard devised the multi-faceted attack which changed the face of college football in the 1970s. In 1975, Bellard received the Gold Cup Award from the Academy of American Football for his innovation. Four years later in 1979, Bellard became the head coach at Mississippi State.

After his first season in Starkville ended with a disappointing 3-8 record, Bellard came up with another new offense, the "Wingbone"; a multiple formation, triple-option scheme, that added a wing back to the right or left of the wishbone. Behind freshman quarterback John Bond, and an offensive line dubbed "The Bulldozers," the 1980 MSU offense broke school records for yards rushing and total offense in a season. They ranked seventh nationally in rushing, averaging 285 yards per game.

Pretty impressive numbers, until they're compared to the 1980 version of the Alabama Crimson Tide. Paul "Bear" Bryant's squad owned the longest winning streak in the country at 28 games. They owned the last two AP National Championships. And they ran the wishbone offense like they owned the patent to it. The top-scoring team in the country, Alabama averaged 425 yards per game, led by leading rusher Major Ogilvie.

Bellard should get some credit for 'Bama's success. In 1971, he got together with Bryant and laid out the blueprint of the wishbone for the Bear to learn...and master. Alabama football was never the same. The Tide (7-0) was the No. 1 team in the country, and 18-point favorites to stay that way when they traveled to Jackson, Mississippi, to face the Bulldogs (6-2). A game which looked like an entertaining offensive show, turned into a rigid defensive war.

Besides designing the wishbone, Bellard also knew how to disassemble it. Man-on-man, he crowded the line of scrimmage, daring the Tide to throw, and choking the option attack. 'Bama's power running machine slowed to a southern grind. "We looked them in the eyes at the line of scrimmage and went after them," said MSU linebacker John Miller.

"They had folks between us and where we were going," said Bryant. Linebacker Johnnie Cooks seemed to be everywhere. He had 11 tackles, so did freshman defensive end Billy Jackson. Amazingly, Alabama rushed for just 116 yards in the game. MSU almost doubled that output with 216 yards on the ground.

But the stingy 'Bama defense, which already had three shutouts in seven games, kept the Bulldogs off the scoreboard in the first half, and kept the Tide in the game.

With the score knotted at 0-0 late in the second quarter, MSU's Marty McDole fumbled a fair catch at the Bulldogs 35-yard line. Mike Pitts recovered for the Tide with just 34 seconds left in the half. 'Bama converted the miscue into a 49-yard field goal by Peter Kim as time ran out in the half and the Tide led 3-0 going into the locker room.

In the second half, 'Bama returned the

Game 17

favor. Reserve QB Alan Gray, in the game after starter Don Jacobs was shaken up, coughed up the ball at the 'Bama 33. The ever present Jackson recovered for the Bulldogs. Sophomore place kicker Dana Moore converted the turnover into three points on a game-tying 37-yard boot with 11:39 left in the third quarter.

Bond, the first-year MSU quarterback, gained 94 yards on 20 carries in the game while orchestrating the Wingbone. As the fourth quarter got underway, he led his team on a 12 play, 67 yard drive that stalled at the 'Bama five-yard line. Moore kicked the 22-yard field goal and MSU surprisingly, led 6-3 with 13:35 left to play.

Both teams' passing offenses were non-existent. Gaining most of his yardage on the ground, Bond was a paltry 2 of 10 for 25 yards through the air. 'Bama's Jacobs faired even worse. As the fourth quarter clock ran down on the Tide's chances, Jacobs was just 1 of 9 for 11 yards in the game.

But then, with just 2:13 left, the Tide defense rose up. Sophomore defensive end Mike Pitts blocked a 49-yard field goal-attempt by Moore. The MSU kicker desperately fell on the loose ball.

On the other hand, the stifling MSU defense wasn't about to give up any ground. The Tide went backwards. Jacobs lost three yards. Jacobs lost seven yards. Alabama was penalized for delay of game.

Third-and-20 back at the UA 43. Suddenly Jacobs became a passer. Out of nowhere, the Tide started to roll. Jacobs connected with Ogilvie for 25 yards. Then he hit Jesse Bendross for 14 more. Alabama was at the MSU 20-yard line.

Forty seconds left and the clock was running. Jacobs got under center and motioned to the officials that he couldn't hear. The boisterous Bulldogs fans were screaming, stomping, and clanging cowbells to try and stop the Tide's desperation drive.

Alabama had no timeouts left. The referees weren't going to give them one. The clock kept running. Jacobs had to snap the ball. He dropped back and found tight end Bart Krout over the middle for 16 yards to the MSU four-yard line.

Suddenly Jacobs couldn't miss. Horror-filled screams echoed through Jackson Memorial Stadium. The crowd got louder. The cowbells clanged harder. The clock kept running.

THE PLAY
CD 1—Track 11—*Jack Cristil,*
Mississippi State University Radio Network

Twenty-one seconds and counting. The MSU fans were deafening.

Jacobs hurried his team to the line, tried to bark out signals, but motioned to the officials again. "It was tough to hear," said halfback Ogilvie. "I'll be honest. I couldn't hear nothin' with all those cowbells," added Bendross.

Jacobs looked to the referees for a timeout. But 'Bama would get no favors. The clock kept running. There was no time to think about a tying field-goal attempt. Jacobs was forced to snap the ball.

He took the snap and faked to fullback Billy Jackson, then kept the ball on the option to his right. All of a sudden, Jacobs was smacked by defensive end Tyrone Keys. All of a sudden, the ball was on the ground. "I don't know if I was supposed to have the quarterback or the fullback," said Keys. "I just tried to take them both."

The ball was loose. MSU's Billy Jackson (yes, the same name, different jersey) quickly pounced on the Alabama fumble. Jackson had his second fumble recovery of the game. Mississippi State had their first win over Alabama in 23 years.

The crowd roared even louder.

The floppy ears of Crimson Tide mascot Big Al must have been ringing. "I thought we were gonna win the game right there at the end," said Bryant, referring to his team's valiant last-minute drive. "But the crowd took care of that."

Six seconds remained. The Bulldogs just needed to snap the ball and fall on it. The MSU faithful were delirious. Then, they almost choked on their cheers. Bond fumbled the last snap of the game at the one-yard line. A scramble ensued, but Mississippi State fullback Donald Ray King recovered.

The game was finally over. So was 'Bama's 28-game winning streak.

THE AFTERMATH

The historic victory for Mississippi State was their first over Alabama since 1957. Their next win over the Tide didn't come until 16 years later in 1996.

The Bulldogs finished the 1980 regular season 9-2, their best record since 1940. But the luster on the season rubbed off a bit when MSU lost to Nebraska 31-17 in the Sun Bowl. They ended up No.19 in the final AP poll.

Emory Bellard enjoyed success in Starkville for just one more year. The Bulldogs went 8-4 in 1981, but then had four consecutive losing seasons under Bellard before he was fired after a 5-6 record in 1985.

The Crimson Tide finished the '80 season 10-2, ranked No.6 after defeating Baylor 30-2 in the Cotton Bowl. Their only other loss was a 7-0 defeat to Notre Dame, a game decided in the second quarter by another Jacobs fumble.

Jacobs botched a handoff at the Tide 12-yard line. Notre Dame then fumbled it back at the one. Jacobs again coughed it up at the four, and Notre Dame's Phil Carter cashed in the second fumble with a two-yard TD run for the margin of victory.

Despite the misfortunes of those two losses in 1980, Jacobs was one of the most successful quarterbacks in Alabama history. During his career, the Crimson Tide won two national championships (1978-79). He played in three Sugar Bowls and one Cotton Bowl (his final game at Alabama), where he was awarded the game ball. Jacobs later became the offensive coordinator and quarterbacks coach at Troy State University in Montgomery, Alabama.

Alabama	0	3	0	0	- 3
Mississippi State	0	0	3	3	- 6

ALA	FG Kim 49
MSU	FG Moore 37
MSU	FG Moore 22

Attendance 50,891

Georgia vs. Florida

"We were doomed.We were done. We were going down the tubes fast."—Lindsay Scott

THE BACKGROUND

In April 1980, Lindsay Scott shoved his academic counselor and lost his scholarship to play football at the University of Georgia. Two months later he broke his right foot and suffered a concussion in an automobile accident. In October, he was late for a team meeting and lost his starting job at wide receiver.

On November 8th, he became a legend in Georgia football history.

Georgia was 8-0, ranked No. 2 in the nation. In his 17th season as head coach, Vince Dooley was in search of the school's first-ever national championship. Florida, ranked 20th, was a surprising 6-1 after finishing 0-10-1 in coach Charley Pell's first campaign in 1979.

Annually, this was the World's Largest Outdoor Cocktail Party in Jacksonville, Florida. Both schools drank toasts to their star freshmen.

Cheers to Herschel Walker. On the fourth play from scrimmage, the freshman running-back took a pitch from quarterback Buck Belue at the Georgia 28, cut right, and zipped by the Florida defense 72 yards for a 7-0 Bulldog lead. Walker rushed for 238 yards on the day.

Cheers to Wayne Peace. After falling behind 14-3, the Gators' freshman quarterback rallied his team, first lobbing a nine-yard TD pass to future NFL player-TV broadcaster Chris Collinsworth. Then, with Georgia up 20-10 to start the fourth quarter, Peace found reserve split end Tyrone Young with a 54-yard completion on third down and five that moved the ball from the UF 35 to the Georgia 11. On the next play, James Jones scampered 11 yards for the score. Peace hit Young again for the two-point conversion and the Gators sliced the lead to 20-18.

The Florida defense forced a punt and Peace moved his team again, connecting with Young on a 19-yard completion to the UGA 30 that put the Gators in position to take the lead. Brian Clark's field goal from 40 yards was good with 6:52 to play and Pell's underdog Gators had rallied with 11 straight fourth-quarter points to take a 21-20 lead.

Georgia took over on their own 20 and went backwards, losing seven yards and punting from their own 13. The Bulldogs' undefeated season was coming to an end.

Now in control of the game with 5:53 to play, Peace threw two third-down daggers into the Georgia hearts. On third-and-three from the UF 38, he hit Young for six yards and a first down. Then facing third-and-six at the UF 47, Peace found Young again for 14 yards (his 10th catch of the day for 183 yards), and another first down.

At the Georgia 36, the Gators looked to run off the final two minutes. "We were down," said Dooley. "I don't think there was any question Florida had the game."

But the Georgia defense came up with a crucial sack of Peace, forcing one last Florida punt, which rolled out of bounds at the Georgia eight-yard line with 1:35 on the clock.

Buck Belue came back on the field. He had completed just one pass the entire second half, a two-yard completion to Walker. He was 6 of

Buck Belue (left) and Lindsay Scott embrace after their 93-yard TD connection with 1:04 to play. Photo courtesy of University of Georgia Athletic Association

14 for a paltry 52 yards and two interceptions for the game. Georgia's offense was Herschel Walker, not Buck Belue. But with 95 seconds left, trailing 21-20, the Bulldogs had no choice but to throw.

On first down, Belue found no one open. He scrambled, losing a yard back to the seven. On second down, he threw incomplete to Charles Junior on the sideline.

Third-and-11. Just over one minute remaining. Ninety-three yards away from the end zone, Georgia was past desperate. Along the sidelines, many Florida players began celebrating the greatest victory in school history. Toasts were being made by thousands of Gators fans.

What happened next, turned their tumblers upside down. It also turned into the most famous play in Georgia football history.

THE PLAY
CD 1 - Track 12 —*Larry Munson,* *Loran Smith,* **University of Georgia/Collegiate Images**

Georgia offensive coordinator George

Haffner called for a possession pass, "Left 76," just trying to pick up the first down and give the Bulldogs some room to operate on the field.

Scott lined up as a split end to the right. Flanker Chuck Jones went wide left. Belue took the snap and dropped back into the end zone.

Lindsay Scott ran a 15-yard curl-in route, sliding left over the middle as Belue drifted to his right, and avoided the rush with the help of a key block from offensive lineman Nat Hudson. Belue then threw high to Scott, who jumped and grabbed the ball at the 25-yard line. With the ball in his left arm, Scott put his right arm to the ground to gain his balance. At the same time, the Florida strong safety coming up to make the tackle, slipped and lost his balance. Scott, the anchor man on Georgia's 440-yard relay team, was off to the races down the left sideline, gripping the football like a relay baton. Jones, who ran a deep post route attracting both a cornerback and the other safety, turned into a pesky moving shield, getting in the way of the Florida defensive backs as they hotly pursued Scott downfield.

Drinks were spilled all over the stadium. This is how Georgia broadcaster Larry Munson called the unforgettable play.

"Florida in a stand up five, they may or may not blitz...they won't. Buck back, third down on the eight...in trouble...got a block behind him...gonna throw on the run...complete to the 25...to the 30...Lindsay Scott thirty-five, forty...Lindsay Scott forty-five, fifty...forty-five, forty...RUN LINDSAY...twenty-five, twenty...fifteen, ten, five, LINDSAY SCOTT, LINDSAY SCOTT, LINDSAY SCOTT...(crowd noise...25 seconds)...I can't believe it...93 yards and Lindsay really got in a foot race...and I broke my chair, I came right through a chair...a metal, steel chair with about a five-inch cushion...I broke it...the booth came apart...the stadium, well the stadium fell down, now they do have to renovate this thing, they'll have to rebuild it now...this is incredible...well, we might call time, we've only got a five-point lead and by the way, there's a minute three and we've got to give the ball back to those guys."

Georgia did give the ball back to Florida, but not for long. After a Belue pass failed on the conversion attempt, the Gators returned the ensuing kickoff to the UF 36. But on the first play from scrimmage Peace was intercepted by cornerback Mike Fisher. Belue downed the ball twice and the game was over.

Georgia 26, Florida 21. Cheers to Lindsay Scott.

THE AFTERMATH

Pell wondered aloud how it slipped away. "All that last play was was a simple curl pattern. It wasn't a double reverse pass or wasn't fancy," he lamented. "It might be the simplest play in football. For us to win, our secondary would have to be good tacklers and we weren't on that play."

"It was actually a first down play but Lindsay turned it into a game winner," said Dooley.

For Georgia, Scott's only touchdown catch of 1980 was the catapult to a national championship, the unforgettable Superman rescue that preserved their undefeated season. On the same day the Bulldogs defeated Florida, intrastate rival Georgia Tech (1-7) tied unbeaten and No.1 Notre Dame 3-3, paving the way for Georgia to move up to the top ranking. Led by Walker, Georgia defeated Auburn 31-21, Georgia Tech 38-20, then Notre Dame 17-10 in the Sugar Bowl to finish No.1 in the country.

Florida ended the season 8-4, losing two of their final three regular-season games to state rivals Florida State 17-13 and Miami (FL) 31-7, then rebounding by defeating Maryland 35-20 in the Tangerine Bowl. It was the first of four consecutive bowl appearances by the Gators before Pell was fired in 1984 when the NCAA placed Florida on probation for violations occurring during Pell's five-year tenure in Gainesville. He left with a 33-26-3 record in five-plus seasons.

In 1997, Lindsay Scott was inducted into the Florida-Georgia Hall of Fame.

Georgia	7	7	6	6	- 26
Florida	3	7	0	11	- 21

UGA	Walker 72 run (Robinson kick)
FLA	FG Clark 40
UGA	Stewart 13 pass from Belue (Robinson kick)
FLA	Collinsworth 9 pass from Peace (Clark kick)
UGA	FG Robinson 24
UGA	FG Robinson 20
FLA	Jones 11 run (Tyrone pass from Peace)
FLA	FG Clark 40
UGA	Scott 93 pass from Belue (pass failed)

Attendance 68,528

Brigham Young vs. Southern Methodist

"I don't believe it. I don't believe it, and yet I saw it."
—broadcaster Al Wester

THE BACKGROUND

Doug Scovil was the architect of the pass-happy offensive machine of the late '70s and early '80s known as the BYU Cougars. Scovil had hopped between the college ranks and the NFL for years, teaching Roger Staubach at Navy, former LA Rams quarterback Bob Lee while he was at Pacific, and spending six years as offensive backfield coach for the San Francisco 49ers. In 1976, LaVell Edwards hired Scovil to be his offensive coordinator at BYU. In both '79 and '80, the Cougars led the nation in passing, scoring, and total offense, first with quarterback Marc Wilson, then with record-setting Jim McMahon.

The Cougars won the Western Athletic Conference for the fifth consecutive year in 1980, as McMahon broke or tied 26 NCAA passing records in only his junior season. He passed for 4,571 yards (no quarterback had reached even 4,000 yards in one season) and 47 touchdowns, shattering the old record of 39 at the time.

Two weeks before BYU's matchup against SMU in the Holiday Bowl, Scovil was named the new head coach at San Diego State. At Scovil's hiring, SDSU athletic director Gene Bourdet quoted Bill Walsh, then the 49ers head coach. "Bill told me that he actually went to Provo to study what Doug was doing with the passing game," Bourdet said. "He sat in on team meetings. He considered Doug one of the few true masters of the passing game."

Scovil would stay on and coach the Cougars offense for one last game.

BYU, which had never won a bowl game, entered the Holiday Bowl 11-1, riding an 11-game winning streak after losing their opener to New Mexico 25-21. SMU was 8-3, and forming the nucleus of an offensive backfield that would dominate the Southwest Conference for the next two years.

Freshman quarterback Lance McIlhenny, and sophomore running backs Eric Dickerson and Craig James put on a Holiday Bowl clinic on "how to pound the ball down your opponents throat." Dickerson high-stepped it into the end zone from 15 yards out. James rumbled for a 45-yard touchdown. The two backs combined for 335 yards rushing in the game. BYU had minus two.

This was an SMU romp from the very start.

The Mustangs stormed out to a 19-0 lead in just the first quarter while Scovil's vaunted aerial attack struggled. It was 29-7 in the second quarter, then 38-19 in the fourth. The game was on ice.

McMahon tried to rally the Cougars with a 90-yard drive. Facing a fourth down near midfield, Edwards sent in the punting team, essentially conceding the game. But McMahon refused to leave the field, demanding to go for it. Edwards reconsidered his strategy, McMahon completed a pass for the first down, and the drive continued. It was capped by a Scott Phillips one-yard TD run to cut the lead to 38-25 with 4:07 to play in the game.

But then after SMU recovered the ensuing onside kick, James took a pitch from McIlhenny on the very next play, headed right, then cut

Somehow, BYU's Clay Brown catches Jim McMahon's 41-yard prayer with no time on the clock. Photos courtesy of Culligan Holiday Bowl

back left behind a wall of Mustang blockers to score untouched from 42 yards out. SMU led 45-25 with just 3:50 left on the clock.

If the game wasn't over before, it surely was now....or was it?

McMahon immediately drove the Cougars downfield. At the SMU 15, he rolled left and threw into the end zone to a sliding Matt Braga who pulled in the low throw off the grasstop with one hand, then immediately showed the ball to the referee as if it was a clean catch. "I guess I did a pretty good acting job, and when I showed the official the ball he took a long time before he raised his arms," said Braga.

It was ruled a touchdown. The lead was 45-31. Even teammate Scott Phillips admitted it wasn't a catch. "The ball bounced into Braga's oustretched hand. Matt jumped up like he caught it and the ref believed him."

Soon after, the Cougars were believing too. After missing the two-point conversion, BYU kicked off with 2:33 left. Lee Johnson tapped another onside kick, this time just barely 10 yards, where BYU's Todd Shell fell on it before

any SMU players had a chance to cover it at the 50-yard line. The Cougars had the ball back.

McMahon scrambled, then launched a bomb over the SMU zone that was caught by Bill Davis at the Mustang one-yard line. Phillips took a sweep right into the end zone with 1:58 to go. Two minutes, two touchdowns. The score was 45-37. McMahon hit Phillips with the two-point conversion pass and the lead was 45-39.

For a third time, Johnson tried the onside kick. It failed. SMU recovered near midfield and with their vaunted ground attack and BYU down to their last timeout, the Mustangs only needed one first down to run out the clock.

They couldn't get it. On third down, Dickerson was stuffed in the backfield for a two-yard loss and SMU was forced to punt from the BYU 48. But just 0:18 remained.

Eric Kaifes took the snap, extended his leg, launched the kick....and it was blocked.

Bill Schoepflin flew in from the right side of the line untouched, and buried Kaifes' kick at the SMU 41. BYU had the ball, but McMahon had just 13 seconds left.

He threw over the middle. Incomplete. He threw long down the right sideline. Incomplete. The Cougars were down to 0:03 and still at the 41.

THE PLAY

CD 1—Track 13—*Tony Roberts, Al Wester*, Westwood One

Scovil, the mastermind behind the Cougars' fourth-quarter blitz, sent in the last play he would ever call for Brigham Young. It wasn't very elaborate.

"We wanna block both backs. Everybody run right for the goal line. All three receivers, the tight end and two wide receivers. Throw it up," he said, pushing a BYU player onto the field.

McMahon took the snap, dropped straight back and threw a towering spiral toward the middle of the end zone where only one BYU player, tight end Clay Brown had a chance to catch it. With three SMU players on his back and three more circling in front of him, Brown leaped for the ball.

Brown came down with the ball. But so did defensive back Wes Hopkins. They fought for it. "It was a dual catch," said Brown. Under college rules, if both the defender and receiver come down with the ball, the catch goes to the offensive team. There was a long pause and then the signal. Touchdown.

"A miracle catch!" screamed broadcaster Tony Roberts.

The game was tied at 45-45 with no time on the clock. Sophomore Kurt Gunther came onto the field and booted the game-winning extra point and incredibly, BYU had completed one of the greatest comebacks in bowl history, winning 46-45.

Edwards was dumbfounded when reporters rushed to interview him on the field. "It's the most unbelievable thing...I...I don't know...I just....It's hard to...I don't know," he stuttered, trying to complete a sentence.

"It was just a prayer," said McMahon who threw for 446 yards, 239 of them in the last quarter. " That's what I told them. Just run to the middle of the field, and I'm gonna throw it up. You guys just go get it."

Scovil had a simple explanation for his last play. "That's what we call 'Save-the-game pass,'" he joked as he left the field.

Brown's interpretation? "It was a 'Hail Mary' pass," he said. "I can call it that because Jim and me are Catholics."

Mustangs coach Ron Meyer wasn't buying the heavenly overtones. "This comeback was no miracle," said the SMU coach. "I'd like to think miracles are used on things more important than football."

THE AFTERMATH

After Scovil's departure from BYU, the Cougars won five more WAC titles in a row, giving them a streak of 10 consecutive championships from 1976-1985.

Scovil coached San Diego State from '81-'85. He was fired after a 24-32-1 record in five years. He later was hired as quarterbacks coach for the Philadelphia Eagles where he tutored Randall Cunningham. On December 9, 1989, Scovil, age 62, died of a heart attack at Veterans Stadium in Philadelphia after his daily workout on a stationary bike ride following a team practice.

Although SMU finished the 1980 season 8-4, the Mustangs would become one of college football's most powerul teams in the next four years. From '81-'84, they were 41-5-1, winning their first SWC title in 16 years in '81, then capturing the conference crown again in '82 and '84. At the same time, they were running into problems with the NCAA. On probation in '81 and barred from post-season play, the SMU program was given the death penalty in '87, university officials chose not to field a team in '88, then restarted the program again in 1989 under new coach Forrest Gregg.

Game 19

SMU	19	10	9	7	-45
BYU	7	6	6	27	-46

SMU	Eric Dickerson 15 run (Garcia kick)
SMU	James 45 run (Garcia kick)
SMU	Safety, ball snapped out of end zone
SMU	Garcia 42 FG
BYU	Brown 64 pass from McMahon (Gunther kick)
SMU	James 3 pass from McIlhenny (Garcia kick)
SMU	Garcia 44 FG
BYU	Sikahema 83 punt return (pass failed)
SMU	Dickerson 1 run (pass failed)
BYU	Brown 13 pass from McMahon (pass failed)
SMU	Garcia 42 FG
BYU	Phillips 1 run (Gunther kick)
SMU	James 42 run (Garcia kick)
BYU	Braga 15 pass from McMahon (pass failed)
BYU	Phillips 1 run (Phillips pass from McMahon)
BYU	Brown 41 pass from McMahon (Gunther kick)

Attendance 50,214

63

Boise State vs. Eastern Kentucky

"I feel 15 feet high."—Jim Criner, Boise State head coach

THE BACKGROUND

It was supposed to be Lehigh and Grambling playing for the national championship in the Camellia Bowl . In the four team I-AA playoffs, Lehigh, unbeaten and rated No. 1 in the country, hosted defending national champion Eastern Kentucky (9-2) in a rematch of the '79 title game won by EKU 30-7. At the same time, heavily favored and No.2-ranked Grambling traveled to Idaho to face the 8-3 Broncos of Boise State.

Surprisingly, the underdogs prevailed. EKU upended Lehigh 23-20, while Boise State knocked off Eddie Robinson's Tigers 14-9. So the two lower-seeded teams met at Hughes Stadium in Sacramento, California, to decide the national championship.

It was a contrast of styles, the conservative Colonels from Richmond, Kentucky, against the renegade Broncos from Idaho. Long time Boise State announcer Paul J. Schneider recalled the teams' demeanors. "At the banquet the night before [the game], Eastern Kentucky showed up in suits and ties and Boise State showed up in long hair and denim," said Schneider. "[Boise State] was kind of an outlaw football team. A lot of people thought they were undisciplined. But that wasn't the case."

The Bronco leader was senior quarterback Joe Aliotti, described by *Idaho Statesman* reporter Jim Poore as, "college football's answer to Minnesota Fats, Amarillo Slim, and every other character who mocks the law of averages." Aliotti, a tobacco-chewing free spirit who led the country in passing efficiency during his junior year, was one of BSU's "Four Horsemen." Mimicking the famous Notre Dame foursome, Aliotti joined senior runningbacks Terry Zahner, David Hughes, and Cedric Minter on horseback in a promotional picture touting the Bronco football program. On the field, it was Aliotti's fourth-quarter flea flicker pass— a handoff to Zahner, a pitchback to Aliotti, then a 63-yard TD toss to wide receiver Kipp Bedard—that beat Grambling in the semifinal.

In the championship game, Bedard again came up big for Aliotti. Besides catching a five-yard TD pass in the second quarter, he corralled 11 catches for 212 of Aliotti's 358 yards passing in the game. Combined with Minter's running (105 yards on 22 carries), the Broncos jumped to a 21-10 lead with 12:25 left in the third quarter.

But the defending national champions stormed back. Quarterback Chris Isaac, a spunky 5-10, 160 lb. junior, ran a keeper around the right side for an 11-yard TD midway through the third quarter to draw the Colonels closer. Then, in the fourth quarter, linebacker David Hill picked off an Aliotti pass and returned it to the Boise State 14. Four plays later, halfback Anthony Braxton scored from the two. With 11:15 left in the game, the Broncos lead was just 24-22.

EKU then moved the ball to the Boise State five-yard line and lined up for the go ahead field goal with just three minutes to play. The Colonels then got their signals crossed. Holder Steve Bird picked up the snap and instead of placing it down for sure-footed kicker David Flores, he tried to run it in for a score. Bird was tackled at the BSU 7. "That wasn't supposed to happen that way," said Flores.

"Steve just didn't get his hands on the ball and thought he could run it in," said coach Roy Kidd. "Three points and we're ahead."

But the Colonels' defense responded, holding BSU deep in their territory. After Tom Spadafore's booming 50-yard punt, EKU took over on their own 40 with just over a minute to play. Isaac's first pass was incomplete. Then on second down, tight end David Booze got behind safeties Larry Alder and Rick Woods. Isaac hit him. Booze streaked 60 yards into the end zone with 55 seconds to play and in stunning fashion, EKU led 29-24.

It was the first long TD pass the Broncos had surrendered all year, and it came at the worst time possible for BSU. "I was feeling as poor as you could, 'cause I let the guys down," said Alder. On the other side, the Colonels sensed back-to-back championships. "All we had to do was hold them for four downs," said Booze.

But then Aliotti took over on his own 20 with no fear. With the Colonels' linebackers protecting the middle of field, Aliotti went to Bedard on the sidelines at the 38. Then he hit Bedard again who took it to the Colonel 48 with 44 seconds left. On the next play, it was Bedard a third straight time. Aliotti scrambled and Bedard turned his out pattern up field. Aliotti found him at the 25, and the smooth receiver made it all the way to the EKU 14 before he was pulled down by George Floyd. First and 10 at the EKU 14 with 0:35 left.

Aliotti, operating with a noticeable limp from an ankle injury sustained in the Grambling game, then came up empty on three straight incompletions. He overthrew Bedard, then missed Hughes, then had his pass over the middle to Bedard broken up by safety Rodney Bird. It was fourth and 10 with just 0:20 on the clock.

THE PLAY

It came down to one play for the national championship. Aliotti dropped back and looked for tight end Duane Dlouhy. "I went to Duane but he was covered so I went right," said Aliotti. The senior dodged EKU nose guard Buddy Moore who broke free into the backfield. Aliotti ran to the far right sidelines. Still no one open.

Then Dlouhy sneaked behind the EKU defense to the left corner of the end zone. Aliotti kept buying time. "I looked back and he was open," he said.

"All I had to do was get open and then he saw me in the corner of the end zone," said the junior receiver. Aliotti floated the ball across the field, the Colonel defense frantically tried to recover. But too late, the 6-5 Dlouhy hauled in the touchdown pass. With 0:12 on the clock, Boise State had driven 80 yards in 43 seconds to take the lead 31-29.

After a desperation pass by the Colonels fell incomplete as time expired, Boise State secured their first-ever national championship. "Never-say-die, that's why we're champions," said Aliotti.

As the final drive unfolded in the broadcast booth, Schneider sensed the winning score. "After two plays you said, 'They're gonna win it.' I don't know if Eastern Kentucky and Roy Kidd and those guys knew it. But I think Boise State, to a man, once they started that drive, knew they were gonna win the ball game."

Kidd didn't expect it. "I knew they'd move the ball but I felt the best they could get was into field-goal range," said the EKU coach.

Broncos coach Jim Criner had a feeling. "We knew we had plenty of time," said Criner.

"That's been a history of Boise State football, even before I got here, of late game comebacks."

It was a good feeling all around the state of Idaho. "If I could bottle the way I feel right now and sell it, I'd be a millionaire," exclaimed Broncos linebacker Ray Santucci.

THE AFTERMATH

Despite losing the final game to Boise State, the 1980 season began a decade of dominance for Eastern Kentucky. The Colonels returned to the national championship game the next two years, losing to Idaho State 34-23 in 1981, then beating Delaware 17-14 in

Boise State's Shawn Beatton hoists the I-AA National Championship Trophy. Photo courtesy of Boise State University, Albertsons Library Archives

1982, marking EKU's fourth consecutive trip to the final game. Roy Kidd's teams had the highest winning percentage among all Division I-AA schools in the '80s (.781) with a record of 88-24-2.

Adding to their national title trophy, BSU coach Jim Criner was named coach of the year in the Big Sky Conference, capping a 20-4 record over the past two years. The Broncos returned to the revised eight-team I-AA playoffs in '81 where they advanced to the semifinals only to be eliminated on their home field by none other than Eastern Kentucky, 23-17.

Boise State	0	14	10	7	-31
Eastern Kentucky	3	7	6	13	-29

EKU   FG Flores 26
BSU   Bedard 5 pass from Aliotti (Camerud kick)
EKU   Braxton 7 run (Flores kick)
BSU   Hughes 1 run (Camerud kick)
BSU   Minter 1 run (Camerud kick)
EKU   Isaac 11 run (run failed)
BSU   FG Camerud 24
EKU   Braxton 2 run (pass failed)
EKU   Booze 60 pass from Isaac (Flores kick)
BSU   Dlouhy 14 pass from Aliotti (Camerud kick)

Attendance 8,157

67

Oklahoma vs. Southern California

"Just another day at the office...Oh boy, what a day."
—USC coach John Robinson

THE BACKGROUND

Number One vs. Number Two. John Robinson vs. Barry Switzer. These were the best of times at Southern California and Oklahoma. Both schools finished in the top three teams in the country in '78 and '79, with USC national champions in the '78 UPI poll. Oklahoma finished third in 1980, and entering the third week of the '81 season, the Trojans (2-0) were ranked No. 1 and the Sooners (1-0) were a close No. 2. The nationally televised game was the first meeting between the top two teams in the country since the '79 Sugar Bowl when No.2 Alabama beat No.1 Penn State.

Oklahoma featured its powerful wishbone attack with Buster Rhymes and Stanley Wilson in the backfield and rotating quarterbacks Kelly Phelps and Darrell Shepard taking snaps. For USC, it was student body right, student body left, with all-American tailback Marcus Allen. The Heisman hopeful had pounded out 274 yards rushing the previous week in a 21-0 victory over Indiana.

From the first play of the game, Oklahoma's offense dominated the line of scrimmage with long touchdown drives of 80, 80, and 74 yards. Using a multitude of offensive sets, Switzer's attack caused problems for USC defensive coordinator R.C. Slocum. "We flat confused them," said Switzer. "They were in a daze. They like to flip-flop people to the weak and strong sides, but they had people running over each other trying to line up in the right place." The Sooners piled up 307 yards rushing in the

game, spreading the yardage evenly among their four elusive backs.

While running the ball was not a problem for Oklahoma, running *with* the ball was. OU fumbled the pigskin a remarkable 10 times on handoffs and pitchouts, losing possession five times, including their first three possessions of the third quarter. Only two fumbles were actually forced by USC tackles. "If we had not had so many turnovers, so many missed snaps, we probably would have had over 600 yards in the ball game," noted Switzer.

Despite themselves, the Sooners still led 24-14 entering the fourth quarter. They had yet to punt all day. Allen kept the Trojans close with 208 yards on the ground, and two touchdowns. The second TD, a short three-yard run on fourth-and-goal, came with 6:37 to play, pulling USC within three points at 24-21.

Oklahoma got the ball back and looked to grind out the last six and a half minutes for the victory. But on a third-down play, Rhymes ran into his own blocker on a blown play and fell one-yard shy of the first down at the OU 40. The Sooners were forced to punt for the first time all day. Boosted by the surge of momentum provided by their first defensive stop of the game, the Trojans took over at their own 22 after the punt with 4:28 on the clock.

Allen and teammate Todd Spencer gained two straight rushing first downs. Allen then broke away for 18 yards, but a holding penalty forced John Robinson to go to the air. He turned to quarterback John Mazur, a redshirt freshman playing only his third game as a Trojan. Mazur

68

quickly found split end Jeff Simmons for a 26-yard completion. After working the ball to the OU 26, USC faced fourth-and-one. Mazur bulled ahead on a sneak for two yards and a game-saving first down.

Then facing third down at the 22, Mazur hit Malcom Moore for 15 yards to the seven-yard line. Just 17 seconds remained.

A pass to Allen in the flat fell incomplete. Twelve seconds left.

On second down, Robinson called in the play, "91 Read-Y," and told tight end Fred Cornwell to delay running his pattern. Mazur saw Allen out of the backfield, wide open in the end zone. He sailed the pass toward the goal line, then raised his hands in victory as the ball approached Allen. But all of a sudden, the late cutting Cornwell, thinking the pass was intended for him, reached up and tipped the ball. It fell incomplete.

"It was my fault," said Robinson. "I screwed up and had Cornwell running a new pattern, and he thought it was for him." The wide open Allen was stunned. "I can't say what I thought," he commented.

The clock showed 0:09.

THE PLAY
CD 1—Track 14—*Tom Kelly,*
University of Southern California
Radio Network

"We were never going for the field goal," said Robinson, bypassing a relatively certain 24-24 tie. "We were going for the win all the way. Too many things were going for us at that time."

Robinson sent in the exact same play again. This time though, Cornwell was to run his regular route, not delaying before slanting across the field.

Mazur found no one open. Then he rolled out to the left and saw some daylight.

"At first I thought I was going to run it in," he recalled, "but then things started happening." Two Oklahoma defenders zeroed in on Mazur. Simultaneously, Cornwell eluded freshman defensive back Keith Stanberry and broke to the left corner of the end zone, waving his arms.

Mazur softly lofted the ball toward the sophomore Cornwell, who had caught exactly one pass in his college career. This would be his first career touchdown. He held on tight as the clock read 0:02.

"When I caught the ball, I didn't know what to think, " said Cornwell. "For an instant I didn't hear anything. I thought there might have been a flag thrown or something."

Perhaps time stood still at the Los Angeles Coliseum. Then it started again. "But when I saw all my teammates charging after me, I knew the touchdown was good. I knew we had won. Not in my wildest dreams did I ever think I'd score the winning touchdown in the final seconds against Oklahoma."

After the PAT, USC led Oklahoma 28-24. The ensuing kickoff was squibbed to Rhymes at the OU 25 and he was quickly tackled at the 40 to end the game.

Long after the game was over, Cornwell still held onto the ball, never wanting to let go.

Switzer couldn't let go either. "We turned a rout into a defeat," he said. "We know we should have beaten the best team in the country. We were the better team."

THE AFTERMATH

Given the lofty early season expectations, the remainder of the year was disappointing for both schools.

Following the loss, Oklahoma went into a tailspin. They turned the ball over seven times the following week and were tied by Iowa State 7-7, then were dominated by rival Texas 34-14. Switzer's Sooners rebounded to finish the season 7-4-1 with a 40-14 rout of Houston in the Sun Bowl.

Southern Cal lost their No. 1 ranking when they were upset by Arizona 13-10 two weeks later. Late in the year, the Trojans missed a shot at the Rose Bowl, losing to eventual Pac-10 champion Washington 13-3. But there was reason to cheer for Trojan fans when they beat both arch-rivals, Notre Dame and UCLA, and Marcus Allen was awarded the Heisman Trophy. The Oklahoma game was the third in a string of five consecutive games of 200 yards or more rushing for Allen, which set an NCAA record. USC finished the year 9-3, with a 26-10 loss to Penn State in the Fiesta Bowl.

Oklahoma	7	10	0	7	-24
Southern Cal	7	7	0	14	-28

OKL	Phelps 11 run (Keeling kick)
USC	Allen 27 run (Jordan kick)
OKL	Wilson 1 run (Keeling kick)
OKL	Keeling 27 FG
USC	Kamana 2 pass from Mazur (Jordan kick)
OKL	Shepard 7 run (Keeling kick)
USC	Allen 3 run (Jordan kick)
USC	Cornwell 7 pass from Mazur (Jordan kick)

Attendance 85, 651

Notre Dame vs. Purdue

"I'm not sure where those plays come from at a time like that. God gives them to you, I guess."
—*Purdue assistant coach Dick Dullaghan*

THE BACKGROUND

Gerry Faust was 173-17-2 as a high school coach. During his 18 years at Cincinnati Moeller, Faust's teams won five state championships, four national titles, and 12 city championships, including nine undefeated seasons.

He was 1-1 as a college coach at Notre Dame.

Following the first loss of his college coaching career (a 25-7 manhandling by Michigan), Faust watched his top-ranked Irish tumble to No.13 in the polls as they traveled to Ross-Ade Stadium to take on intra-state rival Purdue (1-1).

For over three and a half quarters, the game was a defensive struggle. Both teams missed field-goal opportunities. Purdue's Rick Anderson sailed a 31-yard attempt wide left in the first half, while Notre Dame's Harry Oliver was short on two 51-yard tries in the second half (the exact same length that he made to beat Michigan a year earlier).

The score was tied 7-7 when Notre Dame took over from their own 45 late in the fourth quarter. Sophomore runningback Phil Carter then put the Irish on his shoulders and took off. Three runs and he was in the end zone. Carter's nifty 30-yard TD scamper with 2:57 left gave the Irish a 14-7 lead.

Sophomore quarterback Scott Campbell, whose college initiation came at the hands of Notre Dame in a 31-10 loss the year before (as a sub for injured All-American Mark Herrmann), tried one last time to move Purdue downfield.

The Boilers started at their 20. Immediately, ND's Tim Marshall dropped runningback Jimmy Smith for a five-yard loss. On second down, Campbell connected with Smith for a 12-yard gain. Smith then ran for two more, but Purdue was staring at fourth-and-one from their own 29.

Wally Jones kept the Boilers alive with a three-yard run. Still, after Campbell was sacked for a loss of two, it appeared the Irish defense was just too strong for Purdue. But then, hope for the Boilers.

Campbell spotted reserve tailback Eric Jordan who caught his only reception of the game for 28 yards. Purdue was at the ND 42 with the flame still burning.

Irish linebacker Mark Zavagnin was about to snuff it out. On the next play, the junior anticipated Campbell's pass, stepped in front of Smith at the ND 43 and saw the ball go right through his hands. The game-ending interception wasn't game-ending. It wasn't an interception either. The ball fell to the ground.

Campbell entered a second life. He scrambled, avoided the rush, looked into the end zone for receiver Everett Pickens, then let it fly. "We were supposed to throw down the opposite sideline to Eric Jordan," said Young.

Neither Pickens nor Jordan caught the ball. Somehow, senior flanker Steve Bryant found his way to the errant semi-Hail Mary pass and hauled it in before stepping out of bounds at the one-yard line with 0:39 left in the game.

Chasing Bryant was sophomore cornerback

Chris Brown, a replacement for injured starter John Krimm.

"To be honest, the ball wasn't aimed at Bryant. It was a broken play, and I scrambled until I saw Everett Pickens loose in the end zone. The pass was intended for him," explained Campbell.

Notre Dame then staged a goal-line stand. Defensive back Stacey Toran dropped Jones for a six-yard loss back to the seven. After Purdue called timeout with 0:31, Toran knocked down a Campbell pass intended for wide receiver Joe Linville. On third down, linebacker Bob Crable batted down another Campbell pass.

With 23 seconds left, it was fourth down at the seven. Purdue used their final timeout to talk it over.

As Campbell walked over to his coaches, the Boilers' sideline resembled the floor of the NY Stock Exchange. "Five coaches were hollering out which play to use," said Purdue head coach Jim Young, who then chose assistant Dick Dullaghan's advice.

"All the coaches were yelling at Coach Young and he told us to get away. Not that he doesn't want to listen to us, but he can't listen to all of us at once and still think himself," said Dullaghan. "I guess I was just the closest to him...or I was the last one he heard."

What Young heard was, "63 rollout, out of rip, with sail motion."

Cornerback Brown lined up in man-to-man coverage opposite Bryant. The senior flanker went in motion to the left. Out of the shotgun, Campbell took the snap. Bryant broke back to the right and headed for the corner of the end zone. Campbell lofted it up. Brown couldn't reach it. Bryant could. With a leap, he hauled in the touchdown pass, capping a scintillating 80-yard drive laced with fourth-down conversions, improbable receptions, and near interceptions.

Now there was 0:19 on the clock. Purdue trailed by just one point, 14-13.

Like a game show audience egging on a nervous contestant, the Purdue fans, all 70,000 of them, screamed for the two-point conversion attempt.

Young risked it all, and played for two.

THE PLAY

It was the exact same play. Only this time on the opposite side of the field. Bryant lined up to the right. Brown, with one more chance to stop the Purdue flanker, shadowed him across the line of scrimmage.

The Notre Dame defense recognized the play, but Brown didn't. He was on an island all by himself. "The guys were yelling to me, but the crowd was so loud I just couldn't hear them," said the sophomore substitute. "I should've anticipated it."

Hindsight. 20-20.

It was a reverse angle replay. Bryant headed in motion. Campbell took the snap. Bryant cut to the corner. Campbell lofted it up. Brown couldn't reach it. Bryant did. Purdue led 15-14.

"I'm just supposed to loft the ball up and let Steve run under it," said Campbell.

"The ball was high and outside, and I had to leap for it," said Bryant. "It was a much tougher catch than the touchdown."

It sure looked the same to Notre Dame. "It was just a case of two perfect passes, and two perfect catches," lamented Faust.

"I blew it," said Brown. "I had a chance to knock [both the TD and the conversion] down, but I just didn't do it."

Bryant begged to differ. "Number 9 [Brown], well, there was just no way he could stay with me," he said, surprised that he wasn't double-teamed.

The last gasp by the Irish was breathed when Tim Seneff picked off a Tim Koegel desperation pass with six seconds left to seal the unforgettable win by the Boilers.

"I've had many thrills at Purdue, but I don't think I'll ever top this one," said Bryant.

THE AFTERMATH

The upset of Notre Dame was the highlight of a season that started with promise but ended in disappointment for Purdue. After jumping to a 5-2 record, the Boilers lost their last four games to finish the year 5-6. Notre Dame also ended the season 5-6.

Jim Young, just 46-years-old, resigned at

the end of the season with a 38-19-1 record in his five years at Purdue. He took some time off from coaching then accepted the task of re-building the football program at Army in 1983 where he compiled a 51-39-1 record in eight years as head coach. In 2000, Young was inducted into the College Football Hall of Fame with a career coaching record of 120-71-2 at Arizona, Purdue, and Army.

Steve Bryant played in the NFL from 1982-87 with the Houston Oilers and Indianapolis Colts. Scott Campbell, who later in the season broke the school's single-game passing record with 516 yards in a 45-33 loss to Ohio State, also played professionally from 1984-90 with the Pittsburgh Steelers and the Atlanta Falcons. Chris Brown also played with Pittsburgh from 1984-85.

For Gerry Faust, the loss to Purdue was the first time since 1972 that the coach had lost two consecutive football games. It wouldn't be the last time. It happened two more times during the 1981 season and 10 times in Faust's five-year career at Notre Dame. In fact, on only one occasion from 1981-85 did Notre Dame follow an initial loss with a victory.

Faust resigned at the end of the 1985 season with a 30-26-1 record. He went on to coach at Akron where his teams were 42-53-3 in nine years. In 1998, Gerry Faust was inducted into the Ohio High School Football Coaches Association Hall of Fame.

Notre Dame	0	7	0	7	- 14
Purdue	0	0	7	8	- 15

ND	Smith 1 run (Oliver kick)
PUR	Jones 1 run (Anderson kick)
ND	Carter 30 run (Oliver kick)
PUR	Bryant 7 pass from Campbell
	(Bryant pass from Campbell)

Attendance 70,007

Pittsburgh vs. Georgia

"It was a classic situation, things dreams are made of."
—John Brown

THE BACKGROUND

Herschel Walker arrived in Athens, Georgia, in 1980. After finishing third in the Heisman Trophy balloting his freshman year, finishing second his sophomore year in 1981, then winning the Heisman Trophy in 1982, Walker left college for the NFL. The Georgia Bulldogs won three consecutive SEC titles and a national championship during those three years.

It wasn't a coincidence.

Midway through his freshman season of 1979, Dan Marino became the starting quarterback at the University of Pittsburgh. For the next four years, with Marino directing the offense, the Panthers were 42-5 with four Top 10 finishes.

It wasn't a coincidence.

While their respective teams jockeyed back and forth for three years near the top of the polls, Walker and Marino met just one time on the field—the Sugar Bowl at the conclusion of the 1981 season.

Georgia won the national championship in 1980 with a 17-10 victory over Notre Dame in the Sugar Bowl. Pittsburgh finished No. 2 in the final 1980 AP poll. For four weeks toward the end of the 1981 season, the Panthers were the No. 1 team in the country. Then, on the last Saturday in November, their national championship hopes were dashed with a 48-14 shellacking at the hands of Penn State. With Pitt's loss, Georgia, who themselves had lost just once (13-3 to the new No.1 Clemson), moved up to the No.2 spot in the country.

Both Pitt and Georgia entered the 48th annual Sugar Bowl at 10-1. The Bulldogs looked for a victory over the Panthers, coupled with a Clemson loss to Nebraska in the Orange Bowl, to claim their second straight national title. Pitt, which fell all the way down to No.10, hoped to prove that the Penn State loss was a fluke.

Walker gave the Bulldogs a 7-0 lead midway through the second quarter with an eight-yard TD run. But at the half, with Georgia leading 7-3, Walker had just 28 yards on the ground. Marino, despite being 14 of 19 for 100 yards, had yet to lead his team into the end zone.

That changed quickly in the second half.

Just three minutes into the third quarter, Marino found Julius Dawkins with a 30-yard touchdown pass and Pitt led 10-7. It took Walker one play to get the lead back. After Pitt runningback Bryan Thomas fumbled on his own 10-yard line, Walker notched his second TD of the game, bursting to the outside, tossing aside two Pitt defenders, and scoring with 6:42 left in the third quarter. After missing the PAT, the Bulldogs were back on top 13-10.

Statistically speaking, Pitt owned an overwhelming advantage. For the game they racked up 469 yards and 27 first downs to Georgia's 224 yards and 11 first downs. But 14 Pitt penalties (nine of them illegal procedures), accompanied with five turnovers, literally handed Georgia the lead after three quarters.

"We're killing them, but we're losing," bemoaned Panther offensive line coach Joe

Game 23

Pittsburgh quarterback Dan Marino celebrates with tight end John Brown after one of Marino's most famous collegiate passes won the 1982 Sugar Bowl. Photo courtesy of University of Pittsburgh Sports Information

Moore. The Pitt frustration peaked when Georgia's Ronnie Harris picked off a Marino pass at the Georgia goal line for a touchback early in the fourth quarter, kicking off a rollercoaster of events in the final 15 minutes.

On the next play, Pitt linebacker Rick Kraynak returned the favor, jolting the ball loose from Walker, and quickly giving the Panthers possession again at the Georgia 23. Four plays later, Marino hit tight end John Brown from six yards out to give Pitt a 17-13 lead with 11:40 left.

Then Georgia quarterback Buck Belue countered, marching the Bulldogs 80 yards in 10 plays and throwing a six-yard TD pass to Clarence Kay, who made a leaping catch in the corner of the end zone to put Georgia back in front 20-17 with 8:31 to play.

Marino's next drive stalled at midfield, and on fourth-and-three, Pitt's fate seemed sealed when Georgia's Terry Hoage stopped a fake punt attempt short of the first down giving the Bulldogs the ball with 5:29 left.

But Pitt boasted the country's best rushing defense. The Panthers, which held Walker to a season low 84 yards in the game, stymied the Bulldogs on three plays and forced a punt, giving Marino the ball at the Pitt 20 with 3:46 on the clock.

Again Marino took the Panthers to midfield, this time just beyond at the UGA 46, where they faced a potentially game-ending fourth-and-four. In a surprise move, the rarely mobile Marino ran a quarterback draw for an eight-yard gain, breathing new life into the Panther drive.

But two plays later it appeared dead when fullback Wayne DiBartola took a short pass from Marino, was hit by linebacker Will Forts, then fumbled the ball. Fortunately for him, wide receiver Dwight Collins pounced on the loose ball avoiding a fateful sixth Pitt turnover.

Still, as the clock ran down to 42 seconds remaining, Marino was staring at another fourth-and-five from the UGA 33-yard line.

Pitt called their final timeout.

THE PLAY

Marino walked to the sidelines to talk to head coach Jackie Sherrill.

Facing fourth-and-five at the 33, Sherrill could either send in placekicker Snuffy Everett to try and tie the game with a 50-yard field goal, or send Marino back on the field to try and win the game.

Sherrill was leaning toward the field goal. "I'd rather lose than tie," said Marino. "I'm that kind of person." Marino voiced his opinion to Sherrill, who then leaned the other way. "I'll be honest, it was Danny who changed my mind," said the Pitt coach.

Sherrill sent Marino back onto the field with a play. "69-X." "It's a simple crossing pattern by our two backs," said Marino of the play which also sends two wide receivers and the tight end into the pattern. While the Panthers looked to get enough for the first down, Georgia defensive coordinator Bill Lewis looked to disrupt Marino, calling for a blitz by his linebackers.

"I wanted to minimize Marino's chances for a big play," said Georgia head coach Vince Dooley. "It would have worked against most quarterbacks."

But not Dan Marino.

Recognizing the blitzing linebackers, and single coverage on his wide receivers, Marino took a slightly deeper drop back, then spotted tight end Brown streaking down the middle of the field. The two runningbacks, DiBartola and Thomas, stayed in to block, picking off Georgia's blitz. With no linebackers to help out, Georgia safety Steve Kelly tried to pick up Brown. "He looked like he was bending to the outside on a short route to pick up the first down," said Kelly. "I got my shoulders turned around and he broke behind me. When I looked up, there was the ball."

Marino's pass was floating right to Brown, not for a first down, but for a touchdown. "I didn't think that ball was ever going to come down," said Brown. "I just told myself to hang on to it. I couldn't drop that one."

He didn't. A 33-yard touchdown pass with 0:35 on the clock, shattering Georgia's title hopes, and sending the Pitt bench onto the field in a frenetic celebration, piling on top of Brown.

"For the first time in my life, I had claustrophobia...for a few seconds," he said. "I kept yelling, 'Get off me!'"

Marino was enjoying the air at a higher altitude.

"I'm on cloud nine because we won," said Marino. "This feels great."

THE AFTERMATH

Marino was awarded the Sugar Bowl MVP trophy. "I wish I could cut it up and give everybody a piece," he said. "I don't feel like a hero. I'm just fortunate." Marino's performance capped his greatest year as a college player, throwing for 2,876 yards, 37 touchdowns, and a .595 completion percentage.

Pitt finished the year No.4 in the AP poll, while Georgia was No.6. Small consolation for the Bulldogs, but as it turned out a victory over Pitt would not have given them the national title they hoped for, as Clemson defeated Nebraska 22-15 in the Orange Bowl to capture the national championship.

"This was the start of that next year we were all waiting for this season," said Sherrill pointing toward the 1982 season, Marino's senior year, as the Panthers' best shot at a national title. Indeed, Pitt started the following season ranked No.1. They fell in the polls, then regained the top spot in October with a 7-0 record. But for the second year in a row, a November loss, this time to Notre Dame 31-16, knocked Pitt from the top spot, dashing the Panthers' championship dreams.

Coincidentally, Georgia took over the No.1 ranking vacated by Pittsburgh and held it for the final five weeks of the '82 season before returning to the Sugar Bowl for a third straight year with a shot at the national championship, this time against second-ranked Penn State. But in Walker's final game at Georgia, the Bulldogs lost to the Nittany Lions 27-23, giving Joe Paterno his first national championship.

Game 23

Pittsburgh	0	3	7	14	- 24
Georgia	0	7	6	7	- 20

UGA	Walker 8 run (Butler kick)
PITT	FG Everett 41
PITT	Dawkins 30 pass from Marino (Everett kick)
UGA	Walker 10 run (kick failed)
PITT	Brown 6 pass from Marino (Everett kick)
UGA	Kay 6 pass from Belue (Butler kick)
PITT	Brown 33 pass from Marino (Everett kick)

Attendance 77,224

Stanford vs. Arizona State

"I thought my Notre Dame teams had a lock on dramatic comebacks. But Saturday night was the best I've seen."
—*former ASU coach Dan Devine*

THE BACKGROUND

Arizona State had the No. 1 defense in the country. Stanford had the No. 1 quarterback.

Heisman hopeful John Elway led the 3-1 Cardinal into Tempe, Arizona to face No.10-ranked Arizona State (6-0). The Sun Devils were at the end of a two-year NCAA probation period after the firing of Frank Kush in 1979. However, with the probation ending December 31, ASU was eligible for a bowl for the first time in three years, and had hopes of winning the Pac-10 title and making their first-ever Rose Bowl appearance.

Third-year coach Darryl Rogers knew he had his hands full with Elway, who had thrown one of his patented come-from-behind last-second touchdown passes to Emile Harry with 34 seconds left in a 23-20 victory over Ohio State earlier in the season. "God gave him a little more instinct than some others," Rogers said before the game.

Elway's instinct led him to the brink of becoming the all-time Pac-10 leading passer in his senior season. He averaged 386 yards through the air. Arizona State gave up just 102. Something had to give on this clear desert night.

Elway came out on fire. He sliced up the ASU secondary, completing 7 of 8 passes for 72 yards. The Cardinal led 10-0 after their first two possessions. "I've never seen anything like his performance in the first quarter," said Rogers.

Fortunately for Arizona State, they didn't see anything like it for most of the remainder of the game. The Sun Devils employed a double safety blitz to keep Elway in the pocket and not allow him to throw on the run. "When you run the safeties in from both sides, he had great difficulty in seeing what he could do with the ball," said the ASU coach.

While Elway was kept under wraps, ASU quarterback Todd Hons brought his team back with a 31-yard touchdown pass to flanker speedster Ron Brown just 51 seconds before the half. After two quarters, Arizona State led 14-10.

Hons, a redshirt-junior transfer from El Camino Junior College where he won All-America honors, was rushed into the spotlight at ASU during the first game of the season against Oregon when starting QB Sandy Osiecki went down with an injury. Hons actually caught his own first completion at ASU, which bounced off an Oregon lineman, and back to him. Averaging just 110 yards passing, Hons was no Elway. But with the Sun Devil defense giving up a measly six points per game, he didn't have to be.

The fourth quarter wound down with the Sun Devils still leading 14-10. ASU had blown previous scoring opportunities when usually reliable kicker Luis Zendejas missed two field goals. Finally, with just over three minutes to play in the game, it looked like Arizona State would clinch the victory.

After driving to the Stanford one-yard line, fullback Dwaine "Tex" Wright took a handoff and bulled over the goal line....but without the ball. Stanford safety Vaughn Williams recovered

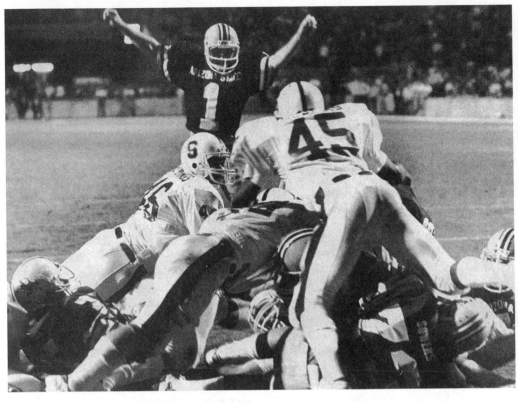

Sun Devil QB Todd Hons (1) drove ASU 80 yards in 38 seconds for the winning TD. Photo courtesy of Chuck Conley

the fumble in the end zone. Stanford had the ball with 3:14 left. They had 80 yards to go.

They also had John Elway, who suddenly out-maneuvered the dominant Sun Devil defense.

He hit flanker Mike Tolliver to the 42, then advanced to the ASU 43 where the Cardinal faced fourth-and-nine with just over 1:00 to play. Elway threw incomplete to his tight end Chris Dressel. But on the play, ASU cornerback Mario Montgomery was flagged for defensive holding. The ball was moved to the ASU 33.

Stanford coach Paul Wiggin sent in a trick play. Elway handed off to split end Emile Harry who threw back to Dressel for 18 yards and a first down at the ASU 15.

It was time for vintage Elway. With 49 seconds on the clock, he zipped a game-winning touchdown pass to Tolliver. Stanford led 17-14 as the Cardinal sideline celebrated another comeback win.

The desert air got chilly....and quiet.

Todd Hons came back on the field. ASU had little hope. It took Hons almost four quarters to rack up 108 yards passing on 8 of 17 attempts. Now he had 80 yards in front of him with only 49 seconds left.

But after watching Elway, Hons suddenly had the naive brashness to think the Sun Devils could race back down the field. "I knew we had a good chance to win," he said.

He may have been the only one among the 70,823 in Sun Devil Stadium with that thought.

On first down, he flipped a screen pass to tailback Willie Gittens out of the backfield for 14 yards to the 34. Then Hons connected again at the 50-yard line with split end Doug Allen who stepped out of bounds. Then a third completion, this time to Jerome Witherspoon over the middle. Witherspoon carried it 22 yards to the Stanford 28.

Twenty-four seconds left. Maybe that wasn't a game-winning touchdown pass by Elway. Maybe Hons took good notes while witnessing the Stanford drive. For 25 seconds, he sure looked like the Stanford quarterback.

Hons then threw for Witherspoon again over the middle. The passed was tipped, nearly intercepted, but fell incomplete. On second down, Hons tried it again. This time he connected with the 6-1, 187 lb. junior. Witherspoon was down at the one-yard line.

First and goal. Thirteen seconds left. Out of nowhere, Hons had traveled 79 yards in 36 seconds. The Sun Devils still needed one more yard.

THE PLAY

Up to this point, Tex Wright wondered if his game-winning touchdown run turned game-losing fumble would blow the Sun Devils' undefeated season. He stood in the huddle like a billy goat, waiting for the play to be called.

"When Willie Gittens came in, he said, 'It's a five-wedge. You're going to get another chance,'" explained Wright.

Five-Wedge. The exact same play Wright fumbled on three minutes before. "It's a quick dive play, strong side, between [center] Mark Shupe and [guard] Ron Sowers," Wright said. "I was going to put it in. They owed it to me."

Hons handed Wright the ball. He blew over the right side. He ended up in the end zone, standing up, with the ball. Redemption for Wright. Touchdown for the Sun Devils. Just 11 seconds left. A remarkable 80-yard drive in 38 seconds.

Hons had pulled an Elway. The Cardinal QB stood helpless on the Stanford sideline, watching the Arizona State quarterback steal his act. "They went down and scored," said Elway, "and there was nothing I could do about it."

Elway did get the ball back with 0:04 on the clock. But he had no chance. Defensive ends Bryan Caldwell and Walt Boyer sacked him at the Stanford 30 as time ran out. Final score: Arizona State 21, Stanford 17.

The Cardinal were crushed. "It was a heartbreaker of a game to lose," said Wiggin. "Everyone is so shattered right now."

Meanwhile, Wright rejoiced in his resurrection. "Not many people get a second chance," he said. " I thank Jesus. It's a miracle."

THE AFTERMATH

Arizona State marched to a 9-0 record before losing a Pac-10 title showdown in Tempe with previously No.1-ranked Washington 17-13. The Huskies had lost their top ranking two weeks prior in a stunning loss to Elway and the Cardinal 43-31. After the Huskies were upset again by Washington State, Arizona State had another opportunity to go to their first-ever Rose Bowl the following week, but lost again to their arch-rivals Arizona 28-18. The Sun Devils, instead ended up in the Fiesta Bowl on New Year's Day, the day after their probation expired. ASU defeated Oklahoma 32-21 as Hons threw for a career best 329 yards and was named the offensive MVP. The Sun Devils ended the season 10-2, ranked No.6 in the AP poll.

Elway had just 209 yards passing against ASU, although his last touchdown broke the Pac-10 career passing record by Washington's Jack Thompson of 7,818 yards. Stanford lost their next two games 41-27 to Arizona and 38-35 to UCLA before ending the season with the most memorable of all finishes in the Big Game against California.

Stanford	10	0	0	7	-17
Arizona State	7	7	0	7	-21

STAN	White 2 run (Harmon kick)
STAN	FG Harmon 24
ASU	Wright 1 run (Zendejas kick)
ASU	Brown 31 pass from Hons (Zendejas kick)
STAN	Tolliver 15 pass from Elway (Harmon kick)
ASU	Wright 1 run (Zendejas kick)

Attendance 70, 823

Southern Methodist vs. Texas Tech

"I can't believe it. It's a miracle."—Bobby Leach

THE BACKGROUND

The Pony Express was rolling through the Southwest Conference.

Southern Methodist's senior backfield tandem of Eric Dickerson and Craig James had led the Mustangs to a 9-0 record, and a nation's best 13-game winning streak that stretched over two seasons. Dickerson and James were one-two in the SWC in combined yards rushing and receiving. Dickerson led the league in rushing (147 yds./game), James was third (85.3 yds./game). When he wasn't handing off to his running backs, junior QB Lance McIlhenny was leading the SWC in passing efficiency with a 133.0 rating. The Ponies had a potent offense.

SMU, directed by first-year coach Bobby Collins, entered Jones Stadium ranked No. 2 in the country behind Georgia, and were heavily favored to beat the 4-7 Red Raiders. But the Mustangs had struggled at Texas Tech over the years, losing the last six matches in Lubbock. Coach Jerry Moore's team was coming off an emotional 16-14 victory over Texas Christian, in which sophomore Ricky Gann booted a 27-yard field goal with 26 seconds left to win the game.

True to form, Tech played the Ponies tough, trailing just 17-10 at the half. But late in the third quarter, SMU's Darin Boone blocked a Dennis Vance punt, setting up the Mustangs at the Tech 16. On the next play, James hit a large hole off right tackle and rambled in for the 16-yard TD run to put SMU up 24-10.

Tech answered right back. On the next drive, quarterback Jim Hart found tight end Buzz Tatom in the end zone from 16 yards out to close the gap to 24-17 at the end of the third quarter.

(In all the excitement following Talom's TD catch, Tech's mascot, the Masked Rider, circled the field on his black quarterhorse, collided with an SMU cheerleader, and knocked her unconscious for a few minutes.)

The Tech momentum maintained. Midway through the fourth quarter, Raider tailback Anthony Hutchison got loose. He broke off right tackle at the Tech 29, crossed midfield, then out ran safety Wes Hopkins to the goal line on a 71-yard touchdown. Hutchison's run topped his huge day rushing, singlehandedly dueling the Pony Express with 206 yards on his own, compared to the Dickerson-James duo's 212 yards combined.

After an SMU tie-breaking field goal with just over four minutes remaining, both Hart and Hutchison carried the load down the stretch as Tech tried to win the game. Hart hit four of five passes, while Hutchison picked up a key first down on fourth-and-two at the Tech 45. The Raiders moved the ball from their 29 to the SMU 11 with time running down. On fourth-and-two, and with no timeouts left, Moore sent in Ricky Gann to try a 28-yard field goal. For the second week in a row, Gann connected in the waning moments, this time with 17 seconds left and the underdog Red Raiders tied the game at 27-27.

SMU's 13-game streak and lofty ranking were in dire straits.

THE PLAY

On the ensuing kickoff, Moore planned for Gann to squib a kick downfield to either side of the field, trying to avoid a long runback and preserve the tie.

Collins had other ideas. He called for the play "kickoff return throwback," sending in wide receiver Bobby Leach and free safety Blane Smith to replace normal deep backs Reggie Dupard and Greg Hubbard. The plan was for Smith to take the kickoff then throw an overhand lateral to Leach on the left sidelines, who would then have a convoy of blockers upfield.

Gann's kick headed left, before bouncing straight down the middle and coming to rest at the 10-yard line. Smith had problems. He couldn't pick up the ball. As he stumbled and fumbled, searching for a handle for at least three seconds, the Tech defenders converged for the kill.

Finally, at the last second before being hit by David Eliff, Smith got control. He then blindly side-armed the ball, past the over-pursuing Raiders, over to Leach. The ball skidded off the astroturf, but Leach scooped it up at the nine-yard line. There wasn't a Red Raider in sight. "I looked to my left and saw nothing but a wall of white (SMU shirts)," said Leach."I kept saying six, six over and over."

Leach streaked up the sideline, right in front of a dumbfounded Tech bench. No one would catch him. A 91-yard kickoff return for a touchdown. Astonishingly, the Mustangs had pulled the great escape. Final score, SMU 34, Texas Tech 27. Jones Stadium was in a state of shock.

"You could look at one sideline and it was just euphoric, and the other sideline was total disbelief," recalled Bob Condron, SMU sports information director from 1971-83.

Leach, a low-key sophomore who had caught a wacky tipped pass off a defender's shoulder pads for a 79-yard TD to break a 10-10 tie versus Texas two weeks prior, was astounded at the play's success. "We practice that play about five minutes every week," he said. "I never thought we would use it. Until now I considered it the most wasted five minutes of the week."

Smith was happy Leach even got the ball. "I really didn't look before I threw," he said. "I got hit when I threw, but Leach can run a 10.2 100-meters, so I knew no one was going to catch him from behind."

Dickerson, who rushed for 115 yards on the cold afternoon, felt it was an act of God. "I always believed in miracles. It was His day. I'm going to church tomorrow," he said.

When he got there he may have seen Smith. "I was a little worried when I bobbled it," said Smith. "But we did it. It's a miracle. I believe in God."

On the other side of the fence, Moore was distraught following the game. He sat outside the Tech locker room sobbing, before having to talk to his team." I couldn't go in and face the players," he said. "This is one of the hardest experiences in the dressing room I have ever had to go through."

THE AFTERMATH

"The Miracle in Lubbock was the single most stunning moment I witnessed in the '80s, including Kirk Gibson's home run (in the '88 World series)," wrote Dallas sports reporter Skip Bayless.

Also known as the "Miracle on Fourth Avenue" at SMU, Leach's TD run kept the Mustangs ranked No. 2, at least for one more week. The following Saturday, ninth-ranked Arkansas tied SMU 17-17 at Texas Stadium when Mustang kicker Jeff Harrell's desperation 52-yard FG attempt with seven seconds left fell short. The tie clinched the Southwest Conference championship and Cotton Bowl bid for SMU, but it also knocked them out of a chance for the national championship which was won by Penn State. The Nittany Lions defeated Georgia 27-23 in the Sugar Bowl. Despite beating Pittsburgh 7-3 in a rainy Cotton Bowl, and being the only undefeated team in the country (11-0-1), SMU finished No. 2 in the polls.

In their final two seasons at SMU, Dickerson, James, and McIlhenny led the Mustangs to a sparkling 21-1-1 record. Dickerson ended his senior season as the SWC career leader with 47 rushing touchdowns. He became the all-time SMU rushing leader, and finished third on the SWC career list, with 4,450 yards. James ranks third on the SMU career rushing list with 3,743 yards. McIlhenny became the SWC's all-time winningest quarterback with a combined record of 34-5-1.

The Red Raiders' bitter defeat was followed by a 24-7 loss to Houston, leaving Tech with a final record of 4-7. Texas Tech athletic director, John Conley, also chairman of the SWC officials committee, was livid the following Monday after the SMU game. "I've been in the conference 21 years and I've never complained to the media about officiating," he said. "But it's a crying shame when a great football game is decided by an official's bad call or lack of call." Conley was particularly upset that no flag was thrown on Leach's run for an apparent illegal block below the knees on Willie Ray Johnson, the last Red Raider who had a remote chance to tackle Leach. "I believe the winners, the teams that have a chance of winning a championship, are protected," he said.

SMU did win the conference championship. Their unbeaten streak came to an end at 21 the following year when lost to Texas 15-12.

SMU	7	10	7	10	-34
Virginia Tech	0	0	7	10	-27

SMU	Dickerson 28 run (Harrell kick)
TT	FG Gann 37
TT	Hart 1 run (Gann kick)
SMU	Dickerson 9 run (Harrell kick)
SMU	FG Harrell 39
SMU	James 16 run (Harrell kick)
TT	Tatom 16 pass from Hart (Gann kick)
TT	Hutchinson 71 run (Gann kick)
SMU	FG Harrell 23
TT	FG Gann 28
SMU	Leach 91 Kickoff return (Harrell kick)

Attendance 45,954

California vs. Stanford 🏈

"We tried to concentrate on being a good band, and at the last possible moment we pull a play that will make us famous for all eternity."—John Howard, student manager of the Stanford band

THE BACKGROUND

The Big Game...The Play...The Trombone.

No game in the history of college football is more synonymous with "magical finish" than the 1982 version of this northern California rivalry, an annual battle overflowing with unforgettable and improbable endings. Consider these dramatic moments. In 1972, Vince Ferragamo hits Steve Sweeney with a seven-yard TD pass on the last play of the game for the 24-21 Cal victory. In 1974, Stanford's Mike Langford kicks a 50-yard field goal with less than a minute remaining and the Cardinal prevail 22-20. In 1976, Stanford triumphs 27-24 when Cal fumbles inside their own five yard line with two minutes remaining, setting up the winning score. Despite the legacy of thrilling climaxes, the 85th rendition of The Big Game remains atop the piles of memories, and can only be described by two words, "The Play."

Joe Kapp was concluding his rookie year as head coach of his alma mater. The 1959 Cal graduate led his team to a 6-4 record, turning around a program that struggled to a 2-9 slate in 1981. Kapp was a somewhat controversial choice to take the job, since he had no previous coaching experience despite many years as a quarterback in the NFL and CFL. At the time, the popular choice for the position among the media was San Jose State coach Jack Elway, father of Stanford's All-American senior quarterback John Elway. The Cardinal, led by third-year coach Paul Wiggin (a 1959 Stanford graduate), were battling for a spot in a post-season bowl game. They had an up and down season (5-5), peaking with a 43-31 victory over then No. 1-ranked Washington at the end of October. With a victory over Cal, they were off to the Hall of Fame Bowl. A loss, and their season was over.

Cal led at the half 10-0, thanks to a stellar defensive effort which forced the Cardinal into six punts on seven possessions. But in the third quarter, John Elway caught fire. He hooked up with Vincent White on two short passes, one a two-yard touchdown pass, the other a short flat pass that White turned into a 43-yard score, and the visiting Cardinal took the lead 14-10. An early fourth-quarter field goal by Cal's Joe Cooper narrowed the gap to 14-13. Two minutes later, Golden Bear quarterback Gale Gilbert found Wes Howell in the left corner of the end zone with a 32-yard touchdown pass and Cal regained the lead 19-14. But Charles Hutchings broke up Gilbert's two-point pass attempt and the lead remained five with 11:24 to play.

Cardinal kicker Mark Harmon booted a 22-yard field goal with 5:32 remaining, to cut the lead to 19-17. Then, after Stanford regained possession, it appeared Elway would march his team for the winning score when, with 2:32 left, he fumbled on the Cal 33 and the Bears recovered. But the Cardinal defense held, and Elway took over for the last time with 97 seconds remaining and one timeout left, deep in his own territory. On a desperation fourth-and-17 play at his own 13-yard line, Elway hit Emile Harry with a 29-yard pass completion, moving

85

EXTRA

THE DAILY CALIFORNIAN

SERVING THE CAMPUS COMMUNITY SINCE 1892

VOLUME XIV, NO. 51   WEDNESDAY, NOVEMBER 24, 1982   BERKELEY, CALIFORNIA

Three days later, it's 20-19

NCAA awards Big Game to Stanford

By BILL KUNS
STAFF WRITER

The National Collegiate Athletic Association (NCAA) has awarded last Saturday's Big Game to Stanford, the Daily Californian was told late last night.

The 85th Big Game, originally a 25-20 Cal win, thus will go down in NCAA record books as a 20-19 victory for Stanford, who, like Cal, will now finish their season at 6-5.

In an unprecedented and sure-to-be-controversial decision, a special NCAA panel, invoking a rarely used amendment to its bylaws, ruled yesterday that Dwight Garner, a Golden Bear freshman involved in the unbelievable five-lateral kickoff return at the end of regulation play at Memorial Stadium, was in fact downed by Stanford defenders at their 45-yard line as the clock ran out.

The commission also found many other irregularities in the play, invalidating those announced by the Pacific-10 Conference yesterday. Although the Pac-10 stated that the final score of the game would not be changed, the NCAA overruled the statement, handing the victory to Stanford.

With four seconds left in the game, Stanford place-kicker Mark Harmon booted a 35-yard field goal to give the Cardinal a one-point edge, culminating a Cardinal comeback that saw it trailing 10-0 at the half.

And so, three days after the Bears' epic play thrilled its fans and started a watching nation, a committee sitting in New York has ruled the touchdown invalid and awarded the win to Stanford, 20-19.

"Damn it," said Richard Davies, the NCAA's chief operating officer, "I've watched that replay a thousand times and if that guy wasn't downed my first name's no't Richard. I put our appeals panel on the case early Sunday

It was this picture, taken by photographer Ari Ray, that persuaded the NCAA to reverse the outcome of last Saturday's Big Game against Stanford. In it, a referee partially obscured by Cal and Stanford players is signaling the play dead (1) while Kevin Moen of the Golden Bears runs with the ball toward the Stanford end zone (2). Moen received a final black (3) as Stanford band members tried to avoid the play (4). The NCAA determined that the play was blown dead before this point and awarded the game to Stanford by the score of 20-19.

morning at the request of Stanford officials, who sent a telegram to my home in New York about 8 o'clock (EST) Saturday night.

"When the committee reported back to me yesterday (Tuesday) that to a man (There are five athletic directors on call for just such an occasion, although this is the first time they've ever been called) they felt that Head Referee Charles Moffett and his crew had blown the call badly, I set the machinery in motion to award the game to Stanford."

Berkeley Athletic Director Dave Maggard obviously was displeased
SEE PAGE 4

Bears shocked, appalled

By ANDY ALLMAN
STAFF WRITER

Officials and players reacted to last night's decision by the NCAA with a mixture of shock and anger.

California Athletic Director Dave Maggard was probably the most poignant.

"Frankly I'm shocked and dismayed," he said late last night. "I know this has got to be a terrible blow both to the team and the fans who have supported the squad all season."

Maggard went on to say that he will fight the decision tooth and nail although he was not exactly sure what recourse was open to appeal the decision.

"This ruling has no precedent," Maggard said. "Right now I'm not exactly sure what options we have open to us."

California players contacted last night thought the ruling was unfair with one player exclaiming: "This can't really be happening."

Although the Bears did not receive a bowl bid, the loss drops their record to 6-5 and certainly puts a damper on one of its most exciting seasons.

Cal receiver Mariet Ford, who made an outstanding (and controversial) catch in the end zone for the Bear's first score and played well all game long, was disappointed and angry at the decision.

"They can't take something like this away from us," he said. "When a game is over, it's over. That's all there is to it.

"What really burns me up is that that a group of people back in New York who weren't even there, have the authority to call this game. It just isn't fair."

Other players were even more to the point. Kevin Moen, who scored the final touchdown called yesterday's decision "a sad moment in college athletics.

"We know we won the game," he said. "There's no way they (Stanford) are going to take the game from us. We won it fair and

square."

After the game, Moen was questioned about the touchdown and he said he didn't even know he scored. Last night, however, Moen said that there was no question that the run was fair.

"I've looked at the replays now, I don't know how many times," Moen said. "There's no question that I wasn't."

The decision by the NCAA claimed that running back Dwight Garner's forward motion was stopped. When contacted by the Californian last night, Garner denied that his knee hit the ground or that his motion was in any way stopped.

Many of the Cal players will not hear about the decision till this morning and one player, quarterback Gale Gilbert, wishes he had been one of them.

"At least I'd be able to sleep tonight," he said when told about the decision. "I can't describe how I feel right now. Lousy just doesn't quite make it."

Even players who did not see action in the game felt the hurt just as much. Reserve quarterback Mike O'Donnel, a walk-on out of Bellarmine Prep in San Jose, said that this was the worst moment in his football career. "Even when I lost in the playoffs in high school (my junior year), it didn't feel this bad.

"I really feel bad for the seniors. This was their last Big Game. What a horrible way to lose."

Decision stuns Joe Kapp

By DREW DIGBY
STAFF WRITER

The phone rang a dozen times before a weary Joe Kapp answered it.

"Hello," he said, still obviously in the throat of sleep. But what might have been a sweet dream before quickly became a nightmare as Kapp heard for the first time of the NCAA's decision to reverse the outcome of Saturday's Big Game.

All the shocked Kapp could muster was a slow, shocked "Oh my God, oh my God." One could almost see the tears brimming in his eyes on the phone.

Then there was silence. A long silence, lasting upwards of

two minutes.

Joe Kapp, the grown man, the head football coach at Cal, and the leader of young men, was crying.

Between the sobs, Kapp began to form words that amounted to more than the two previous "Oh my Gods."

"This has to be the worst moment in my life," he said in a soft, hushed voice. "Why now, why me, why Cal, why Big Game, why in front of 77,666 fans in Memorial Stadium, why did it have to happen to my boys? It's just not fair."

The weeping continued, though Kapp was gradually collecting himself now. The statements became louder, the
SEE PAGE 4

Joe Kapp: "Life isn't fair — I swear to God it isn't."

the ball to the Stanford 42. A sideline pass to Mike Tolliver and a 21-yard sweep by Mike Dotterer and suddenly the Cardinal were perfectly situated in Harmon field-goal range at the Cal 18 with just 31 seconds left . Dotterer took the next handoff which gained nothing, the clock wound down, and Elway hovered near the referee before using his last timeout.

Referee Charles Moffett recalled, "After that last play, he looked at me and said, 'I'm going to call a timeout. ' I said, 'Let me know,' and he called it with eight seconds left as he was looking toward the bench."

If only Elway had waited a few more seconds, his last collegiate game may not have ended like it did.

Harmon trotted onto the field and nailed the 35-yard field goal, seemingly clinching a 20-19 Stanford victory, and igniting a huge Cardinal celebration. Harmon was mobbed by his teammates and a 15-yard unsportsmanlike conduct penalty for excessive celebrating was marked off against Stanford on the kickoff.

A kickoff that started with four seconds left.

THE PLAY
CD 1—Track 15—*Joe Starkey, Jan Hutchins,* KGO Radio

After the penalty, Harmon kicked off from the Stanford 25-yard line. He squibbed the ball along the Astroturf, where it was picked up by senior Kevin Moen at the Cal 43. Moen ran the ball to the Stanford 48 where he pitched it to junior defensive back Richard Rodgers. Rodgers quickly got into trouble and lateraled the hot potato to freshman Dwight Garner. Stanford players converged on Garner and as his knees fell to the turf he desperately flipped the ball right back to Rodgers. At this point, many players and fans thought the game was over. Some of the Cardinal players ran onto the field in celebration. The Stanford band moved onto the field from their position in the end zone.

"I tackled the guy and he was down, and I started running off the field. I ran to Sarge [weight-training coach Steve Schulz] and jumped on him and he was saying, 'Bowl, Baby,'" remembered Stanford's Dave Wyman.

"I was the third person on that pile, and I'm sure he was down. I even saw the referee signal the play over," concurred Cardinal Jack Gilmete.

Garner explained, "I had the ball almost between my legs; my forearm was the only thing free. I remember falling and Rich [Rodgers] calling my name, but they had my arms. At the last moment I got the ball out. People still question me, and, honestly, if you're from Stanford I was down, and if you're from Cal I wasn't."

The play continued.

Rodgers ran the ball to the wide side of the field and found some room before pitching it to wide receiver Mariet Ford at the Stanford 46. Ford continued across field to the southwest corner when he approached the Stanford band, now at least 20 yards on the field of play.

"Richard was definitely setting up the guy in front of him, but when I got it, I see the band and I'm confused," said Ford. "I knew I wasn't going to make it. I knew I was in front of Kevin [Moen], but I never saw him."

Ford ran the ball to the Stanford 25 where he blindly flipped the ball backwards. "I just figured Kevin was there and threw a blind pass. Once it left my hand I was smashed by three guys, and that's the last I saw of the ball," said Ford.

Moen, the original recipient of the kickoff, was alertly following the play as it continued, and found himself with the ball in the middle of the Stanford brass section, 20 yards away from an impossible touchdown.

"I remember seeing the band there and there wasn't really a lane to go through. As far as I was concerned, they were all Stanford players and I just busted through. I got to the end zone and spiked the ball," said Moen.

Moen also flattened Stanford trombone player Gary Tyrrell.

"I had turned around to look at our drum major, and I turned around again to see this guy," remembers Tyrrell. "I had this guy coming at me, and I thought he just wanted to get off the field to avoid the mayhem. And then I said, 'Oh, he has the ball,' and boom! It was a sobering experience, literally."

"The trombone player was just in the wrong

place at the wrong time," said Moen. (Yes and no…. Tyrell's trombone is now displayed prominently in the College Football Hall of Fame.)

After Moen crossed the goal line, confusion reigned. Numerous penalty flags were thrown on the play. Cal announcer Joe Starkey tried to make sense of it all over the airwaves. "It was an overwhelming sensory overload. It was almost too much," he recalled years later.

Now, referee Moffett had a decision to make. "I called all the officials together and there were some pale faces," he said. "The penalty flags were against Stanford for coming onto the field. I say, did anybody blow a whistle? They say no. I say, were all the laterals legal? Yes.

"Then the line judge, Gordon Riese, says to me, 'Charlie, the guy scored on that.' And I said, 'What?' I had no idea the guy had scored." (Moffett's line of vision was completely blocked by the Stanford band.)

"Actually when I heard that I was kind of relieved. I thought we really would have had a problem if they hadn't scored, because, by the rules, we could have awarded a touchdown [to Cal] for [Stanford] players coming onto the field. I didn't want to have to make that call.

"The [other officials] were shook. So I say, 'I can't believe it happened, but we got to make a decision here. We got a touchdown. Anybody disagree with a touchdown?' No one did.

"So I say, 'Here we go.' I wasn't nervous at all when I stepped out to make the call; maybe I was too dumb. Gee, it seems like it was yesterday. Anyway, when I stepped out of the crowd, there was dead silence in the place. Then when I raised my arms, I thought I had started World War III. It was like an atomic bomb had gone off. "

Cal had won 25-20.

At that moment, Starkey breathlessly screamed, "The most amazing, sensational, traumatic, heart wrenching, exciting, thrilling finish in the history of college football!"

It's hard to disagree….unless you're the Stanford quarterback.

"That was an insult to college football. They ruined my last game as a college football player," said Elway.

THE AFTERMATH

Starkey recalled the confused members of the media, who had left the press box after Harmon's last field goal to get post-game interviews.

"An enormous amount of people covering the game didn't see the finish because they were either in the elevator or on their way into the Stanford locker room to talk about the win," remembered Starkey. "They got down to the Stanford dressing room and said, 'What happened here? Why are they so miserable?' They just didn't know."

The Stanford band took the loss hard, feeling they may have contributed to the final play.

"Most members of the band are still in shock. They're hitting themselves. They wish they could do what Superman did in the movie, after the earthquake in California—turn back the clock, reverse time, as if it never happened," said John Howard, student manager of the band, a few days later.

Two days after the game, Wiles Hallock, Pac-10 executive director, reviewed the tapes of the game and announced that California was in illegal formation on the kickoff. They did not have the required five players within five yards of the restraining line. The Bears also started the play with only nine players on the field. The 10th and 11th players actually came onto the field after the play started. On the other hand, Stanford players also ran onto the field during the play when they thought the game was over. Hallock stated the 25-20 Cal victory would stand.

"I looked at the play two days later with the [Pac-10] supervisor of officials and we agreed it was arguable, but a lot of plays are," said Moffett. "Three rules changes resulted from that play, including one that does not allow a band onto the field until the game is over."

Despite losing the game, some Stanford students took the opportunity to get the last laugh on the matter. The following week, members of *The Stanford Daily,* the student newspaper on campus, printed up a phony issue of *The Daily Californian,* the Cal student newspaper. The fake issue had articles proclaiming a landmark decision by the NCAA to reverse the outcome of the game, based on a review of the game films. The perfect replica issue was distributed on the Cal campus, the same day that the real *Daily Californian* was having printing problems. So for a while, the joke tricked quite a few Cal faithful. In the end though, the Cal victory remained.

For Elway, it was the end to a brilliant collegiate career. He finished second in the 1982 Heisman Trophy balloting behind Georgia's Herschel Walker. His father, Jack Elway, became the Stanford coach in 1984 after Wiggin was fired at the end of the '83 season. Unable to be at his son's final game, the elder Elway was on his way to coach San Jose State when "The Play" occurred.

"I was on the freeway driving to our game, listening to the radio. I pulled over and beat my head against the steering wheel. Sixty-two times. I counted," Elway said.

On a bizarre side note, Mariet Ford, who was Cal's MVP in '82 and the player who tossed the last of the five laterals on The Play, was convicted in 1998 of murdering his pregnant wife and three-year-old son in Laguna Creek, California. Ford was sentenced to 45 years to life in prison.

Stanford	0	0	14	6	- 20
California	0	10	0	15	- 25

CAL	Cooper FG 30
CAL	Ford 29 pass from Gilbert (Cooper kick)
STA	White 2 pass from Elway (Harmon kick)
STA	White 43 pass from Elway (Harmon kick)
CAL	Cooper FG 35
CAL	Howell 32 pass from Gilbert (pass failed)
STA	Harmon FG 22
STA	Harmon FG 35
CAL	Moen 57 kickoff return (no kick attempt)

Attendance 75,662

USC vs. UCLA

"When I got him down, I thought, 'It's over. Thank God it's over.'"—Karl Morgan

THE BACKGROUND

UCLA was on the verge of its best season ever under seventh-year head coach Terry Donahue. The Bruins were undefeated in the Pac-10, two games away from capturing the conference title and heading to the Rose Bowl for the first time since the 1975 season when coach Dick Vermeil beat Ohio State 23-10 in his last game as Bruins' coach.

Then, heartbreak in Westwood.

A crushing 10-7 loss to Washington all but killed UCLA's Rose Bowl dreams. Entering the final game of the season against Southern Cal, the Bruins' familiar cross-city foe, UCLA (8-1-1) needed a weak-linked chain of events to occur for them to reach for the roses on New Year's Day. First, they had to beat the Trojans, something Donahue had done only one time in six tries. Second, Washington State, an 18-point underdog, had to upset Washington. And third, the following week, Arizona had to surprise Arizona State on its home field.

"Still a mathematical chance" was the common phrase associated with the Bruins' faded Rose Bowl hopes. In the mean time, UCLA made other post-season plans, set to head to Honolulu for the inaugural Aloha Bowl on Christmas Day.

The USC Trojans were going nowhere for the holidays. Despite a 7-2 record, USC was ineligible for the Pac-10 title or any bowl game because of NCAA sanctions. But nothing could take the tarnish off a season on probation like a victory over the Bruins. The Trojans' fans hoped to repeat a cheer heard from the UCLA faithful during the final seconds of Donahue's only victory in the series in 1980. "Roses are red, violets are blue, we're not going, and neither are you," they shouted, as time ran out in the 20-17 UCLA win. This time, it was USC's chance to douse UCLA's flickering flame of hope.

For the first time in the 52-game history of the rivalry, the game was played inside the Rose Bowl, which UCLA claimed as its new home field in 1982. Led by Tom Ramsey, the nation's No.1-ranked quarterback in passing efficiency, UCLA jumped out to a 14-3 first quarter lead on the Trojans, whose defense was only giving up an average of 12.2 points per game.

The Bruins scored the first two times they touched the ball. Tight end Harper Howell caught a nine-yard TD pass from Ramsey on a third down play capping an 80-yard drive. Then tailback Danny Andrews, on a third-and-13, broke away off left tackle for a 23-yard touchdown.

But that would be the end of the UCLA scoring frenzy. The Bruins managed just two John Lee field goals the rest of the way.

USC closed the gap to 17-10 thanks to a Ramsey fumble recovered by USC's Keith Browner on the UCLA 16 with just over four minutes left in the first half. Five plays later, tailback Todd Spencer scored from the three-yard line.

With UCLA leading 20-10 early in the fourth quarter, the Trojans ran the ball with Spencer and tailback Anthony Gibson trading handoffs from the USC 41 to the UCLA six-yard line. There, the Trojans had it first-and-goal. But linebacker Blanchard Montgomery stood up

November 20, 1982—Pasadena, California

Nose tackle Karl Morgan crashes in on USC's Scott Tinsley on the game's final play. Photo courtesy of UCLA Photography

Gibson twice, and, on third down, QB Scott Tinsley threw incomplete for Mark Boyer, forcing a 21-yard field goal by Steve Jordan. With 8:51 to play in the game, UCLA led 20-13.

The Trojans regained possession with 5:28 left at the USC 34. They held the ball the rest of the game.

Tinsley hit split end Jeff Simmons for 17 yards into UCLA territory at the 48. Then Tinsley found Timmy White for 15 more to the UCLA 31. Tinsley to tight end Pat McCool took the ball to the 15-yard line. Facing third-and-six at the 11, Tinsley went 4-for-4 on the drive connecting with White again for seven yards to the UCLA 4.

First-and-goal. Gibson crashed up the middle for three yards, stopped just shy of the goal line by Montgomery, who dislocated his left shoulder on the play. In pain, Montgomery stayed in the game. Second-and-goal. Gibson tried over the top from the one, but was stopped again by Montgomery. Third-and-goal. Gibson again. Montgomery again. For the sec-

ond time in the fourth quarter, Montgomery had almost single-handedly held the Trojans out of the end zone.

The gallant goal-line stand by the Bruins forced USC down to their final play. Tinsley ran the clock down to 0:03 before taking the snap on fourth down at the one-yard line.

This time, the Trojans avoided Montgomery. Tinsley lobbed a pass to Boyer in the back of the end zone. Touchdown USC!

With no time left on the clock, UCLA's lead was down to 20-19. But to the weary Bruins defense, it felt like the Trojans had won the game. "I didn't realize what the score was," nose tackle Karl Morgan said. "I thought we were trailing and had to hold them. So, when they scored, I thought we'd lost the game. Then, I saw the look in everybody's eyes and I knew we had one more chance."

In a finish wrought with sweaty-palm anticipation as the Trojans pounded on the front step of the end zone, there was still one more climactic play left in the game.

THE PLAY
CD 1—Track 16—*Fred Hessler,*
UCLA Football Radio Network

"A tie was an alternative, but not an acceptable one," said USC coach John Robinson. Indeed, a kicked extra point would have left the 95,763 fans demanding a refund. He called timeout to talk over the game's decisive play with his quarterback. The tension, already at a feverish plateau, escalated as Tinsley broke from his conversation with Robinson, then came back on the field.

Then the Bruins called timeout. The entire defense huddled with Donahue, seeking the general's advice when the final attack was imminent. "I know you've given it your best shot all day," Donahue told his team, "now give it your best shot for one more play, and if they score, they win, but we've given it our best shot."

The Bruins returned to defend their end zone. The drawn out final moments had the drama of a Hollywood whodunnit with all the suspects gathered in one room waiting for the killer to be revealed.

Finally, Tinsley came to the line of scrimmage. The Bruins presented a five-man rush, looking to quickly apply pressure. Tinsley took the snap and dropped back to pass as linebacker Neal Dellocono blitzed. Dellocono was picked up by an offensive lineman with help from the fullback.

But while two players blocked Dellocono, no one stopped Karl Morgan. He stormed through the middle into the backfield. Tinsley had a brief moment to look for a receiver, but it was fleeting.

Simmons was open over the middle, but Tinsley couldn't find him. Instead, he found Morgan pulling him down from the waist. Tinsley was sacked at the 10-yard line. The game was over. UCLA 20, USC 19.

"Tinsley had his arm up in the air and I thought he was going to throw the ball," said Morgan, playing with an injured knee. "But when he tucked it back in, I jumped on him."

"When I got him down, I thought, 'It's over. Thank God it's over.'"

It was over for USC, but not for the Bruins. The UCLA locker room celebration turned even more festive when word trickled in that Washington State had upset Washington.

The Bruins were still alive for the Rose Bowl.

THE AFTERMATH

Three days later, John Robinson resigned as head coach at USC. The Trojans sent him off into the sunset the following week with a 17-13 victory over Notre Dame, giving Robinson a sparkling career record of 67-14-2 and a .817 winning percentage. Robinson rode back into town 11 years later, taking over the Trojan reins once again from 1993-97. While USC was less successful in Robinson's second term, 37-21-2, they still won three consecutive bowl games, including the 1996 Rose Bowl over Northwestern 41-32.

For UCLA, the unlikely "mathematical chance" became reality when Arizona knocked off Arizona State 28-18 the following week, sending the Bruins to the Rose Bowl where they defeated Michigan 24-14. It was the first bowl victory for Donahue and the first of seven consecutive post season wins for the Bruins, including three Rose Bowls in the next four seasons.

When Robinson returned to USC in 1993, Donahue was still at UCLA. The two coaches faced off three more times with UCLA winning all three games before Donahue retired after the '95 season. In fact, Robinson never beat UCLA again, going 0-5 against the Bruins from '93-'97.

November 20, 1982—Pasadena, California

Southern Cal	3	7	0	9	- 19
UCLA	14	3	3	0	- 20

UCLA	Howell 9 pass from Ramsey (Lee kick)
USC	FG Jordan 44
UCLA	Andrews 23 run (Lee kick)
UCLA	FG Lee 45
USC	Spencer 3 run (Jordan kick)
UCLA	FG Lee 42
USC	FG Jordan 21
USC	Boyer 1 pass from Tinsley (attempt failed)

Attendance 95,763

Nebraska vs. Miami 🏈

"Going for the tie never entered my mind."—*Tom Osborne*

THE BACKGROUND

After 11 years as head coach, it was supposed to be Tom Osborne's turn.

The Nebraska Cornhuskers (12-0) were an offensive wrecking crew, averaging a staggering 52 points per game, the consensus No. 1 team in the country. In October of '83, *Sports Illustrated* touted the 'Huskers as "the greatest college football team ever." Nebraska surpassed all other college teams. They were being compared to NFL squads. In a *Time* magazine article, Washington Redskins runningback John Riggins said, "There are no great football teams anymore—except maybe Nebraska. And they're not on our schedule, thank God."

The teams that were on Nebraska's schedule took their punishment, outscored by a margin of 624-186. Average final score? 52-15. They had a 22-game winning streak and would have been defending national champions had it not been for a controversial early season loss in 1982 at Penn State, 27-24.

In that twilight game played with half a bank of portable lights out in the fourth quarter, quarterback Turner Gill scored with 1:18 to play, capping an 80-yard Nebraska march and giving the Huskers a 24-21 lead. But Penn State quarterback Todd Blackledge led the Nittany Lions on a last second drive.

Facing fourth-and-11 at the Nebraska 34, Blackledge hit Kenny Jackson who squeezed past the first-down markers by a foot. After a six-yard Blackledge run to the 17, the Penn State quarterback threw 15 yards to Mike McCloskey on the left sideline. Replays showed McCloskey was clearly out of bounds when he caught the pass with nine seconds left.

"I was worried," said McCloskey. "I saw some of the Nebraska players and they looked pretty confident that I was out. But the ref came over and made the call."

"If McCloskey didn't catch that one, we would have run once to the middle to get into field-goal position, called time and kicked the ball," said Penn State coach Joe Paterno. Instead, with the ball at the two-yard line, Blackledge found tight end Kirk Bowman in the end zone for the winning score with just 0:04 remaining.

Penn State went on to win the national championship. Nebraska had not lost since. One year and three months later, the Huskers entered the 50th Orange Bowl primed for a national title coronation.

Howard Schnellenberger arrived at the University of Miami in 1979. After leaving his position as assistant coach with the NFL Dolphins, Schnellenberger came to Coral Gables boldly predicting a national title for a school whose last bowl appearance was 1967.

In '83, he positioned his young Hurricanes to do just that. Ranked No.5, Miami (10-1) needed a monumental upset of Nebraska on the 'Canes home field, coupled with a Georgia upset of No.2 Texas in the Cotton Bowl, to make Schnellenberger's prediction come true.

Georgia held up their end of the bargain, beating the previously undefeated Longhorns 10-9 earlier in the day. Later that night, Miami,

Game 28

recognizing their opportunity, reeled off a shocking first quarter. It started when Kevin Fagan blocked Scott Livingston's 45-yard field-goal attempt on Nebraska's first possession. Red-shirt freshman quarterback Bernie Kosar then blindsided the Huskers with two touchdown passes to Glenn Dennison and the 'Canes led 17-0 after one period.

They could have had more. But with Miami poised for another score, Dave Burke intercepted a Kosar pass, and returned it to the Nebraska 26. That sparked a Husker rally. After driving to the Miami 19, center Mark Traynowicz faked a snap and left the ball on the ground. Right guard, and Outland Trophy winner, Dean Steinkuhler picked up the ball and rumbled left for the surprising touchdown. A play forever known as the "Fumblerooski."

Nebraska was back in the game. They trimmed the lead to 17-14 at the half. Then Burke made another key play, recovering Keith Griffin's fumble at the Miami 23 on the first play of the third quarter. That set up a Livingston 34-yard field goal, which tied the game at 17-17.

But Kosar led Miami back with two straight third-quarter scores, both keyed by Nebraska pass interference penalties. The first one on Burke, against Stanley Shakespeare in the end zone, led to a one-yard TD plunge by Alonzo Highsmith. The second penalty gave Miami a 29-yard gain to the Nebraska 44, and Albert Bentley capped the 73-yard drive with a seven-yard TD run. Miami had a 31-17 lead with 4:44 to play in the third quarter.

Things got even worse for Nebraska. Heisman Trophy winner Mike Rozier twisted his ankle forcing him to leave the game with 147 yards on 25 carries.

With a determined sense of urgency, the Nebraska offense attacked, but then repeatedly tripped. From the Miami 38, Rozier's replacement Jeff Smith rumbled 36 yards to the Miami 2, but then fumbled and Miami's Fred Robinson recovered. After regaining possession, the Huskers again drove deep into Miami territory. But the drive stalled and Livingston missed a 47-yard field-goal attempt.

Finally, with 6:55 left in the fourth quar-

ter, Gill cracked into the end zone on a one-yard run, narrowing the margin to 31-24.

Then Schnellenberger's squad fought back, driving to the Nebraska 26. But with 1:53 left and an opportunity to seal the win, Miami kicker Jeff Davis missed a 43-yard field-goal attempt.

Down by seven, Nebraska had one last chance to claim their crown. Gill, faked an option, spun around and hit Irving Fryar slicing over the middle. Fryar, just inches from sprinting past the Miami secondary, was narrowly tripped up at the Miami 45 for a 29-yard gain. From there, the Huskers moved the ball to the 24-yard line where they faced fourth-and-eight.

Osborne's offense was down to their last play.

Gill sprinted right on the option, then made a last-second pitch to Smith who rambled to the 20, the 10, the 5, he dove for the corner. Touchdown Nebraska. With 0:48 on the clock, Nebraska trailed 31-30.

THE PLAY
CD 1—Track 17—*Sonny Hirsch*,
University of Miami Football Radio Network

At this point in the evening, at the end of the New Year's bowl games, Nebraska was the only undefeated team remaining in the country. One successful extra-point kick by Scott Livingston could have given the Huskers a 31-31 tie. At 12-0-1, without question, Nebraska would have been voted national champions.

But that wasn't good enough for Tom Osborne and the Cornhuskers. They didn't flinch, immediately preparing for a two-point conversion. "We wanted to win the game. We didn't want to back into anything," Osborne said.

The Miami defense had to act quickly. "We called a coverage right away," said Schnellenberger. "It was a 50 double dog trio coverage. We were going to go into a blitz and three defenders to that side and cover all three receivers on that side."

Nebraska went for it all. "Triple right, 51, I-back fly" was the play. Gill would roll right and look for Fryar cutting over the middle, then Smith in the right flat. If they weren't open, Gill would take it himself.

Literally, one play for the national championship.

Gill lined up over center with the ball on the left hash mark. Kosar, his counterpart, could only watch. "I thought I was going to have a heart attack," he said.

Gill took the snap and rolled five steps to his right. Fryar couldn't get open. Smith slid into the right flat across the goal line. Safety Ken Calhoun was a step behind Smith. Gill immediately fired...slightly behind his receiver who turned back for the ball. Calhoun lunged, tipping the pass with his right hand. It ricocheted off of Smith's helmet. He had no chance. The ball fell to the ground. So did the Nebraska sidelines.

The Orange Bowl burst. The Hurricanes flooded the field, hands high, helmets off, dancing up and down.

"The ball was in front of me all the way," Calhoun said. "I hit it. I saw the play develop and it was my job to cover the back as quickly as possible. I got about four fingers on it. When I hit it, I knew we had it won."

Schnellenberger tipped his pipe to Osborne.

"There's a way to win and a way to gain stature among your colleagues and the public at large," said Schnellenberger. "I would have made the same call. He went for it like a champion."

Nebraska's last flicker of hope was snuffed out when Miami's Danny Brown recovered the ensuing onside kick. The Hurricanes ran out the final few seconds and celebrated the 31-30 upset.

THE AFTERMATH

Miami was voted national champions in the polls. Nebraska finished second. After building the foundation to Miami's success in the 1980s, Schnellenberger left the university and accepted an offer to become the head coach of a proposed Miami franchise in the United States Football league. That franchise never materialized and Schnellenberger's staff stayed at Miami for the '84 season, joined by new head coach Jimmy Johnson.

When Schnellenberger accepted the head coaching position at the University of Louisville after the '84 season, he brought with him many of his Miami assistants.

Eleven years later on New Year's 1995, after losing to Miami in the '89 and '92 Orange Bowls, after two consecutive Orange Bowl losses to Florida State in '93 and '94, there stood Tom Osborne, again trying to win a national championship at the Orange Bowl.

Nebraska No.1 versus Miami No.3. Before the game, Osborne, still chasing that elusive title after 22 seasons, recalled his decision to go for two, which over time had become a hightly respected, stoic move.

"I thought that to win the national championship we had to win the game," Osborne said. "I was not aware of any other option. So what I did wasn't any act of heroism. It wasn't any great fortitude. Just a reflex."

Osborne finally won his much deserved national championship that night with a 24-17 victory over the Hurricanes. The legendary coach won two more national titles in the next three years before retiring after the 1997 season.

Miami	17	0	14	0	- 31
Nebraska	0	14	3	13	- 30

MIA	Dennison 2 pass from Kosar (Davis kick)
MIA	FG Davis 45
MIA	Dennison 22 pass from Kosar (Davis kick)
NEB	Steinkuhler 19 fumble return (Livingston kick)
NEB	Gill 1 run (Livingston kick)
NEB	FG Livingston 34
MIA	Highsmith 1 run (Davis kick)
MIA	Bentley 7 run (Davis kick)
NEB	Smith 1 run (Livingston kick)
NEB	Smith 24 run (pass attempt failed)

Attendance 72, 549

Florida vs. Miami

"Words cannot describe the feeling."—Bernie Kosar

THE BACKGROUND

Miami had five days to celebrate.

The 10th-ranked Hurricanes just knocked off the No. 1 team in the country, the Auburn Tigers 20-18 in the Kickoff Classic on August 27th. Miami, the defending national champion, sporting a nation's longest 12-game winning streak, had to quickly turn around and face 17th-ranked Florida. The Gators were the last team to defeat the Hurricanes, 28-3 in the 1983 season opener.

In his second game as Miami head coach, Jimmy Johnson was just starting out in Coral Gables after five years at Oklahoma State. Across the field, Charley Pell was just ending his stay in Gainesville. Earlier in the week, in the wake of a 20-month NCAA investigation, Pell announced his resignation effective at the end of the season. He had taken the Gators to four straight bowl games in five seasons as head coach.

Pell's quarterback, in this, the Gators' season opener, was Kerwin Bell, a freshman walk-on, forced into duty when senior Dale Dorminey went down with a season-ending knee injury earlier in the week.

Bell played with wobbly legs the first two possessions, throwing wounded duck-like incompletions. Finally, after Miami took a 3-0 lead, Bell got his first collegiate completion and the Gators gained their initial first down of the game with 6:05 to play in the first quarter. It led to a Bobby Raymond 44-yard field goal, tying the game at 3-3 to end the quarter.

Eighty-nine seconds later, Gator tailback Lorenzo Hampton took a pitchout off left tackle on Florida's next possession and rumbled 64 yards for a 10-3 Florida lead.

Tampa Stadium, swamped with Gator fans despite it being officially a Miami home game, went crazy. But Miami stayed cool. Led by ultra-calm and confident sophomore quarterback Bernie Kosar, the 'Canes relentlessly attacked the Gators' defense, piling up yardage through the air all evening long.

But despite numerous trips into Florida territory, **Darryl** Oliver's 21-yard run around right end in the second quarter was the Hurricanes' only touchdown. Four drives stalled at the Florida 12, 3, 10, and 8-yard lines. All four times, freshman Greg Cox came on to convert short field goals. Miami, unable to put the Gators away, still led 19-13 entering the fourth quarter.

A fourth quarter not soon forgotten in the state of Florida.

Bell, gaining confidence as the game wore on, drove the Gators toward a go-ahead score when he found wide receiver Gary Rolle at the Miami 10 with 11:50 to play in the game. But Rolle was stripped of the ball at the four-yard line and strong safety Ken Calhoun recovered at the Miami 1.

The Hurricanes moved it to the 29 and were forced to punt. Miami punter Rick Tuten took the snap, but then dropped it, and ran frantically around right end, before being tackled at the 31 where the Gators took over with seven minutes left.

They could do nothing. Bell threw two incompletions and Raymond's 46-yard field-goal attempt fell short. Miami got the ball back, Kosar was sacked for a huge loss and Tuten had to punt again. This time he held onto the ball and Ricky Nattiel made the fair catch at the UF 48-yard line.

Trailing by six points and with 4:27 on the clock, Bell went from a freshman to a senior in 11 plays and 52 yards. He hit Ray McDonald with a 16-yard completion into Miami territory. Then facing fourth-and-four, Bell hooked up with McDonald again for eight yards to the Miami 28.

Again the Gators faced fourth down, this time fourth-and-five at the Miami 12. Again, Bell came through, scrambling around the left side for the first down at the five-yard line. On the next play, Bell hit Frankie Neal for the Florida touchdown with just 0:41 left. Florida led 20-19.

It would have been a legendary last-second Gators drive witnessed by 71,813 orange-clad fans from both teams, the second largest crowd in Tampa Stadium history.

But while Bell may have matured as a freshman, Kosar, in just his second year, was already a grizzled veteran. After Oliver returned the kickoff 16 yards to the Miami 28, Kosar took the controls with 0:36 on the clock.

He immediately spotted sophomore tight end Willie Smith for a 36-yard gain. Then he zipped a 17-yard pass to split end Eddie Brown who stepped out of bounds with 0:22 left. In the blink of an eye, Miami was at the Florida 19-yard line poised to kick the winning field goal.

Kosar completed a short four-yard pass to Oliver, stopping the clock with 17 seconds left. Then Oliver ran for three yards, to the middle of the field, perfectly lining up Cox for the game-winning field-goal try.

Kosar called time-out with 12 seconds left.

THE PLAY

"Bernie came over [to the sideline] and we discussed it," said Johnson.

Kosar thrived in these situations. He remembered the '84 Orange Bowl, and even though the 'Canes won that game, Kosar wished

he could have played more of a role in the thrilling finish. "I'd hoped Nebraska would have scored on that two-point conversion, then we could have driven down the field and at least gotten into field goal range," he said.

This time, Kosar wanted more than just a field goal. He wanted to win it himself.

"He thought we could score," said Johnson. "He saw how we had moved the ball downfield to get where we were."

Johnson took the chance. "It was a unanimous decision of the staff, and we felt we could get the touchdown," said the Miami coach. Kosar turned to his coach. "Thank you," he said.

"Running would be the safe thing to do, but that's not the way you win games," said the Miami QB, providing the perfect example of the take-no-prisoners demeanor which exemplified the Miami dominance of the 1980s.

Kosar brought the Hurricanes to the line of scrimmage, took the snap, and lofted a pass into the far left corner of the end zone. Miami's Eddie Brown was there, having gotten behind defensive back Vernell Brown.

"The ball was right where it should be," said Johnson. "If Brown doesn't catch the ball, nobody does."

Eddie Brown made the fingertip catch in stride, with 0:07 on the clock. Touchdown 'Canes. Miami 26, Florida 20. The Gators defense was shocked.

"No other team in America would have thrown the ball down there except Miami," said safety Roger Sibbald. "They caught us off guard."

Bell got the ball back after the kickoff at the Florida 26. With just 0:01 left, his desperation heave was picked off by red-shirt freshman Tolbert Bain, who weaved down the field 59 yards as time expired for another Miami score, making the final tally a deceptive 32-20.

Pell searched for an explanation. "We just couldn't stop them at all," said the Gators coach. "And that's what the game came down to. We just couldn't stop all of them."

THE AFTERMATH

Miami immediately jumped to the No. 1 spot in the country, only to lose it the following

Game 29

week at Michigan 22-14 as the 'Canes turned the ball over eight times.

The loss to Miami was the only defeat of the year for Florida. The Gators tied LSU 21-21, and walloped Tulane 63-21. But then the NCAA notified Florida of 107 alleged violations. Pell's resignation became effective immediately. He was removed as coach and replaced by offensive coordinator Galen Hall.

With a 1-1-1 record, Hall led the Gators to eight straight victories to end the season 9-1-1, and undefeated in the SEC. It would have been Florida's first SEC championship, but when the NCAA placed Florida on probation during the season, the Gators were stripped of their title. In the SEC record books, there is no conference champion for the 1984 season. Florida finished No.3 in the AP rankings, behind Washington and national champion Brigham Young. *The New York Times* final computer rankings listed the Gators No.1.

Miami	3	13	3	13	- 32
Florida	3	7	3	7	- 20

MIA	Cox 29 FG
FLA	Raymond 44 FG
FLA	Hampton 64 run (Raymond kick)
MIA	Cox 20 FG
MIA	Oliver 21 run (Cox kick)
MIA	Cox 27 FG
MIA	Cox 25 FG
FLA	Raymond 30 FG
FLA	Neal 5 pass from Bell (Raymond kick)
MIA	Brown 12 pass from Kosar (Cox kick)
MIA	Bain 59 interception return (no attempt)

Attendance 71, 813

William & Mary vs. Delaware

"I didn't realize we had won the game at first. It didn't hit me until the guys started jumping on me."—Jeff Sanders

THE BACKGROUND

Harold "Tubby" Raymond ranks as the second winningest active coach in Division I-AA, with 277 victories entering the 1999 season. Since 1966, Raymond has directed the Delaware Blue Hens to three national titles and 15 top 10 finishes. In 1984, Raymond's squad was 1-0, ranked No.8 in Division I-AA when they faced the College of William & Mary. The last two times the W&M Tribe traveled to Newark they were trounced 102-21.

"Delaware is a team that has had our number for a lot of years," William & Mary coach Jimmye Laycock said before the game. Sixty-one to be exact. W&M last beat Delaware in 1923. Sixty-one years later, Laycock was starting his fifth year at William & Mary (1-0), hoping to build a solid program for his alma mater. Junior quarterback Stan Yagiello steered the Tribe's attack.

"Stan was a little bit like a I-AA Elway," recalled W&M broadcaster Jay Colley. "He led a lot of last two-minute drives." Sidelined with an intestinal virus in the pre-season, Yagiello was just getting back to full speed.

After the first play of the Delaware game, he may have gotten sick again. Yagiello was picked off by linebacker Darrell Booker on a pass deflected by 6-5, 240 lb. Gary Cannon. Twelve seconds into the game, Delaware had the ball at the W&M 13.

Sophomore QB Rich Gannon ran six yards for the Blue Hen touchdown and Delaware jumped out to a 7-0 lead.

Yagiello immediately responded, driving the Tribe 61 yards in nine plays. He connected with fullback Bobby Wright from six yards out to tie the score at 7-7. The Tribe tacked on 10 more unanswered points capped by Merritt "Dirk" Gibson's 42-yard TD romp on third-and-one with 5:53 remaining in the first half. The surprised Blue Hens trailed 17-7.

Gannon, a future NFL quarterback, brought them back, driving Delaware 66 yards in 64 seconds, then firing a 19-yard bullet to split end Guy Darienzo to make the score 17-14 just before the half. It stayed that way until the fourth quarter.

With 9:56 to play in the game, W&M cornerback Calvin Trivers recovered a Blue Hens fumble at the Delaware 14-yard line. The Tribe moved it to the nine where they faced fourth-and-five. Opting to bypass the short field-goal attempt and a six-point lead, Laycock went for it. They didn't make it. Cannon came up with another big defensive play, knocking down Yagiello's pass, and Delaware took over, still trailing 17-14.

The Blue Hens used that gust of momentum to set sail on a monumental 18-play, 90-yard drive, eating up most of the remaining time. Gannon hit six of seven completions on the drive against a Tribe defense playing without their star safety Mark Kelso who was injured in practice earlier in the week. With 1:03 to play, Gannon pitched to Bob Norris on a sweep left. Norris took it into the end zone from 10 yards out and Delaware re-gained the lead 21-17.

After the kickoff, Yagiello got the ball on

his 30 yard line with 57 seconds left. Gibson took a handoff to the left for 10 yards. Yagiello then hit wide receiver Ron Gillam for 17 to the Delaware 47. But there, it appeared the game ended.

Yagiello threw long downfield for split end Dave McDowell at the 10-yard line. Senior cornerback Jeff Hynoski, looking to seal the victory for Delaware, intercepted the pass... but then dropped it.

With a second life, Yagiello threw complete 20 yards down the left sideline to tight end Glenn Bodnar. The Tribe was at the Delaware 27-yard line. Time was running out.

The Blue Hens defense stiffened, forcing third-and-10. Yagiello flipped to Wright out of the backfield, for nine yards.

Fourth down-and-one at the 18-yard line. More importantly, just 0:07 left. Laycock called time out.

THE PLAY

"Left 87 Z post." Yagiello would look for 5-8 wide receiver Jeff Sanders on a post pattern.

"I just wanted to make sure Stan knew there were seven seconds left," said Laycock. "We wanted to get the ball in the end zone. We didn't want to run the chance of trying to run two plays with only seven seconds left."

Yagiello made quite certain only one more play would be run.

After taking the snap, he saw Sanders covered. Yagiello then started to scramble. Avoiding a three-man rush, pump faking twice, Yagiello ran out the final seven seconds with the ball still in his hands, looking for a receiver.

"We had everything covered," said Delaware defensive coordinator Ed Maley. "I figured that we'd either sack him or that he just wouldn't be able to find anyone."

Yagiello kept looking. Sanders saw the play was busted. "I stopped when I reached the end of my route," said the senior receiver, tightly covered by Hynoski.

From there, it was game of hide-and-seek.

Yagiello changed directions. Sanders did too. "I went to the far corner of the end zone

and he lost me." Hynoski couldn't hold the coverage forever. Sanders was open, wide open in the left corner. Yagiello approached the line of scrimmage, then lofted the ball up.

"I didn't think about it. I just threw it," said Yagiello.

All alone, Sanders bobbled the ball. It would have been one of the most nightmarish drops ever. But he held on. A Tribe touchdown after time had expired. William & Mary 23, Delaware 21.

Hugging, jumping, dancing, the William & Mary players partied in the silent Delaware Stadium. The Blue Hens' defense, scattered across the field, fell on their knees, helmets slung to the ground.

In 19 years at Delaware, Raymond had never lost like that. "This has to be a stunning blow for them," he said about his team. "To pull a game out of the fire like that only to see it blown away..."

Yagiello was modest about the last pass. "I did a lot of things wrong today. That was one of the things I did right." The one thing forever remembered at William & Mary.

THE AFTERMATH

"That was the game that brought on the resurgence of William & Mary football that Jimmye Laycock has brought on," noted Colley.

The following Tuesday, William & Mary received their first-ever national ranking, No. 8 among I-AA schools. Their season ended with a 6-5 record, but in 1985, W&M cracked the final Top 20 poll, finishing No. 16 with a 7-5 record. Laycock then led the Tribe to 9-3 season, a No. 8 ranking, and their first NCAA I-AA playoff appearance in 1986, coincidentally against Delaware. The Blue Hens, led by Gannon in his senior year, won 51-17, gaining revenge for three consecutive losses to the Tribe in the past three seasons.

Laycock's W&M teams got stronger as the years went by, compiling a 116-43-2 record (.727) against fellow I-AA opponents through 1998.

Gannon went on to set 21 Delaware school records, passing for 5,927 yards in his four-year career. He was named the Yankee Conference

Offensive Player of the Year in his senior season and was drafted in the fourth round of the 1987 NFL Draft by the New England Patriots. Gannon was then immediately traded to the Minnesota Vikings where he became the starting quarterback through 1992. The Vikings traded Gannon to Washington in 1993. He later went to Kansas City, then became the starting quarterback for the Oakland Raiders in 1999.

Considered one of the school's all-time greatest quarterbacks, Stan Yagiello set just about every passing record at W&M, and was a I-AA Honorable Mention All-American his senior year. After getting a look from the Washington Redskins, Yagiello latched on to the Arena Football League in 1987, playing for the Pittsburgh Gladiators in the league's inaugural season, as well as the New York Knights in 1988.

William & Mary	10	7	0	6	- 23
Delaware	7	7	0	7	- 21

DEL   Gannon 6 run (Griskowitz kick)
W&M   Wright 6 pass from Yagiello
          (Morris kick)
W&M   FG Morris 31
W&M   Gibson 42 run (Morris kick)
DEL   Darienzo 19 pass from Gannon
          (Griskowitz kick)
DEL   Norris 10 run (Griskowitz kick)
W&M   Sanders 18 pass from Yagiello
          (no attempt)

Attendance 15,928

Clemson vs.
Georgia

"Oh my God! Oh my God!"—Larry Munson, Georgia broadcaster

THE BACKGROUND

From the end of the 1979 season to the beginning of the '84 campaign, Vince Dooley's Georgia Bulldogs owned a sparkling 45-4-1 record, with just two regular-season setbacks—a 13-7 loss to No.3 Auburn in 1983, and a 13-3 defeat at Clemson in 1981.

Early in the 1984 season, the 20th-ranked Bulldogs (1-0) looked to avenge one of those losses when they hosted No.2 Clemson (2-0). The Tigers, finishing their second year on probation by the NCAA and the ACC, were ineligible for a post-season bowl game but still had a chance to earn the national championship in the AP poll if they could finish undefeated at 11-0. Featuring William (the Refrigerator) Perry at middle guard, along with Mike Eppley, the nation's No.3-rated passer from the '83 season, Clemson had gone three straight years unbeaten in the ACC. They were favored to do it again. The Tigers' pre-conference matchup against SEC foe Georgia, between the hedges, was to be their highest hurdle of the year.

Coach Danny Ford's squad came out strong in the 90 degree heat at Sanford Stadium where Georgia had won 25 of its last 26 games.

After the Tiger defense intercepted Georgia QB Todd Williams three times, and Eppley threw two first half TDs, a 16-yarder to K.D. Dunn and a 27-yard connection with Terrence Flagler, Clemson held a commanding 20-6 halftime lead.

But as poor a first half as Williams endured, Eppley, a 6-2, 185 lb. senior, had an even worse second half. He turned the ball over five out of the first six Clemson possessions in the final two quarters, throwing two interceptions and losing three fumbles.

At the start of the second half, Eppley botched a handoff on his own 30. Georgia's Carlyle Hewatt recovered. From there, Williams, who threw a total of five interceptions in the game, eventually connected with one of his own Bulldog receivers, Herman Archie, for a 19-yard TD completion that cut the margin to 20-13.

After Georgia's Kevin Harris recovered another Eppley fumble on a bad pitch at the UGA 34, freshman runningback Cleveland Gary (who later transferred to Miami, FL) capped a 66-yard Georgia drive with a one-yard TD plunge to tie the game at 20-20 near the end of the third quarter.

Then Eppley and Williams sparred back and forth with miscue after miscue. Cornerback Tony Flack intercepted Eppley at the Georgia six-yard line. Williams overthrew a receiver, forcing a punt at the Georgia 8. Flack picked off another Eppley pass at the UGA 47. Williams underthrew a receiver on third-and-eight at the Clemson 40, forcing another punt.

"There were enough mistakes on both teams to lose two games," noted Dooley. "It's a good thing we were playing each other."

Almost on cue, Eppley quickly turned the ball over again. He escaped from the Clemson 24 and rambled 31 yards across midfield. Then, at the end of the magnificent run at the UGA 45, he fumbled. Georgia defensive end Calvin Ruff recovered with 9:29 on the clock.

This time, choosing to move exclusively on the ground, Georgia marched to the Clemson 27 where senior placekicker Kevin Butler nailed his third field goal of the game, a 43-yarder, to put the Bulldogs ahead 23-20 with 6:03 to play.

Clemson took the ensuing kickoff and Eppley suddenly got back on track, hitting four completions to move the ball to the Georgia 32 before Donald Igwebuike connected on a 48-yard field goal, tying the game at 23-23 with 2:10 left.

Dooley's 'Dawgs countered one last time. With 1:19 left, tailback Troy Jackson ran a trap up the middle 24 yards from the Georgia 31 to the Clemson 45. But three downs later, the stubborn Clemson defense had allowed just one more yard.

The clock was under 20 seconds. Georgia was stuck with a fourth-and-nine at the Clemson 44.

THE PLAY

With no timeouts remaining, Dooley had little choice but to send in Butler to try an SEC record-tying 60-yard field goal. "I thought the percentages were against him making it," said Dooley.

So was a 10 MPH wind from the east, blowing in Butler's face.

After missing a 26-yarder in the second quarter, Butler felt a burden for redemption. "I thought I had lost the game when I missed the earlier one," he said. "I work with these guys, eat with them, live with them. I couldn't let them down."

But they probably would have understood if his mammoth attempt fell short. The ball was snapped. Holder Jimmy Harrell placed it down at the 50-yard line. Butler approached the ball.

"When I kicked it, I knew it was going to be long enough," said Butler, "but when there's sixty yards ahead of you, you just kind of wait to see if the ball starts tailing off."

Butler waited. So did everyone else in Sanford Stadium, their hearts rising up into their throats as the ball kept going and going.

Georgia broadcaster Larry Munson couldn't control himself. "Oh my God! Oh my God!" he shouted as Butler's kick soared through the air. That was all he said.

The stadium erupted. "The crowd was so loud that I just took off my headset," said Munson. The Georgia announcer forgot to say whether or not the kick was good. "I don't know how many seconds passed before we told our audience that the field goal was good."

Phil Schaefer, Munson's broadcast partner, actually informed those listening on the radio after several seconds passed.

"My preacher called me Sunday. He said he wondered if I'd had a heart attack or something. I just got so involved emotionally," said Munson.

So did the rest of the Georgia team who got penalized 15 yards for the massive celebration of Butler's miracle kick. "It was a miracle...a real miracle!" said Dooley. "The only thing I can say is the Butler did it again."

Butler streaked down the field to the Georgia 20-yard line, and fell on his knees as if he just kicked the game-winning goal in a World Cup soccer match.

He may as well have, because in Athens, Butler was king of the world. "It was like electricity was going all through my body," said the Georgia hero. "There has never been anything like it in the world."

With Georgia ahead 26-23, Butler kicked off from the UGA 25 and only 11 seconds on the clock. Then, for Georgia fans, the unthinkable almost happened. Ray Williams fielded the kick at the Clemson 20, ran it to the 30, then passed the ball across field to teammate Terrance Roulhac who sprinted all the way to the Georgia 35 before being stopped as the clock ticked to one second, then 0:00.

Ford felt his team should have had a chance for one last field-goal attempt of their own. "I thought there was one second left on the clock when our boy went out of bounds on the kickoff and there was also a flag thrown for a late hit. I tried to find the official [to get an interpretation] but couldn't."

The players and coaches milled around on the field. The officials consulted each other. No penalty was called. The game was ruled over. The fans celebrated. Georgia 26, Clemson 23.

Kevin Butler booted field goals of 34, 51, 43, and 60 yards on the day. Photo courtesy of University of Georgia Athletic Association

THE AFTERMATH

After the game, Butler became the toast of the town. "We just went from party to party and all I saw was happy people," he said. "This whole town was jumping. Needless to say, I didn't get much sleep."

Butler was chosen a consensus All-American in his senior season, making 23 of 28 FG and all 23 PAT attempts. After starting out 7-1, Georgia finished the year 7-4-1, losing their final three games to Florida, Auburn, and Georgia Tech, then tying Florida State 17-17 in the Citrus Bowl, when Butler's 70-yard field-goal attempt as time expired fell just short. It was his last FG attempt in college.

Butler ranks sixth all-time in Division I-A career field goals. From 1981-84 he connected on 77 of 98 attempts (.786), including 50 of 56 inside 40 yards.

The week after the Georgia loss, Clemson lost their first ACC game in four years, with a 28-21 setback to Georgia Tech. After high pre-season expectations, the Tigers' season ended with a disappointing 7-4 record.

Clemson	10	10	0	3	- 23
Georgia	0	6	14	6	- 26

CL	Dunn 16 pass from Eppley (Igwebuike kick)
CL	FG Igwebuike 22
GA	FG Butler 34
GA	FG Butler 51
CL	Flagler 27 pass from Eppley (Igwebuike kick)
CL	FG Igwebuike 43
GA	Archie 19 pass from Williams (Butler kick)
GA	Gary 1 run (Butler kick)
GA	FG Butler 43
CL	FG Igwebuike 48
GA	FG Butler 60

Attendance 82,122

Bloomsburg vs. West Chester

"I said a Hail Mary and then thought 'this is stupid, it's never going to work.'"—Bloomsburg captain Mike Jupina

THE BACKGROUND

The Pennsylvania State Athletic Conference is comprised of 14 Division II colleges from around the Keystone State. Split into two divisions (eastern and western), the conference determines its champion each November in Hershey, Pennsylvania, where the division winners square off in the State Game.

Toward the end of the 1984 regular season, third-year head coach George Landis had his Bloomsburg University Huskies one game away from the school's first-ever eastern division championship and spot in the State Game. The Huskies were in second place (4-1) behind coach Danny Hale's West Chester Rams (5-0), with Bloomsburg travelling to West Chester for the final conference game to determine the division champion. Landis was rebuilding a Bloomsburg program that between 1979 and 1982 had won just four games. The Huskies were saddled with a 2-22 record versus West Chester since 1960.

A wild first half of scoring concluded with Bloomsburg scoring 17 points in the final 4:12 to trail 24-22 at the intermission. Early in the third quarter, West Chester tailback Mike Irving (who led the team in rushing, receiving, kickoff, and punt return yardage) scored on a three-yard run, his third TD of the game, and the Rams took a 31-22 lead. Brian Scriven's one-yard plunge with 5:12 to play in the game brought Bloomsburg to within 31-28. But Todd Sullivan's PAT was blocked and West Chester held a three-point lead and the ball until they were forced to punt with under a minute left.

From the Bloomsburg 37, Rams punter Charles McDermott perfectly placed the kick deep into Husky territory and Bloomsburg was forced to take over on their own five-yard line with just 0:45 remaining and no timeouts left.

Onto the field came quarterback Jay Dedea, a 24-year-old sophomore who quit his job in Altoona, Pennsylvania, in 1983 to enroll at Bloomsburg, play football, and get a degree. Dedea was starting just his second game of the year, substituting for injured starter Mike Glovas.

From the Bloomsburg five-yard line, the Huskies gained just six yards on the first two plays. But on third down, Dedea found Ken Liebel for 18 yards to move the ball to the Bloomsburg 29 with 0:22 left. Then Kevin Grande caught a short six-yard pass from Dedea and got out of bounds at the 35. Just 14 seconds remained.

With time running out, a pressured Dedea scrambled out of the pocket for 15 yards to midfield before stepping out of bounds and stopping the clock with only 0:05 remaining.

West Chester called time out.

THE PLAY
CD 1—Track 18—*Jim Doyle, Charlie Chronister,* **WHLM-Radio**

Rams coach Danny Hale was concerned.

"Our sidelines are going crazy. The fans are going crazy. They think they have it won.

Unfortunately, I did not have that sense. It ain't over til it's over, " he said.

Bloomsburg captain Mike Jupina knelt down and said a prayer on the field as his teammates were on the sideline during the timeout. "Jay came in the huddle and called the play, 'Hail Mary on one,'" said Jupina.

Hale recalled the defensive set. "We ran prevent defense, your standard lay back, fourteen million people in the end zone.... [We] rushed three."

As they came to the line of scrimmage, Landis noticed a mistake by his offense. "We gave Jay the basic formation on the timeout," he explained. "We wanted three receivers on the right, but with all the excitement Joe [Dowd] ended up on the left."

The plan was for the Huskies' receivers to run into the right corner of the end zone where Dedea would throw it and 6-5 Kevin Grande would tip the ball to another teammate. But Dedea took the snap and ran the wrong way, to the left side of the field.

"It was my fault because I started left and everybody was going right so I just came back to it," said Dedea.

Dedea then scrambled, and scrambled, and scrambled, avoiding the three Rams' pass rushers.

"Jay had the ball a long time back there," said Landis. "It seemed like he had the ball for at least 20 seconds."

Hale thought it was longer. "It seemed like an eternity. It just took forever that he scrambled around."

Finally Dedea launched the pass, roughly 60 yards in the air into the end zone where freshman Curtis Still, one of four receivers on the route, was blanketed by three West Chester defenders.

Somehow, Still came down with the ball. No time on the clock. Ninety-five yards in 45 seconds with no timeouts. Miraculously, Bloomsburg won the game, 34-31.

"I had three guys. Three of my players are there... and their one, and it wasn't like he out jumped them," recalled Hale. "The ball somehow got between them all and fell in this kid's hands. It was his third reception of the year, and his first touchdown of the year."

It was also the first time Still was on the field all afternoon. Plagued with an ankle injury, the wide receiver sat on the bench the entire game until the final play.

Bloomsburg announcer Jim Doyle recalled the moment. "In the press box it was at least 10-15 minutes before we knew who caught it. There was a big stack and no one came out holding the ball," he said. As it happened, Doyle thought Grande was the recipient of the pass, only to find out later it was Still.

"All I saw was the ball coming. It seemed like it was taking forever to get to me. The catch really makes me feel great," said Still.

"I'll tell you, Curtis made one helluva catch," said Dedea.

THE AFTERMATH

The West Chester game was the last victory of the year for Bloomsburg who finished the season 6-5, 5-1 in the conference. They suffered a major letdown the following week, losing to Division III power Lycoming 24-14 in their final regular-season game. The Huskies then lost the Pennsylvania Conference Championship game 21-14 to the Vulcans of California University, when Dedea, attempting to duplicate the West Chester miracle, threw a last-play desperation pass to Still from 58 yards away. This time it was knocked down. However, the following year, Bloomsburg was the only Division II team to finish the regular season undefeated (10-0). They won the State Game, and advanced all the way to the semifinals of the Division II championship playoffs before being ousted by North Alabama 34-0.

For the Rams of West Chester, the '84 season ended at 7-3, 5-1 in the conference. After taking his alma mater to the Division II playoffs for the first time ever in 1988, coach Danny Hale took some time away from football.

He returned to football in 1993, oddly enough as head coach for Bloomsburg University, where memories of the '84 game never fade. "When I took the job up here, I re-live it. Almost every week somebody brings it up," said Hale.

Has he changed his defensive philosophy on last second plays?

Bloomsburg quarterback Jay Dedea (2) gets a hero's ride while teammate Curtis Still (82) clutches the ball after his miracle last-second catch. Photo courtesy Kevin Lynch

"Ever since then, I don't just rush three [players]... We're gonna bring that extra guy. It doesn't matter how many you have, you need some pressure. You can't let a guy sit back there and throw all day."

Under Hale, Bloomsburg went on to win four straight Pennsylvania Conference Championships from 1994 to 1997. After the '97 season, Hale ranked as the fifth winningest active Division II coach by percentage with a record of 80-27-1 (.745).

The State Game has since been dropped by the conference in order to give both division winners a better chance of making the Division II playoffs.

Bloomsburg	3	19	0	12	-34
West Chester	17	7	7	0	-31

BL	Sullivan 33 FG
WC	Irving 20 pass from Horrocks (Wentling kick)
WC	Wentling 20 FG
WC	Minnino 44 fumble return (Wentling kick)
BL	Horrocks tackled in end zone by Heckman
BL	Grande 5 pass from Dedea (Sullivan kick)
WC	Irving 94 kickoff return (Wentling kick)
BL	Dowd 17 pass from Dedea (Sullivan kick)
BL	Sullivan 25 FG
WC	Irving 3 run (Wentling kick)
BL	Scriven 1 run (kick failed)
BL	Still 50 pass from Dedea (no attempt)

Boston College vs. Miami

"It's the play that never seems to go away."
—Miami offensive tackle Dave Heffernan

THE BACKGROUND

Doug Flutie versus Bernie Kosar. The game was supposed to have been played two months earlier on September 29th. But thanks to CBS and Rutgers University, this matchup between two of the country's premier quarterbacks became one of the most famous finishes in college football history, witnessed by millions on national television.

CBS paid Rutgers $80,000 to cancel their game with Miami on the Saturday following Thanksgiving so that the earlier scheduled Boston College-Miami matchup could be moved to the Friday after Thanksgiving for a national television audience and hopefully higher ratings for CBS. (Like a side dish to a main course, Miami substituted Rice for Rutgers early in the season, stuffing the Owls 38-3.)

But the Hurricanes' season, which at one point had them ranked No. 1 in the country, hit a Titanic-like glacier the game before the Boston College showdown with a catastrophic 42-40 loss to Maryland. Quarterback Frank Reich engineered a miraculous comeback, at the time the greatest in NCAA history, to overcome a 31-0 Miami halftime lead and give the Terrapins the stunning victory. Miami's record fell to 8-3.

"Unbelievable," said Miami coach Jimmy Johnson following the game. "I can see them scoring a few points in the second half, but so many so quick? Unbelievable."

The Miami defense was in a state of disrepair.

Upon his arrival in Miami in '84, Johnson was told by the school administration to retain former coach Howard Schnellenberger's assistant coaches. Bill Trout, a popular candidate for the head coaching position, but then named defensive coordinator under Johnson, was one of them. As the '84 season wore on, the Hurricanes' 13-game winning streak was halted by Michigan 22-14, Florida State demolished their intra-state rivals 38-3, and the maligned Hurricanes defense collapsed against Maryland. Not coincidentally, Johnson's relationship with Trout wore thin.

By the time Boston College (7-2) arrived at the Orange Bowl, a chasm had developed in the Hurricanes' coaching staff. "There was a great coaching staff prior to my arrival," Johnson said, "but it's the head coach who sets the pattern, the philosophy. I like an aggressive, attacking defense and that was not the style used prior to my arrival."

The players felt the tension too. "We were all pulling in different directions," said running-back Alonzo Highsmith, whose season ended prematurely when he suffered damaged cartilage in his right knee during the Maryland game.

Such was not the state of affairs at Boston College. Propelled by Flutie's march toward the Heisman Trophy, the Eagles were enjoying their best season since 1940 when Frank Leahy led them to a 19-13 Sugar Bowl victory over Tennessee and No.5 ranking.

Given the national holiday spotlight, the 5-9$\frac{1}{2}$-inch Flutie feasted on the Miami defense, completing his first 11 attempts of the game. The Eagles had a quick 14-0 lead.

But back came Kosar. The red-shirt 6-5 sophomore with a national championship ring, matched Flutie with 11 straight completions of his own. His 10-yard strike to tight end Willie Smith tied the game at 14-14 in the second quarter.

Back-and-forth in the rain, across the wet Orange Bowl turf went Flutie and Kosar. For the game, Flutie threw for 472 yards, Kosar for 447. The game was tied 31-31 after three quarters. The lead would change five times in the fourth quarter alone.

With 3:50 to play in the game, fullback Steve Strachan scored from the one-yard line, giving BC a 41-38 lead. On the next possession, Miami teetered on the brink of defeat. Backed up to their own 10-yard line, facing third-and-21 with the clock down to 2:30, the Hurricanes rallied. Kosar dropped back into the end zone, avoided a sack, then found Darryl Oliver for a 20-yard gain to the 31. On fourth-and-one, freshman Melvin Bratton, playing in place of the injured Highsmith, got the first down to keep the Hurricanes alive.

Kosar did the rest, connecting on passes of 15, 10, 15, then 20 to move the ball to the BC five-yard line. Oliver gained four yards to the one. Miami called their last timeout with 0:30 left. Bratton then dived over for the touchdown. The Hurricanes led 45-41 with only 28 seconds left.

After the kickoff was downed in the end zone, out came Flutie, seemingly outdueled and out of time to drive the length of the field. He connected with Troy Stradford for 19 yards to the 39. Then, on the left sideline he found Scott Gieselman who ran out of bounds at the Miami 48.

On first down, Flutie tried for tight end Peter Caspariello at the Miami 25, but overthrew him. The clock stopped with six seconds left and the Eagles half a field away from a score. "I assumed at that point we had lost," said Eagles coach Jack Bicknell. "I'm thinking, 'What am I going to tell these guys?' They had just played a great game."

THE PLAY
CD 1—Track 19
Dan Davis, **Kelley Communications**

Boston College had one play left. They practiced it every Thursday—55 Flood Tip. Three receivers to the right—Stradford, Kelvin Martin, and Gerard Phelan. Six games earlier in the season, Flutie threw the same desperation pass as time expired in the first half against Temple. Phelen, Flutie's roommate, caught it for a 51-yard touchdown.

Miami knew what was coming. "This is something you work on all the time," said Trout, who by this time in the season, had enough of the animosity in the coaching staff and wanted out of Miami. In fact, he couldn't be reached by the Miami coaches on the field to call the last defensive formation. He had already left the press box.

Still, the Miami players weren't surprised when Flutie took the snap, avoided the rush of Jerome Brown, then rolled to his right, drifting back to the BC 37. With only a three-man rush, Flutie had time, lots of time, time for a couch potato to grab a drink out of the 'frig and still see The Pass.

"I always tried to hang on to the ball as long as I can to allow everybody to get down the field," remembered Flutie. "I kind of scrambled out to the right and rolled right. It wasn't a designated roll or anything like that. I was just trying to buy a little time to allow them to get down so I could just throw a jump ball."

Finally, with a hop and a skip, Flutie launched the ball toward the end zone.

This was not a pass. This was more like a baseball, hit high into the Miami evening sky, drifting back to the outfield fence. Three Miami defenders backed up to the goal line like center fielders trying to keep the ball in the park. Phelen had snuck behind the goal line, the forgotten fan standing behind the fence, a couple yards into the end zone, somehow unnoticed by Miami safeties Darrell Fullington and Tolbert Bain, both red-shirt freshmen.

"I ran into the end zone, while everybody else stopped at the 5-yard line. It wasn't going to be a touchdown if I was stopped on the 5," said Phelan.

Game 33

Doug Flutie celebrates "The Pass," his now legendary Hail Mary to Gerard Phelan. Photo courtesy of Boston College Sports Information

Bain jumped. Fullington jumped. Reggie Sutton leaped as well, bumping into his teammates. BC's Strachan was in the mix too, causing turmoil. They all misjudged Flutie's arm. "I was looking for the ball to land at the five or 10-yard line," said Bain. "I never thought it would go that far. I dove, but I couldn't get there. I was praying the ball would hit the ground."

Just beyond the crowded group at the goal line, over the imaginary fence, it hit Phelan right in the gut. A falling star he cradled into his stomach. A meteor, crashing down on Miami. Touchdown Boston College. The clock read 0:00. Boston College 47, Miami 45.

"I didn't really know he [Phelan] was behind us until he caught the ball," said Fullington.

"To think the ball would come to me with eight men standing only 3 yards in front of me and without being batted down or intercepted, that's incredible," said Phelen.

That's also unforgettable.

"I had a lousy seat," said Bicknell who couldn't see the catch from the sidelines. "I couldn't believe it until I saw our kids going

nuts." One after another, the Boston College players tossed themselves on top of a huge mound, a human laundry pile in the right corner of the end zone.

"You just heard a silence you never want to hear in your home stadium," said Miami offensive tackle Dave Heffernan on the other sideline.

"I'm in a state of shock," added Kosar. "I didn't think there was any way Boston College could come back."

They did, with the undivided attention of a national television audience. The Pass became the standard. The one college football play identified with the term "Hail Mary."

THE AFTERMATH

Trout resigned following the Boston College game. He left Miami along with offensive line coach Chris Vagotis and defensive line assistant Danny Brown to join their former boss Schnellenberger at the University of Louisville.

The Miami defense faltered again on New Year's Day as the Hurricanes lost to UCLA 39-37 in the Fiesta Bowl, on a 23-yard field goal by John Lee with 51 seconds left. Miami finished the season 8-5 ranked No. 18. Johnson rebuilt his coaching staff the following year, beginning construction on the middle tier of a three-level Miami dynasty in the '80s and early '90s. From 1983-92, Miami won four national titles ('83, '87, '89, '91) under three coaches (Schnellenberger, Johnson, and Dennis Erickson) while amassing a 107-13-0 record. They finished in the top three in the country each year from '86-'92. Johnson left Miami after the '88 season to become the head coach of the Dallas Cowboys.

Flutie ended the game 34 of 46 for 472 yards, and in the process became the first college quarterback to throw for over 10,000 yards in a career. He easily captured the Heisman Trophy Award and led the Eagles to a 45-10 season-ending victory against Holy Cross, then a 45-28 win over Houston in the Cotton Bowl. Boston College finished 10-2, ranked No.5 in the AP poll.

Ten years later, Flutie, unable to find a home in the NFL after brief stints with the

Chicago Bears, New England Patriots, and New Jersey Generals of the USFL, was a star quarterback with the Calgary Stampeders of the Canadian Football League.

But The Pass followed him wherever he went. "I think it's the one signature play and the thing that people most remember me by and all that," Flutie said. "In a negative aspect, it's the only thing people remember about me."

Probably true until 1998, when Flutie resurfaced in the U.S. as the quarterback for the Buffalo Bills where he finally gained the well-earned respect of the NFL as a talented, but undersized quarterback, with an oversized heart.

Bernie Kosar left Miami after his sophomore season and entered the 1985 NFL supplemental draft, where he was the first pick of the Cleveland Browns. He retired in 1997 after 12 years in the NFL, mostly with the Browns, but also with the Dallas Cowboys and Miami Dolphins. Kosar holds the NFL mark for most consecutive passes without an interception (303).

Boston College	14	14	3	16	- 47
Miami	7	14	10	14	- 45

BC	Martin 33 pass from Flutie (Snow kick)
BC	Bell 1 run (Snow kick)
MIA	Bratton 2 run (Cox kick)
MIA	Smith 10 pass from Kosar (Cox kick)
BC	Flutie 9 run (Snow kick)
MIA	Williams 8 pass from Kosar (Cox kick)
BC	Phelan 9 pass from Flutie (Cox kick)
MIA	Bratton 1 run (Cox kick)
MIA	FG Cox 19
BC	FG Snow 28
BC	FG Snow 19
MIA	Bratton 52 run (Cox kick)
BC	Strachan 1 run (Snow kick)
MIA	Bratton 1 run (Cox kick)
BC	Phelan 48 pass from Flutie (no attempt)

Attendance 30,235

Principia College vs. Illinois College

"It probably was one of the greatest finishes in the history of college football, [but] not many people know about it."—Jon Hinds

THE BACKGROUND

Located in Elsah, Illinois, Principia College has an enrollment of 550 students, all members of the Christian Science church. It is the smallest school in the NCAA that fields a football team. Actually in 1985, only 39 players suited up for the Indians.

"It was really just for guys who loved the game and couldn't give it up after high school and wanted to continue to play," recalled Jon Hinds, the sophomore quarterback of the 1985 squad.

These are the kind of guys who yearn for that one magical moment on the gridiron that they can reminisce about for the next 50 years. The Principia Indians of 1985 have a story to top every washed up college jock sitting in a sports bar west of the Mississippi River. Few finishes compare to what happened when Principia traveled to tiny England Field in Jacksonville, Illinois, to open up their season against the Blueboys of Illinois College (1-0).

The game was no different than any other Division III contest played on a sunny autumn Saturday, in a high school-sized field with scattered cars parked on the grass next to the running track that circled the stadium.

Illinois College took a 15-6 lead into the fourth quarter before Principia rallied to close the gap. Hinds capped a 55-yard Principia drive with a spinning three-yard TD run, and the Indians cut the Blueboys' lead to 15-12 with 6:11 to play. It stayed that way until the final minute of the game when one of the most bizarre endings of all-time took place.

Principia marched downfield to the IC 31-yard line, where the Blueboys were flagged for a 15-yard pass interference penalty. First-and-10 for Principia at the IC 15. Hinds hit wide out Rob Guthrie for three yards out of bounds at the 12. Then, with just 0:28 on the clock, Hinds connected again with Guthrie on a post pattern for the 12-yard touchdown pass. Principia took the lead 20-15.

"We thought we'd won the game with 28 seconds to go," said senior Dan Sellers, the school's all-time leading receiver. They hadn't. In fact, the game was far from over. Further than anyone could imagine.

Taking the kickoff at his three-yard line, Dan Schone raced to the right sideline, broke numerous tackles, and returned the ball to the IC 49-yard line. The Blueboys then moved to the Principia 36-yard line thanks to a 15-yard facemask penalty against the Indians. With the clock under 10 seconds, Blueboys quarterback Joe Killday tossed up a sailing prayer to a heap of players at the Principia three-yard line. Four Indians players crashed into each other. The ball bounced backwards off their outstretched fingertips and right into the hands of halfback Tim Fritzche who was late getting downfield, but right on time to receive the rebound gift. The sprinting Fritzche gladly took the ball in his arms and danced into the end zone. Touchdown Illinois College with 0:02 left.

The boisterous Blueboys cleared the bench, piling on top of Fritzche in that grassy

113

area just beyond the end zone but just inside the asphalt track, just to the left of the minimalist scoreboard which was just big enough to have "IC" painted on one side and "Visitors" just below it.

There was no Jumbotron replay.

The extra point made it Illinois College 22, Principia 20. "I thought the game was over at that point," said Principia coach Todd Small.

No, not yet.

With 0:02 remaining, IC coach Joe Brooks hoped to run out the final two ticks with an onside kick. Sellers was on the Principia front line. "I was hoping they were going to kick it to me and I was going to squirt through and take it to the house for a touchdown," he remembered fondly. Realistically though, Sellers was dreaming. The Blueboys did squib the onside kick right at Sellers. But as he tried to pick the ball up, teammate Will Hagenlocher, Principia's largest player, pushed him down on the ball. The whistle blew. Sellers was disappointed. "I said, 'Will, I was going to score a touchdown on that,'" he recalled telling Hagenlocher. "I was thinking, ahh geeze there goes our only hope."

But thanks partially to his teammate's forcefulness, Sellers inadvertently downed the ball at the IC 48, stopping the clock with 0:01 left, and giving Principia time to run one more play.

THE PLAY

The Indians had never practiced any type of Hail Mary pass. So as his offense huddled on the sidelines, Small called for a scripted post pattern over the middle. Hinds wanted no part of it. "I remember telling him, 'Forget that. We're going to do exactly what they just did,'" said Hinds. "Let's just line up the three receivers on the same side and run just the deep Hail Mary pass."

The sales pitch to Small worked. "He said 'OK, let's give it a shot,'" recalled Hinds.

Sellers, Guthrie, and a third Principia receiver split wide left. With no specific instructions on where to go, Sellers had an idea. "As I was lining up wide to the left, I thought the only way I'm gonna come down with anything

here is if I run behind the pack," said the ever-optimistic wide receiver. "Hopefully the ball was gonna get deflected behind the pack, that was my thinking."

None of the Principia receivers talked to each other. They just guessed what to do next.

Illinois College defensive coordinator Tom Rowland called over his safety Randy Mitchell for a few final words. "I said, 'Randy, they're gonna try this Hail Mary pass,'" recalled Rowland, now the head coach at Illinois College. "Whatever you do, make sure you knock the ball down.'"

Mitchell took Rowland's words to heart.

Hinds dropped back. The final horn sounded on the scoreboard. After the clock expired, Hinds let fly a high looping pass which floated down to the 10-yard line. Mitchell, a star long jumper on the IC track team, out jumped two Principia receivers and two other Blueboys defenders. He cleanly flipped the ball away from the pile with his right hand.

"[Mitchell] came flying over from his left safety position and batted it and it just popped right up in the air," said Rowland.

Right to Sellers, who was trailing the play to the left.

"I never had to break stride for it," said Sellers. "It was the easiest catch I made my whole four years of playing [at Principia]." Sellers waltzed into the end zone, his hands raised high , chest protruding like Moses holding up the Ten Commandments. Ten yards behind him, Mitchell fell to his knees as if he was struck by lightning from above, his hands stuck to his helmet in disbelief. It was an ending of biblical proportions.

Two Hail Mary passes in two seconds. Three touchdowns in 28 seconds. The Christian Scientists won. Believe it. It happened.

"It was just nutty," said Sellers. "I remember running through the end zone and seeing all their fans throwing their hats on the ground, really hacked off."

Rowland fell into a coma. "I just went so numb I didn't hear any noise. I didn't hear anything. I just went into a shell and felt extremely bad because those were my defensive backs," he recalled.

Principia coach Small leaped jubilantly

into the pile of Indians players celebrating the miracle of miracles. At the same time Blueboys' coach Brooks tried to comprehend it all. "I don't know what to say...It was a fantastic finish."

That it was.

THE AFTERMATH

"Unbelievable game. Unbelievable game. Everybody was just in so much shock that we just kind of sat there," said Rowland. "I just can't believe what just happened," he told the other coaches.

With only a Super 8mm film camera capturing the final play, the stunned Illinois College coaches had to wait until the processed film returned from nearby St. Louis later in the week to see exactly what transpired. "It was five days before we really knew what the hell happened," said Rowland.

It was the one lasting memory from a 2-9 season for Principia, a school not known for its gridiron accomplishments."We probably won five or six games my entire college career," said Hinds, who is now a commercial real estate broker. "That was definitely the highlight."

"It probably was one of the greatest finishes in the history of college football, [but] not many people know about it."

Rowland, now the head coach at Illinois College, will never forget it. "From now on, every game that we're in that [last second] situation, I still think of that game every single time. God, could this be another Principia?"

Has Rowland ever used that game as a motivational device in the locker room for his current players? He laughed. "I would have 10,000 times if we had won."

Principia	6	0	0	20	- 26
Illinois College	0	12	3	7	- 22

PR	Guthrie 16 pass from Hinds (kick failed)
IC	Pohlman 10 run (kick failed)
IC	Weiss 24 pass from Killday (kick failed)
IC	FG Engelmann 32
PR	Hinds 3 run (Peterson kick)
PR	Guthrie 12 pass from Hinds (Peterson kick)
IC	Fritzsche 36 pass from Killday (Engelmann kick)
PR	Sellers 48 pass from Hinds (no attempt)

Auburn vs. Alabama 🏈

"To the Alabama and Auburn fans, the game means more than life and death."—ABC commentator Frank Broyles

THE BACKGROUND

The 50th Anniversary of the Iron Bowl. Golden.

Ray Perkins was in his third year of swimming in the unfillable shoes left by Paul "Bear" Bryant. His Crimson Tide squad, after starting the season 4-0, entered Legion Field 7-2-1 and unranked. Auburn, 8-2 and seventh-ranked in the country, was poised to make amends for what happened the year before in the annual season ending war.

In 1984, Alabama led 17-15 late in the fourth quarter when Auburn defensive end Kevin Greene picked off a Mike Shula pass at the Alabama 17-yard line. The Tigers moved the ball to the one-yard line with 3:44 on the clock. Fourth-and-one. Tiger coach Pat Dye opted to go for the touchdown.

Then it happened. Another play known as "The Play," but not for the usual reasons. "We're all looking for Bo on some kind of play," said 'Bama safety Rory Turner. (All-America Bo Jackson, that is.) "Maybe a sweep. Maybe a power play over the top. But we're looking for Bo," said Turner.

Dye called a combo sweep. Combo 56. Surprisingly, the ball went to halfback Brent Fullwood running right. More surprisingly, Jackson was running left, the wrong way as a lead blocker. Turner joined Randy Rockwell, and Vernon Wilkinson to slam Fullwood for a three-yard loss. "I waxed the dude," was Turner's infamous post-game quote about the famous tackle.

Even with the botched play, Auburn got a second chance to defeat their arch nemesis. But with 14 seconds left, kicker Robert McGinty hooked a 42-yard field-goal attempt and Alabama's season, although the first losing one in 27 years (5-6), ended successfully with the 17-15 upset of the 11th-ranked Tigers.

One year later, here was Auburn again, this time trailing 16-10 with just over seven minutes to play in the game, staring at fourth-and-goal at the 'Bama one-yard line.

This time Jackson did get the ball. Playing with two fractured ribs and hoping to solidify his Heisman Trophy chances, Bo leaped over the top for the Auburn touchdown. With 7:03 to play, the game was tied 16-16. Freshman kicker Chris Johnson came on to give the Tigers the lead. But he missed the PAT. Fortunately for the Tigers, Alabama was called for too many men on the field. Johnson got a reprieve. He connected. Auburn led 17-16.

It was the beginning of an unforgettable ending.

Just one minute later at the 'Bama 26, Tide halfback Gene Jelks took a sweep right. "I got a hole that you or I could run through," said Jelks. The 'Bama freshman cut back into the open, chased by Auburn's Tom Powell and Jimmie Warren. He outran them both, 74 yards into the end zone. After missing the conversion attempt, 'Bama led again 22-17 with 5:57 to play.

Back came Auburn. Quarterback Pat Washington led the Tigers on an 11-play drive, eating up the clock. Jackson carried six times on

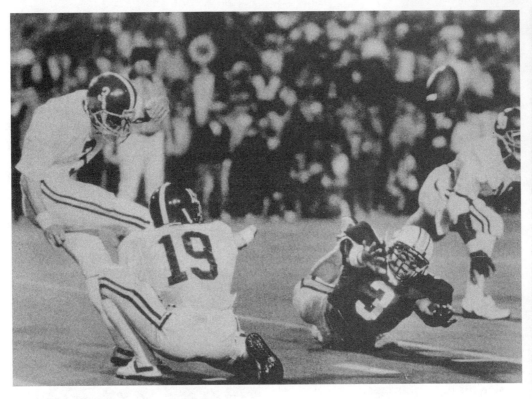

Van Tiffin's kick turned the state of Alabama "crimson." Photo courtesy of Paul W. Bryant Museum

the drive for 26 yards, giving him 142 yards rushing for the day. The Tigers again found themselves at the 'Bama one-yard line. Dye tried to milk the clock as much as he could. "I told the coaches we didn't want to score too quickly," Dye said. Washington ran the play clock down to two seconds before handing the ball to fullback Reggie Ware who plowed into the end zone with 0:57 on the clock. Auburn had the lead again, 23-22. But the two-point conversion pass to Jackson was batted down by linebacker Cornelius Bennett. The lead stayed at one.

The Tide had one chance left.

With 57 seconds, Shula started at his own 20. He threw incomplete on first down. The he was sacked, losing eight yards. The clock was down to 0:37 and Alabama was desperate. But Shula still fought. He found Jelks out of the backfield for 16 yards to the 26, setting up a do-or-die fourth-and-four.

Facing their final gasp, Alabama called timeout with 29 seconds remaining. The play came in from the sidelines. "We thought it was a play that had a chance to pick up 4 yards and get out of bounds," said Perkins.

Shula pitched to Jelks, who had a game-high 192 yards rushing. But Jelks would gain nothing on this play. Instead, he handed to split end Al Bell on the reverse. Bell caught a block from Shula on the corner and rambled for 20 yards. A stunning call by 'Bama offensive coordinator George Henshaw. A stunned Auburn defense.

Still, only 21 seconds were left with the ball at the 'Bama 46. Auburn knocked down the next pass intended for Greg Richardson with 0:15 on the clock. Shula, leading the country in passing efficiency, took a chance. He connected with Richardson over the middle at the Auburn 45. Precious seconds ticked away. "I was just hoping Little Richard would get out of bounds with enough time left to try a field goal," said Shula.

Alabama announcer Paul Kennedy got caught up in the excitement. "Head to the boundary Greg! Head to the boundary!" he called over the radio network.

Richardson was hit by Luvell Bivins at the Auburn 40 but kept moving forward. He lunged for five more yards to the 35 where he did get out of bounds with just 0:06 on the clock.

THE PLAY

CD 1—Track 20—*Doug Layton,*
Paul Kennedy, **Alabama Sports Network**

Junior place-kicker Van Tiffin was watching the last play nervously with the entire 'Bama field-goal unit. "The coaches had the 'white' call on, which means we've got our helmets on and we're all close to the field, ready to run out when it's time."

It was time.

Tiffin had already connected on three field goals from 26, 32, and 42 yards out. He had hit 96 consecutive extra points through three seasons. He had broken his own school record with a 57-yard field goal earlier in the year against Texas A&M.

None of that mattered. This was the Iron Bowl. This was from 52 yards away. This was the Southern version of "The Kick."

Tiffin hurried out and placed his tee down at the 42-yard line. A Birmingham breeze was in his face. "There was a 5-MPH wind blowing and that always messes up my mind," he said.

Tiffin had no time to think. Butch Lewis snapped the ball. Larry Abney placed it down. Tiffin booted it. "When I hit it, I felt it was a good kick. I stayed with the ball and when I saw it rise, I could see it was going to be good."

It was good. Straight through the uprights. "It hit the middle, and that's the best place," said Tiffin. Especially if you're the 'Bama coach.

Perkins jubilantly ran out onto the field looking for his kicker. "Van...Van Tiffin!...Van Tiffin!" yelled Perkins in the post-game melee. "I love ya, Van Tiffin. I love ya."

"The state of Alabama is crimson!" shouted Kennedy over the airwaves.

Tiffin was trying to gather himself. "I guess it was 30 seconds or so after I made the field goal that it sunk in...that we won the game. This is one you dream about," said Tiffin.

Alabama 25, Auburn 23. A surreal nightmare if you're an Auburn fan. "It seemed like a dream, like it wasn't supposed to happen that way," said Washington.

Dye summed it up best. "A game like this, Alabama players will remember it the rest of their lives. Auburn players...it'll eat their guts out the rest of their lives."

THE AFTERMATH

Jackson captured the Heisman Trophy Award the following week, narrowly outpointing Iowa's Chuck Long in the voting. Auburn's season ended at 8-4 after losing to Texas A&M 36-14 in the Cotton Bowl.

Alabama finished 9-2-1, beating Southern Cal in the Aloha Bowl 24-3. At the conclusion of the following season, Perkins left the Tide to coach the Tampa Bay Buccaneers of the NFL. He was replaced by Bill Curry.

Auburn	0	10	0	13	- 23
Alabama	10	6	0	9	- 25

ALA	Turner 1 run (Tiffin kick)
ALA	FG Tiffin 26
ALA	FG Tiffin 32
AUB	Jackson 7 run (Johnson kick)
ALA	FG Tiffin 42
AUB	FG Johnson 49
AUB	Jackson 1 run (Johnson kick)
ALA	Jelks 74 run (pass failed)
AUB	Ware 1 run (Pass failed)
ALA	FG Tiffin 52

Attendance 75,808

Georgia Southern vs. Furman

"We live in an age of miracles, and everybody here just saw one."
—Erk Russell

THE BACKGROUND

They stopped playing football at Georgia Southern in 1941. After World War II ended, they never picked it up again, until 40 years later.

In 1981, the university hired longtime University of Georgia defensive coordinator Erskine "Erk" Russell, to head the newly revived football program in Statesboro, Georgia. In 1982, the Georgia Southern Eagles, entirely made up of walk-on players, took the field as a club sport, playing mostly Division II and NAIA opponents. They finished the season 7-3-1 by defeating the junior varsity squad at Florida State, 31-20.

In '84, the Eagles joined Division I-AA. Just one year later, running an elusive triple-option attack, Georgia Southern made the I-AA playoffs with a 9-2 record. The upstart and ninth-ranked Eagles didn't stop there. They beat Jackson State 27-0, then shocked number-one rated Middle Tennesse 28-21, and continued with a 40-33 semifinal upset of No.4 Northern Iowa on junior quarterback Tracy Ham's 20-yard run with just 34 seconds remaining.

Georgia Southern, in just their second year of I-AA competition, was headed for the national championship game.

The Eagles' opponent, Furman University, was an established I-AA power. Led by coach Dick Sheridan, the second-ranked 12-1 Paladins had one of the best records of any I-AA school from 1980-85 (56-13-2), and were champions of the Southern Conference for the fifth time

in the past six years. In their three I-AA playoff games leading up to the final, Furman steamrolled its opponents by a combined score of 122-27.

With only 5,306 fans in attendance at the Tacoma Dome in Washington, Georgia Southern and Furman, two schools from the deep southeast, faced off in the far northwest for the I-AA national championship.

As many observers expected, the favored Paladins pounded the Eagles early and often, scoring touchdowns on three of their first four possessions. After senior quarterback Bobby Lamb connected on his 11th straight completion, a 33-yard TD pass to Larry Grady with 10:57 left in the third quarter, Furman led 28-6, apparently well on their way to the school's first-ever national title.

Meanwhile, Georgia Southern's vaunted ground attack which featured three players (runningbacks Gerald Harris and Ricky Harris, along with QB Ham) hovering near 1,000 yards for the season, had been stymied.

In a key strategic move, Sheridan had sacrificed one of his safeties, pulled him up to the line of scrimmage, and completely negated the elusive Ham on the option, daring the shifty quarterback to throw the ball.

"We've run [the option] so much," said Ham, "you knew someone would stop it someday." Furman did.

Russell decided to change strategy. He replaced runningback Ricky Harris with freshman backup Frankie Johnson, a better receiver than runner. Ham, who was averaging just 10

Frankie Johnson's leaping touchdown catch with just 0:10 left gave Georgia Southern the National Championship. Photo courtesy of Georgia Southern Athletics

passes per game in the playoffs, abandoned the option, and started throwing and throwing and throwing—37 times in all.

It paid off.

In a whirlwind of a third quarter, the Eagles launched a massive rally. Ham hit wide receiver Monty Sharpe for a 24-yard TD. Then the Eagle defense stopped Furman for the first time since the beginning of the game. Ham took over again, burning the Paladins deep with a 40-yard TD pass to Johnson. It was 28-21 with 4:35 still to play in the third quarter.

Again the Eagles held. Lamb threw three straight incompletions and Georgia Southern immediately got the ball back. They went back to their bread-and-butter. Ham pitched to Gerald Harris who broke free down the left sideline for a 52-yard jaunt to tie the game 28-28.

The Eagles weren't through yet. Again stifling Furman's offense, Georgia Southern got the ball back and marched 60 yards with Ham hitting Herman Barron with a 12-yard touchdown pass.

Four consecutive touchdowns. With 12:21 to play in the game, Georgia Southern led 35-28 in stunning fashion.

The Paladins regrouped.

Pounding the ball on the ground, Furman drove 76 yards in 11 plays, and John Bagwell scored his third touchdown of the game on a seven-yard run with 7:51 left to play. The Paladins had tied it up 35-35.

But with 3:37 left, Tim Foley booted the Eagles back ahead with a 39-yard field goal.

Then Furman regained the lead with another long 80 yard drive. Again it was Bagwell, this time scoring from four yards out with just 1:32 remaining. Sheridan's squad was back on top 42-38.

A blowout had turned into a tug-o-war. Georgia Southern took one last pull.

The Eagles started their final drive with a 10-yard penalty. They went backwards before they went forward.

Facing first-and-20 on their own 18, Ham struck through the air again, connecting with Johnson for 53 yards to the Furman 29. From there, the Furman defense stiffened, forcing the Eagles into a fourth-and-11 at the 30. With 38 seconds to play, it was GSU's last chance.

Ham dropped back, faked left, then looked right and found Tony Belser for a 17-yard gain. The Cinderella Eagles were alive at the 13 with 25 seconds left.

But two incompletions later they were staring at third-and-10, down by four points.

THE PLAY

Russell called for Three-70 Vertical.

Four receivers lined up wide. Johnson was one of them. "Ham just told me to go deep and up the middle," said Johnson, a freshman walk-on who probably forgot the playbook in such a tense moment.

Ham took the snap and glanced the other way. "Coach told me to look backside on the play," said Ham. " I looked play-side until the last minute, then looked backside and there he was."

Johnson, that is. "I just tried to get between the two defenders," said the freshman.

He did. Ham tossed it. Johnson caught it. Who could believe it? Touchdown Georgia Southern. The new kids on the block led 44-42 with only 0:10 on the clock.

Johnson, seldom used during the season, had caught just six passes all year. He snared seven for 148 yards in the final game alone. "We've just been too dumb to use him," said Russell about the 5-9, 175 pounder who didn't even make the press guide before the season.

He certainly did the next year.

"It was a perfect pass by Ham," said Johnson. "It had to be perfect to get between those two defenders."

Three-thousand miles to the southeast, the streets of Statesboro erupted. Even in the Tacoma Dome, the Eagles' fans couldn't help but run onto the field. That cost GSU a 15-yard penalty. Not important at this celebratory moment.

But when Foley missed the PAT and Trey Harold had to kick off from the 25, Furman had a slight chance for a long field goal if they could return the kick into GSU territory. Mark Rudder returned it to their 49 with 0:04. But Lamb's desperation pass fell harmlessly to the ground as time expired.

Georgia Southern had captured an unforgettable championship.

At the same time, Erk Russell had built a national power in the amount of time it takes some coaches to unpack their playbooks. "Nobody in his right mind would have thought this

ever would have happened, and I have no idea how it did, " he said.

THE AFTERMATH

Tracy Ham finished the game with a I-AA championship record 509 yards in total offense. With the loss, Bobby Lamb finished his Furman career as the leading all-time passer in Paladins history (4,594 yards).

"This will hurt a long time," said a disappointed Sheridan following the game.

The highly successful coach resigned at Furman after the championship loss to take the head coaching position at North Carolina State, a team the Paladins blasted 42-20 during the '85 season. He left Furman with the highest winning percentage in the history of the school .734 (69-23-2).

Sheridan's replacement, former assistant Jimmy Satterfield, led the Paladins to the 1988 title when Georgia Southern and Furman met again for the championship. This time, Furman prevailed, winning 17-12 in Pocatello, Idaho.

Georgia Southern and Furman were two of the top three I-AA programs during the 1980s. Second only to Eastern Kentucky, the Paladins finished 83-24-4 (.773) for the decade. Georgia Southern was right behind them with a 68-22-1 (.753) record. If you ignore Russell's first two years when the team was a club sport, Erk's Eagles (55-14-0) carried the highest winning percentage (.797) of all I-AA teams in the '80s.

The Eagles returned to the I-AA championship in 1986 and, led by Ham, captured their second consecutive title by defeating Arkansas State 48-21. In '89 they did it again, knocking off Stephen F. Austin 37-34 to complete a perfect 15-0 season. Four days later, Russell stepped down as head coach, leaving an amazing legacy behind. His teams were an unprecedented 16-2 (.888) in I-AA playoff games.

The next year, under former offensive co-ordinator Tim Stowers, the Eagles won the national championship for the fourth time in six seasons, beating Nevada 36-13.

Georgia Southern's home winning streak, started in their '85 national championship season, reached an I-AA record 38 games until it was broken in 1990 by Eastern Kentucky.

December 21, 1985—Tacoma, Washington

Georgia Southern	0	6	22	16	- 44
Furman	7	14	7	14	- 42

FUR	Bagwell 1 run (Esval kick)
GS	FG Foley 44
FUR	Bagwell 9 run (Esval kick)
GS	FG Foley 33
FUR	Lamb 10 run (Esval kick)
FUR	Grady 33 pass from Lamb (Esval kick)
GS	Sharpe 24 pass from Ham (Ham run)
GS	Johnson 40 pass from Ham (Foley kick)
GS	G. Harris 52 run (Foley kick)
GS	Barron 12 pass from Ham (Foley kick)
FUR	Bagwell 7 run (Esval kick)
GS	FG Foley 39
FUR	Bagwell 4 run (Esval kick)
GS	Johnson 13 pass from Ham (kick failed)

Attendance 5,306

Lycoming vs. Susquehanna

"They were running the ball over us. They were passing over us. They were crushing us."—Rob Sochovka

THE BACKGROUND

Williamsport, Pennsylvania. Home of the Little League World Series. Also home to Lycoming College, a consistent power in the Division III Middle Atlantic Conference. Under the direction of 12th-year head coach Frank Girardi, the Warriors were one of only three Division III schools to finish the 1985 regular season 10-0 before losing their final game of the year in the NCAA Division III playoffs.

The following year, the defending MAC champions took a 1-0 record, a 13-game regular season unbeaten streak, and a 45-minute drive down State Route 15 to Selinsgrove, Pennsylvania, to play their bitter rivals, Susquehanna University at Amos Alonzo Stagg Field. (The legendary Stagg co-coached Susquehanna with his son, Amos Jr., from 1947-52, after completing an NCAA record 57 years as head coach at Springfield, Chicago, and Pacific.)

Rocky Rees was 56 years behind Stagg's record. The Susquehanna coach struggled through a 3-7 season in his first year as head coach in '85. But after a season opening victory over Muhlenberg, 17-7, Rees was hoping his Crusaders could build some confidence against their neighborhood rivals.

Confidence shattered. Lycoming was ruining Susquehanna's homecoming game. "It was a complete ass-whooping for 52 minutes," recalled Susquehanna wide receiver Al Bucci. "We were just getting hammered."

Lycoming senior quarterback Larry Baretta connected with wide receiver James O'Malley for 154 yards and three TDs in the first two quarters alone. The Warriors led 28-7 at haltime.

After Barretta recorded his second rushing touchdown of the day on a five-yard scamper with 8:06 to play in the fourth quarter, Lycoming had a seemingly safe 42-22 lead.

For Susquehanna quarterback Todd Coolidge, this was a learning experience.

Coolidge, a converted safety who led his team in interceptions the year previously, was playing just his second game behind center. Rees switched him to quarterback in '86 to run the Susquehanna Wing-T offense.

But down 20 points to Lycoming, Rees was forced to abandon the Wing-T attack and air it out, in a last ditch effort to win the game.

He took out his tight end and inserted wide out Bucci along with split end Rob Sochovka. Suddenly, with the extra receiver, the field opened up. Coolidge started throwing. Bucci caught a 39-yard pass, then Coolidge hit Sochovka for a 36-yard TD. Seventy-five yards in 25 seconds. Susquehanna trailed 42-29.

After a Lycoming punt, the Crusaders got the ball back at their own 20. Coolidge to Bucci for 23 yards. Then later in the drive, Coolidge to Bucci slicing across the middle for another 20-yard TD. With 4:09 to play, Susquehanna had moved to within one score, 42-36.

Lycoming responded. Chewing up time, Barretta methodically moved the Crusaders to the SU 34. But facing third-and-seven, he overthrew O'Malley down the right sideline. On fourth down, Lycoming punted through the end zone.

With just 1:13 remaining, 80 yards to go, down by six points with no timeouts left, Coolidge tried to run the two-minute offense. One problem. He'd never done it before.

Sochovka explained the simplified set to Coolidge. "We had two receivers on the slot. One guy on each side would always do an out, and the other guy would do a seam down the post. Whatever way the quarterback choosed to roll that's what you did on that side. Then the other guy on the opposite slot would do a drag across the middle."

Coolidge gave it a try. He rolled right. Then he rolled left. He connected to the 37, then out of bounds at the 48. The Crusaders eventually moved to the Lycoming 37.

On third-and-four, with the clock under 30 seconds, Coolidge rolled right, but was chased across the wide side of the field. He tried to get out of bounds, but was dragged down at the 40. A three-yard loss, but more importantly the clock kept running. Fourth down. The Crusaders had to quickly line up.

The clock was down to 10 seconds, 9 seconds, 8 seconds...

THE PLAY

Sochovka lined up in the left slot. Bucci was wide right. Neither one of them had much fuel left. "That last 1:07, myself and Bucci, we were dead because we were doing flys (fly patterns) every play," said Sochovka.

But on the Susquehanna bench, nose tackle Damian Caracciolo, sidelined with a concussion in the second half, wouldn't let Sochovka quit. "He was on the sideline and we were running back ... and he was screaming at me, 'You f...ing get this ball, you get this ball, you can do it!'" remembered Sochovka. "I heard him say that, and he's not even in his pads, he's in his jersey 'cause they pulled him from the game."

While Caracciolo shouted desperately, Coolidge, in the shotgun, took the snap with seven seconds left. He rolled back to his left toward Sochovka. "I was like 'Oh my God, he's

coming my way,' said Sochovka. "My legs were burnt. I just took off down the field."

Out of breath, Sochovka ran 10 yards to the 30 then faded toward the left sideline behind a Lycoming defensive back, but in front of the safety who was playing for a Hail Mary pass.

Coolidge lofted the ball up.

At the 20-yard line, Sochovka looked over his left shoulder. But Coolidge's pass was floating the other way. To try and catch the ball, Sochovka literally did a 360-degree pirouette which confused the safety coming up behind him. Off-balance and back pedaling, he cradled in the ball at the 18. The Lycoming defender grabbed at air, stumbling to the ground.

Sochovka got his balance, turned, and ran for the goal line. Caracciolo was running too. "As I caught the ball, he was running down the sideline yelling at me," said Sochovka. "He was running stride by stride with me all the way to the end zone. I thought for sure he was gonna come out and block the last guy."

Tip-toeing along the sideline, Sochovka avoided one tackler who tried to swipe his feet out from under him. He high stepped to the five-yard line. One final Lycoming defender came screaming over. Sochovka stopped. The last Warrior flew past him. "I just gave him a juke. He went one way, I went the other."

Into the end zone. A 20-yard catch. A 20-yard run. A 40-yard touchdown. A Hail Mary that wasn't even a Hail Mary.

Having never run the two-minute drill in a game, Coolidge misjudged the final seconds. "I knew the out-and-up would go sooner or later," said Coolidge. "And on that last play, I thought we had enough time to get out of bounds."

They didn't. Had Sochovka stepped out of bounds, the game would have been over. "It wasn't even the right play," said Bucci. " It was like a 15-yard out pattern. [Normally] you throw it up in the end zone, you got a 6-2,6-3 guy. You get a touchdown. You win the game."

But nothing was normal about the end of this game.

Out of control and in his shorts, Caracciolo ran into the end zone and lifted Sochovka up in the air in celebration. The

Game 37

September 20, 1986—Selinsgrove, Pennsylvania

clock read 0:00. The game was tied 42-42. But flags littered the field.

Exhilarated but exhausted, Sochovka saw the penalty markers. " I thought, 'Here we go, it's for nothing, it's gonna come back,'" he said.

While Sochovka celebrated in the end zone, Bucci had run over to Lycoming defensive back Joe Harvey. Like many of the players in this small town rivalry, Harvey and Bucci had jostled back and forth, trash talking all game long. This time, Bucci took off his helmet and gave Harvey a few choice words.

"They were taunting us. We were taunting them. I don't know why Bucci took his helmet off," remembered Sochovka. "But he took his helmet off and the guy popped him. [Harvey] popped him in the mouth. He knocked out two of his teeth! "

Actually, Bucci lost one tooth. "It was real heated, spirited. You get so emotionally involved at what's happening at the time," Bucci explained. "[It] spilled over into a dental scenario."

Needless to say, Bucci never took off his helmet during a game again.

After a long conversation among officials, two off-setting personal fouls on Bucci and Harvey were called. But the play stood.

No time remained. But with the extra-point attempt still to come, Girardi called time out to try and ice kicker Randy Pozsar. It didn't work. "I was nervous, but one of their guys got in my face and started taunting me, so I just concentrated on the ball," said Pozsar.

Unlike Bucci, Pozsar kept his helmet on.

Sochovka was the holder. On an earlier muffed PAT, he had taken the fumbled snap and flopped over the goal line for a two-point conversion. This time, Sochovka took the snap cleanly, and placed it down. Pozsar kicked it through. Susquehanna won 43-42.

Girardi had never experienced a loss like this one. "It's new for me, and it doesn't feel good," he said.

Sochovka's emotions were quite different.

Split end Rob Sochovka is hoisted by Charles Buckley in celebration after catching the winning touchdown pass with no time left. Photo courtesy of Putzee Vannucci

125

"It was the greatest feeling," he said. "I could do that a million times over."

THE AFTERMATH

The fairytale victory turned into a textbook football lesson on the power of success.

"If there's one thing that came out of that game it's that winning is contagious in any aspect of life," said Bucci. "We could have just as easily been 3-7 that year as we were the year before when we lost our first six games. It was almost the exact same group of people. It's just that when you get on a streak and you start believing in what your team can do....that carried over to an undefeated season and our best finish ever."

Susquehanna's miracle win launched a memorable season in Selinsgrove. The Crusaders marched through their regular season schedule undefeated at 10-0, winning the MAC championship and receiving the school's first ever bid into the NCAA playoffs. Susquehanna rallied from a 20-7 deficit to defeat Washington & Jefferson 28-20 in the first round of the playoffs before bowing out of the tournament with a 31-17 loss to Salisbury State. As a reward for turning around his program from 3-7 to 11-1 in one season, Rees was named the Kodak Region II College Coach of the Year.

The following year, Lycoming produced their own brand of magic in the re-match between the two schools. Trailing 6-0 in the final seconds, Susquehanna quarterback David Battisti scored on a four-yard run with three seconds left. However, the Warriors blocked the extra point, won the game 7-6, and gained revenge for the stunning finish from the previous year.

From 1990-98, Lycoming had five undefeated regular seasons and played for the national championship twice, losing to Allegheny in the 1990 final game 21-14 in overtime, and to Mount Union in the '97 title game 61-12. Frank Giradi's squads ranked among the top 10 of over 200 Division III schools in total gridiron wins in the 1990s, and appeared in the NCAA playoffs eight times from 1989-1998.

Lycoming	14	14	0	14	-42
Susquehanna	0	7	7	29	-43

LY	O'Malley 25 pass from Barretta (Fricke kick)
LY	O'Malley 60 pass from Barretta (Fricke kick)
SU	Weber 56 run (Pozsar kick)
LY	Kondan 1 run (Fricke kick)
LY	O'Malley 35 pass from Barretta (Fricke kick)
SU	Bucci 18 pass from Coolidge (Pozsar kick)
LY	Barretta 5 run (Fricke kick)
SU	Gormley 51 run (Sochovka run)
LY	Barretta 5 run (Fricke kick)
SU	Sochovka 36 pass from Coolidge (Pozsar kick)
SU	Bucci 20 pass from Coolidge (Pozsar kick)
SU	Sochovka 40 pass from Coolidge (Pozsar kick)

Attendance 3,500

Northern Iowa vs.
Eastern Illinois

"That finish came from the movies."
—*Eastern Illinois linebacker Dan Polewski*

THE BACKGROUND

Darrell Mudra rebuilt the Eastern Illinois football program in 1978.

Known as "Dr. Victory" in the coaching circles, the well-traveled and highly successful coach guided the Blue Panthers (1-10 the previous season) to the Division II National Championship in his first year at EIU. Mudra, who coached his players from the press box and not the sidelines during the game, left EIU at the end of the '82 season with a 47-15-1 record, after advancing the program up to Division I-AA.

In the fall of '83, he landed in Cedar Falls, Iowa, at the University of Northern Iowa. Not unlike his previous stops at Adams State, North Dakota State, Western Illinois, and EIU, Mudra built a winning program. After leading UNI to the I-AA National Semifinals in 1985, his Purple Panthers started the '86 season 3-0-1 and ranked No. 8 in the country. Then UNI travelled to Mudra's old stomping ground, Eastern Illinois, in a showdown of Gateway Conference leaders. It was homecoming not only for Mudra, but also for the EIU alumni who came back to cheer their 11th-ranked Panthers (4-1).

The battle of the Panthers started out a defensive struggle. It wouldn't end that way.

After a scoreless first half marred by penalties and turnovers, UNI took a 16-7 lead with 10:16 to play in the game when quarterback Mike Smith hit Sherrod Howard with a two-yard TD pass on a fourth-down play.

But then EIU exploded. Senior QB Sean Payton's 59-yard TD pass to Roy Banks capped a 21-point outburst in less than five minutes, and gave EIU a commanding 28-16 lead with only 3:39 remaining. Coach Al Molde's squad then appeared to wrap the game up when Jeff Mills intercepted a Smith pass with 2:51 on the clock. But as the crowd was filing out of O'Brien Stadium, with EIU grinding out the remaining time, runningback DuWayne Pitts fumbled a pitch from Payton at the UNI 22. Four plays, 78 yards, and 85 seconds later, UNI cashed in. Smith hit Scott Francke from 22 yards out and UNI cut the margin to 28-23.

Suddenly UNI was within reach.

After a pass interference call on the touchdown play was assessed on the kickoff, UNI kicker Mike Angell lined up at the 50 with 1:25 left. His line drive onside kick smacked off Eastern's Scott Johnson and was recovered by UNI's Pat Williams at the Eastern 39. Smith, the junior QB from Crawfordsville, Florida, ran back on the field. He threw one pass, a 36-yard strike to Luis Gonzalez, and UNI was at the Eastern three.

After Errol Peebles was stopped for no gain on first down, UNI used their final timeout. On second down, Smith was forced to throw the ball away. A trap play to Peebles on third down made it to the one, but time kept running and Mudra's squad had one play left.

Smith threw for Francke in the end zone. The ball was underthrown. It hit the back of EIU's senior defensive back Greg Rhea, who had turned to chase the UNI receiver. Francke reached up and literally took the ball off of Rhea's back for the go-ahead TD with 26 seconds left.

Eastern Illinois kicker Rich Ehmke launches a 58-yard field goal attempt as time expires. Photo courtesy of Eastern Illinois Athletics

"At defensive back there's a fine line between being the goat and the hero," said Rhea. "I thought I was going to get it. I heard 'ball' and turned back the wrong way. He caught it off my back. Then I looked up and saw the official's hands up. At that point my life ended."

It would be revived.

Caught up in the celebration of the UNI comeback, Mudra and his coaches in the press box lost control of their kicking team that immediately ran onto the field and kicked the extra point. Holding a 29-28 lead, Mudra wanted two points to give his team a three-point margin.

"Sure we wanted to go for two," he said. "We [the coaches upstairs] just couldn't get it in. In fact we wanted to take a [delay of game] penalty [to set up a two-point attempt]. One point doesn't do us any good."

Assistant coach Terry Allen shouldered some of the blame. "I lost control of my emotions in the press box when he caught the pass," explained Allen. "By the time I got the head-set back on, the kicking team was on the field."

"We thought we had the game won, we got so excited," said Mudra.

Allen called down to coach Bill Salmon to try and get holder Kevin Willard's attention. But the signal never got through and UNI's lead was 30-28.

With :26 left, UNI kicked off and Eastern returned the ball to their own 44.

On the first play, Payton, who like his counterpart Smith held numerous school passing records, threw deep for Willie Cain. Pass interference on UNI. The 15-yard penalty took the ball to the UNI 41. But two incomplete passes later, Eastern was still stuck at the 41 with only four seconds left.

THE PLAY
CD 1 - Track 21—*Doug Bock,*
Ken Wooddell, **WLBH-Radio**

"I thought I needed to get us one more completion and get inside the 40," said Payton.

So did most everyone else. Afterall, the Division I-AA field-goal record was 58 yards. EIU kicker Rich Ehmke was 1 for 5 over 30 yards for the year. And the junior college transfer's longest kick ever was a 52-yarder at Grossmont Community College in California. This would be a 58-yard attempt.

Eastern radio announcer Ken Wooddell certainly doubted. "Well, there wasn't even a chance. I mean you don't kick those kind of field goals. We said something about there being a wind. Well there was, but it's not going to carry it an additional ten yards. It wasn't a blustery thing. It was just a breeze blowing," he recalled.

Nevertheless, holder Pat Carroll knelt down at the UNI 48. So did Molde. "I saw Rich get ready to kick it and I said a little prayer," said the Eastern coach.

Prayer answered.

Ehmke's boot sailed two yards beyond the crossbar. "It was pretty much straight down the middle," the new EIU hero remarked. No time was left. Final score: Eastern Illinois 31, Northern Iowa 30.

Ehmke was mobbed. "All I remember afterwards was about fifty guys jumping on top of me," he said. "The guys just kept coming and coming, they were all on top of me. I was lucky to get out of there alive."

Down came a goalpost.

"I'm calling that the greatest game in the history of Eastern Illinois University football," said Molde, who happened to capture his 100th career coaching victory at the same time.

"My coaches coached like hell to get us ahead and then they bring a guy out that kicks a 60-yard field goal," mused Mudra.

For Ehmke it was a like dream come true. "It's really funny but I had a dream last night," he said. "I dreamt the score was tied 20-20 with two seconds left and I kicked a 53-yarder to win it. Strange."

Yep.

THE AFTERMATH

Eastern Illinois went on to win their final five games of the season, finishing 11-2, champions of the Gateway Conference. The Panthers ended up ranked #3 in the final I-AA poll. Payton ended his career at EIU with 10,655 career passing yards which still ranks in the top ten all-time among Division I-AA quarterbacks. He played professional football briefly in the CFL, Arena Football League and in 1987 with the Chicago Bears. For the next two decades, Payton flourished as an assistant coach both in college and more notably in the NFL. After being assistant head coach with the Dallas Cowboys from 2003-05, he was hired as the head coach of the New Orleans Saints in January 2006.

Northern Iowa lost two of the next three games and finished the season 7-3-1. They did not make the NCAA playoffs. The following year, UNI reached the I-AA semifinals before losing to eventual national champion Northeast Louisiana 44-41 in double overtime. That game was Darrell Mudra's last as a coach. He retired as one of the most successful coaches in I-AA history with 200 career victories. In the history of the NCAA, only John Heisman coached at more schools (8) than Darrell Mudra.

Northern Iowa	0	0	9	21	-30
Eastern Illinois	0	0	7	24	-31

UNI	Baker 5 pass from Smith (kick failed)
EIU	Marable 1 run (Ehmke kick)
UNI	Angell 39 FG
UNI	Howard 2 pass from Smith (Angell kick)
EIU	Marable 1 run (Ehmke kick)
EIU	Banks 12 pass from Payton (Ehmke kick)
EIU	Banke 59 pass from Payton (Ehmke kick)
UNI	Francke 22 pass from Smith (Angell kick)
UNI	Francke 1 pass from Smith (Angell kick)
EIU	Ehmke 58 FG

Attendance 11,052

South Carolina vs.
North Carolina State

"It was like a fairy tale come true."
—NC State defensive back Derrick Taylor

THE BACKGROUND

If you can't beat 'em, hire 'em.

Furman University, a Division I-AA school (enrollment 2,500), had beaten North Carolina State (enrollment 24,000) two years in a row. In 1984, the Paladins knocked off the Wolfpack 34-30. In 1985, Furman won again, 42-20. In 1986, NC State hired Furman's coach.

Dick Sheridan came to Raleigh, North Carolina, as the 1985 Division I-AA Coach of the Year, narrowly missing a national championship with a 44-42 loss to Georgia Southern in the '85 title game. His task at NC State was to rebuild a program that had three consecutive 3-8 seasons from 1983-85.

Sheridan wasted no time.

The Wolfpack surprised many in 1986 by running out to a 5-1-1 record. NC State was riding an impressive two-game swing, knocking off previously unbeaten and No.17 North Carolina 35-34 on a failed two-point conversion attempt by the Tar Heels with eight seconds left. The Wolfpack then dismantled ACC leader and 16th-ranked Clemson 27-3.

Now, NC State had replaced Clemson at No.16 in the AP poll, and taken over the driver's seat for the ACC championship. All that remained between Sheridan and an unlikely conference title was South Carolina (2-4-1), Virginia (2-5), and Duke (3-4).

"I don't think many people could have predicted we'd be where we are now," Sheridan said.

The Wolfpack momentum rolled on against Joe Morrison's South Carolina Gamecocks as NC State stormed out to a 17-0 lead. Runningback Bobby Crumpler ran for 89 yards and 2 TDs in the first half, while the Wolfpack defense intercepted USC red-shirt freshman quarterback Todd Ellis three times to go along with three sacks, all in the first two quarters. NC State roared into the locker room up 17-3.

Then all of a sudden, something changed.

After a 45-yard field goal by USC's Scott Hagler closed the margin to 17-6 in the third quarter, State quarterback Erik Kramer injured his ankle and had to leave the game. At the same time, Carolina's offense continued to pick up steam, scoring on their next possession as Ellis hit Sterling Sharpe with an eight-yard TD pass to make it 17-13.

Kramer, the Wolfpack's senior leader who threw for 2,092 yards during his final season, re-entered the game later in the third quarter, but he clearly wasn't the same quarterback. After Hagler hit his third field goal of the game to bring the Gamecocks within 17-16, Kramer threw the first of two fourth-quarter interceptions, this one to Ron Rabune, who returned the ball to the State 29-yard line. Ellis, whose 297 yards surpassed the school's season passing record of 2,030 held by Tommy Suggs, cashed in the turnover with a one-yard run to put Carolina ahead 22-17.

The Gamecocks had scored 22 unanswered points, completely dominating Sheridan's squad in the second half.

With the Wolfpack offense unable to move the ball, generating just 59 yards in the final two quarters, State punted to USC with 3:10 left in the game. The Pack defense quickly forced a third-and-12 situation.

From his own 15-yard line, Ellis hit Ryan Bethea for 23 yards and a crucial first down to the USC 38. The Wolfpack then used their last timeout with 2:13 left. With four downs, and State unable to stop the clock, Coach Morrison figured he could run out the final seconds and go home to Columbia, South Carolina, with a 22-17 upset victory.

He figured wrong.

After Raynard Brown was stopped for no gain on first down, Morrison instructed Ellis to take a knee. On second down, Ellis lost four yards. On third down, he danced around in the backfield then fell to the ground for a five-yard loss. A delay of game penalty moved the ball back to the USC 24, but there was still 30 seconds to play.

Morrison was unhappy with the time-keeper. "They stopped the clock after Brown's run for no reason and then just took nine seconds off. We still thought we could run the clock down instead of trying for another first down. It was just a very questionable clock. I'd like to have that clock operator work some of our games in Columbia," Morrison said.

USC's Scott Bame had to punt.

Under pressure, Bame shanked the ball out of bounds. A measly 15-yard punt to the USC 39. With 0:27 on the clock, Kramer and the Wolfpack had a chance.

But they could do nothing with it. Two plays netted one yard. Down to his last gasp, the hobbled Kramer dropped back to pass but couldn't even get rid of the ball. He was buried for a sack. The final seconds ticked off the clock.

South Carolina players and fans streamed onto the field, dancing with joy, celebrating the upset victory. NC State's bubble had been burst.

But wait. There was a flag on the field.

Linebacker Kenneth Robinson, who had blown through the middle of the line on the final play, was called for offsides. The ball was moved to the 33-yard line. With time expired, the Wolfpack were given one additional play.

THE PLAY

Confusion reigned. The previously jubilant South Carolina players were waved off the field. Their celebration put on hold.

Without benefit of a timeout, Sheridan quickly got Kramer over to the sidelines to decide on a play. After order was restored and the field cleared, Kramer brought his team to the line of scrimmage. A simple "trips right" was called. Danny Peebles, Haywood Jeffires, and Frank Harris lined up to the right.

Kramer took the snap and scrambled around until his receivers could get to the end zone. He launched it for the corner, then fell to the ground re-injuring his leg.

Peebles, a 5-11 sophomore, found himself in the middle of a swarm of defenders in the corner of the end zone as the ball spiraled toward him. "That play usually does not work," said Peebles. "You know you're going to pass. The other team knows you're going to pass. The odds are so great against you."

He jumped. He pushed. He beat the odds.

Peebles came down with the ball. Safety Chris Major tried to knock it loose. "The first time I saw the ball it was in his gut," said Majors. "All I could do was try and rip it out." Peebles held on. Touchdown Wolfpack. Now it was NC State that had won 23-22.

The field was swarmed again. This time by Wolfpack fans and players. Unable to walk, Kramer had to be carried away. Meanwhile, the Gamecocks were distraught and disgusted, claiming Peebles pushed off to make the final catch. "I might've pushed," said a gleeful Peebles. "But what's a pushing penalty when there's one second left?"

"This one was taken away from us," Morrison said, "and I feel sorry for those players in the locker room."

His team outplayed for the entire second half, Sheridan felt fortunate. "It was a humbling victory," he said modestly. "A win like this usually makes the law of averages swing the other way."

THE AFTERMATH

The law of averages caught up with the Wolfpack the following week. NC State was upset at Virginia 20-16. Kramer, forced to sit out the first two quarters with his injured ankle, hobbled onto the field in the second half, but had to leave again as the Wolfpack lost their chance for the 1986 ACC title, which was won by Clemson.

NC State ended the season 8-3-1 with a 25-24 loss to Virginia Tech in the Peach Bowl when Tech's Chris Kinzer hit a 40-yard field goal as time ran out. Kramer was named ACC Player of the Year, while Sheridan received ACC Coach of the Year honors.

South Carolina finished the season a disappointing 3-6-2, but Joe Morrison led the Gamecocks to back-to-back 8-4 seasons and two straight bowl appearances in '87 and '88. Then, in February of 1989, he died suddenly of a heart attack at the age of 51. Morrison compiled a record of 39-28-2 during his six seasons at South Carolina, including a school record 10-2 mark in 1984.

Sheridan turned down an offer to replace Morrison as the South Carolina coach. He stayed at NC State until 1993, when coincidentally at age 51, he retired citing health reasons. Sheridan left with a 52-29-3 record and six bowl appearances in seven seasons at NC State.

South Carolina	0	3	13	6	- 22
NC State	3	14	0	6	- 23

NCS	FG Cofer 38
NCS	Crumpler 1 run (Cofer kick)
NCS	Crumpler 26 run (Cofer kick)
USC	FG Hagler 41
USC	FG Hagler 45
USC	Sharpe 8 pass from Ellis (Hagler kick)
USC	FG Hagler 21
USC	Ellis 1 run (pass failed)
NCS	Peebles 33 pass from Kramer (no attempt)

Attendance 50,330

Auburn vs. Florida

"It has to be one of the finest comebacks ever."—Galen Hall

THE BACKGROUND

It was a tremendous season in the works for Auburn's Pat Dye. The fifth-ranked Tigers were 7-0, dismantling every opponent in their path. Their closest game was a 31-10 victory over Georgia Tech. The Tigers averaged more points (39.0) than any other team in the Southeastern Conference, and their defense gave up fewer points (7.6) than any other.

Meanwhile, Galen Hall's Florida Gators were struggling. Hall started his head coaching career at Florida when he took over for Charley Pell amid an NCAA investigation into a recruiting scandal in the middle of the 1984 season. After two years with the Gators under NCAA sanctions, he had compiled a sparkling 17-1-1 record, the seventh best start over two seasons in the history of Division I-A football.

But in '86, with Florida now free to play in bowls and on TV, things changed. The Gators limped to a 1-4 record to start the season. They were winless in the SEC (0-3). In addition, junior quarterback Kerwin Bell, a former walk-on, former SEC Player of the Year his freshman season, potential Heisman Trophy candidate, three-year starter, and all-around team leader, had missed the last two weeks with a sprained left knee ligament. In his place, lefty Rodney Brewer took the snaps for the Gators.

No one gave the Gators much of a chance against Auburn. Even the entire sports staff of their hometown paper, the *Gainesville Sun*, picked the Tigers to continue their winning ways over Florida.

From the start, they looked right on the money.

Florida's offense couldn't have played a worse first half in their last home game of the season. The Gators turned the ball over an astounding six times in the first two quarters. Brewer had an abysmal half. For the record, he was 1 of 6 with two interceptions. He also fumbled twice.

Trailing 14-0 with 5:27 to play in the half, Hall had to make a change. The gimpy Bell returned to the lineup.

The Auburn defense did not take pity. Strong safety Arthur Johnson picked off a Bell pass in his first series back. Then in the third quarter, defensive back Alvin Briggs intercepted another Bell attempt at the AU 22. From there, Auburn senior tailback Brent Fullwood broke off a 41-yard run (he had 168 yards rushing on the day), setting up a 31-yard Chris Knapp field goal with 14 seconds left in the third quarter. Entering the fourth quarter, Auburn was sailing 17-0.

On Florida's next possession, it looked like another Bell interception. Outside linebacker Aundray Bruce had his hands all over a pass intended for running back Wayne Williams. Bruce bobbled, and bobbled, and bobbled it. The ball fell to the ground.

Perhaps something changed. Bell took the second chance to complete five of six passes, marching the Gators 79 yards and scoring on a one-yard keeper to cut the lead to 17-7 with 12:09 left.

Auburn quarterback Jeff Burger couldn't get

the Tigers moving. Three-and-out for the Tigers and the Gators had the ball back. Bell went to work again, moving the ball to the AU 24.

After Bell was sacked for an 11-yard loss, kicker Robert McGinty came on to try a 51-yard field goal. McGinty was a transfer from Auburn, where he was well known for missing the 42-yard field goal in the final seconds against Alabama in 1984, giving the Tide a 17-15 win. After that, Dye literally kicked McGinty off the team. He transferred to Florida and sat out a year.

"I feel certain I won't miss one of those [last second] kicks again," said McGinty. In his first game against his old teammates, the re-juvenated kicker connected from 51 yards out to make it 17-10 with 7:10 on the clock.

But Auburn's offense began to retake control.

For five minutes they held the ball while marching to the Florida 36. Then they fumbled. Fullback Reggie Ware coughed up the ball as he was running through the line and Florida's Webbie Burnett recovered. It was the third Auburn turnover of the game.

With two minutes remaining, Bell tried to move the newly resurrected Gators for a third straight score. He got off to a quick start. Defensive tackle Tracy Rocker was called for a 15-yard facemask and the ball was moved to the AU 49.

Bell then marched the Gators to the Tiger 30. Next, he lofted a pass down the sideline for wide receiver Ricky Nattiel, closely guarded by safety Johnson. Nattiel, playing with a separated shoulder suffered in the third quarter, snared the perfectly thrown ball for a 25-yard completion. The Gators were at the Auburn five-yard line with under a minute left.

Bell threw the next pass away. On second down, Nattiel and receiver Eric Hodges lined up wide left. Hodges cut inside, Nattiel cut outside. Auburn's Johnson tried to follow. "I sorta hesitated because I thought I was going to run into the (other) receiver," said the safety.

Hodges momentarily screened Johnson off the play. Nattiel was wide open in the corner. Pick plays are illegal. "Oh no, it was a fade, not a pick," said Nattiel.

Fade plays are not illegal. Nattiel caught Bell's five-yard fade pass for the touchdown with 0:36 left and the Gators trailed 17-16.

At 0-3 in the conference, Florida had no reason not to go for two.

THE PLAY
CD 1—Track 22
David Steele and Norm Carlson,
Florida Gator Radio Network

Florida had the ball moved to the left hash-mark. Bell sent three receivers to the right.

Nattiel was the main target again. "I was supposed to do whatever it took to get myself free," he said. Bell took the snap and looked for Nattiel. He was covered and couldn't get open.

"If Kerwin had thrown the ball my way, we would've lost," said Nattiel. Instead, Bell stepped up in the pocket. Linebacker Russ Carreker stormed up the middle toward the quarterback. Bell desperately avoided his rush. Then, looking to the left corner of the end zone, with a recuperating left knee, he decided to run.

"I was just hoping I could get there," said Bell. "It seemed like it took me all day. But I was running as fast as I could."

Bell's lack of mobility was no secret. "I was shocked when he ran," said Auburn linebacker Edward Phillips. "Bell never runs."

This time he did. Phillips tried to catch up before he made it to the goal line. "I just forgot about the knee," said Bell. "I was just a second too late," said Phillips.

Bell made it. He crossed the goal line as Florida Field shook. The entire Gator team streamed out onto the field. Florida led 18-17, but it wasn't quite over.

A 15-yard unsportsmanlike conduct penalty was assessed on the kickoff for the massive celebration. After the kickoff, Auburn had the ball at the UF 49. They moved it to the 36 with :06 left. Knapp, who replaced McGinty as Auburn's kicker, tried a 53-yard field goal into the wind. It was short.

Knapp had missed from 53 while McGinty had made from 51. The Gators had won and Auburn's undefeated season was no more.

Game 40

THE AFTERMATH

Florida finished the season 6-5, winning five of their last six games of the year. Auburn lost again two weeks later to Georgia 20-16, falling into a four-way tie in the SEC with Alabama, Georgia, and Ole Miss at 4-2. (LSU won the '86 SEC title with a 5-1 conference record.) Auburn ended the season 10-2 after defeating Southern Cal in the Citrus Bowl, 16-7. The Tigers finished the year ranked No.6 in the AP poll.

Fullwood ended his senior year with the Auburn record for highest yards-per-rush average for a season (8.3), and a career (7.2). He ran for 2,789 yards in just 390 carries. Burger had a razor-sharp season in '87, leading the Tigers to the first of three straight SEC titles, and finishing his career as the all-time leader in completion percentage at Auburn (331-538, .615).

Bell completed his superlative career with the Gators in 1987, as the career passing leader not only for Florida, but for the entire SEC, throwing for 7,585 yards. He bounced around the NFL as a free agent with numerous teams, Atlanta, Tampa Bay, and Indianapolis among them, played in the World League of American Football, but was probably most successful as a quarterback in the Canadian Football League.

Hall remained coach at Florida until 1989 when he was forced to resign, after admitting to violating NCAA rules. He was replaced by interim coach Gary Darnell, then in 1990 by permanent new coach Steve Spurrier. Despite three straight 6-5 regular season finishes from '86-'88, Hall had a 40-18-1 record with the Gators.

Auburn	7	7	3	0	-17
Florida	0	0	0	18	-18

AU	Ware 1 run (Knapp kick)
AU	Fullwood 11 run (Knapp kick)
AU	Knapp 31 FG
UF	Bell 1 run (Dawson kick)
UF	McGinty 51 FG
UF	Nattiel 5 pass from Bell (Bell run)

Attendance 74, 521

Penn State vs. Miami 🏈

> "One club makes the play and they are national champions, the other team makes the play and they're national champions."—*Joe Paterno*

THE BACKGROUND

"It was the classic morality play. Good versus evil, clean versus outlaw," remembered Penn State broadcaster Stan Savron. Indeed, that's the way the 1987 Fiesta Bowl played out in the media, with all the soap opera drama of a pro wrestling championship bout.

In this corner, wearing the army fatigues and combat boots, the top-ranked team in the land, the Miami Hurricanes. "Boooooooooo!!"

Their opponents, wearing the starched collars and khaki pants by day, and the generic football uniforms by night, ranked No.2, the Penn State Nittany Lions. "Yeaaaaaahhhh!"

The winner to be crowned the undisputed national champion.

Miami, the bad boys of college football, were the pioneers of late 20th century trash talking, and proud of it. The Hurricanes walked off their plane in Tempe, like troops invading the desert, stocked with powerful ammunition and a cockiness akin to the World Wrestling Federation.

"We don't care what people think of us as long as we win, our fans are happy, our school is happy and we bring our school more money," said defensive leader and Outland Trophy finalist Jerome Brown. While the overpowering Hurricanes were a dominant 11-0, sporting a 21-game regular-season unbeaten record, their team police record was grabbing more headlines.

Halfback Melvin Bratton, charged with alleged shoplifting. Linebacker George Mira, Jr.,

charged with battery of a police officer following a domestic argument. Sophomore split end Michael Irvin, accused of driving his car over the feet of two university law students. Defensive end Daniel Stubbs, charged with petty theft and resisting arrest. The beat went on.

Sure, they may have been tainted, but they were also tight. During a supposed friendly Fiesta Bowl steak dinner where both teams put on funny skits after the meal, the Miami players walked off the stage, offended by seemingly harmless jokes made by the Penn State players.

"When people poke fun at us, when people poke fun at the head football coach, our people are offended and they want to know it's not fun," said Miami coach Jimmy Johnson.

"There's nothing to say," said Penn State runningback D.J. Dozier. "What happened, happened. I continued to eat my steak. I was hungry."

Perhaps both teams were actually playing along with the hype, welcoming their given roles. "It was great theater," noted Savron. In any case, the heavyweight fight atmosphere kept building.

"When we were down there, Joe used to knock on my door at the motel, and he'd say 'Let's take a walk,'" remembered George Paterno, brother of the Penn State coach. "He'd work off his energy before going to practice. And the local people, the people from Arizona, would be going to work and they'd stop the car and they'd back up on the highway and they'd roll the window down and they'd say, 'Hey Joe, get them son-of-a-bitches.'...It was that symbolic."

Penn State linebacker Don Graham sacks Miami QB Vinny Testaverde. Photo courtesty of Penn State Sports Information

Joe Paterno's Nittany Lions were 11-0 and had their own 22-game regular-season winning streak. With an ugly but efficient offense carried all season by a steel-headed defense, Penn State was perfectly cast in the role of underdog.

Their quarterback, senior John Shaffer, could do nothing on the field but win. Since seventh grade, Shaffer's record as a starting QB was 65-1. His only loss? The 1986 Orange Bowl, when he threw three interceptions as Oklahoma knocked off the undefeated Nittany Lions 25-10 to claim the national championship.

At Penn State, Shaffer was more of a caretaker than quarterback, winning by handing off and protecting the ball, with an average of 158 yards per game through the air. "To suggest that they [Penn State] would win a national championship with John Shaffer at quarterback really was almost absurd," noted Savron. His broadcasting partner George Paterno agreed. "We didn't have a quarterback. We had John Shaffer, they had Vinny Testaverde."

Testaverde, the Heisman Trophy winner, had more touchdowns in the '86 season (26) than Shaffer had his entire career (18). Miami's QB led the nation in passing efficiency his senior season, completing 175 of 276 for a .634 completion percentage. He threw just nine interceptions.

But on this night, Penn State defensive coordinator Jerry Sandusky concocted an elaborate scheme, constantly changing alignments to try and confuse Testaverde. "We had 24 different coverages in the secondary and about 30 different looks including the guys up front, said safety Ray Isom. "We mixed it up as much as possible."

Even with Sandusky's smoke and mirrors, Testaverde still threw for 285 yards. Shaffer had a measly 53. The Hurricanes dominated the statistics rolling up 445 total yards to Penn State's 162. Miami controlled the clock, running 93 plays from scrimmage. Penn State had just 59. The Hurricanes had 22 first downs to Penn State's 8.

January 2, 1987—Tempe, Arizona

"You're out here to win, not to see how many stats you can get," said Lions head coach Joe Paterno.

Indeed JoePa. Miami, averaging almost 40 points per game, a team so talented that 34 of the 91 players on their roster were eventually drafted by NFL teams, led just 10-7 after a Mark Seelig 38-yard field goal with 11:49 to play in the game. Why? Because of two fumbles and three interceptions forced by Sandusky's defense. At key moments, Testaverde misread coverages and Penn State would intercept his passes.

"No doubt about it, the defenses were confusing him," said linebacker Trey Bauer. "He was throwing the ball right into our hands."

Midway through the final quarter, All-America linebacker Shane Conlan collected his second interception of the game, Testaverde's fourth, and returned it 38 yards to the Miami 5. With a golden chance to take the lead, Shaffer fumbled the snap on the next play. But fortunately for the Lions, Keith Radecic recovered. On second down, Dozier scooted up the middle for a six-yard touchdown run. With 8:13 to play, Penn State held an unlikely 14-10 lead.

Overwhelming favorites, Miami came down to their last drive, desperately needing a touchdown for a national championship.

The 'Canes took over with 3:07 to play on their own 23. They quickly faced fourth down at the 26. Testaverde took a short drop and found Bennie Blades cutting across to the left. Blades turned the corner up the left sideline across midfield for a 31-yard gain to keep Miami alive.

Inside Penn State territory, suddenly Testaverde looked unstoppable. He connected five straight times, surgically moving Miami to the Penn State six-yard line with 0:48 left. But then, with the clock down to 25 seconds, defensive tackle Tim Johnson came flying around left end and sacked Testaverde with a hook to the head, dropping him at the 13-yard line.

After a timeout, Testaverde threw to the right on third down, but runningback Warren Williams couldn't hold on. The Hurricanes were faced with fourth-and-goal at the 13. Only 18 seconds remained.

The national championship came down to one play.

THE PLAY

It had happened twice before to Penn State at the end of the '86 season. Against both Maryland and Notre Dame, the Lions' defense needed to defend their goal line in the waning seconds in order to remain undefeated.

When Maryland scored a touchdown with 14 seconds left to close to within 17-15 of Penn State, Sandusky's defense forced an incomplete pass by Dan Henning on the two-point conversion attempt to preserve the victory.

The following week, Notre Dame stood at the Penn State nine-yard line with 0:52 left on the clock, trailing 24-19. But a sack by linebacker Don Graham of quarterback Steve Beuerlein pushed the Irish back to the 18, and Penn State held on downs to win the game.

Now, for the third time in their final four games, Penn State was in the same position. Paterno put his faith in Sandusky.

"I'm not the kind of guy that likes to pray for the Good Lord to take care of a football game. I figure He has better things to do. But I was tempted to pray," said Paterno.

Sandusky had devised a nickel defense that added an extra linebacker instead of a defensive back, befuddling Testaverde on several occasions. But on the final drive, the Miami QB seemed to have solved the puzzle.

"I do remember thinking the bubble was about to burst because how long could you contain Testaverde and that offense," recalled Savron. "I was convinced that they were going to score at the end there and pull it out."

It seemed inevitable. Testaverde dropped back and looked left for split end Brett Perriman in the end zone. Without hesitation, like a quarterback eyeing a wide open receiver, Testaverde fired the pass...right at junior linebacker Pete Giftopoulis covering at the goal line.

Testaverde was stunned. "Like he knew where I was going exactly," said the Hurricanes' QB. Giftopoulis grasped the ball, and quickly fell to the ground at the 11-yard line, protecting the ball like a newborn baby. It was Testaverde's fifth interception of the game, the fourth picked off by Lion linebackers, the one that secured Penn State's national championship.

"Any one of four players could have intercepted it or knocked it down," said Gifto-poulis."I just happened to be in the right place at the right time."

Shaffer took one more snap, kneeling to the ground as the final nine seconds ticked off the clock. Ding, ding, ding. The bell rang. The championship match was over. Ladies and gentlemen, we have a decision. Workman-like Penn State 14, Flashy Miami 10.

After the game, Testaverde was asked to explain Penn State's mysterious pass defense. "If I knew, I would have had no problem," he said.

THE AFTERMATH

Penn State finished No.1 in the polls. Miami was No.2.

"I think historically and emotionally and as far as a legacy, I think that's Penn State and Joe Paterno's greatest win," said his brother George. Joe Paterno was voted Football Writers Association of America Coach of the Year and *Sports Illustrated*'s Sportsman of the Year for 1986. The following season, the Nittany Lions regular-season streak ended with a 24-13 loss to Alabama in the second game of the year. Penn State ended the '87 season with an 8-4 record.

Meanwhile, the talented Hurricanes gained revenge in 1987, picking up right where they left off at the end of the '86 regular season, finishing 11-0, defeating Oklahoma 20-14 in the Orange Bowl, and capturing their second of four national titles from 1983-1991.

Penn State	0	7	0	7	-14
Miami	0	7	0	3	-10

UM	Bratton 1 run (Cox kick)
PS	Shaffer 4 run (Manca kick)
UM	FG Seelig 38
PS	Dozier 6 run (Manca kick)

Attendance 73,098

Northeast Louisiana vs. Northwestern State ⚈

"That was wild, wasn't it ?"—Pat Collins

THE BACKGROUND

Natchitoches, Louisiana, is about 90 miles southwest of Monroe, Louisiana. When Northwestern State joined the Southland Conference in the fall of 1987, the two towns got a little closer.

The Northeast Louisiana Indians traveled from their home in Monroe to Turpin Stadium in Natchitoches to battle their new conference rivals, the Demons of Northwestern State, in their homecoming game. Both teams were ranked in the top 10 of Division I-AA schools (NLU was No.2 in the nation, Northwestern was No.8). Both teams featured potent offensive threats. Senior quarterback Stan Humphries, a transfer from LSU, had thrown for 950 yards without an interception in just three games for the undefeated Indians. Tailback John Stephens was the leading rusher in the conference, averaging 5.2 yards per carry for Northwestern (2-1). Both teams featured overpowering defenses. NLU was second in the country against the rush (47.6 yards/game), Northwestern was second against the pass (70.6 yards/game).

Both teams knew that the winner had the inside track at the conference championship and an automatic bid into the I-AA playoffs.

In the first half, fullback Tommy Minvielle pounded away at the highly touted Demons run defense, racking up 141 yards on numerous draw plays. His 55-yard jaunt in the first quarter led to a short Humphries' TD pass and NLU took the early lead 7-0. But Humphries was then picked off for the first time in 114 attempts (an NLU record for consecutive passes without an in-

terception) by Michael Smith, who returned it 46 yards to the NLU 17. Stephens tied the game up at 7-7 with a one-yard TD run. From there, NLU scored 17 consecutive points, helped by Demon fumbles, and capped by Teddy Garcia's 55-yard field goal, giving coach Pat Collins' squad a commanding 24-7 lead.

Coming out of the locker room for the second half trailing 27-14, Northwestern looked like a new team. Junior flanker Floyd Turner hauled in a 40-yard TD pass from back-up quarterback Scott Stoker on the opening drive. The seldom-used Stoker was thrust into the starting role when Demon QB Rusty Slack tore thumb tendons on the last play of Northwestern's previous game. As it turned out, Stoker carried the Northwestern offense on his shoulders after Stephens was forced to leave the game with a knee injury in the third quarter.

Trailing 27-21 early in the fourth quarter, Stoker drove the Demons downfield and scored on a three-yard TD run with 10 minutes left to play. Keith Hodnett's PAT gave Northwestern the come-from-behind 28-27 lead.

The Demons' defense completely shut down NLU's attack in the second half. After the struggling Humphries was intercepted for the second time, setting up a Hodnett 32-yard field goal, Northwestern regained possession with 5:08 left. They methodically drove into NLU territory, nursing the 31-27 lead.

Facing fourth-and-two at the NLU 14 with under 30 seconds left, coach Sam Goodwin had a decision to make.

"A field goal wouldn't have done us any good in the conference race," said Goodwin. "If

140

Future NFL star Stan Humphries engineers the NLU miracle. Photo courtesty of University of Louisiana at Monroe Sports Information

we had kicked, and they came back and scored a touchdown and kicked an extra point, then it's a tie and we're out of the conference race at 1-1-1. If we get the first down, then that's the last play of the game because they had no timeouts."

With 16 seconds on the clock, Stoker kept the ball on an option run. He was stopped short of the first down.

NLU took over on its own 13-yard line. But needing a touchdown, with no timeouts left, and facing a Demons' defense that had relinquished just 35 yards of offense the entire second half, the Indians' chances of going back to Monroe victorious were practically zero.

Nevertheless, Humphries rifled a pass to T-back Jeff Steele over the middle who collided head on with a Demons' defender, then somehow bounced backward, stayed on his feet, and scrambled for a 39-yard gain to the Northwestern 48-yard line.

Frantically, the NLU offense ran to the line of scrimmage. Humphries took the snap and threw the ball out of bounds with one second showing on the clock.

The previous year in Monroe, Northwest-

ern beat NLU 17-14 with a 27-yard field goal by Hodnett on the last play of the game. This year in Natchitoches, the Indians had the ball for the final play.

THE PLAY

CD 1—Track 23—*Frank Hoffmann*, University of Louisiana at Monroe

Three NLU receivers, Chris Jones, Mike Manzullo, and Jackie Harris lined up on the right side of the field. Five Demons defenders, Adrian Howard, David Chitman, Randy Hilliard, Gary Cater, and Sidney Thissel would be waiting for them downfield.

The play was called "99 Victory." Call it "Hail Mary on the bayou."

Humphries flung a high-arcing pass to the middle of the field that came down around the two-yard line. Four waiting Northwestern players and two Indian receivers jumped for it. At the same time, NLU's Harris, trying to catch up with the pass, ran by the pack in a futile attempt to tip the ball. He ended up falling behind the group into the end zone.

Meanwhile, the ball caromed off a defender's hands, then bounced off a shoulder pad, then got tipped a third time and flicked back to the four-yard line. There, Northwestern's Thissel tried to bat it away for good, but instead flipped it over the pack of players into the end zone...right where Harris, a sophomore tight end, was kneeling by himself on the ground. Harris reached up from his knees and plucked the pass out of the air.

It was like watching a trick shot in billiards that hits four bumpers, avoids five balls, then magically falls in the corner pocket. "I just turned around and grabbed it," said Harris. "I can't believe this."

Incredibly, Northeast Louisiana won 33-31.

"I never saw the catch myself," noted Humphries. " I didn't know it was caught until I saw all our guys jumping and yelling."

"We work on that play every Thursday. It's in the playbook. We practice it. The ball is supposed to be tipped around. That's the way it's designed," said Coach Collins. "Call it a lot of things, but not luck."

Perhaps a lunar eclipse?

"When I saw the film, there's nothing but purple [Northwestern] jerseys around," a befuddled Goodwin commented. "The guy who caught it is lying on the ground in the end zone...I've never lost a game like that."

Neither has most anyone else.

THE AFTERMATH

It was a year of destiny (not luck) for the NLU Indians. After being stunned the following week in a non-conference game by Lamar University 48-28, the Indians finished the season 6-0 inside the conference. In the "Southland Showdown," NLU beat conference foe North Texas State 24-23 when Keith Chapman's PAT hit the right goalpost and bounced back with 1:23 to play. It was North Texas' only missed PAT of the season.

NLU ended the season 13-2, winning the Division I-AA National Championship with a come from behind 43-42 victory over the Marshall Thundering Herd in Pocatello, Idaho. Pat Collins won the I-AA Coach of the Year Award from CBS Sports and *The Football News*.

Stan Humphries was voted first-team All-America and drafted in the sixth round of the 1988 NFL draft by the then-Super Bowl champion Washington Redskins. He was the second straight NLU QB taken in the draft. (Bubby Brister, Humphries' predecessor, was drafted by the Pittsburgh Steelers.)

After taking the San Diego Chargers to the Super Bowl in 1995, Humphries returned to Monroe in 1999 as the quarterbacks coach for the former Northeast Louisiana University, now known as the University of Louisiana at Monroe.

The following season in 1988, Northwestern State won the Southland Conference (6-0) and reached the quarterfinal round of the I-AA national playoffs. Sam Goodwin was named Southland Conference Coach of the Year and Louisiana Coach of the Year. The Demons finished the year ranked No. 8 in the I-AA poll and beat two teams, North Texas State and Stephen F. Austin, which were ranked No. 1 in the country.

NLU	7	20	0	6	-33
NSU	7	7	7	10	-31

NLU	Humphries 1 pass to Johnson (Garcia kick)
NSU	Stephens 1 run (Hodnett kick)
NLU	Humphries 12 pass to Manzullo (Garcia kick)
NLU	Minvielle 11 run (Garcia kick)
NLU	Garcia 55 FG
NSU	Stephens 1 run (Hodnett kick)
NLU	Garcia 17 FG
NSU	Turner 40 pass from Stoker (Hodnett kick)
NSU	Stoker 3 run (Hodnett kick)
NSU	Hodnett 32 FG
NLU	Harris 48 pass from Humphries (no attempt)

Attendance 13,600

Marshall vs. Louisville

"I'm not sure what [Petersen] was doing, but it worked."
—Marshall head coach George Chaump

THE BACKGROUND

The town of Huntington, West Virginia, endured one of the worst stretches in the history of college football. From 1966-83, the hometown Thundering Herd of Marshall University collected 18 straight losing seasons. Finally, in 1984, with a 31-28 win at East Tennessee State in the final game of the season, the Herd squeaked out a 6-5 record.

The streak was over.

Three years later, Marshall, coached by George Chaump, was in the midst of a 2-3 campaign when they traveled to Louisville for a battle with the Division I-A Cardinals. Coach Howard Schnellenberger's team was 2-2-1 coming into the game, smarting from a 65-6 pasting at the hands of Southern Mississippi the previous week. But against Division I-AA Marshall, the Cardinals had an eight-game winning streak, dating back to 1964. In fact, Louisville won the last two games between the teams by a combined score of 92-0.

Marshall lit up the Louisville night sky with 28 first-half points, leading the Cardinals 28-10 at the half on the strength of quarterback Tony Petersen's arm. Petersen was on fire, hitting 15 of 21 passes for 188 yards and two TDs in the first half.

But the Cardinals shut down the Marshall offense in the second half. Petersen's passes suddenly ended up in the wrong hands.

After Louisville cut the lead to 28-18 on a 35-yard TD scamper by Rodney Knighton early in the third quarter, safety Terry Lantz picked off a Petersen pass at the Marshall 30 and ran it back to the 10-yard line. Cardinal QB Jay Gruden took one play to convert. Flanker Anthony Cummings made a diving TD reception of Gruden's pass and Louisville cut the Herd lead to 28-24.

Still trailing by four points with under seven minutes to play in the game, Louisville halfback Deon Booker (who had a career high 196 yards rushing), broke away off the right side for 38 yards down to the Marshall 20. Gruden connected with Joey Hamilton on the next play for the 20-yard touchdown and the Cardinals had their first lead 31-28.

After 18 straight points by Louisville, Marshall was melting.

On the next series, Petersen threw another interception to Lantz and the Cardinals ran the clock down to under two minutes before kicker Ron Bell attempted a 41-yard field goal.

He missed. With 1:51 to play, Petersen and the Herd took over, 76 yards away from a score with just one timeout left. They hadn't scored a point the entire second half.

Out of nowhere, Petersen got his touch back. He hit six short passes, moving the ball down to the Louisville 28. Along the way, Marshall was forced to use their final timeout. They ended up playing a frantic game of beat the clock in the final minute.

With just 32 seconds left, on a first-down play, Petersen rolled out, looking for an open receiver. He scrambled, couldn't find anyone, suddenly saw tight end Sean Doctor, but couldn't get the ball away before junior linebacker Chris Sellars flattened him at the 31.

The clock kept running. Twenty seconds. Fifteen seconds. The Herd couldn't stop the clock. Petersen peeled himself off the ground and scrambled to the line of scrimmage.

THE PLAY
CD 1—Track 24—*Bill Roth,*
Marshall University Thundering Herd Network

"I saw the clock was running out," said tailback Ron Darby. "I was yelling throw the ball out of bounds!" The clock ticked down to 10 seconds.

Marshall could have tried a 48-yard field goal for the 31-31 tie.

Chaump screamed at his quarterback from the sidelines, "Throw the ball out of bounds!" Petersen ignored his coach's instructions. Instead, he called "all-deep," a play where two receivers on each side of the line head toward the end zone.

Five seconds. The Herd still hadn't snapped the ball. "I saw there were four seconds on the clock and thought about throwing it out of bounds. But I figured the clock might run out anyway and it wouldn't do any good," said Petersen.

Marshall snapped the ball at four seconds. The frantic Herd receivers had lined up in the wrong formation. Three receivers, Keith Baxter, Bruce Hammond, and Doctor, were on the right, and only one wide out, leading receiver Mike Barber, was on the left.

Petersen rolled out and looked for Barber to go deep. But in all the confusion, Barber never heard Petersen's "all-deep" call and ran the wrong route, cutting across on a post pattern directly into Louisville's coverage.

The clock ran out. Defensive tackle Chris Thieneman then came barreling in toward Petersen. The Herd quarterback quickly sidestepped Thieneman, giving him one last moment to find a receiver downfield.

In an instant, he spotted Hammond open. Petersen floated the ball deep in the end zone. It was too deep. "When I passed the ball, I thought 'I just overthrew the receiver,'" Petersen said.

He did. But crossing over the back of the end zone was 5-9 Keith Baxter, who had slipped behind safety Lantz. Looking for his third interception of the game, Lantz jumped for the ball with cornerback Gary Warren. Neither one came down with it. Keith Baxter did.

"We jumped and collided," said Warren. "I landed on the ground, heard the crowd roar, looked up and saw him [Baxter] on the ground with the ball. My heart just dropped. I couldn't believe what had happened."

"It was pretty much a 'Hail Mary' pass," said Lantz. "The guy just out-jumped us. When I saw him come down with it, my heart sank."

On Petersen's prayer of a pass, Marshall won 34-31.

Schnellenberger offered his opinion on the catch. "It was a desperation interception ball that the guy went up and made a great play on," said the Louisville coach.

Chaump was honest about it. "We got lucky," he said. "I've had them go the other way so many times and I guess it was our turn."

THE AFTERMATH

Petersen's pass is considered the moment that Marshall football turned around. The Thundering Herd went on to win five of their last six games and gain a spot in the NCAA Division I-AA playoffs, where they advanced all the way to the championship game before losing to Northeast Louisiana 43-42. The recruiting class that followed the '87 season won the 1992 national championship, beating Youngstown State 31-28. It was the second of three straight national title matches between the two schools from 1991 to 1993.

Youngstown State, under coach Jim Tressel, won the titles in '91 and '93, then repeated as champion in '94, and won a fourth title in '97. Marshall appeared in five championship games from '91 to '96, winning a second I-AA title in '96, with a 49-29 win over Montana. The Thundering Herd moved up to the Mid-American Conference in Division I-A in 1997.

Louisville finished the season 3-7-1, losing six of their last seven games. Quarterback Jay Gruden went on to have quite a career in the Arena Football League, winning four championships as a player, then coaching the Orlando Predators to the 1998 Arena Bowl title.

Marshall	7	21	0	6	-34
Louisville	0	10	14	7	-31

MU	Darby 1 run (Mitchell kick)
UL	Knighton 3 run (Bell kick)
MU	Darby 5 run (Mitchell kick)
MU	Barber 14 pass from Petersen (Mitchell kick)
UL	Bell 27 FG
MU	Harris 4 pass from Petersen (Mitchell kick)
UL	Knighton 35 run (Hamilton pass from Gruden)
UL	Cummings 10 pass from Gruden (kick failed)
UL	Hamilton 20 pass from Gruden (Bell kick)
MU	Baxter 31 pass from Petersen (no attempt)

Attendance 21, 658

Texas vs. Arkansas

"Plays like that sure do make you believe. I'll be at church at 8 A.M. tomorrow morning...sharp."—John Hagy, Texas free safety

THE BACKGROUND

For pure hype and hoopla, there is no greater game in the long-standing feud between Arkansas and Texas, than the 1969 epic battle when the No.1 Longhorns met the No.2 Razorbacks.

Texas had an 18-game winning streak. Arkansas had won 15 in a row. ABC television moved the game from October to December 6th for the undivided attention of a national audience. It was a made-for-TV event. Billy Graham gave the invocation. President Richard Nixon attended and praised both teams in an extended Super Bowl-esque televised post-game show.

There was the 1969 version of "The Pass," etched into the collective memory of the entire Southwest. Facing fourth-and-three from their own 43, and trailing the underdog Razorbacks 14-8 with under six minutes to play, Texas coach Darrell Royal shocked everyone by calling "Right 53 veer pass." A pass from the wishbone-happy Longhorns?

Quarterback James Street faded back and tossed deep for tight end Randy Peschel, the lone receiver on the route. Peschel hauled in the exhilarating 44-yard completion to the Arkansas 13 setting up Jim Bertelsen's two-yard TD run moments later. After Happy Feller's extra point, Texas led 15-14 with 3:58 left. Later, when Longhorn Tom Campbell intercepted a Bill Montgomery pass at the UT 39, Texas ran out the clock and won "The Big Shootout."

That was a great game...not necessarily a great finish.

In 1987, both schools longed for those glory days when they ruled the rankings. Arkansas (4-1) was ranked 15th, Texas was struggling at 2-3. Still, this was Texas-Arkansas, a legendary series that began in 1894, and was played annually from 1932 to 1991 until it was stopped in 1992 when Arkansas joined the Southeastern Conference.

Texas held a commanding 51-17 lead in the rivalry, always seeming to find a way to beat the Hogs. Although the Razorbacks won 21-14 the previous year, it had been over 20 years since Arkansas took two straight games from Texas. Current coach Ken Hatfield needn't be reminded. He was a senior on that Arkansas team that won in 1964, then again in '65 and '66.

When Arkansas wide receiver Derek Russell dropped a wide open 53-yard, would-be touchdown pass on the first play from scrimmage, the Razorback fans in Little Rock's War Memorial Stadium must have been thinking, "Here we go again."

Senior quarterback Greg Thomas attempted just three passes in the first quarter before his fourth was intercepted by Texas safety John Hagy who returned it to the Arkansas three-yard line. After a five-yard penalty, Eric Metcalf's eight-yard scamper on the last play of the first quarter gave the Longhorns a 7-0 lead.

Arkansas would not attempt another pass the entire game. Hatfield's Hogs ran, and ran, and ran—62 times to be exact. They rolled up 222 yards on the ground in the first half alone, scoring twice in the second quarter.

The second TD was a costly one.

Thomas ran around left end, scoring from seven yards out for a 14-7 lead. But as he crossed the goal line, he was jolted by cornerback Tony Griffin. Thomas injured his shoulder and left the game.

Freshman Quinn Grovey, himself nursing a groin injury which kept him out of all but one practice during the week, was enlisted to take over the quarterbacking duties. The Arkansas triple-option attack slowed to a halt in the second half, gaining just 66 yards in the final two quarters.

Meanwhile, Texas quarterback Brett Stafford, who threw five interceptions in a 44-9 loss to top-ranked Oklahoma the previous week, got the Horns a bit closer in the third quarter. He completed two big third-down passes, one to Metcalf, the other to fullback Darron Norris, to set up a Wayne Clements 38-yard field goal.

Arkansas still led 14-10 and held that margin in the fourth quarter when Texas drove to the UA 15-yard line with 6:05 to play in the game. On fourth-and-three, first-year coach David McWilliams chose not to kick a field goal, but went for the first down instead. "Arkansas does such a great job of holding on to the football that I was afraid we might not see it again," he explained.

His worst fears were partially realized. The Horns came up empty. Lineman Tony Cherico pressured Stafford into a bad pass intended for Jorrick Battle at the 11, nearly intercepted by linebacker Erik Whitted. Nevertheless, the incompletion gave the Hogs the ball with 5:58 on the clock and a four-point lead. Texas' hopes had dimmed.

Hatfield tried to jumpstart his offense just enough to run out the clock by reinserting the hampered Thomas. The Texas defense crowded the line, daring Arkansas to throw. "I wanted to call a pass, but Greg couldn't raise his shoulder to throw," said Hatfield. Thomas led his team to one first down on the ground. But then he was hurt again. Grovey came back in. The Hogs could get the ball no further than the UA 27, and were forced to punt.

With 1:48 left, Texas took the ball on their own 44. On first down, Stafford found Norris out of the backfield. He was hit by outside linebacker Kerry Owens at midfield. The ball squirted loose and safety Steve Atwater dove for the ball. Then Texas center Alan Champagne jumped in. A pile up ensued. "I had it," claimed Atwater. "Even when he came in, once he got in the pile, we both had it half way. But I had it first."

Apparently Champagne had it last.

In a pivotal call, the officials gave the ball to Texas. Stafford completed three short passes to his runningbacks to move the ball to the Arkansas 32 with 29 seconds to play. Then he threw three straight incompletions. With 14 seconds left, it was fourth-and-10. The Longhorns were down to their first final play of the game.

Stafford dropped back and again looked for his runningback. Somehow, Metcalf escaped wide open down the left sideline. He caught Stafford's toss for a first down at the 13-yard line, his 11th reception of the day.

Just seven seconds remained. Stafford took the snap and killed the clock with a quick incompletion. Four seconds left.

McWilliams took his final timeout. He had another final play to call.

THE PLAY

After the timeout, Stafford, with one TD pass and 10 interceptions to his name in the first five games of the season, stood over center. Something was wrong. "We were in the wrong formation," he said.

Then a flag, an official's whistle, and a twist of fate. Someone jumped offsides. Texas was called for illegal procedure.

The "fortunate" five-yard penalty moved the ball to the 18-yard line. It also gave the Longhorns a chance to regroup. McWilliams then called a play that had never been run before. It wasn't even in the UT playbook.

"We felt like they would be looking for Eric [Metcalf], so we went looking for the seam," said McWilliams, who, like Hatfield, was a player in the Horns-Hogs series, as a co-captain for the 1963 Longhorns.

Sophomore wide receiver Tony Jones lined up wide left. Metcalf became a decoy.

Stafford took the snap and looked at only one receiver, Jones, who ran a post pattern right over the middle of the end zone. "Brett just told me it was coming to me," said Jones.

Stafford threw it right over linebacker Whitted. Atwater closed on Jones from his safety position. Cornerback Anthony Cooney zeroed in from the other side. Jones caught it....then was blasted from both sides.

"Steve and I hit him at the same time hoping we could jar it loose," said Cooney.

Jones, only five feet-seven inches tall, was viciously spun around 360 degrees in the air like a helicopter propeller. He crash landed on the turf.

"I saw Tony catch the pass, but he took a tremendous hit," said McWilliams. " I held my breath until I saw the official signal that it was a catch. Then I went crazy just like everyone else on our sideline."

His bones jarred, Jones somehow held onto his helmet, his consciousness, and the ball. No time was left on the clock. For the 52nd time in 69 games, Texas figured out a way to beat Arkansas. This time it was a back-breaking 16-14 victory.

Hatfield watched the play in disbelief, threw off his hat, then sank to the ground. "We tried to force them to throw underneath, and didn't want to get beat deep," he said. "They just executed extremely well."

"It was the last play of the game and we had to execute," said Atwater. "Unfortunately, they executed a little better."

"It was just one hell of a catch," added Cooney.

THE AFTERMATH

Stafford's pass to Jones was the first time in the storied history of Texas football that the Longhorns won on the game's final play. Eight years later, it happened again in 1995 when Phil Dawson kicked a 50-yard field goal as time expired to defeat Virginia 17-16 in Austin.

The Longhorns finished the '87 season 7-5 after beating Pittsburgh 32-27 in the Blue-bonnet Bowl. Arkansas ended the year 9-4, los-ing to Georgia 20-17 in the Liberty Bowl. The two teams split the remaining four games of the series that ended in 1991 when Arkansas won 14-13.

From 1984-1989, Hatfield compiled the best winning percentage in Arkansas history. Before leaving the program to coach at Clemson in 1990, he took the Razorbacks to six consecutive bowls, winning two SWC championships.

In 1998, the two schools announced that the series would resume in 2003. " It will be as big a game as ever," Arkansas athletic director and former coach Frank Broyles said. "You can't get 70 years out of your system in a few years."

Texas	7	0	3	6	-16
Arkansas	0	14	0	0	-14

UT   Metcalf 8 run (Clements kick)
ARK   Foster 11 run (Trainor kick)
ARK   Thomas 7 run (Trainor kick)
UT   Clements 38 FG
UT   Jones 18 pass from Stafford
          (no attempt)

Attendance 54, 092

Iowa vs. Ohio State

"I think I made it by an inch."—Marv Cook, Iowa tight end

THE BACKGROUND

The Ohio State football season was going downhill fast. Two straight losses, one to Michigan State 13-7, followed by a 26-24 upset at the hands of Big Ten cellar-dweller Wisconsin, and the 5-3-1 Buckeyes were struggling to stay in contention for a bowl bid. The week before their final home game of the year versus 7-3 Iowa, coach Earle Bruce met with athletic director Rick Bay and university president Edward Jennings to discuss his future in Columbus.

"He's my coach," said Bay. "I'm solidly behind him." In nine years as coach, Bruce had compiled the best record in the Big Ten (80-25-1) since 1979. That was the same year that Hayden Fry took over as head coach in Iowa City. Under Fry's direction, Iowa had gone to six straight bowl games and two Rose Bowls since 1981.

In 1987, the Hawkeyes were riding a three-game winning streak, with the arm of Chuck Hartlieb leading the way. Hartlieb, the third-string quarterback at the beginning of the year, who took over the starting job six games into the season, set a Big Ten record the week before the OSU game by throwing seven touchdown passes in a 52-24 rout of Northwestern. But despite the Hawkeyes' recent successes, Iowa had only beaten OSU once in Fry's tenure and hadn't won in Ohio Stadium since 1959.

The Buckeyes jumped ahead early 14-3 on the strength of two Tom Tupa to Everett Ross touchdown passes, the last one covering 60 yards. But Kevin Harmon's 50-yard TD sprint with 9:10 left in the second quarter, combined with Rob Houghtlin's second and third field goals (the last one from 22 yards as time expired in the first half), gave Iowa a 15-14 lead entering the third quarter.

A third Tupa TD pass, this one a 20-yarder to tight end Jeff Ellis, put the Buckeyes up 21-15 after three periods. But then Iowa's Marshal Cotton blocked a Tupa punt that was recovered by Mike Burke at the OSU 37. With 9:11 to play in the game, fullback David Hudson dove in from the one-yard line and Iowa regained the lead 22-21. Again, the Buckeyes answered back, as freshman runningback Carlos Snow scored on a 14-yard run to put Ohio State back on top 27-22 with 2:45 to play.

Ohio State's defense needed one more stop. Led by senior linebacker Chris Spielman (who would win the Lombardi Award at the end of the season), the Buckeyes had not surrendered a passing touchdown in 13 quarters. They completely eliminated Iowa's star receiver, Quinn Early, from the game. Early, who had caught four touchdowns for 256 yards versus Northwestern the previous week, was shutout by the Ohio State defense. That left tight ends Marv Cook and Mike Flagg as Hartlieb's main targets.

Harmon took the ensuing kickoff back to the Iowa 36. On second-and-five, Hartlieb hit Flagg for 14 yards. On the play, Ohio State was flagged 15 yards for 12 men on the field placing the ball at the OSU 30. But from there, the Hawkeye drive hit the skids. After a holding penalty, Hartlieb was sacked by Ray Holliman, the ball squirted loose, but was recovered by

November 14, 1987—Columbus, Ohio

fullback Hudson. Still, the 11-yard loss set up a second-and-31 play back at the Iowa 49.

On a critical play, Hartlieb found Cook for 27 yards moving the ball to the OSU 24 with 1:24 remaining. On third-and-four, Harmon (who had 151 rushing yards on the day) was stuffed. Fourth-and-three.

Hartlieb went to Cook again, this time in the left flat for eight yards. The drive was alive at the OSU 15.

But back came Bruce's Buckeyes. Defensive end Eric Kumerow jolted Hartlieb from the blindside eight yards behind the line of scrimmage, cutting Hartlieb's chin, and forcing Fry to use his last time out with 47 seconds left. Then Harmon lost more yardage, slipping on a sweep right. Now facing third-and-23 at the OSU 28, Hartlieb threw too low for wideout Travis Watkins.

The Iowa rally seemed doomed—16 seconds left, no timeouts, and fourth-and 23. The Hawkeyes were down to their last play.

THE PLAY
CD 1—Track 25—*Jim Zabel,* WHO Radio

With the play clock running, Fry had to make a quick decision. "Mike Flagg had gone on the field," he said. "But something told me to call him back. I did and sent Cook in."

Cook, a smaller, quicker tight end than Flagg, ran into the huddle. "It was total chaos," he said.

The Buckeyes, blitzing on the last four plays, changed their strategy. "We were playing three deep so they wouldn't get the big one," said Bruce. Hartlieb noticed. "I was shocked they weren't coming," noted the Iowa quarterback.

With Early stymied at the line of scrimmage, Hartlieb had time, looked and threw to Cook at the nine-yard line. The 6-4, 232 lb. junior caught the pass near the sideline, turned inside, and bulled toward the goal line. At the two, he was hit by Buckeyes Sean Bell and Ray Jackson. One hit him high, the other wrapped him low. Cook barreled forward. His knee fell to the ground with six seconds left... just as

he crossed the goal line. "I was an inch over. It wasn't by much," said Cook.

Hartlieb couldn't tell as he rushed down field . "I wasn't sure he was in the end zone," he said. "So I hustled back down there in the event we needed another play."

There wasn't need for one. The Hawkeyes had won 29-27.

"You have to give credit where credit is due," said Bruce. "He [Hartlieb] passed the ball one more time than I would have liked to have seen."

"We knew what they were going to do," said Buckeye cornerback William White. "The tight end ran that play six or seven times. They just made the play and we didn't."

It was mayhem for Jim Zabel in the Iowa radio booth. "Ed Podolak [Zabel's broadcast partner] was hugging and kissing me," he said. Meanwhile Zabel was screaming over the air, "It's an Iowa touchdown, it's an Iowa touchdown!" His voice skied into a new range.

Des Moines songwriter Roger Maxwell was driving home listening to the dramatic ending played over and over on the radio. He couldn't believe how high Zabel's voice got.

"It was a high A-flat. That's where soprano's sing!" Maxwell said. Inspired by Zabel's call, Maxwell wrote a hilarious classical music accompaniment to the play called "It's an Iowa Touchdown," with Zabel's actual words sung by a female vocalist. Hayden Fry heard the tune and asked Maxwell to put the song over the video replay of the catch. It became quite a popular clip across the state of Iowa.

THE AFTERMATH

"Whew boy! I think I'll just go ahead and retire right now," said a jubilant Hayden Fry after the game. "I've been associated with some great games in 36 years of coaching, but I've never had one that was more meaningful to a group of players and assistant coaches."

The Hawkeyes finished the season 10-3, with a 34-20 win over Minnesota in their annual battle for Floyd of Rosedale, and a 20-19 come-from-behind victory against Wyoming to capture their second consecutive Holiday Bowl title.

Game 45

Fry waited 11 more seasons before really retiring, after the 1998 season. After Fry's 20-year tenure ended, Zabel reflected back on Hartlieb's pass that beat Ohio State. "It's the single most important play in the Hayden Fry years at Iowa," Zabel noted, after calling almost five decades of Hawkeye games. "The most exciting game finish that I've ever seen. Of all the games I've done, nothing has been as dramatic as that single play."

For Earle Bruce, Cook's last second catch triggered a series of unsavory events in Columbus. The highly successful coach was fired the following Monday with the second highest winning percentage (.755) in school history, next to Woody Hayes (.761).

Big Ten coaches were livid about Bruce's dismissal. Michigan's Bo Schembechler called it "a sad day for college football." Fry himself, was very vocal in his disgust about the situation. "Woody Hayes," he said, " is probably rolling over in his grave." Separating himself from the Ohio State administration, OSU athletic director Rick Bay resigned in protest over the firing. Even members of the Ohio State marching band backed Bruce, gathering at his home to play the "Buckeye Battle Cry." Tears streamed down Bruce's face.

In his last game the next week, Bruce was carried off the field by his players after a 23-20 upset victory over Michigan. The Buckeyes finished the season 6-4-1.

Following the victory, Bruce filed a $7.44 million dollar lawsuit against Ohio State University and its president Edward Jennings, claiming his constitutional rights were violated by the firing and that Jennings libeled and slandered him by circulating rumors about his personal character.

A week later the suit was dropped by Bruce in return for the $471,000 he would have earned during the rest of his contract.

Iowa	3	12	0	14	-29
Ohio State	7	7	7	6	-27

OSU	Ross 24 pass from Tupa (Frantz kick)
UI	FG Houghtlin 39
OSU	Ross 60 pass from Tupa (Frantz kick)
UI	Harmon 50 run (pass failed)
UI	FG Houghtlin 41
UI	FG Houghtlin 22
OSU	Ellis 20 pass from Tupa (Frantz kick)
UI	Hudson 1 run (Houghtlin kick)
OSU	Snow 14 run (run failed)
UI	Cook 28 pass from Hartlieb (Houghtlin kick)

Attendance 90,090

151

Florida State vs. Clemson

"Y'all wanna sell the farm?"—Bobby Bowden, to his assistant coaches

THE BACKGROUND

This game was big. So big that both Clemson and Florida State surprisingly unveiled stylish new pants during warmups. The Tigers brought out their special orange pants which were 14-1 in the 15 important games that they had previously been worn. Not to be outdone, coach Bobby Bowden dressed his FSU Seminoles in spiffy new white pants supplied by actor and FSU alumnus Burt Reynolds. It was the first time since Reynolds played in the 1950s that FSU had worn white pants.

As it turned out, both teams were overdressed. The steady rain that had fallen the night before, continued in the first half at Death Valley, making for a sloppy, wet field. Florida State, pre-season No. 1, but now ranked 10th after a 31-0 loss to Miami, was 1-1, desperate for a win, with the entire season on the line in just their third game. Clemson, coached by Danny Ford in his 10th full season at the helm, was 2-0 and sitting at No. 3 in the country after two early home wins over Virginia Tech and soon-to-be Division I-AA national champion Furman.

Clemson controlled the first half on the ground, taking a 14-7 lead on quarterback Rodney Williams' seven-yard keeper with 2:45 to go in the second quarter. That touchdown run capped a lengthy 99-yard drive, giving the Tigers an enormous 232 to 71 yard advantage in total yards after two quarters.

The FSU offense was struggling, so the Seminoles looked for help elsewhere in the second half. They got it in the name of Deion Sanders. With the Clemson bench taunting the flamboyant Sanders, and Sanders playing along with the chants of "Prime Time, Prime Time" (his proud nickname), the defensive back took an early third quarter punt from Chris Gardocki and headed upfield. Straight upfield. "It was a big hole, and I figured, you know, I could hit the seam," said Sanders. He flew by the Tiger coverage, then juked a helpless Gardocki. Seventy-six yards later in the end zone, Prime Time had tied the game at 14-14 and was yelling to the crowd, "How you like me now?"

The punt return ignited the Seminoles offense. Well, at least the passing attack. FSU was without a first down rushing in the game to this point. After getting the ball back on downs, quarterback Chip Ferguson led FSU from their 23. He hit Victor Floyd for 34 yards, then Terry Anthony for 10 more. After a holding penalty temporarily slowed the drive, Ferguson found 6-4 Bruce LaShane high over the middle and just beyond the hands of All-American cornerback Donnell Woolford for a 36-yard completion to the Clemson one-yard line. Fullback Dayne Williams carried it over from there and FSU's second TD in three minutes gave them a 21-14 lead.

A short Florida State field-goal attempt at the end of the quarter would have solidified the lead. But Clemson's James Lott kept the margin at seven and quelled the FSU attack by blocking Richie Andrews' kick. The FSU kicker had yet to make a field goal in his brief career. With 7:28 to play in the game, Clemson began

Game 46

to drive from their own 34. Five minutes later, with 2:32 remaining, Clemson fullback Tracy Johnson took an off-tackle play outside and scored from 19 yards out to tie the game at 21-21. Death Valley became deafening.

With the boisterous crowd imploring the Tiger defense, Florida State began to crumble. A clipping penalty on the kickoff put FSU in a hole at their own 15. Dexter Carter got six yards on first down, but then LaSane dropped a pass and on third down Ferguson's pass was nearly intercepted by two Clemson defenders who collided going for the ball. With 1:33 to play, on their own 21, FSU dropped back to punt on fourth-and-four.

THE PLAY

The dangerous Woolford dropped back to receive Tim Corlew's punt. With the game tied, and facing the prospects of his team being at best 1-1-1 on the season, or worse 1-2 with a last-second Clemson field goal, Bowden made a radical decision. "We were going to sell the farm," he said.

As the Seminoles lined up to punt, junior safety LeRoy Butler ran onto the field late and lined up as a blocking back alongside Alphonso Williams, just behind the center. The third back, Dayne Williams, stood two steps behind Butler, while Corlew awaited the ball. As the snap came, Corlew jumped high to his right in frightened desperation, searching for a ball soaring over his head. The CBS cameras searched for the ball too.

It was in the hands of Dayne Williams who had taken the short snap. He took a step up and sneakily stuffed the ball like a loaf of bread between Butler's legs. Butler hunched over motionless in a blocking position. Williams then acted like he had the ball and ran right. The rest of the Florida State offense rolled right as if to try and block for him. Corlew was still searching for the lost ball. It was a three-act play and Clemson fell for it. The Tiger defense followed to the right, chasing Williams. Even Woolford moved up field to make a play.

Still frozen, Butler started counting to three before running with the ball , in order to allow the Clemson defense to run themselves

out of position. "I got to the one and a half, and then I said,'You gotta go man,'" said Butler.

Off ran Butler down the left sideline, unnoticed by fans, TV cameras, and most importantly, half the Clemson defense. By the time the Tigers reacted, the only person who had a chance to stop him from running 79 yards for the touchdown was Woolford. He finally dragged Butler down at the Clemson one-yard line. "I was shocked. I've never seen anything like that," said Woolford.

"The man [Bowden] has no conscience," said Clemson strong safety Gene Beasley. "I couldn't have called that play." Butler himself was stunned and nervous when the play was called. "Nervous ain't the word," he said. "I didn't have butterflies. I had lizards."

The score was still tied, but the now famous "puntrooski" set Florida State up for the knockout blow. Dayne Williams ran over from the one on the next play, but it was nullified due to a delay of game penalty. Bowden took no more chances and sent Andrews on to kick the winning field goal (his first made attempt of his FSU career) with 32 seconds left . Clemson's last desperation plays were unsuccessful and Florida State slithered out of Death Valley, 24-21 winners.

"Basically, we got out-tricked," said Clemson receiver Ricardo Hooper.

THE AFTERMATH

"I wish now I could go back and call timeout and alert our people for the fake," said Clemson's coach Ford after the game. The Tigers, in fact were quite aware of Bowden's propensity to call trick plays, especially fake kicks. "We knew they had a fake and we talked about it," said Ford."We wanted to save our timeouts for our drive for a winning field goal."

Actually, the fake punt was a borrowed recipe. FSU's first-year graduate assistant Clint Ledbetter had informed Bowden of the play's success when it was used while he was a defensive tackle at Arkansas State. After receiving film of the play, Bowden put it into the FSU repertoire.

The high-stakes coach knew the consequences if the gutsy call failed. "I would have been the goat of the whole stinking world," he said. Instead, it propelled the Seminoles to 10 straight wins, finishing the season 11-1 with a 13-7 victory over Auburn in the Sugar Bowl, and a No. 3 national ranking behind Notre Dame and Miami.

Clemson recovered well from the surprising loss. The Tigers finished 10-2 on the season, No.9 in the AP poll, with their only other defeat being a 10-3 setback at 24th-ranked N.C. State. Clemson won the ACC Championship for the third straight year with a 6-1 league record, then went on to beat Oklahoma 13-6 in the Florida Citrus Bowl.

Florida State	0	7	14	3	-24
Clemson	7	7	0	7	-21

CL   Cooper 61 pass from C. Davis (Seyle kick)
FSU   D. Carter 40 pass from Ferguson (Andrews kick)
CL   R. Williams 7 run (Seyle kick)
FSU   D. Sanders 76 punt return (Andrews kick)
FSU   D. Williams 1 run (Andrews kick)
CL   Johnson 19 run (Seyle kick)
FSU   Andrews 19 FG

Attendance 84,576

Princeton vs. Holy Cross

"That was about as low, about as sick a feeling as I can ever remember. You're in shock and disbelief."
—*Princeton head coach Steve Tosches*

THE BACKGROUND

In 1869, the Princeton Tigers played the first intercollegiate football game versus Rutgers in New Brunswick, New Jersey. One-hundred-nineteen years later, Princeton fans may have witnessed the most memorable finish in school history. Tiger coach Steve Tosches certainly won't forget about it anytime soon.

The College of Holy Cross Crusaders had never scored a point in four previous meetings with Princeton. In the four games played between 1910 and 1916, the Crusaders were outscored 112-0. Times had changed at Holy Cross, however, and head coach Mark Duffner led the Crusaders to a sparkling 21-1 record in his first two seasons beginning in 1986. They ended the 1987 season 11-0, ranked No. 1 in Division I-AA, and Duffner won the Eddie Robinson Award as I-AA Coach of the Year.

Princeton's second-year coach Steve Tosches brought his team into their home opener of the '88 season at Palmer Stadium, well aware of the Tigers' underdog status. "We had a chance to pull a tremendous upset," he recalled.

Led by a defense which forced three interceptions of Holy Cross quarterback Jeff Wiley, the Tigers took a 20-17 lead with 3:27 left in the third quarter on a 15-yard pass from Jason Garrett to Dave Wix. The score was set up when linebacker Franco Pagnelli forced a fumble by Crusaders runningback Joe Segretti at the Holy Cross 41-yard line.

Sophomore kicker Chris Lutz booted his third field goal of the day from 34 yards out with 12:11 left in the fourth quarter and Princeton led 23-17.

With six minutes remaining, Holy Cross regained possession on their own 17. A few plays later, faced with fourth down and 18 at the HC 39, Wiley's last-ditch desperation pass to flanker Viv Washington fell incomplete. But a pass interference call on junior safety Brian Wietharn moved the ball all the way to the Princeton 28. From there, the Holy Cross running game, led by Joe Segretti, Tim Donovan, and Daren Cromwell took over. The three combined for 199 yards rushing on the day and Segretti's five-yard jaunt with just 73 seconds left gave the favored Crusaders a 24-23 lead.

But back clawed Tosches' Tigers.

Princeton's Garrett (23-34 for 223 yards) engineered a frantic 52-yard drive that ended up at the Holy Cross 18-yard line. He then called time-out with seven seconds left, making way for Lutz, who calmly kicked his fourth field goal of the game, leaving just two seconds on the clock.

The home crowd celebrated the apparent 26-24 Princeton victory.

"This was a tremendous upset on our part, that we were about to pull off. God, we played such great football," recalled Tosches. "For 59 minutes and 58 seconds we played as well as any Princeton team I've ever seen. We lined up and kicked off with two seconds to go and then that's when all the entertainment took place."

The Princeton sidelines, in a state of shock, after the Tigers' kick off to Holy Cross with just two seconds to play. Photo courtesy of Paul Huegel

THE PLAY

CD 1—Track 26—*Bob Fouracre,*
WWTM Radio

On the kickoff to end the game, Lutz only had to dribble the ball to one of Holy Cross' front-line players, making sure to avoid return man Tim Donovan, whose 50-yard kickoff return toward the end of the first half set up an earlier Crusader touchdown.

"We squibbed it, probably kicked it a little harder than we should have, and it went in to the second line, and they picked it up and started up field," said Tosches.

The ball ended up in the hands of Darren Cromwell at the Holy Cross 25. Cromwell ran up field, slanting left toward the Holy Cross sideline. As he crossed the Holy Cross 42, he was met head on by Princeton's Wietharn who wrapped both hands around Cromwell's shoulder pads and spun him around. Instantaneously, Vince Avallone, the closest Princeton defender to the sideline, moved in to finish the tackle. As Cromwell's body was being slung around, he flipped the ball out of his right hand

and lateraled to the dangerous Donovan who was three feet directly to his left, along the Holy Cross sideline. Donovan took the ball and sprinted past Avallone, who turned and chased him downfield to the Princeton 25 before lunging in despair. The rest of the over-pursuing Princeton defense couldn't catch Donovan who ended up running 55 yards untouched into the end zone for the unthinkable touchdown and the 30-26 Holy Cross win.

Tosches was shocked.

"You know you squib it and you basically think you're going to create one of those rugby type of situations where bodies just all pile into each other and eventually the play's over, and all of sudden you see the ball and the runner going all the way," he said.

Donovan believed in his partner Cromwell. "We talked about being ready to pitch it to each other before the kickoff," he said. "So when Darren started to go down I yelled, 'Darren, pitch it! Pitch it! Once I got it, I said to myself, 'this guy can't catch me.'"

Duffner called it a planned play, but recognized his team's fortunes. "I wouldn't say the chances of that kick return working are real good. We could probably run it another hundred times and it wouldn't work," he remarked after the game. "That winning touchdown was the most exciting play I ever saw in college football."

Longtime Crusader announcer Bob Fouracre recalled the scene on the field. "Holy Cross had 90 kids on the sideline and they all ran into the end zone into a heap a mile high."

One after the other, Crusader players and coaches launched themselves onto a pile of celebration in the end zone.

The Princeton players slumped to the ground. On the radio, a shocked Fouracre yelled, "The Tigers are stunned! The Tigers are stunned!"

As time passed and he reviewed the play on film, those words rang true to Tosches. "You had to watch it about 25 times to try and convince yourself it was real, " he said.

THE AFTERMATH

Holy Cross took the momentum from the Princeton game and reeled off eight consecutive victories to end the season with a 9-2 record. Between 1986 and 1991, Duffner orchestrated five Colonial Conference championships (now known as the Patriot League) in six years at Holy Cross, amassing a 60-5-1 record before moving on to become head coach at the University of Maryland.

Princeton finished the season 6-4. As the years passed, Tosches, who coached the Tigers for 13 years, was able to laugh about the game as he remembered a humorous anecdote.

"That was my second year [at Princeton]. The one thing I did was to go in on Monday [after the game] and see the Associate Athletic Director who was in charge of schedules, and I said that I would play anybody in the country with the exception of any more Catholic schools. [laugh] There's a tremendous advantage right there and it all came out in that two seconds!"

Holy Cross	0	14	3	13	-30
Princeton	10	3	7	6	-26

PRI FG Lutz 28
PRI DiFelice 3 run (Lutz kick)
HC   Segretti 9 run (Keegan kick)
PRI FG Lutz 37
HC   Gallagher 3 pass from Wiley (Keegan kick)
HC   FG Keegan 33
PRI Wix 15 pass from Garrett (Lutz kick)
PRI FG Lutz 34
HC   Segretti 5 run (Keegan kick)
PRI FG Lutz 35
HC   Donovan 55 run with lateral on kickoff return (no attempt)

Attendance 10,220

September 25, 1988—Princeton, New Jersey

Miami vs. Notre Dame

"This has been a war in South Bend."—broadcaster Brent Musburger

THE BACKGROUND

November 30, 1985. The day Notre Dame fans would never forget. Miami 58, Notre Dame 7. It was the fourth worst loss in Notre Dame history, and the worst defeat in 41 years.

Trying to impress the pollsters, coach Jimmy Johnson's squad thoroughly humiliated the Irish in Gerry Faust's last game as Notre Dame coach. Up 51-7 with less than five minutes to play in the game, the Hurricanes blocked a punt and ran it back for a touchdown. They ran a reverse with 1:15 left.

The following Wednesday, departing senior tailback and career rushing leader Allen Pinkett addressed the underclassmen at Notre Dame's football banquet. "Always remember what happened in Miami," he said. "And remember the beauty of sports is you always have a second chance. And when you get that chance, do it for me. Please."

Two years later in 1987, under second-year coach Lou Holtz, the Irish traveled again to Miami. Again, the Hurricanes blew away Notre Dame 24-0, on their way to the national championship. The wounds grew deeper for Irish fans.

In 1988, Miami, the defending national champs, still ranked No.1, ventured into Notre Dame Stadium for the first time since the '85 fiasco. It was a picture perfect, sunny autumn day.

The Hurricanes (4-0) hadn't lost a regular season game in over three years, covering 36 games. They owned a 16-game winning streak, and a string of 20 straight road games without

a loss. They were the undisputed team of the '80s. Meanwhile, Holtz had taken Notre Dame from the smoldering ashes of the '85 game to No.4 in the nation in his third year as coach. The Irish were 5-0.

T-shirts on the Notre Dame student body read "Catholics vs. Convicts." The resentment and bitterness, built up for three years, was bubbling at the top of the kettle. It overflowed before the game even started.

As Miami left the field, on their way to the locker room after pre-game warm-ups, the Hurricanes crossed paths with the Notre Dame players in the north end zone. Words and fists were exchanged. A melee broke out in front of the tunnel to Notre Dame Stadium. Like every fight, there were two sides to the story. "They attacked us," said Johnson. "They taunted our players and hit our players," countered Holtz.

The game began. Miami quarterback Steve Walsh blistered the Irish defense all day long, throwing for 424 yards, a record for a Notre Dame opponent. But in the same breath, hounded by a swarming, swatting Notre Dame defense, the Hurricanes turned the ball over seven times.

A wild first half ended 21-21 after Walsh threw two quick TD passes in the final 2:16 of the half to erase a 21-7 Irish lead.

Despite Miami gaining the momentum at the half, Holtz jogged his team's memory in the locker room. "Wouldn't you like to have been here this time last year, tied at halftime?" The Hurricanes had buried the Irish by a combined score of 133-20 over the last four meetings.

Game 48

The Irish fought back in the third quarter gaining a 31-21 edge. They then scrambled to hold off a ferocious Miami onslaught in the fourth quarter. Four times, the Hurricanes drove inside the Irish 25 in the final 15 minutes. The first time, they made it to the six-yard line before Carlos Huerta booted a 23-yard field goal with 13:07 left to make it 31-24.

Minutes later, the Hurricanes threatened again, facing fourth-and-seven at the ND 11 with 7:04 remaining. This time, Johnson went for the touchdown. "I thought that if we ever got in the lead, we would have the game won," the Miami coach remarked.

Walsh found fullback Cleveland Gary inside the five. Gary caught the ball behind him, turned clockwise to the right, and dove for the goal line. In a desperation attempt, strong safety George Streeter dove for Gary, sticking his right hand on the ball as Gary lunged it forward. The ball popped loose. Irish linebacker Mike Stonebreaker fell on it at the one.

Was Gary down before the ball came loose? Johnson stormed the sidelines, arguing vehemently, but to no avail. "First Down, First Down, First Down," he screamed, ironically looking like a Florida State fan with his right arm mimicking the famous Tomahawk chop.

Still trailing by seven points, the Hurricanes regained possession at midfield with 3:52 left to play. For the third straight time they marched inside the Notre Dame 25. In fact, Miami punted just one time all afternoon. It was turnover or score.

On first down at the ND 24 with 3:37 left to play, Walsh was blindsided by linebacker Frank Stams who slapped the ball out of his right hand. It rolled forward and Chris Zorich pounced on it. Miami turnover number seven.

Notre Dame just needed a first down. Instead, they fumbled it back to Miami. Facing third-and-17 at the 21, quarterback Tony Rice (whose thrifty eight completions for 195 yards keyed the Irish throughout the day) was stripped of the ball at the ND 15 by blitzing defensive back Randy Shannon. Lineman Greg Mark recovered with 2:10 left.

Miami had one last chance to score at point-blank range, their fourth shot of the quarter. They gained just four yards in three plays and quickly faced fourth down at the 11. The clock read 0:51.

Walsh dropped back and threw a fade pass to the right corner of the end zone. A perfect toss to Andre Brown, who faked inside, then turned out, came back for the ball, and made a diving TD catch in front of defensive back Todd Lyght with 0:45 left. The score was Notre Dame 31, Miami 30.

For Johnson, there wasn't a thought of sending kicker Carlos Huerta on to the field. "We always play to win," he said. The Hurricanes were going for two.

THE PLAY

CD 1—Track 27—*Tony Roberts,*
Tom Pagna, Westwood One Radio

Notre Dame's defense, opportunistic if not stingy all day long, gathered on the sidelines. "Coach Holtz called us over and just said we've got to believe," said linebacker Wes Pritchett.

Expecting the pass, defensive coordinator Barry Alvarez dropped eight men deep, and rushed three. Miami sent two wideouts, Brown and Dale Dawkins, to the right.

Walsh faded back to pass. He had time, maybe too much time. "Our outside guys were supposed to come in, but their cornerbacks were jamming them," he said. Walsh looked elsewhere.

Runningback Leonard Conley broke out of the backfield to the right corner. "The halfback was open for a split second," said Walsh.

With lineman George Williams now approaching, the Miami QB lofted a high pass almost exactly where the previous touchdown was caught.

This time however, the Irish had a defender ready. As Walsh was looking off his primary targets, safety Pat Terrell had slid over to pick up Conley. Terrell had a beat on the ball, as well as position on Conley.

" I just jumped in front of him," said Terrell. "I don't think Walsh saw me coming, and I followed his eyes the whole way and knew where he was going to throw the ball."

"I floated the ball too much," said Walsh, who perhaps waited too long to release it, giving Terrell an extra second to react.

159

Terrell played it like a volleyball player blocking a spike. He batted the ball away with both hands above his head. The one-point Irish lead was preserved.

The collective inhale of 59,000 fans turned into a riotous celebration and a moment frozen in Notre Dame folklore. After Anthony Johnson recovered the ensuing onside kick for Notre Dame, the Irish fell on the ball to run out the clock and Notre Dame won 31-30.

The fragile Holtz was physically swept away in the tidal wave of students who rushed the field. Trying to conduct a post-game television interview for CBS, he had to scream at the mob around him to "Shut up!" then said, "This was a win by the Notre Dame spirit." The crowd erupted again.

"They're sick, I'm sick," said Johnson about his team. "As many mistakes as we made, and we made a ton of them, in my mind, I felt we should have won the game," he said.

"There's no doubt that we're the better team," added Gary, maintaining the trademark Hurricane brashness.

Sometimes the best teams don't always win.

THE AFTERMATH

The Miami game was the catapult to Notre Dame's drive to the national championship. The Irish remained undefeated over 10 contests, beat No.2 USC 27-10 in their last regular-season game of the year, then captured the Fiesta Bowl and national championship with a 34-21 victory over No.3 West Virginia. The Hurricanes also won the rest of their games, beat Nebraska 23-3 in the Orange Bowl, and finished No.2 in the country.

"I think the two schools really and truly need to talk about playing in the future," said Holtz, referring to the animosity that had grown to troubling proportions. "I'm talking about next year. I think we need a cooling-down period."

Holtz didn't get one. In '89, the Hurricanes got their revenge.

Notre Dame continued their winning ways the next season, building a 23-game winning streak that ended when the two schools met

again. In the rematch at Miami, the Hurricanes marched 98 yards in a remarkable 22-play drive that consumed 10 minutes and 47 seconds of the third quarter, leading to a 27-10 win over the Irish. The drive was highlighted by an astounding third-and-44 conversion pass from Craig Erickson to Randall Hill from Miami's own seven-yard line.

It was Dennis Erickson's first year as coach, taking over for Johnson who left to replace Tom Landry as the new coach of the Dallas Cowboys. Miami won the '89 national championship, their third of the decade, by beating Alabama 33-25 in the Sugar Bowl, while Notre Dame finished No.2 in the polls.

Miami	0	21	0	9	-30
Notre Dame	7	14	10	0	-31

ND	Rice 7 run (Ho kick)
UM	Brown 8 pass from Walsh (Huerta kick)
ND	Banks 9 pass from Rice (Ho kick)
ND	Terrell 60 interception return (Ho kick)
UM	Conley 23 pass from Walsh (Huerta kick)
UM	Gary 15 pass from Walsh (Huerta kick)
ND	Eilers 4 run (Ho kick)
ND	Ho 27 FG
UM	Huerta 23 FG
UM	Brown 11 pass from Walsh (pass failed)

Attendance 59,075

Washington State vs. UCLA

"This is huge for me. I'm just about to explode."—Rich Swinton

THE BACKGROUND

UCLA quarterback Troy Aikman was the Heisman Trophy candidate. Washington State's junior signal caller Timm Rosenbach led the nation in passing efficiency. Aikman completed 66.5 percent of his passes for 1,708 yards and 19 touchdowns. Rosenbach connected on 70.6 percent of his passes for 1,883 yards and 18 touchdowns.

That's about where the similarities ended between UCLA and Washington State.

The Bruins were 7-0 (4-0 in the Pac-10), the top-ranked team in the country, fresh off a 24-3 thrashing of Arizona, and headed for an end of the year winner-take-all showdown with undefeated USC. Coach Dennis Erickson's Cougars were 4-3 (1-3 in the Pac-10), limping into Pasadena on the heels of two straight losses, 45-28 to Arizona and 31-28 to Arizona State. Despite having the conference's best offense, WSU also sported the league's worst defense.

The Arizona State game turned nightmarish for the Cougars. Not only did they give up 31 points to ASU, a team which hadn't scored in 10 straight quarters, but the Cougars lost running back Steve Broussard, the Pac-10's leading rusher, to an ankle sprain.

WSU hadn't won at UCLA since 1958. The 30-year drought looked to extend another year as the Bruins pounced on the WSU defense for 20 unanswered points, taking a 20-6 lead into halftime.

In the third quarter, the UCLA offense picked up right where they left off in the first half. On their first possession, Aikman drove the Bruins 71 yards in seven plays. Eric Ball ran the last eight yards for the touchdown, and the Bruins pulled away 27-6.

The Cougars could have quit.

But Rosenbach, sacked four times at the end of the second quarter, went 4-for-4 on the next drive, hitting split-back Tim Stallworth from 15 yards out to slice the lead to 27-13. Washington State was still in it.

Even more so when, two plays later, Ball was hit by defensive back Artie Holmes and coughed up the football at the UCLA 37. WSU recovered. Rosenbach scrambled twice, down to the 13-yard line. Then sophomore Rich Swinton, subbing for Broussard, took two plays to crash in from the six-yard line. The Cougars had scored 14 points in under two minutes to only trail 27-20.

They weren't through. After a UCLA punt with 1:00 left in the third quarter, Rosenbach connected with Stallworth again for 25 yards, then Stallworth broke away , turning the reception into a stunning 81-yard touchdown. Twenty-one unanswered points and the score was tied 27-27 entering the fourth quarter.

Coach Terry Donahue's No.1-rated Bruins were in trouble.

A determined Aikman (27 of 44 for 325 yards) took his team immediately from the UCLA 27 to a first-and-10 at the WSU 15. But the Bruins drive stalled at the 13 and a 30-yard field goal gave them a slim 30-27 advantage.

Still, Washington State's offense couldn't be stopped. For the fourth time in five second-

With his father Pinky at his side (far left), WSU head coach Dennis Erickson celebrates as the Cougars hold on to upset top-ranked UCLA. Photo courtesy of Washington State University Athletic Media Relations

half possessions, they hit paydirt. Rosenbach and Swinton traded carries for 80 yards over the next five minutes, and when Swinton bullied in from the one-yard line, the underdog Cougars led 34-30 with 6:21 to play.

Things turned from bad to worse for UCLA. Brian Brown fumbled the ensuing kickoff. WSU kicker Jason Hanson recovered at the UCLA 37, but then missed a 33-yard field-goal attempt a few plays later. The Bruins had new life.

With the clock down to 3:16, Aikman began a final march, hitting three short passes to the WSU 45. But then it ended. Holmes picked off an Aikman toss at the 38-yard line, the third Bruins turnover of the second half. The Cougars sidelines bubbled over with joy.

WSU had just 1:59 left to kill before they partied back in Pullman.

Erickson played it conservatively on the ground, but couldn't gain a first down and run out the clock. So WSU punted back to UCLA with just under a minute to play. After a 31-yard return, the Bruins, left for dead only moments before, now had the ball again at the WSU 39.

Forty-four seconds were left. Time enough for UCLA, trailing by four points, to make amends for their second half flubs. It looked like Aikman would only need half of it. With no timeouts, he wasted no time. On the first play he fired a laser to Charles Arbuckle for a 33-yard gain to the WSU six-yard line.

Suddenly, things looked bleak for the Cougars. "We were so nervous," Swinton said. "To have Aikman in that situation, with that amount of time, on your 6-yard line . . . sheesh! We were over there shaking."

They had good reason. With first-and-goal from the WSU 6, Aikman, the prized pick in the upcoming NFL draft, was pitted point blank against the Pac-10's basement defense, last in passing, last in total defense. This was like a skilled marksman shooting at plastic sitting ducks in the arcade.

On first-and-goal, Aikman wasted a pass to stop the clock at 0:32. Second-and-goal. With nothing to lose, the Cougars blitzed. Aikman quickly tried split end David Keating. Incomplete, broken up by the ever present Holmes. Still, third down-and-goal. Aikman had two bullets left in his chamber.

WSU blitzed again. Aikman fired to the end zone. Incomplete, broken up by Ron Lee. Suddenly, the Cougars' defense had some bite. Aikman's aim had gone south. Shockingly, the Bruins were down to their final play.

Fourth-and-goal from the six and 0:26 on the clock.

THE PLAY

The week before against Arizona State, the Cougars' offense faced an almost identical situation. They failed. Rosenbach threw an interception with a minute to play inside the ASU 10-yard line and WSU lost 31-28. Now, it was the defense's turn. Could they dodge Aikman's bullet one more time?

For a third straight play, the Cougars blitzed, trying to disrupt the UCLA quarterback. Aikman dropped back and looked for Keating in the right corner of the end zone. Defensive back Vernon Todd had the coverage. Aikman threw it high.

Both Keating and Todd went up for the final pass, but neither one came down with it. The ball fell incomplete, broken up by Todd, the third-string defensive back on the league's last-place defense. The Bruins players fell to their knees, while the Cougars jumped for the sky. Somehow, the woeful WSU defense had stopped the heralded Heisman hopeful. Washington State took over on downs. Rosenbach took a knee and the upset was complete. Washington State 34, UCLA 30.

Aikman couldn't figure it out. "More times than not, we get the ball on the [six-yard line]

and have three chances to score," he said, "more often than not, we're going to. For whatever reasons, we weren't able to get it done today."

Donahue stood by himself, trying to come to grips with what happened. "It's like the old saying, I guess, that victory has a thousand fathers, but defeat is an orphan," he said.

Even Holmes couldn't explain it, though he tried. "I think we've played good defense all year. We've just allowed too many points," he said.

Ironic, but somehow true.

THE AFTERMATH

"Maybe the No. 1 ranking stimulates the opponent," said Donahue following the loss. "but I don't think, in terms of walking around being No. 1, that it's a particularly heavy burden to carry. I'd sure like to carry it again—someday."

He never got that chance again.

The Bruins lost the battle for the Rose Bowl in '88, falling to Rodney Peete and the Trojans 31-22 in the season finale. UCLA finished 10-2, ranked No.6, after defeating Arkansas 17-3 in the Cotton Bowl. Donahue stepped down in 1995 after 20 years as UCLA head coach, compiling a record of 151-73-8 since taking over for Dick Vermeil in 1976.

Aikman finished third in the Heisman Trophy balloting behind Rodney Peete and Heisman winner Barry Sanders. He was the top pick in the '89 NFL Draft , and signed with the Dallas Cowboys for $11.2 million over six years (a record rookie contract at the time).

The monumental victory for WSU triggered a five-game winning streak, and No.16 ranking in the final AP poll. After a 32-31 triumph over state rival Washington, the Cougars knocked off Houston 24-22 in the Aloha Bowl to end the year 9-3.

Rosenbach skipped his senior season in Pullman and entered the supplemental NFL draft in July '89 where he was selected in the first round by the Phoenix Cardinals and signed a five-year $5.3 million contract. After the '92 season, disillusioned with the NFL despite some success as the Cardinals' QB, Rosenbach quit football, left behind $1.05 million for the final year of his contract, and returned to WSU to finish his college degree.

Dennis Erickson left WSU after the '88 season to become the head coach at Miami (FL), where, the following year, the Hurricanes went 11-1 and captured the national championship. Erickson led Miami to another title in 1991, then returned to the state of Washington to become the head coach of the Seattle Seahawks in the NFL.

Washington St.	3	3	21	7	- 34
UCLA		3	17	7	3	- 30

WSU	FG Hanson 48
UCLA	FG Velasco 47
UCLA	FG Velassco 23
UCLA	Estwick 1 run (Velasco kick)
UCLA	Thompson 1 pass from Aikman (Velasco kick)
WSU	FG Hanson 51
UCLA	Ball 8 run (Velasco kick)
WSU	Stallworth 15 pass from Rosenbach (Hanson kick)
WSU	Swinton 6 run (Hanson kick)
WSU	Stallworth 81 pass from Rosenbach (Hanson kick)
UCLA	FG Velasco 30
WSU	Swinton 1 run (Hanson kick)

Attendance 51, 970

Colorado State vs. New Mexico

"This is the most exciting thing that's ever happened in any game I've ever played."—Mike Good, New Mexico linebacker

THE BACKGROUND

Somewhere along the line, things had to get better for New Mexico coach Mike Sheppard. They really couldn't get much worse.

In 1987, Sheppard, in his first year as head coach of the Lobos, suffered through an 0-11 season. The one bright spot on the team was wide receiver Terance Mathis. A third-team All-America in '87 (73 receptions 1,132 yards), Mathis was 10th in NCAA Division I-A career receiving yards (2,939) after just two seasons.

But in 1988, Mathis was sidelined with academic difficulties, unable to play. In addition, New Mexico was the only Division I-A school to start the season with a true freshman at quarterback. Jeremy Leach called the signals for the Lobos, and although he threw for 1,986 yards during the season (more than any other freshman in the country), New Mexico mustered just one victory entering the last two games of the year.

Their only win of the year, the only win of Sheppard's tenure so far, was a 36-34 nailbiter over New Mexico State. Lobos' kicker Rick Walsh hit a 34-yard field goal with 0:02 left for the winning margin. Knowing that the Lobos' victory was part of a 27-game New Mexico State losing streak from 1988-90, puts things in proper perspective when talking about the state of football in the state of New Mexico during the late '80s.

Not good.

This was a battle for the basement of the Western Athletic Conference. The Colorado State Rams were 1-8, 1-6 in the WAC. New Mexico (1-9, 0-6) was trying to shake a 16-game WAC losing streak, outscored 110-3 in their previous two losses to BYU and Hawaii. Sheppard hoped that at some point, he could treat the few Lobos fans that still showed up at University Stadium to his first home victory.

The first half lived up to the advanced billing. Botched snaps from center, missed tackles, fumbled punt returns and mindless penalties highlighted the unremarkable first two quarters. Colorado State held the 17-9 halftime lead. After three quarters, the score remained the same, and it looked like the same old story for New Mexico.

But this time the Lobos rallied.

A Walsh 35-yard field goal with 13:45 to play, followed by a three-yard TD run by Lobos running back Andre Wooten, gave New Mexico an 18-17 lead with 8:04 remaining in the fourth quarter. Could it be? New Mexico was about to break their losing streak?

But in the final minute of the game, it was the Lobos' hearts that were broken instead. Colorado State had the ball at their own 41 with just over a minute to play when quarterback Scooter Molander found wide receiver Tony Branch (a native of New Mexico) on a crossing pattern. Branch took in the pass and took off for the end zone. Fifty-nine yards later Colorado State had the lead 23-18 with 0:57 on the clock.

New Mexico was devastated. "There was that feeling of 'There it goes again,'" said Sheppard. With their tails between their legs, the Lobos got one more chance to stop their endless tailspin.

After the CSU kickoff, Leach got the ball back on the UNM 19 with just 52 seconds left. The Lobos had zero timeouts and even less of a chance to end their woeful WAC losing streak. But Leach, the wide-eyed freshman, gave it his best shot. He hit tight end Mitch White with two short completions to set up a third-and-one near the UNM 30-yard line.

Leach then threw two completions to fifth-year senior runningback Tony Jones, who zipped down the right sideline on both plays, then out of bounds to stop the clock with 0:10 remaining. Suddenly, the Lobos had the ball at the CSU 28-yard line. Still, they needed a touchdown.

Leach threw deep into the end zone for wide out Al Owens. The ball glanced off his hands. The Lobos were down to their final play.

Three seconds left.

THE PLAY

Sheppard sent Jones back in the game with one last offensive call. "All-streak."

"My assignment is to run a post pattern," said Jones. "If there's one safety on me, I just try to beat him. If they're in a four-deep, I try to split the two safeties." Colorado State lined up in a four-deep defense.

Sheppard wanted the ball thrown to Jones. "We felt like the weakness of the defense they were in was in the middle of the field," said the Lobos' coach.

Jones translated that strategy as he came into the huddle. "Tony just told me to throw it to him," said Leach. Simple enough. But remember, these were the Lost Lobos.

Leach took the snap, then stumbled backwards with the ball in his hands. No one would have been too surprised had he fallen to the ground. He didn't. Leach righted his ship, then threw to the end zone, over CSU linebacker Lance Ane, between the safeties, right to the "W" in New Mexico painted in the end zone.

Right to Tony Jones. Touchdown New Mexico. No time on the clock. No time for the Lobos to figure a way to lose. This time, they

had figured a way to win. New Mexico 24, Colorado State 23.

"They made a great pass and we didn't go to the football," lamented Rams coach Leon Fuller. The entire New Mexico team stormed into the end zone. The WAC streak was over. The Lobos finally won a home game for Sheppard.

"It's one step," Sheppard said of the thrilling finish. "It's a small one, but at least it's a step."

THE AFTERMATH

"Hopefully this is the turning point," said UNM safety Brett Heber after the game.

It wasn't. The Lobos lost their final game of the season 18-10 to San Diego State (2-8). New Mexico finished 2-10 on the year. Colorado State ended 1-10 with a 32-28 loss at Tulsa.

Leach had his 15 minutes of national fame the following year when he narrowly missed breaking the NCAA single-game passing record by throwing for 622 yards (41 of 68) against Utah. At the time, the record was 631 yards set by Leach's counterpart, Scott Mitchell of Utah.

Leach ended his four-year career at New Mexico ranked in the Top 20 all-time in career passing yardage. His total of 9,382 yards places Leach slightly ahead of John Elway (9,349) in that category.

Terance Mathis returned to the New Mexico lineup in 1989 and finished his stellar college career with 263 receptions for 4,254 yards and 36 TDs. He is third all-time in NCAA Division I-A career receptions.

By the time Mike Sheppard was fired at the end of the 1991 season, New Mexico had sunk to the bottom of the 106 Division I-A schools. Actually, they had been there for a while. After five years in Albuquerque, Sheppard's Lobos were a dismal 9-50. (Four of those victories were over their brothers in misery, New Mexico State.)

When Dennis Franchione took over as head coach in 1992, Sheppard moved on to California where he became offensive coordinator for the Bears. He later turned into a successful offensive assistant coach in the NFL, first as tight ends coach with the Cleveland Browns in

'93, later as offensive coordinator for the San Diego Chargers in '97, and also quarterbacks coach for the Seattle Seahawks in '99.

Leon Fuller was only slightly more successful at Colorado State than Sheppard was at New Mexico. After a 1-10 season in '88 and a 25-55 record from 1982-88, Fuller was replaced as the Rams head coach by former Ohio State leader Earle Bruce.

Colorado State	10	7	0	6	- 23
New Mexico	0	9	0	15	- 24

CSU	Whitehouse 1 run (Brown kick)
CSU	FG Brown 26
UNM	FG Walsh 49
UNM	Owens 15 pass from Leach (pass failed)
CSU	Yert 2 run (Brown kick)
UNM	FG Walsh 35
UNM	Wooten 3 run (pass failed)
CSU	Branch 59 pass from Molander (pass failed)
UNM	Jones 28 pass from Leach (no attempt)

Attendance 8,180

167

North Texas vs. Kansas State 🏈

"I was paralyzed. I felt like crying, I felt like laughing. It's the greatest feeling in the world."—Carl Straw, Kansas State quarterback

THE BACKGROUND

Twenty-seven consecutive games over two and a half seasons without a victory. The losingest program in the history of college football. Unquestionably, the worst team in Division I-A. That is what Bill Snyder inherited when he left his job as offensive coordinator at Iowa to become the head coach at Kansas State in 1989.

During the losing streak, in which the only non-loss was a 17-17 tie in '87 to their cross-state rivals Kansas, K-State certainly had their chances to bring home a victory. They blew a 28-7 halftime lead against Louisiana Tech in '88. That same season, Tulane scored a TD with 14 seconds left to beat them 20-16. In '87 Austin Peay hit a 35-yard TD pass with 10 seconds left to win 26-22. Later that year, Iowa State kicked a 39-yard field goal in the final minute to beat the Wildcats 16-14.

"They had unbelievable bad luck," said Nebraska coach Tom Osborne. "They had three or four games during that period that they just flat had locked up that somehow got away from them." On the other hand, all the games weren't that close. K-State was blown out by 30 points or more on five different occasions in '88.

Three weeks into Snyder's first season in Manhattan, Kansas, the country's longest streak had grown to 30 games without a win (16 consecutive losses). Despite changing the school's logo and closing practices to the media, it was the same old K-State leading the country in the United Press International's Bottom 10.

With one final non-conference game remaining at the beginning of the season, K-State's chances at breaking the streak in '89 were dwindling. Fortunately, their opponent was a Division I-AA school. Unfortunately for the Wildcats, it was the North Texas Mean Green Eagles (3-0), the No. 1-ranked team in Division I-AA. North Texas was the second I-AA opponent of the season for K-State. The Wildcats had already lost to Northern Iowa 10-8.

As usual, K-State fell behind. Darrin Collins' 32-yard TD run late in the first quarter put North Texas on top 7-0. But then the Wildcat defense gave the home faithful (these fans redefined the word "faithful") something to cheer about. Defensive end Maurice Henry partially blocked a North Texas punt with 2:48 left in the half, setting up the K-State offense at the Eagle 39. Two minutes later Curtis Madden barreled in from the one-yard line with 0:48 left in the half. David Kruger then made the PAT to tie the game 7-7. After three and a half games, the K-State kicker finally got his first point of the season.

It was halftime and the Wildcats weren't losing. The fans were applauding. K-State quarterback Carl Straw noticed a change. "When we came off the field at halftime, it was the first time I had heard the fans cheering us so much," said Straw. "We got the feeling then that they believed in us."

The good vibes carried over into the third quarter. Two plays after a long K-State drive ended when Straw was sacked and fumbled at the North Texas 10, tackle Anthony Davis hit

KSU coach Bill Snyder and the Kansas State team pour onto the field after breaking a 30-game winless streak. Photo courtesy of Rod Makinski

Eagle QB Scott Davis, forcing another fumble, which was recovered by K-State's Ekwensi Griffith at the North Texas two. A short TD run by fullback Sonny Ray Jones and the 'Cats led 14-7.

As time ran down in the fourth quarter at KSU Stadium, the K-State lead was 14-10. North Texas had one last chance when they took the ball at their 23-yard line with 2:59 left to play. After struggling all day on offense (the Eagles were 1 of 15 on third-down conversions) Davis led his team to the K-State 47 with under two minutes left. But there the drive stalled.

Fourth-and-19. The Wildcats winless streak was seemingly over. Just one more play. With very few options left, Davis dropped back, scrambled away from the rush, then threw a prayer into the end zone.

Unbelievably, it happened again.

Wide receiver Carl Brewer caught Davis' desperation fling among three defenders. North Texas took the lead, 17-14, with 1:35 to play. The Eagles celebrated wildly while the winless Wildcats were distraught. "I'm just devastated," said Henry. "I figured if we're not going to win there, we're never going to."

K-State took the kickoff and could only return the ball to their 15. Straw was sacked on the next play. He sat on the ground at the K-State 8. The clock ticked down to 1:00 and the Wildcats, one play away from a victory just seconds ago, now appeared doomed to another week with the streak.

But on the next play, North Texas got called for pass interference to move the ball to the 23. The Straw found Michael Smith for 26 yards to the KSU 49. The flicker of hope which remained seemed doused the next play when Straw was sacked again back to the KSU 38. Just 38 seconds on the clock.

The, almost magically, wide receiver Smith got open again, and again, and again. Three consecutive completions of 20, 20 and 11 yards from Straw. Stunningly, the Wildcats were at the North Texas 12 with just 0:14 left.

Then an incomplete pass, followed by another incompletion. Straw was hit hard by lineman Roderick Manning. Snyder called time-out with 0:04 left. A woozy Straw teetered over to the sideline. "I thought about pulling him," said the Wildcats coach. Straw, who had already replaced starter Chris Cobb in the second

169

quarter, shook his jammed right thumb. Cobb ran onto the field to take over for the last play.

THE PLAY
CD 1—Track 28
Stan Weber, Mitch Holthus,
Kansas State University Radio Network

At this point, Snyder could have gone for the tie with a field goal. But with their current streak, the question was moot. "It wasn't a tough decision," said the new coach. "They've had ties before. Ties don't count. We came to win."

Snyder then decided to keep Straw in the game. His quarterback came back on the field replacing Cobb. "There was no way someone was going to take me out 'cause of a little injury," said Straw, who was almost pulled earlier in the game after fumbling twice.

Straw took the snap. Split end Frank Hernandez broke open in the end zone. He cut to the corner behind defender Isaac Barnett. Straw lofted the ball. A perfect pass. Hernandez cradled the ball in his stomach. He made sure both feet were in bounds. Could it be?

Yes. A touchdown. With no time remaining, Kansas State had beaten North Texas 20-17. The streak was over.

KSU stadium erupted into a melee of celebration. The goalposts came tumbling down. Two-hundred-eighty-pound center Paul Yniguez jumped on the victory bell and rang it furiously for the first time in three years. "We won, damnit," he screamed, crying. "We won. We won." The players were mobbed.

"I thought we won the damned Super Bowl," said Henry. "There were people jumping over the bench, people tackling me. Little kids were biting me on the ankles."

That's how hungry Wildcat fans were for a win.

They took part of the goalpost out of the stadium and paraded it down Main Street. Car horns blared, people partied. Finally, after 1,071 days without a victory, Kansas State had won a game.

THE AFTERMATH

"That's the day that the whole program changed," said K-State broadcaster Mitch

Holthus, who spontaneously called it a "big, big, big, big, big, big win!" [That became his announcing signature for years to come.] It didn't happen overnight though. The Wildcats were pummeled the following week by perennial Big Eight conference giant Nebraska, 58-7. In fact, the Wildcats lost the rest of their games during the '89 season, finishing 1-11.

But Snyder had laid the foundation for possibly the greatest turnaround in college football history. The '89 team finished No. 1 in the nation in passing defense, as team defense became a staple of the Snyder-led K-State teams of the '90s. From '93 to '98, the Wildcats went to six straight bowl games, finished in the top 20 all six years, and in the top 10 in three of those seasons. Perhaps the pinnacle came in 1998 when K-State was undefeated and just one game away from a national title match, before a heartbreaking overtime loss to Texas A&M in the Big 12 conference championship game.

For North Texas, the bottom fell out on a promising season. After ending K-State's 30-game winless streak, the Mean Green lost their next four games. North Texas finished the season 5-6. In 1995, North Texas joined Division I-A and began play in the Big West Conference in '96.

North Texas	7	0	0	10	-17
Kansas State	0	7	7	6	-20

NT	Collins 32 run (Chapman kick)
KS	Madden 1 run (Kruger kick)
KS	Jones 1 run (Kruger kick)
NT	Chapman 51 FG
NT	Brewer 47 pass from Davis (Chapman kick)
KS	Hernandez 12 pass from Straw (no attempt)

Attendance 26,564

Moravian vs. Juniata

*"When he threw it, the ball was wobbling, and I said,
'Ugh, not a shot.'"—Moravian coach Scot Dapp*

THE BACKGROUND

Juniata College sits just 45 miles south of State College, Pennsylvania, in the shadow of Penn State University. In 1988, the Division III school unveiled Chuck Knox Stadium, named after the longtime NFL coach and Tribe alumnus. The next season, new coach Brad Small was seeking his first victory at Juniata after the Indians struggled to an 0-4 start.

Traveling three hours west by bus from their home in Bethlehem, Pennsylvania, the Moravian Greyhounds looked to improve on a 3-1 record, coming on the heels of the school's first ever NCAA Division III quarterfinal playoff finish in '88. Moravian was contending for their second straight Middle Atlantic Conference title, and coach Scot Dapp's team was heavily favored to run over the winless Indians.

But things went bad in Huntingdon, PA, for the Greyhounds. "For some reason, seems like every year that we've gone out there, we just struggle a little bit," recalled Dapp. "They played very well and things weren't working for us." In fact, Juniata was dominating the game. Benefiting from four Moravian fumbles and two interceptions, the Tribe led 10-0 early in the second half. Juniata's big score came when quarterback John Spahr flipped a screen pass to conference rushing leader Dennis DeRenzo on a second-and-long play. DeRenzo, with a caravan of blockers in front of him, rumbled 51 yards for the early third quarter touchdown.

Things got worse for Moravian. Kicker Tim Cunniff, on his only attempt of the day, sailed a 30-yard field goal wide left in the third quarter, keeping the Juniata lead at 10. Finally, after Spahr's errant pitch was fumbled and recovered by Moravian at the Juniata 28, the favored Greyhounds got on the scoreboard. Senior QB Rob Light hit tight end Craig Cunniff with an 11-yard TD pass on the first play of the fourth-quarter and Moravian cut the lead to 10-7.

But despite numerous fourth-quarter opportunities, the Moravian offense, top-ranked in the conference, could not get over the hump.

The Greyhounds defense kept giving the ball back to their offense, which kept turning it back over to Juniata. After Tony Carasia barreled downfield 27 yards on three plays, Light made a bad pitch that was recovered by Indians linebacker Dan Jones, stopping the drive at the Juniata 32 with 12:37 left to play.

Juniata lost 10 yards in the next four plays. Back came Moravian. Driving to the Juniata 39, the Greyhounds stalled again when Light's fourth-and-four pass fell incomplete with eight minutes left. Once again, three and out for Juniata. After a 10-play drive, with just three minutes remaining, Moravian faced a fourth-and-21 at the Juniata 36. Light found Bill Fitzell on a 19-yard completion, stopped two yards shy of the first down. Juniata took over again with only 2:43 left, leading 10-7.

As the Indians ran down the clock and the Greyhounds ran out of timeouts, Dapp thought about the long bus trip back to Bethlehem. "[We were] losing a game to a team we felt we should've won, knowing that we sputtered on offense, that the offense should've been scoring definitely more points. The defense probably would've been mad [on the bus ride home] because I know there were times throughout the course of that game that we botched up opportunities with a fumble or a dropped pass. You know the defensive players probably would've been looking at the offense [saying] 'Way, to go, six points against this team, that's all you can do?'"

Spahr drove Juniata on the ground to the Moravian 43. On fourth down, the quarterback, who doubled as the team's punter, pooched a kick that was fair caught by Joe Thomas at the Moravian 25-yard line. The Greyhounds had no timeouts and only 0:13 left.

THE PLAY

" I can literally say that I was thinking about what I was gonna tell the team after the game that was gonna make the long ride home easier," said Dapp.

Moravian had one play left, 75 yards to cover, not much strategy, and very little hope.

"We never practiced a Hail Mary," said the coach, resigned to the loss. He shouted an improvised play to his players across the field. "I just told the guys to line up. I put three guys on this side and I said, 'You guys just go straight downfield.' I told the one guy in the middle, 'You lag back about five yards in case it's tipped this way.'"

It was the play that every kid makes up in his backyard. "The only difference was we didn't have a stick drawing it up on the ground," joked Dapp. "Luckily, you've got college kids and they're supposed to be able to visualize this stuff, so we didn't have to draw it."

Light dropped back to pass. With the wind at his back, he let it fly. It was a wobbly floater down the left sideline that only made it to the Juniata 30-yard line. Senior wideout Mike Howey jumped for the ball flanked by two Indian defenders.

The ball tipped off Howey's hands. As the two Juniata defenders lunged for the ball, they collided, knocking the pigskin back to Howey. Still on his feet, Howey snatched the ball, quickly turned, jumped over one last tackler, and raced the remaining 30 yards for the im-

probable 75-yard touchdown as time expired.

Dapp went crazy.

" I was just jumping up and down in the middle of the field. I didn't know who to grab," he recalled. " The rest of the team was halfway on the field before (Howey) was even in the end zone and my assistant coach came up to me afterwards and said, 'I'm there trying to get everybody back, everybody back, and I looked and I saw you were out in the middle of the field.'"

Juniata's winless coach was crushed. "I've never felt worse for a bunch of kids in my whole life," said Small. "We lost a game that we thought was ours."

Dapp commiserated. "I felt bad for their coach. Because I can't say we deserved to win that game. (However) I wasn't about to give it back to him. But it was one of those plays that we could've practiced 35 times and it would've never worked. I guess sometimes you're just not supposed to win."

THE AFTERMATH

Brad Small had to wait four more weeks before notching his first victory as Juniata coach. Losses to conference foes Lycoming, Albright, and Susquehanna preceded the Indians first victory of the season, a 21-7 win over Wilkes. Juniata finished 2-8. After his third season in 1991, Small was replaced as head coach. Juniata later changed their mascot to the more politically correct Fighting Eagles.

In Bethlehem, PA, Scot Dapp became the most successful coach in Moravian football history, approaching 100 victories in 13 seasons and still counting. Quarterback Rob Light set the school record during the '89 season for career touchdown passes with 37.

From 1995 to 1999, Moravian and Juniata played five games in consecutive seasons that ended tied in regulation. Four of them were settled in overtime, one finished in a tie.

October 7, 1989—Huntingdon, Pennsylvania

Moravian	0	0	0	13	-13
Juniata	0	3	7	0	-10

JC	O'Neill 22 FG
JC	DeRenzo 51 pass from Spahr (O'Neill kick)
MC	Cubbin 11 pass from Light (Cunniff kick)
MC	Howey 75 pass from Light (no attempt)

Attendance 700

173

Southern Mississippi vs. Louisville 🏈

"Face it, what are the odds of that play working?"
—*Brett Favre, Southern Mississippi quarterback*

THE BACKGROUND

Brett Favre started the 1989 season at Southern Mississippi with a bang. The junior quarterback orchestrated a stunning 30-26 upset of Florida State in the first game of the season, throwing for 282 yards and two TDs. But despite Favre's prolific passing (he already had amassed 37 touchdowns and 4,855 yards in just 27 career games at USM) the Golden Eagles fell into a slump, losing their next four games.

Up in Louisville, Kentucky, coach Howard Schnellenberger had rebuilt the U of L program in just four years. The Cardinals finished the 1988 season 8-3, their first winning season in a decade, but then were snubbed by all the bowls and spent the holiday season at home for the 11th straight year. Louisville fans hoped 1989 would be the year to break the bowl drought when U of L started strong with a 3-1 record.

But as Louisville entered their homecoming game at Cardinal Stadium with Southern Mississippi (2-4), memories of past defeats at the hands of the Golden Eagles were fresh in their minds. In 1987, Southern Miss destroyed Louisville 65-6, and the final score did not sit well with the U of L players. "They had the game won, and they just kept pouring it on trying to embarrass us," Cardinal tight end Chad Fortune said. "I'm still sore about that."

In 1988, U of L lost 30-23 in Hattiesburg, when the clock expired with Louisville on the USM 10-yard line after driving from its own 18 in the final minute. That game was played in what Cardinal defensive tackle Ted Washington called, "hurricane conditions."

"They should have stopped the game," Washington said. "I was in mud up to my elbows. Southern Miss is used to playing in that stuff, but we aren't. Every time we moved our feet we went down."

The Golden Eagles had beaten Louisville seven consecutive times. "Southern Miss has to believe there's no way we can beat them," Schnellenberger said. "They have to think we don't have the character and guts to sustain an offense and that we'll find a way to lose."

Washington vowed revenge. "This time they're up here and things are going to be different."

For most of the autumn afternoon and up to late in the fourth quarter, it appeared Washington was right. With the score tied 10-10, Louisville took the ball from their own 20 with 2:30 left to play in the game, and methodically marched downfield. Junior quarterback Browning Nagle hit six passes to take Louisville down to the USM 26, where they set up for the game-winning field goal.

With the second largest crowd in U of L history sensing a Cardinal victory, kicker Ron Bell lined up for the 43-yard attempt. As Bell approached the ball, USM freshman Vernon Collins swept in from the right side of the line and deflected the kick. Collins had tipped Bell's 26-yard FG earlier in the quarter, but the ball still went through the uprights. Not this time. The kick was blocked and it appeared the game would end in a 10-10 tie.

174

Southern Miss took over with just 0:13 left on the clock at their own 26. On the first play, Favre dropped back to pass and was promptly sacked by defensive end Mike Flores for a five-yard loss.

Coach Curley Hallman called one last timeout, stopping the clock with 0:06 left.

THE PLAY

"The only thing you can do is drop back and throw it as far as you can," said Favre.

So the Golden Eagles came up to the line of scrimmage with three wide receivers lined up on the left side, and one receiver, senior Darryl Tillman, lined up to the right. After taking the snap, Favre scrambled toward the right sideline, trying to avoid the rush. But defensive end Washington had the USM quarterback within reach. Washington lunged, into a chin-high left stiffarm by Favre. Washington fell to the ground. Favre wobbled. Staggering backwards like a boxer hit by an uppercut, Favre desperately caught his balance. Just before falling out of bounds, he righted himself at the 10-yard line.

"I got a hand on him," Washington said, "but he slipped away. I got to him again, but he threw the ball. I couldn't look. I closed my eyes." Favre launched the pass to the middle of the field at the Louisville 35.

Four Louisville players surrounded one USM receiver.

The play was designed for 6-4 Michael Jackson to tip the ball, and for Tillman to come behind the pack and grab it in mid-air.

Jackson jumped, reached up to tip the ball, but missed. It slipped right through his hands. But it bounced right off his helmet.... directly into the arms of Tillman, who caught it in full stride 10 yards behind Jackson, splitting two Cardinal defenders at the 25-yard line.

Immediately, free safety Derek Hawthorne turned backwards and threw both arms around Tillman, but couldn't hold onto the Golden Eagle receiver who had a full head of steam heading straight to the left corner of the end zone. Cornerback Art Alexander was the Cardinals' last hope, chasing after a runaway miracle.

"I gave it my best effort, but I just couldn't catch the guy," Alexander said.

With no time left on the clock, Tillman streaked across the goal line with an unbelievable 79-yard touchdown reception. Southern Miss had beaten Louisville for the eighth consecutive time, 16-10.

"One hundred percent luck," Cardinal defensive coordinator Rick Lantz said. "Everything had to be perfect. If it had hit any other part of his helmet or body, [Tillman] couldn't have caught it."

Alexander was dumbfounded. "It was a fluke. We had practically the whole team back there," he said.

A wild celebration, or dirge, ensued depending on which side of the field you were on. Jackson was so excited jumping up and down, that his leg got stuck in the bass drum from the Cardinal marching band which had assembled near the end zone before the final play.

After the game, Favre was still in disbelief of his own accomplishments. "I can't believe it happened," he said. "The odds of that play working are probably slim to none."

Schnellenberger was slightly more precise.

"The odds of that happening are about one in umpteen to the second power," he said.

THE AFTERMATH

Southern Miss ended the season 5-6, while Louisville finished 6-5. The end of the season was especially frustrating for Schnellenberger's Cardinals. "I've never had a year where we've lost so many games we should have won," Schnellenberger said after U of L's 24-13 season ending loss to Syracuse in the Tokyo Dome in Japan. Louisville lost three games on the final play during the '89 season. The week following the Southern Miss loss, tight end Fortune couldn't hold on to a deflected pass in the end zone as time expired, and Tulsa knocked off the Cards 31-24. The next week, Virginia's Jake McInerney booted a 37-yard field goal as time ran out, giving the Cavaliers a 16-15 victory, and the Cards' their third straight loss on the last play of the game.

The next season, Schnellenberger's program peaked. The Cardinals finished 10-1-1 and defeated Alabama 34-7 in the Fiesta Bowl.

In Hattiesburg, Southern Miss announcer

John Cox tells the story of a Golden Eagle fan who had listened to Cox's call of the "Miracle of Louisville" so many times that when he met Darryl Tillman one day, he started the conversation by saying, "Hey, aren't you 'Tipped-and-caught by Tillman'?

"I've been around some weird ones and I've seen Favre pull out games time and time again. But that was the only one that I would say was a miracle," remembered Cox.

The following year, Favre pulled off another dramatic finish in his senior season by throwing an 11-yard TD pass to Michael Welch with no time remaining to give Southern Miss a 14-13 win over Southwestern Louisiana.

Southern Miss	7	0	3	6	-16
Louisville	0	7	0	3	-10

USM	Jackson 5 run (Davis kick)
LOU	Gardner 2 run (Bell kick)
USM	Davis 32 FG
LOU	Bell 26 FG
USM	Tillman 79 pass from Favre (no attempt)

Attendance 34,484

Florida vs. Auburn

"It's a game that leaves you numb…without feeling."—*Gary Darnell*

THE BACKGROUND

The 12th-ranked Auburn Tigers entered this nationally televised Saturday night game at Jordan-Hare Stadium with a 5-2 record, 3-1 in the SEC, seeking a third-straight SEC championship for coach Pat Dye. Florida, although 6-1, ranked No. 19, and riding a six-game winning streak on the field, was a program in turmoil off the field.

Five weeks into the season, Arden Czyzewski's 41-yard field goal as time expired gave the Gators a dramatic 16-13 victory over LSU in Baton Rouge. Florida was 4-1. Things looked bright.

The next day, in the wake of the second NCAA investigation into the school's football program in five years, head coach Galen Hall resigned. Defensive coordinator Gary Darnell was appointed interim coach."In one day we went from what was billed as one of the greatest wins in Florida history, to where everything stopped," said Darnell.

The Gators, however, continued to win with two main weapons. The nation's top-rated defense, and the country's leading rusher, junior tailback Emmitt Smith.

Smith entered the Auburn game fresh off a 316-yards rushing performance against New Mexico to raise his nation's best average to 161 yards per game.

But things were different this night.

Neither the Gators nor the Tigers could muster much offense. Auburn managed just 87 yards and three first downs in the first half. Florida only 98 yards. The Gators scored the only touchdown of the first half after Auburn quarterback Reggie Slack fumbled on his own five-yard line. Defensive end Brad Culpepper recovered. On the next play, Smith took it up the middle for the 7-0 Florida lead.

The third quarter started and Auburn had yet to cross midfield. But the Tiger defense, led by linebacker Quentin Riggins (13 tackles and seven assists in the game), was keeping Smith in check. He had just 39 yards on 16 carries in the first half.

"We were playing so well that I don't think they would have ever scored if they hadn't got the ball at the five," said Riggins.

Finally, late in the third quarter, the Tiger offense squeezed into Gator territory. Fullback James Joseph's 14-yard run across midfield set up a Win Lyle 47-yard field-goal attempt. It hit the crossbar, then bounced through. With 2:18 left in the third quarter, Auburn trailed 7-3.

The Tiger defense held, forcing a Gator punt to the AU 28. Then Auburn took a nine-minute journey into frustration. From their own 28, the Tigers ran off 18 plays to the Florida five-yard line, by far their most successful drive of the night.

They got nothing out of it. Lyle's 22-yard field-goal attempt was blocked.

The long drive left just 5:53 on the clock. The Florida defense would not break. But their offense couldn't move either. Starting from the UF 20, Smith was stuffed twice. Three downs garnered just five yards. The Gators were forced to punt the ball back to Auburn, who had moved the ball into Florida territory just twice all night. But those were the last two drives.

November 4, 1989—Auburn, Alabama

Shayne Wasden found himself all alone in the end zone. Photo courtesy of Auburn Athletic Media Relations

They had one last shot at the end zone.

Starting at the AU 47 with 3:56 left, Slack threw to Joseph for six yards. Then Alex Strong burst up the middle for 11 yards to the UF 36. Darrell Williams got eight more around left end. After an illegal procedure penalty, Slack rolled out and ran for nine yards for a first down at the 24.

The fans at Jordan-Hare who booed Slack and his listless offense in the first half, were desperate for a score. But time was running out and Auburn had just one timeout left.

Then, Darnell's defense rose up.

Defensive tackle Mark Murray sacked Slack for a 14-yard loss back to the 38. The Tigers had to use their last timeout. A minute 20 remained.

Facing second-and-24, Slack connected with Greg Taylor for 15 yards to the 23. But then an ill-fated pass to Strong in the right flat lost two yards.

It may have been the most valuable two-yard loss in Auburn football history. Running down the field on the play, sophomore receiver

Shayne Wasden was left uncovered. The Florida defense didn't notice him. The Auburn coaches did.

THE PLAY

CD 1—Track 29
Jim Fyffe, **Auburn Network**

The clock was running with 45 seconds left. Auburn faced fourth down and 11 at the 25. Wasden came back to the huddle. "The coaches up in the box had picked it up. I didn't have to say anything," he recalled.

The call came in from the sidelines. Slack relayed the play to his offense. "60 Rail." A four wide receiver set. "Everyone just straight down the field," explained Wasden. "Four Go routes."

Slack took the snap, avoided a strong rush, then looked Wasden's way. He was wide open in the right corner of the end zone. "They had a busted coverage and no one around," said Wasden. Perhaps they just forgot about him. He hadn't caught a pass all night long.

Slack lofted the pass.

Auburn announcer Jim Fyffe saw Wasden all by himself. "It was such an easy pass to catch that I could have probably caught it," said Fyffe. "Things were going through my mind as I'm describing it. I'm thinking 'Oh my God don't let him drop it.' How bad would that be?"

"It was an eternity...it took forever for the ball to come down," said the 5-8, 174 lb. Wasden.

Only the referee standing by could have stopped him. Wasden caught it with both hands, head high, then fell backwards to the turf. Jordan-Hare Stadium erupted. So did Fyffe in the radio booth with 0:26 on the clock.

He sounded like a magical Tiger toy that, when you press its tummy, yells, "Touchdown Auburn, Touchdown Auburn, Touchdown Auburn." Fyffe repeated it over and over to make sure it was true.

The Tigers led 10-7. Florida freshman quarterback Donald Douglas was left with 23 seconds to move the Gators from his own 21-yard line. But he had just one completion for six yards the entire game. Two scrambles and an incomplete Hail Mary later, the game was over.

It was Darnell's first loss as a head coach. "Auburn turned a Cinderella night into a nightmare," he said.

Certainly a dream come true for the Auburn faithful. "It was truly a miracle finish because neither team had been able to move on each other," remembered Fyffe. " It was one of those prayers that are answered."

"I don't believe in miracles, but I believe in not giving up and having faith," said Dye.

Ten years later, most Auburn fans remember where they were when Wasden, now a high school football coach in Opp, Alabama, made the catch.

"I've had several people tell me they were walking out of the stadium and missed the play. And I've had several people tell me they were standing in the breezeways fixing the leaves and turned around to watch the last play. And that they were watching it from the aisles [in the stadium]. Everywhere but their seats, because they were leaving. They had given up on us," he recalled.

Wasden laughed. "You make one play in your career and people tend to remember that. If I hadn't caught the ball, I'd be infamous."

THE AFTERMATH

The victory over Florida catapulted Auburn to a share of their third-straight SEC championship. The Tigers won their final three regular season games, including a historic 30-20 victory over previously undefeated Alabama in the first game of the rivalry ever played at Jordan-Hare Stadium, which celebrated its 50th birthday in 1989. Auburn then defeated Ohio State 31-14 in the Hall of Fame Bowl to finish 10-2 and No.6 in the country.

The Gators slid downhill after the Auburn loss, losing three of their last four games, including a season ending 34-7 defeat to Washington in the Freedom Bowl.

Former Gator quarterback and Heisman Trophy winner Steve Spurrier left his head coaching position at Duke to take over the Florida program in 1990, leading them to a decade of unprecedented success in Gainesville.

The Gators were hit with a one-year probation and banned from any bowl appearances in 1990. The probation denied Florida of its first-ever SEC title after they finished 6-1 in the conference. Spurrier made up for lost time in the following years. From 1991-96, the Gators were 64-12-1, captured five SEC titles, and won the 1996 national championship.

Gary Darnell left Florida and became defensive coordinator at Notre Dame in 1990. He later moved on as an assistant coach at Texas before taking the head coaching position at Western Michigan in 1996.

Florida	7	0	0	0	-7
Auburn	0	0	3	7	-10

UF	Smith 5 run (Francis kick)
AU	FG Lyle 47
AU	Wasden 25 pass from Slack (Lyle kick)

Attendance 85,214

Utah vs. Minnesota

"It was a fitting end to a crazy game."
—Minnesota head coach John Gutekunst

THE BACKGROUND

The Utah Utes were dead last in the nation in defense at the end of the 1989 season. Finishing 4-8 that year, Utah hired Ron McBride, the former assistant head coach at Arizona as its new leader to turn around the program.

McBride gave his players a new coaching acronym, MAFU, which stands for "mental toughness, aggressiveness, fanatical effort and unity." The first game results of McBride's new philosophy were impressive. A shutout, 49-0, against in-state rival Utah State to start the '90 season.

They then traveled to Minneapolis where it was opening night for coach John Gutekunst's Minnesota Golden Gophers. Only 32,229 fans bought tickets, the smallest crowd ever to watch a Minnesota home game in the Metrodome. And after the Utes ran out to an overwhelming 19-0 first-quarter lead with the help of two Minnesota turnovers, the Gopher faithful may have wondered why they even bothered to show up.

But then Minnesota came to life in the second quarter. Ben Williams sacked Utah QB Mike Richmond, stripped the ball loose, and John Lewis recovered for UM. Gutekunst switched quarterbacks. Two plays later, newly inserted QB Marquel Fleetwood, who replaced starter Scott Schaffner, ran 24 yards for a score. Then Minnesota linebacker Pat Wright picked off a Richmond pass and returned it to the Utah 40. Fleetwood cashed in again with a 29-yard strike to Pat Tinglehoff. Utah's lead shrunk to 19-14.

The sloppily played contest, in which each team committed five turnovers, went back and forth until Fleetwood hit tight end Pat Evans with a three-yard TD pass with 0:38 remaining in the third quarter. UM's Marcus Evans ran off right tackle for the two-point conversion and the game was tied 29-29.

It remained tied until late in the fourth quarter.

With 2:27 to play, Utah's Wayne Lammle attempted a 51-yard field goal that sailed wide. After the Utes defense held, McBride's squad got the ball back but could do nothing with it. On fourth down, Utah's Lammle dropped back to punt with just over a minute to play in the game. Gophers freshman Drinon Mays blocked the punt and Minnesota took over at the Utah 35 with just 1:04 left.

On first down, Evans rumbled for 21 yards. The Gophers were sitting pretty at the Utes 14. After two running plays to set the ball up in the middle of the field, senior kicker Brett Berglund came on to try a chip shot 29-yard field goal with eight seconds left.

The Gopher fans were ready to celebrate.

THE PLAY
CD 1— Track 30 —*Bill Marcroft*, KALL 910 Radio

Greg Reynolds was the strongest player on the Utah team. The 6-2, 240-lb. senior, bench-pressed 550 pounds. When Utah special teams coach Sean McNabb called the play "middle block," designed to stack the middle and push

Game 55

back the line, nose guard Reynolds stood directly over center.

The snap was good, but holder Dean Kaufman bobbled the ball momentarily before placing it down. Reynolds roared in. "I just bowled over their center, stuck my arms up and it happened," said Reynolds.

What happened? Pouring through the middle, Reynolds whacked down the Gophers' supposed winning kick. The ball popped loose at the nine-yard line.

LaVon Edwards, a 5-10, 176-lb. defensive back, scooped it up. "I turned around and the ball was right there," said Edwards. All of a sudden, he took off for the Utah end zone.

"I may not be the fastest defensive back in the world, but I'm not going to get caught from behind," he said.

Kicker Berglund was Minnesota's only hope. As he approached Edwards at the Utah 45, Gopher Mark Swanson knocked him off his feet. Edwards was in the clear.

He crossed the Minnesota 30 and time expired. He crossed the goal line and the game was over. Utah had won in stunning fashion, 35-29. The Gopher fans stood shocked.

Coach McBride joined the delirious Utes in a huge pile on the Metrodome turf. The party moved to the Utes' locker room where the tearful coach shouted, "I told you we would find a way to win!"

Just two games into his Utah coaching career, McBride experienced one of his most memorable moments. "I've been in a lot of crazy games," he said, "but never one like this."

THE AFTERMATH

After coming down off their cloud, the Utes were dominated the following week by 23rd-ranked Fresno State, 31-7. They then lost their next three games to Hawaii, Wyoming, and Colorado State, finishing the season 4-7 after the promising 2-0 start.

But the Utah program had been turned around. McBride led Utah to eight consecutive winning seasons after 1990, highlighted by a school record 10-2 finish in 1994, and a No.8 ranking in the final USA Today/CNN Coaches poll.

Minnesota came back and finished the year 6-5 overall, a solid 5-3 record in the Big Ten, and a surprising 31-24 upset of Rose Bowl bound Iowa. At the end of the season, Gutekunst signed a three-year extension to his contract. But after a disastrous 2-9 record just one year later, the sixth-year coach resigned under pressure and was replaced by Jim Wacker.

Utah	19	3	7	6	-35
Minnesota	0	14	15	0	-29

UT	Witkin 22 run (Lammle kick)
UT	Anglesey 7 pass from Richmond (kick failed)
UT	Abrams 2 run (pass failed)
MN	Fleetwood 23 run (Berglund kick)
MN	Tingelhoff 29 pass from Fleetwood (Berglund kick)
UT	Lammle 30 FG
UT	Abrams 2 run (Lammle kick)
MN	Tingelhoff 20 pass from Fleetwood (Berglund kick)
MN	P. Evans 3 pass from Fleetwood (M. Evans run)
UT	Edwards 91 blocked field-goal return (no attempt)

Attendance 32,229

Mississippi vs. Arkansas

September 22, 1990—Little Rock, Arkansas

"It hurt when I hit him. It hurt bad. But it feels good now."
—*Chris Mitchell*

THE BACKGROUND

On January 22, 1990, Jack Crowe became the head coach at the University of Arkansas, taking over for Ken Hatfield, who left Fayetteville to become the head coach at Clemson. Crowe's initial debut was a success, defeating Tulane 28-3, and leading the Razorbacks (1-0) to a No.13 ranking as they hosted Ole Miss at War Memorial Stadium.

Billy Brewer's Rebels (1-1) were coming off a 24-10 loss to Auburn. Ole Miss was without their starting quarterback, Russ Shows, who was injured with a pulled abdomen muscle. In his place, backup Steve Luke stepped in.

It was a long afternoon for Luke. He completed just 3 of 11 pass attempts in the game for 59 yards. He lost a fumble at the Ole Miss 20.To make matters worse, the Rebels ground game was slowed to a trickle—32 rushes for just 52 yards. Ole Miss had an anemic 111 yards in total offense.

The Arkansas defense dominated the line of scrimmage. The Arkansas offense controlled the ball for nearly three quarters. The Hogs led Ole Miss 427 to 111 in total yards, 40:30 to 19:30 in time of possession.

On paper, this was a blowout. On the scoreboard, it was a surprise.

Arkansas pounded on the Ole Miss front door time and time again. Four times in the first half, they stood at the Rebels' doorstep. A fumble and three 20-something field goals by Todd Wright were all they had to show for it.

Like a sparring partner, the Rebels took Ar-

kansas' best punches all afternoon. But they refused to go down. In fact, they snuck in a few of their own jabs.

Arkansas punter John Baxter's 17-yard shank in the second quarter gave Ole Miss the ball at the Hogs' 25. From there, Luke hit flanker Vincent Brownlee in the end zone with one of his three completions. Ole Miss led 7-6. Then Baxter punted again, this time a low-liner 33 yards to Brownlee at the Ole Miss 11. Brownlee raced 89 yards past the entire Arkansas team for a second Rebel score. Somehow, Ole Miss was in front 14-6.

The Arkansas fans were left scratching their heads at the half. But in the third quarter, Quinn Grovey finally broke through for the Hogs. The Arkansas QB scrambled 11 yards for a touchdown, then tacked on the two-point conversion to give the Razorbacks a 17-14 lead. "He's slippery as an eel," was defensive tackle Kevin Pritchett's description of Grovey.

While Arkansas grabbed the lead, the floundering Ole Miss offense could muster only 30 total yards in the second half. But like a penny-wise spinster, they used them judiciously, again manufacturing something from nothing. Jim Earl Thomas scored on a 13-yard TD run with 13:45 to play in the game. Ole Miss had their third thrifty touchdown of the game. The Rebels were back on top 21-17.

The Razorbacks, frustrated all day, got the ball back once, twice, three more times in the final period. But they couldn't crack the Rebels defense.

With 59 seconds left, trailing by four,

Arkansas got their fourth and final chance of the quarter.

From the UA 36-yard line, Grovey determinedly moved the Hogs downfield. He connected with Derek Russell over the middle on a 34-yard completion. Then, he hit Russell again for 13 more to the Ole Miss 17.

With the Arkansas crowd now in a frenzy, Grovey threw to the end zone for Russell again, but the ball was narrowly batted away by Tyrone Ashley. An illegal procedure penalty moved the ball back five yards to the 22. Then Grovey scrambled out of bounds to the 20 with 0:27 left. On third down, he hit Ron Dickerson for eight yards to the 12.

Fourth down and five.

The Razorback momentum had snowballed to unstoppable proportions. With only 19 seconds left, at the Ole Miss 12-yard line, Brewer tried to stop it. He called time-out, walked out onto the field, and addressed his troops. "I told them it's one play to win or lose, to give me everything you've got, it's a total sellout," he said. "We're either going to come out of here happy or sad and you've played too damn good to lose." The Rebels general walked back to the sidelines.

Arkansas was out of timeouts. This was it...or was it?

Grovey took the snap, rolled left, and threw to Dickerson out of the backfield, complete for a seven-yard gain, and a first down at the five-yard line. The clock stopped momentarily at 0:13 to move the chains.

Brewer was wrong. There were two plays left. For the sixth time in the game, Arkansas had ventured inside the Ole Miss 10-yard line.

The Razorbacks rushed to the line.

THE PLAY
CD 1—Track 31—*Lyman Hellums, David Kellum*, Ole Miss Radio Network

"Our coaches had hollered to watch the dive-option pass," said Ole Miss cornerback Chauncey Godwin. "I wouldn't say I was expecting the pass, but it sure seemed like a good possibility."

More like a high probability. The clock started again. Grovey called a run-pass option.

He took the snap, looked for a receiver, but couldn't find one. So Grovey headed left, then pitched back to Dickerson.

"I saw the end zone and I went for it," said Dickerson. He sprinted toward the pylon, got to the three-yard line, then was hit by Godwin.

"I made the hit, right into his legs, but I felt him try to spin and I went down," said Godwin. Falling to the ground, Dickerson's momentum carried him toward the end zone.

Just as Dickerson was about to cross the plane of the goal line for the winning touchdown, safety Chris Mitchell, who started the play on the opposite side of the field, came flying into the picture.

"I was just thinking 'keep him out of the end zone,'" said Mitchell. "If he scored, I knew we had lost. I ran full speed and hit him as hard as I could."

Mitchell made a mammoth hit, folding Dickerson right at the goal line. Did Dickerson score? Was he out of bounds to stop the clock?

After the collision, Mitchell laid on the ground in a daze. "It rung my bell a little bit when I hit him," said the senior safety. "Somebody said he got to the one-foot line. I don't know how close it was."

Dickerson was equally confused. "I thought my momentum carried me across the goal line," he said. "I saw the end zone, and I thought I had gone out of bounds."

On the sideline, Brewer strained to see what happened. "I didn't exactly have the best view," said the Rebels' coach. "I was scared they were going to say he got in."

He didn't. He was neither out of bounds, nor in the end zone. Dickerson was down just inches short of the goal line. The last few seconds trickled away.

"I guess I was just surprised when I heard the game was over," said Dickerson. " I really didn't know what had happened. Everything was in slow motion. It was like I could feel the seconds ticking off the clock."

Ole Miss had won 21-17.

Rocked from the magnitude of the collision, Mitchell finally came to. "The first thing I knew, [safety] Jeff Carter was jumping on top of me hollering that the game was over and that we won."

They had, thanks to Mitchell's 17th tackle of the game, forever known as "The Hit" at Ole Miss.

"This was just one of those days when we won a football game without an offense," said Red Parker, the relieved Ole Miss offensive co-ordinator.

Luke concurred. "Give this one to our defense. Period. That's the story of the game."

(As a way of honoring former Rebels defensive player Chuckie Mullins, paralyzed on the field after a hit against Vanderbilt in '89, Ole Miss began a tradition in 1990 of awarding Mullins' jersey number to the outstanding defensive player in the Rebels' spring game each year. Mitchell was the first recipient.)

Wearing Mullins' No.38, Mitchell saved the game for Ole Miss.

From his home in Oxford, Mississippi, Mullins watched the final seconds of the Arkansas game on television. "It was great seeing No. 38 make that lick," he said.

THE AFTERMATH

Ole Miss ran off seven straight wins before losing to Tennessee 22-13. The Rebels then ended their season 9-3, losing to Michigan 35-3 in the Gator Bowl. The 1990 season was the most successful of Brewer's first eight years in Oxford, as his squad finished No.21 in the AP poll, marking the first time since 1971 the Rebels ended a season ranked.

For Jack Crowe, the loss was his first at Arkansas. There were many to follow. The Razorbacks tumbled to a 3-8 season record in '90, the school's first losing season in 23 years. After a 6-6 record the following year, Arkansas was stunned in their 1992 season opener 10-3 by The Citadel, a Division I-AA school. Falling out of favor with the fans and athletic director Frank Broyles, Crowe was forced to resign the day after the opening game loss. Defensive coordinator Joe Kines was named interim head coach for the remainder of the season.

After finishing with a 9-15 mark in just over two years, Crowe later became the offensive coordinator at Baylor University before leaving in 1996 to pursue other business interests.

Danny Ford, whom Hatfield replaced at Clemson, became the new Arkansas head coach in 1993, completing the musical chairs coaching switch between the schools.

Ole Miss	0	14	0	7	- 21
Arkansas	3	6	8	0	-17

ARK	FG Wright 24
ARK	FG Wright 29
UM	Brownlee 25 pass from Luke (Lee kick)
UM	Brownlee 89 punt return (Lee kick)
ARK	FG Wright 20
ARK	Grovey 11 run (Grovey kick)
UM	Thomas 13 run (Lee kick)

Attendance 54,890

Colorado vs. Missouri

"We are human. We erred. And we feel terrible in regards to the circumstances at the end of the game."—head referee J.C. Louderback

THE BACKGROUND

On November 16, 1940, coach Carl Snavely's No. 1-ranked Cornell team took an 18-game winning streak into their battle with slumping Dartmouth, losers of four of their previous five games. Trailing 3-0 with 4:30 remaining in the game, Cornell had the ball on their own 48-yard line. The Big Red marched down the field on their final drive as time ticked away and the snow began falling at Dartmouth's Memorial Stadium. A pass from Walter Scholl to wingback Bill Murphy gave Cornell a first down on the Dartmouth five-yard line.

Fullback Mort Landsberg carried on first down to the four-yard line. Then Scholl ran for another short gain. On third down and goal, Landsberg was stopped at the one-yard line, and with just seconds remaining, Cornell called time, even though they had run out of timeouts. They were penalized back to the six-yard line for delay of game and a fourth down pass from Scholl to Murphy was knocked down in the end zone, apparently sealing the upset for Dartmouth.

Head linesman Joe McKenney placed the ball on the Dartmouth 20-yard line for the change in possession, but referee William (Red) Friesell, a well-respected official from Princeton, thought it was still fourth down coming up. The scoreboard mistakenly read third down and Friesell overruled McKenney and placed the ball at the Dartmouth six-yard line with six seconds remaining.

Dartmouth captain Lou Young vehemently protested but Cornell was given one more play.

Scholl took the snap, released the ball with two seconds left, and Murphy caught it in the end zone for the winning TD. Cornell won 7-3...or did they?

After watching the game films the following Monday, Cornell president Dr. Edmund Ezra Day (a Dartmouth graduate) admitted the mistake, and voluntarily forfeited the game to Dartmouth, 3-0. "If we hadn't made that decision, we'd have been explaining that game as long as football has a place in intercollegiate athletics," Day said. Dartmouth coach Earl Blaik gladly accepted the victory.

Twenty-five years later, the two teams met at Dartmouth for an anniversary of the game. Referee Friesell was there too.

"Sure, I pulled a boner. A big one. But the people still are nice to me," he said. "I officiated 575 games. That would have been about 80,000 plays. I made one mistake, but that one was a beauty."

Flash forward 50 years.

Coach Bill McCartney's 12th-ranked, defending Big Eight Champion Colorado Buffaloes (3-1-1) traveled to Faurot Field in Columbia, Missouri, to face Bob Stull's Missouri Tigers (2-2) in the Big Eight Conference opener for both teams. Colorado was without its Heisman Trophy candidate, junior quarterback Darian Hagan, who sat out the first half of the game with a shoulder injury. After Missouri battled Colorado to a 14-14 halftime score, McCartney inserted Hagen into the game in the third quarter, but he could play just two series before having to leave for good. However, his replacement, Charles S. Johnson, hit wide receiver Mike Pritchard for a 70-yard touchdown pass, one minute into the fourth quarter giving Colorado a 24-21 lead.

After the teams traded field goals, Missouri quarterback Kent Kiefer (who riddled the Buffalo defense for 326 yards in the game) found Damon Mays for a 38-yard TD with just 2:32 remaining and the Tigers surged ahead 31-27.

But Johnson calmly led his team down the field in the final moments on a 15-play drive starting at the Colorado 12-yard line. With just 31 seconds left, the Buffs had a first-and-goal at the Missouri three-yard line. From there, a series of events would unfold that indelibly shaped the 1990 Division I-A national championship.

First Down: Johnson spiked the ball at his feet to stop the clock with 0:28 remaining.

Second Down: Runningback Eric Bienemy, who surpassed his school's career rushing record with 217 yards in the game, gained two yards up the middle to the Missouri one-yard line. The Buffaloes then called their final timeout with 0:18 left. At this point, a critical error was made when the chain official failed to flip the sideline marker from second down to third down. With the marker still reading second down, Colorado ran the next play.

Third Down: Bienemy tried to score through the middle of the line where he was stopped short of the goal line by linebackers Tom Reiner and Mike Ringgenberg. With no timeouts remaining, the Colorado offense scrambled to get another play off before time ran out, while the Missouri defense stalled getting off the goal line pile.

Head referee J.C. Louderback stopped the clock with eight seconds remaining. "If you notice through the game, I stopped it anytime there was an unusual delay in a pile up," Louderback said. "That was about the fourth or fifth time that had occurred during the game."

Missouri's coach didn't complain. "We were laying there. We weren't jumping off," Stull said.

Fourth Down: After the ball was set, the clock continued, and Johnson, seeing third down on the sideline marker, took the snap and mistakenly spiked the ball once again to try and kill the clock before it ran out. The clock stopped at 0:02.

Two seconds that had been previously added to the clock by Louderback.

"If you remember," he recalled in an interview one year later, "I had put two seconds back on the clock earlier, at about 36 seconds left. Mizzou had called time out and the clock had kept running. When they dumped it down on third down—which was really fourth down—there were two seconds left."

Thinking the game was over, Missouri fans began charging the field, actually tearing down the goalposts at the opposite end of the stadium.

Meanwhile, one play remained.

THE PLAY

Confusion and chaos reigned on the field. Colorado quickly came up to the line of scrimmage to run the "fifth down" play. Without calling time-out, Missouri had no time to argue.

"Several of our coaches tried to yell at the officials. Fans tried to tell them. But they wouldn't acknowledge us, which they should do," Stull said. "I'm not going to call a timeout to give [Colorado] a chance to talk over a play," he added. "I would rather have them do it in a hectic scene like they did. They called a play and they didn't execute it very well either."

Johnson rolled right and lunged for the end zone. Instantaneously, Missouri's Reiner hit the Colorado quarterback, who then spun, fell on his back, and stretched the ball over the goal line.

Was the ball across the goal line before he was down?

"When I landed on the ground, I looked to the sidelines and the goal line was going right through my body," said Johnson. "There was no question in my mind."

"It looked like he was down and the ref took a while to call it," said Missouri defensive end Rick Lyle.

"That was a very close play," said Louderback. "You'd have to look at it and make your own decision. It was a tough call, no doubt about it."

Even a year later, Colorado coach Bill McCartney still couldn't tell. "I haven't seen any footage yet that's conclusive," he said.

It was ruled a touchdown.

Coaches and officials discussed the disputed ending for about 20 minutes before the Missouri team actually had to return to the field to defend an extra-point try, which if blocked and returned for a score, would have tied the game. But wisely, Colorado's Johnson simply fell on the snap from center and the game was officially over. Colorado had escaped with a 33-31 win.

Then the scene at Faurot Field turned ugly.

Angry fans chased the officials back to their dressing room, then pounded on the locked doors. "We had a good police escort," Louderback said. "There were some rabid fans. There was a lot of shouting outside, but I never was afraid." One person was arrested for knocking down a police officer, another was arrested for running over a woman while fleeing from the police.

As McCartney began his post-game press conference, Missouri fans repeatedly screamed at him, "Five Downs! Five Downs!" Soon after, another Tiger fan rushed to the railing behind the Colorado coach and began yelling at him. The fan was escorted away by authorities, then McCartney moved the press conference inside the visitor's locker room, where he complained about the quality of Missouri's Omniturf playing surface, deflecting all fifth down comments.

"That field is not playable," he yelled. "No one should have to play on that turf. It's a joke. It's a joke to college football to try to run an option attack on that field. We slipped all day on that field." (McCartney and his staff would later "document" 92 slips by his players during the game.)

The next day, after reviewing the tape of the game, McCartney (a graduate of the University of Missouri) re-addressed the game's ending. "Obviously we would rather have won this game without this controversy," he said. "We'd rather have scored in four downs, but I do not feel we should give up the victory. In no way do I feel like that."

THE AFTERMATH

After a review of the game the following Monday, the Big Eight Conference suspended indefinitely the seven officials who worked the game.

"We have no excuses," said John McClintock, the Big Eight's supervisor of football officials. "Our officials made a mistake, and I feel terrible about it. I don't suppose I've ever felt as bad about anything in all my years around football."

Referee Louderback turned 57 the following summer, the mandatory retirement age for Big Eight officials, but his retirement from the Big Eight had nothing to do with the fifth down game. He joined the Midwest Independent Officials Collegiate Association the next year and continued officiating.

David Nelson, the secretary-editor of the NCAA football rules committee, said the outcome of the game would stand. "It's a rule that's over 100 years old, and it's that the team with the greater number of points at the end of the game wins," Nelson said. "It tells you right out-there's no appellate system. Once the game is concluded and the referee determines it's concluded . . . that's it."

Although Cornell did agree to forfeit its 7-3 victory over Dartmouth in 1940, Nelson said a rules change since then made it impossible for Colorado to forfeit even if it wanted. Colorado went on to win six consecutive games after the Missouri victory, won the Big Eight championship, and played Notre Dame in a memorable Orange Bowl climax that rivaled the Missouri conclusion (see Notre Dame vs. Colorado, January 1, 1991).

Missouri ended the season 4-7, finishing 2-5 in the Big Eight. The Omniturf at Faurot Field was replaced in 1995 with natural grass.

Colorado	7	7	3	16	-33
Missouri	14	0	7	10	-31

MU	Bailey 19 pass from Kiefer (Jacke kick)
CU	Bienemy 29 run (Harper kick)
MU	Mays 49 pass from Kiefer (Jacke kick)
CU	Pritchard 68 run (Harper kick)
CU	Harper 35 FG
MU	Jones 13 run (Jacke kick)
CU	Pritchard 70 pass from Johnson (Harper kick)
MU	Jacke 45 FG
CU	Harper 39 FG
MU	Mays 38 pass from Kiefer (Jacke kick)
CU	Johnson 1 run (run failed)

Attendance 46,856

Georgia Tech vs. Virginia

"I could go four years, and I could kick seven game-winners... but it would probably never be the same as that kick."—Scott Sisson

THE BACKGROUND

For the first time ever, Virginia was No.1, with dreams of a national championship.

George Welsh's Cavaliers were 7-0, riding a 13-game regular season winning streak, and powered by two of the most explosive offensive players in the country, quarterback Shawn Moore and wide receiver Herman Moore. The Moore-to-Moore connection led a high octane offense that was churning out an average of 48.1 points per game. The Cavaliers had outscored their opponents 337-80.

Georgia Tech, coached by future NFL head man Bobby Ross, was also undefeated. An early season 21-19 win over Clemson moved the Ramblin' Wreck up to No.11 in the rankings, but a 13-13 tie with North Carolina the following week blemished their otherwise perfect record. Tech (6-0-1), unbeaten in the last 11 games, was ranked No. 16 when they traveled to Charlottesville to face the top-ranked Cavaliers.

The top two teams in the ACC faced off in the most anticipated game ever in Charlottesville. A record crowd of 49,700 packed Scott Stadium along with over 350 media members who were each given T-shirts that read, "I squeezed into the press box at Scott Stadium." The air of excitement around the game turned smoky after vandals broke into the stadium the night before the game and set a portion of the field on fire. Grounds crew members spent the early morning hours replacing an 18 x 32 foot section of artificial turf that

was declared playable after Ross and Welsh examined it just hours before kickoff.

It was the Cavaliers offense that was on fire in the first half. After a 44-yard completion to Herman Moore, Shawn Moore scored on his second one-yard TD run of the game with 6:32 left in the second quarter, and the Cavaliers opened up a 21-7 lead.

But Tech's sophomore QB Shawn Jones kept the Jackets within striking distance. Following Moore's score, he completed three straight passes for 62 yards, the last one a 43-yard touchdown to Jerry Gilchrist to narrow the lead to 21-14.

Back came the Wahoo Express. Moore capped the end of the first half with his third TD, a six-yard run with 0:41 left in the second quarter. Virginia took a 28-14 lead into the locker room.

Then things changed. Shawn Moore fumbled on UVA's first offensive play of the second half. Tech linebacker Calvin Tiggle recovered. The Jackets cashed in the turnover with a 12-yard reverse run by Gilchrist for the touchdown. Later in the quarter, Jones found Emmett Merchant for a 26-yard TD pass and the game was tied 28-28.

But quickly it was untied. Just 86 seconds later it was Moore-to-Moore with a 63-yard TD pass. With 3:08 left in the third quarter, Virginia was back on top 35-28.

The Jackets immediately responded, driving 74 yards in seven plays. Tailback William Bell scored on an eight-yard TD run at the end of the third quarter. The game was tied again 35-35.

Georgia Tech's Marco Coleman sacks Cavalier quarterback Shawn Moore. Photo courtesy of Georgia Tech Athletic Association

After a Scott Sisson 32-yard FG, the Jackets held a 38-35 lead. The clock wound down inside the final four minutes as the Cavs drove to a first-and-goal at the Tech one-yard line. Scott Stadium was poised to erupt.

On first down, running back Nikki Fischer was stopped short of the goal. Then UVA was penalized for illegal procedure. Now, the ball was back at the six-yard line. Moore found Moore back down to the one.

Third down from the one.

With 2:44 left and the No.1 ranking in the balance, Moore hit tight end Aaron Mundy for the go-ahead touchdown. An explosion of emotion. Virginia had the lead.

But wait. A flag on the play. The Virginia coaches, screaming from the sidelines, had tried to get Shawn Moore's attention. The Cavs were missing a second tight end in their formation on the play, leaving just six men on the line of scrimmage. Virginia was penalized five yards for an illegal formation. The go ahead points were taken off the scoreboard.

Back at the the six-yard line, the Cavs faced third down again. Shawn Moore looked for

Herman Moore, but linebacker Tiggle batted the ball away, forcing a critical fourth-down play.

At this point, Herman Moore had nine catches for 234 yards, the second-highest total in school history. Welsh had a decision to make. Give Shawn Moore one more chance to hit his favorite receiver for the go-ahead score, or kick the short field goal for the tie.

Welsh elected to send in Jake McInerney who booted the short 23-yard field goal with 2:34 left. The game was tied 38-38. Herman Moore was disappointed. "I definitely wanted to go for it," he said, realizing that even if they failed, the Cavs had all three timeouts left and Tech would be backed up against their goal line. "I say keep them down deep and force them to kick again. But it wasn't up to me."

True. It was up to the Virginia head coach. "We thought we could stop them and get the ball back," said Welsh.

They couldn't. Given 2:26 to work with, Jones was magnificent, marching the Jackets from their own 24-yard line. He threw to Bell for 23 yards. Then, after Bell ran for 13 more yards,

Jones connected two more times and the Jackets had a first-and-10 at the UVA 20-yard line.

Time was running out. The Cavs' sweet dreams of a national championship were turning rancid.

At this point, Welsh may have second-guessed himself. "I still don't think you go for the touchdown on fourth-and-goal from the six," Welsh said. "My God, what's your chances of that? I would think 99% of the coaches would [kick the field goal]."

Tech ran the clock down, then called time-out to set up a game-winning field goal attempt.

THE PLAY

Six-two, 197 lb. Scott Sisson came onto the field to try the 37-yard kick. He was out there for a while. Virginia called two timeouts of their own to try and tighten up Sisson's leg.

"I didn't want to stay on the field and let them freeze me, so I tried to go over and talk to the guys in the huddle," Sisson said. "Then I went over and talked to Coach Ross."

In the meantime, the Virginia fans had plenty of time to get a good look at the sopho-more placekicker from Marietta, Georgia, who, out of high school, was offered a spot as a walk-on at UVA, but instead took his only Division I-A scholarship offer and enrolled at Georgia Tech.

That's more information about Scott Sisson than any Cavs fan ever wanted to know. Maybe if they knew he would go on to be drafted by the New England Patriots but ultimately be dropped from their roster after missing some key kicks in the NFL, they'd feel better. Prob-ably not.

Scott Sisson is a name they'll never forget in Charlottesville. Like David Gordon in South Bend. Or Van Tiffin in Auburn.

They are the names of the guys who stole your high school girlfriend, and there was noth-ing you could do about it....except weep...and play an endless mind game of "what if."

What if we could've scored from first-and-goal at the one? What if we didn't get two il-legal procedure penalties? What if we would've tried for the touchdown instead of kicking the tying field goal?

What if Sisson misses? Then... your girl-friend comes back to you.

After the long wait, holder Scott Aldredge took the snap and placed it down. Sisson kicked it.

Your girlfriend left the prom hand-in-hand with a sharp dressed Yellow Jacket from Geor-gia Tech. The scoreboard read Georgia Tech 41, Virginia 38.

Left with heartbreak and 0:07, Shawn Moore and the Cavs got the ball back at their 26. Moore threw one last desperation pass. Like an unanswered phone call, it didn't connect, picked off by Erick Fry.

"We had the whole season in our hands and we let it slip away," said Virginia center Trevor Ryals.

The words of the jilted boyfriend.

THE AFTERMATH

"As far as enthusiasm goes, we're devas-tated," Herman Moore said. "But we have some games left. We'll have to get ready."

After three weeks perched atop the AP rankings, the Cavaliers came tumbling down. UVA lost three of their last four regular season games, then lost 23-22 to Tennessee in the Sugar Bowl to finish 8-4, falling all the way down to No.23 in the AP poll. Shawn Moore finished fourth in the 1990 Heisman Trophy balloting while Herman Moore was voted con-sensus All-American along with Tech safety Ken Swilling.

At the top of the polls at the end of the season? Georgia Tech. Yes, they married the girlfriend they stole from Virginia.

The win in Charlottesville was perhaps the most significant in Tech history, because it pro-pelled the Yellow Jackets to the school's first ever national championship. After escaping with a 5-3 win against Virginia Tech the next week (won on another late Sisson field goal), Tech hammered Wake Forest 42-7, then Geor-gia 40-23 to finish the regular season 10-0-1.

Even though Colorado ended up No.1 in the AP poll afer narrowly defeating Notre Dame 10-9 in the Orange Bowl, the Jackets demolished Nebraska 45-21 in the Citrus Bowl, then snuck up to No.1 in the UPI Coaches poll, inching out the Buffaloes by one single vote to claim a share of the national championship.

Sisson made a habit of breaking Cavalier hearts. The following year he kicked a 33-yard field goal as time ran out to give the No. 16 Yellow Jackets a 24-21 victory over UVA. After his senior season ended in '92, Sisson had booted six game-winning field goals, two as time expired, but none more memorable than the one that beat Virginia in 1990. "Every other kick I ever made here at Tech goes down the drain with that kick," he said.

Sisson's stint in New England was not his last in the NFL. He later became a successful placekicker for the Minnesota Vikings.

Georgia Tech	0	14	21	6	- 41
Virginia	10	18	7	3	- 38

VA	S. Moore 1 run (McInerney kick)
VA	FG McInerney 27
VA	FG McInerney 51
GT	Jones 23 run (Sisson kick)
VA	S. Moore 1 run (H.Moore pass from S. Moore)
GT	Gilchrist 43 pass from Jones (Sisson kick)
VA	S. Moore 6 run (McInerney kick)
GT	Gilchrist 12 run (Sisson kick)
GT	Merchant 26 pass from Jones (Sisson kick)
VA	H. Moore 63 pass from S. Moore (McInerney kick)
GT	Bell 8 run (Sisson kick)
GT	FG Sisson 32
VA	FG McInerney 23
GT	FG Sisson 37

Attendance 49,700

Ohio State vs. Iowa

"I went nuts, bananas. It seemed like the impossible dream."
—*Jason Simmons*

THE BACKGROUND

The sixth-ranked Iowa Hawkeyes were packing their bags for Pasadena. Coach Hayden Fry's squad was 7-1, 6-0 in the Big Ten and on the verge of wrapping up the Big Ten title. A stunning 24-23 upset of top-ranked Michigan earlier in the season put the Hawkeyes atop the Big Ten standings. With a win over 5-2-1 Ohio State, Iowa would clinch a tie and virtually assure themselves the conference championship.

In Columbus, the Buckeyes struggled out of the gate with a 2-2-1 record in 1990, but had strung together three straight impressive Big Ten wins over Purdue (42-2), Minnesota (52-23), and Northwestern (48-7). Still, John Cooper had yet to beat a ranked Big Ten opponent in his third year as Ohio State coach. He was hoping to break that string against Iowa, in what would be his 100th career coaching victory.

It looked like he'd be stuck on 99 for another week.

The Hawkeyes controlled the first half, leading 17-7 with 43 seconds left in the second quarter. Ohio State took over at their 25 and moved to the Iowa 48 where quarterback Greg Frey was forced to launch a last second Hail Mary pass as time ran out in the half. Defensive back Merton Hanks zeroed in for the interception , but the ball hit his shoulder pads at the Iowa 17 and bounced right to senior flanker Jeff Graham, who made a one-handed grab, then streaked across the goal line as the half ended.

The Buckeyes sauntered into the locker room down just 17-14.

But the Ohio State offense could not carry the momentum into the second half. Lew Montgomery's one-yard TD plunge with 11 minutes left in the fourth quarter gave the Hawkeyes a comfortable 26-14 lead.

Perhaps too comfortable.

The Iowa defense was confident. And why not? Up to this point, Frey's afternoon was one of his worst—1 for 13 in the second half and 6 for 25 in the game. On the next possession, he was dumped for a 10-yard loss at the Ohio State 22. The Buckeyes had to punt the ball right back to Iowa.

But three plays later, after Iowa quarterback Matt Rodgers was stopped on a third-and-two run by linebacker Jason Simmons, the Hawkeyes lined up to punt at their own 32-yard line. With 7:22 to play in the game, Jim Hujsak's punt was blocked by OSU's Foster Paulk. The Buckeyes took over at the Iowa 24.

Ohio State got just three yards in the first two plays. But on third down, Frey connected. He found Bobby Olive on a quick slant pattern. A startling 21-yard touchdown pass. The sudden strike closed the gap to 26-21. Still 6:34 to play.

Momentum shift.

The Hawkeyes got the ball back, then gave it right back to Ohio State. Lance Price picked off a Rodgers pass intended for Alan Cross near midfield and returned it to the Iowa 44.

Fidgeting in Kinnick Stadium.

The clock—4:37. The Buckeyes looked to

193

take the lead. But on fourth-and-15 from the 34, Frey threw to the goal line where Jason Olejniczak intercepted the pass intended for Bernard Edwards. Just 2:31 remained.

The relieved Hawkeye fans celebrated. But it wasn't over yet. Iowa needed to run out the clock.

Ohio State wouldn't let them. Simmons threw runningback Tony Stewart for a six-yard loss. Then he tackled Montgomery for a gain of one on third-and-15. The Hawkeyes had to punt one final time. From his 21, Hujsak got off a weak 27-yard kick. Graham took the fair catch.

You could sense the nervous tension mounting. Ohio State had the ball at the Iowa 48 with 59 seconds remaining. They had no timeouts left. They trailed by five. Offensive coordinator Jim Colletto told his quarterback, "Get in the hurry-hurry. Make your best decisions."

The Buckeyes hurry-hurried. Frey immediately hit Olive for 23 yards to the 25. Then a short seven-yard pass to Graham. On third down, Frey hit Graham again for 15 yards over the middle to the Iowa three-yard line.

First down Ohio State. The clock kept running. The Buckeyes quickly lined up. Frey looked for Graham on a fade route to the right corner. He overthrew it.

The clock stopped with 0:07 left.

THE PLAY
**CD 1—Track 32—*Jim Karsatos,
Terry Smith*, WBNS Radio**

"Let's Go Hawks. Let's Go Hawks." The crowd urged the Iowa defense as Frey brought his offense to the line of scrimmage. Olive was split wide right. Graham lined up in the slot beside him.

"I saw the free safety overplaying me to the outside," said Olive. "I was supposed to run a pick, to free up Jeff [Graham], but their free safety bit real hard to the outside."

Iowa feared the fade route. Olive changed his path. Frey noticed. "Bobby was supposed to run an outside route," Frey said. "But the safety was overplaying him, and he cut inside."

Frey read the detour and fired the ball to Olive on the post pattern. He dived, catching the ball parallel to the ground in the back of the end zone with just one second on the clock. Touchdown Ohio State.

"I wanted to dance, I wanted to go hug Greg, I wanted to run to the sideline and be with my teammates," said Olive.

He did none of the above. He was mobbed in the end zone by his teammates.

The Ohio State marching band immediately played an adrenaline-filled version of the Buckeye fight song to a silent audience at Kinnick Stadium. When they were done, you could hear the corn blow in the fields.

Ohio State kicked off. Iowa's return fell short. Ohio State 27, Iowa 26.

"It's heartbreaking to lose a ball game like that, where you just completely dominate everything except the dad-gum score board," said Fry who remembered a series of Iowa-Ohio State rollercoaster endings. "It's always been a weird game affected by outside forces like a monsoon, a referee who can't handle crowd noise, a fourth-down touchdown as time runs out. Win, lose, or draw, it's been crazy."

Crazy and memorable for Cooper. "I'll never forget my first victory. Obviously, I'll never forget my 100th," said the Buckeye coach. "You've got to be lucky to win a game like that."

THE AFTERMATH

The Buckeyes defeated Wisconsin 35-10 the following week. Then, needing a victory over Michigan accompanied with an Iowa loss to Minnesota to go to the Rose Bowl, Ohio State hosted the Wolverines in the regular season finale. With the score tied 13-13 and 1:38 to play, Cooper was forced to gamble on a fourth-and-one at the Buckeyes 29-yard line to keep their Rose Bowl hopes alive.

He lost. Michigan defensive tackle Mike Evans stuffed Frey on a quarterback sneak. The Wolverines took over the ball, and moved to the 19-yard line where J.D. Carlson booted a 37-yard field goal as time expired. The 16-13 Michigan victory sent Ohio State to the Liberty Bowl and Iowa to the Rose Bowl, even after the Hawkeyes were upset by Minnesota 31-24. Four teams finished tied for the Big Ten Title in 1990 with 6-2 conference records (Michigan, Iowa,

Illinois, and Michigan State). The Hawkeyes defeated all three teams during the season to earn the trip to Pasadena.

Air Force upset Ohio State 23-11 in the Liberty Bowl, perhaps a low mark in the John Cooper era in Columbus. The Buckeyes ended the year 7-4-1. Iowa lost 46-34 to Washington in Hayden Fry's third and last Rose Bowl appearance as the Iowa coach. The Hawkeyes finished 8-4 and ranked 18th in the AP poll.

Ohio State	0	14	0	13	- 27
Iowa	7	10	3	6	- 26

IOWA	Rodgers 3 run (Skillett kick)
OSU	Frey 1 run (Williams kick)
IOWA	FG Skillett 34
IOWA	Montgomery 1 run (Skillett kick)
OSU	Graham 48 pass from Frey (Williams kick)
IOWA	FG Skillett 37
IOWA	Montgomery 1 run (run failed)
OSU	Olive 21 pass from Frey (Williams kick)
OSU	Olive 3 pass from Frey (run failed)

Attendance 70,033

Stanford vs. California 🏈

"Over 27 years I've been involved in a lot of football games that have been painful. I can't remember any quite this painful."—Bruce Snyder

THE BACKGROUND

Eight years had passed. The Big Game had come and gone each season. With each passing year, The Play of '82 was recalled. It became an annual nightmare for Stanford fans to toss and turn through, reliving the impossible reality of the infamous ending.

Well, choose your favorite déjà vu cliche here, because the "Ghost of Big Game Past" visited again in 1990. Only this time, he was dressed in Cardinal.

It was a rollercoaster season for Stanford. They were 4-6, with two heartbreaking losses in the final seconds to Colorado and UCLA for starters, then a shocking upset of No.1 Notre Dame 36-31 in the middle of the year, followed by a three-game losing streak. There would be no bowl game for coach Dennis Green's Cardinal. The Big Game was their last game.

Bruce Snyder's Golden Bears were enjoying their first winning season since 1982. At 6-3-1, Cal was tied for second place in the Pac-10, and had already accepted their first bowl bid in 11 years to appear in the Copper Bowl on New Year's Eve.

The Bears jumped out to a 17-3 lead behind the running of Russell White, who gathered 177 yards on the day. White was dueled by Stanford's Glyn Milburn whose 196 yards rushing and Pac-10-record 379 all-purpose yards helped the Cardinal slowly chip away at the lead.

When Milburn broke away on a 53-yard touchdown run with 4:16 left in the third quarter, the Cal lead was trimmed to 17-15. In re-sponse, Cal quarterback Mike Pawlawski immediately marched the Bears to the Stanford 12-yard line but then fumbled. Cardinal Jono Tunney recovered and Stanford took it the other way.

The Cardinal drive stalled at the Cal 10, where John Hopkins attempted to give Stanford the lead with a 27-yard field goal. It was blocked by Cal's Joel Dickson.

Back came the Bears, but not for long. On the second play after the block, a Pawlawski pass was picked off by Darien Gordon at the Cal 36. That set up another Hopkins attempt, this one good from 22 yards, and Stanford finally had the lead 18-17 with 9:56 left in the game.

But the Bears marched right back down the field, driving 88 yards in 10 plays. White scored from the eight-yard line, and after Pawlawski hit Greg Zomalt for the two-point conversion, Cal led 25-18 with 6:03 on the clock.

After exchanging possessions, Stanford started from their own 13 with just 1:54 to play. Quickly it was fourth-and-six at the Stanford 35. Quarterback Jason Palumbis converted, hitting Chris Walsh for the first down. The Cardinal moved downfield.

With 22 seconds left, it was first down at the Cal 19. Palumbis looked for Milburn, but Cal's David Wilson read the pass perfectly, stepped in front of Milburn and nearly intercepted the ball. He didn't. Stanford was still alive.

On second down, Ed McCaffrey ran a corner route to the right side of the end zone. He

Game 60

Ed McCaffrey's touchdown grab with 0:12 left was just the beginning of a wild finish to the Big Game. Photo courtesy of Rod Searcy

was open. Palumbis connected. Touchdown Stanford with just 0:12 on the clock.

Trailing by one, 25-24, the Cardinal lined up for the two-point conversion. Palumbis looked for McCaffery again, this time in the back of the end zone. He tried to thread it threw the middle. But there was John Hardy, who stepped in front and picked off the pass. The Bears had stopped Stanford. Cal still led by one point.

Memorial Stadium erupted. The Cal fans, thinking the game was over, flooded the field in celebration. Bear players joined them too. "Haven't they learned?" said Cal announcer Joe Starkey, recalling the '82 finish.

"California had quite a few players on the field," referee Pat Flood said. "The coaches were trying to hold them back. They thought the game was over for some reason."

Flags flew.

Starkey expressed the feelings of the Cal faithful. "This is an enormous thing for 19- and 20-year-old kids. It's the biggest game of their life every year with Cal and Stanford. So they did what you expected them to do, they were celebrating like crazy. The official immediately assessed a 15-yard penalty on the kickoff just because they enjoyed what you're supposed to enjoy, success in a college football game in a very dramatic way."

The field had to be cleared. After the penalty, instead of kicking off from the 35, Stanford would try an onsides kick from the 50.

"If we just got the ball back, we'd pretty much be in field goal range," said Hopkins, confident of his range of about 55 yards.

After order was restored, from midfield, with 12 seconds left, Hopkins squibbed the onsides kick towards the Stanford bench. For the Bears, the unthinkable happened. The ball slipped through a couple of Cal players to the 37-yard line where Stanford's Kevin Scott and Dan Byers both scrambled for it.

Byers came up with it. Suddenly the Cardinal had the ball again with just nine seconds left. They were at the very edge of Hopkins' range. Green tried to run one more play to get his kicker closer.

Palumbis again looked toward McCaffery who was running down the sideline. But being pressured by noseguard John Belli, Palumbis intentionally threw it out of bounds.

Then Palumbis was hit.

"I was going full steam. I really didn't hit him, I sort of ran through him," Belli said. With just five seconds left, Flood assessed a 15-yard roughing the passer penalty.

"The penalty was because it was a late hit. It wasn't a violent hit. He didn't try to hold up," referee Flood said. "I wouldn't call it violent, but it was late."

Did Palumbis think it was a penalty ? "The referee is a ref and I play," he said. "He made the call and I'm not questioning it."

Snyder was more to the point. "It wasn't a good call," he said.

Like all Cal-Stanford debates, no one agreed. "It was clean [an obvious penalty]. I thought everybody saw it," said Green.

Nevertheless, it was undeniably costly. The ball was placed at the Cal 22-yard line with five seconds left. Surprisingly, the Cardinal had a shot to steal the Big Game.

THE PLAY

The Bears called their final timeout.

Hopkins, who already hit four field goals, went through his normal sideline procedure by himself. "It's kind of like a pitcher. When a pitcher's having a game, you don't talk to him," he said. He went over to kick a few balls into the practice net behind the bench. But the net was missing. So Hopkins promptly kicked a couple into the crowd behind Stanford's bench.

Meanwhile, Green peered down the field. The Stanford band lined up just beyond the back of the end zone. Eerily, they had gathered in the exact same spot as they did eight years ago, waiting to go onto the field for a post-game performance.

"Denny Green sent his bodyguard down to remind the band to stay off [the field], to get some security guys in front of them," remembered Hopkins. " He was definitely aware of that situation and wanted to make sure history didn't repeat itself."

It seems everyone was aware of the history. Stanford radio announcer Bob Murphy had

moved down to the field for post-game interviews. He stood right under the goalposts.

"I'm talking to the band...I'm walking up and down the back of the end zone line and I'm saying, 'Now look you guys you understand what this line is? Do you understand where that ball is? You know what happened here eight years ago? Now, I would suggest you stay behind this line....You will not move. You will not take one step in any direction until that ball goes between those two posts...and then you can have some excitement and do whatever you want to do,'" remembered Murphy. "It was comical. They were laughing. These kids were laughing 'cause they all knew what the hell was going on."

What was going on, was that Stanford was about to scratch an eight-year old itch.

Hopkins came on the field. "I wasn't thinking about anything," he said. "I blocked everything out. I was really focused. I was hitting the ball well. I looked up, I saw the ball down the middle, I knew it was over." The 39-yard field goal was good.

Stanford won 27-25 as the clock read 0:00. This time there would be no kickoff.

THE AFTERMATH

In all the confusion, two San Francisco television news shows, signing off their 6:00 newscasts just before the game ended, reported that California had won 25-24. When the remarkable footage returned from Memorial Stadium, they had to recant their stories on the 11:00 report.

"Over 27 years I've been involved in a lot of football games that have been painful. I can't remember any quite this painful," Snyder said.

"I don't feel any better today," Belli said the day after the game. "This is something I'll remember for a long time."

The Bears took some time to regroup after the loss before taking on Wyoming in the Copper Bowl. Six weeks later they found themselves in a familiar situation. Leading 17-9 with 49 seconds to go, Cal punted to Wyoming's Robert Rivers, who promptly returned the kick 70 yards down the right sideline for a stunning touchdown, making the score 17-15.

Game 60

Strangely enough, Cal was forced to defend a two-point conversion to preserve the game again. But this time Wyoming was flagged for excessive celebration after the TD, and penalized five yards for delay of game. On the conversion attempt from the eight-yard line, defensive tackle Joel Dickson sacked Cowboys QB Tom Corontzos, and (without any more penalties called) the Bears hung on to win 17-15.

Hopkins' winning kick set a Stanford record for most field goals in a game. In addition, it gave him, at the time, the record for most career points at Stanford, surpassing kicker Mark Harmon. Palumbis also set a school passing record in '90, with a season completion percentage of .686 (234-341).

Stanford	0	6	9	12	-27
California	3	14	0	8	-25

CAL	Keen 50 FG
STAN	Hopkins 26 FG
CAL	White 2 run (Keen kick)
CAL	Dawkins 15 pass from Pawlawski (Keen kick)
STAN	Hopkins 29 FG
STAN	Hopkins 47 FG
STAN	Milburn 53 run (run failed)
STAN	Hopkins 22 FG
CAL	White 8 run (Zomalt pass from Pawlawski)
STAN	McCaffery 19 pass from Palumbis (pass failed)
STAN	Hopkins 39 FG

Attendance 75,662

USC vs. UCLA 🏈

November 17, 1990—Los Angeles, California

"You're so drained as an announcer and fan, that [you're thinking] 'This is crazy.'"—USC broadcaster Pete Arbogast

THE BACKGROUND

Todd Marinovich and Tommy Maddox.

Marinovich was a sophomore. Maddox, a redshirt freshman. Two highly publicized young quarterbacks. Two "can't miss" pro prospects. Despite all the Maddox-Marinovich hype, the cross-town rival quarterbacks faced off just one time during their brief careers.

It turned into a fabled fourth-quarter shootout at the Rose Bowl between two college cowboys who faded into the sunset far sooner than most people expected.

Neither UCLA nor USC was having a championship season in 1990. The Trojans were 7-2-1 and assured a bid to the John Hancock Bowl on New Year's Eve. Terry Donahue's Bruins, just 5-5, had to beat USC in their final game of the season to keep their slim bowl hopes alive.

On the strength of 157 yards rushing from Mazio Royster and some timely defense, USC held a 24-21 margin entering the fourth quarter. It was perhaps the wildest 15 minutes in the history of the storied rivalry.

The two marching bands played endlessly.

With 12:02 left in the game, USC's Jason Oliver picked off a Maddox pass intended for Reggie Moore at the UCLA 34 and ran it back for the second Trojan interception return for a touchdown in the game. USC led 31-21.

The Trojan fans sang along, "Fight on for old SC, Our men fight on to victory..."

After a dead ball personal foul on the kick-off gave the Bruins great field position at the 'SC 39, Maddox went to work. Four plays later,

he connected with senior flanker Scott Miller, splitting two USC defenders for a 29-yard touchdown. In just 76 seconds, the USC lead was trimmed to 31-28.

Cymbols crashed. Trumpets blared. "We are the sons of Westwood, And we hail the Blue and Gold..."

Three plays later, the Bruins had the ball again.

After the kickoff, Trojan runningback Scott Lockwood fumbled on third down and one. Bruin cornerback Dion Lambert recovered at the 'SC 38.

In seven seconds, the Bruins scored.

Maddox found Miller at the goal line on the next play. He bobbled it in the end zone but held on for the touchdown. "We are the sons of Westwood, And we hail the Blue and Gold..." UCLA took the lead 35-31. Nine minutes and 17 seconds remained.

After an exchange of punts, the Trojans started at the Bruin 47 with 6:31 to play. It was Southern Cal's turn. Marinovich had thrown for just 105 yards passing to this point. He would double that before the game ended.

On third-and-10, Marinovich hit redshirt freshman Johnny Morton on the left sideline for 14 yards. Then at the 21, he found Morton again, who made a leaping catch in the right corner of the end zone. Trojans 38. Bruins 35.

"Fight on for old SC, Our men fight on to victory..."

With 3:09 left, Maddox loaded his holster and shot back. From the UCLA 26, he tossed a

Game 61

Johnny Morton makes the first of two acrobatic TD catches in the waning minutes. Photo courtesy of USC Athletics

bullet to Miller for 29 yards to the 'SC 46. He took a naked bootleg 11 yards, then from the shotgun, hit Reggie Moore at the 10-yard line. Sean LaChapelle caught another Maddox pass at the one-yard line. From there, fullback Kevin Smith got the last yard for the score. Seven plays, 75 yards, in under two minutes. Only 1:19 remained on the clock.

"We are the sons of Westwood, And we hail the Blue and Gold..." The Bruins led again 42-38.

"It was like a *Rocky* movie," said Trojan coach Larry Smith. "Back and forth. Back and forth. One team gets knocked down and then the other gets knocked down."

The band played on. But it was far from over. "It was never over," recalled USC announcer Pete Arbogast. "Nobody could stand up, they were so tired."

Actually, Marinovich was hobbled with a sprained ankle. Morton had re-injured a sepa-rated shoulder, to go along with a torn tendon on his left pinkie finger. The battered Trojans fought on.

Curtis Conway returned the kickoff to the 'SC 25. With 1:13 left to play, trailing by four, Marinovich, the left-handed gunslinger, saddled up for a frantic gallop downfield. Quickly, he faced third-and-10 at the 'SC 28 with 0:44 on the clock. Marinovich spotted Gary Wellman over the middle for 27 yards to the UCLA 45.

Thirty-six seconds left. On the next play, Marinovich hit Wellman again over the middle for 22 more yards to the UCLA 23.

Timeout USC. Just 26 seconds remained.

Marinovich came to the sidelines. "I got tired of hearing that UCLA fight song," he said. "I just wanted to shut them up. I never get tired of our fight song."

That's a good thing because an Associated Press reporter counted the number of times the

USC fight song was played during the game...85.

Marinovich had one more chance to strike up the band.

THE PLAY
CD 1—Track 33—*Pete Arbogast,*
Univ. of Southern California Radio Network

Morton lined up wide left. Cornerback Lambert stood across from him. Lambert knew the ball was coming his way. Morton noticed Lambert playing tight to the line of scrimmage.

"We knew if they were in bump-and-run what play we would use," said Morton. "When I got to the line, I saw the bump-and-run and winked at Todd. That was our sign, a wink."

Marinovich, who must have had superior eyesight to see a wink inside a helmet from across the field, did recognize the coverage. He pointed toward the Bruins' cornerback. "[Lambert] knew it too. He shook his head [as if to say], 'No, you're not going to get it,'" said Marinovich.

Marinovich dropped back. Morton took off. "I was supposed to run an 18-yard comeback [route]," Morton said. "But versus that coverage, we adjusted to a post corner route."

Morton slanted over the middle, then cut to the outside. Lambert got caught off balance. He slipped and fell.

Free safety Michael Williams was left to rescue the Bruins. Williams, forced into duty after saftey Eric Turner hyperextended his left elbow and sat out most of the second half, picked up Morton as he sprinted toward the corner of the end zone.

Linebacker Roman Phifer bore down on Marinovich. "I knew I had to get rid of the ball in a hurry. I got rid of it just in time and got leveled," said Marinovich.

The ball floated into the left corner of the end zone. Williams couldn't catch up with it. "My heart dropped to the pit of my stomach," said Williams. "I felt like I had died."

With Marinovich on the ground, Morton leaped into the air. "I looked up and saw our crowd jump up, saw about 10 players jump on top of me and knew it was good," Marinovich said. "I don't know what happened. I guess he made a great play."

He did. With 16 seconds left. Touchdown USC.

"Fight on for old SC, Our men fight on to victory..."

The Trojans led 45-42. Maddox got one more chance to fire his gun with 11 seconds left on the UCLA 39. He was out of ammunition. A long pass over the middle for Miller fell incomplete, as did a Hail Mary at the buzzer. The Trojans prevailed.

The Bruins were overcome with grief. "To have it taken away hurts worse than anything you can ever explain to anyone," said Maddox.

"From our standpoint, it was a real tragedy to lose the game," said Donahue. His senior wide receiver concurred. "This was the most exciting game, start to end, I've ever been involved in," lamented Miller. "And then to lose, well, it's just too much to deal with."

On the other side of LA, legendary tales were being hatched. "It was the greatest feeling ever," said Morton. "When I got up and saw it was a touchdown. I mean, you dream about catches like that."

Wellman, his fellow receiver, sat next to him. "It will go down as one of the greatest [catches] in school history," he said.

THE AFTERMATH

The 87 total points were the most in the 61-year history of the Los Angeles rivalry. Maddox's performance set a UCLA single-game passing record of 409 yards. He left UCLA after his sophomore year and was the 25th player selected in the 1992 NFL draft, a first-round choice of the Denver Broncos. Broncos coach Dan Reeves nurtured Maddox in the NFL, but he never bloomed. Maddox later followed Reeves to the New York Giants and the Atlanta Falcons, playing the role of back-up quarterback before he was released in 1997.

Maddox then took up a career as an insurance agent for Allstate. In 2000, he resurfaced on the gridiron, playing a season for the New Jersey Red Dogs of the Arena Football League. Then in the spring of 2001, the dawn and dusk of the XFL reignited Maddox's career. He was the fledgling league's one and only MVP. A few months later, Maddox got a call from the Pittsburgh Steelers, and in 2002, at the age of 31,

Game 61

started his first NFL game. He led Pittsburgh into the 2002 playoffs with a 10-5-1 record, and remained the starter until injuring his arm in 2004. The Steelers released Maddox in March 2006.

Marinovich also left college after his sophomore season, but on different terms. He was benched in the fourth quarter of the Trojans' 17-16 Hancock Bowl loss to Michigan State, ending the '90 season. Smith then suspended Marinovich from the USC football team for missing a meeting and failing to register for classes. Nine days later, Marinovich was arrested for possession of cocaine and marijuana. He decided to bypass his final two seasons of eligibility at USC and entered the 1991 NFL draft, the first sophomore quarterback to ever enter the draft (Maddox became the second). Marinovich was the 24th player selected in the first round by the Oakland Raiders. After seven starts and two seasons, Marinovich was released by the Raiders in 1993.

He toiled in the CFL and Arena Football League briefly, but was later arrested multiple times between 1997 and 2005 on drug related charges. The police report of his last arrest listed Marinovich's occupation as "unemployed musician".

November 17, 1990—Los Angeles, California

USC	14	7	3	21	- 45
UCLA	7	7	7	21	- 42

USC	Pace 27 interception return (pass failed)
UCLA	Maddox 9 run (Daluiso kick)
USC	Royster 7 run (Lockwood pass from Marinovich)
UCLA	LaChapelle 47 pass from Maddox (Daluiso kick)
USC	Marinovich 1 run (Rodriguez kick)
USC	FG Rodriguez 20
UCLA	Brown 5 run (Daluiso kick)
USC	Oliver 34 interception return (Rodriguez kick)
UCLA	Miller 29 pass from Maddox (Daluiso kick)
UCLA	Miller 38 pass from Maddox (Daluiso kick)
USC	Morton 21 pass from Marinovich (Rodriguez kick)
UCLA	Smith 1 run (Daluiso kick)
USC	Morton 23 pass from Marinovich (Rodriguez kick)

Attendance 98,088

Colorado vs. Notre Dame 🏈

"Without the flag it was one of the most incredible plays you ever saw."—Lou Holtz

THE BACKGROUND

Call it what you want, but Colorado's 1990 season was either positively magical, fatefully pre-determined, or plain old lucky.

Three times during the regular season, the football gods smiled kindly on the Golden Buffaloes.

They survived a 21-point fourth quarter rally by Tennessee in the season opener when the Volunteers chose to kick an extra point instead of go for two points with two minutes remaining. The game ended in a 31-31 tie.

They scored on a fourth-and-goal one-yard leap by Eric Bienemy with 0:12 left to beat Stanford in Boulder. Whether Bienemy actually broke the plane of the goal line was up for debate. "In my opinion, if we were at home, they don't get that call," said Stanford coach Dennis Green.

They escaped Columbia, Missouri, with a 33-31 victory when Charles Johnson squeezed into the end zone with no time left on a fifth down mistakenly awarded by the officials.

Then, as the season ended, they found one last shiny penny of good fortune in Miami.

Coming into the New Year's night Orange Bowl against Notre Dame, Colorado was 10-1-1, had played the nation's toughest schedule, and was ranked No. 1 in the AP poll.

The Irish had surrendered the top spot in the country to Colorado on November 17th when Penn State's Craig Fayak, following a Darren Perry interception with 59 seconds left, kicked a 34-yard field goal with 0:04 remaining to beat Notre Dame in South Bend, 24-21.

It was a rematch of the 1990 Orange Bowl in which third-ranked Notre Dame ruined No.1 Colorado's undefeated season and national championship hopes by defeating the Buffaloes 21-6. One year later, CU had a second chance. A Colorado win over the fifth-ranked Fighting Irish (9-2), and coach Bill McCartney's Buffaloes would surely be the national champions.

Notre Dame led 6-3 in the second quarter after Ricky Watters scored on a two-yard run. But when Ronnie Bradford blocked Craig Hentrich's extra-point attempt, breaking his school record streak of 73 consecutive extra points, the margin stayed at three.

Things took a turn for the worse for CU when quarterback Darian Hagan went down with a ruptured tendon in his left knee late in the first half.

But in the second half, helped by a defense which forced three Notre Dame turnovers in four plays from scrimmage, Hagan's replacement, Charles Johnson, finally got the Buffalo offense on track.

After a Hentrich field goal made it 9-3, linebacker Paul Rose, playing for an injured Kanavis McGhee, recovered an Irish fumble at the ND 40. Johnson then led the Buffaloes on a 40-yard drive that was capped by a one-yard Bienemy TD run. With 4:26 to play in the third quarter, Colorado led 10-9.

From there, the CU defense took over.

Colorado held Notre Dame without a first down for the rest of the second half, until the

Game 62

Raghib Ismail rockets 91 yards down the right sideline with nothing behind him but a yellow flag. Photo courtesy of Michael and Susan Bennett

Buffaloes had the ball themselves, first down at the ND 27 with 2:15 left in the game. Colorado was primed to put the Irish away and claim the school's first national title.

But then, the Notre Dame defense rose up.

Fullback George Hemingway was stopped for a 2-yard loss on first down. Then Johnson was sacked for another 10-yard loss. On third down, Johnson again was thrown for a loss, this time nine yards and Colorado was facing fourth down at the ND 48.

The Buffaloes ran the clock down to just over a minute to play, then mistakenly took a delay of game penalty, moving the ball back to the CU 47. On fourth-and-36, coach Bill McCartney sent in the punting team. The way Colorado's defense had shut down the Notre Dame attack, realistically, the only Irish threat to score stood waiting outside the Notre Dame goal line.

Raghib "Rocket" Ismail was the Walter Camp Player of the Year in 1990. He finished second in the Heisman Trophy balloting behind BYU's Ty Detmer and had a total of six kick returns for touchdowns in three years at Notre Dame.

The Rocket waited for a punt no one thought he would receive.

THE PLAY
CD 1—Track 34—*Jack Ham,*
Tony Roberts, Westwood One Radio

With 1:05 on the clock, NBC broadcaster Bill Walsh said on television what 77,062 people in the Orange Bowl (author included) were thinking. "I'm sure Rouen will kick it out of bounds," remarked Walsh. "He has to."

Astoundingly, he didn't. "I was worried about getting beat by a field goal," McCartney said. "Rouen has never really been effective at angling the ball out of bounds. I was afraid he might knock it out at the 30 and they could get in field goal range."

So Rouen, the nation's best punter in 1989, kicked the ball high and straight down the middle of the field. Right to the Rocket at the nine-yard line. There was a collective inhale, or was it a gasp?

Ismail took off from the nine. As he crossed the 18-yard line, four Colorado players surrounded him like a quartet of cats cornering a mouse. Somehow, he eluded them all. Ismail danced over two lunges at his feet. He bounced off of a high shot to the body, moved forward to the 25, and freed his leg from a seemingly inescapable ankle trap. It was Houdini with a gold helmet.

Then the engines kicked in. Approaching the 30, Ismail burst into the open. Now being trailed by Colorado's Tim James, the Rocket angled toward the Colorado sideline while teammate Greg Davis ran from behind to help out.

As Ismail crossed the 30-yard line, Davis threw a block at James' right side, trying to knock him off course. James stumbled forward, grazing Ismail's jersey at the 35. An official, running parallel to the play at the 30, did nothing.

Looking forward, one Colorado player remained in Ismail's path. Rouen, the punter.

He had no chance. The Rocket blew past Rouen along the Colorado sideline at the ND 41. Simultaneously, he also passed the last official on the play, standing in front of the Buffaloes' bench like a state trooper on a highway.

As Ismail zoomed by, a yellow penalty marker went flying. It was as if the gust of wind stirred up by the passing speedster blew the flag right out of the official's back pocket.

Notre Dame coach Lou Holtz could only wish that were true.

The Rocket sailed ahead into the end zone, ending the 91-yard journey. It was a stunning feat. Even the timekeeper was astonished as the clock kept running from 0:50 to 0:35.

Irish fans were screaming, Buffalo fans weren't breathing, the Colorado team was pointing...to the flag.

"I was in the end zone when I heard the public address announcer," said Ismail. "I heard the public address announcer say there was a flag on the play. I was just hoping the flag was on them and not on us."

The referee stood at the ND 40. James stood next to him, hands on hips, breathing deeply. The signal was made. Clipping against Notre Dame. A giant Buffalo exhale was heard from Miami to Boulder.

It was perhaps one of the greatest plays in the history of college football that never counted.

"I would have never forgiven myself if the punt had been returned for a touchdown," said McCartney.

Did Davis' block make a difference on the run back? "Tim James had a legitimate chance

to make the tackle on Rocket, or, if not tackle him, slow him down," said McCartney.

"I don't think I clipped him," Davis said. "I'm pretty sure I would have gotten him," countered James.

No one will ever know.

After the penalty was assessed, the clock was reset to 43 seconds, and Notre Dame had the ball at their own 21. Three unsuccessful plays were followed by a 17-yard completion from sophomore QB Rick Mirer to Irv Smith to the ND 38. But only 0:13 remained. With no timeouts left, Mirer threw long over the middle to Smith. Safety Deon Figures picked off the pass, the fifth Irish turnover of the game, and ran out the remaining seconds near midfield.

The state of Colorado celebrated as the Buffaloes, seemingly blessed from above one last time, took home the Orange Bowl trophy, 10-9.

THE AFTERMATH

Years later, Davis discussed the pivotal penalty.

"I did not think it was a clip when it happened. However, when I looked back at the tape, it was a much closer call than I remembered during the game. It could have gone either way and unfortunately it went the other way," he recalled.

He also good-naturedly remembers leaving the stadium that night, suddenly a household name among Irish fans.

"I was thinking that I would just walk out, greet my family and leave before anyone noticed me. My mother and sister didn't really watch football unless I was playing on TV so they did not know all the rules. When I got about five yards away from my sister, she screamed out, 'Hey honey, what did you do?!!!' Of course, I felt those eyes that did not know it was me start looking my way."

Davis, now the answer to a sports trivia question, takes the infamy in stride. "The funny thing is that after the game I knew it was a big play but I never, in my wildest dreams, thought people would still be remembering that play almost 10 years later. I thought in a year or two it would all be forgotten. Everyone remembers the play, but no one remembers my name."

They do now, thanks to his close friends.

"My friends won't let me forget and are quick to tell anyone who doesn't know," he said. This is a typical introduction: "Hey, this is my friend Greg Davis. Do you remember the Orange Bowl game between ND and Colorado? Blah, blah, blah, well, he is the one that clipped."

The day after the game, the votes were tallied and Colorado was crowned the national champion in the writer's Associated Press poll, capping their remarkable season. Georgia Tech (11-0-1), which dismantled Nebraska 45-21 in the Citrus Bowl and finished as the country's only undefeated team, was given the title in the Coaches UPI poll. How close was the coaches voting?

"We lost the UPI poll by one vote," McCartney said. "That's a very fragile thing. If one coach had voted differently, we wouldn't have shared that thing. We lost by one point."

For Raghib "Rocket" Ismail, the famous punt return was the last time he ever touched the ball in a Notre Dame uniform. Unable to get his hands on the ball during ND's final drive, Ismail finished his career at Notre Dame after his junior year, entered professional football in the Canadian Football League with the Toronto Argonauts, then later wound up in the NFL with the Oakland Raiders, Carolina Panthers, and Dallas Cowboys.

Colorado	0	3	7	0	- 10
Notre Dame	0	6	3	0	- 9

CU	Harper 22 FG
ND	Watters 2 run (kick blocked)
ND	Hentrich 24 FG
CU	Bienemy 1 run (Harper kick)

Attendance 77,062

Southwestern Louisiana vs. Central Michigan

"This is like kissing your sister again and again and again."
—*Billy Smith, Central Michigan runningback*

THE BACKGROUND

In 1991, the phrase "fit to be tied" was probably the most tired, worn-out euphemism heard in Mount Pleasant, Michigan, for a long time. In fact, the overused pun should of have been banned when talking about the Central Michigan Chippewas, a team that "accomplished" a feat the equivalent to getting a basketball stuck between the rim and the backboard and not being able to get it down...over and over again.

You see, the '91 Chippewas, appropriately enough, tied the NCAA record for most ties in a season.

It's hard to interpret a 6-1-4 record. It's somewhere between 10-1 and 6-5. For a major Division I-A school, that would be somewhere between the Sugar Bowl and home for the holidays. For Central Michigan fans, it was somewhere between ecstasy and heartache. A feeling usually associated with an on-again-off-again long distance romance. It was one of the most nerve-wracking, thrilling, unfulfilling seasons ever.

CMU opened the season with a 17-17 tie versus Ohio University. Chippewas quarterback Jeff Bender hit Bryan Tice with a four-yard TD pass with no time remaining on the clock and Chuck Selinger kicked the extra point as CMU salvaged the deadlock. It was the perfect appetizer to a season peppered with salty finishes.

Central Michigan (0-0-1) returned the following week to Kelly/Shorts Stadium for their home opener against the Ragin' Cajuns of

Southwestern Louisiana (0-1). USL was supposed to be an early season sparring partner for the Chippewas as they prepared to open up the Mid-American Conference portion of their schedule. "It's good to have a non-conference opponent because it gives us an opportunity to utilize more people," said CMU head coach Herb Deromedi. "In an early conference game, you're not given that luxury."

After USL lost their opener to Northeast Louisiana 21-10, they sure looked like a certain "W" for the homestanding Chippewas. But nothing this season was certain for Central Michigan.

It took a while, but after senior Ken Ealy gathered a handoff on a reverse and jetted 78 yards for a touchdown in the third quarter, the Chippewas led 21-10 and began to look forward to their matchup the following week against 18th-ranked Michigan State.

Naturally, the Ragin' Cajuns took advantage. They sliced the lead to 21-17 at the end of the third quarter on a 23-yard sprint by Damon Denaburg. In the fourth quarter, with just under eight minutes to play, USL took over at their own 11-yard line. Quarterback Tyjuan Hayes then led a drive that must have sent the CMU fans digging for their antacids. Facing third-and-six at the USL 15, Hayes connected for a 23-yard completion to the USL 38. The Cajuns kept moving downfield. A 15-yard pass interference penalty took the ball into CMU territory at the 47.

Then on fourth-and-six from the 43, USL pulled a fake punt, gaining 10 yards and a first down at the 33. The USL drive continued. It carried on for 18 plays. Finally, with only 0:53 left, and the Chippewas fans sick to their stomachs, Hayes sneaked over from the one-yard line. The marathon drive gave USL the lead for the first time in the game, 24-21.

Central Michigan got the ball back at their own 20. Bender, the school's all-time passing leader and Mid-American Conference Player of the Year from the previous season, had to rescue his team from the sinking ship. The Chippewas mastered the art of staying afloat in '91, never quite swimming to shore, but always finding a way to keep their heads above water.

Immediately, they faced fourth-and-three at the CMU 27. Bender tossed a life-preserver to Darian McKinney for six yards and the first down at the 33. But only 15 seconds were left.

The Chippewas, gasping for air, then caught an ocean rush that carried them to the brink of another tie. Bender broke the backs of the USL defense by hitting Ealy for a 55-yard completion to the USL 12-yard line. Only four seconds remained.

Deromedi sent in Sellinger to try a game-tying 29-yard field goal. USL called time-out, giving Sellinger time to think about his kick.

Instead it was the CMU coach who thought things over. Deromedi had a change of heart. Back came Bender. With one play left, the Chippewas were going for the win.

Bender threw to the end zone where senior Bob Kench looked for the ball. Time ran out. Cornerback Craig Roberts swarmed Kench. The pass fell incomplete. A penalty flag fell to the ground.

Pass interference on USL. The ball was moved to the two-yard line. Time had already expired, but there would be one more play.

THE PLAY

Given another reprieve, Deromedi could have sent in Sellinger to kick the tying field goal for a second time and (in hindsight) the Chippewas would have owned the NCAA record for most ties in a season (5). But he didn't.

He went for the win again. "We didn't do it for our fans," said Deromedi. "We did it for our football team."

This time the Chippewas wouldn't just stay afloat. They'd either sink or swim with Bender. The record-setting QB dropped back and threw to seldom used senior L.J. Muddy at the goal line. "The play wasn't going to me," said a surprised Muddy.

But it did. Muddy caught the ball, was hit by two USL defenders at the goal line, then flopped into the end zone. "I tried to avoid the first man, and I stretched the ball to the goal line." Like a long lost castaway reaching dry land. Touchdown Central Michigan.

Final score CMU 27, USL 24. In their typical dramatic fashion, the Chippewas drove 80 yards in nine plays and 53 seconds to capture the win, and avert yet another tie.

THE AFTERMATH

L.J. Muddy, used primarily as a kick returner, never caught another pass the rest of the year at CMU. The winning touchdown grab against USL was also his only career touchdown reception.

The next week , CMU shocked Michigan State 20-3 in one of the school's landmark victories. After that, the Chippewas' stomach-churning season resumed as Sellinger kicked a 26-yard FG with 0:03 left to beat Akron 31-29.

Then came another tie. Selinger hit a 22-yard FG in the waning seconds to tie Toledo 16-16. That kick came after an apparent TD pass from Bender to Ealy was ruled out of bounds. The Chippewas tied Miami (OH) 10-10 and later Eastern Michigan 14-14, prompting running back Billy Smith to comment, "This is like kissing your sister again and again and again."

USL ended up losing the first seven games of the season before finishing with a 2-8-1 record. The school changed its name at the end of the decade to the University of Louisiana-Lafayette.

Southwestern Louisiana	0	10	7	7	- 24
Central Michigan	7	7	7	6	- 27

CMU	Ealy 3 pass from Bender (Sellinger kick)
CMU	White 1 run (Sellinger kick)
USL	Butler 64 pass from Hayes (Cunningham kick)
USL	FG Cunningham 27
CMU	Ealy 78 run (Sellinger kick)
USL	Denaburg 23 run (Cunningham kick)
USL	Hayes 1 run (Cunningham kick)
CMU	Muddy 2 pass from Bender (no attempt)

Attendance 17,116

Tennessee vs. Notre Dame

"I thank my mom for giving me a big butt."—Jeremy Lincoln

THE BACKGROUND

The 300th game played at Notre Dame Stadium. Since it opened in 1930, "The House That Rockne Built" had been the home to numerous "miracle" comebacks by the Fighting Irish. The cliches collected over the years. "The Luck of the Irish," "Touchdown Jesus," and the "ghosts" of Rockne, the Gipper, and the Four Horsemen supposedly swirled around the sidelines at key moments in famous Notre Dame victories.

It would only make sense that all the fabled icons would gather for an anniversary game, right ? Well...

The 13th-ranked Volunteers of Tennessee (5-2) traveled to No. 5 Notre Dame (8-1) for just the second time in the history of the school. A 31-14 loss in 1978 to the Irish in South Bend was the first meeting ever between the two teams who had played just three times before.

The last time being a thrilling 34-29 Notre Dame victory in 1990 at Knoxville when ND's Rod Smith intercepted an Andy Kelly pass in the end zone with 45 seconds left, thwarting a furious Vol rally. Kelly tossed a 23-yard TD pass to Alvin Harper with 1:44 left, then the Vols' Carl Pickens recovered an onside kick and UT marched to the Irish 20 before the final interception preserved the win for the top-ranked Irish.

The following season, Notre Dame blasted the Vols early and often, in a devastating first half for Johnny Majors' mistake-ridden squad. "I was in shock," said the UT coach, trailing 21-0 in the first quarter, after a fumbled punt

by Dale Carter turned into an Irish score, and a Kelly interception was returned 70 yards for a touchdown by ND's Tom Carter.

With the Irish leading 31-7, and just 40 seconds remaining in the first half, ND's Craig Hentrich lined up to kick a 32-yard field goal.

As Hentrich got ready to move the Irish even further ahead, to beat the crowd, the famed Notre Dame spirits shook hands, packed their bags, and took off for an early winter vacation after watching the final home victory of the season for the Irish.

How else do you explain what happened next?

Linebacker Darryl Hardy blocked Hentrich's kick. Cornerback Floyd Miley pulled the ball out of a pile and raced 85 yards for a stunning Tennessee touchdown with 0:14 left to make the score 31-14. Perhaps more significant, Hentrich was hurt. The Irish kicker sprained his knee on the pivotal play and was helped off the field.

The half ended but the game had just begun.

Tennessee's defense simply took over in the second half, slowing Notre Dame's offense to a halt. "They shut down our running game and forced us to pass," said ND quarterback Rick Mirer. "They gave us looks I've never seen before. They changed on every series so we could never adjust." The Irish amassed 233 yards rushing in the first half, but just 82 after that.

Meanwhile, Kelly and the Vols picked apart the Notre Dame defense. Tight end Von Reeves caught a four-yard TD pass midway through the

Jeremy Lincoln sweeps in to block Rob Leonard's kick. Photo courtesy of Michael and Susan Bennett

third quarter to make it 31-21. Freshman tailback Aaron Hayden scored from two yards out to cap a brief 45-yard drive with 9:03 left in the fourth quarter.

The Volunteers had closed the gap to 34-28.

Sandwiched in-between the two UT scores, Hentrich came back to make a short 20-yard field goal. In the process, he realized his knee could take no more. Hentrich headed for the locker room and was done for the day.

Stuck in neutral, Notre Dame's offense then shifted to reverse. A Mirer pass near midfield was picked off by UT's Carter, and with 5:09 left in the game, the Vols had the ball at the ND 45.

Three plays later they struck again. Burning the over-pursuing Irish defense, Kelly hit Hayden on a 26-yard screen pass to shock the home crowd and give the Vols the lead 35-34 with 4:03 remaining.

After the kickoff, Notre Dame took the ball for the fifth and last time in the fourth quarter. The previous four times they couldn't even muster a first down. But then, with 3:57 to play, the Irish began to drive.

Perhaps the legendary ghosts heard the score on the radio and came back.

As if they were writing another magical chapter to the Notre Dame history books, the Irish offense awakened. They methodically gained four first downs, marching the ball down to the UT nine-yard line.

Miley, whose blocked field goal return had triggered the Vol comeback, recognized the seemingly inevitable scenario. "I kept thinking about the Gipper, about all that other mystique stuff you hear about Notre Dame," he said while watching the Irish position themselves for the winning score. "I was saying to myself on the sidelines, 'Damn, we were so close, but we're so far away.'"

Majors declined an ND holding penalty on third down at the UT 9 which would have pushed Notre Dame back 10 yards, but also given the Irish one more shot at the end zone. "I didn't want to give Mirer another pop at us," explained Majors.

Notre Dame faced fourth down and three at the nine. They ran the clock down, calling time-out with four seconds left.

Game 64

THE PLAY

CD 1— Track 35—*John Ward,*
USA Vol Network

Irish coach Lou Holtz had a decision to make. Hentrich, the second most prolific field goal kicker in Notre Dame history, was injured. His replacement would be one of two walk-ons, Rob Leonard or Drew Marsh.

Leonard, a sophomore from Decatur, Georgia, got the call. His career resume included just one extra point. This 27-yard attempt was essentially another PAT. He was ready. "As we got closer to the end zone, I kept picturing myself making the last-second field goal to win the game," he said.

Vols defensive coordinator Larry Lacewell, who had orchestrated his team's second half defensive surge, felt helpless. "I put my head on my hands and said, 'Lord, let somebody miss one of these things once.'" Then he remembered where he was. "But that's unfair . . . He doesn't get involved in football, otherwise we wouldn't have had a chance," added Lacewell.

The ball was on the right hash mark. The snap was slightly low to holder Jim Sexton. This was Leonard's moment to become a Notre Dame legend.

"Right when I hit it, before I looked up, I thought it was good . . . I hit it well," Leonard said. "It's something I've always dreamed about."

The dream turned into a nightmare. Slicing from the right end, senior defensive back Jeremy Lincoln flashed in front of Leonard. In fact, Lincoln got into the Irish backfield so fast that he over ran the play, mistiming his dive.

He flew horizontally past Leonard as the substitute kicker approached the ball.

Leonard booted it...into Lincoln's booty! The ball deflected off of Lincoln's butt. Literally, a kick in the ass to the Notre Dame mystique.

Sliding off course, the ball sailed wide right. Time expired. Tennessee won 35-34. Scratch that chapter in Notre Dame folklore. Add one to Tennessee's.

Volunteers announcer John Ward couldn't believe it. He repeated the words, "It is no good," a half dozen times in the next minute.

"On behalf of all the Protestants in the country, I think we deserved a little help," Lacewell said with a smile.

"They say there's a Notre Dame god," added Vol tackle Shazzon Bradley. "There must be a Tennessee god, too." Yes, somewhere on Mount Rocky Top.

Lincoln gave credit to his mother. "Whenever I go home, my mom teases me about my big butt," he said. "Today, that big butt paid off for us."

Stunned by the turn of events at the end, Holtz was beside himself. "This is the most disappointed I've been in my entire life."

Just the opposite for Tennessee's coach. "The University of Tennessee has not had a more important, or bigger, comeback in our school's history," exclaimed Majors.

THE AFTERMATH

In Knoxville, the game is forever known as "The Miracle at South Bend."

It was a crushing defeat for Notre Dame who had entertained national championship hopes until the Tennessee game. The Irish were blasted the following week at Penn State 35-13, then had to struggle to hold off Hawaii 48-42 in the season finale. Leonard missed a 24-yard field-goal attempt in that game, the only other field goal attempt of his career. He did connect on seven of eight PATs.

Ranked 18th, the Irish accepted a controversial bid, perhaps one they didn't deserve, to play No.3 Florida in the Sugar Bowl. Trailing 16-7 at the half, Holtz turned to his power running game led by Jerome Bettis, Rodney Culver, and Tony Brooks. Notre Dame ran up 32 points in the second half to upset the Gators 39-28.

The Vols rolled on, finishing the season 9-2 with a 45-0 demolition of Vanderbilt. They played sixth-ranked Penn State in the Fiesta Bowl. Leading 17-7 in the third quarter, the wheels came off the Volunteer train as Penn State scored five TDs in just under eight minutes, thanks to three UT turnovers inside their own 30. Despite Tennessee outgaining the Nittany Lions by an amazing 441-226, Penn State won 42-17. Tennessee ended the season ranked 14th in the AP poll while Notre Dame was 13th.

The '91 season established Kelly as the Vols' all-time leading passer at the time, with records in just about every season and career passing category (6,397 career yards, 36 TDs). He was 24-5-2 as a starter.

Tennessee	0	14	7	14	-35
Notre Dame	21	10	3	0	-34

ND	Brooks 12 run (Hentrich kick)
ND	Carter 79 interception return (Hentrich kick)
ND	Mirer 10 run (Hentrich kick)
UT	Fleming 21 pass from Kelly (Becksvoort kick)
ND	FG Hentrich 24
ND	Bettis 2 run (Hentrich kick)
UT	Miley 85 return of blocked field goal (Becksvoort kick)
UT	Reeves 4 pass from Kelly (Becksvoort kick)
ND	FG Hentrich 20
UT	Hayden 4 run (Becksvoort kick)
UT	Hayden 26 pass from Kelly (Becksvoort kick)

Attendance 59,075

Northeast Louisiana vs. Eastern Kentucky

"You should all sneak out of bed early tomorrow. There are several churches around town."—EKU coach Roy Kidd after the game

THE BACKGROUND

Eastern Kentucky's Roy Kidd is a coaching legend in Richmond, Kentucky.

Since becoming head coach in 1964, Kidd's Colonels have had the highest winning percentage in Division I-AA in the 1980s (.781), are in the top 10 schools for the 1990s, and won two national championships (1979, 1982). Kidd is the winningest active Division I-AA coach. But as he approaches his 300th career coaching victory, Kidd may look back on the 1992 game against national power Northeast Louisiana as the most bizarre finish of them all.

The Colonels (1-0), ranked No. 5 in Division I-AA, hadn't lost a home opener since 1962 in Roy Kidd Stadium, but coach Dave Roberts' 10th-ranked NLU Indians (1-1) posed a serious threat as one of the country's top teams. Roberts was returning to the Bluegrass State where he had previously taken Western Kentucky to the I-AA playoffs in 1987 and 1988, only to be knocked out of the championship tournament both years by Kidd's EKU teams.

When EKU's Leon Brown returned the opening kickoff 98 yards for a touchdown, Roberts saw the beginning of a total collapse in his special teams and kicking game. But despite having an extra point blocked, a missed two-point conversion attempt, a botched fake punt attempt, and watching EKU's holder Jason Thomas run in a fake field goal for a touchdown, the Indians still only trailed 20-15 early in the third quarter. Their strong ground game, led by Greg Robinson (23 carries, 140 yards)

and Roosevelt Potts (20 rushes, 75 yards), was complemented by a short passing game from QB Ches Liles to Vincent Brisby (8 receptions, 102 yards) When the Colonels' star running back Markus Thomas (16 carries, 166 yards), who finished his senior season in '92 as the I-AA career rushing leader, left the game with a mild concussion midway through the second half, NLU began to rally.

The Indians' John Brown picked off a Joey Crenshaw pass and returned it 26 yards to the EKU 36. That set up three Robinson runs, the last one, a one-yard TD plunge giving NLU a 21-20 lead with 8:14 left in the game. But again, the Indians' two-point attempt failed.

Eastern's offense responded, but Thomas' replacement, Mike Penman, playing with pulled ligaments in his left hand, fumbled at the NLU 16-yard line and the Indians recovered. After holding NLU, the Colonels had one more chance with 2:28 to play. But Penman fumbled again, this time the first play of the series at midfield, Curtis Harrison recovered for NLU, and the Indians simply needed to run out the clock for the 21-20 victory.

That didn't happen.

Not able to gain a first down and facing a fourth-and-11 at their own 49-yard line, NLU chose to let the clock run down to 0:06 and take a five-yard delay-of-game penalty.

The ball was moved back to the NLU 44.

Northeast coach Dave Roberts called a timeout to decide whether to punt or call a running play in hopes of eating up the final six seconds. "The [players] wanted to run the clock out," he said. But Roberts worried that a quick tackle could give EKU a long field goal attempt at the buzzer.

The Indians decided to punt.

EKU put all 11 players on the line of scrimmage hoping for a block. There were no Colonel players back to return the punt. All punter Chad McCarty needed to do was kick it...anywhere.

Just before the last snap, an offensive lineman jumped, putting the ball five yards further back at the NLU 39.

THE PLAY
CD 1—Track 36—*Webber Hamilton, Greg Stotelmyer*, EKU Radio Network

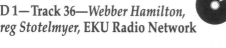

Standing at the 25-yard line, McCarty called for the last snap.

NLU center Chandler Tatum snapped it...over McCarty's head!

In fact, the ball was so far over McCarty's head, it skidded toward the end zone.

"I felt like I was watching a movie," McCarty said. "When I saw the ball come high, I knew my only hope was to pick it up or kick it out [of bounds]. It was going into the end zone pretty quick, and I didn't have much room to work with."

It was a foot race between EKU's Brad Ladd and Sean Little, and the panicked McCarty, to recover the bouncing ball which was perilously close to the end zone. If the ball reached the end zone, EKU would win by safety or touchdown. If McCarty could stop it before the goal line, NLU would win because time would expire.

Out of desperation, McCarty dove for the ball on the one-yard line. Almost simultaneously, Ladd (who had already blocked an extra point and broken up a two-point conversion attempt) pounced on McCarty. The ball squirted free and rolled innocently onto the punter's white towel just beyond the goal line. The clock read 0:00. Then the speedy Little (who runs a 4.45 second 40-yard dash) neatly scooped up the ball and began a wild victory lap with his teammates through the end zone, circling across the field, and over to the sideline, where they were met by the rest of the delirious Colonel players and coaches. EKU 26, NLU 21.

"I couldn't believe it. I was screaming all the way down in the end zone," said EKU defensive tackle Chad Bratzke.

Eastern's radio announcer Greg Stotelmyer recalled the confusion in the press box.

"When I called it first, I saw one of the officials indicate a safety because the ball looked like it may not make the end zone, and then it kind of squirted in the end zone and I thought a Northeast player had covered it up," he said. "The instant that it happened you couldn't believe it, because all they needed to do was down the football. On a fourth down, time was gonna run out, and then the snap went high. Nobody expected it. It was like something made out of a movie. It wouldn't really happen in real life."

It did.

After Stotelmyer's broadcast partner Webber Hamilton spotted the touchdown, Stotelmyer called it, "A gift from high above!"

Bradd Ladd believed. "Right when we had the time out, I kneeled down and I prayed to the Lord. You know, I still had hope," he said.

So did Little. "What really turned me on was how the ball kept rolling. And rolling. He jumped on it, it popped out and I just picked it up. All praises are due to Allah," he said.

"The Lord was with us tonight," said Kidd.

Roberts, however, downplayed the divine intervention.

"All we have to do is get a foot on the ball and we win," he said. "We got what we deserved....I'm sick, and I hurt."

Runningback Potts was more extreme. "I might jump off the plane on the way home," he pondered. "There's nothing else to say."

THE AFTERMATH

Northeast Louisiana did not lose another regular season game. They finished the season 9-2, Southland Conference champions, and ranked No. 1 in Division I-AA, before losing in the I-AA playoffs to Delaware 41-18. Dave Roberts was named Southland Conference Coach of the Year.

EKU finished the season 9-3, ranked 12th, and lost 44-0 to eventual national champion Marshall in the first round of the playoffs.

Game 65

Interestingly enough, a couple years after the wild NLU finish, Coach Kidd started the annual Roy Kidd's Kicking and Longsnapping Academy each summer in Richmond, Kentucky.

"To have a successful football program, you have to have a good kicking game. That's why we stress that at EKU and why we began Kentucky's first-ever kicking instructional school on our campus," said Kidd.

Dave Roberts probably couldn't agree more.

NE Louisiana	12	3	0	6	-21
E. Kentucky	7	7	6	6	-26

EKU	Brown 98 kickoff return (Duffy kick)
NLU	Brisby 8 pass from Liles (kick blocked)
NLU	Brisby 4 pass from Liles (pass failed)
EKU	Thomas 71 run (Duffy kick)
NLU	FG Tallent 35
EKU	Thomas 3 run (run failed)
NLU	Robinson 1 run (pass failed)
EKU	Little fumble recovery (no extra-point attempt)

Attendance 17,200

San Jose State vs. Wyoming 🏈

"If I make it, it's going to be awesome and, if I miss it, I don't think anybody is going to blame me."—San Jose State kicker Joe Nedney

THE BACKGROUND

The altitude in Laramie, Wyoming, is 7,277 feet above sea level.

One week before they hosted San Jose State, the Wyoming Cowboys galloped out of Louisville, Kentucky, with a 26-24 victory and a 2-2 record, when Louisville's sophomore kicker Brandon Brookfield missed a 23-yard field goal with just over a minute left in the game.

The Spartans of San Jose State (2-2) were also having kicking woes. Sophomore Joe Nedney was a paltry 3 of 7 in field-goal attempts for the year and coach Ron Turner decided to pit the inconsistent Nedney against teammate Juan Zumudio in a competition during the week for the starting kicking chores. Even through the warmups before the Wyoming game, they still battled it out until the 6-5 Nedney finally got the nod from the coaching staff to start the game.

Early in the game, Nedney responded to the week-long challenge. He drilled his first field-goal attempt, a 45-yarder in the first quarter, to give the Spartans the early 3-0 lead.

Meanwhile, Wyoming's second-year coach Joe Tiller had personnel problems of his own. Starting quarterback Joe Hughes was having a schizophrenic game for Tiller's team. He brought the Cowboys back from the early deficit with a 52-yard TD pass to junior Ryan Yarborough, and led Wyoming to a 17-3 second-quarter lead. But in the second half, Hughes was picked off twice (three times for

the game), and San Jose crept back into the game on the strength of runningback Nathan DuPree (29 carries, 191 yards).

With the Cowboys still leading 17-12 in the fourth quarter, Hughes committed his fourth turnover, fumbling the ball at the UW 29. During the play, he suffered a deep thigh bruise and was lost for the remainder of the game. The Spartans recovered the fumble and scored soon after on a DuPree two-yard TD run. QB Jeff Garcia rambled in for the two-point conversion and suddenly San Jose State led 20-17 with 6:31 on the clock.

On came Tiller's second-string QB sophomore John Gustin. His third play from scrimmage resulted in another San Jose State interception at the UW 29. That led to Nedney's second FG of the day, from 26 yards out, and the margin was 23-17.

Now, with just 3:14 left in the game and his anemic offense without a second half completion, Tiller threw caution to the wind. Eighty yards away from the goal line, he called in third stringer Scott Jones to quarterback the Cowboys. It was the first time the red-shirt freshman from Anaheim, California, had ever taken a snap in a game. But like a calm senior, the green Jones clicked on his first play, a 20-yard pass to Eric Edmond. Then he hit Edmond again for 10 yards.

The War Memorial Stadium crowd came alive.

Jones drove the Cowboys down the field, and with just 0:34 left, the ball was on the Spartan 15 when the unlikely hero found tight end Matt Swenson wide open over the middle on a delayed screen pass. Swenson scored and dramatically the game was tied at 23-23. The freshman had rallied the Cowboys. Kris Mindlin's successful PAT then gave Wyoming the 24-23 lead.

But San Jose State still had one last chance.

The Spartans took the ball at their own 23 to start the final drive. Garcia quickly found Scott Reese for 23 yards, then escaped on a 12-yard run to the Wyoming 42. Suddenly Jones' heroics were in jeopardy. But the Cowboy defense stopped Garcia on two incompletions and the clock read 0:06.

THE PLAY
CD 1—Track 37—*John Shrader*,
San Jose State University Football Network

Just a reminder. The altitude in Laramie, Wyoming, is 7,277 feet above sea level.

Coach Ron Turner sent Nedney out onto the field. "He had been kicking well. He's got a strong leg and I just thought 'let's give him a chance,'" said Turner.

Tiller called time out. "I didn't think we'd need a lot of luck," he said, remembering his good fortunes from the previous week. "The guy's 2 for 10 and he's trying from 60 yards."

Actually Nedney's stats were slightly better than that. But his longest field-goal was from 49 yards. This would be from 60 yards.

Tiller called another time out. "If a 60-yard field goal has got to beat you every week, I'd like to step to the plate and take my shots at that every week," noted the Cowboy coach.

Nedney stood on the field talking to himself. "Look how high you're up," he thought. "I'm at 7,200 feet, the wind's blowing my direction. I got everything going for me."

For the third time in a row, Tiller called time out.

"The first one was understandable," said Nedney, referring to the timeouts. "The second one was okay, but the third one was just funny. I was giggling."

Finally, with Tiller out of timeouts, center Mike Gardner snapped the ball. It bounced to holder Garcia. The quarterback scooped it up,

placed it on the grass, and the left-footed Nedney smacked it.

It sailed through the thin Wyoming air.

"It was true, straight as an arrow. No hook. No nothing," said Nedney. It was also good. Time expired. A new Big West Conference record, a new San Jose State record, and a 26-24 victory for the Spartans over Wyoming.

"I feel great. I feel wonderful. I don't think I could feel any better than this right now," said Nedney after a delirious Spartan celebration.

Tiller was rather blunt about the result. "It came down to a 60-yard field goal, and he kicked it."

THE AFTERMATH

Two weeks later, Nedney kicked a 32-yard FG with 0:06 left to beat California. He missed just one field goal attempt the remainder of the year, ending up 14 of 19 in FG attempts, and was named first team All-Big West Conference. The 60-yard kick against Wyoming was, at the time, the second longest field goal on a natural surface without a tee in NCAA history. San Jose State finished the '92 season at 7-4.

Wyoming ended the season 5-7. The next year, coach Joe Tiller led his Cowboys to the WAC championship and a birth in the Copper Bowl. After taking his team to a 10-2 record in 1996, Tiller was selected as one of six finalists for the Paul "Bear" Bryant Coach of the Year Award and one of 10 finalists for the Football News National Coach of the Year. He then left Wyoming and took the head coaching job at Purdue in 1997.

San Jose State	3	2	7	14	-26
Wyoming	7	10	0	7	-24

SJS	Nedney FG 45
WY	Yarborough 52 pass from Hughes (Mindlin kick)
WY	Mindlin FG 33
WY	Driver 1 run (Mindlin kick)
SJS	Safety, O'Connell blocked punt out of end zone
SJS	DuPree 9 run (Nedney kick)
SJS	DuPree 3 run (Garcia run)
SJS	Nedney FG 26
WY	Swenson 15 pass from Jones (Mindlin kick)
SJS	Nedney FG 60

Attendance 15,543

Appalachian State vs. James Madison

"Wow! It hadn't worked all week in practice."—Craig Styron

THE BACKGROUND

Parents' Weekend at Bridgeforth Stadium on the James Madison University campus. The Dukes of JMU were 3-2 in coach Rip Scherer's second season. The year before, in 1991, Scherer had turned around the JMU program, leading the Dukes to a 9-4 record and quarterfinal finish in the I-AA playoffs. Despite losing to Virginia Tech and Richmond at the outset of the '92 season, the high-powered Dukes had an impressive 52-49 win over defending national champion Youngstown State.

Coach Jerry Moore's Appalachian State Mountaineers had made the I-AA playoffs in two of Moore's first three seasons in Boone, North Carolina. But ASU struggled out of the gate in '92, averaging just 14 points per game with a 1-3 record.

Continuing the momentum of their three-game winning streak, James Madison built a late 21-7 lead after quarterback Eriq Williams scored on his second TD run of the game, this one from three yards out, with 7:58 to play in the fourth quarter.

ASU senior quarterback D.J. Campbell tried to rally the Mountaineers when he hit Anthony Smith on a fourth-and-21 TD pass with 3:02 left to play. After missing the two-point conversion, ASU trailed 21-13. But on the next JMU possession, back-up tailback Charles Bankins, who entered the game in the fourth quarter for injured starter Kenny Sims, fumbled a Williams pitch on the option play. ASU's Kevin Sikorski pounced on it and the Mountaineers had the ball at the JMU 37.

On the first play, Campbell found Smith again. This time, a 37-yard TD pass with 2:30 remaining. Junior Craig Styron then caught the two-point conversion pass over safety Robert Smart just inside the goal line to tie the game 21-21.

In 32 seconds, JMU's 14-point bulge had been erased.

But Scherer's Dukes, starting from their own 20, methodically marched downfield to set up an apparent winning score. With under a minute to play and the ball at the ASU 29, David McCloud caught a 12-yard pass from Williams, moving the ball to the ASU 17-yard line. Forty-nine seconds remained.

But on first down, instead of playing conservatively to set up a game-winning field goal, Williams tried to throw an ill-fated out-pass to the sidelines. ASU defensive lineman Avery Hall tipped the pass straight up in the air where a group of players waited for it to come down. Linebacker Tony Davis wrestled the ball away in the crowd for the interception.

The Dukes' gamble had misfired. "We had passed our way down there," said Scherer. "We were trying to get down as close as we possibly can."

Appalachian State now had the ball on their own 18-yard line with 39 seconds and one timeout left. The game was still tied at 21-21.

Campbell rolled left and hit Smith on the sidelines for eight yards to the 26. His second pass was incomplete, stopping the clock with 0:26 left. On third down, Willie McClean took a handoff on a draw play and burst up the middle for 18 yards to the 44, getting out of bounds with 0:19 on the clock. ASU used their final timeout.

On first down, Campbell scrambled, then took off down the right sideline. Crossing midfield, he ran out of bounds with just 0:08 left at the JMU 44. A quick pass to Styron fell incomplete. With only 0:05 remaining, ASU's Moore had a choice to make.

"Is Tom Dempsey in the house?" joked ASU broadcaster Steve Brown. Mountaineer kicker Jay Millson was, but he wasn't coming onto the field to attempt what would have been a 61-yard attempt. Instead, Moore left Campbell in for one final play.

THE PLAY
CD 1—Track 38—*Brian Estridge,*
Steve Brown, **Appalachian Sports Network**

"Right Heavy Victory." It was a play that ASU practiced all week. Receivers Smith, Styron, and Ray Gama lined up wide right. Campbell dropped back to pass. He let it fly toward the end zone. Time ran out. "It was your basic Hail Mary. Throw it up and pray," said Campbell.

"We have a tipper, and Ray and myself are on each side of the goalpost," said Styron, whose stepfather Rob Best was the ASU offensive coordinator and designed the play. "We're supposed to get about five yards deep in the end zone and look for a deflection."

Campbell overthrew all of his receivers.

The ball came down in a crowd of three James Madison defenders who jumped for it. Styron, the first receiver to arrive, threw his body into the mix late. "I jumped into the pile, back-first with the idea that, 'What the heck, maybe I can make something happen,'" he said. The ball was tipped up, but Styron fell down, smacked flat on his back in the middle of the end zone by a fourth JMU defender.

A fifth JMU defensive player flew into the end zone, grasping the floating ball. Instantaneously, ASU's Gama hit him in the back.

"The next thing I knew I was lying on the ground and I looked up in time to see Ray knock it away from one of their guys," said Styron.

The ball fell. Everyone was face down.

Styron was face up. It bounced off a JMU player.

Then...."It landed in my chest, I guess," said a flabbergasted Styron. "I just knew it was in my chest, and they kept trying to strip me." He held on desperately as the JMU defenders scratched and clawed for the ball.

"I said please just let the officials hurry up and get there because I don't know how much longer I can hold onto the football." A few seconds seemed like a few seasons. On the Appalachian Sports Network broadcast, Brian Estridge's voice cracked like a choir boy hitting puberty. "It's caught!" he screamed.

Smith stood over Styron in shock. Anxiously stuttering his feet up and down, he looked for an official to confirm what he saw. Finally, a call was made. Touchdown Appalachian State.

The JMU defenders were beside themselves. "He was lying there and the ball just went in his hands," said strong safety Pat Carrey. "He was on the damn ground," added free safety Chris Parrott.

The play's success was just as shocking to Styron. "To tell you the truth, [in practice] it has not worked yet," he said. Moore was also surprised. "We got it picked [intercepted] every time."

For the first time, the play was successful. By scoring 20 points in the final 3:02, Appalachian State had won 27-21.

A happy ASU linebacker Rico Mack recognized his team's good fortune. "Somebody wanted us to win," he noted, running off the field into the locker room.

THE AFTERMATH

Years later, Styron, now a high school football coach in North Carolina, still recalls the wild finish with affection. "You can't describe it. It's something I'll remember forever." So will his wife, who was dating another student at the time, but often tells the story of hearing Styron's catch over the airwaves, jumping for joy, and then a few years later, marrying the wide receiver.

The amazing Mountaineer rally carried over to the rest of the season as ASU won six of their

Game 67

last seven regular-season games, including a 37-34 upset victory on the road versus Marshall. In that game, Campbell again rallied his team with a nine-yard TD pass to Gama with just eight seconds remaining to defeat the Thundering Herd. It was Marshall's last defeat of the season, as they went on to win the I-AA national championship, beating Youngstown State 31-28 in the title game. Appalachian State lost their first round I-AA playoff game to Middle Tennessee State 35-10.

James Madison only managed one more victory the rest of the season, finishing 4-7. However, Scherer returned the Dukes to the I-AA playoffs in 1994, reaching the quarterfinals for the second time in his four-year tenure, before losing to Marshall 28-21 in OT. He left JMU at the end of the season to take the head coaching position at the University of Memphis in Division I-A. In 1996, Scherer notched the greatest victory in Memphis history by upsetting sixth-ranked Tennessee, 21-17.

Appalachian State	0	7	0	20	-27
James Madison	0	7	7	7	-21

JMU	Thurman 14 run (Weis kick)
ASU	Hooks 20 run (Milson kick)
JMU	Williams 2 run (Weis kick)
JMU	Williams 3 run (Weis kick)
ASU	A. Smith 21 pass from Campbell (pass failed)
ASU	A. Smith 37 pass from Campbell (Styron pass from Campbell)
ASU	Styron 44 pass from Campbell (no attempt)

Attendance 14,000

Maryland vs. Duke

"The one in a million happened."
—Andy Geiger, Maryland Athletic Director

THE BACKGROUND

In 1989, Duke coach Steve Spurrier led the Blue Devils to a share of the ACC title, their first in 27 years. Spurrier then moved on to coach Florida in 1990 while assistant coach Barry Wilson took over the reins in Durham.

Wilson's teams struggled to an 8-13-1 record in his first two years, a lowly 2-12 within the conference. In '92, the Blue Devils were 2-4 (0-3 in the ACC), seeking their first conference victory against equally awful Maryland (1-6, 0-4).

Like Duke, the Terrapins were searching for answers under new head coach Mark Duffner, who had lost more games in half a season at Maryland than he did in his previous six years at Holy Cross (60-5-1). The Terps led the entire conference in total offense averaging 466.5 yards/game. They were first in passing offense with 329.8 yards/game. But unfortunately for Duffner, they were also last in total defense (474.2 yards/game), last in rushing defense (204.4 yards/game) and last in scoring defense (33 points/game). Duke was just one notch ahead of them, sharing the basement of the ACC with the Terps in each category.

So two terrible teams played each other. Big deal. How exciting could that be?

Just remember that this was homecoming at Duke. And if you've read carefully throughout the book, you've noticed that for some reason, homecoming games produce miraculous finishes.

So read on.

The Blue Devils scored on their first three possessions of the game. Two Randy Gardner field goals and a seven-yard burst by Randy Cuthbert gave Duke a 13-7 lead. But with 5:14 remaining in the half, on third-and-13 from midfield, Maryland quarterback John Kaleo launched a soaring pass that floated down to wide receiver Marcus Badgett at the four-yard line. Badgett took it into the end zone and Maryland took a 14-13 lead.

The Terps struck again before halftime, quickly driving 75 yards in two minutes as Kaleo connected on seven straight passes. Frank Wycheck capped the drive with a four-yard TD run with 0:39 left. Maryland led 21-13 at the half.

That's the way it stood entering the fourth quarter when Duke grabbed a handful of momentum that multiplied into a bushel full. Quarterback Steve Prince marched the Blue Devils 80 yards and Cuthbert scored on a one-yard TD run with 12:53 to play in the game, pulling Duke to within 21-19.

As Duke rallied, Maryland came apart at the seams.

Kaleo was intercepted at the Duke 24, and Prince immediately took the Blue Devils 76 yards downfield for the go-ahead touchdown. Cuthbert's third TD run of the game put Duke back on top 25-21 with 6:45 to play in the game.

The fourth-quarter nightmare continued for the Terps. Duffner's offense again moved the ball to the Duke 29. But Scott Berdan intercepted another Kaleo pass at the 21-yard line,

Game 68

October 24, 1992—Durham, North Carolina

returned it 15 yards to the 36, and the Blue Devils seemed to have the game in hand with 3:48 left.

For the sixth time in eight games, Maryland had blown a fourth-quarter lead.

After forcing Duke into a fourth-and-one situation with 1:50 remaining, the Terps blew another chance, jumping offsides, and giving the Blue Devils a first down.

But as much as Maryland tried to hand the game to Duke, the Blue Devils just wouldn't take it. After all, neither team knew how to win an ACC game.

Leading by four, but unable to gain a first down again, Duke's Tim Davis punted from the Blue Devils 46 to the Maryland 8. Richie Harris returned it three yards to the 11 with 24 seconds left.

Out of timeouts, the Terps took possession. Duffner, a tireless optimist, exhorted his run-and-shoot troops as they lined up. "Keep on believing!" he yelled to his offense.

After Kaleo threw incomplete to Wade Inge on first down, and defensive back Jamal Ellis nearly intercepted the Maryland quarterback on second down, no one in Wallace Wade Stadium believed the Terps could travel 89 yards with only 13 seconds left.

No one except Duffner, who had witnessed his 1988 Holy Cross squad score on a wild 70-yard kickoff return with no time remaining to beat Princeton.

With nothing left but chance, on third down, Kaleo threw a Hail Mary pass towards Badgett down the right sideline. The ball was tipped into the air. It somehow came down to Badgett, who bobbled the pigskin in his hands, then grasped control, falling out of bounds at the Duke 38 with 0:04 on the clock.

Badgett's remarkable 51-yard reception, his eighth catch of the game, sent both teams running downfield to set up for one final play.

THE PLAY

"When you have just four seconds left on the clock you really don't have any plays—you just tell everybody to run deep and just try to make something happen," said Kaleo.

Actually, Maryland did practice a last-sec-ond play each Thursday. Badgett was supposed to line up on the left, run down the middle, and tip Kaleo's pass to a teammate. But in the confusion as their offense scrambled to put one final play together, Badgett lined up on the wrong side of the field.

Thirty-eight yards away from a score, Kaleo took the snap. He drifted back, looked for Badgett, then waited.

"I held it as long as I could to give Marcus a chance to get into the end zone and I just threw it as high as I could, and as far as I could, because a high ball is a better ball to judge," said Kaleo.

He took a hit from a Duke defender and fell to the turf. Time ran out. Meanwhile, the ball still hadn't come down.

"I'll tell you, the ball looked like it went up and touched the clouds. It looked so small, and I was just waiting for it to come down," said Badgett. As the ball finally fell toward the ground, cornerback Ellis, defending on the play, slipped just as Badgett jumped.

With four Duke players in the vicinity, the 6-1, 185 lb. Badgett soared above them all, grasping the winning 38-yard touchdown pass. "I just jumped as high as I could and I came down with it," he said.

His coach may have jumped higher.

"I had about a 40-inch vertical leap, my watch fell off and I just tried to squeeze every white jersey until it popped," said Duffner.

Maryland 27, Duke 25. Homecoming spoiled in Durham. Wilson was beside himself, with a simple explanation of the stunning finish. "I don't think we had enough guys going for the football."

"This is something you practice when you're younger," said a much more cheerful Kaleo. "But for it to actually happen, I don't know if I can get a better feeling than this...This is a dream come true."

THE AFTERMATH

Badgett caught nine passes for 218 yards in the game (89 yards on the last two plays). After collecting 75 catches for 1,240 yards on the year, both Maryland records and tops in the ACC, he was named all-ACC first team wide receiver. Badgett finished seventh in the country in receptions and second in receiving yards.

Duke's Randy Cuthbert , who scored three TDs in the game, became the only Duke runningback to ever rush for 1,000 yards twice in a career. He ended the season as the second leading rusher in Duke history with 2,771 career yards, just behind all-time Duke rusher Steve Jones (2,951 yards from 1970-72). The Blue Devils lost their remaining four games and finished 2-9 on the year (0-8 in the ACC).

Barry Wilson lasted just one more year at Duke, resigning at the end of a 3-8 campaign in 1993. In four years as head coach of the Blue Devils, he compiled a 13-30-1 record.

After losing their next two games, Maryland beat Clemson 53-23 for their only other conference victory, ending the season 2-6 in the ACC, 3-8 overall. While at Maryland, Mark Duffner never approached the level of success he enjoyed previously at Holy Cross. After a 20-35 record in five seasons, Duffner was fired as Maryland's head coach. He later moved on to the NFL as linebackers coach for the Cincinnati Bengals.

Maryland	7	14	0	6	- 27
Duke	6	7	0	12	- 25

DUKE   FG Gardner 29
MARY   Burnett 8 run (DeArmas kick)
DUKE   FG Gardner 43
DUKE   Cuthbert 7 run (Gardner kick)
MARY   Badgett 50 pass from Kaleo
       (DeArmas kick)
MARY   Wycheck 4 run (DeArmas kick)
DUKE   Cuthbert 1 run (run failed)
DUKE   Cuthbert 2 run (pass failed)
MARY   Badgett 37 pass (kick failed)

Northwestern vs. Illinois

"I'm 20 and I'm a man. But I felt like crying."
—*Robert Crumpton, Illinois defensive back*

THE BACKGROUND

Gary Barnett and Lou Tepper shared the same office as fellow assistant coaches under Bill McCartney at Colorado from 1982-87. Tepper was the Buffaloes defensive coordinator while Barnett was an offensive assistant coach.

In 1992, both of them were head coaches for the first time. Tepper was directing an Illinois squad (3-3) in their homecoming game against intra-state rival Northwestern, headed by Barnett, who had taken on the unenviable task of resurrecting the dead in Evanston, Illinois. The Wildcats were in the midst of their 21st consecutive losing season. From 1989-91, they were 5-28 in France Peay's last three years as coach. In fact, the previous three coaches in Evanston were 24-127-3.

So far in 1992, the Wildcats had lost five of the first six games.

Northwestern was generally considered one of the worst football programs in Division I-A. Their offense ranked last in the Big Ten. So did their defense. They had a knack of being an annual homecoming date for many schools. Actually, three times in '92.

"It's hard to be everyone's homecoming game," said receiver Chris Gamble. However, despite entering the Illinois homecoming with a 1-5 record, the Wildcats did spoil Purdue's festivities with a 28-14 victory to gain their only win of the year.

"The Purdue game got me mad. The fourth game of the season, and they schedule homecoming just because it's us," lamented Gamble.

On the other side of the field, Illinois was seeking revenge. One year prior in 1991, the 17th-ranked Illini were stunned by the lowly Wildcats 17-11 on a dark, rainy day in Dyche Stadium to take back the Sweet Sioux Tomahawk Trophy, given to the winning team in the annual battle. It was the first time Northwestern had beaten a ranked team in 20 years.

"We were shocked, and we were surprised," Illinois fullback Darren Boyer said. "We expected to go up there and dominate." In '92, Illinois vowed revenge. "This is the most important game of the year for us," said defensive lineman Erik Foggey.

The Illini took charge.

Illinois led 19-6 when sophomore running-back Kevin Jackson burst through the Wildcats defense for a 47-yard gain down to the NU four-yard line. Boyer scored from there and Illinois had a commanding 26-6 lead with three minutes left in the third quarter.

But then the tables turned. Northwestern, a team that averaged just 11 points a game, began to move the ball on Tepper's defense. After Illinois, led by Dana Howard and Kevin Hardy, sacked quarterback Len Williams four times in the first half, Barnett's offense made adjustments and the Illini switched to a zone defense.

Williams zoned in.

"All of a sudden Len Williams just started connecting on every pass, and most of them to Chris Gamble," said Wildcat announcer Dave Eanet.

Gamble, a junior from Marietta, Georgia,

Lee Gissendaner's spectacular catch capped the remarkable Northwestern comeback. Photo courtesy of John Freidah/ courtesy of Northwestern University

had never caught more than one pass in a game. By the end of the day, he would have 10 for 146 yards.

Williams, a mediocre 12-21 for 114 yards up until the fourth quarter, suddenly was on fire. He hit his next 11 of 13 for 128 yards. "I felt nothing could go wrong," said the senior quarterback. "It felt like I was somewhere else. I felt like I was the best quarterback in the nation," he said.

Williams hit Gamble on a 31-yard scoring play, capping an 80-yard drive with 13:35 to play in the game. The lead was 26-13.

After linebacker Hugh Williams sacked Illini quarterback Jason Verduzco for a 21-yard loss forcing a punt, the Wildcats got the ball back on their own 35.

"Northwestern completely abandoned the run," noted Eanet.

Instead, Barnett decided to ride the arm of Williams, which had suddenly turned from aluminum to gold. He moved the 'Cats to the Illinois five-yard line where he faced a third-and-goal. This time he found standout receiver Lee Gissendaner, who made a leaping catch for the touchdown with 4:53 left. The Illinois lead was now 26-20.

After the kickoff, the Illini needed two first downs to run out the clock. They couldn't get one.

On third-and-one Jackson took a handoff on the same play he broke for 47 yards earlier in the third quarter. This time he got nothing. Tackle Frank Boudreux stopped Jackson for no gain and the Illini were forced to punt.

Williams got the ball back on his own 32 with 3:23 on the clock. He hit Gamble twice for nine and 21 yards. Then with NU at the Illini 32, Williams tried Gamble again down the left sideline toward the end zone. Defensive back

Game 69

Rod Boykin, who had just replaced injured starter Filmel Johnson was called for interference and the ball was moved to the Illini 17 with 1:16 to play. On a quarterback draw, Williams sprinted for eight yards to the nine. Gissendaner made another acrobatic catch at the four-yard line for a first down with 0:35 left.

The Wildcats scrambled.

With one timeout left, Northwestern rushed to the line of scrimmage. Williams looked for Gamble in the left corner of the end zone, but the high throw fell incomplete as Gamble was tightly covered by sophomore defensive back Robert Crumpton. Eighteen seconds remained.

THE PLAY

CD 1–Track 39—*Dave Eanet,*
WBBM Radio and Northwestern University

Tepper's defense decided to pressure Williams, hoping to force Northwestern into a mistake. Gissendaner lined up wide left, then went in motion to the right. Williams took the snap and sprinted out to the right, directly in line with an untouched blitzing Illinois defender.

But tailback Dennis Lundy stepped up with a last second, crushing block to save Williams, who skirted around the end. Williams quickly looked to Gissendaner, who was running parallel to him with Crumpton desperately chasing behind.

With a confident toss, Williams led Gissendaner high and to the outside. "I had in my mind, if I touch it, I'm not going to drop it," said Gissendaner. Fully extended, he dove sideways for the ball looking like Superman in flight. The "N" on his helmet turned into an "S."

"I couldn't believe he could get up that high," Barnett said.

The leaping Gissendaner snared the pass, fell to the ground, then immediately sprung up with arms high and wide and ran crossways through the end zone with his jubilant teammates trailing in a mini-victory parade.

Touchdown Northwestern. The score was tied with 0:13 left. Kicker Brian Leahy came on and booted the decisive extra point.

"Who would've believed this!" shouted Eanet. "This is the most incredible thing we have ever seen."

Yes, Northwestern, the perennial doormat of the Big Ten, had overcome a 20-point fourth quarter deficit to lead 27-26.

Illinois returned the ensuing kickoff to their 45 with 0:05 left before Verduzco's last gasp pass fell incomplete to end the game. The disgruntled Illinois crowd, embarassed by another loss to Northwestern, booed loudly while the Wildcats celebrated on their own.

"Everybody in that stadium was stunned," said Eanet.

Crumpton was crushed.

"To have the last score scored on you," he wondered. "I'll try to hold my head up a little. I know my mom's going to love me and my father's going to love me."

Tepper was also dismayed. "I don't know that I've been hurt as much by a loss as we were today," he said.

Williams was elated. "Last year, some people thought our win was a fluke, that the rain made it hard for Verduzco to pass," he said.

"This one showed we can play and win—and we did!"

THE AFTERMATH

The magnitude of the win stuck with the Wildcats' head coach. "We pulled out a couple of games in the past [at Colorado]," said Barnett, "but they were never away, where crowd noise was such a factor. And none of them seemed as important as this one does right now."

Perhaps there were purple seeds of success planted below the Astroturf in Champaign that day. Barnett's program at Northwestern took a wild, almost fairy tale-like turn during the next few years. The Wildcats rose from Big Ten toad to conference prince during the next four seasons, winning the conference championship outright in 1995, then sharing the title with Ohio State in '96 after a series of close victories (Michigan 17-16, Minnesota 26-24, Wisconsin 34-30). Northwestern was 15-1 in the Big Ten during those two seasons.

"In '96, Northwestern won all those games in the closing seconds. We started calling them the 'Cardiac Cats'. But [the '92 Illinois win] was really the first hint of that [future success]," said Eanet.

After the 1998 season, Barnett left Northwestern to become the new head coach at Colorado.

The Illini bounced back to finish the '92 regular season 6-4-1 with three conference wins and a 22-22 tie vs. Michigan, which earned them a spot in the Holiday Bowl against Hawaii. The Rainbows, however, beat Illinois 27-17.

Unrelated to the '92 game, both Chris Gamble and Dennis Lundy were part of a major gambling scandal at Northwestern involving the 1994 season. Among other things, Lundy admitted to fumbling on purpose in a '94 game against Iowa to ensure the Hawkeyes would cover the point spread.

Northwestern	3	0	3	21	-27
Illinois	6	13	7	0	-26

NU	FG Leahy 46
ILL	Verduzco 2 run (kick blocked)
ILL	FG Richardson 25
ILL	Jackson 8 run (Richardson kick)
ILL	FG Richardson 37
NU	FG Leahy 35
ILL	Boyer 4 run (Richardson kick)
NU	Gamble 31 pass from Williams (Leahy kick)
NU	Gissendaner 5 pass from Williams (Leahy kick)
NU	Gissendaner 4 pass from Williams (Leahy kick)

Attendance 52,332

Virginia Tech vs. Rutgers

"If you're a college football fan and you didn't enjoy that game, you need to go to another sport someplace."—Doug Graber

THE BACKGROUND

Brian Fortay was in his first season at Rutgers since transferring from the University of Miami after two years as a back-up QB.

Fortay felt he should have been the Hurricanes' starting quarterback.

In fact, he said coach Dennis Erickson promised it to him. Fortay was so sure, that upon his transfer, he filed a $10 million lawsuit against Miami claiming Erickson reneged on his commitment.

In 1992, Fortay became the starting quarterback for the Rutgers Scarlet Knights.

He led the Knights (4-3) into their homecoming matchup against Virginia Tech (2-4-1) on Halloween day. For the native of East Brunswick, it was also his own personal homecoming in his first year back home in New Jersey.

It turned out to be one of the worst games of Fortay's career. It was also perhaps the best game of his career. You decide.

On the first snap from scrimmage, Fortay was sacked and fumbled the ball. Virginia Tech's P.J. Preston recovered. The Hokies immediately converted the turnover into seven points on a one-yard run by Mark Poindexter.

The game then got wacky. Tech led 21-7 after Tony Kennedy scored on a three-yard run with 51 seconds left in the first quarter. On the next play from scrimmage, Fortay was picked off by Ken Brown who ran it back 18 yards for another Tech TD. Fourteen points in seven seconds and the Hokies led 28-7.

Eighteen seconds after that, Rutgers tailback Craig Mitter ran 66 yards for a TD on the next play from scrimmage. Tech 28, Rutgers 13, still in the first quarter.

From there, it was a shootout. Fortay threw another interception and was yanked by coach Doug Graber in favor of freshman Ray Lucas. Then Fortay would return, throw an interception and get benched. Then return. Then get benched.

Fortay threw four interceptions, three TD passes, and was replaced by Lucas three times in the game. Meanwhile, Tech's sophomore QB Maurice DeShazo was having a career day. He hooked up with future Green Bay Packer Antonio Freeman for a 49-yard TD, to make it 42-23 Tech in the third quarter.

DeShazo threw for a personal best 302 yards. Fortay would return to throw for more. After Lucas injured his ribs in the third quarter, Fortay returned for good.

He brought the Knights back to trail 49-44 with under three minutes left in the game. When Tech's Poindexter was stopped short by the Rutgers defense on a fourth-and-one with 2:36 left, the Knights had the ball at their own 45.

Then nine seconds later, Fortay threw interception number five. Safety Kirk Alexander picked it off near midfield and it looked like the Hokies had the wild affair wrapped up.

But using all of their timeouts, Rutgers forced a Hokie punt and took over with 1:32 left on the RU 22. Fortay, playing a Jeckyl & Hyde game, came back on the field with one more chance.

231

Rutgers Stadium erupts after the Scarlet Knights score with no time left. Photo courtesy of Rutgers Sports Media Relations

He started the final drive as Dr. Jeckyl, stumbling over his own lineman's foot before dumping the ball to runningback Bruce Presley who barely got back to the line of scrimmage. The clock kept running.

Then Fortay found Jim Guarantano who stepped out of bounds after only a six-yard gain with 1:01 remaining. Now facing third-and-four at the RU 28, Fortay scrambled. Finding no one downfield, he desperately flung an outlet pass to Presley who began retreating to the 18 as he tried to outrun a Tech linebacker. Finally turning the corner, Presley got a crushing block from Eddie Walker, and was able to weave his way up to the 36 for a first down. Still, the clock was down to 0:48.

Fortay then threw a meaningless three-yard pass to Mario Henry who was immediately wrapped up by Tech's Ken Brown. The clock dwindled to 23 seconds. At the drive's current turtle pace, the Knights would need four more minutes on the clock to score.

From the RU 39, Fortay finally threw long down the sideline for Guarantano. Three Hokie defenders converged. The ball was tipped by

Tech's Tyrone Drakeford and P.J. Preston, who along with safety Alexander, dove for the floating ball, only to watch a game-ending sixth interception of Fortay slip through their hands.

At 0:14, Tech called their final timeout. As Fortay huddled with his coaches, apparently someone on the Rutgers' bench summoned Mr. Hyde to replace Dr. Jeckyl on the overcast Halloween afternoon. Fortay came back on the field a changed man.

On third-and-seven from the RU 39, Rutgers spread four receivers across the field. Fortay took the snap out of the shotgun and threw a perfect high floating bomb to sophomore Mario Henry at the Tech 15. Henry, with a 40-inch vertical leap, out-jumped the defenders and gathered in the 46-yard completion with just 0:07 left.

Suddenly, Rutgers had hope. The clock stopped to move the chains. Fortay rushed his teammates downfield to line up. The chains got tangled along the Tech sideline forcing a further delay. Once the clock was restarted, Fortay spiked the ball to stop it with 0:05 remaining.

THE PLAY
CD 1—Track 40
Pat Scanlon and Bob Casciola,
New Jersey Network

From the Tech 15, Fortay's last play from scrimmage would be dramatically different than his first.

Guarantano, Henry, and Chris Brantley (who already had three TDs on the day) lined up wide right. Fortay was in the shotgun. No one lined up in front of Brantley, the middle receiver. Finally, safety Alexander drifted over, seven yards off the line of scrimmage.

Fortay took the snap. Guarantano broke to the inside, while Brantley faked inside and went outside. "It was a post-corner route, same as I'd run on a couple of the other touchdowns earlier in the game," said Brantley. " I faked inside, the defender went inside, I think, then I broke outside and that's the last I saw of him."

Alexander tried to catch up with Brantley as he ran to the right corner of the end zone. Fortay lofted it high. Drakeford, seeing Alexander beaten, sprinted over to try and stop Brantley. He dove. Brantley looked over his right shoulder. Drakeford was too late.

"I just ran to the corner and Bryan made a great throw, right on my numbers," said Brantley. "When I came out and saw the coverage, when I saw there was nobody near me except one guy about 10 or 12 yards away, I knew I'd have a clear shot to the corner."

Just as the clock hit 0:00, the ball simultaneously fell into Brantley's hands. He grabbed the picture perfect toss in his arms, fell into the end zone, then did a somersault out of bounds. The Rutgers receiver jumped up holding the ball at his waist, launched it skyward with both hands, then thrust his arms high like a gymnast finishing a dismount.

The Jersey judges gave Brantley a perfect 10. A Rutgers touchdown. After throwing for 338 yards, tossing five interceptions, and losing a fumble, Fortay had amazingly rallied the Scarlet Knights to an improbable 50-49 victory.

"I didn't see the ball, I didn't see the catch, I didn't see the official. All I saw was the crowd," Fortay said. "It was like it was in slow-motion. First there was no reaction, then all of a sudden everyone was up and cheering and going crazy."

Actually they were on the field, mobbing the team which was mobbing Brantley. "I think I established a new record for vertical jump for myself," laughed Graber who whimsically predicted the final score before the game. "On Tuesday night, at the end of practice, I was a little bit upset. But I meant it and I said, 'I don't care what it's going to take,' but I gave them the score of 50-49. That's the God's truth."

THE AFTERMATH

Brantley's catch was his fourth TD of the game, setting a Rutgers school record for touchdown receptions in a game.

Rutgers was brought down to earth the following week when Cincinnati knocked off the Scarlet Knights 26-24, as Brian Whitlow booted a 34-yard field goal with 0:17 left in the game for the victory.

However, the Knights bounced back to win their final two games of the season, 13-9 over West Virginia and 35-10 versus Temple, to finish the season at 7-4. Fortay set a Rutgers season record in '92 with 16 TD passes. It was Doug Graber's best season as head coach. But after a 4-7 slate in 1995, his sixth season with the Knights, Graber was fired with a 29-36-1 record and replaced by Terry Shea.

Ironically, after graduating and playing in the World League of American Football, Fortay, viewed as a traitor by many fans in south Florida, was signed by the Miami Hooters Arena Football team in 1995. A year later, Fortay and the University of Miami settled their longstanding differences out of court.

For Tech, bad things got worse as the Hokies slid downhill the remainder of the season, losing their final three contests to end the season 2-8-1. That's where the Hokies bottomed out. Coach Frank Beamer then turned the program around, leading Virginia Tech to five straight bowl appearances from 1993-97.

In '93 they were the country's most improved football team, turning in a 9-3 record and Independence Bowl victory over Indiana 45-20.

October 31, 1992—Piscataway, New Jersey

Rutgers	13	10	7	20	- 50
Virginia Tech	28	7	7	7	- 49

VT	Poindexter 1 run (Williams kick)
RU	Brantley 22 pass from Fortay (Benestad kick)
VT	Hebron 1 run (Williams kick)
VT	Kennedy 3 run (Williams kick)
VT	Brown 18 interception return (Williams kick)
RU	Mitter 66 run (kick failed)
RU	Bratley 26 pass from Fortay (Benestad kick)
RU	Benestad 37 FG
VT	Campbell 48 pass from DeShazo (Williams kick)
VT	Freeman 49 pass from DeShazo (Williams kick)
RU	Brantley 3 pass from Lucas (Benestad kick)
RU	Mitter 1 run (Benestad kick)
VT	Poindexter 5 run (Williams kick)
RU	Evina 7 pass from Fortay (Benestad kick)
RU	Brantley 15 pass from Fortay (no attempt)

Attendance 28,432

Penn State vs. Notre Dame

"Let's put it this way, Reggie Brooks is not the first guy I would throw to."—Lou Holtz

THE BACKGROUND

It was the end to a great series. Penn State would join the Big Ten in 1993 and leave behind a growing rivalry with Notre Dame that, while short in numbers (only 17 games were played between the two schools), was long on memorable finishes, mostly in favor of the Nittany Lions.

Four times, the game had come down to the final minute. Four times, Penn State had won. In 1983, Penn State rallied to score with 0:19 left in Happy Valley to beat Notre Dame 34-30. In 1986, the first matchup between Joe Paterno's Lions and Lou Holtz' Fighting Irish, third-ranked Penn State prevailed with a fourth-quarter goal line stand to win 24-19 on their way to the national championship. In 1987, Pete Curkendall tackled Tony Rice on a two-point conversion attempt with 31 seconds to play as the seventh-ranked Irish were upset 21-20 in Beaver Stadium. In 1990, top-ranked Notre Dame was toppled by Penn State 24-21 after Darren Perry intercepted a Rick Mirer pass with 59 seconds left, setting up Craig Fayak's 34-yard field goal with 0:04 on the clock to win it for the Lions.

Entering the series finale, Penn State held a slim 8-7-1 margin in victories. But Notre Dame had never won a game decided by fewer than seven points.

This would be their last chance. The Irish (7-1-1) were ranked No.7. Penn State (6-3) was No. 23. The weather was first in everyone's minds.

Official Tom Ransom remembered the weather conditions well. "It snowed so hard at one point in time, I could hardly see the Notre Dame sideline on the other side of the field. You knew the ball was some place, but you didn't know for sure what was going on."

After a first half of frequent snow squalls, the flurries subsided in the second half with Notre Dame leading 9-6 on the strength of three Craig Hentrich field goals.

But then in the fourth quarter, Penn State threatened to take control. Quarterback Kerry Collins connected with Troy Drayton for a 22-yard completion down to the ND one-yard line.

On first-and-goal from the one, running-back Richie Anderson tried the center of the line. He was met short of the goal line by middle linebacker Demetrius DuBose. Then Anderson lost two on his second attempt to score. Collins threw a third-down incompletion out of the back of the end zone, leaving the Lions with fourth-and-goal.

Midway through the final stanza, Notre Dame's successful goal line stand forced Penn State to settle for a V.J Muscillo field goal. The game was tied 9-9 with 8:35 left.

A minute later, the Lions got the ball right back. Stretching for a first down after a completion, Irish tight end Irv Smith fumbled at the ND 44 with 7:11 remaining. Penn State recovered and capitalized. With 4:25 on the clock, Brian O'Neal broke free up the middle for a 13-yard TD run. Penn State led 16-9. With a defense that had shut down Notre Dame's

With the snow falling in the fourth quarter, ND's Demetrius DuBose stops Richie Anderson at the one-yard line. Photo courtesy of Michael and Susan Bennett

November 14, 1992—Notre Dame, Indiana

high-powered offense (averaging 40.1 points per game) without a touchdown all day, the Lions were primed for the upset.

Notre Dame had time for one last drive, and the senior backfield of quarterback Rick Mirer, and runningbacks Jerome Bettis and Reggie Brooks had one final chance to win their last home game in Notre Dame Stadium.

Starting at their own 36 with 4:19 on the clock, Mirer hit Bettis on a second-down screen pass for a 21-yard gain to the Penn State 43. Bettis injured his ankle on the play but later returned. After being sacked by Rich MacKenzie, Mirer rolled left, then reversed field and scrambled right for a 15-yard gain to the Penn State 32 with 2:42 left. Later, on a third-down play, he hit Ray Griggs for a 17-yard completion across the middle. Notre Dame was at the Penn State 21, at the end of the field where the slick wet snow still remained.

Brooks ran for five yards. Then Mirer scrambled again. He slid out of bounds at the nine-yard line with 1:14 to go. First-and-goal, and Penn State stiffened. Brooks ran for the left corner but was tripped at the four by Phil Yeboah-Kotie. Mirer was stopped at the three on an option play. The clock kept running down to 0:30. Mirer's third-down pass to Brooks was underthrown and incomplete.

Only 25 seconds left. Fourth-and-three, Notre Dame trailed by seven. The Irish used their last timeout. They were down to one final play.

Mirer dropped back looking for Smith. He was covered. Bettis was supposed to wait in the backfield to block, then break out over the middle if Mirer yelled "Go."

"He says it so many times in practice," Bettis said, "it became second nature, when to stay and when to go." Without hearing his quarterback, Bettis left on his own around the left side of the line, then over the middle. As soon as he got to the goal line, Mirer's pass met him there. Touchdown Notre Dame. With 0:20 left, the score was 16-15.

Holtz, who was criticized for conservatively playing for a 17-17 tie in the first home game of the '92 season versus Michigan, decided to go for two in the last home game against Penn State.

THE PLAY

CD 2—Track 1—*Tony Roberts,* *Tom Pagna,* **Westwood One Radio**

Three receivers lined up to the left. Lake Dawson and Adrian Jarrell were wide, while

Brooks was in the slot. Bettis set up wide right. No one was in the backfield.

Mirer faded back. He looked for Dawson. He faded back some more. He looked for Jarrell. He faded back some more. He looked for the tight end Smith. He drifted further. He looked for Bettis. He rolled right. Mirer was at the 16-yard line still looking as the Penn State defense finally caught up to him, forcing a decision.

Brooks, meanwhile, broke from the left side of the field all the way over to the right side of the snow-covered end zone. Weaving through linebackers and cornerbacks, he suddenly broke open, running toward the sideline.

"I don't think Rick saw me until the last minute," said Brooks.

Maybe Mirer didn't want to throw it to him. Brooks had caught just one pass his entire career at Notre Dame.

"We've run that play 100 times, but I'd never gotten to the point where I had to look for Reggie," said Mirer.

This time he had no choice. He had to throw the ball. Mirer lofted it up high, leading Brooks to the corner. With arms fully extended, the senior runningback made an acrobatic horizontal leap for the ball.

Official David Witvoet had to make the call. "All I remember thinking was 'Either drop it, or hang onto it please.' Don't make it one of these little bobble things that I've got to decide whether or not you really caught it or didn't catch it," he said, recalling the play years later.

The ball hit Brooks' fingertips. He bobbled it momentarily, then grasped it with outstretched hands as he fell to the ground. "There wasn't any doubt that he hung onto it," said Witvoet, who signaled the score. In breathtaking fashion, Notre Dame had rallied to lead 17-16.

Amid the snow and slop, there was mayhem on the field. Fans joined in the players' celebration in the south end zone, mobbing Brooks. Notre Dame was penalized for unsportsmanlike conduct and forced to kickoff from their own 20. It could have been a crucial penalty. It ended up being a moot one.

Penn State returned the ensuing squib kickoff to midfield with 0:15 left, but three Kerry Collins incompletions down the right sideline ended the game.

Notre Dame had finally beaten Penn State with their own dramatic ending. "You really couldn't write a better script," said Mirer.

"It's probably as fine a comeback as I've ever seen by a football team," said Holtz. "I've never had a team drive the length of the field to score to win in the last minute of the game and have to make two and do it. So this one was a new one for me."

As it was for Notre Dame over Penn State.

THE AFTERMATH

The Irish finished the season 10-1-1 and ranked No.4 in the AP poll after defeating USC 31-23, then Texas A&M 28-3 in the Cotton Bowl. The victory over Penn State was part of a 17-game Irish winning streak that ended suddenly in the final home game of the '93 season when the top-ranked Irish were stunned at home by Boston College, 41-39.

Penn State rebounded from the heartbreaking loss by pummeling rival Pittsburgh 57-13, but then lost to Stanford 24-3 in the Blockbuster Bowl to end the season 7-5, ranked No.24. The Lions debuted in the Big Ten in '93, finishing 6-2 in the conference. They captured their first Big Ten title in '94, beat Oregon 38-20 in the Rose Bowl, finished the season undefeated at 12-0, but were voted second in the polls to eventual national champion Nebraska.

On a sad note, Irish co-captain Demetrius DuBose, triumphantly carried off the field on the shoulders of the Notre Dame student body after the win over Penn State, his last game at Notre Dame Stadium, was shot and killed in San Diego during the summer of 1999 during a confrontation with police.

November 14, 1992—Notre Dame, Indiana

Penn State	6	0	0	10	-16
Notre Dame	3	3	3	8	-17

ND	Hentrich 26 FG
PS	Anderson 1 run (kick blocked)
ND	Hentrich 31 FG
ND	Hentrich 37 FG
PS	Muscillo 22 FG
PS	O'Neal 13 run (Muscillo kick)
ND	Bettis 4 pass from Mirer
	(Brooks pass from Mirer)

Attendance 59,075

Mississippi State vs. Mississippi

"I guess we're blessed."—Cassius Ware, Ole Miss linebacker

THE BACKGROUND

The Battle of the Golden Egg, or simply The Egg Bowl.

The annual season-ending state of Mississippi grudge match between the Bulldogs of Starkville and the Rebels of Oxford. For the first time since 1972, the Rebels played host to MSU at Vaught-Hemingway Stadium on the Ole Miss campus.

Between 1973 and 1990, the game was played in Jackson, MS, until '91 when it returned to the respective campuses and Mississippi State won 24-9 in Starkville. The following year, the entire city of Oxford was waiting for the Bulldogs and second-year coach Jackie Sherrill. Both teams shared identical 7-3 records, but MSU was ranked 16th while Ole Miss was rated 24th.

In the first half, Ole Miss played the role of gracious host, turning the ball over six times in the first 30 minutes of play. Fortunately for coach Billy Brewer's squad, MSU fumbled three times themselves, unable to take full advantage of the Rebel miscues in the chilly 32 degree weather.

Still, the Bulldogs held a 10-7 lead at the half.

The third quarter was a battle for field position with Ole Miss gaining the edge, repeatedly pinning MSU deep in their own territory, and finally cashing in with 2:00 left in the quarter. Senior tailback Cory Philpot capped a brief 40-yard drive with a seven-yard TD run and Ole Miss took the lead 14-10.

Brian Lee's 22-yard field goal gave Ole Miss a 17-10 edge with 10:50 remaining in the game.

With 5:47 to play, State had the ball at the Ole Miss 41 poised for one last drive. Throughout the game, the Rebels' defensive front had manhandled the more heralded State offensive line. The Bulldogs, averaging 204 yards rushing per game, were held to just 39 yards on 41 carries.

So coach Jackie Sherrill switched quarterbacks, and inserted junior backup Todd Jordan to try and pass the Bulldogs to a victory. Jordan moved the ball through the air. In eight plays, MSU was at the Ole Miss 6.

Then with, under three minutes remaining, Jordan threw for the end zone. His pass was picked off by Rebels free safety Michael Lowery, who then made a big mistake and tried to run the ball out of the end zone.

"I knew I was in the end zone, but when I looked down, my momentum had already taken me out," said Lowery. Instead of taking the touchback, he ran the ball out, only making it back to the Rebel three-yard line. Still, with only 2:27 left and a seven-point lead, the home crowd began celebrating.

But then, two plays later, disaster struck for Ole Miss. Philpot, needing just six yards to surpass the 1,000-yard mark for the season... fumbled.

For the fifth time in the game, the Rebels coughed up the ball, and for the fifth time a Bulldog recovered it. This time it was safety Franki Luster. Once again, the Bulldogs were sitting pretty inside the Rebels 10-yard line. This time at the eight with 1:49 on the clock.

Without a running attack, Jordan went to the air again. But two incompletions and a sack by linebacker DeWayne Collier, and the Bulldogs were forced into one last fourth-down attempt.

Jordan dropped back and threw for Olanda Truitt in the end zone.

Incomplete. But a flag. Safety Tony Collier was penalized for pass interference. The ball was placed at the Rebels two-yard line. For the third time in the final three minutes, State had four shots to score inside the Rebel 10-yard line. This time, right at the doorstep of the goal line with under one minute to go.

Sherrill decided to run the option. He sent in starting QB Greg Plump, hampered by a sprained left shoulder, to replace Jordan. On first down, halfback Randy Brown was stopped at the one. 54 seconds left. On second down, Plump faked the handoff to fullback Michael Davis and pitched to Brown. Rebels tackle Chad Brown read the play perfectly. "I saw the guard getting ready to pull, and I knew what the play was going to be," he said. The 6-7 senior then stuck the Bulldogs halfback for a three-yard loss.

Suddenly it was third down from the four. The Rebels defense had withstood nine plays inside the 10-yard line. After a timeout, Plump ran a bootleg to the right. But safety Johnny Dixon threw him for a two-yard loss back to the six.

Ten plays inside the 10. No touchdown. The Bulldogs were now truly down to their last chance.

THE PLAY
CD 2—Track 2
David Kellum, Lyman Hellums,
Ole Miss Radio Network

The Bulldogs running attack was futile. It was apparent that Plump had to try and throw for the score. Sherrill and offensive coordinator Watson Brown called "Read," a quick slant pattern designed for receiver Willie Harris.

Plump took the snap. Harris cut over the middle in front of cornerback Lance Whiteside. For a moment he was open. Plump released the ball.

"I didn't see the ball from the release," said Harris. "I saw it about middle ways. I tried to adjust to it. I was hoping he'd lead me inside."

He didn't. Being pressured by the Rebels line, Plump threw it slightly behind Harris. The Bulldogs' receiver reached back and got both hands on the ball. But he couldn't hold on. It fell incomplete.

With 0:19 left, the Rebels took over, downed the ball once and the game was over. Ole Miss had stopped MSU an astounding 11 times inside the 10-yard line to win the Golden Egg, 17-10.

It will forever be known in Oxford as "The Stand."

Ole Miss quarterback Russ Shows, who stood helplessly on the sidelines exhorting the Rebels' defense, was beside himself. "This was one of the most intense, greatest games ever played at Ole Miss," he said. "I saw fans throwing people in the aisles. I saw one goal post come down. This is the best."

Rebels defensive coordinator Joe Lee Dunn, in his first year at Ole Miss, was a proud man. "I told these guys when I got here I didn't come here to have a good defense, I came here to have a great defense. And they probably played great today," said Dunn.

Probably? Definitely.

THE AFTERMATH

Dunn's defense continued their dominating ways by shutting out Air Force 13-0 in the Liberty Bowl to end the season. It was the Falcons' first shutout in 150 games. Ole Miss, a pre-season pick to finish last in the SEC Western Division, ended up 16th in the nation, with a 9-3 record and second to national champion Alabama in the SEC West.

Mississippi State ended the season with a 21-17 loss to North Carolina in the Peach Bowl. The Bulldogs had a 14-0 halftime lead that could've been 28-0, but two Plump touchdown passes (82 and 21 yards) to Olanda Truitt were called back because of holding. The Tar Heels rallied in the second half to hand MSU a third consecutive loss, ending their season at 7-5. MSU finished 23rd in the final AP poll, making Sherrill just the seventh collegiate head coach

November 28, 1992—Oxford, Mississippi

One-eleventh of "The Stand," Ole Miss' Chad Brown tackles MSU's Randy Brown for a three-yard loss as quarterback Greg Plump looks on. Photo courtesy of Bruce Newman

ever to take three different schools (MSU, Texas A&M, and Pittsburgh) to year-end national rankings.

Mississippi State	0	10	0	0	-10
Ole Miss	0	7	7	3	-17

MSU	Davis 7 run (Gardner kick)
MSU	FG Gardner 22
UM	Courtney 7 pass from Shows (Lee kick)
UM	Philpot 7 run (Lee kick)
UM	FG Lee 22

Attendance 41,500

South Carolina vs. Georgia

"Taneyhill is Dead."—a marquee in Athens, Georgia, the day before the game

THE BACKGROUND

Midway through the 1992 season, the South Carolina Gamecocks were pathetic, 0-5, ranked 103rd out of 106 Division I-A teams, with an offense averaging a paltry 7.8 points per game in their first season as a member of the SEC.

The players revolted, demanding the resignation of coach Sparky Woods. Standing firm, Woods remained, but he made one key maneuver, installing freshman Steve Taneyhill as the new Gamecock quarterback.

The cocky, brash Taneyhill picked up the Gamecocks. He slung them over his shoulder, carrying South Carolina to four consecutive victories. In his first game, Taneyhill led the Gamecocks to a stunning 21-6 upset of 15th-ranked Mississippi State. Two weeks later they shocked No.16 Tennessee, 24-23. They finished the season 5-6 by defeating rival Clemson 24-13. The players believed again. Hopes were higher than high for the '93 season.

"I'm not like anybody else, and I don't try to be like anyone else," commented Taneyhill, known for his long ponytailed hair, and celebratory home run baseball swing everytime he threw a touchdown pass. When the Gamecocks traveled, Taneyhill typically drew the ire of the hometown crowd because of his on-field antics and unstoppable mouth.

Ray Goff's Georgia Bulldogs were fresh off their best season (10-2) in a decade, finishing No.8 in the final 1992 AP poll. They entered their '93 home opener between the hedges ranked No.14, with a backfield loaded with talent in junior quarterback Eric Zeier and junior tailback Terrell Davis. On the other hand, they were missing two key offensive stars from the previous year in Garrison Hearst and Andre Hastings, both gone to the NFL.

Talent aside, the Bulldogs made mistakes in the first game of the season. Lots of mistakes.

Late in the first quarter, Zeier fumbled the ball after being hit by South Carolina's Stacy Evans. On the next play Taneyhill connected with freshman Corey Bridges for a 41-yard touchdown pass. Then, toward the end of the second quarter, a Gamecock punt bounced off of Georgia's Charles Pledger and was recovered by USC. Freshman Reed Morton converted the turnover into a 33-yard field goal as time expired in the first half. Georgia trailed 10-7 at intermission.

It got worse for Goff. On the first play from scrimmage of the third quarter, Davis fumbled at the UGA 32. Two plays later, USC's Brandon Bennett ran from the 26 to the five-yard line where he lost the ball, only to have wide receiver Toby Cates recover in the end zone for a 17-7 Gamecocks lead.

Nothing was going right for Georgia. They had two field-goal attempts blocked and missed a third. "Never in my wildest dreams did I think we'd get two field goals blocked," said Goff. "Sometimes your wildest dreams come true."

Just ask Steve Taneyhill.

After Zeier rallied the 'Dogs with 211 second-half yards through the air, and two fourth-quarter touchdowns, Georgia had a 21-17 lead. But with three minutes left, they punted from their own 14 to the USC 45.

With 2:52 on the clock, Tanneyhill took over, tantalizing the Sanford Stadium crowd with a series of key completions. He found tight end Mathew Campbell for nine yards on third-and-seven at the 48. On second-and-17 at the 50, he flipped a short pass to fullback Stanley Pritchett that turned into a huge 35-yard gain down to the UGA 15. Facing third-and-10 with the clock now under a minute, he hit his other tight end Boomer Foster for 13 yards down to the two-yard line.

Thirty-six seconds were left. After Georgia jumped offsides, the ball was moved to the one and a half.

Taneyhill took the snap and gave it to power back Brandon Bennett. He dived. He didn't make it .

The Gamecocks had no timeouts remaining—21 seconds and the clock was running.

THE PLAY
CD 2—Track 3
Bob Fulton, Tommy Suggs,
Gamecock Sports Network

The Gamecocks furiously tried to unpile and run another play. "I looked up at the clock and there were 10 seconds left," Taneyhill said.

Georgia had seen this scenario before. The previous season against Auburn, with 19 seconds left, Auburn was at the UGA one-yard line, trailing 14-10. With no timeouts left, Auburn's Stan White tried to handoff to tailback James Bostic, but the ball fell to the ground. Bostic pounced on the bungled handoff just outside the goal line. The Georgia players fell on Bostic. They wouldn't get up. The clock ran down. The officials wouldn't stop it. It ran out. Auburn never got another play off. Georgia won 14-10.

"We don't coach our guys to jump right up so they can line up and run another play," said Goff after that game.

A year later Georgia was in no hurry either. But this time, the Gamecocks were able to pry themselves away from the pile. They lined up.

The Bulldogs were forced to get set on defense. "Same play, same play," yelled Taneyhill

to his teammates. South Carolina just wanted to get a play, any play, off before the clock ran out.

"Their guys knew what we were doing," said USC center Vincent Dinkins. "They were coming at us, and we were coming at them." The clock was down to five seconds and Sanford Stadium was in a panic. "I just yelled go and hit Vincent Dinkins in the butt," said Taneyhill.

He got the snap. The 205 lb. Bennett got the ball. He leaped over his left guard James Dexter. He wasn't quite over. Then Bennett made a desperation twist to the right. Did he make it?

The signal came. Touchdown South Carolina. Just 0:02 on the scoreboard. South Carolina 23, Georgia 21.

"Everybody was so intense," said Bennett of the final drive. "They knew we were going to win."

No one knew more than the never shy Taneyhill who taunted the stunned crowd on the sideline. "Fourth quarter baby!" he yelled to the stands as he was being pelted with programs and paper cups. "I knew that on that last drive everyone in the stadium except for the 10,000 South Carolina fans wanted me to do bad," Taneyhill said.

Taneyhill did gain the respect of Georgia linebacker Mitch Davis. "He's not a quarterback who has all the ability in the world, but he wins football games," said Davis, who sacked Taneyhill twice only to have the Gamecock quarterback get up and tell him, "we still weren't going to win the football game."

It was Taneyhill's first last-second march in a Gamecock uniform. "I did it in high school. The last six games, I did it five times," said the Altoona, Pennsylvania, native. "It's nothing new to me."

The 23-21 loss was crushing in Athens. Bulldog play-by-play announcer Larry Munson, never one to understate the drama of a game, told his listeners that they may be in for "a dying, gasping, struggling season."

Goff tried to downplay the upset loss. "We've only played one game," he said the week after the game. "It would be easy to sit back and jump off a cliff. But I'm not ready to slit my throat yet."

Game 73

THE AFTERMATH

Georgia did fall off the cliff the following week with a 38-6 thrashing at the hands of Tennessee. Munson was right. It was a tough season in Athens as the Bulldogs finished 5-6. Goff, who undertook the unenviable task of following Vince Dooley as head coach in 1989, was fired two years later at the end of the 1995 season after seven years and a 46-34-1 record.

Taneyhill came back to Columbia after the Georgia win, and was promptly arrested at a student apartment the following night and charged with possession of alcohol by a minor. Essentially, he had a beer in his hand at a fraternity party. Taneyhill was sentenced to 30 hours of community service. He started the next week against Arkansas.

The Gamecocks got bumped up to No.19 in the polls before Taneyhill's magic ran out, as South Carolina lost to Arkansas 18-17. They finished 4-7 after losing the final three games of the season to Tennessee, Florida, and Clemson. (A 17-6 loss to Alabama was later deemed a victory by forfeit because the Tide used an ineligible player. So the official South Carolina record stood at 5-6.)

Sparky Woods was fired at the end of the season after five years in Columbia. He then moved around the ranks as offensive coordinator at Memphis, Virginia, then Mississippi State.

Taneyhill ended his college career by shattering school passing records his senior season in 1995 with 261-of-389 passes (67.1 percent) for 3,094 yards, 29 TDs, and just nine interceptions. He held the record for most completions in a SEC game with 39, and led South Carolina to their first-ever bowl victory, a 24-21 win over West Virginia in the 1995 Carquest Bowl. Despite his impressive numbers, Taneyhill was left undrafted by the NFL. He tried to hook onto the Jacksonville Jaguars as a free agent but was released. Taneyhill then spent a season playing for the Frankfurt Galaxy of the World League in 1997, followed by a brief two-week stint with the New York City Hawks of the Arena Football League. In 1998, he returned to the state of South Carolina as a high school football coach at Cambridge Academy in Greenwood, South Carolina.

South Carolina	7	3	7	6	- 23
Georgia	0	7	0	14	- 21

SC	Bridges 41 pass from Taneyhill (Morton kick)
UGA	Hunter 14 pass from Zeier (Parkman kick)
SC	FG Morton 33
SC	Cates recovered fumble in end zone (Morton kick)
UGA	Zeier 22 run (Parkman kick)
UGA	Harvey 8 run (Parkman kick)
SC	Bennett 1 run (run failed)

Attendance 84,912

September 4, 1993—Athens, Georgia

245

Florida vs. Kentucky 🏈

"It's sort of amazing how it happened."—*Steve Spurrier*

THE BACKGROUND

Since Steve Spurrier arrived in Gainesville in 1990 as head coach, the Florida Gators had never lost to an unranked team. Spurrier reignited the Florida football program, putting the Gators back in the top 10 in both '91 (No. 7) and '92 (No. 10). Entering their '93 SEC opener with unranked Kentucky (1-0), the seventh-ranked Gators (1-0) were looking forward to playing fifth-ranked Tennessee the following week in Gainesville. They played like it too.

Redshirt junior QB Terry Dean, who waited three years for his chance behind starter Shane Matthews, was Florida's starting quarterback against Bill Curry's Wildcats, who had lost five straight games to end the '92 season. Dean completed his first three passes of the game to extend his streak of consecutive completions to 14 in a row over the first two games (second best in school history behind Spurrier himself with 16).

But then the wrong players started catching Dean's passes.

Dean threw four interceptions in less than three quarters while the Gators fell behind. Spurrier's patience with his starter shriveled up and Dean was replaced by freshman Danny Wuerffel once in the second quarter (which lasted long enough for Wuerffel to throw an interception of his own), and then for good late in the third quarter with UK up 17-9.

The 'Cats were spurred on by a 70-yard TD run straight through the middle by true freshman Mo Williams with less than two minutes gone in the second half.

With 10 minutes left in the game, the 19-year-old Wuerffel, playing in only his second game, took the Gators from their own 12 and marched them downfield. He hit junior Chris Doering on three big completions, 26 yards, 17 yards, and then a touchdown grab of 19 yards with 7:36 left. Doering, who walked on to the team in 1991 after not being recruited, was starting his first game after earning a scholarship in '93.

Now trailing 17-15, Wuerffel connected with Willie Jackson, who squeezed into the end zone on the two-point conversion to tie the game at 17-17.

Then, when the Gators regained possession with 5:57 left, Wuerffel lost it.

He was picked off by UK, their sixth interception of the game. But the Florida defense held and the Gators got the ball back with three minutes remaining. Again, Wuerffel threw an interception, number seven on the day, this time at the UF 15-yard line. Combined with Florida's 127 yards in penalties, as compared to UK's 15, it was a wonder the game was tied.

It wasn't for long. The Gator defense, which kept their team in the game all evening long, held UK to a Juha Leonoff 25-yard field goal and Kentucky led 20-17.

"Kentucky completely outplayed us, outcoached us, outhustled us," Spurrier said.

Florida had one last chance when Harrison Houston took the ensuing kickoff to the UF 42 with 1:14 remaining to play. Playing with the consistency of the freshman that he was, Wuerffel, with three interceptions under his belt, suddenly regained his stroke. He found tailback Errict Rhett for nine yards, then Jack Jackson for nine yards with 0:36 to play at the UK 40. Rhett caught another 12-yarder to move the ball to the UK 28 and Florida took their final timeout with 0:17 on the clock.

On first down, Wuerrfel looked to Jackson down the right sideline. But free safety John Hall knocked the ball away. With 13 seconds left, Wuerffel found Doering over the middle. He was bumped by a UK linebacker and, fortunately for Florida, dropped the ball short of the goal line. Without a timeout, time may have expired without the Gators running another play.

Eight seconds remained with the ball still at the UK 28.

THE PLAY
CD 2—Track 4
Mick Hubert, Lee McGriff,
Florida Gator Radio Network

Free safety John Hall was a sophomore cornerback playing safety for the first time in place of injured starter Melvin Johnson. Johnson's normal backup, Salim Shahid, was not with the team due to personal reasons.

Hall's partner in the defensive backfield, strong safety Marcus Jenkins, already had three interceptions on the day for Kentucky. So it wasn't a mystery where Spurrier was going to go with the Gators' last shot at victory.

Spurrier sent two receivers to the left, Jenkins' side of the field. He sent two to the right, Hall's side. Jackson was wide right, Doering was in the right slot. Jackson was covered by a cornerback, Doering by a linebacker. As the ball was snapped, Jackson broke down the sideline, while Doering broke over the middle. Hall had a decision to make. "They kind of put me in a bind," said Hall. "They threw to the sidelines once before, and I broke on the ball and almost had an interception," he said remembering the incompletion to Jackson only seconds previously. "So I kind of cheated over there."

As Jackson got double coverage, Doering

found himself wide open over the middle, after running by the linebacker in coverage.

"I didn't see Chris, but I knew where he was going," said Wuerffel. "The safety was cheating toward Jack, so I gave a pump like I was going to Jack, and then turned and went down the middle." He lofted it up.

"When the ball was thrown, it seemed like it hung in the air forever. I couldn't believe there was no one near me," said Doering, who gathered it in with 0:03 left.

Touchdown Florida. Commonwealth Stadium froze in the middle of September. The Gators had escaped with the 24-20 victory.

"It's just a terrible feeling to have it in your hands and let it slip away," Curry said the day after the game.

Spurrier had a different feeling. "I still don't know how we won that game. It was a miracle. Somebody besides ourselves was looking out for the Gators," he said.

"That play changed my football career," added Doering, who went on to finish the season as one of the SEC's top receivers. The play was also the first crowning moment in Wuerffel's illustrious college career that ended in 1996 when he won the Heisman Trophy and the Gators captured the national championship.

THE AFTERMATH

The seven interceptions tossed by Wuerffel and Dean tied an NCAA record for most interceptions thrown by a winning team. (In 1980, Pittsburgh beat Army 45-7 while throwing seven interceptions.) The next week, Wuerrfel took over the starting QB job and led the Gators to a 41-34 win over Tennessee. Florida finished the season 11-2, with the most wins in one season in the school's history. Dean came back at the end of the season to take over as starting quarterback when Wuerffel struggled against Georgia. He led the Gators to a 28-13 victory over Alabama in the SEC title game, then a 41-7 demolition of West Virginia in the Sugar Bowl. Florida ended the season ranked No. 5 in the AP poll.

"Without that Wuerffel-to-Doering pass there at the end, we don't win the Eastern Division, we don't win the conference, we don't go to the Sugar Bowl," Spurrier said. "We don't have our biggest year ever. That one play." Of course, Spurrier would have even bigger seasons, namely '95 when they finished No. 2 behind Nebraska and '96 when they defeated Florida State 52-20 to win the Sugar Bowl and national championship.

Kentucky's '93 season ended up being Curry's only winning campaign in his seven-year tenure in Lexington. The 'Cats finished the regular season 6-5 and earned a Peach Bowl bid opposite Clemson.

Leading 13-7 with under a minute to play, UK linebacker Marty Moore intercepted a Clemson pass at the Kentucky five-yard line to apparently seal the Wildcat victory. But tempted by a possible return for a touchdown, Moore raced upfield, was hit by Clemson halfback Rodney Blunt, and fumbled the ball. Clemson recovered on the UK 21 with 44 seconds to play.

Three plays later, Tiger QB Patrick Sapp hit Terry Smith with a 21-yard touchdown pass with just 20 seconds left and the 'Cats had lost 14-13 in an almost mirror image of the Florida game.

"This one will hurt for a long time," Curry said.

"I really can't put my finger on it," said senior tight end Terry Samuels. "We just have a habit of losing big games."

Florida	3	6	0	15	-24
Kentucky	7	0	7	6	-20

UF	Davis 31 FG
UK	Browning 3 pass from Jones (Leonoff kick)
UF	Dean 1 run (pass failed)
UK	Williams 70 run (Leonoff kick)
UK	Leonoff 22 FG
UF	Doering 19 pass from Wuerffel (Wuerffel pass to Jackson)
UK	Leonoff 25 FG
UF	Doering 28 pass from Wuerffel (Davis kick)

Attendance 58,175

Illinois vs. Michigan

"I was on my knees praying."—Lou Tepper

THE BACKGROUND

Nineteen ninety-three couldn't have started out any worse for Lou Tepper's Fighting Illini. Three straight losses to Missouri, Arizona, and Oregon, left Illinois winless at 0-3 as they entered Big Ten conference play. Finally, with a 28-10 win over Purdue and a 49-3 triumph over Iowa, Illinois began to gain confidence early on in their conference schedule.

Homecoming in Ann Arbor. The Michigan Wolverines had won at least a share of the Big Ten title for five consecutive seasons. They were coming off back-to-back Rose Bowl appearances in 1991 and 1992. But in '93, Gary Moeller's troops (4-2, 2-1 Big Ten) had already lost one conference game at Michigan State 17-7. Any more stumbles along the road to Pasadena, and the 13th-ranked Wolverines' odds of a Rose Bowl three-peat would reach lottery proportions.

But the odds of Illinois (2-4, 2-1) coming into Michigan Stadium and leaving with a victory in front of 106,385 Maize and Blue clad patrons might have been even steeper. The Illini hadn't beaten the Wolverines in a decade, and hadn't won in Ann Arbor since 1966. So to try and change their luck, right before kickoff, the Illini changed pants. They took off their old orange ones and slipped into new blue bottoms, and hoped that "something new and something blue" would give them the superstitious good fortune of a bride on her wedding day.

After driving 80 yards in nine plays on their first possession, capped off by a Johnny

Johnson 17-yard TD pass to tight end Ken Dilger, the Illini led 7-0 and the Illinois equipment managers started looking for new blue jerseys to match their pants.

But as the game wore on, the honeymoon wore off.

Michigan, unable to establish a consistent running attack against the best defense in the Big Ten, struck through the air with three Todd Collins touchdown passes. The Michigan wideouts broke down the Illini secondary twice for long scores. Amani Toomer took a 10-yard pass from Collins and turned it into a 56-yard TD midway through the second quarter to give Michigan a 14-7 lead.

Then Derrick Alexander broke loose for a 90-yard score, the longest pass play in Michigan history. With 7:35 remaining in the third quarter, the Wolverines were up 21-10.

That's where it stood when Illinois took their first possession of the fourth quarter and scored on a one-yard burst by freshman Ty Douthard, whose 27 carries for 123 yards almost doubled the Wolverines' 76 yards rushing for the entire game.

Michigan played conservatively, trying to protect the 21-17 lead. But on third-and-one from the UM 26, a big stop by linebacker Kevin Hardy on senior runningback Ricky Powers, forced a Michigan punt. The Illini had momentum.

With 4:15 to play, Illinois took over on their own 45-yard line. On first down, Johnson found Dilger over the middle for 38 yards. But just as the Illini train chugged toward a go-ahead score, Dilger coughed up the ball at the end of the run and Michigan recovered at the 17-yard line.

Relief in the Big House. The last Illini threat had fizzled.

As the clock wound down from the 4:08 mark, and with the air sucked out of the Illinois balloon, the Wolverines were able to successfully chew up time with short gains by Powers. On third-and-one he busted over right tackle for a crucial first down. The Illini used their remaining timeouts. But then on third-and-six, Collins connected in the flat with Che Foster for eight yards and another first down at the UM 41.

The lights went out on Illinois.The clock was under two minutes. Leading by four points, the Wolverines kept handing to Powers, who got the majority of his carries after Heisman hopeful Tyrone Wheatley left the game with a shoulder injury early in the fourth quarter. Powers muscled over left tackle for three yards. The clock dwindled toward one minute left.

Then Powers tried right guard where he was met by Hardy again. The mundane moments of running out the clock instantly turned into panic in Ann Arbor. The ball popped loose. Simeon Rice scooped it up for the Illini, and with 1:13 on the clock, Illinois had the ball at the Michigan 44-yard line. Maybe there was still some life in those blue pants.

Johnson, the sophomore QB from North Chicago, quickly connected on two straight passes. An 11-yard completion to Douthard stopped the clock momentarily with a first down at the Michigan 19-yard line. After it restarted, Johnson downed the ball. On second down he threw incomplete for tight end Jim Klein. Forty-seven seconds remained.

On third down, Johnson dumped off to Douthard who was run out of bounds at the 15-yard line. With 41 seconds left, trailing by four points, Illinois faced fourth-and-six. Needing one defensive stop, Michigan used their final timeout.

THE PLAY
CD 2—Track 5—*Neil Funk,*
Jim Grabowski, **Illini Sports Network**

Out of the shotgun, Johnson took the snap. He stepped up then ran left out of the pocket. Two Wolverine defenders, Buster

Stanley and Shonte Peoples, converged. One grabbed for his ankles. Johnson looked like he was hopping through an obstacle course. He kicked out, tripped up, then instantly shed the other off his shoulder. "They brought the house, but I wasn't going down," said Johnson.

After dancing for his life, it certainly appeared as if Johnson was just getting rid of the ball in desperation. Just before being thrown to the ground, he flung a toss toward the left corner of the end zone.

"I thought the ball was going out of the end zone," said Tepper. But Johnson had a purpose behind the pass. Tight end Klein, a former walk-on transfer from Western Illinois, was waiting beyond the goal line as the ball floated toward him. Between two Michigan defensive backs, Clarence Thompson and Jean-Agnus Charles, Klein jumped for the ball.

"It was definitely slo-mo," said Klein. "I probably could have watched the stripes on the football. I looked it in. I cradled it."

He caught it, right in his chest, then was sandwiched to the ground, but held on. Touchdown Illinois. The Illini led 24-21.

Hands on their helmets, mouths draped open, the Michigan players and fans stood in stunned silence.

Meanwhile, the Illinois bench emptied, running onto the field in a moment of unabated celebration. Of course, the excessive celebration flags came with them. "We haven't won up here since 1966," offensive coordinator Greg Landry told an official. "You could allow for some levity."

College football's most archaic 15-yard penalty (how 'bout changing it to a five-yard penalty?) moved the Illini back to their own 20 on the kickoff, and set up the Wolverines for a last-second dash down the field.

Alexander took the kick at his 26 and returned it to the UM 42. With 0:30 left, Collins fired to Alexander for 22 yards to the Illini 36. The Wolverines rushed to the line. Collins spiked the ball. With 0:21 left, Collins threw to Alexander again down the right sideline, but defensive back Robert Crumpton batted it away. At 0:15 Michigan wished they had that last timeout back.

Collins then tossed a short completion to

Walter Smith who fell just one yard short of a first down at the 25-yard line. Michigan scrambled. The clock kept ticking. Kicker Peter Elezoic couldn't get on the field fast enough. Time ran out on Michigan. Illinois had broken 27 years of frustration.

"We believed when we came here that we could do this," said Illinois offensive lineman Randy Bierman, decked out in his blue digs. "Now that we've done it, I can't believe it."

THE AFTERMATH

The Wolverines' season bottomed out the following week with a 13-10 loss to Wisconsin. At 4-4, Michigan salvaged a respectable 8-4 season by winning their final three conference games (including a 28-0 skunking of Ohio State), then trouncing North Carolina State 42-7 in the Hall of Fame Bowl.

Despite a 3-4 record, at 3-1 in the Big Ten, the Illini found themselves battling for the conference lead and a trip to the Rose Bowl. They survived two more narrow conference victories over Northwestern and Minnesota to go 5-1. Then reality came knocking. Losses to Penn State 28-14, and a 35-10 collapse against Wisconsin ended the rosy Illini dreams as they finished with a 5-6 overall record.

Illinois	7	3	0	14	- 24
Michigan	0	14	7	0	- 21

ILL	Dilger 17 pass from Johnson (Richardson kick)
MICH	Alexander 13 pass from Collins (Elezoic kick)
MICH	Toomer 56 pass from Collins (Elezoic kick)
ILL	FG Richardson 25
MICH	Alexander 90 pass from Collins (Elezoic kick)
ILL	Douthard 1 run (Richardson kick)
ILL	Klein 15 pass from Johnson (Richardson kick)

Attendance 106,385

Thomas More vs. Defiance

"If you've ever heard of divine intervention, that's it."—Greg Stofko

THE BACKGROUND

It was a bye week for the Thomas More College football team, a Division III school located in Crestview Hills, Kentucky. With no game to play that Saturday, senior wide receiver Greg Stofko was relaxing, watching a Notre Dame football game on TV. His dad was raking the leaves at home in nearby Cincinnati.

They got a phone call.

Greg's younger brother Mike, a freshman walk-on player for Thomas More, had been killed in a one-car accident.

Devastated by the loss of his brother, Greg took some time away from football as his teammates prepared to play undefeated Defiance College in a game which would determine the Association of Mideast Colleges conference champion.

The following Wednesday, Stofko got another phone call. It was defensive coordinator Joe Schlager. "I'll never forget getting the phone call," remembered Stofko. "He said you've got to move on. Mike would want you to play. Let's get on out here and let's get you prepared and let's win this league championship." Stofko rejoined the team that same day.

The 8-0 Defiance Yellow Jackets were ranked third in the NCAA North Region, and had won 25 of 28 games in the last three seasons. Coach Malen Luke's squad was looking forward to getting revenge on Thomas More, which had given the Yellow Jackets two of those three losses.

Thomas More, however, had never lost a game in the tiny four team AMC (Wilmington and Bluffton rounded out the conference). Head coach Vic Clark's Blue Rebels (5-2 overall, 2-0 conference) were competing in just their fourth season since launching a new football program in 1990.

With Defiance's stadium under renovation, the game was played at nearby Defiance High School, on a sloppy turf, wet from the morning snowfall. The entire Stofko family made the trip north, including Greg's uncle, former major league baseball player and coach Buddy Bell.

Defiance took control early. Led by the passing of quarterback John Smith, the Yellow Jackets held a 10-0 lead midway through the second quarter. But Thomas More's defense turned the game around. Three interceptions by Blue Rebel defensive backs Brian Kenny, Chris Haliburton, and Greg Ivey, were converted into three touchdown runs. Two 20-plus romps by Dan Calhoun and one short burst by Carlton Carter put Thomas More in charge 18-10 with 10 minutes to play in the game.

However, the Rebels missed all three extra-point attempts. That would come back to haunt them.

With a chance to increase the Thomas More lead later in the fourth quarter, Erik Ward's 44-yard field-goal attempt was blocked. Defiance rallied, immediately driving 60 yards in 11 plays. Quarterback Smith hit his favorite receiver Sammy Williams (9 receptions, 98 yards) with a five-yard TD pass and the TMC lead was cut to 18-16. After a pass interference penalty on the conversion attempt, it was Smith to

Game 76

Greg Stofko shares a tearful moment with his father after scoring a bizarre touchdown on the game's final play. Photo courtesy of Don Weber

halfback Raheem West for the two-point conversion and the game was tied 18-18 with 2:22 left.

John Paul Case had entered the game at quarterback for TMC during the third quarter, replacing starter Larry Hutson. Case, Thomas More's all-time leading passer, hadn't played all year, but rather was a student coach. Midway through the season, he was awarded an extra year of eligibility by the NCAA for a medical hardship he suffered at Wittenberg College before transferring to TMC. Case was just now ready to take the field again.

The senior QB marched the Blue Rebels down the field in the final two minutes.

He hit fullback Derrick Jett for 34 yards on a crucial third down play to move the ball to the Defiance 24. Then a questionable pass interference penalty on the Jackets' Jason Besgrove advanced the ball down to the nine. Three short runs brought the ball to the six-yard line where Defiance called time-out with only 0:04 on the clock.

Blue Rebels' coach Vic Clark had a decision to make. Kicker Erik Ward had missed one extra point, had another extra point blocked, and also had a field-goal attempt blocked. With their kicking game failing miserably in the sloppy field conditions, should the Rebels just try to score from the six-yard line? Or should they attempt another kick, normally an easy chip shot field goal from only 23 yards out?

THE PLAY
CD 2—Track 6
Gary Ball, Bill Herman,
Northern Kentucky Sports Network

Greg Stofko was having a quiet day in his first game back after the family tragedy. As a receiver, he caught only two passes for 12 yards. But Stofko also doubled as the holder for the placekicker, so he remained on the field when Clark decided to give Ward one more chance.

The ball was snapped. Stofko caught it cleanly and placed it down.

Just then, Defiance defensive back Jim Berner swept around the left end of the line completely untouched, launched his body in the air, and blocked Ward's kick.

The fourth botched Blue Rebels' kick of the game. Time expired. The Defiance fans celebrated, as did Berner who raised his hands in triumph toward the home crowd, and joyfully skipped away toward the sidelines.

Meanwhile, the ball fell into the pack of linemen directly in front of holder Stofko. As Stofko got up off the ground to try and cover the ball so Defiance couldn't advance it, the ball somehow squirted out, took one high bounce, and landed directly in his hands. "I got a hop from above I guess," said Stofko. "It popped right to me."

Just 10 yards away from the goal line, he immediately began running to the right corner of the end zone. Stofko turned the corner, raised the ball above his head, and dove inside the right pylon, just over the goal line. It was a miracle touchdown. Thomas More had won 24-18.

"That's one of the greatest plays I've ever seen in college football," screamed Thomas More broadcaster Gary Ball.

Utter amazement reigned on both sides of the field. Clark literally staggered across the field in a daze, looking for someone to hug, and repeating out loud, "I can't believe these kids. I cannot believe these kids. I cannot believe it."

After being mobbed by his jubilant teammates, a sobbing Stofko, overcome by the week's events, engaged in a long, emotional embrace with his father who had rushed onto the field.

Sixteen-year veteran Kentucky sports reporter Don Weber remembered it well. "That's right up there with the most emotional moments I've ever covered," said Weber. "With the circumstances being what they were, that's about as dramatic an ending as you could have."

"It was like a storybook," said Clark after regaining his composure. "It was like we were pre-destined to win that game."

Defiance's coach echoed those thoughts, but with an opposite view. "I guess it just wasn't meant to be," said a dejected Malen Luke. "It just wasn't meant to be for some reason."

Stofko felt a special presence on the play. "I think my little brother helped me on that one, 'cause heaven knows I wouldn't have gotten to the corner [of the end zone] in time," he said after the game. "Maybe he was up there giving me a little hand."

THE AFTERMATH

Thomas More went on to win the AMC conference championship, beating Bluffton 45-0 to finish the season 8-2. For the Defiance Yellow Jackets, which ended the season 9-1, the improbable loss dashed their hopes of making the Division III playoffs.

But Defiance got a measure of revenge five years later in 1998 when an 0-6 Yellow Jacket squad beat Thomas More on an eerily similar ending to the game. With 52 seconds remaining, Thomas More's 31-yard winning field-goal attempt was blocked by Defiance, but then picked up by a Blue Rebel who raced to the end zone, just like Stofko did five years prior. This time however, he was tackled at the five-yard line and Defiance held on to win the game 29-27.

For Greg Stofko, the '93 game was the pinnacle of a storybook career at Thomas More. He was a member of the first football team at the school in 1990. He caught the school's first touchdown pass in a 30-0 win over Kentucky Wesleyan. And he will always be remembered in Blue Rebels folklore for one of the most amazing finishes in college football history.

"I never in my lifetime have seen, and don't plan to see, another play like that," said Stofko.

Thomas More	0	6	6	12	-24
Defiance	7	3	0	8	-18

DEF	Manders 7 pass from Smith (Wooden kick)
DEF	FG Wooden 27
TM	Calhoun 22 run (kick failed)
TM	Calhoun 25 run (kick failed)
TM	Carter 3 run (run failed)
DEF	Williams 5 pass from Smith (Williams pass from Smith)
TM	Stofko 6 blocked kick return (no attempt)

Attendance 1,809

Nevada vs. Arkansas State

"I guess you can tell I'm a little discombobulated."
—*Arkansas State head coach John Bobo*

THE BACKGROUND

Chris Ault built a dynasty in Reno, Nevada. From 1976-92, he coached the Wolf Pack of Nevada-Reno, compiling a 145-58-1 record, winning four Big Sky conference championships, and making the I-AA playoffs six times. He was I-AA Coach of the Year in 1978 and '91. In 1992, he took his program to Division I-A. The Wolf Pack dropped the "dash Reno" in their name, joined cross-state rival Nevada-Las Vegas in the Big West conference, and promptly won the conference title in their first year.

Then Ault called it quits. He remained athletic director at the school, and named six-year assistant Jeff Horton as the new head coach. Horton had previously left Reno to be assistant head coach at UNLV for two years, only to return back to Reno.

The new coach kept the high-powered offensive machine that Ault had finely tuned over the years. Guided by senior QB Chris Vargas, the Wolf Pack led the nation in offense, averaging an eye-popping 582.7 yards per game. Vargas himself had built quite a reputation in Reno. Known as the "Magic Man," he had rallied the Wolf Pack from behind 12 times in the fourth quarter. His most amazing feat came in a 1991 win over Weber State where the No. 1-ranked Wolf Pack trailed 49-14 in the third quarter, then scored the final 41 points of the game to win 55-49; the biggest comeback in NCAA history.

When Nevada traveled to Arkansas State, the 7-3 Wolf Pack needed a win to gain a share of yet another conference title and a shot at the Las Vegas Bowl. Their opponents, the 1-8-1 Indians were ending another dismal season. Arkansas State was 4-26-1 over the past three years, and first-year coach John Bobo's squad was winless in the Big West. This was the last game of the year for Arkansas State, a team disregarded so much, they were listed No. 6 in the the *Los Angeles Times'* "Bottom Ten" teams in the country rankings.

Perhaps that last distinction was motivation for Arkansas State. Or maybe it was the celebration of the 100th game in Indian Stadium. Maybe Nevada was flat. Whatever the reason, the Indians roared out to a 10-0 second-quarter lead. But Vargas, true to form, led a late second-quarter drive that culminated in a three-yard TD pass to Fred Williams with 39 seconds left in the half and the ASU lead was 10-7.

However, on the last play of the half from the ASU 47, Indians' sophomore QB Johnny Covington threw a pass tipped by Nevada's Steve Bryant, and caught one-handed by freshman runningback Marquis Williams over the middle at the Nevada 22. Williams then broke two tackles and scored on the spectacular 53-yard pass play, as the horn sounded ending the first half. In stunning fashion, ASU led 17-7.

Remember that sequence of plays.

Playing without their top receiver Bryan Reeves (also the nation's second leading receiver), who was out with a shoulder injury, the Wolf Pack had their backs to the wall. ASU held on to a 17-14 lead with 3:14 to play in the game, and had the ball on the Nevada 17. On fourth-and-10, knowing Vargas' history of comebacks, Coach Bobo bypassed a field-goal attempt (which would have given ASU a six-point lead) and went for the touchdown. "I knew they wouldn't be content for a tie," he said. But Covington's fourth-down pass was incomplete and Nevada took over.

Vargas went to work.

Hoping to take his team to a bowl with one more late comeback, he hit Shawn Price for a 30-yard completion on a third-and-20 play, quickly moving the ball down to the ASU 35 with two minutes remaining. Then five plays later, with just 0:46 left, Vargas did it again. He found Michael Stephens with an 18-yard TD pass and Nevada led 21-17. The drive covered 83 yards in 11 plays, the 13th fourth quarter rally by Vargas. "Once you watched him, you know why they call him 'The Magic Man,'" said Bobo.

Facing the identical situation as the end of the first half, Covington tried to rally the Indians against a loose Nevada prevent defense. Starting from the ASU 26, he hit Clark McBride for eight yards, then Reginald Murphy got open for 20 more and Arkansas State was at the Nevada 46 with 0:12 seconds left. On a risky play, Derrick Austin crossed over the middle and snatched a 16-yard pass for a first down to the Nevada 30.

The Indians tried to call time-out. The clock wound down. Then it ran out.

But the officials ruled an ASU time out had been called. Three seconds were put back on the clock.

THE PLAY
CD 2—Track 7—*Randy Rainwater,*
Arkansas State University Radio Network

With ASU 30 yards from the end zone, offensive coordinator Jody Allen mapped the last play. "Reggie [Murphy] was the first read. The safety, if he jumps Reginald, [then] Johnny throws to Derrick [Austin]. If he doesn't jump Reginald, then that's the first place Johnny looks," explained Allen. "We instructed Reggie on the sidelines to run his route deeper than he normally runs to make sure he got in the end zone."

Murphy interpreted those instructions lit-

erally, and the freshman ran to the back of the end zone, past cornerback Bernie Chapman.

Covington took the snap and rolled right. Just avoiding a sack and getting a key block from lineman Jessie Miller, he fired the ball deep over the middle to Murphy.

Vargas stood on the opposite sideline, helpless. "I didn't even watch the last play," he said. "I got a little nervous, but still, I was thinking no way it could happen."

No way it could happen twice in the same game.

The 5-8 Murphy, who had made two critical fumbles the previous two weeks, watched the ball all the way to his hands. "I was thinking, 'I have to redeem myself for the last two weeks,'" he said.

"I saw his eyes when the ball was coming down and I knew right then he would catch it," said teammate Austin.

He did, barely keeping his feet in bounds. With no time left, Arkansas State had pulled off the remarkable upset, 23-21. Pandemonium on the field. The Indians piled on Murphy beyond the end zone, their season of frustration redeemed with one catch on the final play of the year.

"I didn't see it at first, but then everybody started to run on the field," said Covington. "It was one of the greatest moments of my life."

Not for Vargas, who ended his career as the NCAA all-time Division I-A record holder in total offense per game (320.9). "I can't believe this is my last game," he remarked immediately after the shocking defeat. "It hasn't hit me yet that we lost. I haven't had time to cry or mourn. I just want to get out of here."

THE AFTERMATH

The loss triggered a series of bizarre events at Nevada. The following Tuesday, after just five and a half months as head coach, Horton left Reno, took the head coaching job at rival UNLV, and brought with him seven of the Wolf Pack's nine assistant coaches who had built Nevada's successful program. When Horton informed his team of the decision, a boisterous meeting ensued.

"There was a lot of yelling and screaming

and arguing going on in there," said defensive end Jeff Kondra. "People were asking, 'Where's your loyalty?! What about that?!'"

"It's like you're with your girlfriend, and all of a sudden she up and leaves you for another dude," said quarterback Todd Floyd, a redshirt freshman.

Athletic Director Ault was furious. Players and fans begged him to return as the Wolf Pack leader. The next day he came back as head coach again. "When someone starts to burn your house down, you go put water on it," said Ault.

A year later, Ault looked back at what happened. "When they didn't win the championship, I felt responsible," he said. "Maybe that's ego, maybe that's something else. But we wouldn't have lost that last game on that last play, and I can never give that back to those kids."

The following season, Horton's UNLV Rebels won the eagerly awaited matchup between the two feuding coaches 32-27 on a DeJohn Branch four-yard TD run with 58 seconds left, giving Nevada its only conference loss of the year.

Then in '95 Horton returned to Reno for the first time to face Ault's Wolf Pack again. This time it got ugly. UNLV was assessed a 15-yard penalty during a pre-game brawl in which several punches were thrown. During the game, a UNLV defensive back threw his helmet at Ault. Nevada won the game 55-32. QB Mike Maxwell threw his seventh TD pass, on the last play of the game as payback for the pre-game fight. That move launched a post-game brawl. Reno fans doused Horton and other UNLV players with beer and threw objects at players and Rebels fans. Two players from each team were suspended for one game by the Big West conference.

Chris Ault retired from coaching for good after the '95 Las Vegas Bowl, which the Wolf Pack lost to Toledo 40-37 in overtime. Jeff Horton never beat Nevada again. He coached UNLV through the '98 season, after which he was re-assigned at UNLV with a 6-39 record in his final four years. He was replaced by former USC coach John Robinson.

Meanwhile in Jonesboro, Arkansas, John Bobo was named Big West Coach of the Year in 1995, when he led Arkansas State to their first winning season (6-5) since 1987. However, his contract was not renewed following the '96 season. He finished with a 13-30-1 record at Arkansas State.

Nevada	0	7	7	7	-21
Arkansas St.	7	10	0	6	-23

ASU	M.Williams 7 run (Caldwell kick)
ASU	Caldwell 33 FG
UN	F. Williams 3 pass from Vargas (Avina kick)
ASU	M. Williams 53 pass from Covington (Caldwell kick)
UN	Stephens 28 pass from Vargas (Avina kick)
UN	Stephens 8 pass from Vargas (Avina kick)
ASU	Murphy 30 pass from Covington (attempt failed)

Attendance 10,094

257

Boston College vs. Notre Dame 🏈

"I'm basically in shock right now."—Jim Flanigan

THE BACKGROUND

The Game of the Century. November 13, 1993.

No.2 Notre Dame hosted No.1 Florida State in the latest remake of the "Game of the Century," a much anticipated, much ballyhooed battle (over 700 media credentials were issued for the game) that actually lived up to the over-hype. Both teams were undefeated, 9-0, sporting the nation's best 16-game winning streaks.

The Irish took a seemingly insurmountable 31-17 lead with 6:53 to play in the game on a 11-yard TD run by Jeff Burris. But eventual Heisman Trophy winner Charlie Ward rallied the Seminoles.

With 2:26 left, on a desperation fourth-and-20 play, Ward miraculously connected with Kez McCorvey on a TD pass deflected by safety Brian Magee to pull FSU within 31-24. After holding ND on downs, the 'Noles got the ball back on their own 37 with 51 seconds left, and no timeouts. In three plays, Ward had them at the Irish doorstep. Ten seconds remained. From the ND 14, Ward looked to the end zone. But his pass was batted down by defensive end Thomas McKnight.

That left 0:03 on the clock. On the final play of the epic battle, Ward rolled left and threw to the end zone for Kevin Knox. But defensive back Shawn Wooden stepped up, knocked the ball away, preserved the 31-24 victory for Notre Dame, and unleashed a massive party inside Notre Dame Stadium. Notre Dame was now No.1.

Like the day after a Don King heavyweight fight, arrangements were already being made for a national championship rematch between the two teams in the Fiesta Bowl on New Year's Day.

That was the week before Boston College came to town.

Boston College was quietly 7-2, ranked 16th, and riding a seven-game winning streak. Fresh in their minds was a 54-7 humiliation at the hands of the Irish the year before, in which Notre Dame faked a punt leading 37-0. Fresh in the minds of the Irish was the celebration the previous Saturday.

Notre Dame had a bad hangover, while Boston College played the role of the chirpy, sober guest to perfection, cleaning up after a wild party. The Eagles came out of the gate re-freshed, energized, motivated, dominant. The Irish searched for a trash can to lean over.

Led by senior quarterback Glenn Foley, Boston College outplayed top-ranked Notre Dame in every facet of the game, building a 38-17 lead after Foley hit tight end Pete Mitchell from one-yard out with only 11:13 to play in the fourth quarter. That was Foley's fourth TD pass of the game. This was a shocking blowout.

It turned into a shocking finish.

One minute later, ND runningback Lee Becton broke away for a 29-yard touchdown run. Then Becton took a handoff from quarterback Kevin McDougal, and threw back to McDougal for the two-point conversion. The score was 38-25. The dormant crowd, half frozen from the mid-30 temperatures, half

258

stunned in disbelief for most of the game, suddenly thawed out.

Still, Foley wasn't fazed. He calmly marched the Eagles downfield like he had all afternoon. But at the ND 31, he fumbled the snap. Jim Flanigan recovered for the Irish. Sixty-seven yards and six plays later, fullback Ray Zellars was in the end zone with a four-yard TD run. The lead had diminshed to 38-32 with 4:02 left. That hangover had finally blown over.

The Irish defense, dissected all day by Foley, caught another break. Facing third-and-nine on the next possession, the Boston College quarterback fumbled the snap again. This time he recovered on the BC 30, but the Eagles were forced to punt. The Irish had the ball again at their 33 with 2:51 remaining.

McDougal wasted no time, connecting with Derrick Mayes on a spectacular 46-yard completion to the BC 21. Notre Dame swiftly (perhaps too swiftly) moved to the four-yard line where they faced an all-or-nothing fourth-down play. McDougal then perfectly threaded a touchdown toss to Lake Dawson in the back of the end zone. Kevin Pendergast's extra point gave the Irish a remarkable 39-38 lead.

A 22-point barrage in nine minutes. One minute nine seconds was on the clock. The Notre Dame momentum seemed insurmountable. Even more so, after Anthony Comer muffed the ensuing kickoff at the BC 3 then was buried at the 10-yard line. But a crucial personal foul penalty for an illegal forearm hit was called on the exuberant Irish after the play, moving the ball to the 25.

A fortuitous break for Foley, who now had some breathing room and 61 seconds to rekindle the Eagles' flame. But just as the final drive started, the flame appeared snuffed out. On second-and-10, Foley threw over the middle, right to a wide open receiver...ND linebacker Pete Bercich. Incredibly though, the ball slid threw Bercich's grasp. "I just flat-out dropped it," said Bercich. "It didn't touch anybody. It hit me in the hands."

The Boston College flicker of hope still had a spark left. It ignited Foley, who completed two brief passes, moving the ball to the BC 43 with 0:27 left. Then, in the shotgun, Foley stepped up in the pocket, slid to his left, and just before running with the ball, spotted Mitchell cutting across the middle. He connected with the tight end to the ND 33 with only 0:18 left, Mitchell's 13th reception of the day for a total of 132 yards.

Screams of horror filled Notre Dame Stadium, their undefeated dream season was being dismantled by an unfathomable drive in the last seconds of the last regular-season game.

Meanwhile, Foley felt Flutie-like, brilliantly orchestrating an incredible reversal of momentum. The Eagles were at the brink of field-goal range and the brink of a historical upset.

After throwing the ball away to avoid a blitz, Foley tossed his fourth completion of the drive, a middle screen to Ivan Boyd who moved the ball nine more yards to the ND 24. With 0:05 on the clock, the Eagles called time-out.

THE PLAY
CD2—Track 8
Dick Lutsk, Peter Cronan,
Kelley Communications

Boston College had never beaten Notre Dame (0 for 4). Senior walk-on David Gordon had never made a field-goal attempt longer than 39 yards.

Earlier in the season, his 40-yard kick with 1:07 left to play against Northwestern sailed wide right. BC lost 22-21. The season before, his 43-yard game-winning attempt against West Virginia was blocked. Earlier in this game, he missed a 40-yard attempt.

This final try was from 41 yards.

BC coach Tom Coughlin stopped Gordon on his way onto the field. "He grabbed me and stared into my eyes," said Gordon. "He said, 'David, all I want you to do is make good contact with the ball and good things will happen. I know you can make it.'"

"That really sunk in," said Gordon, a soccer player-turned-placekicker, who transferred to BC from the University of Vermont.

The left-footed Gordon lined up the kick. Hands were held. Knees were bent. Catholic prayers rose from both sidelines.

The ball sat slightly left of center. The holder was Foley. The snap was high.

Foley snatched it. Then placed it. Gordon kicked it. The gasp was deafening.

The ball immediately hooked to the right. "His ball travels from right to left," Foley said. "It started out way wide of the post... and then it started back in."

It locked itself dead center. Straight between the uprights. Straight into the chest of Touchdown Jesus.

The Kick. Boston College 41, Notre Dame 39.

"It had a funny rotation," said Gordon about the kick. "It wasn't like I'd nailed it. I didn't hit it that good." He did hit it hard enough to knock over about a dozen Notre Dame players who laid strewn across the field like wounded soldiers, their national championship hopes shot through the heart.

Foley looked like he won the lottery. "I didn't know what to do when that thing went through," he said. " I started running around like an idiot." So did all of his teammates, except the newest Boston College hero.

The delirious Eagles raised Gordon high, then piled on top of him. "There must have been about 90 guys on top of me, " said Gordon. "Those guys were big guys. I'm like 'Guys, let me breathe.'"

Notre Dame had voluntarily stopped breathing, crushed by the stunning upset. "It would have been an unbelievable victory," Irish coach Lou Holtz said. "To be down so far and to come back and have it within your grasp with a minute to go, it's heartbreaking.

"I don't know what else to say, except that we all hurt."

One man's pain is another man's glory. "You couldn't ask for a better ending to a football game," said Coughlin.

THE AFTERMATH

While the goalposts at Notre Dame Stadium remained upright, the ones at Boston College came down. The win was so thrilling back in Chestnut Hill, that students crashed the gates of Alumni Field and tore down their own goalposts. A party of 5,000 greeted the victorious Eagles back to campus later that evening.

BC moved to No.11 in the polls but still had one last game of their own, hosting another undefeated team, fifth-ranked West Virginia (10-0). But like Notre Dame, the Eagles followed their monumental win with a sluggish perfor-

mance, and a humbling loss. With the benefit of five Eagles turnovers, West Virginia knocked off Boston College 17-14 to gain a spot in the Sugar Bowl.

"Now I know how Notre Dame feels," said a dejected BC flanker Keith Miller. Boston College went on to defeat Virginia 31-13 in the CarQuest Bowl to end the season 9-3, ranked 13th in the AP poll.

Instead of playing for the national championship, Notre Dame settled for the Cotton Bowl where they defeated seventh-ranked Texas A&M 24-21. Despite finishing with the identical 11-1 record as Florida State, the Irish finished second in the AP poll while the Seminoles captured the national championship after beating Nebraska 18-16 in the Orange Bowl.

Tom Coughlin left Boston College at the end of the season to take the head coaching job with the NFL expansion Jacksonville Jaguars.

Boston College	10	14	7	10	- 41
Notre Dame	0	14	3	22	- 39

BC	FG Gordon 28
BC	Boyd 4 pass from Foley (Gordon kick)
ND	Zellars 39 pass from McDougal (Pendergast kick)
BC	Boyd 36 pass from Foley (Gordon kick)
ND	Burris 1 run (Pendergast kick)
BC	Mitchell 3 pass from Foley (Gordon kick)
BC	Campbell 21 run (Gordon kick)
ND	FG Pendergast 29
BC	Mitchell 1 pass from Foley (Gordon kick)
ND	Becton 29 run (McDougal pass from Becton)
ND	Zellars 4 run (Pendergast kick)
ND	Dawson 4 pass from McDougal (Pendergast kick)
BC	FG Gordon 41

Attendance 59,075

Beneath the pile of joyous Eagles lies David Gordon, whose 41-yard kick crushed Notre Dame's title hopes. Photo courtesy of Matt Cashore

Colorado vs. Michigan

"Like the dark, it never goes away."—Gary Moeller, two years after

THE BACKGROUND

Homecoming for Bill McCartney. From 1974-1981, McCartney was an assistant coach under Bo Schembechler at Michigan. He left Ann Arbor in 1982 to rebuild the Colorado football program. That process climaxed in 1990 with the school's first national championship.

As a head coach, this was his first trip back to the old stomping grounds. McCartney brought his 2-0 Buffaloes (ranked No.4 in the country), back to Michigan Stadium to face the No. 7-ranked Wolverines (also 2-0), coached by Gary Moeller. It was televised nationally by ABC.

Led by quarterback Todd Collins , the Wolverines overcame a 14-3 first-half deficit with 23 unanswered points. Tailback Tyrone Wheatley, a pre-season Heisman Trophy candidate playing his first game of the season after recovering from a knee injury, gave Michigan a 17-14 lead with a five-yard TD run in the third quarter.

Collins then hit Amani Toomer with a 65-yard TD pass with 2:43 left in the third quarter, and the Wolverines led 26-14. It stayed that way until Colorado drove to the Michigan goal line with under six minutes to play in the game.

Attempting to cut the 12-point margin in half, CU quarterback Kordell Stewart tried to reach the ball over the goal line, but instead, fumbled into the Michigan end zone. Wolverine Clarence Thompson recovered with 5:08 left. Michigan still led by 12 points.

But on the next possession, the Buffs held Michigan to three plays and a punt. Getting the ball back at their own 28, Stewart then drove his team downfield once again. This time, tailback Rashaan Salaam (who would win the '94 Heisman Trophy) scored from one yard out, capping a 72-yard drive with 2:16 to play. The Michigan lead was 26-21.

Colorado attempted the onside kick, but was unsuccessful. Michigan simply had to run out the clock. But facing third-and-two at the CU 38, the Wolverines jumped, causing a procedure penalty that moved them back five yards. Tim Biakabutuka could only muster three yards on third-and-seven. It was fourth-and-three for the Wolverines. They were forced to punt with 21 seconds on the clock.

With the ball on the CU 42, Michigan punted to the Colorado 15, where a fair catch by Chris Hudson gave the Buffaloes the ball with 0:14 remaining, down by five, with no timeouts left.

On first down, Stewart hit Michael Westbrook cutting over the middle of the field. Westbrook reached the 36-yard line where he was tackled with 0:08 left. The clock stopped to move the first-down markers. Stewart quickly brought his team to the line of scrimmage, immediately took the snap when the clock was started, and downed the ball with 0:06 left.

Even though it was first down, with time for only one play, Colorado essentially had fourth-and-64 to go.

Game 79

THE PLAY
CD 2—Track 9
Larry Zimmer,
Colorado Football Network

"Rocket Left." Sounds like an instant lottery game. In a way, it was. The Buffaloes tried it at the end of the first half. It was intercepted by safety Chuck Winters. Now, at the end of the game, they scratched off another circle.

Three receivers. Rae Carruth, Blake Anderson, and Westbrook, lined up wide left. Receiver James Kidd was split to the right. Stewart took the snap and retreated to the 25. Fortunately for Colorado, Michigan rushed just three linemen. Dancing back and forth with no pressure, Stewart ran the clock down, waiting for his receivers to sprint toward the end zone.

As the clock struck 0:00, the fifth-year quarterback stepped up to the 27-yard line and launched the ball 73 yards in the air, surprising even his own coach. "I didn't think he could throw it that far," remarked McCartney.

"Kordell can throw the ball 85 yards on his knees," Westbrook said. "Ask him."

"Today," said Stewart, "I could have thrown it the whole field."

The ball came down right on the goal line.

Like the end of the first half, Winters was there again, along with defensive back Ty Law. They hovered on top of Anderson. Carruth was behind the Michigan defenders who both jumped high and appeared to have the best shot at the ball.

"I saw the ball the whole way," Winters said. "I was coming down with it in my hands, but their guy tipped it up." Anderson got a piece of the pigskin.

As Carruth fell to the side, the ball popped straight up in the air, over Law's head, and into the end zone. Seemingly ignored, and trailing the play in stride just to the left, Westbrook found himself all alone with a football falling right into his hands.

He cradled it in. Law scrambled to try and rip the ball away. It was too late.

"Never in my life has that ever happened before," said Westbrook. "I couldn't believe it. I still can't."

Three Cherries, Lucky Four, Instant Powerball, Touchdown Colorado. The Buffaloes were winners, 27-26.

Colorado announcer Larry Zimmer (who also called Wolverine games from 1966-70) vividly remembered the scene."There were 106,000 people there... and you could have heard a pin drop."

Actually, it was the sound your heart makes when it hits the bottom of your stomach.

"All of a sudden it was like somebody flipped a switch. It went quiet, and nobody moved," remembered official David Witvoet. "It was eerie."

The Colorado bench poured onto the field. It took Stewart a while to join his teammates. After his mammoth launch, he had to run 75 yards to catch up with the celebration.

"I kissed the end zone, I licked the grass, I kissed my teammates on the lips, I was going to kiss anyone who came close to me," said the delirious Stewart.

"We ran that play in practice and we never got it to work," noted Kidd who was five yards behind the play, with four other Michigan defenders, trying to catch up to Stewart's throw, when the reception was made.

"I'm supposed to be the tip man," Westbrook said. "But the ball was thrown away from me. Blake Anderson hit it up and I just happened to be in the back."

"I don't know if it will ever sink in, but I do know I'll never forget it. I was glad to be a part of it," added Anderson.

For Michigan, it was a bitter pill. "This was a sad one, one of the toughest ones," Moeller said. "You can never say you have a football game won."

"We work against that play all of the time, it's not a miracle. Everybody did everything right, the ball bounced up and they caught it."

THE AFTERMATH

Ten years after Flutie found Phelen with "The Pass," the nation had their next nationally televised Hail Mary. Stewart-to-Westbrook simply became known as "The Catch."

The following week, the Buffaloes defeated Texas 34-31 when Neil Voskeritchian hit a 24-yard field goal with one second on the clock. At that point, McCartney had just about enough of the drama. "I'll take a boring win any time," he said. " I feel like I've aged 10 years in seven days."

Colorado ended the season 11-1, with the one loss coming at Nebraska 24-7. They defeated Notre Dame in the Fiesta Bowl 41-24 in McCartney's last game as head coach. He retired with a 93-55-5 record after 13 seasons at CU. McCartney was succeeded by Colorado quarterbacks coach Rick Neuheisel.

After defeating Colorado State 24-14 in the Holiday Bowl, Moeller and the Wolverines finished the year 8-4 in what turned out to be the last season in Ann Arbor for the Michigan head coach. He resigned the following May after an altercation with police in a restaurant resulted in his arrest on charges of disorderly conduct and assault and battery. Moeller had a 44-13-3 head coaching record at Michigan where he served as a member of the Wolverine staff for 24 years.

When the two teams met again, two years later in Boulder, it happened again.

This time the score was 20-13 Michigan. This time the Buffs' quarterback was Koy Detmer. This time Rae Carruth was diving for the batted ball in the end zone.

This time it fell incomplete. The underdog Wolverines knocked off No.5 Colorado 20-13.

The following season, when Colorado returned to Ann Arbor for the first time since "The Catch," announcer Zimmer decided to venture onto the field before the game to see just how far Stewart actually threw the miracle pass. He stood dumbfounded at the spot, gazing 75 yards ahead of him.

"I still don't know how he threw it that far," he wondered.

Colorado	7	7	0	13	- 27
Michigan	0	9	17	0	- 26

CU	Salaam 2 run (Voskeritchian kick)
UM	Hamilton 33 FG
CU	Westbrook 27 pass from Stewart (Voskeritchian kick)
UM	Biakautuka 4 run (pass failed)
UM	Wheatley 5 run (Hayes pass from Collins)
UM	Hamilton 20 FG
UM	Toomer 65 pass from Collins (run failed)
CU	Salaam 1 run (Voskeritchian kick)
CU	Westbrook 64 pass from Stewart (no attempt)

Attendance 106,427

Virginia vs. Michigan

"It's never over until it's over, and it wasn't over."—George Welsh

THE BACKGROUND

The Pigskin Classic kicked off the '95 season for both Michigan and Virginia. For the Wolverines, it was an unveiling of the new guard. New head coach Lloyd Carr brought his first team into The Big House, and he also brought with him a new quarterback, redshirt freshman Scott Dreisbach. After beating out back-up Brian Griese for the starting job, the untested Dreisbach was a bit queasy about his opening day performance.

"I had the worst butterflies I've ever had in my life," Dreisbach said. "I almost threw up in the hotel before the game." Carr was nervous too. "I woke up at 4:30 this morning and I never went back to sleep," he said.

George Welsh was celebrating his 62nd birthday by coaching the 17th-ranked Cavaliers against the No. 14 Wolverines. Virginia had high hopes for the '95 campaign after finishing 9-3 in '94 and winning the Independence Bowl 20-10 over TCU.

The Cavaliers dominated most of the game as Dreisbach struggled to jump start a woeful Wolverines' offense. Early in the third quarter, runningback Tiki Barber took a handoff at the UVA 19 and rambled 81 yards for a Cavaliers' touchdown. Virginia led 14-0. Rafael Garcia hit a 30-yard field goal with 12:55 left in the game and the UVA lead was 17-0.

It could have been worse for Michigan. Garcia missed two first-half attempts of 30 and 39 yards.

Meanwhile, Dreisbach and Carr were hearing it from the crowd. After Dreisbach was picked off for the second time (this one in the Virgnia end zone late in the third quarter), boos flooded Michigan Stadium. "They were booing [Dreisbach]?" Carr said. "I thought they were booing me."

Probably both. Griese, the backup, started warming up.

Then, for a moment, Dreisbach silenced his own fans with a 41-yard completion to Mercury Hayes at the UVA 35. Seconds later, Ed Davis, subbing for injured tailback Tim Biakabatuka, finally got the Wolverines on the scoreboard with a two-yard TD plunge with 11:36 left. Remy Hamilton missed the extra point and the score was 17-6.

After Virginia was forced to punt on their own 24, Carr's offense turned into Air Dreisbach. Six straight completions covered 75 yards, the last pass a short one to Hayes who turned it into a 31-yard touchdown. Suddenly, it was 17-12 with 7:47 left. The Wolverines threw the ball 21 of their final 23 plays in the game.

Not a boo to be heard.

After the missed two-point conversion, Virginia looked to rebound. Quarterback Mike Groh, who had just been taken out for cramps and dehydration, returned to march the Cavaliers down to the Michigan 28 with under three minutes left. But on second down and two, Groh audibled from a run to a pass, the Cavaliers got confused, and the result was a four-yard loss. After an incomplete pass to Pete Allen, Welsh chose to punt from the Michigan 32 instead of trying a 49-yard Garcia field-goal attempt.

265

But instead of pinning the Wolverines deep in their own territory, Will Brice's punt took a wacky bounce, right over the head of UVA's Sam McKiver, who was ready to down it inside the Michigan 5. It landed in the end zone for a touchback.

Trailing by five, Dreisbach had 80 yards to go with 2:35 on the clock. With 1:06 left, Michigan was at their own 40. With 12 seconds left they were at the UVA 15 after Dreisbach dived for a first down. Then two incompletions.

Third-and-10. Six seconds left. Michigan had no timeouts left.

Receiver Tyrone Butterfield got open over the middle. But UVA cornerback Anthony Poindexter was waiting for Butterfield five yards shy of the first down at the 10. "I tried to wave [Dreisbach] off to not throw the ball," said Butterfield.

But the freshman threw it anyway.

"[It] was a mistake on my part," Dreisbach said. "I was supposed to throw the ball into the end zone or throw it away, and I didn't do either."

Instead, the ball came right to UM's Butterfield, who dropped it...intentionally, he claimed. "I tried to knock it down," he said, "but I made a mistake and tipped it up. I looked up and thought maybe somebody might catch it."

Had anyone caught it, on either team, the game would have been over as time would have run out. But no one did, leaving Michigan with four seconds and one last gasp remaining.

THE PLAY

CD2—Track 10
Larry Henry, Jim Brandstatter,
WWJ Newsradio 950

It was fourth down, but it didn't matter. From the UVA 15, this was the game's final play.

Split end Amani Toomer went wide left alongside the tight end. Hayes lined up wide right. Dreisbach took the snap and looked left.

Michigan's Mercury Hayes tries to stay in bounds on the game's final play. Photo courtesy of Bob Kalmbach

Game 80

"Amani had single coverage. After the snap, the coverage rotated to Toomer and that freed Hayes up. Hayes was wide open, I just had to get the ball to him," said Dreisbach, who set a Michigan record for passing yards (372) and attempts (27 of 52).

"I knew what I had to do," added the freshman QB.

Virginia defensive back Ronde Barber, the 1994 ACC Rookie of the Year, found himself alone against Hayes. He broke inside. Hayes went outside.

"I just made a wrong decision," said Barber. "I was playing the slant and I wasn't prepared for the corner. . .When he cut outside, there was nothing I could do."

Dreisbach threw the ball to the corner. Hayes, open on the sideline, reached for it and tried to keep one foot in bounds. He planted his left foot and dragged his right.

"We always talk about never giving up," Hayes said. "The game's never over until the clock goes zero, zero, zero."

The clock was at zero, zero, zero. Did Hayes get one foot down in the end zone?

For a second, 100,000 people went silent. Field judge Collin McDermott pointed down to the sideline where Hayes' foot came down, then made the signal. Hayes was inbounds. Touchdown Michigan. One hundred thousand people went nuts, pouring onto the field. "I was ecstatic...feeling good," said Hayes. "Then everybody swarmed me at one time."

Michigan had scored 18 unanswered points in the final quarter to win 18-17. On the last drive, Dreisbach squeezed 16 plays into 2:35, covering 80 yards, to cap the greatest comeback in 116 years of Michigan football.

"I don't ever remember losing a game like that," said Welsh, who was in his 23rd year as a head coach.

Carr's view was blocked on the winning pass. "I never saw [the play], but I'll never forget it," he said, following his first collegiate coaching victory.

THE AFTERMATH

Michigan won their first five games of the '95 season, but then Dreisbach broke his thumb and Griese became the starter. The Wolverines faltered with losses to Northwestern, Michigan State, and Penn State before shocking undefeated Ohio State 31-23. They finished the season 9-4 after losing to Texas A&M 22-20 in the Alamo Bowl.

After Griese was suspended in the spring of '96 for an off-campus altercation, Dreisbach regained his starting job until the end of the '96 season when he injured his arm against Ohio State. Griese again came on in relief, rallying Michigan from a 9-0 deficit to upset the undefeated Buckeyes for the second year in a row, 13-9. Griese returned for a fifth-year in '97, beating out Dreisbach for the starting role and leading UM on a wonderous 12-0 journey as Michigan won the national championship by beating Washington State 21-16 in the Rose Bowl. Griese was the game's MVP.

The '95 season became one that most Virginia fans will never forget, if nothing else than for the sheer torture of excruciating finishes almost every time the Cavaliers took the field. To mention a few, UVA scored on a one-yard TD run with 13 seconds left to beat NC State. They lost to Texas 17-16 on a 50-yard field goal with no time remaining, then later blew a 15-point second-half lead to Virginia Tech as the Hokies hit a 32-yard TD pass with 0:47 left and won 36-29.

Virginia alumnus Mark Bain eloquently and humorously summed up what it was like to be a Cavaliers fan at the Michigan game—a microcosm of the whole season.

"During the intermission between quarters three and four, the full weight of what our football team was doing dawned on us. We were dominating this traditional powerhouse on both sides of the ball in their own absurdly huge stadium, and the scoreboard showed it, 17-0. It was a beautiful sunny day in late August and the mix of the taste of imminent victory and bourbon was nothing short of exhilarating.

"The fourth quarter progressed, and our situation became more and more unpalatable as the excitement of the Michigan fans grew and the differential on the scoreboard shrank. Our navy-and-orange-bleeding Cavalier hearts found their usual lodgings up in our throats for Michigan's final and decisive possession. When

Mercury Hayes' foot came down and the officials' arms went up, I felt like I had just heard the shots ring out for my own execution. Shock, disbelief, disorientation, emptiness. These feelings stayed fresh with me for a good three hours following the game as I wandered the streets of Ann Arbor. When a semblance of normal brain function returned, I made it home. The devasted feeling has faded but will always be there."

That depressed state must have been cured a few weeks later when the Cavaliers hosted Florida State.

Virginia	0	7	7	3	-17
Michigan	0	0	0	18	-18

UVA	Groh 1 run (Garcia kick)
UVA	T. Barber 81 run (Garcia kick)
UVA	FG Garcia 30
UM	Davis 2 run (kick failed)
UM	Hayes 31 pass from Dreisbach (conversion failed)
UM	Hayes 15 pass from Dreisbach (no attempt)

Attendance 101,444

Arkansas vs. Alabama

"I think maybe we had a little bit of [divine intervention] today."—Barry Lunney

THE BACKGROUND

Danny Ford's first trip back to Alabama to coach against his alma mater was not a pleasant one. The Crimson Tide pummeled Ford's Razorbacks in 1993, 44-3. In fact, entering Bryant-Denny Stadium two years later, Arkansas had never beaten Alabama in their five previous meetings.

Well, actually they had. At the beginning of the '95 season, Alabama was hit hard by the NCAA, placed on probation, and forced to forfeit 11 games from the '93 season because of penalties stemming from player Antonio Langham's dealings with an agent and improper loans received by former player Gene Jelks. The '93 rout became an Arkansas win with an asterisk.

"That doesn't help us now, does it?" Ford said of the forfeit. "If it helped us two years ago, that would mean something, but it's just history now. We still got beat, and we got beat bad."

In '95, despite the turmoil in Tuscaloosa (athletic director Hootie Ingram had just resigned), the Tide was 2-0 and ranked 13th as they opened their SEC conference schedule. Arkansas was 1-1, their loss coming to Southern Methodist in the opener when quarterback Barry Lunney, who had driven his team 79 yards to the SMU one-yard line with 56 seconds left, fumbled the ball. SMU recovered and won the game.

"I fumbled the ball, it was a clean snap," Lunney said. "I feel bad about it. Obviously, you can't forget something like this. It hurts."

Lunney, a left-handed senior, would remember that play two weeks later.

Brian Burgdorf's 40-yard scoring pass to Curtis Brown before halftime gave the Crimson Tide a 17-10 lead heading into the locker room. But the 'Bama offense came to a halt in the second half. Gene Stallings' squad managed just one first down in the last two quarters. Still their defense put two more points on the board when Razorback sophomore running-back Madre Hill (who set an SEC record with six touchdowns the week before) was tackled in the end zone with 9:48 left in the third quarter. The safety was setup by a 'Bama punt that hit at the Razorback 18 and rolled to the one-yard line. J.J. Meadors called for a fair catch but let the ball roll. Hill was tackled on the next play.

"I was thinking I had pretty much lost the game for us after we had worked so hard," said Meadors. The Alabama lead was 19-10.

With 'Bama at midfield on the next series, Arkansas linebacker Mark Smith picked off a Burgdorf pass and returned it 48 yards to the 'Bama 8. The Tide defense held, forcing a 21-yard field goal by redshirt freshman Todd Latourette to make the score 19-13. Still, Arkansas had gained some momentum which was fueled by their stingy defense. The Razorbacks continued to shut down 'Bama's offense, rationing the Tide to just three yards of offense in the fourth quarter.

With both defenses dominating, Arkansas gained some field position and started from

Arkansas' Barry Lunney threw quickly...

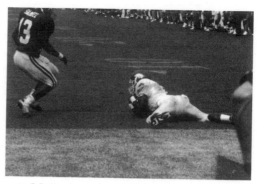

...to J.J. Meadors, who slid his hands between the ball and the grass. Photos courtesy of University of Arkansas Sports Information

their own 43 with 3:13 remaining in the game. They went backward. After Lunney was sacked for a 13-yard loss, the Razorbacks faced third-and-24 on their 30, and the clock under two minutes. Lunney hit Hill for 15 yards to set up fourth-and-eight.

At the Arkansas 45, down by six points, the Hogs needed one play to stay alive.

The 'Bama defense attacked Lunney. "We couldn't hardly hold them out," said Ford about the Tide's defensive line. In fact, Arkansas didn't have a first down in the last seven possessions. Facing his last chance, Lunney scrambled. He bounced off two tacklers avoiding a sack, then found freshman Anthony Lucas on the sidelines for a 31-yard completion to the 'Bama 24 with 1:34 left.

New life for the Hogs. "They thought Barry was going to get sacked, and Barry got out of it," said the Razorbacks' coach.

"[Lunney] made a great escape," said Stallings.

The drive continued.

After a false start penalty on Arkansas, Hill took an option pitch for 10 yards to the 19. Then Meadors ran a slant pattern, caught Lunney's throw inside the 10 and took it to the 'Bama three-yard line. Fifty seconds left and the clock was running.

First and goal at the three. Lunney had been there before. "I was thinking, 'Don't throw an interception—four downs and you're bound to score,'" he said.

Lunney tried to get in on an option left but was stopped for a one-yard loss. Twenty-three seconds left. After a timeout by both teams,

the senior QB found Cory Nichols out of the backfield over the middle, but the freshman runningback was upended at the three. Arkansas was forced to use their last timeout with 0:13 on the clock. The Tide defense was making a gallant final stand.

On third down, Lunney took a quick drop and looked to Anthony Eubanks. The pass was broken up just beyond the goal line. Fourth down at the three. Ten seconds to go.

THE PLAY
CD 2-Track 11
Paul Eels, Rick Schaefer,
Arkansas Razorback Sports Network

Meadors, whose mistake led to the last 'Bama score, lined up to the left. Lunney, whose fumble gave SMU the victory two weeks prior, stood over center. Everyone else in Bryant-Denny Stadium stood with him.

"The coaches called an option route, which is whatever the defense does, you do the opposite, just like backyard football," explained Meadors. Alabama's free safety Cedric Samuel guarded Meadors. "He went inside and I came out," said the senior flanker. Meadors was open in the flat just over the goal line.

Lunney rolled left and had one thing on his mind. "I was just thinking J.J., J.J., J.J.. You don't have time to look for four guys in that situation."

He flung a left-handed low line drive to the end zone. "I remember seeing it coming low and thinking, 'Get your arms around, get your arms around it,'" said Meadors.

Game 81

Meadors slid and scooped the ball into his hands. Did he catch it before it hit the ground? To this day, many Alabama fans don't think so. "I made the catch and rolled over to see the ref's arms go up. I did make the catch. It was low, but I caught it," he said. It was a touchdown Arkansas. Lunney had come through. The score was tied 19-19 with 0:06 left.

"He's been to the mountain several times and couldn't make the play," said Ford about his quarterback. "Today he climbed the mountain."

Latourette came in and calmly booted the game-winning extra point. Was Ford concerned that the freshman would miss the PAT? "No way he was going to miss that kick," said Ford. "I didn't even look at it. I was just worried about having too many men on the field and getting a 15-yard penalty."

THE AFTERMATH

Ford had good reason to worry about having too many men on the field. The Wednesday following the game, the entire officials' crew was suspended by the SEC for, among other things, missing a crucial detail in the final drive.

Ford acknowledged the Razorbacks had 12 men on the field on the second-and-goal play from the Alabama 4 when Lunney threw to Nichols for a one-yard gain. If Arkansas had been flagged for having 12 players on the field, it would have been a 15-yard penalty and loss of down. The Hogs would have faced third-and-goal from the 18 instead of third-and-goal from the three.

"That ain't a break. That's just luck," Ford said of not being penalized. "But we'll take it and be glad to take it."

The Razorbacks' win propelled them to the SEC western division title after victories over No. 11 Auburn, 30-28, and Mississippi State, 26-21, both thrillers that also went down to the final play. The Hogs moved to 8-2 and were ranked 13th. But then three straight losses, to LSU 28-0, Florida 34-3 in the SEC title game, and to North Carolina 20-10 in the Carquest Bowl, ended their season on a down note with a 8-5 record.

The season was a record-breaking one for the two stars of the 'Bama victory. Lunney 's TD pass was his 335th completion, breaking Bill Montgomery's Arkansas career record. Meadors, only 5-6 and 152 lbs., became the school's career leader for receptions.

'Bama finished 8-3 with losses to Tennessee 41-14 and Auburn 31-27. They were banned from appearing in a post-season bowl game.

September 16, 1995—Tuscaloosa, Alabama

Arkansas	10	0	3	7	-20
Alabama	3	14	2	0	-19

Ark	Latourette FG 21
Ala	Proctor FG 43
Ark	Kunney 3 run (Latourette kick)
Ala	Riddle 1 run (Proctor kick)
Ala	C. Brown 40 pass from Burgdorf (Proctor kick)
Ala	Hill tackled in end zone for safety
Ark	Latourette FG 23
Ark	Meadors 3 pass from Lunney (Latourette kick)

Attendance 70,123

Auburn vs. Louisiana State

"I didn't do anything spectacular. I just didn't throw six interceptions."—Jamie Howard

THE BACKGROUND

The Earthquake game in 1988. The Jamie Howard game of 1994. The Bring Back the Magic Game in 1995. All part of the unforgettable recent history when Auburn and LSU faced off.

In 1995, Gerry DiNardo ran onto the field at Tiger Stadium in Baton Rouge for the first time ever as head coach of LSU. Fireworks exploded and 80,559 fans roared. The second-largest crowd ever in Death Valley witnessed a new era for the LSU program. DiNardo promised to "bring back the magic" to LSU football.

Terry Bowden knew how that felt. In 1993, he started his Division I-A coaching career by winning 20 straight games as head coach at Auburn, the most consecutive victories ever by a new Division I-A coach. Coming into the third game of the '95 season, Bowden, in his third year at Auburn, had lost just one game.

He should've lost two.

The season before, LSU held a 23-9 lead at Auburn with 13 minutes to play in the fourth quarter when the inexplicable happened. Jamie Howard's worst nightmare came true. In fact, this was a dream so horrific that no quarterback could conjure it up. Howard, the junior signal caller at LSU, was intercepted by strong safety Ken Alvis who ran the ball back 42 yards for a touchdown, cutting LSU's lead to 23-16. A minute later, Howard threw again. Auburn intercepted again, and ran it back for a touchdown again. Fred Smith's 32-yard return made it 23-23. Then, with 1:55 to play, after LSU had regained the lead 26-23, someone should have awakened Howard before he threw again.

They didn't. It happened a third time. Auburn's Brian Robinson intercepted a third Howard pass and ran it back 41 yards for the winning score. Howard threw six interceptions in the game, three returned for touchdowns in the fourth quarter. Auburn won 30-26 in a game that ultimately sunk LSU coach Curley Hallman's flailing ship. He was fired at the end of the season and replaced by DiNardo, former coach at Vanderbilt.

The following year, Bowden's Tigers came to Death Valley 2-0, ranked No. 5 in the country. Dinardo's Tigers were 1-1, hoping for their first winning season since 1988, the year of the Earthquake game. Coincidentally, that was the last time LSU beat Auburn. In that game, trailing 6-0 with 1:41 left, LSU QB Tommy Hodson threw a 10-yard touchdown pass to Eddie Fuller on fourth down, giving LSU the 7-6 victory. The crowd in Baton Rouge exploded into an earthshaking frenzy so loud that it registered on a seismographic record in a LSU science hall.

In 1995, seven years after the last rumblings were heard from LSU football, DiNardo's team hoped to rock Death Valley once again. They stormed out of the gate with a dominating first-half performance, holding the ball for for 21:33 compared to Auburn's 8:27, and outgaining Auburn 225-74.

Determined to scare away the ghosts of the '94 game, Howard connected with tight end Nicky Savoie for a four-yard touchdown in the first quarter. Then with LSU leading 10-3, defensive end James Gillyard tackled Auburn QB Patrick Nix in the end zone to make the score 12-3. On the play, Nix and a confused Auburn offense stopped in their tracks after hearing a false whistle blown from the LSU crowd. Gillyard took advantage, burying the quarterback for two points.

But LSU's scoring stopped after the first quarter, and for a brief moment in the second quarter, flashes of Howard's Hell returned. With two minutes to play in the half and LSU at the Auburn eight-yard line, Auburn's Dell McGee picked off a Howard pass at the one-yard line and streaked 66 yards before being run down by Savoie at the LSU 33.

But the LSU defense held, the half ended 12-3, and Howard took a huge sigh of relief.

Auburn's Matt Hawkins kicked a 28-yard field goal at 9:44 of the third quarter to make the score 12-6. Placekicker Andre LaFleur blew two chances to increase the margin for LSU, missing field-goal attempts of 36 and 39 yards. The last one hit the left upright midway through the fourth quarter, giving Bowden's Tigers new life.

But the Auburn offense failed. A Nix pass to Robert Baker on fourth-and-long fell incomplete and LSU took over. Still, DiNardo's offense couldn't run out the clock, however, and Auburn got one last chance from their 26-yard line with 2:19 left in the game.

Nix began a determined march downfield. Fourteen plays later, the ball was at the LSU 11-yard line, Auburn was out of timeouts, the clock was running down, and Nix quickly brought his team to the line of scrimmage.

He spiked the ball, stopping the clock with four seconds left. Facing fourth down and three, Nix had time for one more play.

THE PLAY

CD2—Track 12
Jim Hawthorne, LSU Sports Network

Auburn had scored 17 TDs in their first two games of the season. This night, they had none.

Down by six, they needed a touchdown. LSU needed some magic. The Tiger Stadium crowd reached back to 1998, roaring to earth shaking proportions. Even the LSU defensive

huddle was loud. "Everybody was yelling," said linebacker Pat Rogers.

"We can either run a vertical out or a vertical in," Bowden said, looking to exploit the LSU secondary. Auburn wide receiver Tyrone Goodsen broke to the right corner of the end zone. The same corner where Eddie Fuller's catch rocked the LSU campus in '88. This time, LSU was on defense.

Nix floated it toward Goodsen. Sophomore cornerback Troy Twillie was the defender. "Please, please knock it down," thought Rogers, along with 80,000 others.

"It was a deep outside zone," said Twillie. "We practiced that play all week. I just said, 'I'm going to get it, I don't care who's out there.'"

He leaped. Time expired.

Twillie outfought Goodsen for the ball, intercepting it, preserving a 12-6 LSU victory, and igniting a celebration in Baton Rouge not seen in many years.

Howard, the goat from 1994, was now the golden calf, hoisted on his teammates shoulders after the victory. With modest passing numbers (16 of 26 for 198 yards and one TD), his most important statistic was the one interception he threw...five less than the '94 game.

"That was the happiest moment I've ever had in Tiger Stadium," Howard said. "I didn't want to leave the field."

Bowden could only ask "what if," wondering what would have happened had Goodsen run to the inside of the field instead of the corner. "We outguessed ourselves and ran the vertical out. If it had been a vertical in, it would have been right there."

For LSU, it was a new beginning. "This is a new era," said kicker Lafleur. "The magic is back. The fans are there. The offense is kicking. It's like the Tigers of old."

THE AFTERMATH

DiNardo's first home victory did launch a three-year turnaround in the LSU program. They ended the '95 season 7-4-1 (4-3-1 in the SEC),with a 45-26 victory over Michigan State in the Independence Bowl.

The LSU coach enjoyed early success in Baton Rouge, leading the school to three straight bowl victories, a 10-2 record in '96 and a 9-3 slate in '97. But then LSU spiraled downhill in 1998 and '99, going 6-15 under DiNardo. Eight straight losses during the '99 season and DiNardo was fired as head coach before the last game of the regular season. He compiled a 32-24-1 record at LSU.

Like DiNardo, Bowden's early success at Auburn met a similar fate in the following years.

Auburn finished the 1995 campaign 8-4 (5-3 SEC), losing to Penn State 43-13 in the Outback Bowl. After an unparalleled start, Bowden's tenure at Auburn ended abruptly in 1998, when he was essentially forced to resign after Auburn fell to 1-5 during the season. He owns the highest winning percentage (.731) among all Auburn coaches since 1900 with a record of 47-17-1.

Auburn	3	0	3	0	- 6
LSU	12	0	0	0	-12

LSU	Savoie 4 pass from Howard (LaFleur kick)
AU	FG Hawkins 41
LSU	FG LaFleur 41
LSU	Safety, Nix tackled in end zone
AU	FG Hawkins 28

Attendance 80,559

Cincinnati vs. Miami (Ohio)

"Honestly, I thought…we'd need a miracle like we got last week."—*Randy Walker*

THE BACKGROUND

This was the 100th meeting between these two southwestern Ohio schools, an annual battle dating back to 1888, the sixth most played rivalry in Division 1-A.

As gut-wrenching as the first few weeks of the season had been for Cincinnati, they were equally as spine-tingling for Miami. UC opened their season by losing at Kansas 23-18 when quarterback Eric Vibberts' 20-yard pass into the end zone with no time left fell incomplete. The next week versus No. 21-ranked Kansas State, the Bearcats' opponent scored on the exact same play UC had failed on. K-state's Kevin Lockett caught a 22-yard TD pass from Matt Miller on the last play of the game to beat the Bearcats 23-21. Head coach Rick Minter's squad entered the Miami game 1-2 after knocking off highly regarded Virginia Tech 16-0. It was Tech's last loss of the season as they marched on to a No. 10 ranking and Sugar Bowl victory over Texas.

Miami (2-1) opened their season with a 17-15 loss to Ball State when Chad Seitz' 51-yard field-goal attempt hit the right upright and bounced away with 0:03 left. But Seitz and the Redskins came back to pull off a stunning victory over Northwestern. The Wildcats, fresh off a shocking upset of Notre Dame, led 28-7 before Miami rallied to pull within 28-27 with 0:43 left. Northwestern was set to punt the ball away when back-up long snapper Larry Curry snapped the ball low and through the legs of punter Paul Burton, who chased the ball all the way down to his own one-yard line. From there, Miami's Seitz kicked the game-winning 20-yard FG as time ran out for the 30-28 victory. Like UC's win over Tech, Miami's triumph was Northwestern's last regular-season loss in a Cinderella season that led Gary Barnett's team to a Big Ten title and Rose Bowl appearance.

Not only were both Cincinnati and Miami inclined to heart-stopping 1995 finishes, the previous year's matchup between the two was perhaps even more remarkable. After UC's walk-on kicker Jon Bacon (who had never made a field goal in his career) booted a dramatic 58-yard field goal with 1:19 to play (the longest kick in the school's history), the Bearcats led 17-14. Miami drove to the UC 20. With just 0:05 on the clock, Miami quarterback Neil Dougherty lofted a high pass toward the left sideline for receiver Scott Trostel. The ball came down at the three-yard line and two UC defenders batted the ball away. It seemed like time ran out. It didn't. There was one second left on the Yager Stadium (Miami's home field) scoreboard. Seitz ran onto the field, kicked the 37-yard field goal, and the game ended in a tie, 17-17.

UC coach Minter was furious. "Who's keeping the . . . clock?" he screamed at referee J.C. Louderback . Yes, the same J.C. Louderback who officiated the infamous Colorado-Missouri fifth-down game from 1990.

"They're keeping it up there," Louderback said, pointing at the press box where Miami timekeeper Eldon Wyckoff controlled the clock.

"I'm not here to criticize the timekeeper, but I will say this—I'd never run a play with five seconds to go. Obviously they know something we don't," noted Minter after the game. (After looking at the videotape, UC's film crew later claimed that the final two plays, which ran from 0:11 to 0:01, actually took 13.5 seconds.)

"Nobody didn't win and nobody didn't lose," said UC receiver Anthony Ladd.

When the two teams met one year later in 1995, it shouldn't have surprised anyone when the Bearcats, trailing 16-6 in a mistake-filled defensive struggle, staged a late fourth-quarter rally destined for a dramatic finish. With just over five minutes to play, Vibberts took over on his own 22 and marched UC to the Miami 20 in just five plays. He then found Ladd with a 20-yard TD pass to cut the Miami lead to 16-13 with 3:39 left.

The Bearcats' defense held on downs, forcing Miami to punt. The Redskins would then pay for their punting fortunes from the previous week at Northwestern. Déjà vu. Punter Jason Cheney watched the snap sail over his head. He scrambled for the ball, picked it up, and then desperately threw a wild pass. It was intercepted by UC's Ivan Fulton at the Miami 40. Fulton returned it to the Miami 20 and the Bearcats had a chance to win the game with 1:19 on the clock.

After two plays, UC was facing third down and five at the 16. Vibberts, in the shotgun, looked toward the sidelines, relayed signals to his wide receiver, and then....the ball hit him in the helmet. The center snapped it before Vibberts was looking. Stunned, Vibberts recovered to fall on the ball at the 27. Now facing fourth-and-17, Minter had no choice but to send in Eric Richards to kick a 45-yard field goal. He did, and the game was tied at 16-16 with only 0:32 left.

For the second straight year, it looked like no one would win the battle for the Victory Bell.

THE PLAY

Miami coach Randy Walker expected Minter to play for the win. He sent in his "hands" unit to try and recover an onside kick. Of the 11 players on the regular kick-return team for Mi-

ami, only four were on the field. The other players were receivers, sure-handed backs, and even quarterback Sam Ricketts. The Redskins had nine men within 10 yards of the 45 where the expected kick would come. The other two men were deep.

To Walker's surprise, Minter had Richards kick the ball deep, a high pooch kick that came down to the left side at the 18-yard line.

"We rehearse a run-back in case they kick deep," said Walker. "It's not a great run-back, but we have ten guys out there, and they can all block."

Ty King, a junior back-up tailback to all-time MAC rushing leader Deland McCullough, caught the ball at the 18. The other Redskins retreated quickly and tried to form a "double wedge" to block for King. They hadn't rehearsed blocking much out of that formation.

"I can't say that I was too upset when they didn't kick it to me," said quarterback Ricketts, not excited by the thought of being piled on. "When they kicked it deep, I was supposed to run down and form sort of a wall, but I didn't touch a soul."

He didn't need to. King burst upfield untouched. "There were all these red Miami jerseys and all of a sudden there was a hole there like the gates of heaven opened up," said King. "Someone from UC didn't fill their lane or something."

"He looked like he was running a 100-meter dash," said Walker. Not a coincidence. King, a sprinter on the Miami track team, would break the school record in the 100-meter dash (10.4 seconds) the following spring. If they clocked this kickoff return, it may have been faster.

Kicker Richards took a shot at tackling King. "No offense to the guy," said King, "but no stupid kicker is going to stop me there."

That left one Bearcat player with a chance to stop him. It was Anthony Ladd. The two had met before, in the past year's indoor track season. King beat Ladd in the 55-meter dash. This time it would be the final 40 yards of King's return. Ladd chased him down inside the UC five-yard line. He dove for King, wrapped his arms around him, and pulled him down. But it was too late. King fell into the end zone with

September 23, 1995—Oxford, Ohio

0:19 left, an 82-yard touchdown run. Miami won the game 23-16.

Minter wasn't too pleased with his team's coverage. "We're allowed to have 11 [players] out there, any one of which is allowed to make a tackle," he sarcastically commented after the game.

When King felt Ladd on his back at the end, he wasn't stopping short. "Once I got that far, the only thing that would have stopped me was a natural disaster or a sniper in the crowd," he said.

THE AFTERMATH

The Redskins, now known as the RedHawks, ended the season 8-2-1, losing the week after the UC game to Michigan 38-19, but winning their final four games of the season. UC finished the season 6-5, winning five of their last seven games.

As if the last two games of the series weren't thrilling enough, the following two battles in '96 and '97 simply played along with the old phrase "Can you top this?" With the advent of overtime play in the '96 season, the Miami-UC game took full advantage of the extra periods. UC got revenge in '96 with a 30-23 triple overtime victory when linebacker Brad Jackson forced a fumble at the goal line just as Miami's Nod Washington was about to score. UC's Artrell Hawkins recovered the ball in the end zone for the Bearcat victory. In '97, it was a 34-31 double overtime win for UC.

"This is a great rivalry, one of the better ones in college football," said Minter. "It's truly for local bragging rights. People talk about it long after they graduate."

Cincinnati	0	6	0	10	-16
Miami (OH)	3	3	10	7	-23

MU	Seitz 19 FG
UC	Richards 39 FG
MU	Seitz 32 FG
UC	Richards 27 FG
MU	J. Hall 8 pass from Ricketts (Seitz kick)
MU	Seitz 32 FG
UC	Ladd 20 pass from Vibberts (Richards kick)
UC	Richards 45 FG
MU	King 82 kickoff return (Seitz kick)

Attendance 21,124

Florida State vs. Virginia 🏈

November 2, 1995—Charlottesville, Virginia

"It's a feeling of ecstasy."—*Tiki Barber*

THE BACKGROUND

In 1992, Florida State played their first football game as a member of the Atlantic Coast Conference. The other eight conference schools must have been thrilled.

The Seminoles football team dominated the ACC, reeling off 29 straight conference victories over the next four years. From '93 to '95, the closest any ACC team came to beating Florida State was a 31-18 FSU win over North Carolina in '94. Hardly a nail-biter.

While the second-ranked Seminoles were rolling right along through their schedule as usual in '95 (7-0 overall, 5-0 in the ACC), 24th-ranked Virginia (6-3 overall, 5-1 in the ACC), was trying to regroup from a heartbreaking 17-16 loss to Texas two weeks prior. Phil Dawson's 50-yard field goal into the wind as time expired gave Virginia its second loss of the season on the game's final play (See Michigan-Virginia '95).

Both teams had an extra week off to prepare for the nationally televised Thursday night battle. "We dubbed this the 'ACC Championship Game,'" said Cavaliers runningback Tiki Barber, eternally optimistic despite being an 18½-point underdog.

An early weekend party atmosphere prevailed at Scott Stadium as the Virginia fans took quarterback Mike Groh's pre-game comments to heart. "I hope they leave the wine and cheese at home and bring the domestic beer," said Groh.

They probably drank a toast to Groh after his 72-yard TD pass to Demetrius Allen gave the Cavaliers a surprising 24-14 lead with 3:05 left in the first half.

Despite trailing by 10, the Florida State offensive machine was clicking on all cylinders. Seminoles QB Danny Kanell shredded the Cavs' defense, throwing for 320 yards and three touchdowns in the first two quarters alone. How fast could they strike? Eighty yards in 52 seconds. Kanell's 38-yard TD pass to E.G. Green made it 24-21.

The powerful FSU offense should have scored more. But at key moments throughout the half, the Seminoles' motor stalled, thanks to a deafening Cavaliers home crowd and some key defensive plays. "We had some communication difficulties," FSU coach Bobby Bowden said. "That crowd was as vocal as any crowd. I didn't think they could make that much noise."

The Virginia defense was contributing too, thwarting two FSU threats deep in UVA territory, one with an interception by safety Percy Ellsworth at the two-yard line, the other with a fourth-and-two stop at the UVA 17. They also blocked an FSU punt to set up a score. After a Rafael Garcia 48-yard field goal, the Wahoos led 27-21 at the half.

Helped by the booming punts of Will Brice, which pinned FSU inside their 10-yard line three times in the second half, Virginia kept the Seminoles at bay. Garcia's fourth field goal, with 6:57 left in the fourth quarter, gave UVA a 33-21 lead.

Then a blast of momentum blew up from Tallahassee.

Game 84

Florida State came roaring back, eating up 80 yards in 44 seconds. Tailback Warrick Dunn threw a 33-yard halfback option pass to Andre Cooper, then scored on a seven-yard run himself with 6:13 left to cut the lead to 33-28.

The Seminoles' defense subsequently forced a punt and Kanell had the ball again at his 16-yard line with 3:29 left. But after moving to the 27, the FSU quarterback was picked off for the third time in the game. Another huge Cavaliers takeaway. It was Ellsworth's second interception, this time at the UVA 45.

With 2:36 left, Virginia just needed a first down. They couldn't get it. Three and out and Florida State had the ball again at their own 20 with 1:37 to play. A lifetime for Bowden's wide open attack.

As another tidal wave of Seminoles offense came ashore, the Cavaliers desperately struggled to hold on in the waning seconds.

Kanell completed 5-of-8 passes, hitting Andre Cooper three times for 11, 16, and 9 yards. The Seminoles briskly moved to the UVA 33. Then out of the backfield, Dunn took a Kanell pass and rambled to the 13-yard line. Kanell quickly moved up to spike the ball and stop the clock. He did with 0:09 left.

A flag flew and Virginia was called for illegal participation. The ball was moved half the distance to the goal to the six-yard line. Kanell then tried for the end zone, found no one open, and threw the ball out of the back end zone.

With 0:04 on the clock, the ball was still at the UVA six-yard line.

THE PLAY

CD 2—Track 13—*Frank Quayle,* *Warren Swain,* **The Virginia Sports Network**

It seemed inevitable. Virginia coach George Welsh saw the familiar poison arrow of fate headed straight for the Cavaliers' hearts. "Honest to God, I thought, 'Oh my God, another one,'" Welsh said. "I thought for sure we were going to lose," he added, remembering last-play losses to Michigan and Texas during the season.

This was a moment made for Bobby Bowden, the legendary gambler in these types of situations. "I figured they'd play 100 percent for the pass," Bowden said.

Offensive coordinator Mark Richt came up with the play. Bowden approved. Four receivers split wide. Dunn was the lone runningback with Kannell in the shotgun.

Kannell never got the ball. Dunn did.

A direct snap from the center to Dunn. A trick play used by Bowden only one other time early in the second quarter. Bowden's move even caught Dunn off guard. " I was surprised by the play. It was the last one I thought we'd call," he said.

With the Virginia defense spread out, Dunn bolted up the middle hoping to catch the Cavaliers by surprise.

He stormed to the three-yard line where freshman safety Adrian Burnim tried to halt him. Slowed but not stopped, Dunn was still going forward to the goal line. Anthony Poindexter, also a freshman, desperately joined in to help Burnim.

"I saw [Dunn] going down, someone was on him," said Poindexter. "Adrian, I guess. I just tried to hit him again . . . stop him from going forward."

But the 178-lb. Dunn , now fighting off two tacklers, lunged for the end zone. Then, as Dunn reached for paydirt, linebacker Melvin Jones hit him.

Right at the goal line.

"I lost control of the ball," said Dunn. "But I felt I had crossed the goal line and I thought I was in."

The officials thought otherwise. In the mayhem, Dunn was ruled down just inches from the end zone. The clock read 0:00. The inevitable never happened. Virginia won.

Almost instantly the stands emptied, flooding the field with fans as Dunn laid at the goal line. Burnim ran off the field squeezing the ball. The goalposts had no chance of survival.

Barber, who racked up 193 yards rushing and two touchdowns in the game, was too scared to watch at the end. "During the last play, I was looking at the ground ... By the time I opened my eyes, I was swarmed."

The Seminoles were shocked. "It's something we probably wouldn't have expected in a million years," FSU linebacker Daryl Bush said.

Two raucous parties of delirious Virginia students paraded sections of the goalposts

November 2, 1995—Charlottesville, Virginia

The Virginia faithful at Scott Stadium stood throughout the game...

...then celebrated wildly after Warrick Dunn's run came up inches short. Photo courtesy of Dan Millin—The Cavalier Daily

around campus, past the statue of Thomas Jefferson, founder of the school, and surely over to a wild fraternity bash.

Meanwhile Bowden was searching for answers. "I don't know how close it was," he said.

"One-foot line," answered UVA linebacker Jamie Sharper, also near the pile at the goal line. "As close as you get without doing it."

Florida State had lost an ACC game for the first time ever. "I'm not happy," lamented Bowden. "But this is good for the conference."

THE AFTERMATH

Florida State and Virginia shared the ACC title in '95 with identical 7-1 conference records. The Seminoles lost to Florida 35-24 to end their regular season 9-2, then rallied to beat Notre Dame 31-26 in the Orange Bowl and finish No. 4 in the AP poll.

The Cavaliers' heart-pounding season ended fittingly in the Peach Bowl. With 1:15 to play, leading Georgia 27-20, Groh completed a pass to tight end Walt Derey deep in his own territory. Derey then fumbled at the Virginia 10-yard line. Georgia defensive lineman Jason Ferguson scooped up the loose ball, rumbled into the end zone and tied the game 27-27 with 1:09 on the clock.

On the ensuing kickoff, UVA's Demetrius Allen took the Georgia kickoff at the 17-yard line. He bolted to the right side, wavered along the out-of-bounds line like a circus tightrope walker, then regained his balance to finish an 83-yard touchdown return with 57 seconds left. Virginia beat Georgia 34-27 in Ray Goff's final game as Bulldogs coach. The Cavaliers' unforgettable year ended 9-4 with a No. 16 ranking.

The Virginia win over Florida State hardly signaled an era of parity in the ACC. Three more years and 18 straight conference wins passed before the Seminoles lost another ACC game, a 24-7 stunner to North Carolina State in 1998.

Florida State	14	7	0	7	- 28
Virginia	7	20	3	3	- 33

FSU	Riley 35 pass from Kanell (Bentley kick)
VA	Barber 64 run (Garcia kick)
FSU	Dunn 14 pass from Kanell (Bentley kick)
VA	Barber 1 pass from Groh (Garcia kick)
VA	FG Garcia 35
VA	Allen 72 pass from Groh (Garcia kick)
FSU	Green 38 pass from Kanell (Bentley kick)
VA	FG Garcia 48
VA	FG Garcia 41
VA	FG Garcia 35
FSU	Dunn 7 run (Bentley kick)

Attendance 44,300

November 2, 1995—Charlottesville, Virginia

281

Penn State vs. Michigan State

"If you had a bad heart condition, you'd probably have had a heart attack."—Derrick Mason, Michigan State receiver

THE BACKGROUND

Michigan State hadn't had a winning season since 1990. After the '94 season, amidst an investigation which ultimately led to the forfeiture of their five victories in 1994 and an 0-11 record, head coach George Perles stepped down, making way for former defensive coordinator Nick Saban to come in and relight the flame that once burned bright under the legendary MSU coach Duffy Daugherty.

Saban's first game as head coach at Michigan State was no surprise. Left with a major rebuilding project in his first year in East Lansing, Saban watched his young Spartans get destroyed 50-10 by Nebraska, the eventual national champions.

But as the season evolved, so did Saban's vision for the MSU program. Sparked by quarterback Tony Banks, a monumental 28-25 conquest of No. 7 Michigan turned Saban's first season from promising to historic. Even at 6-3-1, Michigan State football was back.

Penn State football had never left.

Joe Paterno's Nittany Lions were 11-0 during the '94 regular season. A 38-20 Rose Bowl win over Oregon capped a perfect year for the Nittany Lions. Perfect yet empty. The Nebraska Cornhuskers, also undefeated, were voted national champions, leaving those in Happy Valley, not so happy.

Nineteen-ninety-five was a year to prove the voters wrong. But gone were Kerry Collins and Ki-Jana Carter to the NFL, and although the Lions couldn't match the magic of '94 (a 20-

game winning streak came to an end at the hands of Wisconsin 17-9), entering the last game of the season, Penn State (7-3) was 14th-ranked and primed for a New Year's Bowl invitation. But first, they had to beat Saban's Spartans, who also were looking for a bowl bid themselves.

The chilly Saturday evening in November provided few offensive thrills for the 66,189 bundled fans. After three quarters, the score was knotted at a rather dull 10-10. Michigan State had played an unforgettable 10-10 tie in its history. This wasn't it.

But the fourth quarter in Spartan Stadium was worth the extra cup of hot chocolate.

It started with a 16-yard touchdown run by MSU runningback Scott Greene (19 carries for 95 yards) to give the Spartans the 17-10 advantage. But just over three minutes later, Penn State junior quarterback Wally Richardson hooked up with speedster Bobby Engram, who flew down the left sideline for a 53-yard score and the game was tied at 17-17 with 9:48 left.

The Spartans struck back. After driving to the Penn State 16, Greene broke loose for a 15-yard gain to the one-yard line. But a critical holding penalty negated the run and MSU settled for a Chris Gardner 28-yard field goal to regain the lead 20-17 with 5:13 remaining.

Penn State looked to be losing its grip on a New Year's Bowl invitation. On third-and-six from the PSU 43, Richardson dropped back to pass and was swarmed under by three Spartans back at the 34-yard line. The clock dipped under the 3:00 mark. Paterno waved out his punting team on fourth-and-15 and Penn State kicked the ball away. Perhaps never to see it again.

Michigan State took over on their own 29-yard line with 2:19 left. The Spartans just needed one first down. They ended up getting just one yard.

Greene tried the left side twice, but only mustered five yards. On third-and-five, Banks rolled right on a quarterback sweep, then covered up the ball as he was hit from behind by cornerback Mark Tate for a four-yard loss. "We didn't want to throw the ball in that situation," said Saban of the conservative play-call. "We wanted them to use their last timeout."

Well, the Spartans did succeed on that count. Penn State used all three of their timeouts on the series to preserve time. Then, after a Chris Salani punt was returned five yards by Mike Archie, the Lions took over on the PSU 27-yard line with 1:45 remaining and no timeouts.

Just one minute previously, it looked like the Penn State offense had taken their last snap of the '95 regular season. Who would have thought that Richardson would run 15 more plays?

In one of the more remarkable time conserving drives, Richardson picked at the Spartan defense like it were a turkey carcass the day after Thanksgiving. Penn State ran 12 straight plays, dump offs to fullback Brad Milne, flat passes to Mike Archie, first-down completions to Freddie Scott and Engram. The clock stopped after each one.

"We let them get out of bounds too many times when they shouldn't have gotten out of bounds," Saban said. The Lions also got a fortuitous referee's whistle which stopped the clock after the first play of the drive to measure for a first down.

Somehow, Penn State squeezed 12 plays into 71 seconds. When tight end Keith Olsommer caught a 13-yard pass and bullied his way out of bounds at the MSU three-yard line, only 0:34 remained.

Saban called time-out to regroup his defense. Penn State set up their strategy, a play called "50-scud pass," an inside screen pass

designed for Richardson to choose from Archie on his right or Engram to his left, both breaking to the inside.

On first down from the four, Richardson took a quick drop and fired to his right. Archie took the pass but was immediately wrapped up for a one-yard loss. For the first time on the drive, the clock kept running. The Lions hurried as time ticked away. Richardson spiked the ball with 13 seconds left.

Third-and-goal. Another play like that and time would expire on the Nittany Lions.

THE PLAY
CD 2—Track 14
Fran Fisher, George Paterno,
Clear Channel Sports

Paterno could have played for the tie and taken a sure field goal from Brett Conway. But he didn't.

Instead, Richardson and the offense stayed on the field. Surprisingly, Penn State did call "another play like that," in fact the exact same play, "50-scud pass."

"They used what they call 'an underneath screen' which you don't usually use on about the 4 or 5-yard line because you don't have that much real estate to clear it out. But they tried it," recalled Penn State broadcaster George Paterno.

Gambling on one play, win or lose, Paterno called Richardson over to the sidelines for specific instructions. "Joe told me, 'Look for Bobby on this play, nobody else, he's been wide open,'" Richardson said.

Richardson hustled back into the huddle, brought the Lions to the line of scrimmage, then took the snap. This time he faked right to Archie, then threw left to Engram who was cutting inside near the three-yard line.

But the Spartans played it perfectly.

MSU's Robert Shurelds and Raymond Hill converged on Engram at the three-yard line, one behind him, the other in front. "Once I got my hands on the football, it was just a matter of getting to the goal line," said Engram. Easier said than done. In fact, he looked trapped.

"I got my head down and just toughed it out," said Engram. Actually, he escaped. Engram

283

ducked down at the three, while both MSU defenders went for his head, crashing into each other like evil tag team partners at a professional wrestling match. Then the future Chicago Bear receiver lunged for the goal line, just beating a last-ditch dive by Demetrice Martin to stop him from the end zone.

"It was one football's length in there," Engram said. "It got in there." Somehow, Engram scored. Eight seconds were on the clock. Penn State was on their way to a New Year's bowl.

"Unbelievable. Unbelievable," said PSU announcer Fran Fisher over the airwaves. "I give credit to Fran Ganter, the offensive coordinator," said George Paterno. "The call was unbelievable to do that with time running out at that position on the field."

Even referee David Witvoet was amazed. "That last play, they should never have scored. He caught a little flip pass to the left side of the line and he went to cut back inside and there were two Michigan State players there, and they both went to hit him high, and he ducked underneath them."

If Ingram hadn't made it into the end zone, the game would have been over. "There's no way that they would've got a play off again," said Witvoet.

While Penn State celebrated, Michigan State was crushed.

"When I saw the ball cross the goal line, it was like somebody kicked me in the head," MSU defensive tackle Chris Smith said. "As hard as we've worked, it was like the whole season came down to the last play."

Banks got one final play from his 34-yard line after the kickoff, but he couldn't even get a pass away as the Penn State defense flushed him out of bounds. The game was over. Penn State 24, Michigan State 20.

THE AFTERMATH

"It's a very, very disappointing, gut-wrenching loss," said a somber Saban.

The Spartans wound up in the Independence Bowl where they lost to LSU 45-26 and finished the season 6-5-1. In his first year at MSU, Saban came in third place in the Big Ten Coach of the Year balloting behind Gary Barnett (Northwestern) and John Cooper (Ohio State).

Saban coached at Michigan State for five years, compiling a 34-24-1 record, before leaving at the end of the 1999 season to become the new head coach at LSU.

The Nittany Lions went on to defeat Auburn 43-14, in the Outback Bowl on January 1. Penn State ended the season 9-3, ranked No.13 in the final AP poll.

Engram finished his Penn State career as the Lions' all-time leading receiver with 167 career catches for 3,026 yards and 31 TDs. He was voted second-team All-America by UPI and *Football News*, was an all-Big Ten first-team selection, and a finalist for the Biletnikoff Award (given to the nation's top wide receiver).

Penn State	0	7	3	14	- 24
Michigan State	0	10	0	10	- 20

PSU	Milne 1 run (Conway kick)
MSU	FG Gardner 32
MSU	Greene 3 run (Gardner kick)
PSU	FG Conway 43
MSU	Greene 16 run (Gardner kick)
PSU	Engram 53 pass from Richardson (Conway kick)
MSU	FG Gardner 28
PSU	Engram 4 pass from Richardson (Conway kick)

Attendance 66,189

Army vs. Navy

"We should have gone for the win, not for the jugular."—Charlie Weatherbie

THE BACKGROUND

It all started in 1992. The streak. The luck. The nightmare.

If you root for Army or Navy in the country's most celebrated rivalry, you have your own name for it. That series of unforgettable finishes by the Black Knights that left the Midshipmen feeling, ugh, navy blue.

With 12 seconds left in 1992, and the underdog Middies (1-9) leading 24-22, Army kicker Patmon Malcolm lined up to kick a 44-yard field goal. The snap was good. The hold was good. The kick was good. But while the Cadets celebrated wildly, the referees disallowed the points. The snap was a second late. Army was penalized for delay of game.

Malcolm had to try again. This time from 49 yards away. His career best was 46 yards. Not anymore. The second kick was good too. Army, rallying from a 17-point deficit, beat their archrivals 25-24. "We were in complete control when we had a 24-7 lead," said Navy coach George Chaump. "To lose like that is heartbreaking."

To lose like they did the next year was even worse.

In 1993, trailing 16-14, Navy drove from its 20 to the Army seven-yard line with 55 seconds left. They conservatively moved the ball into position for freshman Ryan Bucchianeri to attempt the game-winning 18-yard field-goal attempt. But after Navy called time with 0:06 left, and Army followed with another timeout, Bucchianeri's seemingly easy kick sailed wide right.

The Cadets had won again. "Heartbreaking," said Chaump for a second year in a row. "Sometimes you think someone wants to see how much adversity we can stand."

More than they ever could have imagined.

In 1994, down 20-19 with just over six minutes to play, Army sent in kicker Kurt Heiss to try an unlikely 52-yard field goal. Heiss, who had astigmatism, couldn't even see the goalposts clearly from over 40 yards away. He kicked the ball, then looked at his holder Derek Klein to see if it was good.

It was. Army 22, Navy 20. "Snakebit?" said Chaump. "Yeah." For the third straight year an improbable field goal had beaten Navy. The next day Chaump was fired.

Charlie Weatherbie took over the coaching duties for Navy in 1995. He immediately turned the fortunes of the Middies around with a respectable 5-5 record. Navy was on the brink of their first winning season since 1982 when they tried to break the Army jinx in the last game of the season.

Midway through the fourth quarter, Navy held a 13-7 lead after holding the nation's second-ranked rushing offense (339.3 yards per game) in check. Then Navy caught the break that would break the jinx. Army back-up quarterback Adam Thompson came into the game for one play, replacing starter Ron McAda. He fumbled. Navy linebacker Fernando Harris recovered at the Army 16.

The Middies looked to clinch the victory.

Navy quarterback Chris McCoy ran for six yards to the Army 10. On second down, he gained seven down to the three-yard line. First-and-goal for Navy.

Then the Middies' motor stalled. Three running plays netted just two yards. Navy faced fourth-and-goal from the one. With 8:26 remaining. Weatherbie had a decision to make. Kick the field goal for a nine-point lead or go for the six points to gain a two-touchdown advantage. Given Army's land-based, time-consuming offense, the answer seemed obvious. Kick the field goal.

But like a rogue general, Weatherbie chose a different strategy. Perhaps he remembered the plight of freshman Ryan Bucchianeri. Certainly the Navy fans did. This would have been another 18-yard field-goal attempt, this time by another freshman, Tom Vanderhorst, playing his first varsity game ever. This would have iced the game.

"I don't know if, subconsciously, I just didn't want it to come down to a kick," Weatherbie said. Makes sense, given what happened to Navy the last three years. Maybe the new Navy coach didn't want to put the Midshipmen through that agony again.

Instead, he provided them with a whole new kind of pain. Navy went for it.

McCoy took the snap and looked for slot back Cory Schemm just over the goal line. Schemm was open over the middle. Weatherbie looked like a genius...until McCoy threw the ball. It fell behind his receiver. The Army defense celebrated the goal-line stand. The Navy sidelines got that sinking feeling again.

"We felt like our inside receiver would be open, and he was open," Weatherbie said later. "We just didn't execute the play."

Ninety-nine yards away, the Cadets took over. From their own one-yard line, Army began a march that would have made General William Tecumseh Sherman proud.

It started with six consecutive runs moving the ball to the Army 23. After advancing to the 44-yard line, McAda, on third-and-seven, avoided a crucial sack, then hit fullback Demetrius Perry with a nine-yard completion into Navy territory.

The drive was alive. Down to the 17-yard line, the Cadets maneuvered with under two minutes on the clock. Then a major setback. McAda was sacked for a 12-yard loss on third down.

Army's lengthy drive had come down to one moment of truth. Fourth down-and-24 at the Navy 29-yard line.

THE PLAY

"We got in the huddle and Joel Davis (Army's 300-lb. offensive guard) said, 'Who's going to make the play?'" explained McAda. "And I said, 'It's the last one, so let's make it.'"

With that, the Cadets QB dropped back to pass. McAda, who had only thrown for 46 yards in the game, looked for senior receiver John Graves down the left sideline. Graves faked inside then broke to the sideline with Navy's strong safety in pursuit.

"I dipped in and out and Ron McAda threw it perfect," Graves said. Just before running out of room along the sideline, McAda's pass arrived in Graves' hands. At the brink of defeat once again, the Cadets had somehow survived. A 28-yard completion. Army was at the Navy one-yard line.

That was the play that sunk the Middies ship.

Two plays later, John Conroy bulled over left tackle for the touchdown. Only 63 seconds remained. The game was tied. Would Army miss the extra point? No. Had it been Navy, with their string of luck, the PAT probably would have been blocked and returned for two points. Instead, Army's J. Parker booted it through for the 14-13 Army lead.

An exhaustive 19 play, 99 yard drive. While the Cadets kicked the Middies to defeat the previous three years, this time they simply stomped on their pride with a grinding beat of a drum and another unexpected, last-ditch effort.

"I imagine that it will go down as one of the greatest drives in Army history," remarked Army coach Bob Sutton.

Navy did have one last shot. But quarterback Ben Fay, the Middies' passing QB, launched a last-second desperation scud into the end zone that was intercepted by Donald Augustus as time expired.

For the fourth consecutive year, Army beat Navy. Four victories by a combined total of six points. One more year of heartbreak for the Midshipmen.

THE AFTERMATH

Weatherbie unequivocally took the blame for the loss. "If I had to do it over, I would have kicked it, no doubt about it," Weatherbie said. "Hindsight is 20/20. A very poor decision. I apologize to the Navy fans. I apologize to the players. It was a tactical error on my part. To let a coaching error like that destroy a winning season really hurts me on the inside."

Despite the deflating loss which denied the Middies their first winning season in 13 years, Weatherbie turned the Navy football program around in the following years. After a 9-3 season in 1996, capped by a 42-38 victory over California in the Aloha Bowl, Weatherbie received a 10-year extension to his contract that runs through 2006.

But even despite Navy's stellar season in '96, the losing streak to Army continued. Army overcame a 21-3 deficit to defeat the Middies 28-24, helped by a game-saving interception by defensive back Garland Gay at the goal line with 10 seconds left.

Finally in 1997, the Midshipmen broke the five-game losing streak to Army with a 39-7 victory.

Army	7	0	0	7	- 14
Navy	7	0	3	3	- 13

NAVY	Butts 22 pass from Fay (Vanderhorst kick)
ARMY	Conroy 1 run (Parker kick)
NAVY	FG Vanderhorst 39
NAVY	FG Vanderhorst 22
ARMY	Conroy 1 run (Parker kick)

Attendance 68,853

Colorado vs. Air Force

"If I drop it, I'm dead."—Jeremy Calhoun

THE BACKGROUND

The Western Athletic Conference was formed in 1962. The legendary tales of offensive shootouts in the league have piled up for 36 years, creating enough stories to fill any ghost town library from southern Utah to northern Wyoming, not to mention every dusty watering hole in-between.

The pistol-packing quarterbacks from the league's past occupy quite a few pages in the NCAA record books. But while gunslingers from BYU, Utah, San Diego State, and other high flying offenses are renowned for their passing proficiency, the quarterbacks of Air Force gained most of their yardage on the ground. And few ran the wishbone offense better than Beau Morgan.

In three years behind center for the Falcons, Morgan averaged 96.5 yards per game rushing, the third highest average ever for a QB in Division I-A. The second coming of Dee Dowis (the Air Force QB from '86-'89 and NCAA record holder for career yards rushing by a quarterback), Morgan scampered for 183 yards against Notre Dame, leading Air Force to a 20-17 overtime upset of the eighth-ranked Irish. Two weeks later, coach Fisher DeBerry's Falcons (5-2, 4-1 WAC) returned home to play their final home game of the season against conference foe Colorado State (5-4, 4-1).

Morgan's last game in front of the home crowd would be his best.

The Falcons took a 21-7 lead with 6:39 left in the second quarter when Morgan sent sparks flying in Falcon Stadium with a dazzling 77-yard touchdown run, his second score of the game.

There was more to come. Another two-yard TD dash capped a 65-yard drive before halftime and the Falcons led 28-14 going into the locker room.

Third Quarter. More Morgan.

After Air Force recovered a fumble by Rams runningback Calvin Branch at the CSU 22, Morgan scored in one play, another 22-yard scamper around the CSU defenders. The Air Force lead was 35-14 . Morgan had four touchdowns. By the end of the game he amassed a career high 243 yards rushing.

The Falcons, who had lost four consecutive times to Colorado State, kept pouring it on. Steve Fernandez sacked Rams QB Moses Moreno, forcing a fumble that was picked up by Steve Pipes and returned for yet another Air Force score. After a missed extra point, the Falcons led 41-14.

With 5:48 to play in the third quarter, the game was over.

No, in the shoot-'em-up WAC, this is where the story begins.

As if they got on their horses, rode out of town, then returned with guns ablazing, the Colorado State Rams performed an ambush worthy of tall tale status in small town saloons for years to come.

Moreno, himself a record-setting quarterback in Ft. Collins, Colorado, was the general. First, he led the Rams 80 yards in 1:19 to cut the lead to 41-21. Then, he hit five-of-six targets on a 10 play, 85-yard drive, connecting with Ronald Antoine on a 15-yard TD pass to make it 41-28.

The Falcons fumbled the kickoff. CSU recovered at the AFA 28.

Branch galloped 17 yards, then 11 more for another Rams score. Two scores in 34 seconds. Incredibly, with 11:01 to play in the fourth quarter, the score was 41-35.

Morgan tried to settle down his offense. But after gaining two first downs, Air Force punted back to the Rams. With 5:55 remaining, Moreno saddled up again, taking Colorado State from the CSU 25 to the AFA 21.

The clock was down to 0:57. CSU coach Sonny Lubick called time-out. The Rams faced third-and-10. Moreno (31 of 48 passing for 358 yards) threw incomplete, setting up a fourth-and-10 showdown at the Air Force 21. As the clock neared midnight, it might as well have been high noon. The Rams were down to their last play.

THE PLAY

CD 2—Track 15—*Steve Anderson,* **Colorado State Sports Network and Clear Channel Sports**

With dusty boots and silver spurs, Moreno came to the line of scrimmage and grabbed for his holster. Split end Jeremy Calhoun ran toward the right corner of the end zone. Moreno drew his gun and fired one last time into the thin 38-degree mountain air.

"As soon as I turned, I saw the ball fall out of the sky," Calhoun said. He had beaten cornerback Mike Walker to the end zone. But was he able to catch up with Moreno's desperation heave?

"I thought it was overthrown and there was no way he could catch it," said Lubick.

The ball hung up just long enough for Calhoun to make a last-ditch head-first dive. "If I drop it, I'm dead," thought Calhoun.

He didn't drop it, but rather made a fingertip grasp just before it hit the ground. A dramatic, impossible catch. A fatal bullet to the chest of Air Force.

The clock showed 0:45. Moreno was the gunfighter left standing in the middle of the road. The game was tied at 41-41.

While the Falcons laid wounded on their backs, the Rams rejoiced. A massive celebration in the end zone drew blank stares from the Air Force cadets in the stands and yellow flags from the referees on the field, who assessed the almost mandatory 15-yard excessive celebration penalty after the miracle touchdown. (Could someone please change that rule?)

That left kicker Matt McDougal with a 35-yard extra-point attempt to try and win it for the Rams. The kick was good. Twenty-eight unanswered points. Colorado State 42, Air Force 41.

Morgan got the ball back at the AFA 20. But without time to run the ball, he was helpless. On the second play, CSU's Erik Olson picked off his pass near midfield and the game was over.

THE AFTERMATH

Morgan, distraught over his team's collapse, uncharacteristically lashed out at CSU after the game. "Their fans, their coaches and their players have absolutely no class. Early in the game I'm a good 3 yards out of bounds and a guy tees off on me and hits me as hard as he can. At the end of the game a guy hits me from behind. I'm getting up and he pushes me back down and stands on top of me. There's a point where enough's enough," said Morgan.

"I don't know if we took cheap shots," Lubick said. "We didn't tackle him all day." AFA officials claimed the CSU players taunted the downtrodden Falcons as they stood at attention for their traditional post-game alma mater. The sore feelings carried over into the crowd as CSU later reported that the Rams' student mascot was punched in the stomach by an Air Force cadet.

The Falcons never quite recovered from the devastating loss. The following week Air Force lost to unbeaten Army 23-7 as Morgan managed just six yards rushing in the game. Air Force ended the year 6-5.

By the end of the '96 season, Morgan had broken the NCAA record for yards rushing in a single season by a quarterback (1,494), and average yards rushing per game in a season (135.8). He is the only quarterback to ever throw for 1,000 yards and rush for 1,000 yards in two different seasons. His 3,379 career yards rushing ranks third all-time among Division I-A schools. But in his brilliant WAC career, Morgan never was able to beat Colorado State.

With a shot at playing in the WAC conference title game, CSU rallied from a 13-0 deficit against Wyoming, only to lose 25-24 to the Cowboys in the final game of the '96 season. Colorado State rebounded the following year to win their third WAC title in four years. The Rams only conference loss in 1997? A 24-0 whitewash at the hands of Air Force.

In July 1999, the core schools identified with the WAC left to form the Mountain West Conference.

Colorado State	0	14	7	21	- 42
Air Force	14	14	13	0	- 41

AFA	Morgan 1 run (Thompson kick)
AFA	Alexander 30 pass from Morgan (Thompson kick)
CSU	Branch 2 run (McDougal kick)
AFA	Morgan 77 run (Thompson kick)
CSU	Antoine 20 pass from Moreno (McDougal kick)
AFA	Morgan 2 run (Thompson kick)
AFA	Morgan 22 run (Thompson kick)
AFA	Pipes 21 fumble return (kick failed)
CSU	Branch 2 run (McDougal kick)
CSU	Antoine 15 pass from Moreno (McDougal kick)
CSU	Branch 11 run (McDougal kick)
CSU	Calhoun 21 pass from Moreno (McDougal kick)

Attendance 51,116

Ohio State vs. Arizona State

"We're at the back door of Hollywood, and I don't think they could have come up with a better script."—Ryan Miller, OSU linebacker

THE BACKGROUND

Arizona State entered the '97 Rose Bowl undefeated, 11-0, second-ranked, just one game away from possibly their first-ever national championship. Orchestrated by head coach Bruce Snyder, the '96 ASU season featured one of the most shocking upsets of the decade as the unheralded Sun Devils knocked off two-time defending national champion Nebraska 19-0 in Tempe, snapping the Huskers' 26-game winning streak.

Ohio State was also undefeated and seeking a national championsip. That is, until they played Michigan in the Big Ten finale of the regular season. The Buckeyes saw their dream season come crashing down to the ground with a 13-9 loss to the Wolverines. Still, the Big Ten champions were 10-1, No.4 in the country, and Rose Bowl-bound.

John Cooper, in his ninth season in Columbus, was going to the Rose Bowl for the first time as the Buckeyes' head coach. But he'd been to Pasadena before.

As the coach of Arizona State.

This was the 10th anniversary of Arizona State's only Rose Bowl appearance, a 22-15 victory over Michigan in 1987. A year later, Cooper replaced Earle Bruce at Ohio State.

The Buckeyes had a two-headed quarterback. The fleet-of-foot Stanley Jackson on one shoulder. The drop-back passer Joe Germaine on the other.

Arizona State's quarterback, Jake "The Snake" Plummer, had only one head, but a heart the size of a Tournament of Roses parade float.

Plummer, who shattered career records at ASU for yards passing (8,827) and TD passes (65), was a wizard at finding ways to salvage unsalvageable situations. The John Elway of the desert.

But Plummer's New Year started like many Americans,' with a bad headache. Freshman linebacker Andy Katzenmoyer led a ferocious Buckeyes' defensive charge that sacked Plummer four times in the first half. Meanwhile, Jackson got the Buckeyes on the board first with a third down, nine-yard TD pass to Darryl Boston in the right corner of the end zone. Ohio State led 7-0 at the end of the first 15 minutes.

With five minutes to play in the half, Plummer finally cracked the Buckeye safe, lofting a 25-yard pass to Ricky Boyer down the right sideline. Boyer, bumped by cornerback Antoine Winfield, launched himself into the end zone, then snared the ball just above the blades of grass as he fell to the ground. After watching the replay, Ohio State fans thought Boyer trapped the ball. ASU fans thought Winfield interfered. The officials thought it was a touchdown. The score was tied 7-7 at the half.

Germaine replaced Jackson in the second quarter, then connected with Dimitrius Stanley on a 72-yard strike midway through the third quarter. The Buckeyes led 14-10.

It stayed that way until six minutes remained in the game. Josh Jackson lined up for a 38-yard field-goal attempt to give Ohio State a seven-point lead. The drama began.

Defensive end Brent Burnstein blocked the kick, safety Damien Richardson picked up the

Mesa, Arizona, native Joe Germaine orchestrated Ohio State's comeback against his hometown school.

ball, then quickly pitched it to Derrick Rodgers who ran the length of the field into the end zone. Arizona State had suddenly gone ahead.

No they hadn't.

Richardson's pitch was ruled an illegal forward lateral. The ball was brought back to the ASU 42. The score was still 14-10.

So with 5:29 remaining, Plummer, harassed all day by the blitzing Buckeyes, had one more chance in his final collegiate game to pull off another come-from-behind victory.

He moved the Devils to the OSU 36, then was faced with a do-or-die, fourth-and-three situation. With the Ohio State defense in his face, Plummer lofted a perfect fade pass to Lenzie Jackson at the eight-yard line. Jackson hauled it in. The Sun Devils were still alive.

After barely eluding defeat once, ASU soon faced third-and-goal at the Ohio State 11. It was here, that Plummer performed the great escape.

The senior quarterback dropped back, looked up, and immediately faced Katzenmoyer, the oncoming train in his path. Narrowly avoiding the seventh sack of the day by Ohio

State, Plummer sidestepped the OSU linebacker, then took off for the end zone, sliding by Matt Finkes, juking Luke Fickell, diving over the goal line past Winfield Garnett.

An astounding touchdown scramble. Dodging four Buckeyes, the Snake had struck. ASU led 17-14.

It would have been the greatest play in Arizona State history. The play that gave the Sun Devils a 17-14 Rose Bowl victory. The play that won them the national championship.

Except there was still 1:40 on the clock.

Germaine, a sophomore whose roots were in Mesa, Arizona, just a six-minute drive from the Arizona State campus, gathered his teammates with 1:33 left in the game.

"He got us in the huddle and told us, 'This will be the biggest drive of the season. This will be the biggest drive of your lives,'" said flanker David Boston.

It *was* the biggest drive of Germaine's career. The Buckeyes started at their 35 with one timeout left.

After two plays, they faced third-and-10. Germaine hit Stanley for 11 yards to the 46.

Game 88

Photos courtesy of Tournament of Roses Archives

THE PLAY
CD2 - Track 16—*Jim Karsatos, Terry Smith*, **WBNS Radio and The Ohio State University**

Germaine called the play "Swarm Route." On first down, Boston lined up to the right, alongside Stanley. Both were primary receivers.

Stanley ran a slant to the inside, drawing double coverage in the end zone. Boston broke to the inside as red-shirt freshman cornerback Courtney Jackson followed...a little too much. Boston cut back to the outside, and Jackson was left behind.

Germaine read the coverage. He threw to Boston in the flat. Wide open, Boston caught the pass, backpedaled, turned and crossed the goal line with 0:19 left. In a whirlwind 12-play drive, Ohio State covered 65 yards in 90 seconds for the 20-17 lead.

Germaine had out-snaked the snake.

With the few seconds that remained, the never-say-die Plummer actually tried to top his own previous magic trick. With 14 seconds left from his 34, he hit tight end Steve Bush for 13 yards, then 17 yards to Lenzie Jackson. But then time ran out on Plummer, with the ball at the Buckeye 36. This time, the rabbit wouldn't come out of the hat.

Ohio State won the Rose Bowl 20-17. The Buckeyes have never won a bowl game in a more dramatic fashion.

"That was a hell of a drive that late in the game. It was big time, and I admire Joe," said Snyder, who had recruited Germaine as a defensive back out of high school.

Germaine chose to play quarterback in Columbus, instead of cornerback in Tempe. He ended up on the right side of Ohio State's first victory at the Rose Bowl in two decades.

The roses smelled sweet to Cooper. "I've been coaching for 35 years. Greatest victory in history," he said.

But the petals were sour to Plummer. "It's tough to take this in my last game as a Sun Devil," Plummer said. "We just ran out of time."

THE AFTERMATH

In his 12 years of announcing Buckeyes football, Smith called the '97 Rose Bowl his

Again they faced third-and-10. Again, Germaine to Stanley for 13 yards to the ASU 41. The next play, Germaine found Stanley a third time for 13 more yards. Ohio State was at the ASU 29 with 46 seconds left.

As if he was sticking needles into his boyhood buddies from Mesa, who faithfully followed the Sun Devils while they were growing up, Germaine surgically threaded the ASU defense.

"You could sense that the [Arizona State] secondary was in complete chaos," remembered Buckeye announcer Terry Smith. Germaine kept attacking. The Sun Devils defense got desperate.

First, defensive back Jason Simmons was flagged for trying to stop Stanley. The pass interference call moved the ball to the 19. Then, facing another third-and-10, Germaine threw for Boston at the goal line. He was mugged by ASU's Marcus Soward. The ball fell incomplete. Another flag flew. Another pass interference against Arizona State.

The officals moved the ball to the five-yard line. Just 28 seconds remained.

greatest moment in the broadcasting booth. "That was number one, absolutely," he said.

Smith remembered the scene after Plummer's TD run in the opposing school's broadcasting booths, which sat side-by-side in the press box. "They [the Arizona State broadcasters] were high-fiving each other and were as excited as can be because they thought that was probably going to win the game."

Then, after Boston's winning score, "Our guys were jumping around in our booth. I immediately looked over into their booth. They were so devastated. I kind of felt sorry for them because they had all that exhilaration less than two minutes earlier and then all of a sudden the shoe was on the other foot."

It was a nausea-to-nirvana moment common to most every great finish.

The Buckeyes finished 11-1, along with Arizona State. "I think we definitely deserve the national championship," Boston said after the game. But the Florida Gators, 12-1 after their 52-20 drubbing of previously unbeaten Florida State in the Sugar Bowl, were crowned national champions in both the AP and *USA Today*/CNN polls. Ohio State finished second, while Arizona State was fourth.

Ohio State	7	0	7	6	-20
Arizona State	0	7	3	7	-17

OSU	Boston 9 pass from S.Jackson (Jo.Jackson kick)
ASU	Boyer 25 pass from Plummer (Nycz kick)
ASU	FG Nycz 37
OSU	Stanley 72 pass from Germaine (Jo.Jackson kick)
ASU	Plummer 11 run (Nycz kick)
OSU	Boston 5 pass from Germaine (kick blocked)

Attendance 100,645

Wisconsin vs. Northwestern

"The lead changed eight times, that is why 50,000 people came out to watch this football game. It's what makes football exciting."—Gary Barnett

THE BACKGROUND

The two Cinderella teams of the Big Ten in the 1990s.

At the start of the decade, both Barry Alvarez and Gary Barnett entered the Big Ten together, determined to turn around the conference cellar-dwellars. Alvarez resurrected a dead Wisconsin program in just four years, winning the 1993 Big Ten title and defeating UCLA 21-16 in the Rose Bowl. Barnett performed miracles at Northwestern, leading the once laughable Wildcats to back-to-back Big Ten titles in '95 and '96.

In 1997, Wisconsin traveled to Evanston, IL for a Saturday night game with the Wildcats, the first sellout at the newly remodeled Ryan Field. The Badgers were 4-1 (1-0 in the Big Ten), while Northwestern was 2-3 (0-1 in the Big Ten). Both teams still had Rose Bowl hopes early in the conference campaign.

Wisconsin was coming off a dramatic high from the week before against Indiana.

With six seconds remaining in Madison, Wisconsin center Mike Schneck snapped the ball back to holder Tim Rosga who placed it down. Matt Davenport kicked it. The 43-yard field goal was true, giving the Badgers a dramatic 27-26 victory.

Euphoria for the Badgers. Schneck ran back to celebrate, tackling Davenport with joy. Overly ecstatic in the pile of happy players, Schneck ended up dislocating his elbow. The Badgers' long snapper was unable to play the following week.

Enter Mike Solwold, a red-shirt freshman, former Gatorade Wisconsin State player of the year in high school. That is, as a tight end, not a long snapper. Solwold had never played a game in college. Against Northwestern, he would be the appointed long snapper.

His debut was shaky. His finale unforgettable.

The Badgers' first punt came in the second quarter with Wisconsin leading 13-6. Solwold's snap was slow, allowing Northwestern safety Rashad Morton to rush in and block Kevin Stemke's kick through the Wisconsin end zone for a safety. Wisconsin 13, Northwestern 8.

In the third quarter it happened again. This time from the Wisconsin 25, Solwold snapped it over Stemke's head. Northwestern's John Burden recovered in the end zone for the touchdown and the lead. Northwestern 22, Wisconsin 16.

"It was pretty much a snapper's nightmare," said Solwold. Misery loves company, and Solwold had plenty of it. The game slid into an abyss of turnovers at the most unpredictable moments in a second half which featured five lead changes and enough ups and downs to make the sellout crowd seasick.

On the next Wisconsin possession, after driving 67 yards to the Northwestern one-yard line, the Badgers were on the verge of taking the lead. But then, heralded sophomore runningback Ron Dayne fumbled just outside the goal line. Jeff Dyra recovered for the Wildcats.

A few plays later, Northwestern gave it right back. Quarterback Tim Hughes was jolted

October 4, 1997—Evanston, Illinois

from behind, popping the ball into the air where defensive end John Favret intercepted it at the NU 6.

Dayne got a second chance.

This time, the 5-10, 261 lb. back who broke the NCAA record with 1,863 yards rushing as a freshman, bowled into the end zone on the next play. Wisconsin led 23-22.

But not for long. Chris Hamdorf took over for Hughes at quarterback and led Northwestern to a Brian Gowens 48-yard field goal at the end of the quarter, a low kick that sneaked inside the left upright. Northwestern regained the lead 25-23.

With 6:04 left in the fourth quarter, Wisconsin took over at their 25. On third-and-eight, QB Mike Samuel hit Tony Simmons for 24 yards to the NU 49. The Badgers appeared ready to move in for the go-ahead score. But on the very next play, Samuel lost the ball. Northwestern's Kevin Buck recovered the fumble. The Wildcats now had possession with 3:59 to play, nursing a two-point lead.

Runningback Adrian Autry rumbled for 17 yards to the UW 30. Two plays later, after a four-yard gain gave him 103 yards rushing on the day, Autry hurt his ankle. Northwestern's starting runningback had to leave the game.

Back-up tailback Faraji Leary replaced him. He took a handoff and squirted eight yards down to the Wisconsin eight-yard line. With under two minutes left and leading 25-23, the Wildcats were on the verge of clinching the victory. But then, on the next play, after gaining four yards, Leary fought for one more yard and made a fatal mistake.

"I faked left and went right," said Leary. "When I went right, my arm came out and somebody hit me from behind." That somebody was linebacker David Lysek who stuck his helmet on the ball, knocked it loose, then fell on it. Wisconsin had the ball.

It was déjà vu reversed. One year before, Dayne and Samuel had botched a handoff in the final minute as the Badgers tried to run out the clock against Northwestern. The Wildcats recovered and quarterback Steve Schnur hit D'Wayne Bates for a 20-yard TD pass with 37 seconds left, giving Northwestern the improbable 34-30 victory.

With those memories freshly stirred and buzzing about Ryan Field, the Badgers had just 1:16 left with the ball sitting on their four-yard line. They needed over 60 yards to get into field-goal range.

Samuel scrambled for 23 on first down. Then on third-and-seven, he found Simmons (6 catches, 158 yards) on a slant pattern for a pivotal 28-yard gain to the NU 42. The clock was down to 0:30. The Badgers drive then began to stall. Samuel ran for two yards. His pass to Simmons fell incomplete.

But on third-and-eight at the NU 40, Wisconsin caught a break. While Samuel's completed pass fell well shy of the first down, cornerback Fred Wilkerson was called for defensive holding, moving the ball to the 30. "That's a heck of a time to call that, because it happens on every play," argued Barnett. With 20 seconds left, the Badgers had crept to the edge of kicker Matt Davenport's range.

They would get no further. Two Samuel sideline passes to Donald Hayes fell incomplete. Eleven seconds on the clock. Alvarez sent in Davenport...and perhaps more importantly Solwold, the snapper, for a 48-yard attempt.

THE PLAY

CD 2—Track 17—*Matt Lepay***, Wisconsin Badger Network from Learfield Sports**

Northwestern called a timeout. Davenport had some time to think about his kick, the longest of his career. Solwold had time to think about his snap, which if bad, would precipitate the longest bus ride back to Madison in the history of Wisconsin football.

"We've done it a zillion times in practice, and I just had to relax," said Solwold. Davenport walked up to his snapper. "You get it down, I'll knock it in," said Davenport. Meanwhile, the Northwestern players held on by a thread.

"Everyone was just praying on the sideline that that field goal wasn't going to go in," said NU's Hamdorf. On the Wisconsin sideline, everyone was praying Solwold could make a clean snap.

"It wasn't just could [Davenport] cover 48 yards, but [also] was the snap going to be

Game 89

good," recalled Wisconsin broadcaster Matt Lepay.

After the wait, Solwold leaned over the ball. He snapped it to Rosga. "It floated, but it got there," said Lepay. It did get there. And so did Davenport's kick, with plenty of room to spare. Two last-second game winners over 40 yards in two consecutive weeks. Wisconsin 26, Northwestern 25.

"A kicker usually gets one chance to do this in his life," said Davenport. "I've gotten to do it two weeks in a row."

After the kick, Rosga lifted Davenport skyward. He was careful. "I was just focusing on not getting hurt," he laughed. Solwold shied away. "I tried to stay out of the pile." No one got injured.

THE AFTERMATH

The Badgers ran their record to 8-2 before faltering at the end of the season with three straight losses to Michigan (26-16), Penn State (35-10) and Georgia (33-6) in the Copper Bowl. Wisconsin finished 8-5, but the following season won the Big Ten title and the Rose Bowl (a 38-31 victory over UCLA) for the second time in the Barry Alvarez era. In 1999, Dayne won the Heisman Trophy and the Badgers captured their third Rose Bowl victory of the '90s, defeating Stanford 17-9.

Dayne ended his four years at Wisconsin as the Division I-A all-time career leading rusher.

Northwestern finished a disappointing 5-7 in '97, a year that marked the beginning of the end of Gary Barnett's rise to the top of the Big Ten. The Wildcats skidded to a 3-9 record in 1998 and Barnett then left Evanston to become the head coach at Colorado in 1999.

Wisconsin	13	3	7	3	- 26
Northwestern	6	8	11	0	- 25

WIS	Dayne 2 run (kick blocked)
NU	Autry 1 run (kick failed)
WIS	Simmons 38 pass from Samuel (Davenport kick)
NU	Safety, blocked punt through the end zone
NU	Stuart 6 pass from Hughes (pass failed)
WIS	FG Davenport 32
NU	Burden fumble recovery in end zone (Musso pass from Hughes)
WIS	Dayne 6 run (Davenport kick)
NU	FG Gowins 48
WIS	FG Davenport 48

Attendance 47,129

Carthage vs. Millikin 🏈

"My dad said he about had a heart attack in the stands."
—Carthage quarterback Eric Corbett

THE BACKGROUND

Eight Division III schools play football in the College Conference of Illinois and Wisconsin (CCIW). Seven teams are from Illinois; one is from Wisconsin—Carthage University in Kenosha. With an enrollment of just over 1,500 students, Carthage was a football power in the conference during the early 1970s. The Redmen won five straight conference titles from 1969-1973.

But times had changed. Entering the '97 campaign, Carthage had just one winning record in the past 15 years, and the last 13 consecutive seasons included their annual drubbing at the hands of Millikin University. The Big Blue pounded Carthage from 1984-96 by a combined 516-118. That's an average final score of 39-9.

Third-year Carthage head coach Tim Rucks (an '83 grad) played on the last Redmen team to win at Millikin back in 1982. Fifteen years later, he brought his squad to Frank M. Lindsay Field in Decatur, Illinois, well aware of the long winless streak. The Redmen were supposed to be their usual passive homecoming guests for the Big Blue, who were 3-0 in the conference and rolling toward a season-ending showdown with perennial power Augustana College. But this year Carthage was 2-1 in the CCIW and had a chance to move into second place with an upset.

Nevertheless, from the first play of the game, it appeared this would be the 14th consecutive Millikin blowout. Carthage's Cameron Ridley fumbled the opening kickoff and Millikin recovered at the Redmen 38. But it took the Big Blue 10 plays to go just 35 yards and their drive stalled at the three-yard line. John Hughbanks converted the 21-yard field goal. Millikin led 3-0, but the Carthage defense had made a statement. This would not be another Decatur debacle.

All-Conference sophomore runningback Kevin Burris capped a 74-yard Carthage drive with a one-yard plunge at the end of the first quarter and Carthage jumped in front 7-3. From there, both defenses took over.

Carthage's Jeff Fursch recovered a Millikin fumble at the end of the first half, setting up Marty Schager's 33-yard field-goal attempt. It sailed wide right. In the second half, linebacker John Sedeska broke up a fourth-and-one pass attempt at the Carthage 26 to stop a Millikin drive. Later, Carthage cornerback Jack Prall picked off a Tim Brylka pass in the end zone, preserving the 7-3 lead.

But then Millikin's defense struck back. Early in the fourth quarter, Redmen quarterback Eric Corbett fumbled deep in his own territory. Senior linebacker Ryan Knox scooped the ball up from three yards out and took it into the end zone. Just like that, Millikin led 10-7.

Carthage regrouped.

Unlike past years, Rucks' Redmen answered the challenge. On the next drive, Burris broke into the clear on a 45-yard TD run and with 8:30 left, Carthage regained the lead 14-10.

The Carthage defense held. But then disaster struck the Redmen again. After their offense sputtered, Redmen punter Terry Filippis dropped back to kick, and for the second time in the game, Millikin's Mike Hyland blocked it. The Big Blue recovered at the Carthage 31 with 5:50 on the clock. Just 31 seconds later, Brylka scored on a nine-yard run and Millikin again had the lead 17-14.

One last drive remained for Carthage to break the streak.

From their 33, the Redmen marched downfield. After reaching the Millikin 37, Corbett hit Burris for 27 yards down to the 10. Millikin's defense then surrendered nine yards on three downs. Facing a fourth down from the one-yard line and time running out, Rucks chose to bypass the game-tying field goal and go for the win. Burris dove over the top. Carthage came up short. Burris was stuffed by an inspired Big Blue effort and Millikin took over, much to the delight of the homecoming crowd.

Rucks second-guessed his call. "I probably should have called a timeout before Burris didn't get the touchdown," he said. "I still would have given him the ball, but in retrospect, we could have run that play differently."

Carthage, though, still had all three timeouts left. They quickly used them in a desperate attempt to get the ball back as Millikin tried to run out the clock. With 0:09 left, Millikin faced fourth down at its own five. Carthage used their final timeout.

Big Blue coach Dough Neibuhr took a calculated gamble. Leading by three, he ordered his center to snap the ball through the end zone and take a safety. Millikin 17, Carthage 16, 0:07 left. Now, Neibuhr hoped punter Jacob Newkirk could kick the ball, from his own 20, deep enough to give Carthage no chance to score on the game's final play.

"I would have done exactly the same thing Millikin did," said Rucks of the safety.

Unfortunately for Neibuhr, Newkirk shanked the kick. It landed out of bounds at the Millikin 45. Carthage had one more chance, (albeit a slim one) to return to Wisconsin a winner for the first time since Rucks last put on a Redmen helmet.

THE PLAY

QB Corbett ran onto the field flanked by four wide receivers. "We lined up in a formation called 'Bif Red' which we practice at the end of practice every Friday," explained Rucks.

The play had never been used in a game during Rucks' tenure at Carthage. "We take two [of our] defensive backs and one regular wide receiver, [three tall guys], and put them on one side of the formation, and a single wideout on the other side," said Rucks. "The idea is the quarterback heaves the ball into the end zone and one of the three guys tips it back to the lone receiver."

Junior Kris Norton was the lone receiver. Three weeks earlier, the 5-10 sprinter on the Carthage track team had dropped two touchdown passes in a 32-26 loss to Lakeland College. Norton's confidence was not high. "I remember thinking my career at Carthage was over," he recalled. He hadn't caught a pass all day.

As the teams came to the line of scrimmage, Corbett recognized the Millikin defense. "Millikin came out in their base defense. They were not in their basic prevent [defense] which most teams would be in. I could not believe it," he said.

With an eight-man front, Millikin looked to pressure Corbett before he could throw the ball. But the senior took the snap and quickly sprinted right, attempting to avoid the rush. On the run, avoiding a Millikin lineman, the transfer from Iowa's Waldorf Junior College launched a wobbly spiral towards the end zone. The scoreboard siren went off as time expired. Somehow, downfield, no one had covered Norton. He found himself standing alone behind the pack of receivers. Corbett's pass came floating down. Falling in the back of the end zone, Norton cradled in the ball. Touchdown Redmen. An unfathomable Carthage comeback. The Big Blue turned blue, their defensive players stood motionless.

"When I landed on the field I looked to the left and all I could see was the pylon," said Norton. "I then heard lots of cheering and I thought it was Millikin, and I had been [down] on the one yard line."

In fact, Norton was looking at the back end line where he caught the winning touchdown. He soon realized it. "My whole team and fans joined in a pile with me on the bottom. Some of the guys picked me and Corbs up and carried us around for a while," he said. We knew that it had been 15 years since we defeated Millikin."

Rucks was overcome with joy. "It was complete pandemonium on the field. There were a thousand hugs," he said. "I remember a Millikin assistant coach, who is a friend [of mine], came over, put his arms around me, smiled and said, 'Tim, I'm really happy for you'. I knew he meant that, and it hit me that we beat Millikin...and tears filled my eyes."

THE AFTERMATH

Norton's memories of his catch will always be attached to a story of Rucks' fortune-telling. "The night before the Millikin game, Coach Rucks wrote everyone on the team a card about the game we were going to play," remembered Norton. "The thing that I will forever have embedded in my head was that coach said, 'You are a big play kind of guy in a big game. I know tomorrow you will make the big play for us.' He couldn't have said it better."

After the Millikin upset, Carthage lost their next two games but finished the season 4-3 in the CCIW (5-4 overall), with their second winning season since 1981. Millikin lost their last two games to finish 4-3 in the conference (4-5 overall). The following year, the Big Blue won the CCIW title (6-1), Doug Neibuhr was named CCIW coach of the year, and Millikin received a berth in the Division III playoffs for the first time since 1989. Their only conference loss of the year was to Carthage 12-7.

Carthage	7	0	0	15	-22
Millikin	3	0	0	14	-17

MIL	Hughbanks FG 21
CAR	Burris 1 run (Schager kick)
MIL	Knox 3 yd fumble recovery (Hughbanks kick)
CAR	Burris 45 run (Schager kick)
MIL	Brylka 9 run (Hughbanks kick)
CAR	Safety (ball snapped through end zone)
CAR	Norton 45 pass from Corbett (no attempt)

Attendance 3,700

The Millikin defense stands dumbfounded as the entire Carthage team piles on in jubilation. Photo courtesy of WAND-TV Decatur, Illinois

Amherst vs. Williams

"I'm just some punk freshman. What do I know about Williams-Amherst?"—Collin Vataha

THE BACKGROUND

The 112th meeting between Williams and Amherst. "The Biggest Little Game in America." The most played rivalry in Division III, perhaps the most heated rivalry in the history of college football.

In 1821, Williams College president Zepheniah Swift Moore, upset at the school's board of trustees, resigned from the college, took some Williams faculty members, students, and library books with him over the mountains into the Connecticut Valley, and founded Amherst Academy, later known as Amherst College.

Only the alumni of Williams were left to save the school, which they did by forming the country's first college alumni society.

Such are the makings of bitter rivals. The Ephs of Williams first played the Lord Jeffs of Amherst in football in 1884. Early on in the series, the two schools couldn't even agree who won the contests. The outcome of the first half-dozen games was disputed with each team reporting different won-loss totals for their seasons. Only in 1964 did the two schools get together to resolve the scores of the games played in the late 1800s.

Frankly, they don't like each other. So intense is the animosity between the two schools, that on the Williams campus, Amherst teams are simply known as "The Defectors," not the Lord Jeffs.

Entering the 1997 season, Williams coach Dick Farley, in his 11th season as head coach,

was eighth all-time among coaches in NCAA football winning percentage (.844) 66-11-3. The Ephs did nothing but improve that percentage in the '97 season, going 6-0 before losing to Wesleyan 28-14. (Williams, Amherst, and Wesleyan make up The Little Three conference). The Ephs stood at 6-1 as they entered their traditional season-ending confrontation with Amherst.

In 1996, Williams spoiled Amherst's perfect 7-0 season with a 19-13 upset victory. In '97, the Lord Jeffs again were undefeated (7-0). Amherst led the nation in scoring defense (6.4 ppg) among Division III schools. "Defense Wins" was the Jeffs' chant each time they ran onto the field. But in the first half against Williams, the normally dominant Amherst defense turned dormant.

The Williams offense cranked out 24 first-half points, jumping out to a 24-7 lead against an Amherst defense that had given up only 45 points the entire season.

The Jeffs trimmed the lead to 24-14 with 0:07 left in the half as quarterback Rich Willard connected with wide receiver Shaun Quigley for a 36-yard TD pass. But entering the locker room, Amherst still trailed 24-14.

Up in the press box, the Williams student radio station was having as many problems as the Amherst defense. Student broadcaster Jason Hehir and sidekick Matt Marvin were without a microphone.

"The [radio] equipment in the first half was being used by the soccer team," recalled Hehir. The Ephs morning soccer game with Amherst had run into overtime and overlapped the football game. So the only account of the football game to be heard on the radio came via a dorm room phone that alumnus Steve Epstein (returning to campus after 15 years as a guest announcer) used to call the first half by himself.

Hehir and Marvin were left without a microphone. "Steve stayed with half a pizza and a phone and called the first half," explained Hehir. "Me and Matt were tailgating behind the end zone in the first half. We went up and called the second half when the equipment came."

The two student broadcasters brought a new perspective to the game in the second half. "We went up there with equipment and as many beers as we could fit in our jackets," laughed Hehir. "Epstein [seeing his well-stocked partners] opened up the second half [on the air] by saying, 'I can see it's going to be a different game in the second half.'"

It was, in more ways than one.

With Hehir and Marvin now behind the mics, Amherst left the Williams announcers speechless by reeling off 17 third-quarter points. Willard's four-yard TD pass to Todd Haggerty gave Amherst a 31-24 lead with 5:16 to play in the third quarter. But an interception by the Ephs' Graham McPhail at the Williams 22 near the end of the quarter stopped another Jeffs drive and launched a flurry of offensive fireworks.

The fourth quarter turned into a scoring bonanza, unlike any Williams-Amherst game of the past.

The Ephs, two touchdown underdogs, tied the game at 31-31, then took advantage of two key Amherst mistakes to take a commanding 45-31 lead. First, a roughing the kicker penalty gave Williams a first-and-goal at the Amherst two-yard line, setting up a Paul Bethe TD run. Then the Jeffs fumbled the ensuing kickoff and Fred Storz scored on another short burst, giving the Ephs a two touchdown advantage.

But in the final six minutes, the Lord Jeffs retaliated.

Willard broke the Amherst school record for touchdown passes (5) in a single game with two more scoring strikes. He capped a 10-play, 86 yard drive with a 19-yard TD pass to Quigley. The Williams lead was trimmed to 45-38 with 4:23 left.

The Ephs went three-and-out. Amherst took over at their 49-yard line with 2:22 remaining. Willard wasted no time. Two plays later, he tossed a 34-yard TD strike to freshman Matt Hall. With 1:49 to play, the Lord Jeffs had closed the gap to one, 45-44.

First-year Amherst coach E.J. Mills then elected to kick the extra point and tie the game. Or so everyone at Weston Field thought.

Hall, the holder on the PAT, picked up the snap and threw to a wide open Haggerty for the two-point conversion, stunning the Ephs, and giving Amherst the 46-45 lead.

After the kickoff, things looked good for Amherst when they sacked the Ephs' senior QB Peter Supino for a 13-yard loss back at the Williams seven-yard line. Time was running out on the Ephs. After an 18-yard jaunt by Storz, Williams faced fourth-and-seven at the 25.

With 0:57 left, the Lord Jeffs defense needed one final stop. Instead, the Ephs got one enormous reception. Supino found junior receiver Matt Sigrist over the middle at the 42-yard line. He was run out of bounds at the 50 for a 25-yard gain. It turned into a 40-yard play when the Lord Jeffs were flagged for a late hit. Williams was at the Amherst 35-yard line.

On the next play, Supino rumbled 22 yards on a quarterback draw. With 28 seconds left, the Ephs had moved to the Amherst 13-yard line.

Sold out and overstuffed, Weston Field was in a frenzy. Storz took a pitchout for three yards to the 10. A handoff up the middle went nowhere. Eleven seconds remained.

On third down, Supino looked for Sigrist in the end zone but as he threw, the ball was tipped at the line of scrimmage and fell just out of the reach of two Jeffs defenders. Amherst narrowly missed a game-ending interception.

With 0:07 left, Farley, wary of a shaky Ephs' kicking game, sent in his field-goal unit.

THE PLAY
CD 2—Track 18
Steve Epstein, Matt Marvin and
Jason Hehir, WCFM Radio

Actually, the Williams kicking game was awful. Worse than awful. The Ephs hadn't made a field goal in 17 games, dating back over two years.

Game 91

A few weeks earlier, Farley, searching for any answer to his kicking dilemma, turned to back-up freshman wide receiver Collin Vataha (son of former New England Patriots receiver Randy Vataha). Farley noticed Vataha, a former soccer player in high school, booting a 50-yard field goal while joking around in practice.

That was enough for the Williams' coach. Vataha got his chance.

Against Wesleyan, Vataha got one opportunity to kick, an extra-point attempt in the mud. It was blocked. But Farley had faith in his frosh. He stuck with Vataha for the season-ending battle with Amherst, and Vataha delivered, connecting on a 34-yard field goal in the second quarter.

The freshman was perfect on the day. Six-of-six PATs, one-for-one on field goals. He hit a second field goal that was taken off the board when Amherst was penalized for roughing the kicker.

Still, this was asking too much. Sure it was a 27-yard attempt. But to beat Amherst ? The pressure on Vataha was enormous. "I was nervous, sure," Vataha admitted. "I realized how important this game was to all of us."

McPhail, a senior co-captain, was the holder. He looked at his freshman kicker. "You're the man," he said.

McPhail took the snap. Vataha never flinched. The kick was good. Williams 48, Amherst 46.

The Williams student announcers lost control. "Williams Wins! Williams Wins! Oh my God, I can't believe it!" The three broadcasters trampled on each others lines. They bellowed out the press box window. They probably shotgunned a beer. It was the most unprofessional, homer radio call ever heard. It also was one of the most entertaining.

"I recall hanging by the waist out of the window, as the kick was in the air," said Hehir. "Most of both of our bodies were hanging out the window rather than being in the booth."

Williams sports information director Dick Quinn had predicted to Hehir before the game that Vataha, who had never kicked a point in a football game at any level, would beat Amherst with a last-second field goal. To that Hehir replied, "If that happens, I will jump nude out of the Weston Field press box."

Perhaps some lucky Williams fan caught a mound of happy flesh.

THE AFTERMATH

"These kids will take the memory of this game to their grave. It's something they'll talk about at their 5th, 10th and 15th reunions. This kind of thing only gets bigger the further away from it you get," said Farley. "A lot of people were saying afterwards that this was the finest football game they'd ever seen and I'd have to agree."

For the second year in a row, a loss to Williams was the only blemish on Amherst's 7-1 record, marking the 11th straight year the Lord Jeffs couldn't find a way to beat the Ephs. That streak stayed intact through 1999 as Williams won 35-16 in '98 and 10-7 in '99. The last Amherst victory in the series was a 10-7 win in 1986.

Hampered by a leg injury, Collin Vataha kicked just two field goals the next season at Williams and none during the 1999 campaign.

Rich Willard ended a four-year career at Amherst with his best game ever, completing 26 of 44 for 378 yards and five TDs. He is the leading passer in Amherst history with 4,387 career yards.

November 8, 1997—Williamstown, Massachusetts

Amherst	7	7	17	15	- 46
Williams	14	10	0	24	- 48

WIL   Supino 10 run (Vataha kick)
AMH   Byrne 3 run (Fleming kick)
WIL   McAdam 1 run (Vataha kick)
WIL   Cleary 5 pass from Supino
        (Vataha kick)
WIL   FG Vataha 35
AMH   Quigley 36 pass from Willard
        (Fleming kick)
AMH   FG Fleming 34
AMH   Barnicle 15 pass from Willard
        (Fleming kick)
AMH   Haggerty 4 pass from Willard
        (Fleming kick)
WIL   Supino 2 run (Vataha kick)
WIL   Bethe 2 run (Vataha kick)
WIL   Storz 10 run (Vataha kick)
AMH   Quigley 19 pass from Willard
        (Fleming kick)
AMH   Hall 34 pass from Willard
        (Haggerty pass from Hall)
WIL   FG Vataha 27

Attendance 11,500

Nebraska vs.
Missouri

"The game's over, man."—a Missouri student being forced off the field at the end of regulation

THE BACKGROUND

Number one, undefeated, and untouched in regular season conference play for almost five years, the Nebraska Cornhuskers (8-0) took their biannual trip to Columbia, Missouri, as 29-point favorites to beat up on Missouri.

It had become a ritual pasting over the years—51-7, 57-7, 42-7, 49-7...should I continue? Nineteen years had passed since Missouri last beat Nebraska in 1978.

However, Larry Smith, in his fourth year as head coach, had put some of the bite back into the Missouri program. With victories over Texas, Oklahoma State, and Colorado, the 6-3 Tigers, although unranked, were still poised for their first winning record and bowl trip since 1983.

Determined to prove his team's mettle against the mighty Huskers, Smith immediately gambled on Missouri's first possession of the game. He went for a fourth-and-one at his own 41. He got it. Fullback Ron James burst ahead for three yards.

The Tigers then burst down the field.

Quarterback Corby Jones connected with tight end Eddie Brooks for a 34-yard completion. Then Jones scrambled for 17 more to the Nebraska one-yard line. Brock Olivo pounded it in from there and the Tigers led 7-0.

Smith had made his statement. It was echoed by the boisterous Missouri fans. The top-ranked Cornhuskers were in for a battle.

After Jones and Nebraska quarterback Scott Frost traded a barrage of big plays in the first two periods (Jones threw for two TDs, Frost ran for two), Missouri entered the locker room with a 24-21 lead. For the first time in nine years, the Tigers had a lead at the half against Nebraska.

Frost's one-yard run with 3:00 to play in the third quarter put Nebraska ahead again, 28-24. But Missouri refused to succumb. Jones got the lead right back with an acrobatic six-yard tumble into the end zone. The Tigers led 31-28 at the end of the third quarter.

Kris Brown's 44-yard field goal tied it up at 31-31 with 10:50 to play. Then Jones drove the Tigers to the Nebraska 15. With 4:39 left to play, he rolled right and hit Brooks for the go-ahead touchdown. Missouri was back in front 38-31.

The Tiger defense held, and with three minutes to play, Jones and company had the ball at the north end of the field trying to run out the clock.

Suddenly, the sprinkler system kicked on in the south end zone. A bizarre 30-second shower took place. Perhaps it was a sign of future inexplicable events.

Missouri tried to keep possession, but with 1:13 left, Jones was stopped for no gain on a third-down run, forcing a final punt by the Tigers. With one final chance to avert the upset, Nebraska took possession at their 33-yard line with 62 seconds on the clock.

Frost, who rushed for 141 yards in the game, went to the air. He hit Kenny Cheatham for 27 yards down the sideline. Then, from the Missouri 40, he threw incomplete. On second down, Missouri's Al Sterling just barely missed a game-saving interception that sent the frenzied Missouri student section boiling to the brim, ready to overflow onto the field.

Frost maintained his poise, hitting a key third-and-10 pass to freshman Matt Davison for 13 yards to the 27-yard line. Cheatham caught two more receptions. Trailing by seven, the Huskers were at the 12-yard line.

But only seven seconds remained.

THE PLAY
CD2—Track 19—*Adrian Fiala, Warren Swain*, Pinnacle Sports Network

Four receivers were split out. One back in the backfield. Shotgun, 99, Double Slant. "Both sets of receivers were running toward the football, kind of like a line-drive Hail Mary," said Nebraska receivers coach Ron Brown.

Frost took the snap out of the shotgun. He looked left. He looked left. He looked left. He looked for receiver Lance Brown who was open, but short of the goal line. Frost looked over the middle. He could have said seven Hail Marys in the time he had to throw.

Maybe he did. Finally, as Shevin Wiggins slanted in from the right, Frost unleashed the pass straight over the middle. Safety Julius Jones was wrapped around Wiggins' back just beyond the goal line. The ball hit Wiggins in the chest. He couldn't hold it as Jones yanked him backwards to the turf.

The ball popped forward and headed for the ground. The exuberant Missouri students couldn't take the suspense anymore. They began crashing onto the field in celebration. They tried to tear down the goalposts.

But it wasn't over.

Missouri's Harold Piersey reached down with two hands to catch the ball off the top of the grass. But just as he grasped it, Wiggins, being wrestled on his back, flung his right foot up, kicking the ball back up in the air toward the back of the end zone.

For Missouri fans, this was a moment from a horror film. The left-for-dead, drowned killer had just stuck his head up from underneath the water.

Piersey, looking stunned at the turn of events, followed the flighty ball backwards. It appeared it would fall harmlessly to the turf. But sliding from the left came The Freshman, Matt Davison.

"I saw the ball get deflected off Shevin," Davison said. "It was floating like a punt, kind of end over end. It just seemed like it took forever to get there. I dove, and I guess the Lord was watching over me."

Davison snatched the ball, and essentially the game, right out from underneath Faurot Field. "It was probably a few inches off the ground when I caught it," he said.

With no time on the clock, Nebraska trailed by one point, 38-37.

For the disbelieving Missouri faithful, Davison was the Grinch in Whoville on Christmas Eve. In Lincoln, Nebraska he was Santa Claus, bringing the greatest gift of all...a possible overtime.

This was the first and only time in his career Tom Osborne had the luxury of not having to go for two at the end of regulation. With the advent of overtime in 1996, Osborne wouldn't need to relive Missouri '73, or Miami '84. No anguishing decision, just Kris Brown kicking the extra point, tying the score at 38-38, and sending the game into overtime. Brown's successful kick came after the disoriented Missouri fans had to stop partying, get off the goalposts, and clear the field.

The overtime was anti-climactic, a foregone conclusion. Fate.

On Nebraska's possession at the 25, two Ahman Green runs gained 13 yards (giving him 189 yards for the game). Frost then ran the final 12 yards on an option to put the Huskers ahead 45-38.

Missouri got the ball back. It had no air in it.

After the Tigers gained just three yards in three plays, Mike Rucker and Grant Wistrom sacked Jones on fourth down to end the game. The Miracle at Missouri was complete. Davison's catch had saved the season for Nebraska.

"It's just one stinking play," said a dejected Smith.

"It's a one-in-a-thousand play," said Osborne.

More like a one-in-a-million play.

THE AFTERMATH

"That Missouri game is the damnedest finish I've ever seen," remarked Nebraska announcer Warren Swain. For Missouri fans, it

Game 92

Freshman Matt Davison (3) clutches Scott Frost's deflected pass for the amazing Husker touchdown. Photo courtesy of Lincoln-Journal Star

brought back nightmares of the 1990 Colorado game, decided on fifth down int he same end zone, with the same result, and a few days later, a similar controversy.

The following week, Wiggins admitted to intentionally kicking the ball. "I looked down and saw the Missouri guy about to catch it, and I just wanted to keep it alive," he said. "It wasn't an accident." Had the officials ruled Wiggin's kick was intentional, the Huskers would have been assessed a 15-yard, loss of down penalty and the game would have been over.

No solace to Missouri. they knew from past experience, no one was going to reverse the outcome of the game.

The win actually dropped Nebraska to No. 3 in the polls as Michigan overtook them atop the ratings. On December 10, 1997, after Nebraska finished the regular season 12-0, up a notch to No. 2 in the polls, Tom Osborne announced his retirement.

After 25 years leading Nebraska, his last game would be against No. 3 Tennessee in the Orange Bowl. Osborne's Huskers routed the Volunteers 42-17 and inched ahead of undefeated Michigan by four points to gain the USA Today/ESPN Coaches poll national championship. Nebraska's third title in four years, Michigan, 21-16 victors over Washington State in the Rose Bowl, maintained their No. 1 ranking in the Associated Press poll.

Osborne retired with a record of 255-49-3, the fifth highest winning percentage (.836) in the history of Division I-A, and the highest winning percentage of all I-A coaches with more than 200 victories.

After losing to Colorado State 35-24 in the Holiday Bowl, Missouri finished 7-5 and ranked No. 23 in the AP poll, the first time since 1981 that the Tigers were ranked at the end of the season.

Nebraska	14	7	7	10	7	- 45
Missouri	7	17	7	7	0	- 38

MU	Olivo 1 run (Knickman kick)
NEB	Frost 16 run (Brown kick)
NEB	Frost 1 run (Brown kick)
MU	Coleman 18 pass from Jones (Knickman kick)
NEB	Green 7 run (K Brown kick)
MU	FG Knickman 39
MU	Olivo 34 pass from Jones (Knickman kick)
NEB	Frost 1 run (Brown kick)
MU	Jones 7 run (Knickman kick)
NEB	FG Brown 44
MU	Brooks 15 pass from Jones (Knickman kick)
NEB	Davison 12 pass from Frost (Brown kick)
NEB	Frost 12 run (Brown kick)

Attendance 66,846

Washington vs. 🏈 Arizona State

"That's the most unbelievable football game I've ever seen."
—Brock Huard

THE BACKGROUND

In 1996, trailing 42-21 to Arizona State with 12 minutes to play in the game, Washington coach Jim Lambright replaced senior quarterback Shane Fortney with a redshirt freshman by the name of Brock Huard.

Huard threw a 55-yard bullet to Jerome Pathon, putting the Huskies near the end zone. Then he ran 10 yards for the touchdown. Then he got the ball back and hit Gerald Harris with a 67-yard TD bomb. It was 42-35. Then Washington forced a Sun Devils' fumble and Huard marched the Huskies inside the ASU 10 again. Then Corey Dillon scampered eight yards for the TD, capping a furious four-minute 21-point UW rally.The score was 42-42.

Then, enter stage left, Jake Plummer.

The Arizona State quarterback dramatically scrambled the Sun Devils downfield and into field-goal position. Then Robert Nycz booted the game-winning 38-yard field goal with 0:02 left and Arizona State won 45-42.

That was then.

September 7, 1996, the beginning of Plummer's glorious senior season that led the Sun Devils to the Rose Bowl and the very brink of a national championship which just eluded them.

That was also the first game of Huard's memorable Washington career.

Two years later, the Huskies and Sun Devils, both Pac-10 title contenders, met again in Sun Devil Stadium to open the 1998 campaign.

Arizona State was ranked No.8 in the pre-season AP poll. Washington was No. 18.

The two teams combined for a whopping 561 yards in offense in the first two quarters alone. ASU took a 28-21 lead into the locker room. But then Huard brought Washington back in the third quarter, throwing his third TD pass of the game and steering the Huskies to a 35-28 lead entering the fourth quarter.

After a Mike Gauthier 42-yard field goal cut the lead to 35-31, pre-season Heisman Trophy candidate J.R. Redmond struck gold for the Sun Devils. Late in the fourth quarter, Redmond took a Huskies' punt at his own 19-yard line and burst upfield. Sixty-one yards later, Arizona State was setting up shop at the Washington 20-yard line after Redmond's electric punt return.

A short fourth-down conversion run by Redmond gave ASU first-and-goal at the UW 9. But the Devils could muster just one yard in three plays. It was fourth-and-goal at the eight. Just 2:06 on the clock.

Sophomore quarterback Ryan Kealy sent four receivers wide. He zipped a pass to Tariq McDonald who caught it in the end zone despite being closely covered by UW's Jermaine Smith. In comeback fashion, the Sun Devils led 38-35. It was just like 1996. Jake Plummer would have been proud.

Still, two minutes remained.

After the ensuing kickoff, Washington started on their own 20. With help from an ASU personal foul, they moved to the Sun Devil 49 where they faced third-and-three with 1:18 on the clock.

Disaster struck. A bad option pitch from Huard to Jason Harris went awry. It bounced off the referee. Harris scrambled and pounced on it. The result was a devastating 14-yard loss back to the UW 37.

Now Huard and the Huskies were in a desperate situation—fourth-and-17 and the clock was still running.

THE PLAY
CD 2—Track 20—*Bob Rondeau,* KOMO Radio and the Husky Football Network

"I didn't even think about the down and distance," said Huard. The unfazed junior quarterback brought his team to the line of scrimmage with 40 seconds left.

Looking across the line, Huard recognized ASU in man-to-man coverage. Cornerback Phillip Brown, a converted safety, was on top of tight end Reggie Davis who lined up in the slot.

Huard suddenly changed the play. "Copper!" he yelled. A post-corner route for Davis.

Huard took the snap. Davis broke to the middle, faking Brown inside, then faded outside as Brown got caught behind trying to catch up. Huard floated the ball downfield.

The pass met Davis at the ASU 30-yard line.

"It was like NFL Films, the ball just coming out of the lights," said Davis. Perhaps the tight end even heard the biblical voice of the late John Facenda as he rumbled across the sun drenched blades of grass, barreling toward a glorious entrance into the golden gridiron gates of Husky lore...or something like that.

Davis still had one man to beat, all-Pac 10 senior safety Mitchell Freedman, who was chasing frantically behind. Perhaps the Devils' best defensive player, the 6-2, 207 lb. Freedman was known as "Fright Night," for his wicked hits on opposing players.

Davis got to the 10-yard line when the scary Freedman suddenly made a weak shoulder-high attempt to strip the ball away from Davis, instead of making a touchdown saving tackle. The tight end brushed off Freedman's swipe and made it into the end zone for the stunning touchdown. A 63-yard TD reception with just 0:28 on the clock.

Washington announcer Bob Rondeau's voice cracked. "I don't tend to get oftly nuts but I sure did on that one," said Rondeau.

The Huskies had shocked the home crowd. Washington 42, Arizona State 38.

"It was divine intervention," said a flabbergasted Huard. "What a tremendous rush and swing of emotion," added Huskies coach Jim Lambright.

ASU did get the ball back at its 46 with 21 seconds left. They moved to the Washington 40 with six seconds remaining, but a Kealy Hail Mary pass fell incomplete as time expired.

While the Huskies celebrated, the Sun Devils were despondent. "It's a huge letdown," said Kealy. ASU coach Bruce Snyder concurred. "It's a terrible loss. It's terribly disappointing to all."

Except to those in purple and gold.

"I don't think any of us in this room could have written a better script," said Huard.

THE AFTERMATH

It was a great beginning to a year that ended sadly for the Huskies. After high expectations, they finished the season just 6-6, losing to Air Force 45-25 in the inaugural Oahu Bowl to close out the year. Even though the ASU win will be remembered as one of the most exciting victories in Huskies history, the lackluster season was the first time in 22 years that Washington did not produce a winning record.

On December 31st, after six years as head coach and 30 years as a member of the Washington coaching staff, Lambright was fired by athletic director Barbara Hedges. He had a record of 44-25-1. Lambright was replaced by former Colorado head coach Rick Neuheisel.

Arizona State's season was equally disappointing, if not more so. Picked by many as national title contenders, the Sun Devils floundered after the opening-game setback. Redmond and Kealy were both hindered by injuries later in the season and ASU stumbled to a 5-6 record.

Like identical bookends, ASU's last game ended just like their first. Kealy's 28-yard desperation pass into the end zone fell incomplete as the Devils lost to arch-rival Arizona 50-42.

"It would involve almost a book to talk about the things that have happened to us," said Snyder at the end of the year.

Washington	7	14	14	7	- 42
Arizona St.	14	14	0	10	- 38

ASU   Bates 13 pass from Kealy
          (Gauthier kick)
WASH   Davis 5 pass from Huard (Skurski kick)
ASU   Heap 15 pass from Kealy
          (Gauthier kick)
WASH   Conniff 16 run (Skurski kick)
ASU   Hightower 2 run (Gauthier kick)
ASU   Redmond 22 run (Gauthier kick)
WASH   Looker 3 pass from Huard
          (Skurski kick)
WASH   Looker 9 pass from Huard
          (Skurski kick)
WASH   J.Harris 5 run (Skurski kick)
ASU   FG Gauthier 42
ASU   McDonald 8 pass from Kealy
          (Gauthier kick)
WASH   Davis 63 pass from Huard
          (Skurski kick)

Attendance 72,118

Penn vs. Brown

"Do you call that a track meet?"—Brown head coach Phil Estes

THE BACKGROUND

Entering the 1998 season, Al Bagnoli was the second winningest active coach in Division I-AA, with a career record of 125-39-0 (.762). After 10 successful seasons with Division III Union College (NY), Bagnoli was in his seventh year at Penn, seeking his third Ivy League title with a strong defense ranked 12th in I-AA. The Quakers (4-1, 2-0) traveled to Brown Stadium to take on the Brown Bears (2-3, 0-2) for their homecoming game.

Welcome home Brown alumni. No graduate in the history of the school had ever witnessed a game like this one.

Penn led 17-14 at the half. But Brown quarterback James Perry threw two perfectly executed TD passes in the third quarter to give the Bears a 28-17 lead. From the Penn 17, he pump faked once on a hitch-and-go route, hitting a wide open Sean Morey, Division I-AA's leading receiver, for the first score. Then Perry rolled right and threw back to his equally wide-open tight end Zach Burns on an 18-yard screen pass for the other TD. Neither receiver was touched. The Penn defense was struggling.

But the Quaker offense wasn't. Senior runningback Jim Finn swam downstream most of the day, accumulating 129 yards through the first three quarters. After the Quakers closed the gap to 28-23 to end the third quarter, Finn shifted gills.

"I didn't really feel warmed up until the fourth quarter, which is when I felt my best," Finn said. Not hard to believe after what happened.

The fourth quarter was unheard of. Mind boggling. The field-goal kickers may as well have been in the stands. They weren't needed. This was basketball on grass. Here's the blow-by-blow description of the final round.

With 14:54 left to play, Morey catches a 13-yard TD pass. Brown leads 36-23. At 11:07, Finn crashes in for a five-yard TD. Penn cuts the lead to 36-30. Brown's Stephen Campbell then fumbles the kickoff. Clock reads 9:10. Finn again. This time from 10 yards. Penn leads 37-36. Perry retaliates with his own flurry. At 7:07, the Brown QB throws seven yards to junior full-back Rob Scholl. Brown back on top 44-37 and 3:48 on the clock. Finn again, capping an eight-play drive from one yard out. Penn ties the game 44-44. But Brown barges back downfield. Sixty-five yards in three plays. Only 2:13 left. Perry to Campbell from 17 yards out. Brown leads 51-44. With just 0:44 remaining, it's Finn a fourth time in the fourth quarter. A five-yard TD caps a 65-yard drive.

The game is tied 51-51. Take a deep breath.

"It got to the point where we were looking at each other in the press box and saying, 'Are you believing this? Are we seeing the same thing? Somebody pinch me,'" said Brown announcer John Rooke.

What had happened to the Penn defense? "We tried three, four, five and six man pressure. We used every defensive back we traveled with," said Bagnoli.

Maybe they needed a bigger bus.

Game 94

Stephen Campbell grabs a 17-yard TD from Brown QB James Perry with 2:13 left. Photo courtesy of John Freidah— The Providence Journal

Brown got the ball with 44 seconds left at their own 20. Had Perry picked the Quaker defense apart so much they couldn't piece together a final stand and force an overtime?

Here's the answer. Three Perry completions moved the ball to the Brown 40. Then, the junior quarterback dropped back in the pocket and zipped a pass to Morey over the middle at the Penn 34.

Eighteen seconds were left on the clock. Perry threw 10 yards to Burns, his eighth reception of the day, to the Penn 24.

Ten seconds remained.

THE PLAY

Five straight completions. The score was still tied 51-51. Why bother with a field goal attempt?

In the shotgun, Perry barked signals. Three receivers lined up wide right. Perry took the snap and immediately rolled right.

"I was in the slot position," Campbell said. "I broke it outside and saw that nobody was there." He was ridiculously wide open behind the helpless Quaker defense. Perry lofted the ball up to the right. Campbell brought it down with four seconds left. Touchdown Brown. Eighty yards in 40 seconds.

Jumping up and down with papers flying all over, the Brown press box burst into celebration. "It was like the entire radio booth got goosed by an electrical charge," said Rooke. "It was truly an amazing day. I've done college basketball games that were slower paced."

Unfortunately for the Quakers, 0:04 wasn't enough time to get Finn back in the end zone. Quarterback Matt Rader's Hail Mary attempt was batted away by Morey. Brown won 58-51.

An NCAA record 58 points were scored in the breathtaking fourth quarter. The 109 total points set the Ivy League record for most points in a game.

Finn finished with 259 yards on 43 carries,

and six touchdowns, also an Ivy League record. He ran for 130 yards on 17 carries in the fourth quarter alone. In contrast, the Brown offense rushed for just 45 yards in the entire game.

On the other hand, they didn't need to run.

Perry's passing statistics were staggering—470 yards, five TDs, no interceptions, no sacks. Morey had nine receptions for 146 yards, Campbell caught nine for 119 yards, Burns gathered eight for 115 yards.

"The offensive line was pretty damn good," Perry said. "I didn't feel pressure all day, and I was able to make all the throws that I wanted to."

The Penn offensive front was equally dominant. "We basically felt that if we got out on the field that we were going to score, so all we had to do was keep scoring," Finn said. "Hopefully there would be one stop on defense where we would have the opportunity to go ahead, but it didn't happen."

No, it didn't. With the exception of the fumbled kickoff, Brown scored a touchdown on every possession of the second half.

"Was it a beautiful win or an ugly win? It doesn't really matter," said Brown's first-year coach Phil Estes. "We will take them any way we can." It was the first Ivy League victory of his head coaching career. He may never experience another one like it.

THE AFTERMATH

The Quakers solved their defensive woes and didn't lose another game the rest of the year, finishing 8-2 (6-1) and Ivy League champs. Brown finished in second place.

Jim Finn was the last player chosen in the 1999 NFL draft, selected by the Chicago Bears with the 253rd and final pick.

Perry set an Ivy League record with 274 completions in the '98 season. The following year, in his senior season, Perry became the all-time leading QB in Ivy League history eclipsing nearly every passing record. He also continued his affinity for leading the Bears to "are-you-kidding-me?" finishes. None more astonishing than the '99 Ivy League opener against Yale.

Trailing 24-17 with 3:32 left, Perry completed 10-of-10 passes on a desperation drive downfield. On fourth-and-one from the Yale 7-yard line, Perry pushed a pass to tight end David Bookman for the touchdown that brought Brown within one at 24-23 with 0:14 left. But Yale blocked the extra point, seemingly clinching the victory for the Bulldogs. That is, until Brown's Michael Powell picked up the ball, headed for the end zone, then pitched to Rob Scholl who crossed the goal line with the two-point conversion that gave Brown the 25-24 lead. The Bears were so over-zealous in their celebration, they garnered two penalties, kicked off from their 10-yard line, then held their breath as Yale missed a 47-yard FG attempt as time expired...exhale, and the Bears prevailed.

Penn	7	10	6	28	-51
Brown	7	7	14	30	-58

BRO	Powell 2 run (Jensen kick)
PEN	Finn 31 run (Fienberg kick)
PEN	FG Fienberg 21
BRO	Powell 1 run (Jensen kick)
PEN	Finn 12 run (Fienberg kick)
BRO	Morey 19 pass from Perry (Jensen kick)
BRO	Burns 18 pass from Perry (Jensen kick)
PEN	O'Neill 18 pass from Rader (run failed)
BRO	Morey 13 pass from Rowley (Campbell pass from Perry)
PEN	Finn 5 run (Fienberg kick)
PEN	Finn 10 run (Fienberg kick)
BRO	Scholl 7 pass from Perry (Burns pass from Perry)
PEN	Finn 1 run (Fienberg kick)
BRO	Campbell 17 pass from Perry (Jensen kick)
PEN	Finn 5 run (Fienberg kick)
BRO	Campbell 24 pass from Perry (Jensen kick)

Attendance 4,438

Virginia Tech vs. Syracuse

"There's 50,000 people in there. How many were jumping on me?"—Stephen Brominski

THE BACKGROUND

The Big East championship and a major bowl bid were on the line when the 12th-ranked Virginia Tech Hokies traveled to the Carrier Dome to face the 25th ranked Orangemen of Syracuse. Tech (6-1, 4-1 Big East) could virtually wrap up a bid to the Orange Bowl with a win. Syracuse (5-3, 3-1) needed a win over Tech, then beat Miami (FL) in the season finale to win the conference.

Virginia Tech boasted the fifth best total defense in the country, compared to Syracuse which ranked number 72. But it was the Orangemen who shut down Tech's offense, limiting coach Frank Beamer's team to just six first downs and 152 yards of offense for the entire game. It was Tech's lowest output in 134 games, dating back to 1987. Syracuse ran an astonishing 50 more offensive plays (88-38) in the game than Virginia Tech.

Then how could the halftime score be Virginia Tech 21, Syracuse 6?

Three plays.

Tech fullback Jarrett Ferguson ran 76 yards for a touchdown on a third-and-two play at the end of the first quarter. (Ferguson ran the last 50 yards without a left shoe after it was pulled off by linebacker Stan Gibbs.)

On Syracuse's next possession, VT's Anthony Midget blocked Doug Dunkin's punt attempt and Ricky Hall recovered the ball in the end zone for the Tech touchdown. It was Tech's 10th blocked kick of the season.

Then, with Syracuse driving deep in Tech territory in the second quarter, SU's Maurice Jackson took a reverse hand off, cut back, and had the ball knocked out of his grasp by the Hokies' Keion Carpenter. The ball popped up into the air and into the hands of Loren Johnson who scampered 78 yards for the second defensive TD of the game for Virginia Tech.

For Syracuse offensive coordinator Kevin Rogers, the first half was a nightmare.

"It was a very frustrating game for us offensively," he recalled. "It was three and a half hours of agony. We're gaining yards [420 total], [but] we got sacked [seven times in the game], and drives would be delayed."

Rogers knew the Syracuse fans were restless too. "You can almost see in the press box at Syracuse," he said. "The people in the crowd were standing up. They're pointing and saying, 'Hey Rogers, the end zone's that way!'"

In the second half, the Orange offense led by senior QB Donovan McNabb continued to chew up yardage. But now the yards were accompanied by points. After narrowing the margin to 21-16 in the third quarter, Rob Konrad's one-yard TD plunge, with 12:23 remaining in the game, gave Syracuse its first lead 22-21.

A lead they held for zero seconds.

Coach Paul Pasqualoni decided to go for the two-point conversion and a three-point lead. McNabb's pass to Kevin Johnson was picked off by Tech's Loren Johnson who once again ran the length of the field, but this time was caught by McNabb at the Syracuse eight-yard line. Before falling to the ground, Johnson tossed the ball forward, perhaps intentionally, where it was recovered in the end zone by VT's Jamel Smith. Two more defensive points for Tech and suddenly Syracuse trailed again, 23-22.

"It was unbelievable how they scored with absolutely no offense," remembered Rogers. "They did absolutely nothing on the offensive side of the ball and had 23 points."

After Tech's All-Big East kicker Shayne Graham booted a 49-yard field goal with 4:42 left to make the score 26-22, a frustrated Syracuse fan turned his attention to Rogers.

"Towards the end of the game, they sell those little individual pizzas in those triangular boxes," Rogers explained. "Some guy wrote a play down on it and smacked it up in front of my face in the press box window...I remember it was an option pass or something like that. It shook us up up there, you know. It wasn't funny at the time but you think back at it...it was an unbelievable day."

It got more unbelievable.

After the kickoff, Syracuse started the final drive on their own 17-yard line with 4:33 left. The Orangemen methodically moved the football. "The way we were having success in moving the ball was in small increments. And the small increment deal was really burning up the clock," said Rogers.

So much so, that Rogers sent his offense into their two-minute drill as they approached midfield. With 1:45 left, McNabb was faced with a fourth-and-seven at the Syracuse 44. Recognizing a Hokies blitz, he raced up the center of the field for a dramatic 44-yard run down to the Tech 15.

After getting up, McNabb suddenly got sick and threw up on the field.

Trying to preserve his final timeout, and seeing his quarterback sick, Rogers called for a McNabb sprint-out pass to avoid a rush. It was incomplete. McNabb went back to the huddle and promptly vomited again. This time on the shoes of tight end Stephen Brominski.

But McNabb continued to play. On the next down he hit Maurice Jackson who scampered 14 yards down to the Tech one-yard line. Again McNabb vomited.

As offensive coordinator, Rogers had a dilemma. "They're screaming he's sick, he's sick. And we've got one timeout. Do we call it then? What do you do? Do you put the second string guy in? I don't think so!"

Fifty-one seconds remained.

With first-and-goal at the Tech one-yard line, Syracuse used their final timeout to give McNabb a few moments to collect himself. "[McNabb] was putting such maximum effort into winning the game," said Rogers. "He legitimately put the football team on his back."

Now, without a timeout, down by four points, the Syracuse offense suddenly hit a wall. On first down, Tech stopped Konrad on a running play at the one. Time ran down.

Quickly the Orangemen got to the line and tried a "pop" pass to the tight end Brominski. McNabb was forced to throw the ball away when Brominski was blanketed by defensive end John Engelberger. But Tech was called for roughing the passer, giving Syracuse another first down at the one.

Twenty-one seconds left.

McNabb dropped back on a bootleg pass, Brominski got wide open in the left flat, but Tech's Corey Moore got to McNabb first, sacking him back at the 13. The clock kept running, a disaster for the Orangemen.

One of the Syracuse staff then looked up from the field toward the press box and saw several unforgiving fans pointing their middle fingers at Rogers.

Syracuse scrambled to get to the line. McNabb spiked the ball to stop the clock with 0:05 left.

"The sack was something that was an absolute taboo. We were gonna throw the ball so we didn't have to burn too much time on the clock," said Rogers. "We didn't run the ball for fear that we would get held out and run out of time."

There was time for one play from the 13-yard line. Virginia Tech called time-out to set their defense. Walking to the sidelines, McNabb had one more chance to pull his weary body together.

THE PLAY
CD 2—Track 21—*Jim Ridlon,*
Doug Logan, **WSYR Radio**

Frank Beamer knew which play was coming. He told his defense to look for the throwback play to the tight end. "We had worked on that play time after time in practice, because we know that is their favorite play," said the Tech coach.

"We wanted to try and get [McNabb] on the corner with as many options as we possibly could have," said Rogers. With one receiver, two tight ends, and two runningbacks in the game, the offensive coordinator detailed the plan.

"We're gonna run an out-cut to the field with a wide receiver. We're gonna delay the tight end to the call side of the play and gonna run him back across the back of the end zone. And then the back side tight end is gonna run a cross route in the back of the end zone. And we're gonna sprint McNabb out to the right, toward the field. So his read progression would've been throw the out-cut, or throw it to the backside tight end who's dragging delayed and went backside, or throw it to the back of the end zone."

In layman's terms, Rogers called the throwback play to the tight end.

McNabb took the last snap and rolled to the right-hash mark. His first wide receiver option was covered. Then the 6-5 tight end Brominski made his cut from the right side of the field to the left, covered by 6-0 linebacker Michael Hawkes who turned his back on McNabb to chase Brominski. McNabb saw it, stopped, and threw off his back foot toward the end zone.

"I threw it right at the back of [Hawkes'] helmet, then hoped he wouldn't turn around," said McNabb.

Brominski made like a basketball center, boxing out Hawkes from the pass. With no time left on the clock, he gathered the floating pass in his arms. Syracuse won 28-26.

The Carrier Dome exploded.

Player-after-Syracuse-player piled onto the joyful Brominski. Hundreds of tension riddled Syracuse fans poured onto the field. The coaches in the Syracuse press box celebrated. "It was a love fest up there. Seven men hugging each other all at the same time," said Rogers.

Down on the field, Brominski's joy turned to fear as the pile on top of him got larger.

"I thought I was out at one point. Somebody rolled off the top and fell right on my chest. It was just the fear that there was nothing you could do. I'm not a very claustropho-bic person, but at that point I was," said Brominski.

Finally, Syracuse players began yanking people from the pile and the celebration moved off the field.

Rogers will never forget it. "Down in the locker room a lot of emotions flowed. Tears of joy," he said. "I remember he [McNabb] hugged me. We actually sobbed. It was such a tremendous effort and relief. That was our whole season. That was our whole season."

THE AFTERMATH

Syracuse went on to win the Big East championship with a 66-13 dismantling of Miami (FL). Donovan McNabb ran for three touchdowns and threw for two more in the senior's last home game. The Orangemen finished the season 8-4, losing 31-10 to Florida in the Orange Bowl in McNabb's last collegiate game. He left Syracuse as the only man to be named Big East Conference Player of the Year three times, holding seven school offensive records. The Orange Bowl was also the last game at Syracuse for Rogers, who left to become the offensive coordinator at Notre Dame the following year.

After beating Rutgers the following week 47-7, Virginia Tech blew a 29-7 halftime lead to rival Virginia in the regular-season finale, losing 36-32. They then accepted a bid to the inaugural Music City Bowl in Nashville, where they finished the season 9-3 with a 38-7 shellacking of Alabama.

| Virginia Tech | 7 | 14 | 0 | 5 | -26 |
| Syracuse | 3 | 3 | 10 | 12 | -28 |

SU	FG Trout 43
VT	J Ferguson 76 run (Graham kick)
VT	Hall recovered blocked punt in end zone (Graham kick)
VT	L Johnson 74 fumble return (Graham kick)
SU	FG Trout 36
SU	Brominski 1 pass from McNabb (Trout kick)
SU	FG Trout 30
SU	Konrad 1 run (2-point conversion failed)
VT	2-point defensive conversion by J Smith
VT	FG Graham 49
SU	Brominski 13 pass from McNabb (no attempt)

Attendance 49,336

Kansas State vs.
🏈 Texas A&M

"I've had a lot of surgeries in my life, and nothing has ever hurt like this before."—Travis Ochs, Kansas State linebacker

THE BACKGROUND

Tennessee (11-0). UCLA (10-0). Kansas State (11-0). The top three teams in the country's polls (Tennessee was No.1 in the AP, Kansas State No.1 in the USA Today/ESPN Coaches poll). On one last, fateful Saturday of the season, all three would end their regular seasons together, trying to be one of the two teams chosen by a complicated Bowl Championship Series formula to play in the Fiesta Bowl for the national championship.

Tennessee faced Mississippi State in the SEC Championship game. UCLA traveled to Miami to take on the Hurricanes in a game rescheduled from the beginning of the year due to a hurricane. Kansas State faced off against 10th-ranked Texas A&M in the Big 12 Championship game.

The Aggies (10-2) were coming off a crushing defeat to Texas the previous week. After overcoming a 16-point fourth-quarter deficit, which would have been the largest comeback in school history, A&M watched UT's Kris Stockton boot a 24-yard field goal with five seconds left to cap a late Longhorns' rally and give Texas the 26-24 victory in Austin. Not only did A&M lose to their bitter rivals, they also saw Texas RB Ricky Williams rush for 259 yards, breaking the all-time Division I-A career-rushing record of 6,082 yards, previously held by Tony Dorsett.

Even worse, Aggies starting quarterback Randy McCown, who led the dramatic comeback, was diagnosed with a fractured collarbone the following week, and backup Branndon Stewart was forced into the starting lineup. Stewart, a senior transfer from Tennessee, had an up-and-down history at A&M. Most recently, he lost his starting job to McCown in the fifth week of the season.

After K-State's Heisman Trophy candidate QB Michael Bishop hit receiver Darnell McDonald with a 66-yard touchdown pass giving the heavily favored Wildcats a commanding 17-3 second quarter lead, a final score was flashed on the Trans World Dome scoreboard. Miami 49, UCLA 45. The wave of purple clad fans erupted. Suddenly the path was clear for Kansas State to play for the national championship, if they could just finish off the Aggies in the second half and extend their 19-game winning streak.

Bishop continued to lead the dominating K-State offense, which ran up a massive 519 yards on the day. His five-yard TD run in the third quarter gave the Wildcats a comfortable 27-12 margin entering the fourth quarter. They hadn't punted all afternoon.

Meanwhile, Stewart was struggling. He completed just 4-of-11 passes for 89 yards and one interception in the first three quarters.

Finally, with 10 minutes left, A&M forced a punt. Something changed.

Somehow, Stewart magically got on track. He drove his team 78 yards on short passes and capped the drive with a 13-yard touchdown pass to Leroy Hodge.

Now trailing 27-19, A&M again forced a K-State punt with 5:58 to play.

Stewart kept the A&M momentum rolling

319

by hitting Derrick Spiller for 26 yards, then 36 yards, and quickly the Aggies were inside the K-State 20-yard line. But after a sack, the drive stalled when defensive tackle Damion McIntosh batted down Stewart's fourth-down pass. K-State took over on the 26, ahead by eight points, with 3:26 to kill on the clock, and a national championship game on the horizon.

Here the Kansas State nightmare began.

Scrambling on a crucial third-and-six play from the 28, Bishop picked up a first down. But on the tackle, A&M linebacker Warren Holdman knocked the ball loose and Cornelius Anthony recovered for the Aggies on the Wildcat 35 with 2:26 remaining.

Stewart moved the Aggies to the nine-yard line. On third-and-five, he hit backup tailback Sirr Parker on a quick slant for the TD. The Aggies were within two, 27-25. Coach R.C. Slocum called the identical play for the two-point conversion attempt. Again Parker caught Stewart's pass and the game was tied with 1:05 left.

The stunned K-State offense regrouped for a last-second drive. Bishop, who accumulated 101 yards rushing and 324 passing on the day, threw one last pass as time ran out, 54 yards to Everett Burnett. He needed 56 yards for the score. Burnett was tackled on the two-yard line and the game went into overtime, tied at 27-27.

After the teams traded field goals in the first overtime, Martin Gramatica booted a 25-yard kick to give K-State the three-point lead, 33-30, in the second overtime. On A&M's following possession, the Wildcats defense stuffed Dante Hall for a two-yard loss. Then a Stewart incompletion and a false start penalty. The Aggies were pushed back to the 32 and facing third-and-17, desperate to get closer for a tying field goal.

THE PLAY
CD 2—Track 22—*Dave South,*
Dave Elmendorf, **Clear Channel Sports**

"I thought we were just trying to get in field goal range," said Parker. He moved in motion to the outside as Stewart stood over center. Prior to this game, Parker had caught just five passes all season.

On a quick count, Stewart took the snap and threw the quick slant to Parker, guarded one-on-one by freshman cornerback Jerametrius Butler. Parker shook off Butler's attempted tackle. "I felt the corner fall off my body and [I] started racing for the goal line," recalled Parker, who then sprinted for the right corner of the end zone.

It was then a foot race between Parker and Aggies safety Lamar Chapman. Parker got to the five-yard line when Chapman dove for him, grabbing high onto the back of his jersey, desperately pulling him back, trying to save the K-State season from falling off the cliff.

Parker drove ahead, dragging Chapman toward the end zone. Just as Parker was falling to the ground, he reached the ball to the goal line. "I'm only 5-11, but I think I stretched to 6-foot on that one," noted Parker. "I wasn't sure if I made it."

Neither was Aggies announcer Dave South, calling the game from the press box. "When I saw him getting close to the goal line, the only thing I was doing was watching the official who was standing right on the goal line. I never saw the kid go in. I was just watching that official," he remembered.

"All of a sudden he signaled touchdown and the whole place went wild," said South. Texas A&M had beaten Kansas State, 36-33, capturing the Big 12 championship, and crushing the Wildcats' national championship dreams.

Parker couldn't control himself. "I jumped onto one of the [Aggie] Corps guys and almost jumped onto his sword," he said. "Somebody on my team grabbed me and slammed me to the ground, and the pile just jumped on top of me."

An avalanche of emotions ensued. Tears of joy. Tears of anguish.

"I had a guy who was working for me in the booth who was one of our former yell leaders. I turned around and looked at him. He was leaning against the wall and was slowly sliding down the wall going to the floor," recalled South. "And he was crying. He had big tears coming out of his eyes.

"I may [announce] another twenty years, [but] I don't think I'll see another game like that...Our players were rolling around on the field and people were hugging strangers!"

On the other side of the field, Kansas

Game 96

Sirr Parker drags Lamar Chapman into the end zone on the 32-yard pass reception that gave Texas A&M the Big 12 Championship. Photo courtesy of Glen Johnson

State's undefeated season had sorrowfully vanished. Later that evening, Tennessee defeated Mississippi State 24-14 to end any dim hopes for a K-State bid to the national title game.

"It's painful now; it's going to be more painful later this evening; it's going to be more painful in the middle of the night, and tomorrow morning will be the most painful of all," said coach Bill Snyder.

THE AFTERMATH

Snyder forgot about the pain of tomorrow evening. That's when the bowl selections were announced. Inexplicably to those in Manhattan, Kansas, and many others around the country, the Wildcats were snubbed by the Bowl Championship Series games (Orange, Sugar, and Fiesta Bowls), as well as the Cotton Bowl and the Holiday Bowl. The now 4th-ranked Wildcats, on the verge of a national championship game the previous day, were left with a bid to play

unranked Purdue (8-4) in the Alamo Bowl.

K-State begrudgingly agreed, then was upset by the upstart Boilermakers, 34-30, when Purdue QB Drew Brees drove his team 80 yards in 54 seconds, throwing a 19-yard TD pass to Isaac Jones with 30 seconds left to win the game. The Wildcats finished the season ranked ninth in the USA Today/ESPN poll. (Tennessee finished No.1, beating Florida State 23-16 in the Fiesta Bowl.)

Meanwhile, after the town of College Station, Texas, had stopped partying, which wasn't for days, the Aggies went on to face Ohio State in the Sugar Bowl, losing to the Buckeyes 24-14. Nevertheless, according to South, the 1998 Big 12 Championship game will never be forgotten among Aggies fans. "It's the biggest game ever played in A&M history. THE biggest game."

Kansas St	10	7	10	0	3	3	-33
Texas A&M	0	6	6	15	3	6	-36

KSU	FG Gramatica 47
KSU	Swift 16 pass from Bishop (Gramatica kick)
A&M	FG Bynum 25
KSU	McDonald 66 pass from Bishop (Gramatica kick)
A&M	FG Bynum 26
A&M	Toombs 2 run (two-point - conversion failed)
KSU	FG Gramatica 45
KSU	Bishop 5 run (Gramatica kick)
A&M	Hodge 13 pass from Stewart (Bynum kick)
A&M	Parker 9 pass from Stewart (Parker reception for two-point conversion)
A&M	FG Bynum 18
KSU	FG Gramatica 22
KSU	FG Gramatica 25
A&M	Parker 32 pass from Stewart (no attempt)

Attendance 60,798

322

UNLV vs. Baylor

"The million dollar question is 'Why did this happen?'"
—Kevin Steele

THE BACKGROUND

Kevin Steele was a new head coach. John Robinson was a new head coach. Steele had an 0-1 record. Robinson's record was 105-35-4.

After two decades of being an assistant at Tennessee, New Mexico State, Oklahoma State, Nebraska, and the NFL Carolina Panthers, Steele finally landed his first head coaching stint with the Baylor Bears in 1999. His task? Rebuild the Baylor program which had consecutive 2-9 seasons in 1997 and '98.

After two decades of being a head coach at Southern California, then the Los Angeles Rams, then back to USC, Robinson was a new head coach for the fourth time. His task in his first year at UNLV? Break the school's 16-game losing streak. Stop the school's 26-game road losing streak. Try to win more than the three victories the Rebels had accumulated over the past two seasons.

UNLV's opening game, a 26-3 win at North Texas, joyfully ended both losing streaks as Robinson's stint in Vegas got off on the right foot. When the Rebels traveled to Waco, Texas, to start a winning streak of their own the following Saturday night, that right foot turned into a rabbit's foot blessed with more luck than a hundred Keno winners at Caesar's Palace.

Meanwhile, Steele's debut was far less fortunate. After being tied on the road with Boston College 23-23 at the end of regulation, Baylor painfully lost their opener when Kyle Atteberry's extra point in overtime went wide, giving BC the 30-29 victory.

Admirably, Steele didn't blame his kicker. "The snap was good and the hold was good. He's hit a 100 of them...The responsibility falls on my shoulders," said Steele. "The score's the ultimate thing and we need to do a better job stopping the run."

Could a head coach, looking for his first career college win, have a more heart wrenching loss?

Well...yes.

It was a blistering 93 degrees in Waco as UNLV and Baylor kicked off the second game of the '99 season. By the end of the game, no one's face was redder than Steele's.

The Bears jumped out to a 10-0 second-quarter margin. UNLV battled back and took the lead at 14-10 with 4:50 left in the third quarter on a one-yard burst by Jeremy Rudolph. But after UNLV tailback Coury Hankins fumbled at his own 20 and Baylor safety Curtis Henderson recovered, the Bears quickly capitalized with a one-yard keeper by quarterback Jermaine Alfred to start the fourth quarter. Baylor led 17-14.

A seven-yard TD pass from UNLV quarterback Jason Vaughn to Nate Turner in the right flat with 7:07 left in the game capped a 67-yard drive, and put the Rebels back on top 21-17. One minute later, after a 53-yard kickoff return by Elijah Burkins, the Bears regained the lead 24-21, on a nine-yard TD run by junior Darrell Bush.

With 4:33 to play in the game, UNLV punted the ball back to Baylor. The Rebels offense never saw the ball again.

Baylor ground out the clock with Bush and

fullback Derek Lagway trading carries deep into UNLV territory. With 2:21 left, Lagway lunged for a first down at the UNLV 32. The clock kept running. Lagway gained four and UNLV called their final timeout, trying to force a field goal attempt.

But on the next play, Bush reeled off seven more yards for another first down at the UNLV 21. With the clock down to 1:38, UNLV, trailing by three points, was helpless as the Bears got a new set of downs.

"They don't even need to hand the ball off anymore," commented David Hatcher on the Baylor Radio Network. The chains were set. The clock was started. There was nothing UNLV could do to stop it from running out.

Still, Alfred gave it to Bush again. He gained five to the 16. The clock ticked down to 0:48. Hatcher reiterated his comment over the airwaves like a mother warning her curious son not to touch the stove. "They do not even have to hand it off," he repeated. "If they just snap the ball and take a knee..."

Alfred handed to Bush again. Bush rambled up the middle eight yards to the UNLV 8. The clock was under 30 seconds. Baylor had to take one more snap and the game was over.

THE PLAY
CD 2—Track 23
Tony Cordasco, Hunkie Cooper, KXNT Radio

The clock kept ticking, down to 0:08 as Baylor's offense came to the line of scrimmage. For a third time, all Kevin Steele's squad had to do was take the snap and fall on the ball. Just ask former NY Giants quarterback Joe Piscarcik.

Alfred took the snap, and then, as if to test fate one final time, handed to Bush, who burst inside the UNLV 5 to the one-yard line. As he struggled toward the goal line, linebackers Tyler Brickell and James Sunia, along with corner-back Andre Hilliard, attacked Bush, ferociously grabbing at the ball while the Baylor running-back tried to inch across for a meaningless touchdown.

Then, it happened.

Baylor touched the stove. Brickell pried the ball out of Bush's grasp. The bouncing ball plopped across the goal line and was scooped up by defensive back Kevin Thomas. No one was near Thomas. He sped down the left side of the field untouched. The clock ran out. Thomas kept running, past his delirious bench, cruising 101 yards with the fumble recovery. Touchdown UNLV. Meltdown Baylor.

The guy reached out for the goal line," Brickell said. "We had Andre Hilliard and Quincy Sanders out there holding this guy up. They hit him about the 3-yard line. He started chugging toward the end zone and reached out with his arm and I just swatted it out of his hand. Kevin Thomas took it from there."

The absolute astonishment of what transpired turned UNLV radio announcer Tony Cordasco into a hyperactive five-year-old, screaming to anyone who would listen, "The Rebels have the football! The Rebels have the football! The Rebels win the game! The Rebels win the game!" It sounded like Cordasco was yelling out of the press box window to all the fans in the parking lot, to all the media members leaving for locker room interviews, to all the UNLV fans from Texas to Nevada. He had just witnessed a jaw-dropping miracle. His partner Hunkie Cooper laughed hysterically like a lucky game show contestant.

"Talk about some second guessing," said Hatcher in the Baylor radio booth. "Yikes."

Yes, the final score was UNLV 27, Baylor 24. Yes, the impossible happened. Yes, no one watching in Floyd Casey Stadium will ever forget that night in Waco...especially Kevin Steele.

Ready to celebrate his first victory, Steele was left to explain, Why? "It falls on my shoulders," said Steele. "I have an explanation, but it doesn't hold water.

"It was just stupid on my part," he said. "We were trying to create an attitude of toughness and we tried to hammer it in. We got burned and I take full responsibility for it."

The Bears were dumbfounded. Bush, who had a soon-to-be forgotten game high 127 yards rushing, ripped off his jersey and shoulder pads, then wandered around the field sulking in anger and disbelief. His teammates used the field as a temporary morgue, scattering themselves on the turf in various states of disrepair. "It's like being shot in the heart," said Alfred.

Game 97

Three UNLV players strip Darrell Bush of the ball at the goal line...

...and Kevin Thomas races the other way with the unfathomable fumble recovery. Photos courtesy of Ben Becker

The UNLV players piled into the end zone like poker chips tossed on a card table. "I didn't know what the hell to do," Robinson said. "I'm too old to run and jump on the pile. I'd get hurt. I wasn't going to run all the way down. The hell with that. I stood right at the 50-yard line, and I started to walk over toward the middle of the field to [Baylor's] bench. I knew [Steele] was in shock. They didn't move. Their whole bench was just standing there like a painting. They were just really in shock."

While Robinson walked across the field as the lucky lottery winner, in the locker room, the veteran coach wasn't celebrating. "I told the players, 'Don't pray to God for anything else. He gave us more than our share tonight.'"

"When you give the coaches a grade," said a humble Robinson, "give me a 'D' because we weren't as efficient as winners are supposed to be."

Steele's final grade certainly would have been higher, as his team clearly outplayed the visiting Rebels. But he may only be remembered for the "F" he received for forgetting to put his name on the paper before turning it in.

"This will go down in history as one of the most unbelievable 'why-did-you-do-its,'" said the remorseful Baylor coach.

THE AFTERMATH

At 2-0, suddenly the UNLV football program had learned to win again, or rather, "accept victory." But UNLV won just one more time in '99, defeating Wyoming 35-32. The Rebels ended the season with a five-game losing streak and a 3-8 record.

For Kevin Steele, it wasn't until the fifth game of the year that he claimed his first college coaching victory, a 23-10 win over North Texas, the same school that UNLV defeated to start the season. Baylor wouldn't win another game, getting blown away in eight Big 12 games by a combined score of 347-61, and finishing the year 1-10.

UNLV	0	7	7	13	-27
Baylor	7	3	0	14	-24

BAY	O'Steen 5 pass from Alfred (Atteberry kick)
BAY	FG Atteberry 31
UNLV	Turner 4 pass from Vaughan (O'Reilly kick)
UNLV	Rudolph 1 run (O'Reilly kick)
BAY	Alfred 1 run (Atteberry kick)
UNLV	Turner 7 pass from Vaughan (O'Reilly kick)
BAY	Bush 9 run (Atteberry kick)
UNLV	Thomas 99 fumble recovery (no conversion attempt)

Attendance 32,272

Louisiana Tech vs.
Alabama

"If you wrote this script for a movie, no one would go watch it because they would think it so unbelievable."—Jack Bicknell

THE BACKGROUND

The state of Louisiana has never seen a quarterback like Tim Rattay. In his three-year career at Louisiana Tech, the 6-1, 210 lb. gunslinger, a transfer from Scottsdale (AZ) Community College, gobbled up almost every single Tech passing record, along with every passing record for all schools in Louisiana—12,341 career passing yards, 112 career touchdown passes. The 1998 national leader in total offense. Rattay's numbers are mind-boggling.

If ever there was a one-man show on a football field, it was Rattay and his flying pigskin in Ruston, Louisiana.

Tech opened the 1999 season 0-2, losing to eventual national champion Florida State 41-7, then to eighth-ranked Texas A&M 37-17. After pounding Sam Houston State 55-17, the Bulldogs (1-2) traveled to Birmingham, Alabama to face their third powerhouse program in four weeks, the 18th-ranked Crimson Tide of Alabama (2-0). The schools had met three times before 1997. Cumulative score: Alabama 103, Louisiana Tech 3. But in 1997, tiny Tech shocked the mighty Tide on Alabama's homecoming, 26-20.

"It was really weird, looking up at the scoreboard and seeing Louisiana Tech 26 and Alabama 20," said the Tide's All-American tailback Shaun Alexander about the '97 game. "It wasn't supposed to be that way. What made it even tougher to take was that it was our homecoming and Alabama just isn't supposed to lose at homecoming."

Alabama, 15-point favorites, vowed revenge in 1999. "The players who are on the team that year and who are still here sure haven't forgotten it," said Alexander.

They won't soon forget about the '99 game either.

'Bama couldn't corral Rattay. He threw for 368 yards and three touchdowns. Aided by four Tide fumbles, coach Jack Bicknell's Bulldogs blasted out to a 12-3 halftime lead, then tacked on a 42-yard field goal by Kevin Pond on the first drive of the second half to stretch the lead to 15-3.

But on the ensuing kickoff, Alexander, a record holder in his own right, jumped on a surf board and rode the Tide back into the game. He electrified the Crimson crowd with a 76-yard kickoff return to cut the lead to 15-10. Later in the third quarter, one play after Rattay was intercepted by Milo Lewis, Alexander stormed 30 yards through the middle for another score. 'Bama was back on top 18-15.

Rattay struck back. After Foster Bradberry intercepted 'Bama QB Andrew Zow's pass at the Tide 33, Rattay hit James Jordan with a 12-yard TD pass to give Tech a 22-18 lead with 13:31 left in the game.

But Alexander retaliated. His third TD of the game, a 14-yard run over left tackle, made it 25-22 Tide with 9:19 left.

The 'Bama defense finally slowed Rattay, forcing a Tech punt with 6:49 to play. Coach Mike Dubose's squad then ran time off the clock, gaining two first downs to the Tech 20. But three conservative runs forced a Chris Kemp

32-yard field goal, and Bama led 28-22 with 2:36 remaining.

Rattay got the ball back for one final drive. It almost ended as quickly as it started. Three downs and zero yards forced Tech into fourth-and-10 at their own 23. But the Bulldogs stayed alive. Rattay calmly hit Jordan over the middle for 25 yards to the 48-yard line.

Rattay was then sacked for a 12-yard loss by Darrius Gilbert with 1:32 left. Stuck with a third-and-22 back at the Tech 36, Rattay did it again, finding Jordan for 26 more yards to the 'Bama 38. The Bulldogs kept barking.

Rattay found junior wide receiver Sean Cangelosi for 22 yards to the 'Bama 16. The clock ran under one minute.

Rattay was uncanny. Rattay was unstoppable. Then, Rattay was injured.

Bama's Kenny King sacked the Tech QB on the next play. Just 0:39 on the clock. Rattay laid on the ground, his foot badly sprained. Tech's chances were evaporating as quickly as his ankle swelled. "I realized I couldn't put any weight on the foot," said Rattay. " I had hurt it a couple of plays earlier and tried to keep playing. On the last sack, I really never got sacked. I just couldn't put any weight on my foot."

Rattay was finished. So, apparently was Tech. They called time-out. Enter sophomore Brian Stallworth, the Bulldogs' back-up quarterback.

'Bama's Canary Knight greeted Stallworth with another sack, moving the ball back to the 32-yard line.

Facing third-and-26, Stallworth mustered just four yards on a pass to Delwyn Daigre. Seemingly, the game was over. The Tide had risen to the occasion, holding off a valiant Bulldog rally.

Fourth down and 26 at the Alabama 28.

THE PLAY
CD 2—Track 24
Dave Nitz, Dan Newman, KXKZ Radio

The crowd at Legion Field screamed for one final defensive stop. "I couldn't hear the crowd," Stallworth said. "I knew in my heart I had to get the ball in the end zone."

If he didn't, the clock would run out. Stallworth took the final snap. The clock ticked under 10 seconds. An exhausted Cangelosi, running pass patterns for 12 straight plays, sprinted to the goal line.

"After a long drive like we had, you are mainly fighting against yourself to not quit," said Cangelosi. "It's instinctual—you've run that route 100 times before in practice."

Stallworth floated the ball up. The 6-4 Cangelosi jumped for it amidst three 'Bama defensive backs. With 0:02 on the clock, Cangelosi came down with it, in the end zone. A stunning touchdown.

The Tech sidelines went into convulsions, jumping up and down. The 'Bama fans stood frozen. Cangelosi collapsed. "All my teammates ragged me all the next week for not celebrating, but I was too tired," he said. " I'm working on my TD celebrations for next year."

He didn't need to celebrate. The entire Tech contingent was whooping it up for him.

"Touchdown Bulldogs! Touchdown Bulldogs! Touchdown Bulldogs!" screamed Tech announcer Dave Nitz. "You gotta love it!"

Still, the game was tied at 28-28.

In a fairy tale scene, sure to be told and retold over the years at Louisiana Tech, the injured Rattay stopped the trainers carrying him into the locker room, so that he could watch the final extra point.

Afterall, Tech senior kicker Kevin Pond already had one PAT blocked and missed another one. This was no sure thing. In fact, if Rattay had one good foot to stand on, he may have run out to kick the final point. Instead, the unsteady Pond gave it one final shot.

This time, Pond made it count. "It wasn't the prettiest thing I've ever seen," Pond said. The ugly extra point gave the Bulldogs a spectacular 29-28 lead.

Tech had only to kickoff. Somehow, the dangerous Alexander got his hands on the ball one last time. He took the kick at the 24, ran 14 yards to the 38, then lateraled to Santonio Beard who broke away, crossed midfield, but then was finally knocked out of bounds at the Tech 28.

No time for a field goal, 0:00 on the clock. Plenty of time to party at Louisiana Tech.

Game 98

For the second time in three years, Tech had come to Alabama and knocked off the Tide, this time taking a 'Bama fan back with them to Ruston, Louisiana.

"A huge Alabama fan actual wrote me and said that on our final drive, he was actually praying that we'd win because he thought we had outplayed Alabama and that it would be an injustice if we lost," said Cangelosi. "I'm glad God heard his prayers."

THE AFTERMATH

Tech coach Bicknell, the former Boston College center who snapped the ball to Doug Flutie on the famous Flutie-to-Phelen Hail Mary pass in 1984, compared the two endings. "It's, like, exactly the same," he said. "I looked out into the end zone, and it's almost like disbelief. You just don't believe it. That's the same way it was with Flutie, except I was on my butt worried that I had held. Thank God it wasn't called or I'd be hiding out in Europe somewhere."

The upset of 'Bama was the second of eight straight victories for Tech, and the school's first victory ever against a Top 25 team. They finished 8-3, losing the final game of the season at Southern Cal, 45-19.

Tim Rattay concluded his senior year as the nation's total offense leader again with 381 yards per game. He finished his career second in total passing yards for all Division I-A schools behind Ty Detmer (BYU). Rattay holds the career record for yards passing per game (385.7), blitzing the previous record of 326.8 by Detmer. He's also third in career touchdown passes.

In Tuscaloosa, Mike Dubose's career was on the ropes, headed toward the canvas. With an 11-12 record at 'Bama heading into the '99 season, DuBose was already in jeopardy. Then a sexual harassment claim against him subsequently led to the university cutting two years off his contract.

But at the end of the '99 season, he got those years back as the Tide performed a startling turnaround. The loss to Tech may have been a 'Bama blessing as DuBose revamped his offense, the Tide rolled to eight wins in nine games, and then captured the SEC Championship with a 34-7 domination of Florida in the conference title game. Alabama finished the year 10-3 with a heartbreaking 35-34 loss to Michigan in the Orange Bowl when kicker Ryan Pflugner missed an extra-point attempt in overtime.

DuBose was named SEC Coach of the Year, and along with a bonus, got his contract extended by the university for the two years he had previously lost. Shaun Alexander garnered SEC Player of the Year accolades, and finished seventh in the '99 Heisman Trophy balloting while Tim Rattay was 10th.

Louisiana Tech	6	6	3	14	- 29
Alabama	0	3	15	10	- 28

LT	Jordan 4 pass from Rattay (kick failed)
AL	FG Kemp 22
LT	Cangelosi 27 pass from Rattay (kick failed)
LT	FG Pond 42
AL	Alexander 76 kickoff return (Kemp kick)
AL	Alexander 30 run (Milons pass from Zow)
LT	Jordan 12 pass from Rattay (Pond kick)
AL	Alexander 14 run (Kemp kick)
AL	FG Kemp 32
LT	Cangelosi 28 pass from Stallworth (Pond kick)

Attendance 80,312

Arizona vs. Washington State

"This kind of feels the way you feel when you get in a car wreck."
—WSU kicker Rian Lindell

THE BACKGROUND

The Washington State football program teetered on the edge of a new school record, a milestone that no one on the Pullman campus wanted to see them reach. The Cougars lost their first three games of the 1999 season, giving them an 11-game losing streak, and tying the school record for futility on the football field. Coach Mike Price's team hit bottom with their third defeat, blowing a 14-0 lead and losing 28-17 to border rival Idaho for the first time since 1965.

"This is the worst of worst times for Cougar football right now," Price said after the loss. "Right now we're at an all time low. We have never been this low."

While Washington State was at the bottom of the Pac-10 conference at the beginning of the '99 season, Arizona was at the top. The Wildcats, 12-1 in '98, were everyone's pre-season choice to be Pac-10 champions. But two early season blowout losses turned those expectations upside down. Arizona opened the season with a 41-7 shellacking at the hands of Penn State. Then after two unimpressive victories over TCU and Middle Tennessee State, the Wildcats were lashed again by Stanford 50-22. Ranked No.4 in the pre-season AP poll, Arizona had floundered out of the gate with a 2-2 record when they traveled to Pullman, Washington, to face the Cougars.

Arizona piled up 500 yards in total offense to 318 for WSU in the game, but four missed field goals by the Wildcats' Mark McDonald (53 and 40 yards in the first half and 43 and 32 yards in the second half) gave the Cougars hope.

Arizona held a 17-10 lead entering the fourth quarter before the two teams sparred with a flurry of back-and-forth offense. Freshman runningback Deon Burnett capped an 80-yard WSU drive with a two-yard TD run to tie the game at 17-17 with 10:15 left.

Arizona reciprocated with their own 80-yard march. Trung Canidate (who tallied 158 yards in the game) rushed nine times on the 14-play drive, scoring his third TD of the game from four yards out. With 4:39 left, Arizona was back on top, 24-17.

But just two plays later, it was tied again. After the kickoff, on the second play from scrimmage, Burnett burst 55 yards for a touchdown down the left sideline, making the score 24-24.

Finally, the Cougar defense held, forcing an Arizona punt. WSU regained possession in great shape, on their own 47 with 2:43 to play. But after freshman QB Jason Gesser (subbing for the injured Steve Birnbaum) called the wrong play on third-and-two at the UA 45, and Burnett was stopped for no gain, Price was faced with a precarious fourth-and-two.

Only 2:04 remained in regulation.

Had it been a few years earlier, before overtime was introduced, Price may have thrown caution to the wind, a gusty 30 MPH wind, and gone for it. Even a 62-yard field-goal attempt by Rian Lindell, who had already connected

Game 99

from 52 yards, wasn't out of the question when your team has lost 11 straight.

"I had the running play [in mind] that we would have run in that situation," Price said. "I thought about the field goal, and I thought about punting the ball down there."

With the score tied 24-24, Price chose to punt. Arizona took over on their own 20 with 1:56 on the clock. They moved quickly. Facing the stiff wind, the Wildcats pushed their way to the WSU 42 yard-line where they seemingly ran out of time.

Only five seconds remained in regulation. Overtime seemed a certainty.

THE PLAY

CD 2—Track 25
Brian Jeffries, Les Josephson,
KNST Radio, Arizona Wildcat Network

McDonald had no chance of hitting a 59-yard field goal against the wind.

So Arizona coach Dick Tomey sent QB Keith Smith out to throw the predictable Hail Mary pass through an unpredictable maelstrom. Freshman wide out Bobby Wade, along with receivers Malosi Leonard and part-time quarterback Ortege Jenkins, streaked toward the left corner of the end zone. So did the entire Washington State defensive backfield.

As the clock ran out, Smith launched a high arching rocket into the blustery wind and into a pile of players in the end zone. Wade was underneath all of them.

"It went straight up and straight down. I'm in the back of the end zone, and it went through everybody's hands, and I was just sitting at the bottom of the pile," said Wade.

The ball passed through the web of outstretched arms. Somehow Wade had the ball. But how did he get it?

Two officials, field judge Jerry Gastellum and back judge Bob Wucetich, hovered nearby in the end zone. Gastellum raised his hands. Touchdown Arizona. No overtime. Arizona 30, Washington State 24.

"A one-in-a-million shot," Smith said. "It's like going into a casino and hitting the big one."

Arguing vehemently, the unlucky Cougars felt cheated. "There is no way he [Gastellum]

could see the ball being caught," said safety Billy Newman. "If the officials had conferred I guarantee they'd say, 'Go to overtime.' It's a tie ballgame, you just don't make that call." Fifty yards away, Smith couldn't see. "I guess Billy caught it on the ground," he said.

Or the ground caught it before Wade did.

Wade defended his 'catch.' "I caught the ball. I showed the ball right away so I was sure they were going to give it to me. No doubt," the freshman said with confidence.

Leonard, Wade's fellow receiver, wasn't so sure. "To me it seemed like he had it, but I was upside down in the air," Leonard said. "It might have been [incomplete], but the officials called it a touchdown and that's what I'm going with."

Price was perturbed, his team left with broken hearts and a broken school record for most consecutive losses.

"I think we won that football game," he said. "We played like winners. I'm proud of the team, and the effort they gave was tremendous. They had the game taken away from them at the end."

Fans watching at home saw what most everyone on the field did not. The ball appeared to have hit the ground before Wade controlled it. "When I see it on tape, it will be the first time I see it," said Tomey.

After watching the replay, Tomey may have realized that sometimes the best seat in the house is in front of the television.

THE AFTERMATH

Three days later, Verle Sorgren, the Pac-10 supervisor of officials reviewed the play. "It's my own personal opinion that the ball was not held long enough for a touchdown," Sorgren said. But he wouldn't unequivocably say the pass was incomplete. "I want to be fair. I think a case can be made for a catch. The Arizona receiver gets possession of the ball, rolls over on his side, and the ball comes loose and he picks it up." said Sorgren. "How long does he have to hold the ball?"

Tomey was comfortable with the win. "We all accept the fact that there's a human quality in the game, and we'll live and die with that," he said.

331

It was the one sparkling memory in an otherwise dismal season for the Wildcats. Once lofty expectations turned into disappointing results as Arizona lost four of their last five games of the season to finish 6-6.

Left empty-handed, all WSU could do was look forward to the next week. "We have to win," said WSU linebacker Steve Gleason. "I don't care if it's ugly or pretty or if we win by a fluke referee call. Somehow, we've got to find a way to win."

The Cougars bounced back with vengeance, breaking the 12-game losing streak by beating California 31-7 on homecoming in Pullman. They ended the year 3-9 when they beat Hawaii 22-14, denying the Rainbow Warriors an NCAA record for the greatest turnaround in two seasons. Hawaii was 0-12 in '98, then under new coach June Jones, went 8-4 in '99, giving WSU plenty of hope for 2000.

Arizona	7	0	10	13	- 30
Washington State	0	10	0	14	- 24

ARIZ	Canidate 1 run (McDonald kick)
WSU	Zubedi 11 pass from Birnbaum (Lindell kick)
WSU	FG Lindell 52
ARIZ	Safety, Birnbaum tackled in end zone
ARIZ	Canidate 2 run (Manumaleuna reception)
WSU	Burnett 2 run (Lindell kick)
ARIZ	Canidate 4 run (McDonald kick)
WSU	Burnett 55 run (Lindell kick)
ARIZ	Wade 42 pass from Smith (no attempt)

Attendance 26,787

Minnesota vs.
🏈 Penn State

"I think I jumped outside of myself. For real man, my heart dropped through my feet."—Thomas Hamner

THE BACKGROUND

Joe Paterno's 400th game as a head coach. Homecoming in Happy Valley. The 9-0 Nittany Lions, No.2 in the polls, were priming themselves for a national title showdown with top-ranked Florida State in the Sugar Bowl. Indeed, the 1999 season looked strikingly similar to 1978, or 1982, or 1986,when Penn State played for the national championship in a bowl game pitting No.1 vs. No.2.

The Minnesota Golden Gophers were in mourning. Three of the last four weeks they stood on the brink of victory, only to have a win pulled out from under their feet. The Gophers (5-3) began to look like the Hollywood actor always nominated for the Oscar, but never the winner.

Hear the gracious but downhearted comments of third-year coach Glen Mason.

After losing to No.20 Wisconsin, 20-17 in overtime,"Our locker room is full of a bunch of kids that are really down. This is emotionally and physically tough to swallow."

After losing to No.22 Ohio State, 20-17, ""We have to regroup and move on. It was close, but no cigar."

Then after another close defeat, 33-28 to Purdue, "Like I've told my team, I'm starting to sound like a broken record. Today was one heck of a football game."

The last time Minnesota traveled to Penn State in 1997, the Gophers had the top-ranked Lions on the ropes, leading 15-3 late in the game. But after Minnesota runningback Tho-mas Hamner dropped a pitchout on the UM 10-yard line with 4:04 to play, the Lions cashed the turnover in for the winning score. Penn State won 16-15 and Mason, dressed for success in his first year at Minnesota, was left with yet another unread acceptance speech.

"I started thinking that here I am in my best sportcoat, and we're going to win, and I'm going to get Gatorade dumped all over it," Mason said. But then, the Lions pulled it out in the final minutes. "I hate to lose. Our players gave a heck of an effort, but we lost," said Mason.

Paterno commiserated. "It's a shame Minnesota lost that football game," he said. "They had every right to win it. They outplayed us. They outcoached us. We just outlucked them."

So Mason, the surrogate bridesmaid of the Big Ten, brought his unranked Gophers back to State College, PA, in 1999. True to form, the Gophers played tough, trailing by just 17-15 as the fourth quarter unveiled.

"I told them at halftime, we were playing hard, we could have gotten Wisconsin in overtime, we should have beaten Ohio State. Good things will start to happen for us," said the ever-optimistic Mason.

A 44-yard field goal by Travis Forney inched the Penn State lead to 20-15 with 14:17 left in the fourth quarter. Then, on the next drive, Hamner made amends after two years in purgatory. "I felt like I lost the game the last time I was here," he said. This time, Hamner rushed for 96 yards on 38 carries. But his biggest play came on a 49-yard TD reception from

With one prayer already answered, the Minnesota sidelines ask for one more favor... Photo courtesy of Ryan Spivak

quarterback Billy Cockerham with 11:25 to play, giving the Gophers a 21-20 lead.

Quickly, Forney regained the lead for PSU. Another 44-yard field goal at the 9:12 mark and the Lions led 23-21. With six minutes remaining, PSU marched from their 39 toward the clinching score. At the Gophers 33, Penn State faced third-and-10 with just over two minutes to play when Kevin Thompson overthrew Chafie Fields forcing a critical fourth-down decision by Paterno.

Send in Forney for a 51-yard attempt with the wind at his back, or punt the ball to Minnesota. "I wanted to make them go the length of the field," Paterno said. "I didn't think they could do it."

Nothing in the immediate past history of Minnesota football suggested they could do it either. So the Lions' Pat Pidgeon punted into the end zone.

In need of a field goal to win, Cockerham took over at the UM 20 with 1:50 to play. "All of a sudden, things started happening in our favor," said Mason, unaccustomed to fortuitous bounces at the end of games.

On first down, Cockerham went deep down the right sideline. Wide receiver Ron Johnson

leaped high to haul it in at the Penn State 34. Suddenly, the Gophers had a chance. A real chance.

But reality and defensive coordinator Jerry Sandusky's traditionally clutch PSU defense struck back.

Cockerham threw incomplete, then was sacked by junior all-everything linebacker LaVar Arrington for a six-yard loss. The Gophers called time-out with 1:26 left. On third-and-16, Cockerham's pass fell incomplete.

Fourth down-and-16 from the PSU 40. Penn State called time-out with 1:22 on the clock. One more stop and the Lions stay in the hunt for the national championship, while the Gophers suffer again.

THE PLAY

"It may be Hail Mary time," said broadcaster Fran Fisher on the Penn State Sports Network.

It was. Sandusky sent the Lions on a blitz. Cockerham had little time. He lofted up a pass down to the Penn State 10-yard line where Johnson was blanketed by safety Derek Fox.

"The play of the game," said Fisher as

Cockerham's pass sailed through the air, then was harmlessly deflected away from the Gophers receiver.

"It is incomp....he, he caught the ball! " yelled Fisher. The suddenly golden football bounced off Johnson and Fox, tumbled backwards, and fell toward the ground where receiver Arland Bruce dove and scooped it up just before it hit the grass.

I thought we batted it down and the game was over," said Paterno. " Then all of a sudden someone yelled, 'He got it.'"

Fox was miffed. "We knew it was going to be a jump ball, and I thought I tipped it away," he said. "The pass must have dipped down, and the guy went and got it. What are you going to do?"

The fans in Pennsylvania had seen it before,

two decades earlier when Franco Harris caught the "Immaculate Reception" for the Pittsburgh Steelers. "I saw it just hanging in the air like 'Come get me, come get me,'" explained Bruce. "So I just grabbed it. It came down to me like it was meant for us to be on top."

"When things go right for you, they go right for you," lamented Fisher's broadcast partner George Paterno in his best Yogi Berra voice.

First down at the Penn State 13 with one minute and counting. A short run by Hamner lost two. Mason took no more chances. A quarterback sneak. Penn State called their final timeout. Cockerham again inched the ball to the middle of the field at the 15, let the clock run down to 0:02, then called time-out to set up kicker Dan Nystrom, 10 for 14 in field-goal attempts on the year.

...and freshman Dan Nystrom delivers. Photo courtesy of University of Minnesota Men's Athletics

Derek Rackley was the snapper. Ryan Rindels the holder. Nystrom was just a freshman. Surely, if history was on the Penn State sideline, or anywhere inside Beaver Stadium, one of those three would muff the final play.

Or, the 6-3, 220 lb. Arrington would block the kick.

He did it against Pittsburgh to preserve a 20-17 victory. He did it against versus Purdue in a 31-25 Penn State win. Nystrom had practiced kicking all week with a ladder in front of him to simulate the leaping Penn State linebacker. Could he boot this 32-yard attempt high enough?

"I can't lie," said Mason. "I had my eyes closed." So did just about everyone else on both sidelines. Hands were held. Knees bent. Breathing ceased.

"My heart got pounding pretty good," said Nystrom.

The snap was low. Rindels found it, placed it, and Nystrom kicked it...over Arrington, straight through the uprights into the Minnesota history books.

Final score: Minnesota 24, Penn State 23.

And 96,573 blank stares. A few dozen bouncing Golden Gophers. "Penn State is absolutely devastated. This defensive unit is in an absolute state of shock," said Fisher.

"I started crying and laid down," Arrington said. "It is a nightmare," added fullback Mike Cerimile. "You expect to wake up at any second and it will all disappear. Reality is we lost and we must move on."

Glen Mason knew the feeling.

THE AFTERMATH

One play, the "Immaculate Deflection" as some people dubbed it in Minneapolis, turned both teams upside down.

Penn State lost their final two games of the regular season, 31-27 to Michigan, then 35-28 to Michigan State. But after sliding from No.2 to No.17 in the polls, the Lions ended the year 10-3 by dominating Texas A&M 24-0 in the Alamo Bowl.

LaVar Arrington was named the Butkus Award winner as the nation's best linebacker and also received the Chuck Bednarik Award,

given to the top defensive player in the country. Arrington decided to bypass his senior season and entered the 2000 NFL draft.

The Gophers finished off their schedule by defeating Indiana 44-20 and rival Iowa 25-21. At 8-3, Mason's squad leap-frogged up the polls to No.12 before losing to Oregon 24-20 in the Sun Bowl, the Gophers' first bowl appearance since the 1986 Liberty Bowl.

In the Sun Bowl, Oregon's Joey Harrington threw a 10-yard TD pass to Keenan Howry with 1:32 left in the game giving the Ducks the 24-20 advantage. Then, linebacker Dietrich Moore forced a fumble by Cockerham at the Oregon 45, recovered by the Ducks with under a minute left to seal the victory.

"You make the plays and if you don't make the plays, you go home sad," said Mason, aptly summing up the rollercoaster '99 season for the Gophers.

Minnesota	3	6	6	9	- 24
Penn State	7	7	3	6	- 23

PSU	Cerimele 5 run (Forney Kick)
MINN	FG Nystrom 27
MINN	Johnson 25 pass from Cockerham (PAT Failed)
PSU	Johnson 17 pass from Thompson (Forney kick)
PSU	FG Forney 20
MINN	Cockerham 3 run (conversion failed)
PSU	FG Forney 44
MINN	Hamner 49 yd pass From Cockerham (conversion failed)
PSU	FG Forney 44
MINN	FG Nystrom 32

Attendance 96,753

Florida State vs. Miami

"Wouldn't you know it? He's been wide left all year. "
—*Bobby Bowden*

THE BACKGROUND

When ranking great college football finishes, it's hard to ignore the numerous nailbiters involving Miami and Florida State during the Bobby Bowden era. Seems every year we see the same sideline shot of the legendary Bowden, with shades and chapeau, leaning, twisting, wincing, as he watches that final fatal field goal kick sail awry.

Dadgummit, the list is long.

In 1991, Gerry Thomas missed a 34-yard kick with 25 seconds left as top-ranked FSU lost to No.2 Miami 17-16.

Dan Mowry's 39-yard game-tying attempt in the final seconds against the 'Canes in 1992 drifted wide right.

And in 1987, Derek Schmidt missed two field goals and an extra point in third-ranked Miami's thrilling victory over fourth-ranked FSU. In that heart stopper Bowden sent Schmidt onto the field to kick the game-tying extra point with the Seminoles down 26-25 after rallying to score a touchdown with just 42 seconds left.

Then the FSU coach changed his mind. "I didn't want to see him kick and miss," said Bowden. "The poor kid would have been in a psycho ward. I had already seen him miss three, which he doesn't ever do."

In fact, at one time, Schmidt had kicked 108 straight extra points.

But FSU went for two. Danny McManus' pass to tight end Pat Carter fell short of the mark and the 'Canes prevailed on their way to the 1987 National Championship.

Of course, field goal kickers have won games for Bowden over the years as well. Just not against Miami.

Perhaps the most famous winning FSU field goal is Scott Bentley's 22-yard boot in the waning seconds to defeat Nebraska 18-16 in the 1994 Orange Bowl. Even then, the Huskers raced downfield and missed a 45-yarder of their own after the officials put two seconds back on the clock and an already Gatorade drenched Bowden had to wait painfully for the kick to hook badly, before claiming that first national title.

But as Bowden once said about himself, "On his tombstone will read....and then he played Miami."

No other high profile rivalry in college football has been settled more times by more infamous field goal attempts than Florida State vs. Miami. A series best known by two words: Wide Right.

The '91 game was dubbed Wide Right I. The sequel, Wide Right II in '92, was just as compelling. In 2000, a third script in the series was being written.

This version of the Miami-Florida State war was not unlike many of the battles before or after it. Both teams near the top of the polls.

Miami (4-0) was No.7, with a roster that read like a future NFL fantasy football team. Jeremy Shockey, Santana Moss, Clinton Portis,

Dan Morgan, Reggie Wayne, Najeh Davenport, Ed Reed.

Florida State (5-0) was simply the defending national champions, the top-ranked team in the country, riding a 17-game winning streak, 26-game regular season winning streak, and a five-game winning streak over the Hurricanes and their coach, Butch Davis.

But after Florida State failed to score four times in the first half inside the Miami 26-yard line, (two interceptions and two failed fourth down tries) it was the Hurricanes that streaked to a 17-0 halftime lead.

FSU quarterback Chris Weinke then unleashed a passing barrage in the second half, throwing for 299 yards of his game total 496 yards. When Weinke found Anquan Boldin for a 2-yard TD toss with 3:15 left in the fourth quarter, FSU had narrowed the gap to 20-17.

It would have been 20-20 had FSU freshman walk-on kicker Matt Munyon connected on a 22-yard FG attempt earlier in the period. But this was Florida State-Miami. And no field goal is too short to miss.

After FSU cut the gap to 20-17, on the next possession, Miami running back Najeh Davenport caught a short pass from QB Ken Dorsey, then fumbled it. FSU's Brian Allen recovered it at the Miami 48 with 2:14 on the clock, and Weinke quickly struck again.

Four plays later, a 29-yard touchdown pass to Atrews Bell with 1:37 left gave Florida State a 24-20 lead.

But back came the 'Canes. With 97 seconds left, Dorsey directed a remarkably crisp seven-play, 68-yard drive. He hit his tight end Shockey once. Found him a second time. Then connected with Santana Moss for 19 yards. Dorsey then looked for his tight end one more time.

"Every time he (Shockey) came back (to the huddle) he told me he was open," said Dorsey. "This time I listened to him."

Dorsey spotted Shockey open in the left flat, and connected on a 13-yard TD pass with 46 seconds remaining. Miami surged back in front, 27-24.

Still, Weinke managed to put the Seminoles in position to force overtime. He moved FSU from their 22-yard line to the Miami 32 in six plays, leaving five seconds on the clock, and one last chance for the FSU kicker.

THE PLAY

Five seconds left. The 5' 11", 185 lb. freshman Munyon raced onto the field.

"It would have been nice if we could have driven down and won it with a touchdown," Munyon said. "But I wanted to redeem myself for missing the 22-yarder."

49 yards from the left hash mark. Munyon hit it solidly.

"I wasn't thinking about those other wide rights when I was out there." said the freshman. "When it left my foot, I thought it was going to be good."

Holder Keith Cottrell concurred. "It would have been good from 55. When it left my hand, it sounded good off his foot."

I watched it, I watched it," Miami receiver Reggie Wayne said. "The only thing going through my mind was wide right one, wide right two, and I was hoping there would be a wide right three."

Sure enough, another sequel was born. As the clock expired, Munyon's kick missed. Miami won 27-24.

"Wouldn't you know it?" Bowden asked. "He's been wide left all year, and then that happens....I told him after the game it was a good kick. It was just a little right."

A little wide right.

"It's obviously going to be hard, but I have to put it behind me or I'll never be able to kick again," the FSU kicker said.

Munyon left the field. The Miami fans partied at the Orange Bowl, and the scoreboard flashed like a movie house marquee, "Wide Right III".

"That's the way it's supposed to (end), right? " quipped 'Canes coach Davis.

THE AFTERMATH

Despite losing to the Hurricanes and ending the season with the same 10-1 record as Miami, Florida State got the BCS nod to play Oklahoma in the Orange Bowl for the national

Game 101

championship. The Sooners took the title with a 13-2 victory. The Seminoles ended up No. 5 in the AP poll, while Miami beat Florida 37-20 in the Sugar Bowl and ended the season ranked No.2.

Wide Right III wasn't the last of field goal misfortunes for Florida State.

In following years, another kicker joined the annals of field goal futility at FSU. In 2002, Xavier Beitia's 43-yard try sailed wide left as time expired. Miami won 28-27.

The two teams met in the 2004 Orange Bowl. With 5:30 to play, Beitia tried again to beat Miami. But his kick was wide right from 39 yards. Miami won again, 16-14.

The 'Cane curse continued. A six season Miami winning streak stretched from 1999-2004. Then in 2005, Miami coach Larry Coker experienced what if felt like to be Bobby Bowden.

After missing two attempts earlier in the game, UM kicker Jon Peattie lined up for a game-tying 28-yard try with 2:20 left, but holder Brian Monroe dropped a low snap, the ball trickled away, and FSU held on to win 10-7.

"We finally stole one from them like they've been stealing them from us," said Bowden. For once, the FSU coach got to view the anguish on the opposite sideline, instead of his own. "It made up for a lot of them," he said. "...but not all of them."

October 7, 2000—Miami, Florida

Florida State	0	0	10	14	-24
Miami	7	10	3	7	-27

Mia	Davenport 22 pass from Dorsey (Sievers kick)
Mia	DJ.Williams 1 run (Sievers kick)
Mia	FG Sievers 31
FSU	FG Munyon 18
FSU	Boldin 48 pass from Weinke (Munyon kick)
Mia	FG Sievers
FSU	Boldin 2 pass from Weinke (Munyon kick)
FSU	Bell 29 pass from Weinke (Munyon kick)
Mia	Shockey 13 pass from Dorsey (Sievers kick)

Attendance 80,905

339

Northwestern vs. Minnesota

"Someone who invented this game gave us four downs, so you might as well use them."- Randy Walker

THE BACKGROUND

When the Northwestern Wildcats knocked off No.7 Wisconsin 47-44 in double overtime, four games into the 2000 season, something must have clicked inside those purple helmets.

"I expected to win," said second-year coach Randy Walker.

Not many others did. The Wildcats were blown out at TCU 41-14 the week before.

The team was 3-8 the season before. They were 3-9 the season before that.

Northwestern had one win in the Big Ten in the past 16 tries.

Yet here were the Wildcats, celebrating after Tim Long's 46-yard FG split the uprights as time expired, sending the game into overtime. Here were the Wildcats celebrating after Damien Anderson's 12-yd TD romp won it in the second overtime. Here were the Wildcats celebrating in Camp Randall Stadium, on Wisconsin's home turf.

A new Northwestern had arrived, and the Big Ten would soon be catching their breath after seeing the makeover.

Led by Notre Dame transfer QB Zak Kustok, the high-scoring Wildcats (5-2), who hadn't tallied more than 23 points in any game during the entire 1999 season, were suddenly averaging 35.8 points per game in 2000.

New and improved, Northwestern traveled to Minneapolis to take on Minnesota (5-3). Apparently the Gophers didn't take notice, promptly shredding the Wildcats' not-so-special special teams.

An 83- yard punt return for a touchdown by Tellis Redmon and a 45-yard TD catch by Elvin Jones on a fake punt got the Gophers going in the first half.

When runningback Asad Abdul-Khaliq scored on a 7-yard TD run with 5:34 to play in the third quarter, Minnesota had cruised to a 35-14 lead.

But Kustok then led a sustained rally, which followed a perilous path of make-or-break plays that's rarely seen.

The 'Cats took the kickoff and marched from their 23-yard line to the UM 13 before stalling. Facing fourth-and-eight at the 13, Walker kept Kustok on the field. Kustok kept Northwestern in the game.

He connected with Sam Simmons for a 13-yard TD reception to cut the lead to 35-21. After a Minnesota punt, the Wildcats started at their 33 and ended up at the UM 3-yard line.

Again fourth down. Again Walker went for it. Again Kustok scored. This time on a 3-yard scramble into the end zone. Minnesota's lead was now 35-28 with 12:35 to play in the fourth quarter.

With 5:01 left, Gopher kicker Dan Nystrom missed a 43-yard FG attempt. Northwestern took possession at the NW 27. Kustok moved his team to the UM 46.

The clock neared two minutes remaining. A holding penalty and false start forced Northwestern into a fourth-and-20. Again

Game 102

Walker went for it. Again Kustok connected. This time it was Kunle Patrick for a 34-yard catch to the UM 12.

The next play Kustok ran for a 12-yard touchdown. With 1:24 left, the game was tied 35-35, Northwestern had scored 21 consecutive points, and the Gophers were reeling.

Jermaine Mayes took the kickoff and was stopped at the UM 7-yard line. The Northwestern defense held, forcing a punt with just 0:50 left.

A 40-yard punt gave Kustok and his teammates the ball at the NU 47. A scramble, a short pass, and an incompletion later, it was yet another fourth down. This time from the Minnesota 45-yard line.

Just three seconds remained. Fourth down for Fourthwestern.

THE PLAY

CD 2-Track 26—*Dave Eanet,*
Ted Albrecht, **WGN Radio**

Four times previously the Wildcats faced fourth down in the game. Four times they converted. Earlier in the second quarter, Walker gambled on fourth-and-goal at the UM 1-yard line. Damian Anderson converted, bursting over for the score.

"Someone who invented this game gave us four downs," Walker quipped, "so you might as well use them."

Now Northwestern faced a fifth fourth down attempt. Kustok called the play.

"Victory right."

Three receivers lined up wide right, Sam Simmons, Kunle Patrick and Jon Schweighardt.

Kustok took the snap and rolled right. Gophers defensive tackle John Schlect applied the heat on the 'Cats QB, knocking him to the Metrodome turf. But not before Kustok released a high arcing prayer toward the front right corner of the end zone.

"I didn't really see it," Kustok said. "I was laying on the ground."

In most cases, the successful Hail Mary pass never works according to plan. "Usually, in practice, I can't throw the ball that far," said Kustok whose rainbow pass reached the goal line.

This time he threw it far enough. This time the Hail Mary pass followed the blueprint.

Hugging the sideline, Patrick and Shweighardt went for the ball, Simmons stood back away from the crowd. Defensive backs Delvin Jones, Trevis Graham, Mike Lehan and Clorenzo Griffin were positioned to bat the ball down. They weren't positioned to handle Simmons.

"We practice that play every Thursday," said Patrick, a former high school basketball player. "It's my job to tip the ball."

With both hands, Patrick, like a volleyball setter, re-directed the ball backward to the waiting Simmons. "It was just a beautiful tip and I was just waiting," said Simmons. "My job is to sit there and wait."

He waited as the ball tipped right to him.

Fourth down. Touchdown.

Simmons got his feet in bounds, then kept them running straight up the runway to the locker room. "When I got to the hallway, I just fell down because I was so tired," he said.

"We hit that play in practice more than any place I've ever been," said Walker. "I bet we've hit it five out of the last six weeks in practice."

Simmons' estimate was a bit lower. "We don't get the tip right all the time," Simmons said. "Matter of fact, we probably only get the tip right 50 percent of the time."

Sure. And the Wildcats only complete thirty percent of their fourth down conversions. Five times they faced fourth down. Five times they converted. Four of those conversions were touchdowns.

"Some games are harder to lose than others," said Minnesota head coach Glen Mason. "You feel like your guts have been ripped out."

THE AFTERMATH

The next week the Wildcats got wilder. As if the Wisconsin win and the Minnesota miracle wasn't enough, Northwestern, now ranked No. 21, completed their trilogy of heart stoppers the following week against No.12 Michigan.

The two teams combined for a non-Big Ten like 1,179 yards of total offense. Kustok threw for 332 yards. Damien Anderson ran for 268 yards. Michigan's Drew Henson threw for 312 yards. Wolverines RB Anthony Thomas rushed for 199 of his own.

Trailing 51-47 with 1:38 remaining in the fourth quarter, Northwestern's hopes appeared dashed when a wide open Anderson dropped a sure TD pass from Kustok.

Michigan took over, tried to run out the clock, but two plays later hit an iceberg. Thomas fumbled. Safety Sean Wieber popped the ball out of his hands and Northwestern's Raheem Covington recovered at the Michigan 30 with just 46 seconds remaining.

Plenty of time for Kustok to connect with Anderson, then Teddy Johnson to the 12-yard line. Then with 0:20 left, who else but a soaring Sam Simmons caught an 11-yard slant pattern for the TD that gave Northwestern a 54-51 lead.

Ryan Field rocked in Evanston, Illinois. Still, Michigan scrambled downfield and managed a Hayden Epstein 57-yard field goal attempt as time expired. The snap was high, Epstein recovered then completed a pass to Evan Coleman who made it to the NU 33 before being tackled. Finally, the epic offensive battle ended with Northwestern on top.

"I'm almost speechless, and I'm sure that's hard for some of you to believe," said an exhausted Walker.

That was the pinnacle for the 2000 Northwestern squad. They finished the year 8-4 (6-2), capturing a share of the Big Ten title. Their memorable season ended with a forgettable blowout, a 66-17 loss to Nebraska in the Alamo Bowl. After taking his team from last place in the Big Ten in 1999 to first place in 2000, Randy Walker was named Dave McClain Big Ten Coach of the Year.

Minnesota completed the season 6-6 with a 30-28 loss to North Carolina State in the MicronPC.com Bowl.

Kustok's two-and-a-half season career

at Northwestern was long enough for him to shatter eleven school records. In 2001, he became one of only four QBs in the history of Division I-A football to throw for over 400 yards and rush for over 100 yards in a single game. Against Bowling Green, Kustok piled up 421 yards passing and ran for another 111 yards in a stunning 43-42 loss, the last home game of Kustok's college career.

In that game, Bowling Green QB Josh Harris connected with Robert Redd on a 5-yard TD pass with 36 seconds left. Then coach Urban Meyer surprised NU, calling a reverse on the two-point conversion instead of playing for overtime. With Northwestern's kick-blocking team on the field, Cole Magner scored on the play capping a 15-point rally in the final 2:30 to give the Falcons their first win over a Big Ten school since 1972.

Northwestern	7	7	7	20	- 41
Minnesota	7	21	7	0	- 35

NW	Anderson 1 run (Long kick)
MINN	Redmon 83 punt return (Nystrom kick)
MINN	Jones 45 pass from Gruening (Nystrom kick)
MINN	Johnson 32 pass from Cole (Nystrom kick)
NW	Anderson 1 run (Long kick)
MINN	Abdul-Khaliq 6 run (Nystrom kick)
MINN	Abdul-Khaliq 7 run (Nystrom kick)
NW	Simmons 13 pass from Kustok (Long kick)
NW	Kustok 3 run (Long kick)
NW	Kustok 12 run (Long kick)
NW	Simmons 45 pass from Kustok

Attendance 59,004

🏈 Linfield vs. Central College (Iowa)

"This is crazy, it wasn't supposed to end this way."
—*Curt Musser, Linfield quarterback*

THE BACKGROUND

In McMinnville, Oregon, they call it "The Streak". Just about sixty miles southwest of Portland, is where you'll find the school with the most consecutive winning seasons in college football history.

The Linfield College Wildcats hadn't had a losing season since 1955, a span of 46 years, and a record that surpassed the previous high of 42 years set by Harvard and Notre Dame.

In Pella, Iowa they weren't too impressed.

You see, the Central College Dutch had their own streak of 40 consecutive winning seasons.

When the two tradition-rich schools met in the 2000 Division III second round playoff game, both teams were undefeated (Linfield 9-0, Central 11-0), and both teams were ranked in the top ten (Linfield 7th, Central 3rd).

Linfield and Central, two strikingly similar football programs, one from the midwest, the other from the northwest, played this game like fraternal twins, mirroring each other's every move.

When the Wildcats cashed in on their first possession of the game, scoring on a Marty Williams one-yard TD run, the Dutch immediately answered back. Central quarterback Scott Koerselman located a wide open Chris McCullough for a 44-yard touchdown pass on the very next drive and the score was tied 7-7.

Playing on a sloppy, muddy field, both teams squandered scoring opportunities in the first half. Twice, Linfield drove inside the Central 20, only to have Wildcats QB Curt Musser toss interceptions both times. The Dutch likewise blew a golden opportunity at the end of the half. With the ball at the Linfield 14-yard line, QB Koerselman was sacked for a 10-yard loss and then fumbled on the following play. Central turned the ball over four times in the game. Linfield, not to be outdone, coughed it up five times.

The first half ended in a 7-7 deadlock.

More of the same in the third period. Central surged ahead on a one-yard Koerselman sneak, set up by a 32-yard completion to McCullough. Linfield took the ensuing kickoff and drove 69 yards in just four plays. A 26-yard catch and run by Josh Harrison knotted the game at 14-14.

Whatever you do, I'll match it. This was a game of H-O-R-S-E played on the gridiron instead of the basketball court.

As time ticked away at the end of the fourth quarter and the score still tied at 14-14, Central finally took the upper hand. With under 90 seconds to play, Koerselman had the Dutch at the Linfield 25. But just moments later, Linfield's Brady Andrews had his hands on an errant Koerselman pass.

A game saving interception. The Wildcats regained possession at their own six-yard line, took a deep breath, and headed for overtime.

Linfield took the ball in the extra period

at the 25-yard line but could only advance it to the 18. After two Musser passes fell incomplete, Scott Cannon came on to knock through a 34-yard field goal and give the Wildcats the 17-14 advantage.

Central took the ball at the 25 in their OT possession, and again mirroring their opponents, the Dutch mustered just six yards in three downs. Fourth and four. Central had no choice but to try and send the game into a second overtime.

THE PLAY
CD 2-Track 27—*J.B. Connoley,*
Al Dorenkamp, **KRLS Radio**

The Linfield fans turned up the decibels as kicker Tim O'Neil lined up for the 38-yard attempt that would tie the game.

Fullback Joe Ritzert, blocking for the Dutch, thought to himself, "This is going to be an easy chip shot for Tim as long as he doesn't fall down."

Don't fall down...don't fall down. Bad karma was seeping into the Dutch's effort.

Central's snapper, Reid Evans, was having problems. "Our holder, Joe Kain, called out his signals, but I couldn't hear him," said Evans.

Kain called for the snap again...Nothing.

Evans strained his ears. "Finally, on his third try, I heard him and snapped the ball."

Linfield charged up the middle. Ritzert, the left upback, had no one to block. "I really did not have a lot of outside pressure from the rush," he said. "That allowed me to look over my shoulder to witness my worst nightmare. Tim slipped in the mud and kicked the ball into the back of the line!"

Amidst the mudpit in the middle of the field, O'Neil looked like Charlie Brown, flat on his back after Lucy pulled the ball right out from under him.

The pigskin plopped into the quagmire. "I turned away in disgust," said Central coach Rich Kacmarynski. The Linfield fans celebrated the Wildcat win.

Meanwhile...the play was still alive.

Evans found himself next to the ball.

"After the snap, I heard the ball hit someone and began looking for it," said the Central center. "I took a short step backwards, looked down, and the ball was at my feet. I picked it up and started running forward. I was hit almost immediately by about three Linfield defenders. I was turned around so that my back was to the end zone and was going to just throw the ball backwards. Luckily for us, our fullback, Joe Ritzert, was there."

Ritzert had a plan.

"I was actually thinking at that point that we could push the pile forward as long as Reid could stay on his feet to get a first down," said Ritzert. "Then I saw that he had more Wildcats hanging on him, and that he probably would not be able to get away. He had his back to our end zone, and I could see the ball in his arms. I ran towards him, and we both just gave each other the all knowing look of what we had to do to keep it alive. So I ran up to him and grabbed the ball from him."

Ritzert began plunging ahead. "It was like a rugby scrum," said the Dutch fullback, who coincidentally *was* an accomplished rugby player, and knew a thing or two about pushing piles of men forward.

The play looked like something right from a Tudor Electric Football game circa 1975.

With the field vibrating from the overjoyed Linfield team jumping up and down, a mass of Central and Linfield players all huddled in a scrum. They migrated, rotated, and floated five yards toward the goal line. Then, after at least five seconds of this congestion, prying himself away from the pack, Ritzert jiggled free and sprinted the final 15 yards into the end zone.

Touchdown Central.

Ecstasy turned to misery on the Linfield side. The entire team, streaming onto the field to embrace their fellow teammates with hands raised out like wives rushing to welcome home their GI husbands from the war, suddenly stopped in their tracks. Utter disbelief.

"Dutch Win !! Dutch Win!! Dutch Win!! Dutch Win!!" Central announcer J.B. Connoley's voice reverted back to puberty.

November 25, 2000—McMinnville, Oregon

"After our kicker slipped, I looked away and didn't see what happened," said Kacmarynski. "When I looked back, I saw Joe running in the end zone. It reminded me of the Stanford-Cal game in 1982."

Very much so. Except, instead of the Stanford Band occupying the end zone, ecstatic Linfield fans running onto the field suddenly scattered like ants when Ritzert barreled toward the end zone.

The officials huddled to confirm what they saw was legit.

"The final play was an interpretation by the officials," said Linfield coach Jay Locey. "I can't say I heard a whistle."

No one had blown a whistle to stop the play.

"I (was) kneeling on the sidelines and praying that they would make the right decision," said Ritzert.

Yes, the touchdown would count. The Dutch won 20-17. "I was at a loss for words," remembered Ritzert. "I just turned to all of our fans, and remember thinking how great it was to play for the Dutch fans."

The Central faithful then streamed onto the field, as the Wildcat fans wandered off in a daze.

THE AFTERMATH

Despite returning to Pella, Iowa to host the next round of the playoffs, Central fell to St. John's (Minn.) in their quarterfinal matchup, 21-18.

Both Central and Linfield continued their winning ways in the years that followed. Linfield extended their record streak of consecutive winning seasons to 50 with a 10-1 slate in 2005, a year after winning the Division III National Championship in 2004. The top-ranked Wildcats' quest for a repeat championship in 2005 ended with a 44-41 loss to Wisconsin-Whitewater in the quarterfinal round of the NCAA playoffs.

Central's streak of winning seasons reached 45 after the Dutch went 9-2 in 2005. Their season also came to an end at the hands of Wisconsin-Whitewater, in the first round of the playoffs, 34-14.

After graduation, Reid Evans accepted a position as an assistant offensive line coach with Central. Joe Ritzert went on to finish a Mechanical Engineering degree. Both will forever be linked in Central College football history as the stars of the Dutch's unforgettable "Miracle In The Mud".

Linfield	7	0	7	0	3	-17
Central	7	0	7	0	6	-20

LN	Williams 1 run (Cannon kick)
CC	McCullough 44 pass from Koerselman (O'Neil kick)
CC	Koerselman 1 run (O'Neil kick)
LN	Harrison 26 pass from Musser (Cannon kick)
LN	Cannon 34 FG
CC	Ritzert 21 blocked kick return (no attempt)

Attendance 2,500

345

Akron vs. Miami (Ohio)

The most fantastic play I've ever been a part of."
—*Terry Hoeppner*

THE BACKGROUND

Ben Roethlisberger and Charlie Frye.

Two red shirt freshmen quarterbacks who grew up 50 miles apart from each other. One from Findlay, Ohio. The other from Willard, Ohio. Miami was 3-2. Akron was 2-3.

A tale of two super frosh quarterbacks and a tale of two halves. In the first thirty minutes, Miami and Roethlisberger lit up the Akron defense. The RedHawk QB was 14-of-19 for 192 yards and two TDs, leading Miami to a 24-6 halftime bulge.

But trailing by 18 points at the half, the Zips opened up their offense in the third quarter. Frye, who threw mainly short passes for a paltry 55 yards during the first half, scorched the RedHawks defense after the break. The Akron QB set a school single-half passing mark with 254 yards in the second half.

A 72-yard hookup with Matt Cherry cut the lead to 24-16 midway thru the third quarter. Frye and Cherry then connected again in the fourth quarter on a 37-yard TD pass with 5:53 to play. A two-point conversion pass to Junior McCray tied the game at 24-24.

While Frye and Cherry were red hot, Roethlisberger was not. Squandering a big halftime lead, and unable to put any points on the board in the second half, the Miami QB and his teammates started making critical mistakes.

While an earlier interception at the Akron 2-yard line killed a RedHawk drive with 10:13 left in the fourth quarter, Roethlisberger's fumble on a fourth-and-one sneak at midfield gave the Zips the ball with 3:55 to play in Miami territory.

Miami defensive tackle Gino DiGiandomenico then committed a critical personal foul penalty after the Red Hawks defense had stopped Akron on third-and-24 from the Akron 42.

The penalty gave the Zips a first down and new life. And Frye took advantage.

Two sideline completions brought the ball to the Miami 20-yard line where Zips RB McCray took the handoff three times, Miami used their final two timeouts, and Akron lined up for a game-winning field goal at the Miami 11-yard line.

Zac Derr's 27-yard attempt was good. The clock read 0:09 and Akron had taken a 27-24 lead.

"We had seemingly blown a game we should have won," recalled RedHawk coach Terry Hoeppner. "We did not, however, give up. We kept our cool on the sideline and decided to take a knee wherever we caught the ensuing kickoff in an effort to save as much time as possible."

Indeed Korey Kirkpatrick caught the kickoff at the 16-yard line and immediately took a knee. 0:07 left on the clock.

"We sent the offense out and called 'Big Ben Out' into the boundary," recalled Hoeppner.

A quick drop and Roethlisberger fired a laser to Eddie Tillitz on the left sideline. Tillitz quickly stepped out of bounds.

Four Akron defenders tip Ben Roethlisberger's Hail Mary pass right to Miami's Eddie Tillitz. Photo courtesy of Jeff Sabo, Miami University

"This was a crucial play, because it got us to the 30-yard line," noted Hoeppner. "(Ben) made a great throw."

Three seconds remained.

THE PLAY

CD 2-Track 28—*Steve Baker,*
Miami University

Hoeppner recalled the details. "We had one chance and so we called "Big Ben", not in reference to the QB, but rather the big clock in England."

It was the second Big Ben set in a row. This time, Tillitz, Jason Branch and Chauncey Henry lined up right to the wide side of the field. Akron only rushed three men, giving Roethlisberger and Hoeppner time to think about the final pass.

We work on it for five or ten minutes every week," said offensive coordinator Shane Montgomery. " It's not something we practice all the time, but we cover it so everybody knows where they're supposed to go. We might not run it but three times a year. Half the time we don't even throw it."

Hoeppner still had hope.

"As our center Paul Thaler snapped the ball, I took off my head phones and handed them to my son," said Hoeppner. "I thought to myself that Northwestern pulled this off three times last year. We ought to be able to do it once."

No one pressured Big Ben. The Miami QB drifted to his left, waited and waited.

"Akron was in a sound prevent defense, but I'm sure they underestimated how far Ben could throw the ball," said Hoeppner.

Actually Roethlisberger threw a mammoth, towering toss, seventy yards in the air, that pushed four Akron defenders back to their five-yard line.

"We had done everything we could to make sure we had guys in the right spots," said Zips coach Lee Owens.

And Akron had the ball played perfectly. If only they would have let the ball drop to the ground, it would have fallen incomplete. Because all three Miami receivers were still trying to catch up with the play.

Instead, all four Akron players leaped for the ball with no RedHawk receivers fighting them.

Rickey McKenzie, John Fuller and Marcus

Suber had the best shot. Fuller got a hand on it and batted it to the left and up.

Up high enough for the trailing Tillitz, running in stride, to tip it with his right hand, pop it up in front of him, race underneath it, and catch the ball while running into the end zone. All in a fraction of a second.

My plan was to play the tip, even though the chances of me catching it weren't that great," said Tillitz. "But it worked out like I hoped it would. I got to give God credit for that. I saw a tip and it was a little out of my range, so I tipped it back with my right hand. Luckily, I had a good tip back to myself."

Touchdown Miami. Final Score: Miami 30, Akron 27.

While the Miami team flooded the end zone, the Akron players doubled over.

"If anyone has ever just walked up to you and punched you in the gut as hard as they can, you can imagine how hard it is to speak," Akron coach Lee Owens said. "It's that sort of feeling. The breath and life just seem to go right out of you."

Meanwhile DiGiandomenico, staring at a long penance for his personal foul that set up the go ahead field goal, was all smiles after the play. ""It's safe to say Ben and Eddie both made my Christmas list with that play," he said afterward.

THE AFTERMATH

The Miami coach recounted the play often.

"I enjoy telling recruits the details of the play and especially where I calmly walked across the field to shake Coach Owens hand..... no I didn't, I ran the length of the field and jumped on the pile with everyone else," joked Hoeppner. " I finally remembered who I was and found Coach Owens and shook his hand. "

In just his sixth collegiate game, Roethlisberger broke the Miami single game passing record, completing 23-of-40 for 399 yards. Frye's stats were a mirror image, minus the winning Hail Mary pass. He finished 21-of-31 for 309 yards.

The play spawned a new saying in Oxford.

"Around here we say, It ain't over Tillitz over," said Hoeppner, who stayed at Miami until the end of the 2004 season when he left to become the head coach at Indiana University.

Roethlisberger left Miami after his junior year in 2003, a sparkling 13-1 season in which he threw for 4,486 yards and 37 touchdowns, shattering the school single-season records. The RedHawks finished that season ranked No.10 in the AP poll.

Big Ben was the number one pick of the Pittsburgh Steelers in the 2004 NFL Draft, took over the starting QB job and led the Steelers to a 15-1 record and spot in the AFC Championship game in 2004. The following year, with Ben Roethlisberger at the helm, the Steelers marched through the playoffs and onto a 21-10 victory over the Seattle Seahawks in Super Bowl XL .

Charlie Frye finished his Akron career in 2004 ranked No.11 in the NCAA record books for career total offense. He holds 54 Akron records and is one of six QBs in NCAA history to throw for over 10,000 yards and have at least 400 yards rushing. The Cleveland Browns drafted Frye in the third round of the 2005 NFL Draft.

Ben and Charlie finished their college careers with almost identical total passing yardage. Roethlisberger tallied 10,829 career passing yards in three years. Frye finished with 11,049 passing yards in four seasons.

Akron	0	6	10	11	- 27
Miami	10	14	0	6	- 30

MIAMI   Murray 31 pass from
        Roethlisberger
        (Parseghian kick)

MIAMI   FG Parseghian 32

AKRON FG Derr 31

MIAMI   Little 47 run
        (Parseghian kick)

AKRON FG Derr 47

MIAMI   Little 37 pass from
        Roethlisberger
        (Parseghian kick)

AKRON FG Derr 52

AKRON Cherry 72 pass from
        Frye (Derr kick)

AKRON Cherry 37 pass from
        Frye (McCray pass)

AKRON FG Derr 27

MIAMI   Tillitz 70 pass from
        Roethlisberger

Attendance 10,561

Michigan vs. Michigan State

"Oh yeah, I was crying my eyes out." — Jeff Smoker

THE BACKGROUND

Sixth-ranked Michigan boasted the country's best run defense, surrendering just 54 yards per game on the ground. The Wolverines (6-1, 4-0 in the Big Ten) were positioning themselves for a possible shot at the BCS National Championship game in the Rose Bowl. Michigan State (4-2, 2-2) was unranked yet dangerous, specifically on offense, with sophomore wideout Charles Rogers, junior tailback T.J. Duckett, and junior quarterback Jeff Smoker.

To the winner of the annual conference battle? State bragging rights and ownership of the four foot high Paul Bunyan Trophy.

The game was knotted at 17-17 entering the fourth quarter, and Duckett was shredding the vaunted Wolverine run defense. With 181 rushing yards already to his name, Duckett broke off a 27-yard romp down to the UM 16-yard line. That set up a 26-yard Dave Rayner field goal and put the Spartans ahead 20-17 with 7:33 remaining.

Spartan Stadium rocked as the Wolverines went three-and-out in the next possession. Then on the next play, it fell silent.

Smoker took over at the MSU 39 with 6:10 left, and promptly fumbled a bad snap on the first play of the drive. UM's Grant Bowman snatched it up. Three plays later QB John Navarre hit backup quarterback Jermaine Gonzales with a 20-yard TD strike.

Michigan led 24-20 with just 4:44 on the clock.

Herb Haygood's 49-yard return on the ensuing kickoff quickly set the Spartans up at midfield. Smoker then found Haygood for an 11-yard completion down to the UM 40. It appeared MSU was headed for the end zone as the fourth quarter ran down.

But the comeback drive stalled. Three incomplete passes forced a punt. Punter Craig Jarrett pinned the Wolverines at the UM 7-yard line with a 36-yard kick.

Now Michigan had a chance to put the game away with a couple first downs. But the Wolverines couldn't get the ball past the 16-yard line. Navarre's third down pass to Marquise Walker fell one-yard shy of a first down and Michigan's Hayden Epstein shanked a 28-yard punt to set the Spartans up at the UM 44 with 2:09 left.

Still, the Spartans couldn't move the ball.

Smoker was sacked by defensive tackle Shantee Orr. Then two incomplete passes left MSU in dire straits. Fourth-and-16 at midfield with 1:25 left to play.

Smoker looked for Haygood, but the pass fell just out of his reach. Seemingly, the game was over.

Then it wasn't.

On the play, UM cornerback Jeremy LeSueur grabbed Charles Rogers' face mask. A 15-yard personal foul was called. The ball was moved to the UM 35.

Michigan State had new life. Down by four points, the Spartans needed the end zone.

Smoker hit Haygood for 17 yards to the

UM 18. But on the next play, the Spartan QB was sacked for the eleventh time in the game. He lost 64 yards rushing on the day. He probably lost a few teeth too. As the Spartans took their final timeout to stop the clock at 0:36, Smoker looked less like a quarterback and more like Rocky Balboa just trying to go the distance with Apollo Creed.

While MSU called timeout, the officials were marching off an illegal participation penalty on the Wolverines who had twelve men on the field. The second critical penalty against Michigan on the drive moved the ball to the UM 11.

But two incomplete passes forced a fourth-and-three. Down to their last play again, MSU emptied the backfield, and Duckett ran a quick slant. Smoker tossed the ball to his runningback who managed eight yards and a first down at the three-yard line.

The suspense grew.

After the chains moved, Smoker spiked the ball.

0:17 remained. Second down at the three-yard line. Smoker rolled right, but then was caught in bounds by defensive back Brandon Williams. The ball was at the two-yard line. The clock was at 0:12. The crowd was in a frenzy.

Smoker scrambled to get to the line of scrimmage. He had no time outs left. The clock ticked down. Five seconds, four, three. "I just got the guys to the line as quickly as possible and showed them I was spiking the ball," he said.

Frantically Smoker lined up over center Brian Ottney. Two seconds, one second. Ottney snapped it. Smoker spiked it.

Did he beat the clock? Was there time for one more play? Or did the clock run out?

THE PLAY

CD 2-Track 29—*George Blaha, Larry Bielat,* **Spartan Sports Network**

The clock read 0:01. Was it stopped too early? Michigan thought so. The officials did not. One tick remained, and the Spartans got one final play.

Smoker regrouped his offense, then took the snap out of the shotgun. He was quickly flushed out of the pocket.

"We had an empty backfield and T.J. was coming on a slant. That was the play we hit to get the first down before," said MSU coach Bobby Williams.

The Spartans hoped it would work again. But Smoker was in danger of taking a twelfth sack from the charging Michigan defense.

Duckett tried to get his QB's attention. "I was just jumping up and down," Duckett said. "I couldn't say anything, I was just jumping waving my hands...I couldn't talk, I couldn't do anything."

The Spartan QB was out of time. "I was rolling right and looked back and threw it up in the air," said Smoker. He made an off-balance desperation pass. "I got hit and waited for the crowd's reaction, to tell you the truth, because I couldn't see it."

As Smoker lay on the ground, his pass arched high into the air toward Duckett and two Wolverine defenders in the middle of the end zone.

"It seemed like the ball just kept climbing up and getting higher and higher. A Michigan defender jumped high, and it looked like it was coming right to his hands, but the ball just kept going," said Duckett. "For a moment everything was silent and I was hoping I caught it."

He did. Silence turned to hysteria. Touchdown Spartans. No time on the clock. Final score: Michigan State 26, Michigan 24.

The celebration began.

"I thought about running out there and jumping on the pile," Williams said. "But I said, 'No, I better not do that.' So I just watched all those guys jump on each other."

And jump they did. One on top of the other.

"I ran into the pile and almost got suffocated," said Smoker. "It was just a crazy range of emotions. I was overwhelmed. I was crying, but I was happy."

THE AFTERMATH

"That play should never have been allowed to be run," said Michigan coach Lloyd

Carr the following day. "Obviously, the clock in the last ten seconds, there's a major error there and something needs to be done about it."

58-year old Bob Stehlin was the Michigan State clock operator, a job he held for 21 years. But never was he the center of a controversial finish like this one. He avoided reporters after the game. "All I wanted was a beer," he said in an interview two years after the fact.

Stehlin stood behind his one second of fame. "If it had been Michigan in that situation, they would've had the second," he said. Dave Parry, coordinator of Big Ten officials agreed. "We could find nothing that suggested there had been a mistake made," he said.

The following season, the Big Ten changed the way official time was kept in a game, with an on-field conference official now responsible for the clock.

Carr's Wolverines finished the season 8-4, ranked 20th in the AP poll, after a 45-17 loss to Tennessee in the Citrus Bowl.

The win over Michigan was the apex for Bobby Williams and the Spartans, who slid down a murky path on and off the field for the next year.

Michigan State popped up at No. 22 in the polls the next day. But the Spartans fell the next week at home to Indiana 37-29. In fact, MSU dropped three straight games following the triumph over Michigan. They knocked off Fresno State 44-35 in the Silicon Valley Bowl to end the season at 7-5.

After completing his second year as head coach, Williams got a contract extension through the 2006 season for his efforts. He was then fired ten games later, during the 2002 season after Michigan pummeled the Spartans 49-3, leaving MSU with four straight defeats, and a 3-6 record. Williams later became the receivers coach for the Detroit Lions in 2003, associate head coach at LSU under Nick Saban in 2004, then joined Saban on his staff in Miami as the running backs coach for the Dolphins in 2005.

Smoker also had problems the following season, suspended for substance abuse midway through the 2002 campaign. He later returned, and turned his life around. His

senior season in 2003 was a record-breaking one under new coach John L. Smith. Smoker shattered the MSU all-time record for completions, attempts, yards passing, touchdowns, and total offense. He was a sixth round pick of the St. Louis Rams in the 2004 NFL Draft.

T.J. Duckett, who finished with 211 yards rushing in the game, decided to forego his senior season and entered the 2002 NFL Draft where he was selected by the Atlanta Falcons as the 18th overall pick.

Michigan	3	14	0	7	- 24
Michigan State	7	7	3	9	- 26

MSU	Rogers 17 pass from Smoker (Rayner kick)
MICH	FG Epstein 57
MICH	Walker 14 pass from Navarre (Epstein kick)
MSU	Duckett 2 run (Rayner kick)
MICH	Walker 32 pass from Navarre (Epstein kick)
MSU	FG Rayner 27
MSU	FG Rayner 26
MICH	Gonzales 20 pass from Navarre (Epstein kick)
MSU	Duckett 2 pass from Smoker

Attendance 75,262

Wabash vs. ⬤DePauw

"I just happened to be in the right place at the right time."
—*Kurt Casper*

THE BACKGROUND

In 1832, Wabash College opened its doors for the first time in tiny Crawfordsville, Indiana. Five years later, and 29 miles down the road, DePauw University was founded.

The schools first met on the gridiron in 1890, and have met every year since 1911 when the Little Giants of Wabash, coached by soon-to-be Notre Dame head coach Jesse Harper, battled the Tigers of DePauw to a scoreless 0-0 tie. Ninety years later, after 107 contests between the two teams (the 12th most played rivalry in college football), the series was still a virtual deadlock. Fifty wins DePauw, 48 wins Wabash, 9 ties.

When these Division III arch-rivals clash every November, throw out the records, and throw in the Monon Bell. Actually, roll it in. The 300-pound steam locomotive bell, a gift from the Monon Railroad back in 1932 given to the winner of the game, is more coveted in south central Indiana than a Bobby Knight autographed red sweater.

The Monon Bell Game is not just a football game. It's a week filled with tangles between the two schools. The rugby teams square off, the debate squads share barbs, and even the glee clubs chime in with a dual concert. But certainly, ringing the Monon Bell after a victory is the high note of the season for either Wabash (7-2) or DePauw (5-4). Across the country, their loyal alums huddle around televisions in bars and restaurants to watch the rare satellite feed from the small town of Greencastle, Indiana, population 9,000.

DePauw's four previous home games of 2001 attracted a total of 5,000 fans. On this crisp November afternoon, Greencastle nearly doubled in size as a crowd of 7,300 packed the bleachers at Blackstock Stadium.

Aided by two DePauw fumbles in their first three possessions, Wabash jumped out to a 14-0 second quarter lead when quarterback Jake Knott found tight end Rob Short with a 15-yard TD strike. It looked as if that lead would stand going into halftime. But with just under three minutes left in the half, DePauw's Jeremy Legge recovered a fumbled punt return by Stu Johnson at the Wabash 20. Three plays later, Tigers quarterback Jason Lee found Dan Ryan for a 4-yard touchdown pass and the Wabash lead was cut to 14-7 at the intermission.

After DePauw battled back to a 14-14 tie on A.J. Smart's 3-yard TD run at the end of the third quarter, Wabash responded.

Knott, a junior QB already sporting school record passing numbers in just his third year, found Josh Bronaugh on a 48-yard gain to the DePauw one-yard line. After a penalty, Knott connected again with Short for a 6-yard TD pass, putting Wabash ahead 21-14 with 10:44 left in the game.

Excitement on the Wabash sideline grew to a fever pitch. No player on the Little Giants' bench had ever beaten DePauw. Neither had their young coach, Chris Creighton, who was in his first year at a Division III school, moving up after four seasons as head coach at NAIA Ottawa University.

Across the field stood Nick Mourouzis, the seasoned DePauw head coach in his 21st year leading the Tigers. Over two decades, Mourouzis led his teams to a school record 121 victories, with eleven wins over Wabash, including five straight Monon Bell triumphs from 1996-2000, tying a series record for consecutive victories.

Down by seven in the fourth quarter, Mourouzis' troops weren't going to panic. Instead, they turned up the heat, playing the rest of the game on the Wabash side of the field.

Lee, a senior southpaw promptly connected with receiver John Stephens for 30 yards to the Wabash 26-yard line. But DePauw could get no further, turning the ball over on downs after a one-yard gain and three straight incompletions.

They got the ball right back. Cornerback Justin Tillis picked off a long Knott pass and returned it to the Wabash 40.

The Tigers moved to the Wabash 17. But Little Giant linebacker Nate Boulais brought Lee to the ground for a five-yard loss on fourth-and-five, thwarting a second straight DePauw threat.

Wabash took over, then soon punted back to DePauw, setting up one final Tigers drive into Wabash territory. Starting at his own 39-yard line, Lee had 61 yards to travel with no timeouts remaining and just 1:22 on the clock.

He found Smart out of the backfield for 16 yards. Then Stephens for 22 yards. Again to Smart for a gain of 17 on third-and-10. DePauw was at the Wabash 6-yard line. The clock was at 0:36. It stopped to move the chains, then kept ticking.

Lee tossed to Stephens over the middle. He grabbed the ball at the five, then lunged for the goal line, but was desperately wrestled back at the one-yard line by cornerback Artie Montes. The clock continued. Twenty-five, twenty-four, twenty-three seconds left. DePauw frantically lined up. Lee just needed to spike the ball to preserve time.

He didn't.

Instead, he handed off to Smart. A huge risk. If he fell short of the end zone, the game would end without DePauw being able to run another play.

But powering over the left side of the line, Smart cashed in with his second touchdown of the game. DePauw had rallied to tie Wabash at 21-21.

Fourteen seconds remained.

Overtime seemed imminent. So did a DePauw victory. Momentum heavily favored the homestanding Tigers.

"After DePauw scored, I felt the sidelines sigh and you could feel the uh-ohs in the air," said Creighton.

With his team stunned by the last second score, the freshman coach tried some impromptu motivation. "I ran up and down the sideline smiling and clapping, saying it doesn't get any better than this. I didn't want our guys to let negative thoughts take over. I wanted them to believe deep down."

The most the Wabash players could truly believe was that the game was headed for an extra period.

The kickoff squibbed down into the hands of freshman Eddie Garza who returned it to the Wabash 39, leaving 10.2 seconds on the clock.

Knott lined up in the shotgun, then tried a quick underneath route over the middle to Kurt Casper, a senior wide receiver who needed just over 100 yards in his final game as a Wabash player to become the school's all-time leading receiver. Held to only thirty receiving yards on the day, Casper would not break the record.

But on this play, he was nearly broken in two.

Casper caught Knott's nine-yard completion in stride, then was flattened to the ground. "Kurt got crushed," said Knott. " He got creamed," echoed Creighton. "He absolutely got ripped," added fellow receiver Short.

How did Casper describe the belly-to-belly body slam put on him by defensive back Cory Partlow? "Probably the hardest hit of my collegiate career," he said.

The DePauw defense celebrated.

The final seconds ticked away....almost.

Staring at the sky in a haze, at the Wabash 48, Casper somehow peeled his shoulders off the mat and signaled timeout, preserving 2.7 seconds on the clock. Enough time for one final play of regulation.

THE PLAY

Like a wobbly boxer, Casper retreated to his corner, the Wabash sideline. There, he joined Creighton and Knott to discuss what to do. It was a brief discussion.

"I told (Coach Creighton) to run the "hook and ladder" which our #2 receiver hooks up at 15 yards and then I come on the outside and he pitches me the ball," said Casper. "We had almost decided on this play, when Jake told him that he could (throw) it to the end zone. So we decided to change the play."

Choosing between the best of two long shots, Creighton described the plan. " Ever since Colorado beat Michigan on (Kordell) Stewart's Hail Mary to Michael Westbrook, I decided to practice the play in case we were ever in a similar situation. Ever since that game, we practice *Colorado* every Friday," said the Little Giants' coach.

The official name of the play was "Trips Lex Gun Colorado Red".

Creighton gave more specifics. "We get into a Trip open, shot gun formation and put a tall fast tight end at the #2 spot on the trips side. The inside and outside receivers are to run as fast as they can down field, as the middle larger receiver runs as deep as he can. Depending on the score, the clock, and the yard line, the inside and outside receivers yell either 'Catch!' or 'Tip!' to the big man going for the ball."

His offense knew the desperation design quite well.

Short, the 6'5" tight end, was the key to the play's chances. Although optimistic, he was more realistic. "In practice, the play really never worked too well, sometimes I would tip it too far or too short, and sometimes I would just catch it myself," he noted.

Knott was more to the point. "It never worked in practice. Not once. Short would either miss the tip or tip it too far away."

Casper too was doubtful, though hopeful. "In the huddle, Ryan and I looked at each other and said 'We're going to do this'," he remembered. "But I don't think either one of us actually thought it was going to happen."

It was hard for Casper to think at all, his head still reeling from the previous hit. "When we decided on the last play, I was still somewhat dizzy, but I knew what I had to do," he said.

On the DePauw sidelines, there were no surprises.

"Hail Mary is a practiced play. Everyone practices that play. We practice that play," said Mourouzis. "We knew that's all they had left. We call it the Big Bend. We always practice it ourselves once a week, usually on Thursdays."

In fact, DePauw's version actually worked in 1991, against Anderson University, when Steve Broderick caught a desperation pass from QB Brian Goodman that deflected off the hands of an Anderson defender. Broderick hauled it in and streaked 65 yards on a muddy field with no time left as DePauw won 12-7.

This time, however, the Tigers were on defense. "We rushed three and dropped eight," said Mourouzis.

Freshman defensive back Obinna Ugokwe was one of the extra defensive backs inserted to stop Wabash's Hail Mary attempt. He mirrored Casper down the field.

From the shotgun, Knott took the snap and rolled right to the far sideline. The clock reached 0:00. Knott kept rolling. Being rushed from behind, he had no choice but to throw on the run as he was pushed from behind into the Wabash bench.

"I sprinted to the sideline as long as I could and I knew I had to throw it when I got to the 48-yard line," remarked Knott. " I chucked it and got knocked into our bench. I fell onto my hand (and injured it). I never saw the play."

The ball floated to the five-yard line where Short was surrounded by four DePauw defenders. "I misjudged it a little," said the

Wabash tight end. "It was further back when I jumped in the air."

Launching his long arms upward like a volleyball player, Short tried to flip the ball behind him. "I was somewhat falling back when I tipped the ball," he said. "I just remember falling to the ground, not knowing what happened."

The ball deflected straight back toward the goal line.

While Knott laid on the ground out of bounds at midfield, and Short tumbled along the sideline, Casper stood alone in the front corner of the end zone. Ugokwe, his defender, had turned to watch Short's attempted tip, momentarily leaving the Wabash receiver wide open.

The ball fell right into Casper's hands. Touchdown Wabash.

Casper immediately palmed the pigskin in his left hand, the last reception of his Wabash career, then raised both arms in a triumphant "V" for victory.

For a brief second, Casper stood still...so did Monon Bell time.

The Wabash fans, standing in red unison on the bleachers, no more than twenty feet from Casper, flooded the field. The barricades surrounding the end zone collapsed like dominos. Chances are the entire Wabash all-male student body, all 860 of them, flopped onto the frenzied pile that swallowed up Casper.

"I just heard an enormous burst of noise," said Short. "Everyone from Wabash was on the field hugging and cheering in disbelief."

The Wabash players, sprinting from the sidelines, joined in, each one of them experiencing a victory over DePauw for the first time.

Finally, they got to ring the bell.

THE AFTERMATH

What did the DePauw coach tell his team afterwards? "There wasn't too much you could say. We were standing there dumbfounded," lamented Mourouzis. "If you were to run that play ten times with no defense, you're lucky to hit it once."

The DePauw coach was even more flab-

bergasted after seeing the videotape of the game. "My son pointed it out to me. It wasn't a planned play. (Short) missed the ball. It hit his helmet!" said Mourouzis.

In fact, replays appeared to show the ball ricocheting perfectly off of Short's helmet just before he raised his arms to try and tip it back. "I know that it looks like it did," replied Short, "and many people believe it hit off my helmet. But I am quite sure that (I tipped it) with my hands."

Never ask a magician how he performs his tricks. Illusion or not, the spectacular play ended the season for both teams.

Casper now has a lifetime to bask in the glory. " I was hoisted up on the shoulders of past alums who were just as excited as I was to bring the bell back to Crawfordsville," said the victorious receiver.

Mourouzis had nine months without an opponent to let it soak in like a cold rain. "The (Monon Bell) game, if you lose it, you think about it all the time."

But to lose like this, being so close to a record sixth consecutive win in the series?

"I wish I could throw away the memories (of that play)," said the DePauw coach.

After a five year drought, Wabash returned to campus with the Monon Bell. The trip back to Crawfordsville was one to remember for Knott.

"The bus ride is about thirty minutes and the entire trip was exciting," said Knott. "We were all up in the aisles, singing and dancing and making fun of each other as most teams do. The tradition with the bell after it is won is to present it to the senior class in the Chapel here at the college. As we got off the bus, there were parents, fans, alumni and most of the (inebriated) student body. Everyone was waiting for us. We went into the chapel and a student-run organization walked the bell down the aisle much like the bride walks before a wedding. The entire time it was ringing and the place (seats about 1000 people) was going crazy. The bell was presented to the senior class, Kurt (Casper) said a few words, then we sang the school song."

Creighton celebrated his first Monon Bell victory as well. "The Wabash campus was up all night I can assure you of that," said the coach. His quarterback agreed whole-heartedly. "It wasn't exactly an all-male campus that night," added Knott.

Short chimed in with a final note. "The bell really did ring for a week straight at Wabash College, he said. "We just rang it and rang it. Every (fraternity) house got to keep it and the thing just kept ringing. And everyone, including our parents, drank out of the bell. I still remember my mom drinking out of the bell. That was one of the funnier things I have ever seen."

Ah, the taste of victory.

Wabash	7	7	0	13	- 27
DePauw	0	7	7	7	- 21

WAB	Dawson 3 pass from Knott (Olmstead kick)
WAB	Short 15 pass from Knott (Olmstead kick)
DEP	Ryan 4 pass from Lee (Harvey kick)
DEP	Smart 3 run (Harvey kick
WAB	Short 6 pass from Knott (Olmstead kick)
DEP	Smart 1 run (Harvey kick)
WAB	Casper 52 pass from Knott (no attempt)

Attendance 7,300

Furman vs. Appalachian State

> "It was a head-coaching blunder by me."
> —*Bobby Lamb*

THE BACKGROUND

Jerry Moore broke the record at Division I-AA Appalachian State. In his 14th year as head coach at ASU, Moore captured his 111th career win with a victory over East Tennessee State to become the winningest coach in Southern Conference history.

The next week, No.4 ASU (4-1) hosted their rivals from Greenville SC, No.5 Furman (4-1), in a game that will probably be No.1 on the list of great finishes for coach Moore and No.1 on the list of "things in life I'd rather forget" for first year Furman coach Bobby Lamb.

Lamb, a former star QB for the tradition rich Furman Paladins, saw his team chew up the clock for the entire game. They held the ball for over 40 minutes, twice as many as ASU. They had 22 first downs, twice as many as ASU. Yet late in the third quarter all Furman had to show for their offensive dominance was twice as many field goals as ASU, and a 6-0 lead.

Even that vanished on one play when ASU's Jay Lyles intercepted a Billy Napier pass at the Furman 43-yard line and returned it for a Mountaineers touchdown. Appalachian State led 7-6.

As the game entered the fourth quarter, Furman regained the lead on the next possession converting a 48-yard kickoff return by sophomore Brian Bratton into a third Danny Marshall field goal, this one from 36 yards out. With 11:03 to play, Furman led 9-6.

ASU QB Joe Burchette then took his team on its first sustained drive of the game, hitting fullback Joey Hoover with a clutch 24-yard TD pass on third down-and-six. ASU was back on top 14-9 with 5:29 left.

Now trailing by five points, senior quarterback Billy Napier proceeded to take the Paladins on a wild ride downfield worthy of an extra admission charge to the 14,311 in the stands at Kidd Brewer Stadium.

Like an amusement park rollercoaster, it started slowly with small thrills. At the Furman 27, Napier connected with Hindley Brigham for a modest four yards. Then Bear Rinehart caught a 22-yard toss from Napier. Four plays later, Napier found Bratton for 22 more yards.

Furman was at the ASU 15-yard line when the corkscrew twist and turns really got fun. On first down, Napier dropped back and dropped the ball. He fell on it at the ASU 19. On second down, ASU's Josh Jeffries sent Furman backward again, sacking Napier for a four-yard loss. Timeout Paladins. Time to re-group with 1:09 on the clock. Napier sauntered back on the field, and on third-and-18, calmly hit Brigham for 16 yards down to the ASU 7-yard line.

Fourth-and-two. Furman called another timeout, stopping the clock with 0:53 left.

With the game in the balance, Brigham got the call and got the first down, mustering a five-yard run down to the ASU 2-yard line. First and goal for Furman. The clock dwindled.

358

Derrick Black celebrates with his teammates after scoring on a most improbable two-point conversion attempt. Photo courtesy of Appalachian State University

Napier tried to win it himself, running on first down, but was hit by K.T. Stovall. The ball squirted free. But Brigham saved the Paladins again, this time falling on the ball at the ASU 2.

Furman still had the ball. On second down Napier looked for Andy Rump in the end zone. But the ball fell incomplete, leaving third-and-goal with just 0:15 remaining.

Then the rollercoaster Paladins did another loop-de-loop.

A false start moved them back five yards. A delay of game flag pushed them back five more. They were down five points and moving in the wrong direction.

Then suddenly, the Paladins shifted from reverse to overdrive on one play.

Now at the ASU 12, with the Furman faithful hanging on for dear life, Napier found Rinehart in the end zone. He rifled a 12-yard TD pass, splitting two Mountaineer defenders and splitting the hearts of ASU fans.

On the Furman side, screams of joy. Touchdown Paladins.

Furman had the lead 15-14 with just 7.4 seconds on the clock. The fun-filled five minute Paladin ride covered 73 yards. Somewhere on the Furman campus, you could hear the following announcement, "Please stay seated with your seat belts fastened until the ride comes to a complete halt."

No one paid heed.

Indeed, just as the Furman fans stopped celebrating, unbuckled their seat belts, straightened their hair, and jumped out of the rollercoaster car.... The Furman fun ride turned into a house of horrors.

THE PLAY

CD 2-Track 30—*David Jackson, Avery Hall,* **Appalachian Sports Network**

While the Furman players celebrated, their coach contemplated what to do next. Kick the PAT? Go for two? "Eight coaches were shouting in the headsets," Lamb said. "You only had a few moments to decide."

The Paladins didn't need points. They just

needed to make sure that ASU didn't get a defensive score on the conversion attempt. The Furman coach chose to avoid a possible blocked kick. The Paladins lined up for the two-point conversion.

Perhaps Napier would just take a knee. Maybe he'd secure the ball and try and run it in. Maybe he'd pass? What?

"We didn't have a timeout," Lamb explained. "And amongst the bedlam after we scored, we were trying to get the right personnel in the game. We wanted to run a sprint to the right, but by the time the play got to the huddle, we didn't have time to put our back in motion to do that. We just lined up and ran a quick little pass to the left."

A tunnel screen left.

Napier took the snap, dropped back and spotted Bratton. He didn't spot the all-American defensive end Josh Jeffries. "They had been running the tailback out of the backfield," Jeffries said. "I just guessed. I guessed right. "

Napier released the ball. Bratton watched helplessly. "I saw it all happening," said Bratton. "It was like a dream, a bad dream."

Jeffries stepped in front of Bratton, picked off Napier's pass at the goal line then headed the other way. The unthinkable. He got twenty yards downfield before deciding he wasn't going to make it on his own.

"As soon as I caught it I was looking for someone to pitch it to because I knew that I was going to get tackled," Jeffries said.

So Jeffries tossed it back to Derrick Black.

"He turned around, I was there and I caught it in stride," Black said. "I was calling his name, but he said he couldn't hear me. He just turned and pitched it to me."

Jeffries then blocked for Black who suddenly had a potential game-winning two points in his hands.

Black took off down the right sideline. He got a key block by Nygel Rogers at midfield, cut past Napier trying to stop the nightmare, and rambled 80 yards for two points that will never be forgotten at Furman or Appalachian State. Amazingly, the Mountaineers had the lead again 16-15.

Exhausted from the climactic play, Josh Jeffries, began vomiting on the sidelines during the wild celebration. But he managed to come back on the field and recover Furman's onside kick attempt.

ASU took one snap and down came the goalpost. It ended up two miles from the stadium.

THE AFTERMATH

"It was a miracle," exclaimed Moore, who knew the view of a miracle from the other sideline. As coach of Texas Tech in 1982, Moore witnessed SMU's Bobby Leach sprint 91 yards with a botched kickoff return to beat his Red Raiders as time expired.

Meanwhile, Lamb would have to endure his fateful decision for quite some time.

"We probably should have lined up in the I-formation and run a power play, or just taken a knee," thought Lamb. "It was my mistake, and I take the blame for it."

The following day, ESPN featured the winning/losing play as its "Bonehead Play of the Week." The sports network replayed it over and over again. Lamb couldn't get it out of his head. "On Sunday, it was a very long day for me," he said.

The Mountaineers moved up to No.3 in the national polls, but then fell hard the following weeks after a 36-20 defeat at No. 13 Georgia Southern and a 26-19 upset loss to Wofford. They regrouped to finish 8-3, then fell to Maine 14-13 in the first round of the I-AA playoffs.

Furman rebounded to also finish the regular season 8-3, but lost in the first round of the playoffs as Villanova rallied from a 24-7 third quarter deficit to beat the Paladins 45-38.

In 2005, after 17 years as head coach, Jerry Moore led the Appalachian State Mountaineers to the school's first-ever National Championship with a 21-16 victory over Northern Iowa in the title game.

Furman	0	3	3	9	- 15
Appalachian State	0	0	7	9	- 16

FUR	FG Marshall 29
FUR	FG Marshall 46
ASU	Lyles 43 interception return (Wright kick)
FUR	FG Marshall 36
ASU	Hoover 24 pass from Joe Burchette (Wright kick)
FUR	Rinehart 12 pass from Billy Napier (Napier pass intercept)
ASU	Black PAT return

Attendance 14,311

LSU vs. Kentucky

"It feels like getting kicked in the teeth."
—*Otis Grigsby, UK defensive end*

THE BACKGROUND

Twelve straight losses to ranked SEC teams. The Kentucky Wildcats hoped that number thirteen would be lucky for them as they hosted 16th-ranked LSU (6-2) in Commonwealth Stadium.

In his second year as head coach, Guy Morriss seemingly had the UK program on the rise. After consecutive 2-9 seasons and the sting of NCAA sanctions imposed for violations under the watch of former head coach Hal Mumme, Kentucky was an upbeat 6-3, averaging nearly 35 points per game.

But it was LSU that opened up a 21-7 lead in the third quarter before a Wildcat rally led by paunchy junior QB Jared Lorenzen. At 6'4"

and 300 pounds (give or take ten pounds), J. Load was a field general with an appetite.

How did the Pillsbury Throwboy stack himself up against other QBs around the country? "I could out-eat them," noted Lorenzen in a feature for the *Cincinnati Enquirer*. "It sounds bad, but I could. Give me pizza, hamburgers, chicken, anything. That might come across wrong, but look at me. I'm a big guy."

Lorenzen's 44-yard touchdown pass to Aaron Boone with 2:24 to play in the fourth quarter capped an 80-yard drive, bringing UK all the way back to a 27-27 tie. It was Boone's third TD catch of the game and the Hefty Lefty's fourth TD pass.

But it was UK's defense that positioned the Wildcats to pull off the upset.

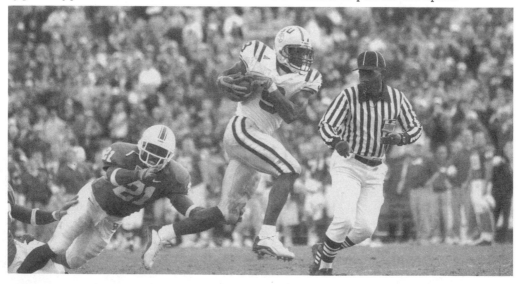

Devery Henderson dashes toward the end zone with the Bluegrass Miracle...then gets a hero's ride afterward. Photos courtesy of LSU Sports Information

On the next possession, Vincent Burns' second down sack of LSU quarterback Marcus Randall, pinned the Tigers back at their own 10-yard line. After an incomplete pass, Donnie Jones' 47-yard punt was returned 21 yards by UK's Derek Abney and the Wildcats were sitting pretty at the LSU 31-yard line with just 0:51 on the clock.

After a pass interference penalty and a 9-yard dash by Artose Pinner moved the ball to the LSU 13, the Tigers called time out with 0:22 left. Lorenzen plowed ahead for one yard, and a first down at the 12-yard line.

The clock stopped momentarily. The chains moved. And Kentucky made a strategic error.

"We had told Jared when he came to the sideline (with 0:22 left), if he makes the first down, we were not going to call a timeout," said Morriss. "When he went into the huddle, he told the team, but apparently they didn't get the message."

With 0:15 left, someone on the UK offense called the 'Cats final timeout.

Morriss was then forced to send in kicker Taylor Begley on first down for a 29-yard field goal attempt with fifteen seconds left instead of four or five seconds on the clock.

As the freshman Begley lined up for the field goal attempt, head coach Nick Saban tried to call LSU's final timeout. But his players didn't see him. UK snapped the ball and Begley's kick snuck inside the right upright with 0:11 left. The Wildcats led 30-27.

Eleven seconds. Enough time to sing a few lyrics of *My Old Kentucky Home*, "By'n by hard times comes a-knocking at the door. Then my old Kentucky home, good night!"

Surely not enough time to stage a miracle in the Bluegrass state. Well, hold that Tiger.

Wide receiver and kick returner Devery Henderson took the kickoff for LSU and quickly ran out of bounds at the 13-yard line. A delay of game penalty then moved the Tigers back to the LSU 8-yard line.

Nine seconds left and 92 yards away.

Randall tossed a short pass to Michael Clayton over the middle. Clayton immediately

363

hit the ground at the 25-yard line and called LSU's final timeout, which wouldn't have been available had Saban's players seen their coach motioning on the sideline moments earlier.

Meanwhile, Lorenzen and two teammates dumped the team cooler of Gatorade on top of Morriss. The 'Cats celebrated on the sideline.

You could here them singing from the downtown bars of Lexington. "Weep no more, my lady, Oh weep no more today! We will sing one song for the old Kentucky home. For the old Kentucky home far away."

But the clock still read 0:02. And there was still some weeping ahead.

THE PLAY
CD 2-Track 31—_Jim Hawthorne,_
LSU Radio Network

During the timeout, while thousands of Kentucky fans primed to rush the field, Saban talked to Randall, an inexperienced quarterback who was thrust into the starter's role after QB Matt Mauck tore ligaments in his foot against Florida four weeks prior.

Dash-right-93 Berlin was the play. "Just throw it as far as you can," were Saban's orders to Randall.

Kentucky rushed three, and dropped eight. Randall rolled to the right with plenty of time to plant his feet firmly at the 17-yard line. As he launched the final pass, the Kentucky student body poured onto the field a few yards behind him. Arms raised, they stormed the goalpost while Randall watched the ball soar over the bluegrass.

The play was designed to have the LSU receivers tip it backward, hoping for a deflection, a catch, and a miracle finish. "Basically, it never worked in practice," remarked Randall. "Our (defensive) guys would always knock it down."

UK's defensive guys looked ready to do the same.

Randall's launch of almost 60 yards, went over the head of the leaping Clayton, into a herd of UK defenders. Wildcat free safety Quentus Cumby tipped it at the 25-yard line. It went over linebacker Morris Lane. Then cornerback Earven Flowers tipped it again at the 21-yard line. But the ball kept going.

In the meantime Devery Henderson was still running full throttle. He zipped into the play at the UK 18-yard line, got his hand on the deflected pass, bobbled it twice, then reeled it in at the 16-yard line.

Cornerbacks Derek Tatum and Leonard Burress were along side of Henderson when he gained control of the ball. But Henderson caught the ball in a dead sprint toward the end zone, splitting the two defenders. Burress and Tatum both lunged after Henderson. No chance.

"When I dove for the tackle and missed, I had a bad feeling," Burress said.

Henderson danced across the goal line right past a delirious UK fan dancing onto the field in celebration. He was at the wrong party. He wasn't alone. Fireworks celebrating the UK "victory" exploded in the air.

As the entire LSU team piled on Henderson in one end zone, the Kentucky students were climbing the goalpost in the other end zone.

For UK, it was painful to watch. Lorenzen and Morris stood side-by-side as the clock hit 0:00, raised their arms in celebration then gnashed their teeth in disbelief as Henderson made the unthinkable catch.

"It was hurtful. It really hurt my heart. It was the most hurtful play in my career," said UK captain Ronnie Riley.

"You may line up and throw that thing a thousand more times and not complete it," noted Morriss.

Lorenzen gave slightly better odds. "If you threw the ball a thousand times, you might complete it once," he said.

"It was just a freak, unbelievable thing," said a stunned LSU offensive coordinator Jimbo Fisher.

An unbelievable thing dubbed "The Bluegrass Miracle", forever a fixture in LSU football lore.

THE AFTERMATH

Three weeks later, the football gods (or odds) caught up with the Tigers.

Then 17th-ranked LSU took on Arkansas in the last regular season game with the SEC West title and a trip to the SEC Championship game on the line. Turn the page to see what transpired.

Kentucky bounced back the following week to beat Vanderbilt 41-21 before losing to Tennessee 24-0 and ending their season at 7-5. After just two years as head coach, Guy Morriss, a Texas native who played at TCU, resigned ten days later to become the head coach at Baylor.

As a four-year starter at UK, Jared Lorenzen set school records for total yards (10,637), passing yardage (10,354), completions (862) and touchdowns passes (78). He holds six NCAA records (set as a freshman), four SEC records and eleven school records.

Lorenzen signed as a free agent with the New York Giants after the 2004 NFL draft.

LSU	0	14	7	12	- 33
Kentucky	7	0	7	16	- 30

UK	Boone 43 pass from Lorenzen (Begley kick)
LSU	Henderson 70 pass from Randall (Corbello kick)
LSU	Henderson 30 pass from Randall (Corbello kick)
LSU	Addai 63 run (Corbello kick)
UK	Harp 3 pass from Lorenzen (Begley kick)
LSU	FG Corbello 49
UK	Boone 25 pass from Lorenzen (Pakulak pass failed)
LSU	FG Corbello 19
UK	Boone 44 pass from Lorenzen (Begley kick)
UK	FG Begley 29
LSU	Henderson 75 pass from Randall

Attendance 66,262

LSU vs. Arkansas

"I don't know that I ever yelled so loud in my whole life."
—Arkansas Athletic Director Frank Broyles

THE BACKGROUND

Arkansas' Matt Jones was no stranger to heart stoppers. LSU's Marcus Randall knew a thing or two about Hail Marys.

In 2001, as a freshman, Jones was the trigger man behind Arkansas' NCAA record setting 58-56 seven overtime victory at Mississippi. In a game of whatever you can do, I can do better with Ole Miss QB Eli Manning, Jones completed the decisive two-point conversion to Decori Birmingham in the seventh OT. He then watched as Razorbacks linebacker Jermaine Petty stopped Ole Miss tight end Doug Zeigler at the 2-yard line on the Rebels two-point attempt to end the longest Division I-A game ever.

The 6'6" Jones did most of the damage with his legs, rushing 18 times for 110 yards after being inserted into the lineup in the fourth quarter by coach Houston Nutt. He ran for two OT scores and threw for two more two-point conversions in the extra periods, which in the end seemed more like boxing rounds than overtimes.

The following season in Knoxville, Jones rallied Arkansas from a 14-point fourth quarter deficit with a 92-yard TD pass to Richard Smith to tie Tennessee 17-17, and send the game into overtime, and then another overtime, and another, and so on, and so on.

Six overtimes later Tennessee pulled out the 41-38 win.

So Jones, only a sophomore, had played in the longest and second longest games in NCAA Division I-A history. He had 13 overtime periods under his belt. "He has ice in his veins," said Nutt.

Marcus Randall had pixie dust in his arm.

Three weeks prior to the Arkansas game, on the last play of the game at Kentucky, LSU's sophomore QB threw a wondrous 75-yard, tip here, tip there, right into the arms of my receiver, Hail Mary touchdown pass to Devery Henderson that magically gave LSU a 33-30 victory.

LSU (8-3) was ranked 18th. Arkansas (8-3) was unranked, but riding a five-game winning streak. To the winner went the SEC West title and a spot in the SEC Championship game against No. 4 Georgia.

The Tigers appeared in control. A 48-yard pass from Randall to Michael Clayton set up Randall's 5-yard TD run with 5:34 left in the third quarter and LSU led 17-7.

But with 6:33 remaining in the game, on a second-and-19 play, Arkansas RB Fred Talley broke free on a draw play. Fifty-six yards later he was in the end zone and Arkansas was back in the game, trailing 17-14.

Still LSU looked to have the game in hand as they marched on a 13-play drive, converting three third downs, eating up most of the remaining clock and all of Arkansas' timeouts. The drive stalled however at the Arkansas 12-yard line and LSU coach Nick Saban chose to settle for a John Corbello 29-yard field goal, seemingly putting the game on ice at 20-14 with just 0:40 on the clock.

Decori Birmingham holds on to Matt Jones' 31-yard game winning pass. Photo courtesy of Arkansas Sports Information

But Corbello wasn't ready to celebrate yet. "After the Kentucky game, I know it's never over until the clock hits zero, zero, zero," said the LSU kicker.

However, things looked pretty good for the Tigers. Jones couldn't have been colder. He had only two completions in thirteen attempts for a lowly 46 yards. It was Jones' worst passing day as Hogs' QB, against an LSU defense that was the nation's second best against the pass.

That didn't bode well for the Razorbacks after they returned the kickoff to their 19-yard line with just 0:34 left on the clock.

Arkansas needed 81 yards. They had no timeouts. But they did have Matt Jones, veteran of thirteen do-or-die sessions.

On first down, LSU rushed three linemen. Jones dropped back, looked up, and to his surprise, saw wide receiver Richard Smith streaking by defensive back Corey Webster down the right side of the field.

"I couldn't believe Richard Smith got behind that guy," Jones said. "That play wasn't even designed to go to Richard. They just let him get behind, and I threw it as far as I could."

Cornerback Randall Gay tried to get over and help. He was too late. Smith caught a stunning 50-yard pass down to the LSU 31-yard line.

"It was just three guys running as fast as they can down the field on the 50-yarder, and we're playing three-deep zone, 3-5-3," said Saban.

"We were in some kind of zone, and I was settling on the second receiver, and I maybe shouldn't have done that," noted Webster, who made a key play earlier in the second quarter, intercepting a Jones pass in the end zone. "The outside one got a little bit over, and he made a good catch."

Quickly the Razorbacks ran downfield. Jones tried a pass to Carlos Ousley that fell incomplete. 17 seconds remained.

THE PLAY

For Jones, this must have felt like overtime. Like the thirteen times before that

367

he had first down at the 25 in a must score situation.

This was second down at the 31. The goal was still the same.

With three receivers to the left and one to the right, Jones lined up in the shotgun and took the snap. Defensive end Marquis Hill rushed Jones from his left, forcing him to roll right.

The Arkansas QB spotted sophomore flanker Decori Birmingham sprinting down to the right corner of the end zone on a post route.

"There may have been ten guys covering me, I don't know," said Birmingham.

Hardly.

Like Smith two plays earlier, Birmingham had mysteriously gotten behind the normally tough LSU pass coverage. Jones threw for the corner. Again, Randall Gay was LSU's last chance. With his back to the ball, Gay lunged for Birmingham. The clock read 0:09.

Birmingham remained focused. "I just had one thing in my eyes and that was making the catch. All I saw was the white circle coming to me."

Falling down in the back corner of the end zone, with the LSU cornerback in his face, Birmingham squeezed the ball as Gay desperately tried to knock it away. Birmingham prevailed. Touchdown Arkansas.

All day long, Jones' accuracy had been awful at best. But not this time. "To throw over the linebackers' heads with that much trajectory, perfect, and then to land it in the back of the end zone to DeCori, that's awesome," said Nutt.

After an excessive celebration penalty, too many Hogs goin' wild, kicker David Carlton booted the 35-yard extra point through the uprights.

Twenty-five seconds. 81 yards. Somehow, some way, Arkansas had the 21-20 lead.

LSU downed the ensuing kickoff at their own 4-yard line, giving the Tigers one last play. Could the Tigers pull off another Hail Mary pass?

No.

Devery Henderson, recipient of the miracle pass at Kentucky, was injured six days prior to the Arkansas contest, and watched as Brandon Holmes sacked Randall, setting off a fumble, a brief game of hot potato, then finally the end to the play and the game at the LSU 7-yard line.

There would be no 75-yard Hail Mary pass this week for the Tigers. The flipside of the Bluegrass Miracle wasn't very pleasant to stomach.

"It happened good for us, then it turned around and happened bad for us," lamented cornerback Corey Webster.

"It's a once-in-a-lifetime thing when you lose a game like this." said LSU offensive tackle Rodney Reed, who had already experienced the once-in-a-lifetime thing from the winning sideline.

"All I can think about is the agony," he added.

LSU safety Jack Hunt was stunned. "I don't think I've ever lost a game anything like this," he said.

Where did the Miracle on Markham Street rank among great finishes in Arkansas football history? "I think it will go down as one of the greatest, if not the greatest of all-time," said athletic director and former coach Frank Broyles. "A finish like that is so rare, I can't remember one like it."

LSU can.

THE AFTERMATH

The win over the Tigers was the pinnacle of the 2002 season for the Hogs. The following week they were manhandled by Georgia 30-3 in the SEC Championship game. Arkansas finished the 2002 campaign at 9-5 after a 29-14 loss to Minnesota in the Music City Bowl.

LSU's 8-5 season ended in the Cotton Bowl with a 35-20 loss to Texas. The following year, in 2003, Matt Mauck regained the starting QB role and led LSU (13-1) to a National Championship. The Tigers were crowned the BCS National Champions with a 21-14 victory over Oklahoma in the Sugar Bowl.

Both Matt Jones and Marcus Randall latched onto NFL teams in 2005, but not as quarterbacks. Jones was a first round NFL draft choice of the Jacksonville Jaguars in

2005, where he was switched from quarterback to wide receiver, and caught 36 receptions for 432 yards and 5 TDS during his rookie season.

Marcus Randall was picked up as a free agent by the Tennessee Titans and switched to safety. He played in three games during the 2005 season.

Randall Gay signed with the Patriots as a free agent in 2004, and by the end of the season, as a rookie, was the starting left cornerback for New England in Super Bowl XXXIX. He had a team high 11 solo tackles in the Patriots' 24-21 championship win over the Philadelphia Eagles.

LSU	7	3	7	3	– 20
Arkansas	0	0	7	14	– 21

LSU	Green 67 pass from Randall (Corbello kick)
LSU	FG Corbello 49
ARK	Pierce 1 run (Carlton kick)
LSU	Randall 5 run (Corbello kick)
ARK	Talley 56 run (Carlton kick)
LSU	FG Corbello 29
ARK	Birmingham 31 pass from Jones (Carlton kick)

Attendance 55,553

Ohio State vs. Miami

"I fell to my knees . . . and then I heard the announcer, 'Wait a minute. There is a flag on the field.' "—*Lydell Ross, OSU*

THE BACKGROUND

Miami was unbeaten. Ohio State was unbeaten. Larry Coker was unbeaten.

The top-ranked Hurricanes (12-0) were riding a 34-game winning streak that included the 2001 National Championship. Their head coach, Larry Coker, a longtime assistant at Miami, was 22-0 in his second year at the helm of the Hurricanes.

Second-ranked Ohio State was 13-0 with it's own 18-game win streak, although head coach Jim Tressel wasn't undefeated. However, he did have four Division I-AA National Championship rings as head coach of Youngstown State in the 1990s.

In fact, Tressel had his Penguins in the I-AA title game six of nine years from 1991-99.

Now he had his defensive minded Buckeyes in the I-A National Championship game as they took the field at the Fiesta Bowl, prohibitive 11 ½ point underdogs to the talent rich Hurricanes.

Does the setup to the championship tilt sound familiar? Then perhaps you watched the 1987 Fiesta Bowl between Miami and Penn State.

If Ohio State QB Craig Krenzel wasn't the new school version of Penn State QB John Shaffer, or Buckeye linebacker Matt Wilhelm the reincarnation of Lions' LB Pete Giftopoulis, then Joe Paterno doesn't wear black shoes and white socks.

Don't be surprised if someday the 2003 Fiesta Bowl is actually discovered to be a scripted Hollywood sequel to the 1987 game played in the same Sun Devil Stadium, sixteen years and one day later. It certainly was a worthy re-make.

In the 2003 version, Ohio State held a 14-7 third quarter lead, and had the ball at the Miami 6-yard line when a clever plot twist was written into the drama.

Krenzel's pass into the end zone was intercepted by Miami safety Sean Taylor, who looked to be sprinting 100 plus yards with a convoy of 'Canes and a game-tying touchdown. But like a police officer chasing a burglar, OSU freshman running back phenom Maurice Clarett flashed onto the scene, and with one motion, tackled Taylor and ripped the ball away from him at the Miami 28-yard line.

Reversal of fortune. The Buckeyes had possession again. Although Ohio State couldn't move the ball from there, that six-point save by Clarett turned into a 44-yard Mike Nugent field goal and a 17-7 Ohio State lead.

Those three points separated the two teams as the fourth quarter unfolded. Sophomore tailback Willis McGahee's 9-yard TD run brought the 'Canes to within 17-14. Then with just over eleven minutes to play in regulation, OSU cornerback Will Allen brought McGahee's college career to an end.

On a third-and-ten screen pass, Allen stopped a potential big gainer for Miami when he burst through and cleanly hit McGahee's left knee. The knee buckled and McGahee (who broke the school's single season rushing record with 1,753 yards in 2002) was through.

The tackle forced Miami to try a 54-yard field goal attempt by Todd Sievers. The kick was wide right. But Sievers would later get one more try to tie the game.

With just over two minutes to play, Miami's Roscoe Parrish atoned for a fumble in the previous possession and returned an Andy Groom punt 50 yards to the OSU 26-yard line. Trailing 17-14, the 'Canes could only manage three more yards and the clock ran down to 0:03.

Sievers came on to try and tie the game with a 40-yard field goal attempt. Ohio State iced him with two timeouts.

Finally, Sievers kicked it. Middle linebacker Matt Wilhelm jumped and got a piece of the ball. A very small piece.

"The ball hit my thumb," Wilhelm said. "How far is it from my thumb to (the rest of) my hand? If it hits solid on my hand, the game's over."

But the ball kept traveling. And the game kept going.

Sievers' 40-yard field goal was just good, sneaking inside the right upright with no time on the clock, and the National Championship game was headed to overtime.

Miami scored first with a 7-yard TD pass from QB Ken Dorsey to tight end Kellen Winslow. Seemingly, the Hurricanes had weathered the storm, kicking the tying field goal to end regulation, going ahead in overtime, then stuffing Ohio State's offense on their first three downs in OT.

The Buckeyes were staring at fourth-and-14 from the 29-yard line. The Hurricanes were staring at a second consecutive National Championship.

Krenzel took the snap from the shotgun, and calmly stepped up in the pocket. Wide receiver Michael Jenkins, played tightly by defensive back Glenn Sharpe, ran straight downfield, then got just enough separation from his defender as he pulled up past the first line marker. Sharpe hit the brakes, then slipped on the turf, leaving Jenkins all alone

on the right sideline. Krenzel delivered a strike. Jenkins hauled it in and was bumped out of bounds at the 12-yard line. It was only the sixth completion of the game for Ohio State. But more importantly, the Buckeyes were still alive.

Now on first down, Krenzel threw incomplete to Jenkins, blanketed by Miami's Taylor who already had two interceptions on the night. Then Krenzel scrambled ahead for seven yards before being smashed by both Jonathan Vilma and Taylor. On third-and-three Krenzel threw incomplete for tight end Ben Hartsock. There was Taylor again to break it up.

Fourth-and-three. Once again, the Buckeyes faced defeat. After a timeout, Krenzel took the snap from the shotgun, dropped back three steps, then fired to Chris Gamble on the right side, three yards into the end zone.

Gamble had one-on-one coverage from Sharpe. No one else was on that side of the field. It was an island with two other inhabitants, linesman Don Kapral and field judge Terry Porter. Kapral stood on the goal line staring directly at the play. Porter was in the back of the end zone, staring directly at the play.

Gamble fought for position, turned his back to Sharpe, leaped, tried to cradle the ball into his right shoulder, but missed. The ball bounced off his right wrist, then his chest, then off the painted Fiesta Bowl turf.

Distraught, the Buckeye wide receiver looked around for help.

Kapral waved incomplete, but his head looked toward Porter as if to say, "What do you think?" Three seconds later, Porter gave his answer.

As Taylor yanked his helmet off and tossed it high into the desert night, Porter quickly checked his short-term memory.

"I replayed it in my mind," he said. "I wanted to make double-sure that it was the right call."

Porter then sent his yellow flag airborne. It probably hit the ground about the same time as Taylor's helmet. Or about the time Krenzel sat up off the turf and removed his helmet in disgust.

371

The state troopers escorting Larry Coker across the field for the post-game handshake, turned the coach back around. The game was not over.

Pass interference was the call. The ball was placed at the two-yard line.

"Everybody thought it was over, me especially," Sharpe said. "I thought I had made a good play and helped my team win the game."

He just stood on the sidelines shaking his head in disbelief. Taylor tried to piece together his broken helmet which came apart in the premature celebration.

It took three more plays, but Krenzel finally pushed the ball into the end zone on a keeper to tie the game at 24-24 and send the title game to a second OT.

As the fans caught their breath, Ohio State took the ball in the next extra period and methodically moved the ball with Lydell Ross getting nine yards around the right side. Then Krenzel forged ahead for a five-yard run. The Buckeye QB hit Jenkins for six more yards. Finally, Clarett sliced through the line and into the end zone from five yards out. Ohio State had the lead 31-24.

Miami took the ball. Then took a huge hit on second down.

OSU's Wilhelm blitzed untouched, straight up the middle, and flattened Dorsey just after he released a pass intended for Winslow. Dorsey didn't get up. Eventually, he was helped to the sideline.

The 'Canes faced third-and-eleven. And now, without their star quarterback.

Derrick Crudup tossed a couple of warmup pitches along the sideline as Dorsey was being helped off the field. Then the backup QB calmly connected with fullback Quadtrine Hill for eight yards, out-of-bounds at the 18-yard line.

Now it was the Hurricanes who were down to their final play. Fourth-and-three. And back came Dorsey onto the field.

After both teams called timeout to strategize, Dorsey took a quick snap and a quick drop, then laced a short strike to Winslow who got the first down. After a five-yard facemask penalty, the ball was placed at the six-yard line.

Dorsey again took a quick three step drop. Then, in a mirror image of the controversial play from the first overtime, 'Canes WR Andre Johnson tried to free himself from (of all people) OSU's Chris Gamble, who also played defensive back.

Gamble draped himself on Johnson. Dorsey's pass sailed high. But a flag fell immediately thereafter. Pass interference on Ohio State.

Needing a touchdown, Miami had the ball first-and-goal at the two-yard line.

Backup runningback Jarrett Payton was stopped up the middle at the one-yard line. Then Dorsey faked to Payton, dropped to pass and spotted a wide open Eric Winston at the goal line. But Dorsey's pass sailed wide of the tight end, who would have taken it into the end zone with the potential tying score.

Now it was third-and-goal. With Winston now sliding in motion to the middle as a lead blocker, Dorsey handed off to Hill. But Wilhelm, OSU's stout middle linebacker, stuffed the Miami fullback just outside the one.

Ohio State's defensive stand needed just one more stop. Miami's offense needed just one more yard.

THE PLAY

CD 2-Track 32—*Paul Keels, Jim Lachey,* **The Ohio State Radio Network**

"Tight Will Tulsa". The defensive call for the Buckeyes.

Outside linebacker Cie Grant lined up on the strong side of the field. Dorsey had a single back, Payton behind him. What he didn't have was a tight end on the side of the line where Grant stood ready to attack.

When Dorsey snapped the ball, Grant blitzed. The Hurricanes were outnumbered on the right side of the offensive line. Four Buckeye rushers against three Miami blockers.

That left Grant unattended and unimpeded, flying straight at Dorsey who was in the process of a five step drop. Meanwhile, Payton vacated the backfield, not picking up the linebacker, but instead running out in the flat for an outlet pass.

"I got probably the best jump off the snap I've ever had," said Grant.

He had a great jump and a free shot at the quarterback. No one touched him. Dorsey faced an oncoming train head on. He had no chance.

"When Dorsey saw me at the last second, I saw his eyes light up," said Grant. "And once I grabbed him, it was slow motion after that."

Grant caught Dorsey by his jersey and flung him around. The Miami QB desperately tossed a prayer somewhere, anywhere. Nothing but Buckeyes surrounded the ball over the middle. It fell incomplete and the party in Tempe (and Columbus) began.

Fireworks exploded as confetti cascaded down endlessly from the Arizona sky. Ohio State had won 31-24, capturing the school's fifth national title, and first since 1968.

For Miami, there were no party favors. It was the school's first loss in nearly two-and-a-half years. "It hurts. Losing hurts," said Dorsey.

THE AFTERMATH

How talented were the teams that night? Ten Miami players from the game were first round draft picks in the 2003 and 2004 NFL Drafts. That included Willis McGahee who despite still recovering from the devastating knee injury, was chosen by the Buffalo Bills in the first round of the 2003 draft.

A year later, Ohio State had a record fourteen players chosen in the 2004 NFL Draft. From 2003-2005, a total of 44 players from the 2003 Fiesta Bowl game (22 from each school) were eventually drafted into the NFL.

One of them was Maurice Clarett. The leading rusher on OSU's national championship team, Clarett was suspended for the entire 2003 season for filing a false police report which claimed he had $10,000 worth of valuables stolen from him.

He then fought the courts and lost a battle to gain exemption from the NFL's rule prohibiting players from entering the draft who haven't been out of high school for at least three years.

Finally in 2005, Clarett became a third round pick of the Denver Broncos. He sat on the sidelines for three preseason games, then was released. A few months later, Clarett was arrested and indicted on two counts of aggravated robbery in connection with an incident outside a Columbus nightclub.

The last time Maurice Clarett touched a football in a game was his winning TD run in the second overtime of the 2003 Fiesta Bowl. He hasn't played a down of football since.

Ohio State	0	14	3	0	14	- 31
Miami	7	0	7	3	7	- 24

MIAMI   Parrish 25 pass from Dorsey (Sievers kick)
OSU   Krenzel 1 run (Nugent kick)
OSU   Clarett 7 run (Nugent kick)
OSU   FG Nugent 44
MIAMI   McGahee 9 run (Sievers kick)
MIAMI   FG Sievers 40
MIAMI   Winslow 7 pass from Dorsey (Sievers kick)
OSU   Krenzel 1 run (Nugent kick)
OSU   Clarett 5 run (Nugent kick)

Attendance 77,502

Columbia vs. Princeton

"That was very Doug Flutie-esque, wasn't it?"
—Bob Shoop

THE BACKGROUND

The Columbia Lions have had a few streaks in their history that they'd just as soon bury in the fine print of the media guide.

From 1983-88, Columbia compiled a 44-game losing streak. At the time, the longest streak in major college football history. (Prairie View later dwarfed that mark by losing 80 in a row from 1989-98.)

On October 8, 1988, the losing Lions finally broke through on the winning end with a 16-13 victory over Princeton. The game ended with Princeton's Chris Lutz kicking a 48-yard field goal that had the mouths of Columbia fans agape as it soared through the air until it eventually fell short, launching a goal post crumbling, streak-purging celebration by a couple hundred loyal Lions supporters.

"This is what you dread," said Princeton coach Steve Tosches who took the honor of being the first coach to lose to Columbia in half a decade. "Life can be very cruel."

Coincidentally, it was Tosches' Tigers that just weeks previously had pulled off a miracle of miracles in a victory over Holy Cross (see game 47).

The Lions' win over Princeton took place at Columbia's Lawrence A. Wien Stadium. But it had been since 1945 that Columbia last won at Princeton Stadium, a road losing streak of 24 games.

The week before the Lions traveled to Princeton in 2003, new head coach Bob Shoop got his first win at Columbia when the Lions beat Bucknell 19-16. Travis Chmelka caught a 5-yard touchdown pass from Jeff Otis with 22 seconds left in the game for the Columbia victory.

Picked to finish last in the league by the media, Columbia entered the Ivy League portion of their 2003 schedule at 1-1 overall, while Princeton struggled to an 0-2 mark to start the season with losses to Lehigh and Lafayette.

However, against the Lions, the Tigers roared to a 20-0 first quarter lead. Princeton quickly rolled up three touchdowns before Columbia could muster one first down.

Time to start the bus for the trip back to New York, right?

Not yet.

Columbia crept closer on a pair of Nick Rudd field goals, to make it 20-6. Then a 57-yard punt return by Chmelka set up a short 2-yard TD run by Ayo Oluwole. Suddenly it was 20-13.

Princeton helped out by missing a 37-yard field goal attempt to end the first half, and failing on a fourth-and-one from the Columbia 22 in their first possession of the third quarter.

Columbia capitalized.

Rudd knocked through his third field goal of the night at 3:34 of the third quarter. Then with 12:37 to play in the fourth quarter, Rudd hit a 20-yard chip shot when the Lions' 14-play, 75-yard drive stalled at the Princeton 3-yard line.

Wade Fletcher snatches Jeff Otis' Hail Mary heave away from a crowd of Princeton defenders. Photo courtesy of W. L. Bill Allen, Jr. - NJ Sport/Action

Princeton's lead had shrunk to 20-19. Three plays later it was in danger of evaporating completely.

The Tigers faced third-and-ten from their own 32-yard line. Junior QB Matt Verbit was sacked by Columbia's Keenan Shaw, the ball came loose, and Chris Sullivan recovered at the 28. Columbia had the ball and a golden opportunity to take the lead.

Sure enough, six plays later from the one-yard line, Jeff Otis improvised on a broken play, and scrambled into the end zone. After a two-point conversion, Columbia had scored 27 unanswered points and taken a 27-20 lead with 8:50 on the clock.

With their offense dormant since the end of the first quarter, the Tigers needed some bite. They got it from junior running back Jon Veach. He snared a 10-yard completion from Verbit. He ran for eleven more. Then a four-yard plunge. Then four more. He made another 11-yard catch.

Veach touched the ball nine times on a 16-play, 66-yard drive which stalled at the Columbia one-yard line with time running out.

Fourth-and-goal. Princeton trailing 27-20.

Give the ball to....not Veach, but Brandon Benson. The Tigers' one-two punch out of the backfield each had 100 yards for the game. However, Benson hadn't touched the ball since the first drive of the second half. But with the game in the balance, Benson got the call, was hit before the goal line, but used a second effort to break into the end zone for the score from one yard out.

With just 26 seconds on the clock, Elliot Bishop's PAT tied the game at 27-27.

After the kickoff, the Lions started from their own 33 with only 20 seconds remaining in regulation. Almost certainly, the game was headed for overtime.

But instead of downing the ball and letting the clock expire, Columbia's coach Shoop had his QB start throwing. A dangerous ploy, considering Otis had already been intercepted once earlier in the game, by Sam Snyder at the Princeton goal line.

Otis' first attempt fell incomplete. He tried again. This time he connected. An 18-yard strike to Pete Chromiak moved the ball to the Princeton 49.

First down. Timeout Columbia. Five seconds remained.

THE PLAY

CD 2-Track 33—*Phil Wallace, Todd Keryc,* **WKCR Radio**

Essentially, the Lions had two plays in their cupboard from which to choose. But with the ball just inside Princeton territory, the choice was clear.

Trips Right 840 Mary. Translation: the Hail Mary pass.

"The other play we had was the hook and ladder," noted Otis. "But that was only used from the -1 to the -49. From the 50 to the +30, we used Mary as the last play."

The strategy was to run Wade Fletcher, the tallest Lion receiver, to the middle of the end zone with one teammate in front and one behind looking for a tipped ball.

"We usually practiced it every Friday," said Otis. "The guys would just run down, Wade being in the middle with two guys flanking him. The innermost guy was supposed to be about two yards deep (in the end zone). Wade would go about six or seven yards deep and then the outside guy would go to the end line in case of a tip. The play is designed to go to Wade since he's 6'7"."

Otis lined up in the shotgun. Princeton countered with seven defensive backs, including 6'5" wide receiver, B.J. Szymanski. The Tiger WR had already snatched a 71-yard TD pass of his own in the first quarter. This time he tried to prevent one.

With his three receivers wide right, Otis took the snap from the left hash, then rolled right as the final horn sounded inside Princeton Stadium at 9:59 pm. For the Cinderella Lions it turned out to be one minute before midnight.

The Columbia QB switched gears and rolled back to the left, buying time so his receivers could get to the end zone, but at the same time forcing a longer throw. Avoiding the three man rush, Otis got a crucial block from running back Derek Smith, giving him another split second to heave the pass roughly 65 yards through the New Jersey air.

Five Princeton defenders surrounded Fletcher in the end zone. But none could prevent the tall tight end from soaring high above the crowd. Even Princeton's 6'5" Szymanski got boxed out by Fletcher who positioned himself in front of the Tiger wide receiver-turned-defensive back.

Not a Tiger touched the ball. It fell directly into Fletcher's hands.

"When the ball was in the air I was pretty much ready to take the interception and get mentally ready for OT," recalled Otis. "And then as I was walking to the sideline everybody started going nuts and started to storm the field. I was in shock when I looked down there and realized Wade had caught it about eight yards deep in the end zone."

Fletcher was just as surprised.

"I don't know where everyone was," he said. "It just seemed like the ball just came to me. It's kind of surreal."

THE AFTERMATH

With the stunning victory, Shoop joined Aldo "Buff" Donelli as the only Columbia coaches to win their Ivy League debut. However, the opening league win wasn't indicative of things to come.

Columbia ended the season at 4-6 overall, 3-4 in the Ivy League. But the following year, the Lions dipped to 1-9. In 2005, after a 2-8 slate, Shoop was shipped out. Fired after three seasons.

The 2003 season was a rough one for coach Roger Hughes and his Princeton Tigers. They ended the season 2-8, not only losing the heartbreaker to Columbia, but also dropping a 43-40 overtime thriller to Harvard and a 27-24 double OT nailbiter to Yale. In the Yale game, the Bulldogs' Alvin Cowan tossed a 22-yard touchdown pass to Chandler Hendley in the left corner of the end zone with no time left to tie the score at 17-17. The touchdown capped a 92-yard drive in the final 1:03 of regulation. Then in the second OT, Princeton's Verbit hit Szymanski on a slant pattern, but

he had the ball stripped and recovered by Yale's Bryant Dieffenbacher to secure the win for the Bulldogs.

Columbia	0	13	3	17	- 33
Princeton	20	0	0	7	- 27

PRIN	Szymanski 71 pass from Verbit (Bishop kick)
PRIN	Benson 2 run (pass failed)
PRIN	Veach 5 run (Bishop kick)
COL	FG Rudd 31
COL	FG Rudd 25
COL	Oluwole 2 run (Rudd kick)
COL	FG Rudd 38 FG
COL	FG Rudd 20
COL	Otis 1 run (Pezley pass from Otis)
PRIN	Benson 1 run (Bishop kick)
COL	Fletcher 49 pass from Otis

Attendance 8,575

Iowa vs. LSU

"I can't believe that just happened."
—*Warren Holloway*

THE BACKGROUND

It's a safe to bet that LSU coach Nick Saban couldn't imagine a final game like this.

The Capital One Bowl capped the 2004 season for 12th-ranked LSU and 11th-ranked Iowa. It also capped the five-year coaching tenure for Saban in Baton Rouge.

On Christmas night, the LSU Tigers arrived in Orlando to begin bowl preparations. What they weren't prepared for was the announcement from their coach that he'd be leaving for the NFL, to take the head job for the Miami Dolphins.

Saban's last hurrah as LSU head coach left a lasting impression...at least in Iowa.

The Hawkeyes built a 24-12 advantage on the strength of two sustained second half drives. As the Iowa offense convincingly moved downfield, the LSU offense was stuck in the second half.

Starting QB Marcus Randall suffered injured ribs in the second quarter and was replaced by redshirt freshman Matt Flynn. After Flynn failed to move the Tigers in the third quarter, Saban turned to another freshman, JaMarcus Russell, with 12:48 left in the fourth quarter.

Eleven plays, 74 yards, and 4:27 later, LSU crept closer as Russell hit Skyler Green with a 22-yard TD strike. Iowa's lead was trimmed to 24-19.

The Tigers defense then stood strong, limiting the Hawkeyes to just one first down on the next drive, and forcing a punt.

Trailing by five, LSU took over at their 31-yard line with 5:06 remaining in the fourth quarter. Again, Russell methodically marched his team downfield, connecting on his first four passes of the drive to get to the Iowa 41. There, the Tigers faced fourth-and-one with 2:16 left.

Saban called timeout, then called Alley Broussard's number. The LSU running back knifed ahead for nine yards and a first down at the Iowa 32.

Russell then found Dwayne Bowe for 18 yards to the Iowa 14. Three plays later, the backup QB connected with Joseph Addai and LSU was at the Iowa 3-yard line with the clock ticking under a minute to play. Russell quickly spiked the ball.

Now, with 0:46 on the clock, Russell the replacement QB, completed the inspired Tiger rally. He fired a 3-yard TD pass to Green in the back of the end zone. LSU led 25-24.

Russell's two-point conversion failed, but his comeback had not. The Tigers looked to send Saban out on top with an inspired fourth quarter performance.

But Iowa still had two timeouts, and they had first team all-Big Ten quarterback Drew Tate.

After the kickoff, the sophomore QB started at the Iowa 29. He found Ed Hinkel for 11 yards to the 40-yard line. Then Tate spotted Warren Holloway for 9 yards to the 49. Quickly the Iowa QB moved to the line of scrimmage. In fact, too quickly.

The clock momentarily stopped to advance the chains. As soon as the ball was spotted and the clock wound, Tate swiftly spiked the pigskin before all his teammates were set.

The clock stopped again at 0:14. A flag flew.

A false start penalty before the snap was called, moving the ball back to the 44. The referee walked off the infraction, then unbeknownst to Tate, started the clock.

Down it went, 11 seconds, 10 seconds. Tate had two timeouts in his pocket, but didn't realize the sand was still running out of the hourglass. As he called for the snap with nine seconds remaining, it was quite apparent. This was the last play of the game.

THE PLAY

CD 2-Track 34—*Gary Dolphin,*
Ed Podolak, **Hawkeye Sports Properties/**
Learfield Communications

The dwindling clock also caught the LSU defense off guard.

"The offense was rushing to the line of scrimmage right as we got the call in from the sideline," said LSU cornerback Corey Webster.

Defensive coordinator Will Muschamp signaled the coverage. The Tigers were to cover man-to-man downfield. But as the defensive secondary matched up, junior safety Ronnie Prude didn't get the message.

"I was just in the wrong place at the wrong time," Prude said. "I never got the coverage call. I didn't know what I was supposed to do. We were all just looking around in a daze."

If only Iowa wasn't flagged for a false start. If only Tate stopped the clock by spiking the ball. If only the clock wasn't running, Prude may have been covering Warren Holloway.

Instead, Prude lined up in the right flat and played short pass coverage, thinking the Hawkeyes would try to get into field goal range.

Think again. Iowa ran four streaks down the field. And the Tigers essentially covered with three defensive backs.

Tate explained the play, "All Up X Glance".

"We just called four verticals and (Clinton) Solomon was supposed to run a skinny post," he said. "They had a safety on him. I was going back to (Scott) Chandler, but the safety playing that side of the field jumped on him."

As Chandler and Solomon were blanketed, Tate noticed the 5-foot-10, 180-pound Holloway. "Warren's guy ran over to the flat," said Tate.

Holloway, a senior, was running the last pass pattern of his Iowa career. Running downfield in the slot unattended.

He had never caught a touchdown pass. This was his last chance.

Tate felt no rush. "That was probably the most time I had to throw all day," he said. "I just threw it up to Warren."

Tate launched a laser that hit Holloway in stride at the 17-yard line. He gathered it in over his right shoulder and shrugged off a last ditch lunge by defensive back Travis Daniels, who turned off his man near the sideline to try and save the day.

"I was scared I overthrew him," said Tate. "But he did an unbelievable job not going down." Holloway found the end zone on the final play of his collegiate career and Iowa found a way to win the 2005 Capitol One Bowl, 30-25.

"We were playing for a field goal," said a happy Iowa coach Kirk Ferentz. "But nobody's complaining about the outcome."

Except perhaps Nick Saban.

THE AFTERMATH

"It's my first touchdown ever, I couldn't top it," Holloway said. "(It's) the best day of my life."

His Iowa teammates, like ice cubes from a hotel vending machine, came pouring down on top of Holloway in the end zone. The celebration was exhilarating and suffocating all at once.

"I was thinking breath slow," he said. "I don't know how many guys were on top of me, but I had to take my time and slow down. Just calm down, take slow deep breaths because it's too good a day to die."

While the Hawkeyes finished the season at 10-2, ranked No. 8, Saban's Tigers ended 9-3, 16th in the country.

"The disappointing thing is that the last fourteen seconds of this game tarnishes what a lot of good football players and seniors on this team have been able to accomplish in their career here," Saban said.

But in truth, the fourteen seconds failed to tarnish what Saban had achieved during his tenure in Baton Rouge. He ended five successful years with the Tigers amassing a 48-16 record, including the 2003 BCS National Championship.

Holloway tried to latch on to an NFL team the following spring, but got no offers. He queried the Canadian Football League, the Arena Football League, then finally got an offer to play for the Ohio Valley Greyhounds of the United Indoor Football Association midway through their 2005 season. In April 2006 he signed with the Sioux City Bandits of the same league.

LSU	0	12	0	13	- 25
Iowa	7	7	3	13	- 30

IOWA	Solomon 57 pass from Tate (Schlicher kick)
LSU	FG Jackson 29
LSU	FG Jackson 47
IOWA	Considine 7 yd blocked punt return (Schlicher kick)
LSU	Broussard 74 run (kick failed)
IOWA	FG Schlicher 19
IOWA	Simmons 4 run (Schlicher kick)
LSU	Green 22 pass from Russell (Jackson kick)
LSU	Green 3 pass from Russell (pass failed)
IOWA	Holloway 56 pass from Tate

Attendance 70,229

Texas Tech vs. ⚈Nebraska

"Moses was in high school the last time these guys lost a homecoming game."—Mike Leach

THE BACKGROUND

70-10.

Very few Nebraska fans don't recognize that score. 114 years of Nebraska Cornhuskers football and never had they been beaten as badly as they were October 9th, 2004.

The perpetrators? The Red Raiders of Texas Tech. "We were just trying to play efficiently," said coach Mike Leach, whose team racked up 28 points in the final twelve minutes after leading 42-10.

A 1983 graduate of BYU, Leach knows a bit about breaking records. Besides breaking Nebraska's record for most points allowed in a game, as offensive coordinator, his past teams own 26 NAIA records (Iowa Wesleyan), seven Division II marks (Valdosta State), and 41 SEC records (Kentucky). In 1999 as Oklahoma's offensive coordinator, the Sooners went from last to first in the Big 12 in passing yards and 107th to ninth nationally.

In 2005, another 70-point outburst versus Nebraska wouldn't be too far from Tech's average Saturday afternoon. However, it would be far from what the suddenly stingy Nebraska "Blackshirt" defense was surrendering.

Leach's offensive juggernaut, averaging 57 points and 449 passing yards per game, was ranked second nationally in total offense (585 yards). Meanwhile coach Bill Callahan's Huskers gave up a measly nine points per game, also second nationally.

The demanding yet uniquely polite Husker Nation showed up in force (an NCAA record 273rd consecutive sellout at Memorial Stadium) for a visit from the Red Raiders. It was homecoming Saturday, a day normally reserved for a Nebraska victory, at least for the past 36 years.

Both teams were 4-0 entering the game. But sure enough, the 15th-ranked Red Raiders picked up right where they left off in 2004, mercilessly marching up and down the field. Quarterback Cody Hodges was a near perfect 14-of-16 through the air for 164 yards, and a touchdown...in the first quarter.

When Joel Filani caught his second TD from Hodges with 9:25 left in the first half, Texas Tech led 21-0, Hodges had three TD tosses and Nebraska fans had recurring nightmares.

Another 70? This time in Lincoln? The thought of a second slaughter at the hands of the lads from Lubbock surely turned a few of the 77,580 Big Red stomachs pink... as in Pepto Bismal.

But this was a different Blackshirt defense from the previous year. And soon it would be different from the one that started the game. After witnessing the leaky performance in the first twenty minutes, Nebraska defensive coordinator Kevin Cosgrove switched his entire alignment into a 3-4 base defense.

The move worked. Tech's next seven possessions netted just 57 yards total. Despite three Husker turnovers that gave the Red Raiders the ball at the NU 11, 20, and 44 in the second half, Texas Tech could only muster two Alex Trlica field goals.

Meanwhile, between the turnovers, Nebraska QB Zac Taylor rallied the Huskers. His four-yard TD pass to Terrence Nunn capped a remarkable comeback for Callahan's offense, in its second year of transformation from option to West Coast attack. With 10:10 to play in the game, Nebraska led 28-27.

A 27-yard FG by Jordan Congdon with 5:10 left put the Huskers up 31-27.

Back onto the field came Leach's suddenly limp offense, with one first down to show for itself in the second half. Somehow, the Red Raiders needed a jumpstart. From the Tech 33, they got it on the first play.

Hodges threw the Tech offense back into high gear with a 31-yard completion to Filani. Suddenly, the Nebraska defense was on its heels. Two more Hodges completions and the Red Raiders were at the Husker 26-yard line.

Then Nebraska linebacker Bo Ruud sacked the Tech QB back at the 35. But Hodges regrouped. He found Jarrett Hicks for 11 yards, then Bristol Olomua for six yards. Then on fourth-and-two, with the game in the balance (for the first time), Hodges hit Filani for six yards and a first down.

Now at the Nebraska 12-yard line, with the clock at 1:20, Hodges' first down pass looked like his last. The errant throw was tipped by linebacker Corey McKeon and picked off at the 5-yard line by senior nose tackle Le Kevin Smith.

There went Smith, all 305 pounds, rumbling with the clincher for the Huskers.

"I saw the interception, and I was hoping he would go down," said coordinator Cosgrove, praying that his large lineman would just fall to the ground with the ball.

Nope. Smith had big eyes and big hopes for his return. Instead it became an infamous Leon Lett moment.

"Defensive linemen get so excited sometimes when they get the ball that they don't always think and make the best decisions," said Cosgrove.

This was a runback of diminishing returns.

Tech offensive guard Bryan Kegans did all he could to bring down the runaway nose tackle. The 286-pound Kegans caught Smith from behind at the 19-yard line, jarred the ball loose, and dropped the jaws of the Husker Nation. Red Raider receiver Danny Amendola fell on the football.

Nebraska literally had victory in its hands, then had it stripped away. The interception turned fumble gave Tech the ball and new life at the Nebraska 18 with 73 seconds left.

Disheartened but not defeated, the Nebraska defense stiffened. A seven-yard pass, a one-yard run and an incomplete pass to Filani forced a fourth-and-two at the NU 10-yard line.

Leading 31-27, The Huskers called time-out with 0:19 left. Hodges went over to talk to his offensive leader.

THE PLAY

CD 2-Track 35—*Brian Jensen,* *John Harris,* **Texas Tech Sports Network**

During the timeout, Leach discussed the options. "We thought they were going to either blitz or drop so we had a play where we felt good about the zone to one side and the blitz to the other. We weren't sure what they were going to do," he said.

Filani went in motion to the right.

"It's a play that we run every day in practice as a two-point conversion play," noted Hodges. "I started (by looking) at (Jarrett) Hicks, but he was covered."

So Hodges scampered left, buying precious seconds. Meanwhile Filani cut left across the middle of the end zone. " I was trying to find a spot to get open," he said.

Seeing Filani maneuvering, the Red Raider QB then tossed the ball to an open space. "There was kind of a patch of grass and I pretty much threw at that patch, and let Joel go get it," said Hodges, who was promptly pasted to the turf by the Nebraska rush.

Facing the clouds, Hodges listened for signs. "I was on my back and heard 'ohhhh' (from the crowd). I figured he caught it and we'd won the ballgame."

Correct.

Touchdown Texas Tech. The Red Raiders

Game 113

took the lead with only 0:12 left. A final desperation play by the Huskers went nowhere as the clock expired and Texas Tech won 34-31.

It was a crushing loss for the Huskers, who had the win in their hands. "Last year's loss was an embarrassment," said linebacker Ruud after the game. "This year's loss was a heartbreaker."

THE AFTERMATH

It was not a good weekend for Smith. Besides the fumbled interception, he was cited for third-degree assault and disturbing the peace after allegedly squeezing the neck of a university parking officer who issued him a ticket for parking illegally the day before the Tech game.

Two months later, Smith was just putting the nightmare behind him after re-living it over and over in his head. "I just stopped playing that play a couple weeks ago," he told reporters as the Huskers prepared to face Michigan in the Alamo Bowl. "That was a big burden."

A wild 32-28 win over the Wolverines helped lift his spirits.

Smith ended his senior season with a career-high five sacks and 37 tackles as part of the Nebraska defense which led the nation in sacks (46). The Huskers finished 8-4 overall, No. 24 in the polls.

The Nebraska finish was just the start of a wild series of heart stoppers for Texas Tech during the 2005 campaign. The final three games of the season saw the Red Raiders lose twice in the final seconds, and win once as time expired.

Rallying from a 17-0 third quarter deficit, Tech tied Oklahoma State at 17-17 in the fourth quarter, only to see the Cowboys' Al Pena score on a 1-yard touchdown run with 23 seconds to play for the OSU 24-17 win.

The next week against Oklahoma, trailing 21-17, Taurean Henderson took a Tech handoff at the Sooners' two-yard line with 0:02 on the clock. He plowed up the middle, and desperately stretched the ball toward the goal line as time expired.

"I started out to score the touchdown, got hit, was laying on top of someone and just stretched out," said Henderson.

Touchdown Texas Tech. But wait. Officials decided to review the play to see if Henderson crossed the goal line before his knee touched the ground. The call was upheld and Tech won 23-21.

Texas Tech finished the season with a 13-10 loss to Alabama in the Cotton Bowl. 'Bama kicker Jamie Christensen kicked an ugly, low, line drive, somehow-it-made-it-through-the-uprights field goal as time expired for the win. The Red Raiders ended the 2005 year 9-3, ranked No. 19 in the USA Today poll.

Texas Tech	7	14	6	7	- 34
Nebraska	0	14	7	10	- 31

TT	Henderson 23 pass from Hodges (Trlica kick)
TT	Filani 14 pass from Hodges (Trlica kick)
TT	Filani 19 pass from Hodges (Trlica kick)
NEB	Glenn 5 run (Congdon kick)
NEB	Glenn 1 run (Congdon kick)
TT	FG Trlica 37
TT	FG Trlica 26
NEB	Nunn 15 pass from Taylor (Congdon kick)
NU	Nunn 4 pass from Taylor (Congdon kick)
NU	FG Congdon 27
TT	Filani 10 pass from Hodges (Trlica kick)

Attendance 77,580

Penn State vs. Michigan 🏈

"I have had a number of wild games in the past few years, but I have never had a wilder game than this one."
—*Lloyd Carr*

THE BACKGROUND

October 15, 2005. It was a great day for great finishes. A scintillating Saturday when college football gave us its own version of March Madness, with mouth dropping endings, one after the other.

In Minneapolis, Wisconsin trailed Minnesota 34-24 with just 3:27 left, when QB John Stocco drove the Badgers 71 yards, hitting Brandon Williams with a 21-yard TD pass. The Badgers defense then forced a punt from deep in Minnesota territory. Wisconsin's Jonathan Casillas blocked Justin Kucek's kick. The ball rolled into the left corner of the end zone where Ben Strickland pounced on it with just 30 seconds remaining, giving Wisconsin an improbable touchdown and a 38-34 victory.

"Just when you think you've seen everything, you haven't," said Badgers coach Barry Alvarez, who had yet to see the end of the Notre Dame-USC game that same day (see game 115).

On the same day, West Virginia rallied from 17 points down in the fourth quarter to beat Louisville 46-44 in three overtimes. UCLA overcame the same 17-point deficit in beating Washington State 44-41 in OT.

Substitute QB Matt Ryan threw two TD scores in the frantic final 2:30 to save Boston College against Wake Forest, giving the Eagles a 35-30 victory. "It was a crazy game," said Wake Forest coach Jim Grobe.

It was a crazy day.

A crazy day that couch potato's dream of. A day of thrilling, screaming, "did-you-see-that?" moments back-to-back-to-back-to-back. A day that could spawn a baby boom of new college football fans all born around July 15, 2006.

Many of them Michigan Wolverine fans.

79-year old Joe Paterno had suffered through a pair of miserable 3-9 and 4-7 seasons the past two years. The clock was ticking as to when the legendary coach would call it quits after a Hall of Fame career. At least on the sports talk shows.

But inside the Penn State program, JoePa wasn't done.

Left off the pre-season radar, Paterno took his 2005 team on a surprising six-game win streak. Atop the Big Ten standings, and fresh from a 17-10 home victory over Ohio State the previous week, eighth-ranked Penn State (6-0) had dreams of a magical season when they traveled to Ann Arbor to tangle with a disappointing Michigan team.

Lloyd Carr's Wolverines were ranked fourth in the AP poll entering the season. After six games, they were in danger of losing their fourth game.

Now 3-3 and unranked, Michigan saw Penn State's visit as their last chance to turn the season around. And it appeared they would do just that.

A Mike Hart two-yard scamper gave the Wolverines a 10-0 lead with 11:10 remaining in the third quarter. But then, a tightly

Game 114

fought defensive battle turned into a wildly swinging affair dotted with huge plays.

Near the end of the third quarter, a 56-yard completion from Penn State QB Michael Robinson to Terrell Golden, combined with a roughing the passer penalty, brought the ball to the Michigan 6-yard line. But Penn State could go no further and settled for a Kevin Kelly 25-yard field goal to make it a 10-3 score.

After forcing a Michigan punt, PSU running back Tony Hunt took the first handoff of the next series at the PSU 37, and burst for 61 yards to the UM 2-yard line. Robinson scored three plays later and suddenly the game was tied 10-10.

The first play after the kickoff, from the UM 28, Michigan QB Chad Henne snuck ahead for seven yards only to have Alan Zemaitis strip the ball and rumble 35 yards into the end zone. After kicker Kelly ran a botched PAT attempt in for a two-point conversion, Penn State led 18-10.

In a stunning three and a half minutes, the Lions had scored 18 points. In two more minutes, the Wolverines would tie it up again.

Steve Breaston returned the ensuing kickoff 39 yards to the UM 45. Soon after, Henne hit Mario Manningham with a 33-yard TD pass. Mike Hart ran for the two-point conversion and the score was 18-18 with 9:32 remaining in the fourth quarter.

Just two minutes later, Breaston again set up the Michigan offense with a 23-yard punt return to the UM 42. Henne moved his team to the PSU 30 where Garrett Rivas kicked a 47-yard field goal with 3:45 left, giving the Wolverines a 21-18 edge.

Then moments later, it appeared Michigan would salt the game away.

Cornerback Leon Hall intercepted a Robinson pass. With 3:14 on the clock, Michigan was at the Penn State 40. However, the Penn State defense held their ground.

When defensive end Matthew Rice and linebacker Paul Posluszny stopped Hart on third down at the PSU 34, Carr sent out his field goal unit. But the Michigan coach then had kicker Rivas pooch a punt instead of risking a long FG attempt or going for it on fourth-and-four.

A weak 15-yard punt went out-of-bounds at the 19-yard line.

So with 2:46 left, quarterback Robinson had one task. March his Lions 81 yards into a storm of 111,249 screaming Michigan fans.

And in thirteen plays, that's what he did.

Aided by a critical pass interference call on Leon Hall on third-and-ten at the UM 15, Robinson then sucked the air out of The Big House with a 3-yard touchdown keeper, scoring with only 53 seconds remaining. Penn State 25, Michigan 21.

Apparently forgetting Breaston's last few kick returns, the Nittany Lions gave him another chance to return a kickoff. Breaston then inflated the home team's hopes with a blistering return, taking the ball at the UM 6 and returning it 41 yards to the UM 47-yard line. For the game, he returned four kickoffs for 128 yards.

Henne quickly found Jason Avant for 17 yards. Then Carl Tabb caught a short 4-yard completion. The Wolverines called timeout with the ball at the PSU 32 and 0:28 on the clock.

Carr lobbied for a few more seconds. "When I asked for the timeout and I looked at the scoreboard, it said 32 seconds," he said. "I was lobbying for four (added), but the ref saw two."

Before the timeout had ended, the officials put two more seconds back on the clock. The Penn State sidelines disagreed. "They said they were putting two seconds back on the clock," commented Paterno. "I said baloney. They walked away."

Five plays later, with 0:06 remaining, on third-and-four from the PSU ten-yard line, Henne found Breaston, but the ball fell incomplete.

Everyone looked at the clock. 0:01 remained. One second for one more play.

THE PLAY

CD 2-Track 36—*Frank Beckmann,* **Host Communications and The Michigan Sports Network**

Michigan used their final timeout. Fourth down at the ten-yard line.

Penn State needed one more stop. Paterno injected himself into the defensive huddle. "The thinking was, hey, everybody suck it up," he said.

Breaston lined up slot right. Manningham was wide right.

"We checked the play for protection and there was no blitz," Henne said. "They had one-on-one coverage on the outside. That was what we wanted."

He took the snap. A quick drop back and Henne noticed his first read, Breaston, had yet to break open. Then he spotted the freshman Manningham cutting inside the senior cornerback Zemaitis.

"We were trying to play [a defense] where half of the field was zoned up and half of the field was man," Penn State safety Chris Harrell said. "There was a little error there with which side was which."

As Manningham slid inside across the goal line, Henne zipped a strike to him. Touchdown Michigan. It was that fast. Final Score: Michigan 27, Penn State 25.

Manningham kept running, across the end zone, back on the field. His joyous teammates tried to tackle him. He kept running.

"I was trying to chase him down, but he's just too fast," said running back Hart. "He was running away from everybody."

Finally, the Wolverines caught up with Manningham at the 25-yard line and the celebration pile began.

THE AFTERMATH

"I have had a number of wild games in the past few years, but I have never had a wilder game than this one," said Carr, on a day of wild games. "There's one second on the clock, millions and millions are watching on TV, 111,000 are watching in the stadium, and you take the ball and throw it perfectly with people who are trying to sack you. I'd say that's a lot of poise," said Carr praising his sophomore QB.

All I am right now is 'P-Oed,' " said a disappointed Paterno after the game, his players made unavailable to the media.

Manningham's catch proved to be the one play that separated Penn State from an undefeated season and perhaps a shot at the National Championship game. However, it may have also been the one play that saved the BCS from explaining why the 11-0 Lions weren't playing for a title for the second time in 11 years. In 1994, Penn State beat Oregon 38-20 in the Rose Bowl, but had to settle for a No. 2 ranking behind undefeated Nebraska, who beat Miami 24-17 in the Orange Bowl.

Penn State finished the 2005 season 11-1 after a mind-boggling 26-23 triple overtime triumph over Bobby Bowden's Florida State squad in the Orange Bowl. After missing a 28-yard field goal at the end of regulation, then a 38-yarder in the first OT, Kevin Kelly hit a 29-yard field goal to win the game at 12:57 a.m., after four hours and 45 minutes.

Exhausted by the marathon, the two winningest coaches in Division I-A history met on the field afterwards. "I told him we're too old for this," Paterno said. "It's almost past my bedtime."

For Michigan, a 7-5 season ended with one of the most bizarre game-ending plays ever.

With two seconds left, trailing 32-28 to Nebraska in the Alamo Bowl, Michigan had the ball on their own 36-yard line. Henne took the snap. A short pass caught by Jason Avant at the 48-yard line set off a flurry of seven laterals and a play that took 43 seconds of real time to complete.

Avant lateraled to Breaston who lateraled to Hart who lateraled back to Avant who threw it across field to Manningham who then ran backwards to the original line of scrimmage before tossing back to Avant again who threw it back across the field (now at the UM 25-yard line) to lineman Mark Bihl, who dropped the ball prompting the Nebraska team to douse coach Bill Callahan with Gatorade as they came celebrating onto the field.

Meanwhile, Mike Hart picked up the ball, shed a tackle, then flipped to tight end Tyler Ecker at the UM 24-yard line. Ecker then streaked downfield as most of the Nebraska players stood around assuming the play had been called dead.

"I'm thinking, 'What's this guy doing

running?'" said Husker defensive end Jay Moore.

Ecker, with speedster Breaston right behind him begging for one last lateral, ran along the right sideline where the only two Husker defenders still playing the game, Zach Bowman and Titus Brothers, finally chased him out of bounds at the Nebraska 13-yard line.

And with a deep breath, the Huskers held on for the 32-28 victory.

With no one on the entire left side of the field, all Ecker had to do during the final thirty yards of his run was to flip the ball back to Breaston who surely would have scored...and the Stanford Band play would have been the second most famous ending to a college football game.

Penn State	0	0	3	22	- 25
Michigan	0	3	7	17	- 27

MICH   FG Rivas 35
MICH   Hart 2 run (Rivas kick)
PSU   FG Kelly 25
PSU   Robinson 4 run (Kelly kick)
PSU   Zemaitis 35 fumble recovery
       (Kelly rush)
MICH   Manningham 33 pass from
       Henne (Hart rush)
MICH   FG Rivas 47
PSU   Robinson 3 run (Kelly kick)
MICH   Manningham 10 pass
       from Henne

Attendance 111,249

USC vs. Notre Dame

"I would imagine this will go down as one of the greatest games ever played."—Matt Leinart

THE BACKGROUND

Omens.

Over 40,000 fans showed up at Notre Dame Stadium the night before USC came to town ...for a pep rally. So did Joe Montana, and Tim Brown, and Chris Zorich, and Daniel "Rudy" Ruettiger.

Jesus appeared at the Grotto on the Notre Dame campus the night before....wearing a Rudy jacket. OK, actually it was actor James Caveziel (who portrayed Jesus in the film "Passion of the Christ"),

USC and Notre Dame. When it comes to college football history, this game had biblical implications. Or at least mythical implications.

While Notre Dame brought the legends and some snazzy new green jerseys, USC brought the horses.

With an offensive juggernaut averaging a mind-boggling 640 yards and nearly 52 points per game, USC stood atop the college football world. A Trojan empire firmly entrenched as the number one team in the land. For 23 consecutive Associated Press polls, to be exact.

National Champions in 2003 and 2004, and marching toward an unprecedented third consecutive title, Pete Carroll's squad could hear the whispers and read the internet blogs declaring the Trojans the "greatest team of all time."

While USC scorched opponents during their 27-game winning streak, Notre Dame, lumbered for a decade in mediocrity with little more to show from the past two seasons other than a brand new coach, Charlie Weis.

But with the former offensive coordinator of the three-time Super Bowl Champion New England Patriots directing the ship, the Irish were suddenly a surprising 4-1, ranked ninth in the country.

Irish fans believed another hallowed Notre Dame "moment" was imminent. Students proudly wore their "We-Is ND" T-shirts to the game. On their way into Notre Dame Stadium, they traipsed past tailgating USC students wearing "I wish I were Matt Leinart" T-shirts.

Frankly, what 21-year old male in America wouldn't want to be Matt Leinart, two-time first team All American quarterback? He led his team to consecutive National Championships in 2003 and 2004, won the Heisman Trophy his junior year, was a magnet of the LA paparazzi, and had a cool final semester finishing his Sociology degree by taking one class, Ballroom Dancing, with his girlfriend.

Most Notre Dame students secretly wished they were Matt Leinart too.

While the Pac-10 conference (and eight other major conferences) adopted the NCAA option of using instant replay to help resolve disputed calls, Notre Dame was an independent and played all non-conference games. In a non-conference game, the visiting team received the option of using instant replay or not.

On the road, the Irish had the choice. At home, their opponents made the decision.

Game 115

Reggie Bush gives Matt Leinart the final push into the Notre Dame end zone. Photo courtesy of Matt Cashore

USC coach Pete Carroll wasn't a fan of instant replay. But he lived with it. "I don't like it," he said. "I never have." Carroll had the opportunity to play the Irish without instant replay, and he chose to do so.

"I have heard of no other schools turning down instant replay other than USC," said Dave Parry, national coordinator of officials for the Collegiate Commissioners Association.

"They gave me a choice and I didn't want it," said Carroll the week before the game. "We had a chance to not have it so now we don't have it. I hope it doesn't come down to one of those replay situations."

Omens.

The weather was perfect. 62 degrees and sunny. The grass was thick and plush and... "It seemed obvious to us, at least to me, that they left the grass long on purpose," said USC tailback Desmond Reed, who injured his knee when his cleat got stuck in the turf on a kickoff return early in the game.

"It was a little long, but that's the way it is around here....I don't cut the grass," quipped Weis. But he did call the offensive plays for the Irish, and his game plan was to slow the vaunted Trojan offense by playing keep away.

The Irish held an astounding twelve minute (21 to 9) advantage in time of possession in the first half, and led 21-14 thanks to a 60-yard punt return for a touchdown by junior Tom Zbikowski.

But while Notre Dame had time on their side, USC had tailback Reggie Bush on theirs.

Simply put, Bush was the best player on the field. Fast, elusive, powerful. Bush stuffed the highlight tapes with a first quarter 36-yard TD sprint where he hurdled an Irish defender without breaking stride. He then tied the game at 21-21 in the third quarter with a 45-yard jaunt. And gave the Trojans a 28-24 lead with his third TD, a 9-yard run with 5:09 remaining in the fourth quarter.

It appeared that USC had overcome the upset omens and taken control. But junior QB Brady Quinn then led Notre Dame on an expedient 87-yard drive, capping it off with a five-yard TD run with 2:04 on the clock. The Irish led 31-28.

Replays showed Quinn's knee was down before the ball crossed the goal line. Oops, replays weren't being used in this game.

Down by three, the Trojans started the final drive at their 25-yard line. Leinart threw incomplete, then was sacked by Trevor Laws. Facing third-and-19, Leinart found Bush over the middle for ten yards.

Fourth-and-nine. 1:32 left.

USC's 27-game streak was teetering on the brink. The crowd of 80,000 was screaming it over the edge. They were louder than loud.

USC called their final timeout. Carroll talked it over with assistants Steve Sarkisan and Lane Kiffin.

"We called time out because if you don't make the first down there, then what good is it to have saved a timeout," said Carroll. "We had a chance to talk to Matt. Lane said to Matt, 'Call it, call the play.' We talked about the play to call. We called it."

"Sark and I are standing there and we were like, whoa, here he goes," said Carroll.

Leinart broke the huddle, stood over center and in the most adverse of environments, called an audible. It wasn't a bold move. It was a steel-eyed cold move.

"He checked out of the play and said he's coming to me," commented split end Dwayne Jarrett who was lined up wide left and playing with blurred vision after hitting the ground while diving for a catch earlier in the half.

"You don't know if everybody is going to hear, or if everybody is going to get it," said Carroll. How anyone heard Leinart's call is amazing. You couldn't hear yourself shout.

Leinart took the snap, a quick drop, then threw a fade route to Jarrett speeding down the sidelines. Cornerback Ambrose Wooden ran stride for stride with Jarrett as Leinart's low liner whizzed by his right arm, and with stealth precision, landed right into the arms of Jarrett.

The perfect pass.

Streaking toward a stunning score, Jarrett raced 61 yards before Wooden's desperate dive caught him at the 13-yard line.

USC was in business. Notre Dame Stadium was in shock.

Three plays later, after a Bush run of five yards, USC had a first-and-goal at the Notre Dame two-yard line. The clock was at 0:20 and running.

Leinart rolled to his left, and looked for Bush in the end zone. Cornerback Mike Richardson had a decision to make, stay with Bush or go after Leinart before he runs into the end zone. If he leaves Bush too early, it's an easy touchdown toss.

Leinart faked. He faked again. Richardson stared him down. Leinart dove high for the pylon. Richardson went for his ankles. Leinart reached the ball out over the goal line when suddenly... Bang! Linebacker Corey Mays stuck his helmet on the ball. Leinart was spun like a helicopter. The ball shot out of his grasp and flew backwards out of bounds.

Did Leinart score? Was he ruled down in bounds? Where did the ball go out of bounds?

The clock kept running.

USC assistant coach Brennan Carroll, (Pete's son) desperately motioned for a timeout. The Trojans had none.

The clock inexplicably drained to 0:00. Notre Dame students poured onto the field. Notre Dame players celebrated. Was this USC-Notre Dame or Colorado-Missouri? It had a surreal "Gore defeats Bush" feel to it.

THE PLAY

CD 2-Track 37—*Pete Arbogast, Paul McDonald,* **1540 "The Ticket" and The Trojan Radio Network**

Players, coaches, students. Everyone was on the field. The Notre Dame side celebrated like the ball had dropped at New Years Eve. But the chaos and the karma favored the champion Trojans.

The fortuitous fumble flew out of bounds, stopping the clock. The officials restored order, reset the clock to 0:07, then placed the ball fractions from the goal line. Meanwhile, replays showed the ball going out of bounds around the two-yard line. Oops, replays weren't being used in this game.

While students scattered off the field like cockroaches when the lights turn on, Carroll had to make a quick decision. "The official came down and told me you have three inches. I was pretty confident we had a shot at that one. I wasn't going to kick a field goal from there."

As USC rushed to the line of scrimmage, Weis, hands on hips, stood at the hash mark, a few yards away. Close enough to be part of the Trojans backfield. Close enough to get an unsportsmanlike conduct penalty never called. He argued with the officials like a car salesman closing the deal.

"Well, let me ask you a question," he said. " I mean, who are you going to review whether or not there's any type of time left on the clock? There's no replay here. It says there's no time left on the clock so there's no time left."

No deal.

Carroll decided to put the game in his quarterback's hands. Spike the ball to stop the clock, or sneak it in.

"On that play, I've got the option to either spike it or run with it," Leinart said. "But when I looked at Reggie, he said, 'You've gotta do it, dude.' "

Faced again with one play to win or lose the game, Leinart went for it.

He took the snap and lunged ahead, only to be met by an Irish wall. Just when it appeared he was stopped, Leinart danced to his left, spun around, and got a firm shove from behind courtesy of his dance partner, Reggie Bush.

Into the end zone went Leinart. Into the history books went a Trojan touchdown never to be forgotten. With three seconds left, USC took the lead. The final seconds ticked away on the ensuing kickoff and USC defeated Notre Dame 34-31.

The play will forever be known as "The Bush Push".

"When Matt hit and spun out, Reggie was hitting the line of scrimmage so he gave him a little shot. That is not something we had taught," remarked Carroll. "There is no question that he helped a little bit."

"Is that illegal?" asked Weis. "Yes, it's illegal. Would I do the same thing? Absolutely. They won the game, they made a play and you could say Reggie pushed him, which he did, but that's a heads-up by Reggie and hopefully any runningback I had would be pushing right along with them."

THE AFTERMATH

Amidst the chaos following the game, Weis took a trip across the Notre Dame Stadium tunnel to the jubilant USC locker room. It became a field trip for his son, Charlie, Jr.

"I said, 'Come on, Charlie, we're walking over to the (USC) locker room,' and he thought I was hallucinating when I said that," said Weis. "I was only in there for about 30 seconds. It wasn't like I wanted to be there. I just felt it was the right thing to do."

Weis congratulated the Trojans then had a talk with his son.

"I went back, and sat down with Charlie and explained to him the difference between how it's easy to be nice when you've won versus how tough it is to be nice when you've lost. I thought it was a good lesson for my son."

What he didn't tell his son was what many across the nation were saying. That this was one of the greatest games ever played.

"You can say whatever you want," said Weis. "It's not going to be one of my greatest games because we lost. It will never be one of my greatest games. I'll take any of those games we won over that greatest game that we lost, 100 out of 100 times."

Bush's eye-popping performance that day launched him to the head of the Heisman Trophy race that he eventually won following the regular season. Leinart finished third in the voting, behind Bush and Texas quarterback Vince Young.

The trio would meet again at the end of the season, in the Rose Bowl.

Game 115

USC	14	0	7	13	- 34
Notre Dame	7	14	0	10	- 31

USC	Bush 36 run (Danelo kick)
ND	Thomas 16 run (Fitzpatrick kick)
USC	White 3 run (Danelo kick)
ND	Samardzija 32 pass from Quinn (Fitzpatrick kick)
ND	Zbikowski 60 punt return (Fitzpatrick kick)
USC	Bush 45 run (Danelo kick)
ND	FG Fitzpatrick 32
USC	Bush 9 run (Danelo kick)
ND	Quinn 5 run (Fitzpatrick kick)
USC	Leinart 1 run (kick failed)

Attendance 80,795

Texas vs.
🏈 USC

"He's off the charts."—Pete Carroll (about Vince Young)

THE BACKGROUND

Vince Young had been here before. The Rose Bowl, that is.

At the end of his sophomore season, trailing Michigan 31-21 in the 2005 Rose Bowl with ten minutes remaining in the fourth quarter, the Texas wunderkind QB stood over center, facing third-and-goal from the ten-yard line. Young took the snap and took the ball, galloping into the end zone, and bringing the Longhorns to within 31-28.

After Michigan's Garrett Rivas kicked a 32-yard field goal with 6:09 left to make it 34-28, Young returned, led his teammates to the Michigan 23, then took the snap and took the ball. He rambled all the way in for the score and Texas led 35-34.

Rivas kicked another 42-yard FG with 3:04 left and Michigan re-claimed the lead 37-35.

Young then ran the 'Horns downfield and ran down the clock. He rushed six times, and threw once on a ten-play drive that culminated with Dusty Mangum drilling a 37-yard field goal as time expired. Texas triumphed 38-37.

Vince Young was dominant. He ran for 197 yards and four scores, was given the Rose Bowl MVP award, and instantly became a 2005 Heisman Trophy candidate.

Eleven months later he sat alongside USC's Reggie Bush and Matt Leinart awaiting the announcement of the 2005 Heisman Tro-phy Award. Leinart won the award in 2004. Bush would win it in 2005. A disappointed Young would finish a distant second.

The trio would meet again four weeks later as undefeated No.1 Southern California (12-0) faced undefeated No.2 Texas (12-0) in the Rose Bowl, for the 2006 National Championship.

With two Heisman Trophy winners playing in the same backfield for the first time in the history of college football, USC rode a 34-game winning streak, seeking to become the first team ever to win three consecutive national titles.

Texas had their own 19-game winning streak, as well as the Heisman-less Young, the first NCAA quarterback to throw for 3,000 yards and rush for 1,000 in a season.

The first half featured questionable calls, questionable decisions, and unquestionable sloppiness. Texas fumbled a punt return before their offense could even get onto the field. The Trojans converted with a LenDale White 4-yard TD run for the early 7-0 lead.

Both teams failed at fourth down conversion attempts. Texas turned it over at the USC 48-yard line after being stuffed on fourth-and-one. The Trojans then took the ball, drove to the UT 17, passed on a field goal attempt, and failed on fourth-and-one.

In the second quarter, Bush caught a 27-yard reception to the UT 18-yard line then made a wild lateral attempt that ended up in the hands of Texas' Michael Huff.

On the next Trojan possession, on a

second down play from the UT 25, Leinart threw an interception to Michael Griffin in the end zone.

Texas took the ball downfield and scored on Young's 10-yard run-turned-pitch to runningback Selvin Young. Selvin took it twelve more yards for a touchdown. However replays showed that Vince's knee hit the ground before he made the pitch. The officials neglected to review the play. David Pino missed the PAT.

Nothing was normal.

By the end of the half, Texas led 16-10. It wasn't pretty. But it was exciting.

In the second half, the USC offense was led by the power running of White (124 yards for the game) and the arm of Leinart (365 passing yards in total). The Trojans eliminated their first half hiccups, stormed up and down the field, and when Dwayne Jarrett snagged a 22-yard TD pass, took a commanding 38-26 lead with 6:42 left.

Sure, Texas had Vince Young. He quickly maneuvered the Longhorns 69 yards in eight plays and scored on a 17-yard jaunt to make it 38-33. But Texas had no answers for the trio of White, Bush, and Leinart.

The last four USC possessions? Touchdown. Touchdown. Touchdown. Touchdown.

After coming out of the locker room for the second half, the Trojans offensive machine had yet to be stopped, slowed down, deterred, or even pestered by the Texas defense. Drive after drive.

So USC took over at their 34-yard line with 4:03 to kill. They gave the ball to their workhorse White. Leinart tossed to Jarrett for a nifty sideline reception. White carried again, and again. Until his third-and-seven run came up two yards shy of a first down.

Southern California was at the Texas 45, facing fourth-and-two with 2:13 left.

"First down, the game is over basically," noted Carroll. "That's our moment to seal the win."

On the opposite sideline, Texas coach Mack Brown called timeout, then gave his defense a promise. "I told the team you stop this fourth down play, we're going to win the National Championship," he said.

The fact that Carroll chose to go for it instead of punting wasn't surprising. What was surprising was the stunt performed by Texas defensive end Brian Robison.

"I was supposed to rush between the tight end and the tackle," Robison said. "But I decided to stunt instead and circled around into the middle."

Robison guessed that with LenDale White in the game, and Reggie Bush on the sidelines, and the National Championship in the balance, the Trojans would play power football up the gut.

Indeed, Leinart handed off to White.

Robison joined defensive tackle Larry Dibbles, and cornerbacks Michael Huff and Aaron Ross, stuffing the middle. A wave of Longhorns converged on the USC running back as he approached the line. Still White drove forward.

He needed two yards. He got one and nine tenths.

"If you make that first down, you're squatting on the football to win the game," said Carroll. "We just missed it. By what...two inches?"

Maybe if Bush was in the backfield, he could have pushed White over the threshold. Not this time. Texas took over. Their defense danced off the field as the undaunted Young took the stage, trailing by five points.

He'd been here before. The Rose Bowl. A fourth quarter comeback. One final drive.

Carroll knew it too. "The last thing I want to do is sit back and see what happens," said the USC coach. So he called blitz after blitz trying to stop the unstoppable Young.

At first, it looked like not even Young (who ran for 200 yards and threw for another 267 in the game) could overcome the Trojans, determined to capture their third straight crown.

Young's first pass to Ramonce Taylor lost two yards. The next pass to Limas Sweed fell incomplete. Now it was third-and-12. Young connected with Quan Cosby for a short 7-yard gain. However on the tackle, defensive back Darnell Bing was called for a facemask penalty, giving the Longhorns a first down at the USC 46.

Young hit Brian Carter for nine yards. Then the Texas QB scrambled for seven more.

0:53 remained and Young was reviving his role as Rose Bowl hero. He hit Carter again underneath coverage, cutting across from the left for 17 yards.

Two incomplete passes to Sweed sandwiched between a five-yard keeper, left Young with 26 ticks on the clock, and more importantly a fourth-and-five at the USC 8-yard line.

THE PLAY

CD 2-Track 38—*Craig Way, Keith Moreland,* **Host Communications/The University of Texas/ Collegiate Images**

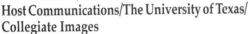

Two wideouts left, one to the right.

In the shotgun, Young took the snap and drifted to the 17-yard line. The Trojans blitzed. Cornerback Josh Pinkard, lined up as an outside linebacker, came flying in. Young quickly went through his progressions, first looking for tight end David Thomas to the left, then Sweed over the middle.

But it was USC defensive end Lawrence Jackson, pressuring hard from the left corner, who immediately forced Young to step up at the 15-yard line, look right, pull the ball down, and sprint for the pylon.

It was run or be sacked.

Young zipped right past the charging Pinkard who quickly turned around and gave chase. That left one hope for the Trojans, defensive end Frostee Rucker who had backed off from rushing the QB. Rucker read Texas RB Selvin Young coming out of the backfield, over the middle. As Selvin Young crossed the line of scrimmage, Rucker turned inside, and popped him. The bump momentarily knocked Rucker off balance, and left an alley behind him to the end zone for the Texas QB.

Rucker valiantly turned back around, sprinted toward the sideline and dived at the streaking Vince Young. But no one touched the Texas superstar as he palmed the ball in his right hand, crossed the goal line, and ran through a sea of photographers. He cradled the football like a precious child, then took in the moment as his teammates swarmed him in celebration. Down by 12 just minutes before, Texas now led 39-38.

Still 19 seconds remained. USC had Leinart and Bush. They also had one timeout remaining. That's like giving Batman and Robin one more commercial break to escape from the Joker.

The Texas coach knew it too. "I was afraid we'd scored too soon," said Brown.

But then as Texas lined up for a two-point conversion attempt, the Trojans made a fateful error. Twelve men on the field. Carroll was huddled with his offense, unaware until defensive line coach Jethro Franklin called USC's final timeout.

After the Trojan defense gathered itself, Young still forged straight ahead for the conversion to make it 41-38.

Saddled without a timeout, Southern California had little hope for even the most magical of Leinart's tricks.

Starting at the USC 31-yard line after the kickoff, Leinart tossed a short pass underneath to Bush who streaked to the sidelines and ran out of bounds at the Texas 42. The 27-yard gain left 0:08 on the clock. Leinart scrambled desperately on the last play, eating up the final seconds before trying to hit Dwayne Jarrett near the UT 25.

His pass was high. The clock was at 0:00, and the Texas Longhorns were National Champions.

THE AFTERMATH

In the midst of a frenzied media throng rushing the field after the final play, Leinart offered this immediate judgment of the game. "We just couldn't tackle him," said Leinart of Young. "I still think we're a better football team. They just made the plays at the end. "

Actually, Young just made the plays at the end.

The pinnacle game of his three years at Texas capped a career where he finished 30-2 as a starter, the winningest quarterback in Texas history. Besides being the Rose Bowl MVP for a second straight year, he also won the 2005 Davey O'Brien Award as the nation's top QB, as well as the Maxwell Award as the nation's best player.

Like Bush, Young decided to forego his senior season and enter the 2006 NFL Draft. Reggie Bush was selected as the second pick overall in the draft by the New Orleans Saints. Vince Young was chosen third by the Tennessee Titans. And Matt Leinart was the tenth pick of the first round, going to the Arizona Cardinals.

The epic Rose Bowl battle drew the highest television rating (21.7) for a college football game since the 1987 Fiesta Bowl (25.1) between Penn State and Miami.

Texas	0	16	7	18	- 41
Southern California	7	3	14	14	- 38

USC   White 4 run (Danelo kick)
UT   FG Pino 46
UT   Young, Selvin 12 run (kick failed)
UT   Taylor 30 run (Pino kick)
USC   FG Danelo 43
USC   White 3 run (Danelo kick)
UT   Young, Vince 14 run (Pino kick)
USC   White 12 run (Danelo kick)
USC   Bush 26 run (Danelo kick)
UT   FG Pino 34
USC   Jarrett 22 pass from Leinart (Danelo kick)
UT   Young, Vince 17 run (Pino kick)
UT   Young, Vince 8 run (Young, Vince rush)

Attendance 93,986

Thanks to the following individuals and publications for their meticulous documentation of the facts and events surrounding the games. Their work was the historical foundation for this book.

The Bugle (Virginia Tech Student Year-book); Bob Croce, *Albany Times Union*; Phil Casaus, Rick Wright, *Albuquerque Journal*; Doug Ireland, *Alexandria Daily Town Talk*; Joe Kunda, Mark Wogenrich, *Allentown Morning Call.*; Bob Cohn, Bob Eger, David Casstevens, Norm Frauenheim, *Arizona Republic*; Bob Moran, *Arizona Tribune*; George Schroeder, Kane Web, Bob Holt, Stephen Caldwell, *Arkansas Democrat-Gazette*; Alan Robinson, Ed Shearer, Harry Atkins, Herschel Nissenson, Howard Ulman, Jenna Halvatgis, John Kekis, Mary Foster, *Associated Press*; Terence Moore, Earnest Reese, Mark Bradley, Marlon Manuel, Matt Winkeljohn, Scott M. Reid, *Atlanta Journal Constitution*; Randy Riggs, *Austin American Statesman*; Dave Moorman, Bud Montet, Scott Rabalais, Lee Feinswog, Joe Planas, Ted Castillo, *Baton Rouge Advocate*; Andy Nuzzo, *Beaver County Times*; Lenn Robbins, Gerry Bourbeau, Ken Davidoff, *Bergen Record*; Loran Smith, *Between the Hedges: 100 Years of Georgia Football (Longstreet Press)*; Charles Hollis, Jimmy Bryan, Kevin Scarbinsky, Wayne Hester, Clyde Bolton, *Birmingham News*; Richard Scott, Bill Lumpkin, *Birmingham Post-Herald*; John Michaels, *Bloomsburg Press Enterprise*; Bob Monahan, Dan Shaughnessy, Ian Thomsen, Michael Vega, Joe Concannon, Mark Singelais, *Boston Globe*; Jason Strauss, *Brown Daily* ; Marcus Prater, *Caspar Star Tribune*; Andrew Joynerm, John Flowers, Sean Green, Shawn Batten, *Cavalier Daily*; Mark Neuzil, *Cedar Rapids Gazette*; Don Hager, Rick Ryan, *Charleston Gazette Mail* ; Lindsey Willhite, *Chicago Daily Herald* ; Jim Spadafore, Len Ziehm, Phil Velasquez, *Chicago Sun Times*; Andrew Bagnato, Bill Jauss, Cooper Rollow, Dave Nightingale, David Condon, Ed Sherman, John Busal, John Husar, Joseph Tybor, Roy Damer, *Chicago Tribune*; Ross Atkins, *Christian Science Monitor*; Neil Schmidt, Paul Daugherty, Tim Sullivan, *Cincinnati Enquirer*; Joe Posnanski, *Cincinnati Post*;

John Walker, Rusty Hampton, John McGrath, Orley Hood, Mike Knobler, *Clarion-Ledger*; Ed Chay, *Cleveland Plain Dealer*; Jimmy Gentry, Tom Marshall, *Columbia Daily Tribune*; George Strode, Mike Sullivan, Ray Stein, Tim May, *Columbus Dispatch*; Bobby Hall, Mike Fleming, Phil Stukenborg, Ron Higgins, Al Dunning, Pete Wickham, *Commercial Appeal*; Kirk Copeland, *Current Sauce*; Mike Haky, Sidney Bell, *Daily Atheneum*; Brian Patterson, *Daily Breeze*; Kevin Modesti, *Daily Bruin*; Brad Young, *Daily Collegian*; Chris Pierle, *Daily Evergreen*; Jody Jividen, *Daily Mail*; Antone Oseka, *Daily Nebraskan*; Paola Boivin, Terry Bowser, *Daily News*; Josh Callahan, Marc Chodock, *Daily Pennsylvanian*; Dave Long, *Dayton Daily News*; Bob Bradley, *Death Valley Days: The Glory of Clemson Football (Longstreet Press Inc)*; Rex Spires, *Decatur Herald and Review*; Jacques Pernitz, *Delaware State News*; Natalie Meisler, *Denver Post*; Angel Hernandez, B.G. Brooks, Randy Holtz, *Denver Rocky Mountain News*; Marc Hansen, Ron Maly, *Des Moines Register*; Doug Robinson, *Deseret News*; Mike McCabe, *Detroit Free Press*; Dave Dye, Angelique S. Chengelis, *Detroit News*; Jonathan Ingram, *Durham Morning Herald*; Neil Cawood, *Eugene Register Guard*; Bob Thomas, Marlon W. Morgan, *Florida Times Union*; Bob Dunkel, Bob Pulley, Bobby Tyler, Paul Jenkins, *Gainesville Sun*; Dave Albee, Rachel Alexander, Rick Brown, *Gannett News Service* ; Bruce Phillips, *Greensboro Daily News*; Mark Berman, *Harrisonburg Daily News Record*; Chick Abadie, *Hattiesburg American*; Jerry Wizig, John Lopez, Terry Blount, *Houston Chronicle*; James Magness, *Huntsville Times* ; Jim Poore, *Idaho Statesman*; Laurie Black, *Jacksonville Journal Courier*; Charles Cromwell, Kevin Turbeville, *Jonesboro Sun*; Mike Vaccaro, *Kansas City Star*; Joel White, Jon Balmer, *Kansas State Collegian*; *Kenosha News*; David Schumacher, *Kentucky Post*; David Comer, *Knight Ridder News Service* ; Jeff Washburn, Paula Waltz,

Tom Kubat, *Lafayette Journal and Courier;* Jim Hersh, *Lancaster Sunday News;* Fred Stabely, *Lansing State Journal;* Bob Hammond, Landon Hall, *Laramie Daily Boomerang;* Mark Anderson, *Las Vegas Review-Journal;* David Reed, Mark Story, Rick Baily, *Lexington-Herald Leader;* Bill Dwyre, Elliott Almond, Gene Wojciechowski, Jerry Crowe, Matt White, Mike Downey, Richard Hoffer, Al Carter, Dwight Chapin, Mal Florence, Tracy Dodds, *Los Angeles Times;* Dick Fenlon, Mark Coomes, Pat Forde, Rick Bozich, Russ Brown, Jim Terhune, *Louisville Courier-Journal;* Norval Pollard, Randy Miller, Ray Glass, *Lubbock Avalanche Journal; Middlesex News;* Jeff Duncan, Jack Mitchell, *Monroe News Star Herald;* Ragan Ingram, *Montgomery Advertiser;* Nate Allen, *Morning News Razorback Bureau;* Mickey Furfari, *Mountaineer Illustrated; Natchitoches Times;* John Kryk, *Natural Enemies: The Notre Dame-Michigan Football Feud (Andrews and McMeel) ;* Dick Weiss, Michael James, *New York Daily News;* Jere Longman, John G. Leyden, Frank Litsky, George Vecsey, Gerald Eskanazi, Gordon S. White Jr., Ira Berkow, Malcolm Moran, Michael Janofsky, Peter Alfano, Tommy Lee Jones, William H. Wallace, *New York Times;* Perr Ballard, *O-A News;* Stewart Mayfield, *Oklahoma Daily;* Doug Thomas, Lee Barfknecht, Steve Pivovar, *Omaha World Herald;* Ed Price, *Palm Beach Post;* Brian Hamilton, *Pioneer Press;* Charley Feeney, *Pittsburgh Post-Gazette ;* Steve Guiremand, *Press-Telegram ;* John Gillooly, *Providence Journal Bulletin;* A.J. Carr, *Raleigh News Observer;* Helen Ross, *Raleigh Times;* Steve McClain, *Richmond Register;* John Markon, *Richmond Times-Dispatch;* Dennis Latta, Doug Soughty, *Roanoke Times and World News;* O.K. Davis, *Ruston Daily News;* Don Bosley, *Sacramento Bee;* Dick Rosetta, Ray Herbat, *Salt Lake Tribune;* Ric Bucher, *San Diego Union Tribune;* Art Rosenbaum, Jake Curtis, Tony Cooper, *San Francisco Chronicle;* John Akers, *San Jose Mercury News;* Allen Gunter, Anthony Stastny, Jim Halley, *Savannah Evening Press;* Bud Withers, *Seattle Post Intelligencer;* Dick Rockne, *Seattle Times;* Scott Ferrell, *Shreveport Times;* Al Lesar, Bill Bilinski, Bill Moor, Joe Doyle, John Finernan, Phil Richards, *South Bend Tribune;* Pat Putnam, *Sports Illustrated;* Bernie Miklasz, Bob Broeg, Jim Thomas, John Sonderegger, Tom Wheatley, Vahe Gregorian, *St. Louis Post-Dispatch;* Charley Hallman, *St. Paul Pioneer Press;* John Romano, Mark Johnson, *St. Petersburg Times;* Mark Craig, *Star Tribune;* Vernon Willis, *Statesboro Herald;* Marty Mule, *Sugar Bowl: The First Fifty Years (Oxmoor House Inc.);* Harold Baker, *Sunbury PA Daily Item;* Dave Rahme, Donnie Webb, *Syracuse Post-Standard;* Don Borst, Bob Condotta, Craig Hill, *Tacoma News Tribune;* Bill McGrotha, George Maselli, *Tallahassee Democrat;* David Whitley, Joey Johnston, *Tampa Tribune;* Bob Petrie, *Tempe Daily News;* Lydia Craver, *The Appalachian;* Patricia K. Ourada, *The Broncos: A History of Boise State Athletics: 1932-1994 (Boise State University);* Doug Waters, *The Collegiate Times;* Tom Harper, *The Comenian;* Mark Froelich, *The Crescent-News;* Gary Sulentic, *The Crusader;* David Sternberg, *The Daily Princetonian;* Larry Bowen, *The Eagle;* Peter Finney, *The Fighting Tigers (LSU Press);* Chuck Wall, *The Flat Hat;* Brian Nielsen, Carl Walworth, J. Michael Flanagan, *The Herald & Review;* David Walsh, *The Herald Dispatch;* Chris Colston, *The Hokie Handbook (Wichita Eagle and Beacon Publishing);* Barry Laswell, *The Independent;* Seth Wickersham, *The Maneater;* Chris Staebell, *The Northern Iowan;* Jason Hehir, *The Record;* Andy West, *The Review;* David Newton, Herman Helms, Randy Laney, *The State;* Charles Johnson, Pat Farnan, Pete Daly, *The State News;* Troy Sellers, *The Voice;* Brian Allee-Walsh, Bob Roesler, *Times-Picayune;* Hendrik Van Leuven, *Touchdown UCLA: The Bruin Football Story (Strode Publishers);* Dan O'Kane, *Tulsa World;* Bill Lohmann, Ira Kaufman, J. Paul Wyatt, Joe Sargis, Mike Tully, Stan Metzler, *United Press International;* Harry Blauvelt, Mike Lopresti, *USA Today;* Steve Carlson, *Virginian-Pilot;* Alan Truex, Byron Rosen, Christopher B. Daly, Gene Wang, J.A. Adande, John Ed Bradley, Ken Denlinger, Mark Maske, Michael Wilbon, Pete Williams, Sally Jenkins, Steve Berkowitz, *Washington Post;* John Hawkins, Tom Knott, *Washinton Times;* Keith Evans, *Waterloo Courier;* Erin Seba, *Wichita Eagle Beacon;* Keith Tresolini, Tom Tomashek, *Wilmington News*

Journal; Andrew Cohen, Andy Baggot, *Wisconsin State Journal.*

Martin Fennelly, *Tampa Tribune;* Tom D'Angelo, Jorge Milian, *Palm Beach Post;* Kevin Record, *The Ledger;* Chris Duncan, Rick Gano, Pete Iacobelli, Larry Lage, Eric Olson, Richard Rosenblatt, *Associated Press;* Brian Landman, *St. Petersburg Times;* Lindsey Willhite, *Daily Herald;* Jeanie Chung, *Chicago Sun Times;* Thomas Martinez, *Statesman Journal;* John Nolen, *The Oregonian;* Marty Williams, *Dayton Daily News;* Eric Lacy, Justin Rice, *State News;* Dave Caldwell, Joe LaPointe, Alex Yannis, *New York Times;* Adam Wire, Scott Mytyk, *Crawfordsville Journal Review;* Josh Dernosek, *Appalachian Online;* Ann Green, *Greenville News;* Jeff Hartsell, *The Post and Courier;* Tommy Bowman, *Winston Salem Journal;* Scott Cain, Dudley Dawson, Wally Hall, Rob Keys, Robert Turbeville, *Arkansas Democrat-Gazette;* Jennifer Smith, Charles Bertram, *Lexington Herald-Leader;* Carl Dubois, Randy Rosetta, William Weathers, *The Advocate;* Ryan Ernst, *Cincinnati Enquirer;* Anuj Basil, Thad Hartmann, *Daily Princetonian;* Rob Oller, *Columbus Dispatch;* Ron Cook, Chico Harlan, *Pittsburgh Post-Gazette;* Brian Christopherson, *Lincon Journal Star;* Emily Badger, *Orlando Sentinel;* Mike Triplett, *Times Picayune;* Glenn Guilbeau, *Shreveport Times;* Natalie England, *San Antonio Express-News;* Randy Riggs, Cedric Golden, *Austin American-Statesman;* Rich Kaipust, *Omaha World-Herald Bureau;* Scott Wolf, *Daily News.*